The All Music Book of Hit Albums

The All Music Book of Hit Albums

Compiled by
Dave McAleer

Miller Freeman Books

First published in the United States in 1995 by Miller Freeman Books
600 Harrison Street, San Francisco, CA 94107
Publishers of GPI Books, Guitar Player, Bass Player and Keyboard magazines
A member of the United Newspapers Group

Distributed to the book trade in the U.S. and Canada by
Publishers Group West, P.O. Box 8843, Emeryville, CA 94662

Distributed to the music trade in the U.S. and Canada by
Hal Leonard Publishing, P.O.Box 13819, Milwaukee, W1 53213

ISBN 0.87930.393.X

Library of Congress Catalog Card Number 95-77071

Executive Editor: Lorraine Dickey
Art Direction: Russell Porter
Editors: Tony Brown, Nigel Matheson, Lol Henderson
Production: Sarah Schuman

Printed and bound in Great Britain

All photographs including cover pictures supplied by London Features International

Author's Acknowledgements
The Billboard Chart Information is copyright © 1960/91 by BPI Communications used courtesy of Billboard, Billboard Æ is a registered trademark of BPI Communications.
The Billboard Chart Information is copyright © 1991/92/93/94 by BPI Communications and Soundscan, Inc. used courtesy of Billboard. Billboard Æ is a registered trademark of BPI Communications.

UK Chart Information 1960-1983 © Music Week
UK Chart Information 1983-1990 © BPI. Compiled by Gallup
UK Chart Information 1990-1993 © CIN. Compiled by Gallup
UK Chart Information 1994 © CIN. Compiled by Milward Brown.

Special thanks to: Derek Brecknock, Tony Brown, Lorraine Dickey, Billie Gordon, the musical McAleers, Jon Philibert, John Tobler and my many friends in the record business and the 'trivia freaks' fraternity.

Contents

INTRODUCTION

The first attempts at producing and marketing long-playing records came in the first years of this century, soon after the dawn of the phonograph age. However by 1910, the idea had been abandoned. The public also showed little interest in the project when RCA launched their 33⅓ LP in 1931. By the end of World War II, record albums were an accepted part of the music business, but in those days the term album meant just that – they were simply collections of 10" or 12" 78 rpm singles which were purchased together in an actual album, hence the name. The situation remained unchanged until 1948 when Columbia Records (CBS) unveiled the 33⅓ microgroove record which could accommodate all the tracks previously sold as a 78 rpm album. This time the idea caught on and by 1956, when sales merited a weekly, rather than bi-weekly, chart, albums were as much an accepted part of the music scene in the USA, as the 45 rpm singles, which RCA had launched at the start of the 1950s. In the UK, albums, and indeed 45 rpm singles, took a little longer to appear on the scene and therefore the first album charts were not seen until late 1958. The first album chart compiled by the record industry's own magazine *Record Retailer* was not published until March 1960, which is where this book starts its coverage of UK album sales.

Most of the world's top album artists in the 35-year period between 1960 and 1994 hailed from either America or Britain. These two countries set the majority of musical trends that keep pop record buyers entertained around the globe. The major musical happening during the period was undoubtedly the growth of rock. It evolved out of late 1940's R&B and C&W music and was spread worldwide in the mid-1950s by Bill Haley and Elvis Presley. In the 1960's, the Beatles and other UK bands, weaned on US rock'n'roll and R&B, gave it a new lease of life. Rock then diversified into scores of successful sub-genres, making many more transatlantic recording artists household names around the globe.

The aim of this book is to try and put the most successful US and UK albums of the rock era into some kind of perspective, and the chart careers of every hit act can be checked in these easy-to-follow, fact-packed charts. At a glance, you can see all the similarities, and indeed differences, between the tastes of record buyers on both sides of the Atlantic.

HOW THIS BOOK WORKS

The chart positions used for compiling the monthly Top 10's were taken from the two best accepted sources; *Billboard* in America, and *Record Retailer* (which later became *Music Week*) in Britain.

CHART FILES

The Top 10 UK and US charts are compiled by means of a complex and comprehensive system which considers not only a record's weekly chart placings and peak position, but also the number of weeks it spent on the Top 10 and the time spent at Number 1 (if applicable).

Apart from the normal chart features, these Top 10's also show:

(a) The aggregate number of weeks a record spent in the country's Top 10 during its total chart run.
(b) The record's equivalent position in the UK/US.
(c) Whether it was the artist's first (F) or most recent (L) Top 10 entry in that country.
(d) Whether it was certified as a million seller (P) in that country (2P indicates two million sales, 3P means three million, etc.).

NB: All the above information is up to December 31, 1994.

CHART COMPILATION INFORMATION

All charts in this book are based on a record's weekly chart performances. This means that the balance is in favour of records that had Top 10 longevity and not those that quickly went in and out – even if they achieved massive sales in doing so. Therefore some top sellers like *Saturday Night Fever* are not placed as high as they would be if the charts were based solely on sales. This is always a problem when calculating a list from chart information, but unfortunately it is impossible to procure accurate sales figures for the last 35 years, so this would appear to be the fairest way.

It is not unusual for an album to have the same title on both sides of the Atlantic but for the content to be different, albeit only slightly. It is also not unheard of for an album to have a different title on both sides of the Atlantic, yet to have identical or almost the same content. In such cases, the rule of thumb has been to call them the same album, when it comes to listing equivalent peak positions, if approximately 80% of the tracks are duplicated. If fewer tracks are the same, as often happened with early Beatles and Stones albums, they are considered to be different records.

Before August 1963, when the US mono and stereo charts were combined, the mono charts (which reflected the bulk of the sales) are referred to. Therefore, albums that only reached the stereo Top 10 are not included. For the record, most stereo-only hits at the time were Easy Listening/MOR products.

In August 1973, *Music Week* decided not to include TV-advertised albums on the chart. This resulted in *That'll Be The Day* vanishing from the top spot and top-selling albums like Elvis Presley's *40 Greatest Hits* not appearing on the chart at the time.

The platinum certification for million-selling albums was not introduced until 1976, and many earlier US million-sellers have never been officially designated platinum, and will therefore be listed without a (P) platinum reference. It is also worth remembering that a handful of labels, most notably Motown, never registered any of their hits for gold or platinum certification.

Various artists and compilation albums were given their own UK chart in 1989. This means that American hits such as *Above The Rim*, *The Bodyguard*, *The Crow*, *The Lost Boys*, *Robin Hood: Prince Of Thieves* and *Wayne's World* do not have equivalent UK peak numbers even though they were British chart hits.

QUARTERLY TRIVIA

Over a thousand record-related trivia items are included in chronological order, to help give an even clearer picture of the events and happenings that shaped the transatlantic music scene. The trivia facts extend the coverage of the book far beyond the realms of the Top 10. Hundreds of less successful but equally important albums are mentioned, and all the successful sub-genres of rock as well as R&B and country are covered. Added to this are regular sales statistics, countless references to Grammy & BRITS winners and numerous mentions of live gigs and music-related TV shows and films.

Please note that references to 'biggest hits' refer to a record's chart placing and not its sales figures. Also remember that, unless stated otherwise, chart positions mentioned refer to an album's weekly chart placings not its monthly position: obviously not every record that reaches the Top 10 will be in the month's Top 10.

NB: The charts referred to in the trivia are those listed in CHART SIZE.

ARTIST INDEX

This easy-to-check index lists an artist's album titles in chronological order and shows the month they entered this book's UK and US Top 10. Therefore, it is a simple matter to check the charts concerned for more information about the album. There is also a short biography of each act which contains such pertinent facts as style of music, year of birth and where born (solo artists), original line-up, where based (groups) and interesting/record breaking feats.

TITLE INDEX

There is also an alphabetical listing of all the album titles in this book with the artist's name. If an album's title was spelt differently in the USA and Britain, it is listed on the chart as it was spelt in that country. However, in the index, it can be found either under the American spelling or separately (if the title is not similar).

Chart Size

UNITED STATES

1960	Top 40 (*Mono*)
Jan-March 1961	Top 25 (*Mono*) Action Albums (*only includes records charted 9 weeks or less*)
3 April 1961-10 August 1963	Top 150 (*Mono*)
17 Aug 1963-25 March 1967	Top 150 (*Mono & Stereo*)
1 April 1967-6 May 1967	Top 175
13 May 1967-Dec 1994	Top 200

UNITED KINGDOM

12 March 1960-7 April 1966	Top 20
14 April 1966 -1 December 1966	Top 30
8 Dec 1966-5 February 1969	Top 40
12 Feb 1969-9 Jan 1971	*fluctuated between* Top 15 *and* Top 77.
16 Jan 1971-28 June 1975	Top 50
5 July 1975-26 November 1978	Top 60
2 Dec 1978-1 August 1981	Top 75
8 August 1981- 7 Jan 1989	Top 100
14 Jan 1989 - Dec 1994	Top 75 (*& compilation LPs given their own separate chart*)

Bob Dylan

the 1960s

The Beach Boys

The Beatles

he Monkees

TOP UK ACTS ON THE US CHARTS IN THE 1960s	
1	The Beatles
2	The Rolling Stones
3	Cream
4	Herman's Hermits
5	Led Zeppelin
6	Tom Jones
7	Dave Clark Five
8	Blind Faith
9	Donovan
10	Mr Acker Bilk

The Sixties was the first decade when the LP became more than just an expensive novelty to be purchased a few times a year, and then only by adults. Not that anyone could predict at the start of the most innovative decade in our lifetime that the LP chart would ever be dominated by anything other than soundtracks or middle-of-the-road (MOR) acts. The Sixties started with *The Lord's Prayer* by the 375-voiced Mormon Tabernacle Choir heading the US chart, and with the soundtrack album to *South Pacific* at Number 1 in the UK – a position that it held for over two years in total.

TOP US ACTS ON THE UK CHARTS IN THE 1960s	
1	Elvis Presley
2	The Beach Boys
3	Bob Dylan
4	Jim Reeves
5	The Monkees
6	Frank Sinatra
7	The Supremes
8	Buddy Holly
9	Diana Ross
10	Ray Conniff

the 1960s

At the start of the decade, it seemed that the only pop/rock acts whose albums were guaranteed a chart placing were Elvis Presley (on both sides of the Atlantic) and Cliff Richard (in the UK only). Teen idols were encouraged to record evergreens and standards to fill out their LPs, which disappointed many of their younger fans and rarely interested the adults these all too familiar tunes were aimed at. Perhaps the first exception to this unwritten rule was Chubby Checker, the King Of The Twist, who monopolized the chart in early 1962. Of much more substance from a musical standpoint was the next US album superstar, blind black R&B performer Ray Charles, whose *Modern Sounds In Country & Western Music*, would have been 1962s top album if not for the *West Side Story* soundtrack, which spent over a year in the top spot and was the most successful LP of the decade in America.

The arrival of the Beatles changed everything, and younger record buyers become more important, as albums began to rival singles in popularity. Many of the top selling album acts of all time first charted in the mid-1960s including Bob Dylan, the Rolling Stones, Simon & Garfunkel, Herb Alpert & The Tijuana Brass, the Beach Boys, Barbra Streisand and Stevie Wonder. By 1967s so-called 'Summer Of Love', the Top 10 of the LP charts on both sides of the Atlantic included little MOR material. Although some of the biggest transatlantic sellers were still soundtrack albums like *Mary Poppins* and *The Sound Of Music*, which returned to the top of the UK chart eleven times between 1965-68. The late 1960s were also the breeding ground for another bumper crop of perennially successful album artists, and it was during the tail end of the Swinging Sixties that US acts such as the Doors, Jimi Hendrix and Chicago debuted alongside British newcomers Cream (with Eric Clapton), Led Zeppelin and Pink Floyd. The latter half of the decade also gave birth to the so-called 'concept' album, theoretically a complete LP of songs relating to a single theme, the most famous example being the legendary *Sergeant Peppers's Lonely Hearts Club Band* LP by the Beatles. By 1967 emerging stars were being judged on their potential as sellers of LPs rather than simply as purveyors of catchy hit singles – a state of affairs that has continued virtually unchanged ever since.

TOP US ALBUM ACTS OF THE 1960s

1. The Beatles
2. Herb Alpert & the Tijuana Brass
3. Elvis Presley
4. Peter, Paul & Mary
5. The Kingston Trio
6. The Monkees
7. Barbra Streisand
8. The Rolling Stones
9. The Supremes
10. Frank Sinatra
11. Andy Williams
12. The Beach Boys
13. Ray Charles
14. Simon & Garfunkel
15. Johnny Mathis
16. Bob Newhart
17. Henry Mancini
18. Allan Sherman
19. Blood, Sweat & Tears
20. Cream

The Doors

TOP UK ALBUM ACTS OF THE 1960s

1. The Beatles
2. Elvis Presley
3. Cliff Richard
4. The Rolling Stones
5. George Mitchell Minstrels
6. The Shadows
7. The Beach Boys
8. Bob Dylan
9. The Seekers
10. Jim Reeves
11. The Monkees
12. Tom Jones
13. Frank Sinatra
14. Val Doonican
15. The Searchers
16. Frank Ifield
17. The Hollies
18. Mr Acker Bilk
19. Led Zeppelin
20. The Supremes

Aretha Franklin

TOP BRITISH ALBUMS OF THE 1960s

1	**The Sound Of Music**	Soundtrack
2	**South Pacific**	Soundtrack
3	**West Side Story**	Soundtrack
4	**The Black & White Minstrel Show**	George Mitchell Minstrels
5	**Please Please Me**	The Beatles
6	**G.I. Blues (Soundtrack)**	Elvis Presley
7	**Mary Poppins**	Soundtrack
8	**Sergeant Peppers's Lonely Hearts Club Band**	The Beatles
9	**Blue Hawaii**	Elvis Presley
10	**The Rolling Stones**	The Rolling Stones
11	**Best Of The Beach Boys**	The Beach Boys
12	**With The Beatles**	The Beatles
13	**Beatles For Sale**	The Beatles
14	**The Best Of The Seekers**	The Seekers
15	**A Hard Day's Night**	The Beatles
16	**Led Zeppelin 2**	Led Zeppelin
17	**Summer Holiday (Soundtrack)**	Cliff Richard
18	**Abbey Road**	The Beatles
19	**Meet The Searchers**	The Searchers
20	**Rubber Soul**	The Beatles

TOP AMERICAN ALBUMS OF THE 1960s

1	**West Side Story**	Soundtrack
2	**The Sound Of Music**	Soundtrack
3	**Peter, Paul & Mary**	Peter, Paul & Mary
4	**Doctor Zhivago**	Soundtrack
5	**The Sound Of Music**	Original Cast
6	**Whipped Cream & Other Delights**	Herb Alpert & The Tijuana Brass
7	**Camelot**	Original Cast
8	**Mary Poppins**	Soundtrack
9	**The Button Down Mind Of Bob Newhart**	Bob Newhart
10	**Blue Hawaii**	Elvis Presley
11	**Blood, Sweat & Tears**	Blood, Sweat & Tears
12	**(Moving)**	Peter, Paul & Mary
13	**Going Places**	Herb Alpert & The Tijuana Brass
14	**Sergeant Pepper's Lonely Hearts Club Band**	The Beatles
15	**The Monkees**	The Monkees
16	**Breakfast At Tiffany's (Soundtrack)**	Henry Mancini
17	**Modern Sounds in Country & Western Music**	Ray Charles
18	**What Now My Love**	Herb Alpert & The Tijuana Brass
19	**Hair**	Original Cast
20	**A Hard Day's Night**	The Beatles

Rolling Stones

Elvis Presley

The Supremes

UK 1960 JAN-MAR

The first album chart published by the British trade paper *Record Retailer* did not appear until March 10, 1960. Therefore there are no monthly charts for January and February 1960.

This Mnth	Last Mnth	Title	Artist	Label	Wks in 10	US Pos	

• Whilst the Broadway cast album of Rodgers and Hammerstein's musical **The Sound Of Music** (starring Larry Hagman's mother, Mary Martin) topped the US chart, the film soundtrack to those composers' musical **South Pacific** (starring Rossano Brazzi and Mitzi Gaynor) held on to the top spot in Britain. It had been the UK's top selling album since 1958 and sales showed no sign of slowing down. It was not the only Hollywood soundtrack album selling well: also listed were the LPs from **Gigi** (Leslie Caron/ Maurice Chevalier), **The Five Pennies** (Danny Kaye) and **The King & I** (Yul Bryner/Deborah Kerr).

•**The Explosive Freddy Cannon** was the first rock album to top the UK charts. The reason for its success was partly due to the inclusion of Cannon's biggest hit, an update of 'Way Down Under in New Orleans', and, perhaps more importantly, because it was a mid-price album - a real rarity in rock 'n' roll in those days.

•Other teen-oriented acts with hit LPs in Britain included "twangy guitar" king Duane Eddy with the biggest of his nine Top 20 entries, **The Twang's The Thang** and Bobby Darin with **This Is**. The only UK rocker riding high was Cliff Richard and **Cliff Sings**. All three albums contained a mix of rock with the obligatory handful of standards.

March 1960

This Mnth	Last Mnth	Title	Artist	Label	Wks in 10	US Pos	
1	-	**South Pacific**	Soundtrack	RCA	179	1	
2	-	**The Explosive Freddy Cannon**	Freddy Cannon	Top Rank	5		FL
3	-	**Gigi**	Soundtrack	MGM	22	1	
4	-	**My Fair Lady**	Original Broadway Cast	Philips	26	1	
5	-	**The Twang's The Thang**	Duane Eddy	London	12	18	
6	-	**This Is Darin**	Bobby Darin	London	6	6	FL
7	-	**Seven Ages Of Acker**	Mr. Acker Bilk	Columbia	2		F
8	-	**Cliff Sings**	Cliff Richard	Columbia	14		
9	-	**The Five Pennies**	Soundtrack	London	4	22	
10	-	**The King And I**	Soundtrack	Capitol	12	1	

US 1960 JAN-MAR

January 1960

This Mnth	Last Mnth	Title	Artist	Label	Wks in 10	UK Pos	
1	-	**Here We Go Again!**	Kingston Trio	Capitol	19		
2	-	**Heavenly**	Johnny Mathis	Columbia	17	P	
3	-	**60 Years Of Music America Loves Best**	Various	RCA	28		
4	-	**Inside Shelley Berman**	Shelley Berman	Verve	3	12	F
5	-	**The Sound Of Music**	Original Cast	Columbia	63	4	
6	-	**Let's All Sing With The Chipmunks**	Chipmunks	Liberty	9		FL
7	-	**Outside Shelley Berman**	Shelley Berman	Verve	13		
8	-	**Fabulous Fabian**	Fabian	Chancellor	10		L
9	-	**The Lord's Prayer**	Mormon Tabernacle Choir	Columbia	5		F
10	-	**The Kingston Trio At Large**	Kingston Trio	Capitol	5		

February 1960

This Mnth	Last Mnth	Title	Artist	Label	Wks in 10	UK Pos	
1	5	**The Sound Of Music**	Original Cast	Columbia	63	4	
2	1	**Here We Go Again!**	Kingston Trio	Capitol	19		
3	2	**Heavenly**	Johnny Mathis	Columbia	17		P
4	3	**60 Years Of Music America Loves Best**	Various	RCA	28		
5	8	**Fabulous Fabian**	Fabian	Chancellor	10		L
6	7	**Outside Shelley Berman**	Shelley Berman	Verve	13		
7	-	**Faithfully**	Johnny Mathis	Columbia	16		
8	6	**Let's All Sing With The Chipmunks**	Chipmunks	Liberty	9		FL
9	-	**Gunfighter Ballads And Trail Songs**	Marty Robbins	Columbia	8	20	FPL
10	9	**The Lord's Prayer**	Mormon Tabernacle Choir	Columbia	5	F	

March 1960

This Mnth	Last Mnth	Title	Artist	Label	Wks in 10	UK Pos	
1	1	**The Sound Of Music**	Original Cast	Columbia	63	4	
2	4	**60 Years Of Music America Loves Best**	Various	RCA	28		
3	7	**Faithfully**	Johnny Mathis	Columbia	16		
4	2	**Here We Go Again!**	Kingston Trio	Capitol	19		
5	3	**Heavenly**	Johnny Mathis	Columbia	17		P
6	-	**Italian Favorites**	Connie Francis	MGM	14		F
7	6	**Outside Shelley Berman**	Shelley Berman	Verve	13		
8	9	**Gunfighter Ballads And Trail Songs**	Marty Robbins	Columbia	8	20	FPL
9	-	**That's All**	Bobby Darin	Atco	8	15	F
10	-	**Belafonte At Carnegie Hall**	Harry Belafonte	RCA	7		

• In the early 1960s the transatlantic LP charts were heavily MOR- oriented because, as a rule, it was only the older and less rock-oriented record buyer who could afford albums. Most teen targeted artists believed the best way to attract album sales was to include a good smattering of "standards" on their LPs. Among the acts successfully following this path were teen queen Connie Francis with a collection of **Italian Favourites** (which included 'O Sole Mio' and 'Sorrento' – both hits for Elvis Presley soon afterwards). Fellow Italian-American pop star Bobby Darin was clicking with a selection of cabaret club popular numbers tagged **That's All** (which featured his recent chart topper 'Mack The Knife'). Even the content of **Fabulous Fabian** by Philadelphian teen idol Fabian included a mix of teen tunes with songs his fans' parents could also relate to.

•Three very different artists had two top hit albums each: Shelly Berman, The Kingston Trio and Johnny Mathis. Humorist Berman scored with his first two releases, **Inside Shelly Berman** and **Outside Shelly Berman**. The high flying folk group, The Kingston Trio, had two successive chart toppers, **At Large** and **Here We Go Again**. Ballad merchant Mathis hit the heights with **Heavenly**, which included 'Misty', and **Faithfully**, which contained 'Maria'.

UK 1960 APR-JUNE

April 1960

This Mnth	Last Mnth	Title	Artist	Label	Wks in 10	US Pos	
1	1	**South Pacific**	Soundtrack	RCA	179	1	
2	5	**The Twang's The Thang**	Duane Eddy	London	12	18	
3	-	**Flower Drum Song**	Original Broadway Cast	Philips	22	1	
4	8	**Cliff Sings**	Cliff Richard	Columbia	14		
5	-	**This Is Hancock**	Tony Hancock	Pye	14		FL
6	3	**Gigi**	Soundtrack	MGM	22	1	
7	6	**This Is Darin**	Bobby Darin	London	6	6	FL
8	4	**My Fair Lady**	Original Broadway Cast	Philips	26	1	
9	-	**My Concerto For You**	Russ Conway	Columbia	4		
10	2	**The Explosive Freddy Cannon**	Freddy Cannon	Top Rank	5		FL

May 1960

This Mnth	Last Mnth	Title	Artist	Label	Wks in 10	US Pos	
1	1	**South Pacific**	Soundtrack	RCA	179	1	
2	5	**This Is Hancock**	Tony Hancock	Pye	14		FL
3	3	**Flower Drum Song**	Original Broadway Cast	Philips	22	1	
4	6	**Gigi**	Soundtrack	MGM	22	1	
5	-	**Can-Can**	Soundtrack	Capitol	19	4	
6	2	**The Twang's The Thang**	Duane Eddy	London	12	18	
7	-	**Songs For Swinging Sellers**	Peter Sellers	Parlophone	9		
8	-	**Follow That Girl**	Original London Cast	HMV	3		
9	4	**Cliff Sings**	Cliff Richard	Columbia	14		
10	-	**The King And I**	Soundtrack	Capitol	12	1	

June 1960

This Mnth	Last Mnth	Title	Artist	Label	Wks in 10	US Pos	
1	1	**South Pacific**	Soundtrack	RCA	179	1	
2	5	**Can-Can**	Soundtrack	Capitol	19	4	
3	2	**This Is Hancock**	Tony Hancock	Pye	14		FL
4	3	**Flower Drum Song**	Original Broadway Cast	Philips	22	1	
5	4	**Gigi**	Soundtrack	MGM	22	1	
6	-	**Oklahoma**	Soundtrack	Capitol	22	1	
7	7	**Songs For Swinging Sellers**	Peter Sellers	Parlophone	9		
8	-	**My Fair Lady**	Original Broadway Cast	Philips	26	1	
9	9	**Cliff Sings**	Cliff Richard	Columbia	14		
10	-	**I Remember Hank Williams**	Jack Scott	Top Rank	3		FL

• After failing an audition to become Billy Fury's backing band, The Silver Beetles toured Scotland with second division British rock star Johnny Gentle. Soon after the group, who would become the era's top selling album artists as The Beatles, performed in Liverpool alongside Gerry & The Pacemakers before heading off to Hamburg for their first overseas work.

• Humorous albums were selling well on both sides of the Atlantic. In Britain **This Is Tony Hancock** and **Songs For Swinging Sellers** by fellow radio star Peter Sellers led the way. Hot on their heels were **Best Of The Goon Shows** – which featured Sellers, Harry Secombe and Spike Milligan – and the American album **An Evening Wasted With Tom Lehrer**. In the USA, funny man Bob Newhart (below) made his debut with **The Button Down Mind Of Bob Newhart**. The album went on to spend three months at the summit and earned Newhart three Grammy awards.

US 1960

APR-JUNE

April 1960

This Mnth	Last Mnth	Title	Artist	Label	Wks in 10	UK Pos	
1	1	**The Sound Of Music**	Original Cast	Columbia	63	4	
2	2	**60 Years Of Music America Loves Best**	Various	RCA	28		
3	-	**Theme From A Summer Place**	Billy Vaughn	Dot	17		
4	3	**Faithfully**	Johnny Mathis	Columbia	16		
5	6	**Italian Favorites**	Connie Francis	MGM	14		F
6	4	**Here We Go Again!**	Kingston Trio	Capitol	19		
7	-	**This Is Darin**	Bobby Darin	Atco	10	4	
8	5	**Heavenly**	Johnny Mathis	Columbia	17		P
9	9	**That's All**	Bobby Darin	Atco	8	15	F
10	7	**Outside Shelley Berman**	Shelley Berman	Verve	13		

May 1960

This Mnth	Last Mnth	Title	Artist	Label	Wks in 10	UK Pos	
1	3	**Theme From A Summer Place**	Billy Vaughn	Dot	17		
2	-	**Sold Out**	Kingston Trio	Capitol	25		
3	1	**The Sound Of Music**	Original Cast	Columbia	63	4	
4	2	**60 Years Of Music America Loves Best**	Various	RCA	28		
5	-	**Elvis Is Back!**	Elvis Presley	RCA	20	1	
6	5	**Italian Favorites**	Connie Francis	MGM	14		F
7	-	**Music From Mr. Lucky**	Henry Mancini	RCA	15		
8	-	**Encore Of Golden Hits**	Platters	Mercury	21		L
9	7	**This Is Darin**	Bobby Darin	Atco	10	4	
10	-	**The Button Down Mind Of Bob Newhart**	Bob Newhart	Warner	43	2	F

June 1960

This Mnth	Last Mnth	Title	Artist	Label	Wks in 10	UK Pos	
1	2	**Sold Out**	Kingston Trio	Capitol	25		
2	5	**Elvis Is Back!**	Elvis Presley	RCA	20	1	
3	10	**The Button Down Mind Of Bob Newhart**	Bob Newhart	Warner	43	2	F
4	3	**The Sound Of Music**	Original Cast	Columbia	63	4	
5	1	**Theme From A Summer Place**	Billy Vaughn	Dot	17		
6	7	**Music From Mr. Lucky**	Henry Mancini	RCA	15		
7	-	**Can-Can**	Soundtrack	Capitol	11	2	
8	4	**60 Years Of Music America Loves Best**	Various	RCA	28		
9	-	**Mario Lanza Sings Caruso Favorites**	Mario Lanza	RCA	13	3	L
10	8	**Encore Of Golden Hits**	Platters	Mercury	21		L

- **Elvis Is Back** was the aptly titled album from the newly demobbed Elvis Presley. The 'King' was only kept from the top spot in the USA by the Kingston Trio's **Sold Out**. For the record, the album did reach Number 1 in the UK.

- Canadian born Percy Faith and his Orchestra may have had America's Number 1 single with 'Theme From A Summer Place' but it was Dot Records' A&R head Billy Vaughn & His Orchestra, the person behind Pat Boone's string of hits, who had the biggest selling album.

- Mario Lanza may have died in October 1959, but the singer who had been the most popular operatic tenor in the Fifties, was not only represented on the Top 10 with his **Sings Caruso** set, but could also be heard on the top selling **Sixty Years Of Music America Loves Best** compilation album.

- Platters lead vocalist, Tony Williams, who had sung on all five of the group's million-selling singles, announced that he was quitting the group as **Encore Of Golden Hits** gave the mixed doo-wop quintet the biggest album of their career.

UK 1960 JULY-SEPT

July 1960

This Mnth	Last Mnth	Title	Artist	Label	Wks in 10	US Pos	
1	1	**South Pacific**	Soundtrack	RCA	179	1	
2	-	**It's Everly Time**	Everly Brothers	Warner	17	9	F
3	2	**Can-Can**	Soundtrack	Capitol	19	4	
4	8	**My Fair Lady**	Original Broadway Cast	Philips	26	1	
5	-	**Elvis' Golden Records Vol. 2**	Elvis Presley	RCA	11	31	
6	4	**Flower Drum Song**	Original Broadway Cast	Philips	22	1	
7	5	**Gigi**	Soundtrack	MGM	22	1	
8	-	**Elvis Is Back**	Elvis Presley	RCA	20	2	
9	-	**The Five Pennies**	Soundtrack	London	4	22	
10	9	**Cliff Sings**	Cliff Richard	Columbia	14		

August 1960

This Mnth	Last Mnth	Title	Artist	Label	Wks in 10	US Pos	
1	1	**South Pacific**	Soundtrack	RCA	179	1	
2	8	**Elvis Is Back**	Elvis Presley	RCA	20	2	
3	2	**It's Everly Time**	Everly Brothers	Warner	17	9	F
4	-	**The Great Caruso**	Mario Lanza	RCA	10	5	L
5	5	**Elvis' Golden Records Vol. 2**	Elvis Presley	RCA	11	31	
6	4	**My Fair Lady**	Original Broadway Cast	Philips	26	1	
7	6	**Flower Drum Song**	Original Broadway Cast	Philips	22	1	
8	3	**Can-Can**	Soundtrack	Capitol	19	4	
9	7	**Gigi**	Soundtrack	MGM	22	1	
10	-	**Come Back To Sorrento**	Frank Sinatra	Fontana	3		

September 1960

This Mnth	Last Mnth	Title	Artist	Label	Wks in 10	US Pos	
1	-	**Down Drury Lane To Memory Lane**	One Hundred & One Strings	Pye Golden Guinea	16		L
2	1	**South Pacific**	Soundtrack	RCA	179	1	
3	2	**Elvis Is Back**	Elvis Presley	RCA	20	2	
4	3	**It's Everly Time**	Everly Brothers	Warner	17	9	F
5	-	**At The Oxford Union**	Gerard Hoffnung	Decca	12		FL
6	6	**My Fair Lady**	Original Broadway Cast	Philips	26	1	
7	4	**The Great Caruso**	Mario Lanza	RCA	10	5	L
8	-	**Oklahoma**	Soundtrack	Capitol	22	1	
9	-	**Oliver**	Original London Cast	Decca	55	4	
10	-	**The Best Of Sellers**	Peter Sellers	Parlophone	4		F

• Budget-priced albums had been instantly successful when introduced to Britain at the end of the Fifties. Pye's Golden Guinea label led the field and America's 101 Strings were their top selling act. The orchestra's biggest seller was a tribute to the British musical stage tagged **Down Drury Lane To Memory Lane**. It temporarily replaced **South Pacific** at the top, and was the first instrumental album to head the UK lists.

• Leather-clad Gene Vincent, who narrowly escaped death in a UK car crash that killed fellow American rocker Eddie Cochran, had his sole British album entry with **Crazy Times,** which peaked just outside the Top 10. It was soon followed onto the chart by the **Eddie Cochran Memorial Album** which included all the late singer's hits.

• As usual, it was a clean sweep for American artists in the annual *NME* readers' poll. The major winners were Elvis Presley (Top Male), Connie Francis (Top Female) and The Everly Brothers (Top Group). Incidentally, Elvis Presley's **Golden Records Vol. 2** joined **Elvis Is Back** on the charts and The Everly's were enjoying the biggest UK chart album of their career with **It's Everly Time**.

US 1960 JULY-SEPT

July 1960

This Mnth	Last Mnth	Title	Artist	Label	Wks in 10	UK Pos	
1	1	**Sold Out**	Kingston Trio	Capitol	25		
2	3	**The Button Down Mind Of Bob Newhart**	Bob Newhart	Warner	43	2	F
3	2	**Elvis Is Back!**	Elvis Presley	RCA	20	1	
4	4	**The Sound Of Music**	Original Cast	Columbia	63	4	
5	6	**Music From Mr. Lucky**	Henry Mancini	RCA	15		
6	7	**Can-Can**	Soundtrack	Capitol	11	2	
7	5	**Theme From A Summer Place**	Billy Vaughn	Dot	17		
8	10	**Encore Of Golden Hits**	Platters	Mercury	21		L
9	9	**Mario Lanza Sings Caruso Favorites**	Mario Lanza	RCA	13	3	L
10	-	**Sentimental Sing Along With Mitch**	Mitch Miller	Columbia	1		

August 1960

This Mnth	Last Mnth	Title	Artist	Label	Wks in 10	UK Pos	
1	2	**The Button Down Mind Of Bob Newhart**	Bob Newhart	Warner	43	2	F
2	1	**Sold Out**	Kingston Trio	Capitol	25		
3	4	**The Sound Of Music**	Original Cast	Columbia	63	4	
4	3	**Elvis Is Back!**	Elvis Presley	RCA	20	1	
5	-	**The Edge Of Shelley Berman**	Shelley Berman	Verve	21		L
6	8	**Encore Of Golden Hits**	Platters	Mercury	21		L
7	-	**Paul Anka Sings His Big 15**	Paul Anka	ABC Paramount	12		F
8	9	**Mario Lanza Sings Caruso Favorites**	Mario Lanza	RCA	13	3	L
9	5	**Music From Mr. Lucky**	Henry Mancini	RCA	15		
10	6	**Can-Can**	Soundtrack	Capitol	11	2	

September 1960

This Mnth	Last Mnth	Title	Artist	Label	Wks in 10	UK Pos	
1	-	**String Along**	Kingston Trio	Capitol	19		
2	1	**The Button Down Mind Of Bob Newhart**	Bob Newhart	Warner	43	2	F
3	-	**Nice 'n' Easy**	Frank Sinatra	Capitol	18	4	
4	7	**Paul Anka Sings His Big 15**	Paul Anka	ABC Paramount	12		F
5	2	**Sold Out**	Kingston Trio	Capitol	25		
6	-	**Johnny's Moods**	Johnny Mathis	Columbia	16		
7	5	**The Edge Of Shelley Berman**	Shelley Berman	Verve	21		L
8	-	**Brenda Lee**	Brenda Lee	Decca	9		F
9	3	**The Sound Of Music**	Original Cast	Columbia	63	4	
10	4	**Elvis Is Back!**	Elvis Presley	RCA	20	1	

• Two teenagers who visited the charts for the first time were 15-year-old Brenda Lee and Paul Anka, who was three years her senior. Brenda's eponymous album included her chart topper 'I'm Sorry'; Anka's Number 1 hits 'Diana' and 'Lonely Boy' were featured on his **Big 15**.

• The fact that an album contained no Top 20 singles did not mean that it could not reach the upper rungs of the album chart; **String Along**, the Kingston Trio's fifth chart topper in less than two years, contained no major hits and neither did Frank Sinatra's **Nice 'n' Easy** or the Johnny Mathis album **Johnny's Moods**.

• In the early Fifties Columbia's A&R executive Mitch Miller produced hit after hit for acts such as Frankie Laine, Guy Mitchell, Johnnie Ray and Doris Day. In 1958 Miller discovered there was also gold to be found in 'Sing-Along' albums and again hit followed hit. **Sentimental Sing Along With Mitch**, the seventh gold album of the series, was a collection of well-known ditties, the most recent of which was a quarter of a century old.

UK 1960

OCT-DEC

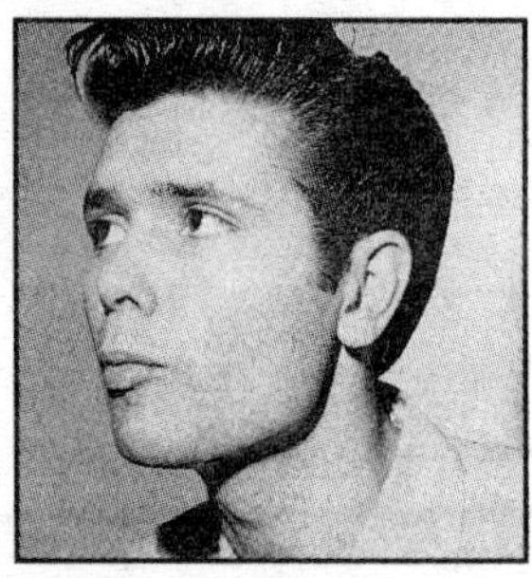

• Britain's top selling act, Cliff Richard returned to the chart with **Me And My Shadows**, which included his Shadows-penned hit single 'Gee Whiz It's You'. Incidentally, The Shadows, who were now popular enough to tour the UK without their famous lead singer, became one of the first acts to make a video-disk. These disks were shown on special juke boxes in Europe. As the year ended Cliff & The Shadows started a six month residency at the prestigious London Palladium.

• The most notable new act on the UK album chart were The George Mitchell Minstrels whose **The Black And White Minstrel Show** was the first British album to top the UK chart and the first on EMI to sell over 100,000 copies. Despite their dated sound and politically incorrect 'blacked-up' appearance, Mitchell's Minstrels were one of the most popular acts in Britain in the early Sixties.

October 1960

This Mnth	Last Mnth	Title	Artist	Label	Wks in 10	US Pos	
1	2	**South Pacific**	Soundtrack	RCA	179	1	
2	1	**Down Drury Lane To Memory Lane**	One Hundred & One Strings	Pye Golden Guinea	16		L
3	3	**Elvis Is Back**	Elvis Presley	RCA	20	2	
4	5	**At The Oxford Union**	Gerard Hoffnung	Decca	12		FL
5	-	**Me And My Shadows**	Cliff Richard	Columbia	28		
6	4	**It's Everly Time**	Everly Brothers	Warner	17	9	F
7	9	**Oliver**	Original London Cast	Decca	55	4	
8	-	**The King And I**	Soundtrack	Capitol	12	1	
9	6	**My Fair Lady**	Original Broadway Cast	Philips	26	1	
10	-	**Fabulous Style Of The Everly Brothers**	Everly Brothers	London	5	23	

November 1960

This Mnth	Last Mnth	Title	Artist	Label	Wks in 10	US Pos	
1	1	**South Pacific**	Soundtrack	RCA	179	1	
2	5	**Me And My Shadows**	Cliff Richard	Columbia	28		
3	3	**Elvis Is Back**	Elvis Presley	RCA	20	2	
4	2	**Down Drury Lane To Memory Lane**	One Hundred & One Strings	Pye Golden Guinea	16		L
5	7	**Oliver**	Original London Cast	Decca	55	4	
6	-	**Oklahoma**	Soundtrack	Capitol	22	1	
7	-	**Button Down Mind Of Bob Newhart**	Bob Newhart	Warner	13	1	FL
8	-	**Swing Easy**	Frank Sinatra	Capitol	5		
9	-	**Buddy Holly Story Vol. 2**	Buddy Holly	Coral	5		
10	10	**Fabulous Style Of The Everly Brothers**	Everly Brothers	London	5	23	

December 1960

This Mnth	Last Mnth	Title	Artist	Label	Wks in 10	US Pos	
1	1	**South Pacific**	Soundtrack	RCA	179	1	
2	2	**Me And My Shadows**	Cliff Richard	Columbia	28		
3	-	**The Black And White Minstrel Show**	George Mitchell Minstrels	HMV	120		F
4	-	**Hi-Fi Companion Album**	Ray Conniff	Philips	25		F
5	-	**G.I. Blues (Soundtrack)**	Elvis Presley	RCA	48	1	
6	7	**Button Down Mind Of Bob Newhart**	Bob Newhart	Warner	13	1	FL
7	-	**Rhythms And Ballads Of Broadway**	Johnny Mathis	Fontana	5	6	
8	-	**Party Time**	Russ Conway	Columbia	7		L
9	-	**At The Oxford Union**	Gerard Hoffnung	Decca	12		FL
10	6	**Oklahoma**	Soundtrack	Capitol	22	1	

US 1960 OCT-DEC

October 1960

This Mnth	Last Mnth	Title	Artist	Label	Wks in 10	UK Pos	
1	1	**String Along**	Kingston Trio	Capitol	19		
2	3	**Nice 'n' Easy**	Frank Sinatra	Capitol	18	4	
3	2	**The Button Down Mind Of Bob Newhart**	Bob Newhart	Warner	43	2	F
4	6	**Johnny's Moods**	Johnny Mathis	Columbia	16		
5	7	**The Edge Of Shelley Berman**	Shelley Berman	Verve	21		L
6	8	**Brenda Lee**	Brenda Lee	Decca	9		F
7	-	**Kick Thy Own Self**	Dave Gardner	RCA	6		L
8	4	**Paul Anka Sings His Big 15**	Paul Anka	ABC Paramount	12		F
9	-	**Rejoice, Dear Hearts!**	Dave Gardner	RCA	8		F
10	5	**Sold Out**	Kingston Trio	Capitol	25		

November 1960

This Mnth	Last Mnth	Title	Artist	Label	Wks in 10	UK Pos	
1	3	**The Button Down Mind Of Bob Newhart**	Bob Newhart	Warner	43	2	F
2	2	**Nice 'n' Easy**	Frank Sinatra	Capitol	18	4	
3	1	**String Along**	Kingston Trio	Capitol	19		
4	-	**G.I. Blues (Soundtrack)**	Elvis Presley	RCA	26	1	
5	4	**Johnny's Moods**	Johnny Mathis	Columbia	16		
6	-	**The Button Down Mind Strikes Back!**	Bob Newhart	Warner	10		
7	5	**The Edge Of Shelley Berman**	Shelley Berman	Verve	21		L
8	-	**Encore Of Golden Hits**	Platters	Mercury	21		L
9	-	**60 Years Of Music America Loves Best, Vol. II**	Various	RCA	6		
10	-	**Wild Is Love**	Nat 'King' Cole	Capitol	3		

December 1960

This Mnth	Last Mnth	Title	Artist	Label	Wks in 10	UK Pos	
1	4	**G.I. Blues (Soundtrack)**	Elvis Presley	RCA	26	1	
2	1	**The Button Down Mind Of Bob Newhart**	Bob Newhart	Warner	43	2	F
3	6	**The Button Down Mind Strikes Back!**	Bob Newhart	Warner	10		
4	2	**Nice 'n' Easy**	Frank Sinatra	Capitol	18	4	
5	3	**String Along**	Kingston Trio	Capitol	19		
6	9	**60 Years Of Music America Loves Best, Vol. II**	Various	RCA	6		
7	5	**Johnny's Moods**	Johnny Mathis	Columbia	16		
8	7	**The Edge Of Shelley Berman**	Shelley Berman	Verve	21		L
9	-	**This Is Brenda**	Brenda Lee	Decca	5		L
10	-	**Say It With Music (A Touch Of Latin)**	Ray Conniff	Columbia	3		

• Tennessee comedian 'Brother' Dave Gardner briefly found himself with two albums simultaneously in the Top 10, **Kick Thy Own Self** and **Rejoice, Dear Hearts!** Fellow funny man Bob Newhart's follow-up, the aptly titled **The Button Down Mind Strikes Back**, quickly followed its predecessor to the top and for a while Newhart held two of the top three rungs.

• Ray Charles, who had been a top R&B star since 1954, was becoming the most talked about artist on the pop scene. The blind singer/songwriter/pianist and band leader had two of his albums in the Top 20, **The Genius Hits The Road** and **Ray Charles In Person**. Charting alongside Charles was relative R&B newcomer Chubby Checker with **The Twist**, an album that would go even higher a year later. Among the other R&B acts creating interest were 18-year-old ex-gospel singer, Aretha Franklin, Detroit group The Miracles and Mary Wells, the latter two giving new labels Tamla and Motown their first hit singles.

• Top DJ Clay Cole replaced payola victim Alan Freed as host of the annual *Christmas Rock & Roll Show* at Brooklyn's Paramount Theater. Headliners included Johnny Burnette, Chubby Checker, Bo Diddley, Dion, The Drifters, Bobby Rydell and Neil Sedaka.

UK 1961 JAN -MAR

• In the early days of stereo, recordings by Massachusetts born Ray Conniff and his Orchestra – not forgetting his Chorus and Singers – were extremely popular on both sides of the Atlantic. In Britain, **Hi-Fi Companion** added to his hit tally whilst in his homeland, a set entitled **Memories Are Made Of This** took him into the Top 10 for the ninth time.

• As The Beatles played their first of 274 shows at Liverpool's Cavern Club, Elvis Presley played his last live show for eight years at the Block Arena in Pearl Harbor, Hawaii. Presley's 17-song show raised $62,000 for the *USS Arizona* Memorial Fund. For the rest of the decade, Presley concentrated on his film career.

• Making her debut on the Top 20 was Shirley Bassey with **Shirley**. It was the first of more than two dozen hit albums for the Welsh song stylist – a total no other British-based female artist has matched.

January 1961

This Mnth	Last Mnth	Title	Artist	Label	Wks in 10	US Pos	
1	5	**G.I. Blues (Soundtrack)**	Elvis Presley	RCA	48	1	
2	1	**South Pacific**	Soundtrack	RCA	179	1	
3	2	**Me And My Shadows**	Cliff Richard	Columbia	28		
4	3	**The Black And White Minstrel Show**	George Mitchell Minstrels	HMV	120		F
5	4	**Hi-Fi Companion Album**	Ray Conniff	Philips	25		F
6	-	**Peter & Sophia**	Peter Sellers & Sophia Loren	Parlophone	9		L
7	-	**Adam**	Adam Faith	Parlophone	16		FL
8	8	**Party Time**	Russ Conway	Columbia	7		L
9	6	**Button-Down Mind Of Bob Newhart**	Bob Newhart	Warner	13	1	FL
10	-	**Nice 'n Easy**	Frank Sinatra	Capitol	22	1	

February 1961

This Mnth	Last Mnth	Title	Artist	Label	Wks in 10	US Pos	
1	1	**G.I. Blues (Soundtrack)**	Elvis Presley	RCA	48	1	
2	2	**South Pacific**	Soundtrack	RCA	179	1	
3	4	**The Black And White Minstrel Show**	George Mitchell Minstrels	HMV	120		F
4	10	**Nice 'n Easy**	Frank Sinatra	Capitol	22	1	
5	3	**Me And My Shadows**	Cliff Richard	Columbia	28		
6	5	**Hi-Fi Companion Album**	Ray Conniff	Philips	25		F
7	-	**Buddy Holly Story**	Buddy Holly	Coral	17	11	F
8	9	**Button-Down Mind Of Bob Newhart**	Bob Newhart	Warner	13	1	FL
9	6	**Peter & Sophia**	Peter Sellers & Sophia Loren	Parlophone	9		L
10	-	**Oklahoma**	Soundtrack	Capitol	22	1	

March 1961

This Mnth	Last Mnth	Title	Artist	Label	Wks in 10	US Pos	
1	1	**G.I. Blues (Soundtrack)**	Elvis Presley	RCA	48	1	
2	2	**South Pacific**	Soundtrack	RCA	179	1	
3	3	**The Black And White Minstrel Show**	George Mitchell Minstrels	HMV	120		F
4	4	**Nice 'n Easy**	Frank Sinatra	Capitol	22	1	
5	-	**A Date With The Everly Brothers**	Everly Brothers	Warner	12	9	
6	5	**Me And My Shadows**	Cliff Richard	Columbia	28		
7	-	**Adam**	Adam Faith	Parlophone	16		FL
8	6	**Hi-Fi Companion Album**	Ray Conniff	Philips	25		F
9	-	**Song Without End**	Soundtrack	Pye	5		
10	-	**Oliver**	Original London Cast	Decca	55	4	

US 1961 JAN -MAR

January 1961

This Mnth	Last Mnth	Title	Artist	Label	Wks in 10	UK Pos	
1	-	**Wonderland By Night**	Bert Kaempfert	Decca	13		F
2	-	**Mantovani Plays Music From Exodus And Other Great Themes**	Mantovani	London	11		
3	-	**Last Date**	Lawrence Welk	Dot	8		
4	-	**Exodus**	Soundtrack	RCA	31		
5	3	**The Button Down Mind Strikes Back!**	Bob Newhart	Warner	10		
6	9	**This Is Brenda**	Brenda Lee	Decca	5		L
7	-	**Belafonte Returns To Carnegie Hall**	Harry Belafonte	RCA	9		
8	-	**The Alamo**	Soundtrack	Columbia	6		
9	-	**Camelot**	Original Cast	Columbia	59	10	
10	-	**Temptation**	Roger Williams	Kapp	3		

February 1961

This Mnth	Last Mnth	Title	Artist	Label	Wks in 10	UK Pos	
1	4	**Exodus**	Soundtrack	RCA	31		
2	1	**Wonderland By Night**	Bert Kaempfert	Decca	13		F
3	-	**Calcutta!**	Lawrence Welk	Dot	23		
4	9	**Camelot**	Original Cast	Columbia	59	10	
5	-	**Great Motion Picture Themes**	Soundtrack (Compilation)	UA	29		
6	2	**Mantovani Plays Music From Exodus And Other Great Themes**	Mantovani	London	11		
7	3	**Last Date**	Lawrence Welk	Dot	8		
8	-	**Sinatra's Swingin' Session!!!**	Frank Sinatra	Capitol	14	6	
9	7	**Belafonte Returns To Carnegie Hall**	Harry Belafonte	RCA	9		
10	-	**Camelot**	Percy Faith	Columbia	4		L

March 1961

This Mnth	Last Mnth	Title	Artist	Label	Wks in 10	UK Pos	
1	3	**Calcutta!**	Lawrence Welk	Dot	23		
2	8	**Sinatra's Swingin' Session!!!**	Frank Sinatra	Capitol	14	6	
3	-	**Make Way!**	Kingston Trio	Capitol	18		
4	4	**Camelot**	Original Cast	Columbia	59	10	
5	5	**Great Motion Picture Themes**	Soundtrack (Compilation)	UA	29		
6	1	**Exodus**	Soundtrack	RCA	31		
7	-	**Memories Are Made Of This**	Ray Conniff	Columbia	5	14	
8	-	**Tonight: In Person**	Limeliters	RCA	4		F
9	-	**Wildcat**	Original Cast	RCA	4		
10	-	**B.M.O.C. (Best Music On/Off Campus)**	Brothers Four	Columbia	2		FL

• In the first quarter of 1961 only records which had spent nine weeks or less on the chart were included in the US Top 10. This temporary change meant that top selling albums from acts such as Elvis, Bob Newhart, Frank Sinatra and The Kingston Trio were excluded. It also meant that several albums that normally would have had a less impressive chart career showed up in the Top 10.

• 1960 was very good for German orchestra leader/producer/arranger Bert Kaempfert. His album and single both entitled **Wonderland By Night** were the first Number 1s of the year, and his composition 'Wooden Heart' was featured on **G.I. Blues**, the Elvis album that he had dethroned at the top. Later in the year, he became the first person to produce British act The Beatles.

• The most successful British-based album act in the States was undoubtedly Mantovani, whose album **Mantovani Plays Music From Exodus And Other Great Themes** earned the Italian-born orchestra leader his fifth US gold record. *Exodus* was one of the most successful movies of the period and it was no surprise that the soundtrack album, which featured The Sinfonia Of London Orchestra, reached the top. It also grabbed the Grammy for Best Soundtrack and its main theme was voted Song Of The Year.

UK 1961

APR-JUNE

April 1961

This Mnth	Last Mnth	Title	Artist	Label	Wks in 10	US Pos	
1	1	**G.I. Blues (Soundtrack)**	Elvis Presley	RCA	48	1	
2	2	**South Pacific**	Soundtrack	RCA	179	1	
3	3	**The Black And White Minstrel Show**	George Mitchell Minstrels	HMV	120		F
4	5	**A Date With The Everly Brothers**	Everly Brothers	Warner	12	9	
5	4	**Nice 'n' Easy**	Frank Sinatra	Capitol	22	1	
6	6	**Me And My Shadows**	Cliff Richard	Columbia	28		
7	-	**Listen To Cliff**	Cliff Richard	Columbia	19		
8	7	**Adam**	Adam Faith	Parlophone	16		FL
9	8	**Hi-Fi Companion Album**	Ray Conniff	Philips	25		F
10	-	**Oklahoma**	Soundtrack	Capitol	22	1	

• Britain's top new teen idol, Adam Faith, scored his only Top 10 album, **Adam**, which included Brook Benton's recent US hit 'So Many Ways' and two Fabian favourites, 'Turn Me Loose' and 'I'm A Man'. It did, of course, also include several standards as did his rival Cliff Richard's fourth LP, **Listen with Cliff** – which gave him his third successive Number 2 album.

May 1961

This Mnth	Last Mnth	Title	Artist	Label	Wks in 10	US Pos	
1	1	**G.I. Blues (Soundtrack)**	Elvis Presley	RCA	48	1	
2	2	**South Pacific**	Soundtrack	RCA	179	1	
3	7	**Listen To Cliff**	Cliff Richard	Columbia	19		
4	3	**The Black And White Minstrel Show**	George Mitchell Minstrels	HMV	120		F
5	-	**Seven Brides For Seven Brothers**	Soundtrack	MGM	11		
6	5	**Nice 'n' Easy**	Frank Sinatra	Capitol	22	1	
7	4	**A Date With The Everly Brothers**	Everly Brothers	Warner	12	9	
8	-	**A Million Dollars' Worth Of Twang**	Duane Eddy	London	6	11	
9	9	**Hi-Fi Companion Album**	Ray Conniff	Philips	25		F
10	-	**His Hand In Mine**	Elvis Presley	RCA	16	13	

• You could say that 1961 was a very good year for Frank Sinatra. In the first six months his albums **Nice 'n' Easy**, **Sinatra's Swingin' Session!!!** and **All The Way** had helped maintain his position as a top transatlantic star. Added to this, **Ring-A Ding Ding!**, the first release on his own label, Reprise, looked set to repeat its American success.

• The big screen still provided many hit albums. Numbered among the best selling movie soundtracks were: **G.I. Blues**, **South Pacific**, **Oklahoma**, **The King And I**, **Song Without End** and **Seven Brides For Seven Brothers**.

June 1961

This Mnth	Last Mnth	Title	Artist	Label	Wks in 10	US Pos	
1	1	**G.I. Blues (Soundtrack)**	Elvis Presley	RCA	48	1	
2	2	**South Pacific**	Soundtrack	RCA	179	1	
3	3	**Listen To Cliff**	Cliff Richard	Columbia	19		
4	4	**The Black And White Minstrel Show**	George Mitchell Minstrels	HMV	120		F
5	10	**His Hand In Mine**	Elvis Presley	RCA	16	13	
6	-	**Best Of Barber And Bilk Vol. 1**	Chris Barber And Acker Bilk	Pye Golden Guinea	22		F
7	5	**Seven Brides For Seven Brothers**	Soundtrack	MGM	11		
8	-	**Music Man**	Original London Cast	JMH	7		
9	-	**Oliver**	Original London Cast	Decca	55	4	
10	6	**Nice 'n' Easy**	Frank Sinatra	Capitol	22	1	

US 1961 APR-JUNE

April 1961

This Mnth	Last Mnth	Title	Artist	Label	Wks in 10	UK Pos	
1	1	**Calcutta!**	Lawrence Welk	Dot	23		
2	-	**G.I. Blues (Soundtrack)**	Elvis Presley	RCA	26	1	
3	6	**Exodus**	Soundtrack	RCA	31		
4	5	**Great Motion Picture Themes**	Soundtrack (Compilation)	UA	29		
5	4	**Camelot**	Original Cast	Columbia	59	10	
6	3	**Make Way!**	Kingston Trio	Capitol	18		
7	-	**The Button Down Mind Of Bob Newhart**	Bob Newhart	Warner	43	2	F
8	-	**Wonderland By Night**	Bert Kaempfert	Decca	13		F
9	-	**The Button Down Mind Strikes Back!**	Bob Newhart	Warner	10		
10	2	**Sinatra's Swingin' Session!!!**	Frank Sinatra	Capitol	14	6	

May 1961

This Mnth	Last Mnth	Title	Artist	Label	Wks in 10	UK Pos	
1	2	**G.I. Blues (Soundtrack)**	Elvis Presley	RCA	26	1	
2	1	**Calcutta!**	Lawrence Welk	Dot	23		
3	5	**Camelot**	Original Cast	Columbia	59	10	
4	3	**Exodus**	Soundtrack	RCA	31		
5	6	**Make Way!**	Kingston Trio	Capitol	18		
6	4	**Great Motion Picture Themes**	Soundtrack (Compilation)	UA	29		
7	-	**All The Way**	Frank Sinatra	Capitol	10		
8	7	**The Button Down Mind Of Bob Newhart**	Bob Newhart	Warner	43	2	F
9	10	**Sinatra's Swingin' Session!!!**	Frank Sinatra	Capitol	14	6	
10	-	**Ring-A-Ding Ding!**	Frank Sinatra	Reprise	7	8	

June 1961

This Mnth	Last Mnth	Title	Artist	Label	Wks in 10	UK Pos	
1	3	**Camelot**	Original Cast	Columbia	59	10	
2	1	**G.I. Blues (Soundtrack)**	Elvis Presley	RCA	26	1	
3	2	**Calcutta!**	Lawrence Welk	Dot	23		
4	6	**Great Motion Picture Themes**	Soundtrack (Compilation)	UA	29		
5	7	**All The Way**	Frank Sinatra	Capitol	10		
6	4	**Exodus**	Soundtrack	RCA	31		
7	-	**Never On Sunday**	Soundtrack	UA	19	17	
8	-	**Genius Plus Soul Equals Jazz**	Ray Charles	Impulse	7		
9	5	**Make Way!**	Kingston Trio	Capitol	18		
10	7	**The Button Down Mind Of Bob Newhart**	Bob Newhart	Warner	43	2	F

- The American album chart was extended to Top 150 mono and Top 50 stereo LPs. Previously there had been a Top 40 mono and Top 30 stereo chart.

- Future superstar Bob Dylan made his album debut playing harmonica on Harry Belafonte's **Midnight Special.** This was soon after he had made his first New York solo appearance at Gerde's Folk City. Dylan, one time member of teen idol Bobby Vee's backing band, was the support act to blues legend John Lee Hooker.

- Lawrence Welk, the polka playing king of 'champagne music', followed his Top 3 album, **Last Date**, with an even more successful selection of songs titled after his chart topping single 'Calcutta', which featured keyboard player Frank Scott. Incidentally, the catchy instrumental, which had given the veteran accordionist his biggest hit, had originally been recorded in the late Fifties under the title 'Tivoli Melody'.

- The half million dollars that CBS had invested in the musical show **Camelot** seemed to be paying off, as Lerner & Loewe's follow up to **My Fair Lady** followed its predecessor to the top. The stars of the Broadway production were Richard Burton, Julie Andrews and Robert Goulet.

UK 1961 JULY-SEPT

July 1961

This Mnth	Last Mnth	Title	Artist	Label	Wks in 10	US Pos	
1	2	**South Pacific**	Soundtrack	RCA	179	1	
2	4	**The Black And White Minstrel Show**	George Mitchell Minstrels	HMV	120		F
3	1	**G.I. Blues (Soundtrack)**	Elvis Presley	RCA	48	1	
4	6	**Best Of Barber And Bilk Vol. 1**	Chris Barber And Acker Bilk	Pye Golden Guinea	22		F
5	-	**Sound Of Music**	Original Cast	Philips	12	1	
6	3	**Listen To Cliff**	Cliff Richard	Columbia	19		
7	5	**His Hand In Mine**	Elvis Presley	RCA	16	13	
8	9	**Oliver**	Original London Cast	Decca	55	4	
9	-	**Tony**	Anthony Newley	Decca	6		F
10	8	**Music Man**	Original London Cast	JMH	7		

August 1961

This Mnth	Last Mnth	Title	Artist	Label	Wks in 10	US Pos	
1	2	**The Black And White Minstrel Show**	George Mitchell Minstrels	HMV	120		F
2	1	**South Pacific**	Soundtrack	RCA	179	1	
3	3	**G.I. Blues (Soundtrack)**	Elvis Presley	RCA	48	1	
4	4	**Best Of Barber And Bilk Vol. 1**	Chris Barber And Acker Bilk	Pye Golden Guinea	22		F
5	8	**Oliver**	Original London Cast	Decca	55	4	
6	6	**Listen To Cliff**	Cliff Richard	Columbia	19		
7	5	**Sound Of Music**	Original Cast	Philips	12	1	
8	9	**Tony**	Anthony Newley	Decca	6		F
9	7	**His Hand In Mine**	Elvis Presley	RCA	16	13	
10	-	**Sound Of Music**	Original London Cast	HMV	37		

September 1961

This Mnth	Last Mnth	Title	Artist	Label	Wks in 10	US Pos	
1	2	**South Pacific**	Soundtrack	RCA	179	1	
2	1	**The Black And White Minstrel Show**	George Mitchell Minstrels	HMV	120		F
3	3	**G.I. Blues (Soundtrack)**	Elvis Presley	RCA	48	1	
4	4	**Best Of Barber And Bilk Vol. 1**	Chris Barber And Acker Bilk	Pye Golden Guinea	22		F
5	-	**The Shadows**	Shadows	Columbia	50		F
6	5	**Oliver**	Original London Cast	Decca	55	4	
7	10	**Sound Of Music**	Original London Cast	HMV	37		
8	-	**When Your Lover Has Gone**	Frank Sinatra	Encore	6		
9	-	**Buddy Holly Story**	Buddy Holly	Coral	17	11	F
10	7	**Sound Of Music**	Original Cast	Philips	12	1	

• Instrumental combo The Shadows, whose single 'Kon Tiki' gave them their fifth successive Top 10 hit, saw their self-titled debut album soar to the top. It was the first album by a British rock act – and indeed the first by any rock group – to top the UK chart. Their long-time partner, Cliff Richard, was the next British artist to reach the summit, which he did a few weeks later with **21 Today**.

• The American music trade paper *Billboard* noted that for the first time since the British single charts had started in 1952, two thirds of the Top 30 records were of local origin. They also noted that the sale of stereo albums in the USA had been much slower than expected. In 1959, 23% of American LP sales had been in stereo; in 1960, this rose slightly to 28% and it was now just 32%.

• The chart was alive with **The Sound Of Music**, as both the London and the Original Broadway Cast of the highly touted Rodgers and Hammerstein musical shared the spoils in the UK. Later in the decade, the film soundtrack fared even better.

US 1961

JULY-SEPT

July 1961

This Mnth	Last Mnth	Title	Artist	Label	Wks in 10	UK Pos	
1	1	**Camelot**	Original Cast	Columbia	59	10	
2	-	**Carnival**	Original Cast	MGM	6		
3	-	**Stars For A Summer Night**	Various	Columbia	11		
4	6	**Exodus**	Soundtrack	RCA	31		
5	7	**Never On Sunday**	Soundtrack	UA	19	17	
6	-	**TV Sing Along With Mitch**	Mitch Miller	Columbia	8		
7	4	**Great Motion Picture Themes**	Soundtrack (Compilation)	UA	29		
8	2	**G.I. Blues (Soundtrack)**	Elvis Presley	RCA	26	1	
9	3	**Calcutta!**	Lawrence Welk	Dot	23		
10	8	**Genius Plus Soul Equals Jazz**	Ray Charles	Impulse	7		

August 1961

This Mnth	Last Mnth	Title	Artist	Label	Wks in 10	UK Pos	
1	3	**Stars For A Summer Night**	Various	Columbia	11		
2	-	**Something For Everybody**	Elvis Presley	RCA	9	2	
3	5	**Never On Sunday**	Soundtrack	UA	19	17	
4	-	**Exodus To Jazz**	Eddie Harris	Vee Jay	7		FL
5	6	**TV Sing Along With Mitch**	Mitch Miller	Columbia	8		
6	1	**Camelot**	Original Cast	Columbia	59	10	
7	-	**Goin' Places**	Kingston Trio	Capitol	8		
8	4	**Exodus**	Soundtrack	RCA	31		
9	-	**Rick Is 21**	Rick Nelson	Imperial	5		L
10	-	**Knockers Up!**	Rusty Warren	Jubilee	10		FL

September 1961

This Mnth	Last Mnth	Title	Artist	Label	Wks in 10	UK Pos	
1	-	**Judy At Carnegie Hall**	Judy Garland	Capitol	26	13	L
2	3	**Never On Sunday**	Soundtrack	UA	19	17	
3	2	**Something For Everybody**	Elvis Presley	RCA	9	2	
4	6	**Camelot**	Original Cast	Columbia	59	10	
5	-	**Yellow Bird**	Lawrence Welk	Dot	5		
6	7	**Goin' Places**	Kingston Trio	Capitol	8		
7	-	**Dance 'til Quarter To Three**	Gary (U.S.) Bonds	Legrand	4		FL
8	-	**Sinatra Swings**	Frank Sinatra	Reprise	6	8	
9	-	**Portrait Of Johnny**	Johnny Mathis	Columbia	15		
10	4	**Exodus To Jazz**	Eddie Harris	Vee Jay	7		FL

• A varied selection of LPs took turns at the top. The Fifties' most successful composer, Bob Merrill, penned **Carnival** which briefly replaced another musical, **Camelot**. Its successor was **Stars For A Summer Night**, a 25-track compilation that cleverly combined pop and classical music. Elvis then took over the helm with a potpourri-of-pop tagged **Something For Everybody** before being dethroned by veteran megastar Judy Garland's **Judy At Carnegie Hall**. Garland's critically acclaimed album won the one-time child star a couple of Grammy Awards – including Album Of The Year. It also proved to be the top album by a female artist in the Sixties.

• Teen idol Rick Nelson scored his third Top 10 album with **Rick Is 21**, which included the high flying tracks 'Travelin' Man' and 'Hello Mary Lou'. To coincide with his coming of age Ricky dropped the 'y' in his name.

UK 1961 OCT-DEC

October 1961

This Mnth	Last Mnth	Title	Artist	Label	Wks in 10	US Pos	
1	5	**The Shadows**	Shadows	Columbia	50		F
2	2	**The Black And White Minstrel Show**	George Mitchell Minstrels	HMV	120		F
3	7	**Sound Of Music**	Original London Cast	HMV	37		
4	6	**Oliver**	Original London Cast	Decca	55	4	
5	3	**G.I. Blues (Soundtrack)**	Elvis Presley	RCA	48	1	
6	1	**South Pacific**	Soundtrack	RCA	179	1	
7	4	**Best Of Barber And Bilk Vol. 1**	Chris Barber And Acker Bilk	Pye Golden Guinea	22		F
8	-	**Button-Down Mind Of Bob Newhart**	Bob Newhart	Warner	13	1	FL
9	-	**Another Black And White Minstrel Show**	George Mitchell Minstrels	HMV	24		
10	-	**Halfway To Paradise**	Billy Fury	Ace Of Clubs	4		F

• Two of the leading lights in the British trad jazz movement, Kenny Ball (above) and Acker Bilk, whose **Best Of Barber And Bilk** was on the chart, appeared at a rock-free Royal Variety Performance. The trad fad never spread to the USA despite the fact that Ball, Bilk and Barber all earned American gold records.

• In America, *Variety* magazine pronounced "Rock and roll is dying" and Frank Sinatra made it clear that no rock'n'roll would ever be released on his label. For the record, later in the decade Reprise signed such rock luminaries as The Kinks, Jimi Hendrix and Fleetwood Mac.

• Britain's Sinatra soundalike Matt Monro appeared on Ed Sullivan's top rated US TV show and in the annual *Billboard* DJ poll Monro was selected as Most Promising Artist and Top International Act. Another British-based artist scoring Stateside was orchestra leader Mantovani, who was presented with five gold albums when he arrived for a US tour.

November 1961

This Mnth	Last Mnth	Title	Artist	Label	Wks in 10	US Pos	
1	9	**Another Black And White Minstrel Show**	George Mitchell Minstrels	HMV	24		
2	-	**21 Today**	Cliff Richard	Columbia	8		
3	-	**Something For Everybody**	Elvis Presley	RCA	10	1	
4	6	**South Pacific**	Soundtrack	RCA	179	1	
5	1	**The Shadows**	Shadows	Columbia	50		F
6	2	**The Black And White Minstrel Show**	George Mitchell Minstrels	HMV	120		F
7	-	**That'll Be The Day**	Buddy Holly	Ace Of Hearts	7		
8	4	**Oliver**	Original London Cast	Decca	55	4	
9	-	**Sinatra Swings**	Frank Sinatra	Reprise	4	6	
10	3	**Sound Of Music**	Original London Cast	HMV	37		

December 1961

This Mnth	Last Mnth	Title	Artist	Label	Wks in 10	US Pos	
1	1	**Another Black And White Minstrel Show**	George Mitchell Minstrels	HMV	24		
2	6	**The Black And White Minstrel Show**	George Mitchell Minstrels	HMV	120		F
3	4	**South Pacific**	Soundtrack	RCA	179	1	
4	3	**Something For Everybody**	Elvis Presley	RCA	10	1	
5	-	**Blue Hawaii (Soundtrack)**	Elvis Presley	RCA	47	1	
6	5	**The Shadows**	Shadows	Columbia	50		F
7	8	**Oliver**	Original London Cast	Decca	55	4	
8	2	**21 Today**	Cliff Richard	Columbia	8		
9	-	**The Roaring Twenties - Songs From The TV Series**	Dorothy Provine	Warner	26	39	F
10	10	**Sound Of Music**	Original London Cast	HMV	37		

US 1961

OCT-DEC

October 1961

This Mnth	Last Mnth	Title	Artist	Label	Wks in 10	UK Pos	
1	1	**Judy At Carnegie Hall**	Judy Garland	Capitol	26	13	L
2	9	**Portrait Of Johnny**	Johnny Mathis	Columbia	15		
3	4	**Camelot**	Original Cast	Columbia	59	10	
4	-	**Jump Up Calypso**	Harry Belafonte	RCA	11		
5	-	**Jose Jiminez - The Astronaut (The First Man In Space)**	Bill Dana	Kapp	7		FL
6	-	**Sixty Years Of Music America Loves Best Vol. 3 (Black Seal)**	Various	RCA	6		
7	8	**Sinatra Swings**	Frank Sinatra	Reprise	6	8	
8	-	**Sixty Years Of Music America Loves Best Vol. 3 (Red Seal)**	Various	RCA Red Seal	4		
9	-	**Great Motion Picture Themes**	Soundtrack (Compilation)	UA	29		
10	3	**Something For Everybody**	Elvis Presley	RCA	9	2	

November 1961

This Mnth	Last Mnth	Title	Artist	Label	Wks in 10	UK Pos	
1	1	**Judy At Carnegie Hall**	Judy Garland	Capitol	26	13	L
2	-	**Blue Hawaii (Soundtrack)**	Elvis Presley	RCA	39	1	
3	3	**Camelot**	Original Cast	Columbia	59	10	
4	2	**Portrait Of Johnny**	Johnny Mathis	Columbia	15		
5	-	**Time Out Featuring 'Take Five'**	Dave Brubeck Quartet	Columbia	21	11	
6	4	**Jump Up Calypso**	Harry Belafonte	RCA	11		
7	-	**Close-Up**	Kingston Trio	Capitol	9		
8	-	**The Sound Of Music**	Original Cast	Columbia	63	4	
9	-	**I Remember Tommy...**	Frank Sinatra	Reprise	7	10	
10	-	**Exodus**	Soundtrack	RCA	31		

December 1961

This Mnth	Last Mnth	Title	Artist	Label	Wks in 10	UK Pos	
1	2	**Blue Hawaii (Soundtrack)**	Elvis Presley	RCA	39	1	
2	1	**Judy At Carnegie Hall**	Judy Garland	Capitol	26	13	L
3	7	**Close-Up**	Kingston Trio	Capitol	9		
4	5	**Time Out Featuring 'Take Five'**	Dave Brubeck Quartet	Columbia	21	11	
5	8	**The Sound Of Music**	Original Cast	Columbia	63	4	
6	3	**Camelot**	Original Cast	Columbia	59	10	
7	-	**Breakfast At Tiffany's (Soundtrack)**	Henry Mancini	RCA	37		
8	4	**Portrait Of Johnny**	Johnny Mathis	Columbia	15		
9	9	**I Remember Tommy...**	Frank Sinatra	Reprise	7	10	
10	6	**Jump Up Calypso**	Harry Belafonte	RCA	11		

- Noted jazz pianist Dave Brubeck and his quartet earned their fourth and biggest Top 10 hit with **Time Out Featuring 'Take Five'**. Lower down the chart another critically acclaimed jazz musician, Miles Davis, debuted with **Miles Davis In Person**.

- Joan Baez narrowly missed the Top 10 with her chart debut, **Joan Baez Volume 2**. At the same time Baez was breaking, fellow folk singers Peter, Paul & Mary were building up a following in Greenwich Village clubs, and Bob Dylan recorded his self-titled debut album which supposedly took only a day and cost under $500.

- Mitch Miller, the undoubted king of the 'sing-alongs' had four albums in the Top 20 over the Christmas period: **Holiday Sing Along With Mitch, TV Sing Along With Mitch, Your Request Sing With Mitch** and the original **Sing Along With Mitch,** which had been a fixture on the charts for three and a half years.

- The American music industry tried unsuccessfully to launch a series of 6-track, 7-inch 33 RPM 'Little LPs'.

- The doo-wop revival spread from the singles to album chart. **Oldies But Goodies Vol. III** entered the Top 20 and Murray The K's **Blasts From The Past** was not far behind.

UK 1962 JAN -MAR

• The first British soundtrack album to pass the million mark world-wide was **The Young Ones** by Cliff Richard & The Shadows. The film meant little in the USA, where it was re-titled *Wonderful To Be Young*. Nonetheless, a song taken from it, 'When The Girl (Boy) In Your Arms', was a Top 10 hit there when covered by Connie Francis. Incidentally, Britain's top selling female singer, 15-year-old Helen Shapiro, reached the runner-up position with her debut album, **Tops With Me** – a collection of recent covers including Connie's 'Lipstick On Your Collar'.

• The Beatles' German recording 'My Bonnie' received complimentary reviews. The combo made their live radio debut and were voted Top Group in the fanzine *Mersey Beat*. On the down side, they failed to pass an audition for Decca, who signed Brian Poole & The Tremeloes instead.

• American actress Dorothy Provine had two Top 10 albums in the UK: **The Roaring Twenties** and **Vamp Of The Roaring Twenties**. The albums were inspired by her character, flapper Pinky Pinkham, in the successful transatlantic TV series *The Roaring Twenties*. The music was not far removed from that on the George Martin-produced **Temperance Seven 1961** by the zany retro-band The Temperance Seven.

January 1962

This Mnth	Last Mnth	Title	Artist	Label	Wks in 10	US Pos	
1	-	**The Young Ones (Soundtrack)**	Cliff Richard	Columbia	30		
2	5	**Blue Hawaii (Soundtrack)**	Elvis Presley	RCA	47	1	
3	2	**The Black And White Minstrel Show**	George Mitchell Minstrels	HMV	120		F
4	1	**Another Black And White Minstrel Show**	George Mitchell Minstrels	HMV	24		
5	3	**South Pacific**	Soundtrack	RCA	179	1	
6	9	**The Roaring Twenties - Songs From The TV Series**	Dorothy Provine	Warner	26	39	F
7	6	**The Shadows**	Shadows	Columbia	50		F
8	10	**Sound Of Music**	Original London Cast	HMV	37		
9	-	**Ring-A-Ding-Ding**	Frank Sinatra	Reprise	4	6	
10	-	**Wimoweh**	Karl Denver	Ace Of Clubs	13		FL

February 1962

This Mnth	Last Mnth	Title	Artist	Label	Wks in 10	US Pos	
1	1	**The Young Ones (Soundtrack)**	Cliff Richard	Columbia	30		
2	2	**Blue Hawaii (Soundtrack)**	Elvis Presley	RCA	47	1	
3	3	**The Black And White Minstrel Show**	George Mitchell Minstrels	HMV	120		F
4	5	**South Pacific**	Soundtrack	RCA	179	1	
5	7	**The Shadows**	Shadows	Columbia	50		F
6	8	**Sound Of Music**	Original London Cast	HMV	37		
7	-	**Oliver**	Original London Cast	Decca	55	4	
8	4	**Another Black And White Minstrel Show**	George Mitchell Minstrels	HMV	24		
9	10	**Wimoweh**	Karl Denver	Ace Of Clubs	13		FL
10	-	**Temperance Seven 1961**	Temperance Seven	Parlophone	3		FL

March 1962

This Mnth	Last Mnth	Title	Artist	Label	Wks in 10	US Pos	
1	2	**Blue Hawaii (Soundtrack)**	Elvis Presley	RCA	47	1	
2	1	**The Young Ones (Soundtrack)**	Cliff Richard	Columbia	30		
3	3	**The Black And White Minstrel Show**	George Mitchell Minstrels	HMV	120		F
4	4	**South Pacific**	Soundtrack	RCA	179	1	
5	-	**The Roaring Twenties - Songs From The TV Series**	Dorothy Provine	Warner	26	39	F
6	-	**Tops With Me**	Helen Shapiro	Columbia	14		FL
7	5	**The Shadows**	Shadows	Columbia	50		F
8	-	**West Side Story**	Original Cast	Philips	3	5	
9	-	**West Side Story**	Soundtrack	Philips	154	1	10
10	6	**Sound Of Music**	Original London Cast	HMV	37		

US 1962 JAN-MAR

January 1962

This Mnth	Last Mnth	Title	Artist	Label	Wks in 10	UK Pos	
1	1	**Blue Hawaii (Soundtrack)**	Elvis Presley	RCA	39	1	
2	-	**Holiday Sing Along With Mitch**	Mitch Miller	Columbia	10		L
3	7	**Breakfast At Tiffany's (Soundtrack)**	Henry Mancini	RCA	37		
4	-	**Your Twist Party**	Chubby Checker	Parkway	27		
5	-	**Doin' The Twist At The Peppermint Lounge**	Joey Dee & The Starliters	Roulette	22		FL
6	-	**Twist With Chubby Checker**	Chubby Checker	Parkway	17	13	F
7	5	**The Sound Of Music**	Original Cast	Columbia	63	4	
8	-	**Bobby Rydell/Chubby Checker**	Bobby Rydell/ Chubby Checker	Cameo	6		L
9	9	**I Remember Tommy...**	Frank Sinatra	Reprise	7	10	
10	2	**Judy At Carnegie Hall**	Judy Garland	Capitol	26	13	L

February 1962

This Mnth	Last Mnth	Title	Artist	Label	Wks in 10	UK Pos	
1	1	**Blue Hawaii (Soundtrack)**	Elvis Presley	RCA	39	1	
2	5	**Doin' The Twist At The Peppermint Lounge**	Joey Dee & The Starliters	Roulette	22		FL
3	4	**Your Twist Party**	Chubby Checker	Parkway	27		
4	3	**Breakfast At Tiffany's (Soundtrack)**	Henry Mancini	RCA	37		
5	2	**Holiday Sing Along With Mitch**	Mitch Miller	Columbia	10		L
6	6	**Twist With Chubby Checker**	Chubby Checker	Parkway	17	13	F
7	7	**The Sound Of Music**	Original Cast	Columbia	63	4	
8	8	**Bobby Rydell/Chubby Checker**	Bobby Rydell/ Chubby Checker	Cameo	6		L
9	-	**For Twisters Only**	Chubby Checker	Parkway	7	17	
10	-	**Time Out Featuring 'Take Five'**	Dave Brubeck Quartet	Columbia	21	11	

March 1962

This Mnth	Last Mnth	Title	Artist	Label	Wks in 10	UK Pos	
1	1	**Blue Hawaii (Soundtrack)**	Elvis Presley	RCA	39	1	
2	3	**Your Twist Party**	Chubby Checker	Parkway	27		
3	2	**Doin' The Twist At The Peppermint Lounge**	Joey Dee & The Starliters	Roulette	22		FL
4	4	**Breakfast At Tiffany's (Soundtrack)**	Henry Mancini	RCA	37		
5	6	**Twist With Chubby Checker**	Chubby Checker	Parkway	17	13	F
6	-	**Let There Be Drums**	Sandy Nelson	Imperial	7		FL
7	-	**West Side Story**	Soundtrack	Columbia	-	1	3P
8	10	**Time Out Featuring 'Take Five'**	Dave Brubeck Quartet	Columbia	21	11	
9	7	**The Sound Of Music**	Original Cast	Columbia	63	4	
10	-	**College Concert**	Kingston Trio	Capitol	16		

• Suddenly everyone was twisting. The R&B dance craze of 1960 had crossed over to the pop market and revitalized a somewhat stagnant scene. People of all ages around the world were cloning Chubby Checker's dance steps. Overnight, Checker – who had borrowed his two-time chart topping single, 'The Twist', from Fifties R&B stalwart Hank Ballard – was America's top selling album act with five albums in the Top 20. Checker proved rock-related albums could sell as well as so-called 'good music'. It was, however, Joey Dee & The Starliters' **Doin' The Twist At The Peppermint Lounge** that was credited as "the album that finally broke the sound barrier between rock and roll and the stereo album market".

• Arguably the most popular non-twist tune of the time was 'Moon River'. It came from Henry Mancini's soundtrack album to the Audrey Hepburn and George Peppard film **Breakfast At Tiffany's**. The song earned composer Mancini a couple of Grammy Awards and the LP was voted Best Soundtrack.

UK 1962 APR-JUNE

• The first British pop film soundtrack to reach the heights was **It's Trad Dad**. The film blended the twist and trad and starred British teen idols Helen Shapiro and Craig Douglas. It also featured guest spots by many top-line US acts including Chubby Checker, Gary U.S. Bonds, Del Shannon and Gene Vincent.

• The Twist, which had taken the world by storm only months earlier, began to lose momentum. As the bandwagon slowed down some of the younger performers jumped off and older acts like Frank Sinatra clambered belatedly on board.

• Jerry Lee Lewis returned to Britain four years after he was ignominiously sent packing when it was discovered that he had a 13-year-old bride. His tour was a great success and **Jerry Lee Lewis Vol. 2** climbed into the Top 20.

• Ex-Beatle Stuart Sutcliffe died in Germany, just days before the band arrived in Hamburg to appear at the Star Club. Meanwhile, in London, fellow R&B enthusiasts Mick Jagger and Brian Jones met for the first time at a blues club.

• The soundtrack album of Leonard Bernstein and Stephen Sondheim's **West Side Story** moved to the top on both sides of the Atlantic. It went on to become the biggest selling album of the decade in America.

April 1962

This Mnth	Last Mnth	Title	Artist	Label	Wks in 10	US Pos	
1	1	**Blue Hawaii (Soundtrack)**	Elvis Presley	RCA	47	1	
2	2	**The Young Ones (Soundtrack)**	Cliff Richard	Columbia	30		
3	6	**Tops With Me**	Helen Shapiro	Columbia	14		FL
4	9	**West Side Story**	Soundtrack	Columbia	154	1	
5	3	**The Black And White Minstrel Show**	George Mitchell Minstrels	HMV	120		F
6	7	**The Shadows**	Shadows	Columbia	50		F
7	5	**The Roaring Twenties - Songs From The TV Series**	Dorothy Provine	Warner	26	39	F
8	4	**South Pacific**	Soundtrack	RCA	179	1	
9	10	**Sound Of Music**	Original London Cast	HMV	37		
10	-	**Wimoweh**	Karl Denver	Ace Of Clubs	13		FL

May 1962

This Mnth	Last Mnth	Title	Artist	Label	Wks in 10	US Pos	
1	1	**Blue Hawaii (Soundtrack)**	Elvis Presley	RCA	47	1	
2	2	**The Young Ones (Soundtrack)**	Cliff Richard	Columbia	30		
3	4	**West Side Story**	Soundtrack	Columbia	154	1	
4	-	**It's Trad Dad**	Soundtrack	Columbia	17		
5	5	**The Black And White Minstrel Show**	George Mitchell Minstrels	HMV	120		F
6	3	**Tops With Me**	Helen Shapiro	Columbia	14		FL
7	6	**The Shadows**	Shadows	Columbia	50		F
8	7	**The Roaring Twenties - Songs From The TV Series**	Dorothy Provine	Warner	26	39	F
9	8	**South Pacific**	Soundtrack	RCA	179	1	
10	9	**Sound Of Music**	Original London Cast	HMV	37		

June 1962

This Mnth	Last Mnth	Title	Artist	Label	Wks in 10	US Pos	
1	1	**Blue Hawaii (Soundtrack)**	Elvis Presley	RCA	47	1	
2	3	**West Side Story**	Soundtrack	Columbia	154	1	
3	5	**The Black And White Minstrel Show**	George Mitchell Minstrels	HMV	120		F
4	4	**It's Trad Dad**	Soundtrack	Columbia	17		
5	9	**South Pacific**	Soundtrack	RCA	179	1	
6	2	**The Young Ones (Soundtrack)**	Cliff Richard	Columbia	30		
7	8	**The Roaring Twenties - Songs From The TV Series**	Dorothy Provine	Warner	26	39	F
8	6	**Tops With Me**	Helen Shapiro	Columbia	14		FL
9	7	**The Shadows**	Shadows	Columbia	50		F
10	-	**Sinatra And Strings**	Frank Sinatra	Reprise	9	8	

US 1962 APR-JUNE

April 1962

This Mnth	Last Mnth	Title	Artist	Label	Wks in 10	UK Pos	
1	1	**Blue Hawaii (Soundtrack)**	Elvis Presley	RCA	39	1	
2	2	**Your Twist Party**	Chubby Checker	Parkway	27		
3	4	**Breakfast At Tiffany's (Soundtrack)**	Henry Mancini	RCA	37		
4	7	**West Side Story**	Soundtrack	Columbia	-	1	3P
5	10	**College Concert**	Kingston Trio	Capitol	16		
6	3	**Doin' The Twist At The Peppermint Lounge**	Joey Dee & The Starliters	Roulette	22		FL
7	-	**A Song For Young Love**	Lettermen	Capitol	7		F
8	5	**Twist With Chubby Checker**	Chubby Checker	Parkway	17	13	F
9	-	**Camelot**	Original Cast	Columbia	59	10	
10	8	**Time Out Featuring 'Take Five'**	Dave Brubeck Quartet	Columbia	21	11	

May 1962

This Mnth	Last Mnth	Title	Artist	Label	Wks in 10	UK Pos	
1	4	**West Side Story**	Soundtrack	Columbia	-	1	3P
2	3	**Breakfast At Tiffany's (Soundtrack)**	Henry Mancini	RCA	37		
3	1	**Blue Hawaii (Soundtrack)**	Elvis Presley	RCA	39	1	
4	5	**College Concert**	Kingston Trio	Capitol	16		
5	2	**Your Twist Party**	Chubby Checker	Parkway	27		
6	-	**West Side Story**	Original Cast	Columbia	19	3	
7	7	**A Song For Young Love**	Lettermen	Capitol	7		F
8	6	**Doin' The Twist At The Peppermint Lounge**	Joey Dee & The Starliters	Roulette	22		FL
9	-	**Judy At Carnegie Hall**	Judy Garland	Capitol	26	13	L
10	-	**Modern Sounds In Country And Western Music**	Ray Charles	ABC Paramount	33	6	

June 1962

This Mnth	Last Mnth	Title	Artist	Label	Wks in 10	UK Pos	
1	1	**West Side Story**	Soundtrack	Columbia	-	1	3P
2	10	**Modern Sounds In Country And Western Music**	Ray Charles	ABC Paramount	33	6	
3	2	**Breakfast At Tiffany's (Soundtrack)**	Henry Mancini	RCA	37		
4	3	**Blue Hawaii (Soundtrack)**	Elvis Presley	RCA	39	1	
5	6	**West Side Story**	Original Cast	Columbia	19	3	
6	5	**Your Twist Party**	Chubby Checker	Parkway	27		
7	4	**College Concert**	Kingston Trio	Capitol	16		
8	-	**Stranger On The Shore**	Mr. Acker Bilk	Atco	11	6	FL
9	-	**Time Out Featuring 'Take Five'**	Dave Brubeck Quartet	Columbia	21	11	
10	-	**No Strings**	Original Cast	Capitol	4		

• Ray Charles continued to grow in status. A collection of his Fifties R&B classics, reissued under the cash-in title **Do The Twist**, including his often covered compositions 'What'd I Say' and 'I Got A Woman', narrowly missed the Top 10. Shortly afterwards, his newly recorded selection of Fifties country songs rocketed to the top. He was the first R&B artist to ever reach the Number 1 spot on the pop album chart.

• Clarinettist Acker Bilk's album **Stranger On The Shore** managed to repeat the feat of its title track by climbing into the US Top 3. Bilk's trad jazz cohort Kenny Ball was only slightly less successful with **Midnight In Moscow**. The title track reached the Top 3 but the album stalled just outside the Top 10.

• At the Grammy Awards top album sellers Chubby Checker and Ray Charles both picked up trophies. Checker took the award for Best Rock And Roll Record ('Let's Twist Again') and Charles grabbed the one for Best R&B recording ('Hit The Road Jack').

UK 1962 JULY-SEPT

• The trad jazz craze reached its peak as its foremost exponents Kenny Ball, Chris Barber and Acker Bilk topped the chart with a **Best Of** collection. For the record, it was the first jazz item to reach the summit.

• Top British songsmith Lionel Bart followed the very successful *Oliver!* with *Blitz,* a musical about London during World War II. Sadly for the composer, who had recently penned chart toppers for Cliff Richard and Anthony Newley, the show bombed out and its original cast recording spent only a brief time in the Top 10.

• Lonnie Donegan, the only British male singer at the time to boast two American Top 10 singles, was relishing his first album chart entry, **The Golden Age Of Donegan**. Simultaneously, over on the singles chart, 'Pick A Bale Of Cotton' was giving the 'Sultan of Skiffle' the last of his 28 successive Top 30 hits.

• Making his only visit to the Top 10 was the unmistakable cockney singer/songwriter Joe Brown with **A Picture Of You**. The record contained not only his chart topping single of that name but also his version of 'I'm Henry VIII, I Am' – a song which later earned Herman's Hermits a gold record.

July 1962

This Mnth	Last Mnth	Title	Artist	Label	Wks in 10	US Pos	
1	2	**West Side Story**	Soundtrack	Columbia	154	1	
2	1	**Blue Hawaii (Soundtrack)**	Elvis Presley	RCA	47	1	
3	3	**The Black And White Minstrel Show**	George Mitchell Minstrels	HMV	120		F
4	-	**Pot Luck**	Elvis Presley	RCA	20	4	
5	5	**South Pacific**	Soundtrack	RCA	179	1	
6	4	**It's Trad Dad**	Soundtrack	Columbia	17		
7	10	**Sinatra And Strings**	Frank Sinatra	Reprise	9	8	
8	-	**Stranger On The Shore**	Mr. Acker Bilk	Columbia	10	3	
9	6	**The Young Ones (Soundtrack)**	Cliff Richard	Columbia	30		
10	-	**Blitz**	Original London Cast	HMV	6		

August 1962

This Mnth	Last Mnth	Title	Artist	Label	Wks in 10	US Pos	
1	4	**Pot Luck**	Elvis Presley	RCA	20	4	
2	1	**West Side Story**	Soundtrack	Columbia	154	1	
3	3	**The Black And White Minstrel Show**	George Mitchell Minstrels	HMV	120		F
4	5	**South Pacific**	Soundtrack	RCA	179	1	
5	2	**Blue Hawaii (Soundtrack)**	Elvis Presley	RCA	47	1	
6	8	**Stranger On The Shore**	Mr. Acker Bilk	Columbia	10	3	
7	-	**The Shadows**	Shadows	Columbia	50		F
8	6	**It's Trad Dad**	Soundtrack	Columbia	17		
9	10	**Blitz**	Original London Cast	HMV	6		
10	7	**Sinatra And Strings**	Frank Sinatra	Reprise	9	8	

September 1962

This Mnth	Last Mnth	Title	Artist	Label	Wks in 10	US Pos	
1	2	**West Side Story**	Soundtrack	Columbia	154	1	
2	-	**The Best Of Ball, Barber And Bilk**	Kenny Ball, Chris Barber & Acker Bilk	Pye Golden Guinea	17		F
3	1	**Pot Luck**	Elvis Presley	RCA	20	4	
4	-	**The Golden Age Of Donegan**	Lonnie Donegan	Pye Golden Guinea	20		FL
5	3	**The Black And White Minstrel Show**	George Mitchell Minstrels	HMV	120		F
6	-	**A Picture Of You**	Joe Brown	Pye Golden Guinea	19		FL
7	5	**Blue Hawaii (Soundtrack)**	Elvis Presley	RCA	47	1	
8	4	**South Pacific**	Soundtrack	RCA	179	1	
9	7	**The Shadows**	Shadows	Columbia	50		F
10	-	**Twistin' & Twangin'**	Duane Eddy	RCA	6	82	L

US 1962

JULY-SEPT

July 1962

This Mnth	Last Mnth	Title	Artist	Label	Wks in 10	UK Pos	
1	2	**Modern Sounds In Country And Western Music**	Ray Charles	ABC Paramount	33	6	
2	1	**West Side Story**	Soundtrack	Columbia	-	1	3P
3	8	**Stranger On The Shore**	Mr. Acker Bilk	Atco	11	6	FL
4	3	**Breakfast At Tiffany's (Soundtrack)**	Henry Mancini	RCA	37		
5	5	**West Side Story**	Original Cast	Columbia	19	3	
6	-	**Peter, Paul & Mary**	Peter, Paul & Mary	Warner	84	18	F2P
7	4	**Blue Hawaii (Soundtrack)**	Elvis Presley	RCA	39	1	
8	-	**Moon River & Other Great Movie Themes**	Andy Williams	Columbia	16		F
9	-	**Rome Adventure**	Soundtrack	Warner	6		
10	-	**The Midnight Special**	Harry Belafonte	RCA	2		L

August 1962

This Mnth	Last Mnth	Title	Artist	Label	Wks in 10	UK Pos	
1	1	**Modern Sounds In Country And Western Music**	Ray Charles	ABC Paramount	33	6	
2	2	**West Side Story**	Soundtrack	Columbia	-	1	3P
3	-	**The Stripper And Other Fun Songs For The Family**	David Rose	MGM	11		FL
4	-	**Pot Luck**	Elvis Presley	RCA	9	1	
5	3	**Stranger On The Shore**	Mr. Acker Bilk	Atco	11	6	FL
6	6	**Peter, Paul & Mary**	Peter, Paul & Mary	Warner	84	18	F2P
7	5	**West Side Story**	Original Cast	Columbia	19	3	
8	-	**Vincent Edwards Sings**	Vincent Edwards	Decca	5		FL
9	9	**Rome Adventure**	Soundtrack	Warner	6		
10	4	**Breakfast At Tiffany's (Soundtrack)**	Henry Mancini	RCA	37		

September 1962

This Mnth	Last Mnth	Title	Artist	Label	Wks in 10	UK Pos	
1	1	**Modern Sounds In Country And Western Music**	Ray Charles	ABC Paramount	33	6	
2	2	**West Side Story**	Soundtrack	Columbia	-	1	3P
3	6	**Peter, Paul & Mary**	Peter, Paul & Mary	Warner	84	18	F2P
4	3	**The Stripper And Other Fun Songs For The Family**	David Rose	MGM	11		FL
5	-	**Roses Are Red**	Bobby Vinton	Epic	7		F
6	-	**The Music Man**	Soundtrack	Warner	14	14	
7	4	**Pot Luck**	Elvis Presley	RCA	9	1	
8	-	**Ray Charles' Greatest Hits**	Ray Charles	ABC Paramount	10	16	
9	-	**It Keeps Right On A-Hurtin'**	Johnny Tillotson	Cadence	2		FL
10	7	**West Side Story**	Original Cast	Columbia	19	3	

• Folk music was making its presence felt on the album chart. Peter, Paul & Mary's eponymous debut LP headed to the top spot, Harry Belafonte's **Midnight Special**, which featured Bob Dylan, briefly entered the Top 10 and Joan Baez had two albums in the Top 40.

• Producer/conductor/arranger and Columbia A&R head Mitch Miller was presented with ten gold albums for his amazingly successful **Sing Along** series.

• Ray Charles, who headed both the singles and albums charts, was not the only performer singing country songs in the Top 10. Both Bobby Vinton and Johnny Tillotson had some Nashville numbers on their albums, **Roses Are Red** and **It Keeps Right On A-Hurtin'** respectively. In fact, they both included the Hank Williams song 'I Can't Help It' and Patsy Cline's recent smash 'I Fall To Pieces'.

• Ray Stevens, made his album chart debut with **1,837 Seconds Of Humor** which included his single success 'Ahab, The Arab'.

UK 1962 OCT-DEC

October 1962

This Mnth	Last Mnth	Title	Artist	Label	Wks in 10	US Pos	
1	1	**West Side Story**	Soundtrack	Columbia	154	1	
2	2	**The Best Of Ball, Barber And Bilk**	Kenny Ball, Chris Barber & Acker Bilk	Pye Golden Guinea	17		F
3	4	**The Golden Age Of Donegan**	Lonnie Donegan	Pye Golden Guinea	20		FL
4	6	**A Picture Of You**	Joe Brown	Pye Golden Guinea	19		FL
5	3	**Pot Luck**	Elvis Presley	RCA	20	4	
6	-	**Out Of The Shadows**	Shadows	Columbia	29		
7	-	**32 Minutes And 17 Seconds**	Cliff Richard	Columbia	13		
8	5	**The Black And White Minstrel Show**	George Mitchell Minstrels	HMV	120		F
9	7	**Blue Hawaii (Soundtrack)**	Elvis Presley	RCA	47	1	
10	8	**South Pacific**	Soundtrack	RCA	179	1	

November 1962

This Mnth	Last Mnth	Title	Artist	Label	Wks in 10	US Pos	
1	6	**Out Of The Shadows**	Shadows	Columbia	29		
2	1	**West Side Story**	Soundtrack	Columbia	154	1	
3	3	**The Golden Age Of Donegan**	Lonnie Donegan	Pye Golden Guinea	20		FL
4	-	**On Stage With The George Mitchell Minstrels**	George Mitchell Minstrels	HMV	17		
5	2	**The Best Of Ball, Barber And Bilk**	Kenny Ball, Chris Barber & Acker Bilk	Pye Golden Guinea	17		F
6	4	**A Picture Of You**	Joe Brown	Pye Golden Guinea	19		FL
7	7	**32 Minutes And 17 Seconds**	Cliff Richard	Columbia	13		
8	-	**Bobby Vee Meets The Crickets**	Bobby Vee & The Crickets	Liberty	21	42	
9	8	**The Black And White Minstrel Show**	George Mitchell Minstrels	HMV	120		F
10	5	**Pot Luck**	Elvis Presley	RCA	20	4	

December 1962

This Mnth	Last Mnth	Title	Artist	Label	Wks in 10	US Pos	
1	9	**The Black And White Minstrel Show**	George Mitchell Minstrels	HMV	120		F
2	1	**Out Of The Shadows**	Shadows	Columbia	29		
3	2	**West Side Story**	Soundtrack	Columbia	154	1	
4	4	**On Stage With The George Mitchell Minstrels**	George Mitchell Minstrels	HMV	17		
5	8	**Bobby Vee Meets The Crickets**	Bobby Vee & The Crickets	Liberty	21	42	
6	6	**A Picture Of You**	Joe Brown	Pye Golden Guinea	19		FL
7	-	**South Pacific**	Soundtrack	RCA	179	1	
8	-	**Rock 'n' Roll No. 2**	Elvis Presley	RCA	14		
9	3	**The Golden Age Of Donegan**	Lonnie Donegan	Pye Golden Guinea	20		FL
10	5	**The Best Of Ball, Barber And Bilk**	Kenny Ball, Chris Barber & Acker Bilk	Pye Golden Guinea	17		F

• American teen idol and Buddy Holly (above) fan, Bobby Vee, had the biggest British album of his career with **Bobby Vee Meets The Crickets**, on which he was backed by Holly's old band. The set contained several rock'n'roll oldies including, naturally, a couple of Holly songs. Among the other tracks was Vee's version of 'Bo Diddley', a song which co-incidentally also appeared on The Shadows' second successive Number 1, **Out Of The Shadows**. Amazingly, Vee's original backing group were also called The Shadows!

• The Beatles, whose debut single, 'Love Me Do', had been a mid-table hit, supported rocker Little Richard on their first UK tour. Richard raved about them saying "they sounded like a black American act". Incidentally, in the annual *NME* Readers Poll, the Liverpool lads were voted fifth Best Vocal Group.

• For the third year in succession, The George Mitchell Minstrels made it a Black and White Christmas in Britain, by putting three of their LPs into the Top 10.

US 1962 OCT-DEC

October 1962

This Mnth	Last Mnth	Title	Artist	Label	Wks in 10	UK Pos	
1	2	**West Side Story**	Soundtrack	Columbia	-	1	3P
2	3	**Peter, Paul & Mary**	Peter, Paul & Mary	Warner	84	18	F2P
3	1	**Modern Sounds In Country And Western Music**	Ray Charles	ABC Paramount	33	6	
4	6	**The Music Man**	Soundtrack	Warner	14	14	
5	-	**Ramblin' Rose**	Nat 'King' Cole	Capitol	14		P
6	8	**Ray Charles' Greatest Hits**	Ray Charles	ABC Paramount	10	16	
7	-	**I Left My Heart In San Francisco**	Tony Bennett	Columbia	26	13	F
8	-	**Hatari!**	Henry Mancini	RCA	6		
9	4	**The Stripper And Other Fun Songs For The Family**	David Rose	MGM	11		FL
10	-	**Jazz Samba**	Stan Getz/Charlie Byrd	Verve	25	15	F

November 1962

This Mnth	Last Mnth	Title	Artist	Label	Wks in 10	UK Pos	
1	2	**Peter, Paul & Mary**	Peter, Paul & Mary	Warner	84	18	F2P
2	1	**West Side Story**	Soundtrack	Columbia	-	1	3P
3	5	**Ramblin' Rose**	Nat 'King' Cole	Capitol	14		P
4	3	**Modern Sounds In Country And Western Music**	Ray Charles	ABC Paramount	33	6	
5	10	**Jazz Samba**	Stan Getz/Charlie Byrd	Verve	25	15	F
6	4	**The Music Man**	Soundtrack	Warner	14	14	
7	7	**I Left My Heart In San Francisco**	Tony Bennett	Columbia	26	13	F
8	-	**My Son, The Folk Singer**	Allan Sherman	Warner	20		F
9	-	**Sherry & 11 Others**	Four Seasons	Vee Jay	5	20	F
10	-	**Modern Sounds In Country And Western Music (Volume 2)**	Ray Charles	ABC Paramount	11	15	

December 1962

This Mnth	Last Mnth	Title	Artist	Label	Wks in 10	UK Pos	
1	8	**My Son, The Folk Singer**	Allan Sherman	Warner	20		F
2	5	**Jazz Samba**	Stan Getz/Charlie Byrd	Verve	25	15	F
3	2	**West Side Story**	Soundtrack	Columbia	-	1	3P
4	10	**Modern Sounds In Country And Western Music (Volume 2)**	Ray Charles	ABC Paramount	11	15	
5	-	**The First Family**	Vaughn Meader	Cadence	17	12	F
6	1	**Peter, Paul & Mary**	Peter, Paul & Mary	Warner	84	18	F2P
7	-	**Girls! Girls! Girls! (Soundtrack)**	Elvis Presley	RCA	12	2	
8	7	**I Left My Heart In San Francisco**	Tony Bennett	Columbia	26	13	F
9	4	**Modern Sounds In Country And Western Music**	Ray Charles	ABC Paramount	33	6	
10	9	**Sherry & 11 Others**	Four Seasons	Vee Jay	5	20	F

- **Modern Sounds In C&W Music Vol. 2** by Ray Charles followed its predecessor up the chart. Simultaneously, Nashville announced that the term C&W was now old hat and that in future the music should simply be called country. Another black performer who dipped into country music was veteran Nat 'King' Cole for his **Ramblin' Rose** album.

- The first dance craze to catch on with adults since the twist was the bossa nova from South America. The first LP to benefit from the interest was **Jazz Samba** by noted jazz musicians Stan Getz and Charlie Byrd, which topped the stereo lists.

- Comedy albums were never more popular than in the early Sixties. The latest funny man to strike gold was Allan Sherman whose **My Son, The Folk Singer** replaced folk singers Peter, Paul & Mary in the top slot. It was superseded by Vaughn Meader's **The First Family**, an hilarious skit on President Kennedy and his family. Meader's album crushed previous sales records by shipping over three million in its first month!

- Among the artists enjoying their first album chart placing were such varied talents as The Beach Boys, Bo Diddley, Aretha Franklin, Quincy Jones, Marilyn Monroe, Gene Pitney, The Smothers Brothers and Jackie Wilson.

UK 1963 JAN -MAR

• Britain's two premier selling rock acts, Elvis and Cliff, fought for the top spot with the soundtrack albums from their latest films, **Girls! Girls! Girls!** and **Summer Holiday** respectively. This time Cliff, whose LP included the million selling single 'Bachelor Boy'/'The Next Time', pipped Presley at the post. For the record, Elvis, who had just signed to RCA for a further ten years, was also riding high with a re-issue of his second album from 1956, **Rock'n'Roll No. 2**.

• **All Star Festival** was one of the first successful charity albums with the vast majority of people associated with the recording giving their royalties to the United Nations Refugees Fund. Acts contributing included Doris Day, Bing Crosby, Louis Armstrong and Nat 'King' Cole. It is believed to have sold over a million copies worldwide.

• In Britain, the death of top American country singer Patsy Cline went almost unnoticed. However, over the years she has slowly attained cult status and in the Nineties her early Sixties recordings often appeared on the album charts.

• Ed Sullivan came to Britain to film Cliff Richard and Frank Ifield for his top rated US television show.

January 1963

This Mnth	Last Mnth	Title	Artist	Label	Wks in 10	US Pos	
1	2	**Out Of The Shadows**	Shadows	Columbia	29		
2	3	**West Side Story**	Soundtrack	Columbia	154	1	
3	5	**Bobby Vee Meets The Crickets**	Bobby Vee & The Crickets	Liberty	21	42	
4	8	**Rock 'n' Roll No. 2**	Elvis Presley	RCA	14		
5	1	**The Black And White Minstrel Show**	George Mitchell Minstrels	HMV	120		F
6	4	**On Stage With The George Mitchell Minstrels**	George Mitchell Minstrels	HMV	17		
7	7	**South Pacific**	Soundtrack	RCA	179	1	
8	-	**32 Minutes And 17 Seconds**	Cliff Richard	Columbia	13		
9	6	**A Picture Of You**	Joe Brown	Pye Golden Guinea	19		FL
10	-	**Summer Holiday (Soundtrack)**	Cliff Richard	Columbia	31		

February 1963

This Mnth	Last Mnth	Title	Artist	Label	Wks in 10	US Pos	
1	10	**Summer Holiday (Soundtrack)**	Cliff Richard	Columbia	31		
2	-	**Girls! Girls! Girls! (Soundtrack)**	Elvis Presley	RCA	18	3	
3	2	**West Side Story**	Soundtrack	Columbia	154	1	
4	1	**Out Of The Shadows**	Shadows	Columbia	29		
5	3	**Bobby Vee Meets The Crickets**	Bobby Vee & The Crickets	Liberty	21	42	
6	7	**South Pacific**	Soundtrack	RCA	179	1	
7	4	**Rock 'n' Roll No. 2**	Elvis Presley	RCA	14		
8	5	**The Black And White Minstrel Show**	George Mitchell Minstrels	HMV	120		F
9	6	**On Stage With The George Mitchell Minstrels**	George Mitchell Minstrels	HMV	17		
10	-	**I'll Remember You**	Frank Ifield	Columbia	32		F

March 1963

This Mnth	Last Mnth	Title	Artist	Label	Wks in 10	US Pos	
1	1	**Summer Holiday (Soundtrack)**	Cliff Richard	Columbia	31		
2	2	**Girls! Girls! Girls! (Soundtrack)**	Elvis Presley	RCA	18	3	
3	10	**I'll Remember You**	Frank Ifield	Columbia	32		F
4	-	**Sinatra - Basie**	Frank Sinatra & Count Basie	Reprise	15	5	
5	3	**West Side Story**	Soundtrack	Columbia	154	1	
6	4	**Out Of The Shadows**	Shadows	Columbia	29		
7	-	**All Star Festival**	Various	Philips	12		
8	5	**Bobby Vee Meets The Crickets**	Bobby Vee & The Crickets	Liberty	21	42	
9	6	**South Pacific**	Soundtrack	RCA	179	1	
10	7	**Rock 'n' Roll No. 2**	Elvis Presley	RCA	14		

US 1963 JAN - MAR

January 1963

This Mnth	Last Mnth	Title	Artist	Label	Wks in 10	UK Pos	
1	5	**The First Family**	Vaughn Meader	Cadence	17	12	F
2	1	**My Son, The Folk Singer**	Allan Sherman	Warner	20		F
3	3	**West Side Story**	Soundtrack	Columbia	-	1	3P
4	2	**Jazz Samba**	Stan Getz/Charlie Byrd	Verve	25	15	F
5	7	**Girls! Girls! Girls! (Soundtrack)**	Elvis Presley	RCA	12	2	
6	6	**Peter, Paul & Mary**	Peter, Paul & Mary	Warner	84	18	F2P
7	4	**Modern Sounds In Country And Western Music (Volume 2)**	Ray Charles	ABC Paramount	11	15	
8	8	**I Left My Heart In San Francisco**	Tony Bennett	Columbia	26	13	F
9	-	**Pepino The Italian Mouse & Other Italian Fun Songs**	Lou Monte	Reprise	6		FL
10	-	**Stop The World-I Want To Get Off**	Original Cast	London	5	8	

February 1963

This Mnth	Last Mnth	Title	Artist	Label	Wks in 10	UK Pos	
1	1	**The First Family**	Vaughn Meader	Cadence	17	12	F
2	2	**My Son, The Folk Singer**	Allan Sherman	Warner	20		F
3	-	**My Son, The Celebrity**	Allan Sherman	Warner	10		
4	3	**West Side Story**	Soundtrack	Columbia	-	1	3P
5	-	**(Moving)**	Peter, Paul & Mary	Warner	50		
6	4	**Jazz Samba**	Stan Getz/Charlie Byrd	Verve	25	15	F
7	6	**Peter, Paul & Mary**	Peter, Paul & Mary	Warner	84	18	F2P
8	5	**Girls! Girls! Girls! (Soundtrack)**	Elvis Presley	RCA	12	2	
9	8	**I Left My Heart In San Francisco**	Tony Bennett	Columbia	26	13	F
10	9	**Pepino The Italian Mouse & Other Italian Fun Songs**	Lou Monte	Reprise	6		FL

March 1963

This Mnth	Last Mnth	Title	Artist	Label	Wks in 10	UK Pos	
1	-	**Songs I Sing On The Jackie Gleason Show**	Frank Fontaine	ABC Paramount	18		FL
2	3	**My Son, The Celebrity**	Allan Sherman	Warner	10		
3	5	**(Moving)**	Peter, Paul & Mary	Warner	50		
4	1	**The First Family**	Vaughn Meader	Cadence	17	12	F
5	4	**West Side Story**	Soundtrack	Columbia	-	1	3P
6	2	**My Son, The Folk Singer**	Allan Sherman	Warner	20		F
7	-	**Richard Chamberlain Sings**	Richard Chamberlain	MGM	9	8	FL
8	6	**Jazz Samba**	Stan Getz/Charlie Byrd	Verve	25	15	F
9	-	**Moon River & Other Great Movie Themes**	Andy Williams	Columbia	16		F
10	7	**Peter, Paul & Mary**	Peter, Paul & Mary	Warner	84	18	F2P

• British stage musicals were having a relative boom period in the USA. The Original Cast album of Anthony Newley's **Stop The World I Want To Get Off** was in the Top 10 and close behind was the Original Cast recording of Lionel Bart's **Oliver!**

• The effect of television on album sales was evident. Frank Fontaine – who played Crazy Guggenheim on Jackie Gleason's top rated TV show – took his album of songs from that programme right to the top, and TV's Doctor Kildare, Richard Chamberlain, was not far behind.

• *Billboard* pointed out that not only were there more British records making it to the US charts but also hits were coming from other overseas countries such as Denmark, Germany, Italy, Canada and Brazil.

• The hit-packed album, **The Ventures Play Telstar The Lonely Bull & Others** and Johnny Mathis' (above) five-year-old **Johnny's Greatest Hits** were among the albums that bubbled under the Top 10.

UK 1963 APR-JUNE

• Liverpool groups The Beatles and Gerry & The Pacemakers toured the UK with American star Roy Orbison, who felt both British groups had what it took to make it in the States. The Beatles' first British album, **Please Please Me**, amassed record advance orders of over 100,000 copies. It quickly went to the top where it stayed until their second album, **With The Beatles**, replaced it in December. The group were also given their own radio show Pop Go The Beatles, recordings of which were finally released on their 1994 chart topping album **The Beatles At The BBC**.

• Despite the fact that he had died more than four years before, Buddy Holly's **Reminiscing** album was the biggest-selling album by an American artist this quarter. Other acts flying the stars and stripes included Brenda Lee with **All Alone Am I** and Elvis Presley whose soundtrack album to **It Happened At The World's Fair** was, as usual, a Top 10 hit on both sides of the Atlantic.

• R&B music was quickly becoming popular in Britain. Pye rushed out albums by early American R&B exponents Chuck Berry and Bo Diddley, and London R&B band The Rolling Stones cut their first single, a cover of Berry's 'Come On'.

April 1963

This Mnth	Last Mnth	Title	Artist	Label	Wks in 10	US Pos	
1	1	**Summer Holiday (Soundtrack)**	Cliff Richard	Columbia	31		
2	-	**Please Please Me**	Beatles	Parlophone	63		F
3	-	**Reminiscing**	Buddy Holly	Coral	26	40	
4	2	**Girls! Girls! Girls! (Soundtrack)**	Elvis Presley	RCA	18	3	
5	4	**Sinatra - Basie**	Frank Sinatra & Count Basie	Reprise	15	5	
6	5	**West Side Story**	Soundtrack	Columbia	154	1	
7	3	**I'll Remember You**	Frank Ifield	Columbia	32		F
8	7	**All Star Festival**	Various	Philips	12		
9	6	**Out Of The Shadows**	Shadows	Columbia	29		
10	9	**South Pacific**	Soundtrack	RCA	179	1	

May 1963

This Mnth	Last Mnth	Title	Artist	Label	Wks in 10	US Pos	
1	2	**Please Please Me**	Beatles	Parlophone	63		F
2	1	**Summer Holiday (Soundtrack)**	Cliff Richard	Columbia	31		
3	3	**Reminiscing**	Buddy Holly	Coral	26	40	
4	7	**I'll Remember You**	Frank Ifield	Columbia	32		F
5	6	**West Side Story**	Soundtrack	Columbia	154	1	
6	8	**All Star Festival**	Various	Philips	12		
7	4	**Girls! Girls! Girls! (Soundtrack)**	Elvis Presley	RCA	18	3	
8	-	**It Happened At The World's Fair (Soundtrack)**	Elvis Presley	RCA	17	4	
9	10	**South Pacific**	Soundtrack	RCA	179	1	
10	-	**All Alone Am I**	Brenda Lee	Brunswick	4	25	FL

June 1963

This Mnth	Last Mnth	Title	Artist	Label	Wks in 10	US Pos	
1	1	**Please Please Me**	Beatles	Parlophone	63		F
2	2	**Summer Holiday (Soundtrack)**	Cliff Richard	Columbia	31		
3	3	**Reminiscing**	Buddy Holly	Coral	26	40	
4	8	**It Happened At The World's Fair (Soundtrack)**	Elvis Presley	RCA	17	4	
5	5	**West Side Story**	Soundtrack	Columbia	154	1	
6	4	**I'll Remember You**	Frank Ifield	Columbia	32		F
7	-	**Billy**	Billy Fury	Decca	13		L
8	-	**Sinatra - Basie**	Frank Sinatra & Count Basie	Reprise	15	5	
9	-	**Greatest Hits**	Shadows	Columbia	41		
10	-	**Hats Off To Del Shannon**	Del Shannon	London	6		FL

US 1963 APR-JUNE

April 1963

This Mnth	Last Mnth	Title	Artist	Label	Wks in 10	UK Pos	
1	5	**West Side Story**	Soundtrack	Columbia	-	1	3P
2	1	**Songs I Sing On The Jackie Gleason Show**	Frank Fontaine	ABC Paramount	18		FL
3	3	**(Moving)**	Peter, Paul & Mary	Warner	50		
4	9	**Moon River & Other Great Movie Themes**	Andy Williams	Columbia	16		F
5	7	**Richard Chamberlain Sings**	Richard Chamberlain	MGM	9	8	FL
6	10	**Peter, Paul & Mary**	Peter, Paul & Mary	Warner	84	18	F2P
7	-	**I Left My Heart In San Francisco**	Tony Bennett	Columbia	26	13	F
8	-	**The Kingston Trio No. 16**	Kingston Trio	Capitol	9		
9	4	**The First Family**	Vaughn Meader	Cadence	17	12	F
10	-	**Big Girls Don't Cry & 12 Others**	Four Seasons	Vee Jay	2		

May 1963

This Mnth	Last Mnth	Title	Artist	Label	Wks in 10	UK Pos	
1	-	**Days Of Wine And Roses**	Andy Williams	Columbia	25		
2	1	**West Side Story**	Soundtrack	Columbia	-	1	3P
3	3	**(Moving)**	Peter, Paul & Mary	Warner	50		
4	8	**The Kingston Trio No. 16**	Kingston Trio	Capitol	9		
5	-	**It Happened At The World's Fair (Soundtrack)**	Elvis Presley	RCA	8	4	
6	2	**Songs I Sing On The Jackie Gleason Show**	Frank Fontaine	ABC Paramount	18		FL
7	-	**I Wanna Be Around**	Tony Bennett	Columbia	10		L
8	-	**Lawrence Of Arabia**	Soundtrack	Colpix	14		
9	6	**Peter, Paul & Mary**	Peter, Paul & Mary	Warner	84	18	F2P
10	4	**Moon River & Other Great Movie Themes**	Andy Williams	Columbia	16		F

June 1963

This Mnth	Last Mnth	Title	Artist	Label	Wks in 10	UK Pos	
1	1	**Days Of Wine And Roses**	Andy Williams	Columbia	25		
2	3	**(Moving)**	Peter, Paul & Mary	Warner	50		
3	2	**West Side Story**	Soundtrack	Columbia	-	1	3P
4	8	**Lawrence Of Arabia**	Soundtrack	Colpix	14		
5	-	**The First Family Vol. 2**	Vaughn Meader	Cadence	6		L
6	7	**I Wanna Be Around**	Tony Bennett	Columbia	10		L
7	5	**It Happened At The World's Fair (Soundtrack)**	Elvis Presley	RCA	8	4	
8	-	**Surfin' U.S.A.**	Beach Boys	Capitol	9	17	F
9	6	**Songs I Sing On The Jackie Gleason Show**	Frank Fontaine	ABC Paramount	18		FL
10	9	**Peter, Paul & Mary**	Peter, Paul & Mary	Warner	84	18	F2P

• Among the stars of the Newport Folk Festival were Peter, Paul & Mary, Joan Baez and Bob Dylan. The latter being described by *Billboard* as "The stuff of which legends are made". They also said "He is not just an individual; he is an absolute original", and prophesied "He will be around for a long long time".

• Andy Williams followed his **Moon River And Other Great Themes** album with the even more successful **Days Of Wine And Roses**. The latter LP, which topped the chart for four months, contained not only the Academy Award winning title song but also the million selling single 'Can't Get Used To Losing You' and his theme song 'May Each Day'.

• The Beach Boys followed their Top 40 debut album, **Surfin' Safari**, with **Surfin' USA** – the first surf album to crash the Top 10. Further down the chart, fellow surfers Jan and Dean debuted with **Jan and Dean Take Linda Surfin'**, which included the Beach Boys' breakthrough song 'Surfin' Safari'.

UK 1963 JULY-SEPT

• In America, Cliff Richard was voted Most Promising Male Vocalist in the prestigious teen magazine *16*. In Britain, neither **Greatest Hits** packages from Cliff or his backing band, The Shadows, could overtake The Beatles' debut album, **Please Please Me**. Another act that had to content themselves with the runner-up position behind the 'mop-tops' were another new Liverpool band, The Searchers, with **Meet The Searchers**.

• The release of the album **Introducing The Beatles** received little media attention in America. When re-issued in 1964 it reached the runner-up rung.

• As top pop TV show *Thank Your Lucky Stars* celebrated its 100th show, a new pop music show *Ready Steady Go* was launched. Early guests were Pat Boone, The Searchers, Kenny Ball and The Rolling Stones. The latter group also embarked on their first UK tour as support act to top-line US artists The Everly Brothers, Little Richard and Bo Diddley.

• In the hope of cashing-in on the success of Andy Williams' TV series youthful group The Osmonds released an album of songs that they had sung on the show. It failed to lift six-year-old Donny and his brothers onto the charts.

July 1963

This Mnth	Last Mnth	Title	Artist	Label	Wks in 10	US Pos	
1	1	**Please Please Me**	Beatles	Parlophone	63		F
2	9	**Greatest Hits**	Shadows	Columbia	41		
3	2	**Summer Holiday (Soundtrack)**	Cliff Richard	Columbia	31		
4	3	**Reminiscing**	Buddy Holly	Coral	26	40	
5	4	**It Happened At The World's Fair (Soundtrack)**	Elvis Presley	RCA	17	4	
6	5	**West Side Story**	Soundtrack	Columbia	154	1	
7	6	**I'll Remember You**	Frank Ifield	Columbia	32		F
8	-	**Cliff's Hit Album**	Cliff Richard	Columbia	14		
9	7	**Billy**	Billy Fury	Decca	13		L
10	-	**South Pacific**	Soundtrack	RCA	179	1	

August 1963

This Mnth	Last Mnth	Title	Artist	Label	Wks in 10	US Pos	
1	1	**Please Please Me**	Beatles	Parlophone	63		F
2	2	**Greatest Hits**	Shadows	Columbia	41		
3	8	**Cliff's Hit Album**	Cliff Richard	Columbia	14		
4	6	**West Side Story**	Soundtrack	Columbia	154	1	
5	5	**It Happened At The World's Fair (Soundtrack)**	Elvis Presley	RCA	17	4	
6	4	**Reminiscing**	Buddy Holly	Coral	26	40	
7	-	**Meet The Searchers**	Searchers	Pye	37	22	F
8	7	**I'll Remember You**	Frank Ifield	Columbia	32		F
9	3	**Summer Holiday (soundtrack)**	Cliff Richard	Columbia	31		
10	-	**Concert Sinatra**	Frank Sinatra	Reprise	9	6	

September 1963

This Mnth	Last Mnth	Title	Artist	Label	Wks in 10	US Pos	
1	1	**Please Please Me**	Beatles	Parlophone	63		F
2	7	**Meet The Searchers**	Searchers	Pye	37	22	F
3	2	**Greatest Hits**	Shadows	Columbia	41		
4	3	**Cliff's Hit Album**	Cliff Richard	Columbia	14		
5	4	**West Side Story**	Soundtrack	Columbia	154	1	
6	-	**Kenny Ball's Golden Hits**	Kenny Ball	Pye	18		L
7	6	**Reminiscing**	Buddy Holly	Coral	26	40	
8	8	**I'll Remember You**	Frank Ifield	Columbia	32		F
9	10	**Concert Sinatra**	Frank Sinatra	Reprise	9	6	
10	-	**Steptoe And Son**	Wilfrid Brambell & Harry H. Corbett	Pye	8		FL

US 1963 JULY-SEPT

July 1963

This Mnth	Last Mnth	Title	Artist	Label	Wks in 10	UK Pos	
1	1	**Days Of Wine And Roses**	Andy Williams	Columbia	25		
2	2	**(Moving)**	Peter, Paul & Mary	Warner	50		
3	8	**Surfin' U.S.A.**	Beach Boys	Capitol	9	17	F
4	3	**West Side Story**	Soundtrack	Columbia	-	1	3P
5	-	**Live At The Apollo**	James Brown	King	12		F
6	4	**Lawrence Of Arabia**	Soundtrack	Colpix	14		
7	10	**Peter, Paul & Mary**	Peter, Paul & Mary	Warner	84	18	F2P
8	-	**I Love You Because**	Al Martino	Capitol	6		F
9	5	**The First Family Vol. 2**	Vaughn Meader	Cadence	6		L
10	-	**The Barbra Streisand Album**	Barbra Streisand	Columbia	6		F

August 1963

This Mnth	Last Mnth	Title	Artist	Label	Wks in 10	UK Pos	
1	1	**Days Of Wine And Roses**	Andy Williams	Columbia	25		
2	2	**(Moving)**	Peter, Paul & Mary	Warner	50		
3	-	**Little Stevie Wonder/ The 12 Year Old Genius**	Stevie Wonder	Tamla	8		F
4	4	**West Side Story**	Soundtrack	Columbia	-	1	3P
5	5	**Live At The Apollo**	James Brown	King	12		F
6	-	**Trini Lopez At PJ's**	Trini Lopez	Reprise	21	7	FL
7	7	**Peter, Paul & Mary**	Peter, Paul & Mary	Warner	84	18	F2P
8	-	**My Son, The Nut**	Allan Sherman	Warner	12		L
9	-	**Shut Down**	Various	Capitol	5		
10	-	**Bye Bye Birdie**	Soundtrack	RCA	16		

September 1963

This Mnth	Last Mnth	Title	Artist	Label	Wks in 10	UK Pos	
1	8	**My Son, The Nut**	Allan Sherman	Warner	12		L
2	6	**Trini Lopez At PJ's**	Trini Lopez	Reprise	21	7	FL
3	10	**Bye Bye Birdie**	Soundtrack	RCA	16		
4	2	**(Moving)**	Peter, Paul & Mary	Warner	50		
5	7	**Peter, Paul & Mary**	Peter, Paul & Mary	Warner	84	18	F2P
6	4	**West Side Story**	Soundtrack	Columbia	-	1	3P
7	3	**Little Stevie Wonder/ The 12 Year Old Genius**	Stevie Wonder	Tamla	8		F
8	-	**Sunny Side!**	Kingston Trio	Capitol	4		L
9	-	**Ingredients In A Recipe For Soul**	Ray Charles	ABC Paramount	14		
10	1	**Days Of Wine And Roses**	Andy Williams	Columbia	25		

• The sales of mono and stereo albums in America were amalgamated for the first time and the first new Number 1 on the combined chart was **Little Stevie Wonder/The 12 Year Old Genius**. The young Motown artist, who was inspired by Ray Charles, was the first act to simultaneously hold the top spots on the singles and album charts. After a week at the summit, the 13-year-old was replaced by Alan Sherman, 25 years his senior, with his third successive chart topper in nine months, **My Son, The Nut**.

• After three months climbing the chart, **The Barbra Streisand Album** finally introduced the highly touted new vocalist to the Top 10.

• As new folk hero Bob Dylan enjoyed his first Top 40 entry with **The Freewheelin' Bob Dylan**, the older folk fans' favourites The Kingston Trio visited the Top 10 for the 14th and last time with **Sunny Side!**

• James Brown's self-financed **Live At The Apollo** album narrowly missed the top and became the first R&B album to sell over a million.

UK 1963 OCT-DEC

• New British groups reaching the album Top 10 for the first time included Brian Epstein's acts Gerry & The Pacemakers and Billy J. Kramer & The Dakotas, and Manchester's zany Freddie & The Dreamers.

• As the word 'Beatlemania' was added to the dictionary, the group's sophomore set, **With The Beatles**, shot to the top to round off an amazing year for Liverpool acts. With Merseybeat ruling the airwaves there was little room in Britain for the type of folk/protest music that was so popular across the Atlantic. In fact the only message song that made any noticeable dent was the Trini Lopez dance version of Peter, Paul & Mary's 1962 hit 'If I Had A Hammer'.

• For the first time British artists were voted World's top Male Singer and World's Top Group in the *NME* poll. The winners were – Cliff Richard & The Beatles. Incidentally, Cliff was second to The Beatles as the year's most successful singles act in the UK and his group, The Shadows, held off Merseybeat opposition to grab third place.

October 1963

This Mnth	Last Mnth	Title	Artist	Label	Wks in 10	US Pos	
1	1	**Please Please Me**	Beatles	Parlophone	63		F
2	2	**Meet The Searchers**	Searchers	Pye	37	22	F
3	3	**Greatest Hits**	Shadows	Columbia	41		
4	-	**Born Free**	Frank Ifield	Columbia	28		
5	6	**Kenny Ball's Golden Hits**	Kenny Ball	Pye	18		L
6	10	**Steptoe And Son**	Wilfrid Brambell & Harry H. Corbett	Pye	8		FL
7	5	**West Side Story**	Soundtrack	Columbia	154	1	
8	4	**Cliff's Hit Album**	Cliff Richard	Columbia	14		
9	-	**Chuck Berry On Stage**	Chuck Berry	Pye International	7	29	F
10	-	**When In Spain**	Cliff Richard	Columbia	3		

November 1963

This Mnth	Last Mnth	Title	Artist	Label	Wks in 10	US Pos	
1	1	**Please Please Me**	Beatles	Parlophone	63		F
2	2	**Meet The Searchers**	Searchers	Pye	37	22	F
3	-	**How Do You Like It?**	Gerry And The Pacemakers	Columbia	27		FL
4	3	**Born Free**	Frank Ifield	Columbia	28		
5	6	**Kenny Ball's Golden Hits**	Kenny Ball	Pye	18		L
6	4	**Greatest Hits**	Shadows	Columbia	41		
7	-	**Freddie And The Dreamers**	Freddie And The Dreamers	Columbia	22	19	FL
8	8	**Chuck Berry On Stage**	Chuck Berry	Pye International	7	29	F
9	-	**With The Beatles**	Beatles	Parlophone	44		
10	-	**Sugar And Spice**	Searchers	Pye	7		

December 1963

This Mnth	Last Mnth	Title	Artist	Label	Wks in 10	US Pos	
1	9	**With The Beatles**	Beatles	Parlophone	44		
2	1	**Please Please Me**	Beatles	Parlophone	63		F
3	3	**How Do You Like It?**	Gerry And The Pacemakers	Columbia	27		FL
4	2	**Meet The Searchers**	Searchers	Pye	37	22	F
5	4	**Born Free**	Frank Ifield	Columbia	28		
6	-	**West Side Story**	Soundtrack	Columbia	154	1	
7	10	**Sugar And Spice**	Searchers	Pye	7		
8	7	**Freddie And The Dreamers**	Freddie And The Dreamers	Columbia	22	19	FL
9	-	**In Dreams**	Roy Orbison	London	20	35	F
10	-	**Trini Lopez At P.J.'s**	Trini Lopez	Reprise	4	2	F

US 1963

OCT-DEC

October 1963

This Mnth	Last Mnth	Title	Artist	Label	Wks in 10	UK Pos	
1	1	**My Son, The Nut**	Allan Sherman	Warner	12		L
2	3	**Bye Bye Birdie**	Soundtrack	RCA	16		
3	9	**Ingredients In A Recipe For Soul**	Ray Charles	ABC Paramount	14		
4	5	**Peter, Paul & Mary**	Peter, Paul & Mary	Warner	84	18	F2P
5	2	**Trini Lopez At PJ's**	Trini Lopez	Reprise	21	7	FL
6	4	**(Moving)**	Peter, Paul & Mary	Warner	50		
7	-	**Elvis' Golden Records, Vol. 3**	Elvis Presley	RCA	13	6	
8	-	**The Second Barbra Streisand Album**	Barbra Streisand	Columbia	18		
9	-	**Live At The Apollo**	James Brown	King	12		F
10	6	**West Side Story**	Soundtrack	Columbia	-	1	3P

November 1963

This Mnth	Last Mnth	Title	Artist	Label	Wks in 10	UK Pos	
1	-	**In The Wind**	Peter, Paul & Mary	Warner	27	11	
2	8	**The Second Barbra Streisand Album**	Barbra Streisand	Columbia	18		
3	7	**Elvis' Golden Records, Vol. 3**	Elvis Presley	RCA	13	6	
4	5	**Trini Lopez At PJ's**	Trini Lopez	Reprise	21	7	FL
5	4	**Peter, Paul & Mary**	Peter, Paul & Mary	Warner	84	18	F2P
6	3	**Ingredients In A Recipe For Soul**	Ray Charles	ABC Paramount	14		
7	6	**(Moving)**	Peter, Paul & Mary	Warner	50		
8	-	**The Singing Nun**	Singing Nun	Philips	18		FL
9	2	**Bye Bye Birdie**	Soundtrack	RCA	16		
10	-	**Surfer Girl**	Beach Boys	Capitol	4	13	

December 1963

This Mnth	Last Mnth	Title	Artist	Label	Wks in 10	UK Pos	
1	8	**The Singing Nun**	Singing Nun	Philips	18		FL
2	1	**In The Wind**	Peter, Paul & Mary	Warner	27	11	
3	2	**The Second Barbra Streisand Album**	Barbra Streisand	Columbia	18		
4	4	**Trini Lopez At PJ's**	Trini Lopez	Reprise	21	7	FL
5	3	**Elvis' Golden Records, Vol. 3**	Elvis Presley	RCA	13	6	
6	5	**Peter, Paul & Mary**	Peter, Paul & Mary	Warner	84	18	F2P
7	-	**Washington Square**	Village Stompers	Epic	2		FL
8	6	**Ingredients In A Recipe For Soul**	Ray Charles	ABC Paramount	14		
9	-	**West Side Story**	Soundtrack	Columbia	-	1	3P
10	10	**Surfer Girl**	Beach Boys	Capitol	4	13	

• 1963 was the year that protest songs went pop, and the artists most responsible were Peter, Paul & Mary. Their third album, **In The Wind**, rocketed them to the top pushing their eponymous debut LP into the runner-up position. The new album included their two Bob Dylan composed Top 10 singles, 'Blowin' in The Wind' and 'Don't Think Twice, It's All Right'. Joan Baez, the queen of Sixties folk/protest music also reached the Top 10 with her two **In Concert** albums. However, it was not all good news in the folk camp as influential pioneers The Weavers announced they were disbanding. The group had included Pete Seeger and Lee Hays; composers of Peter, Paul & Mary's first major hit 'If I Had A Hammer'.

• Arguably the year's biggest left-field hit was a collection of religiously slanted, folk-oriented songs performed in French by Belgian nun Sister Luc-Gabrielle, who was known simply as The Singing Nun. The Nun's sweetly innocent single 'Domenique' and her self-titled album headed both charts as the year closed and the nation mourned the loss of President Kennedy. Incidentally, ten tribute albums to the President reached the Top 200, including one retailing at 99 cents that is said to have sold over four million copies in less than a week.

UK 1964

JAN-MAR

• The American success of The Beatles was greeted with unprecedented media coverage in Britain, where the act hogged the top two places on the LP chart for the entire quarter.

• Britain's longest running pop music TV show *Top Of The Pops* was launched. The show, which based its content on the week's Top 20 singles, was also very influential on album sales. Radio Caroline was another helpful promotional tool for album sales. The pirate radio station, which broadcast its programmes from the North Sea to the London area, was the UK's first Top 40 radio station.

• The interest in the roots of R&B music continued to grow in the UK with both Chuck Berry and label-mate Bo Diddley having two albums in the Top 20. Also reaching the Top 20 were the compilation albums, **Folk Festival Of The Blues** and **The Blues**, which both included cuts by Howlin' Wolf, Muddy Waters and Sonny Boy Williamson. Among the American R&B and blues acts who successfully toured Britain in 1964 were Chuck Berry, Jimmy Reed, John Lee Hooker, Howlin' Wolf and Sonny Boy Williamson. Fifties rock'n'roll also enjoyed a UK comeback this year with sell-out tours by Little Richard, Bill Haley and Carl Perkins.

January 1964

This Mnth	Last Mnth	Title	Artist	Label	Wks in 10	US Pos	
1	1	**With The Beatles**	Beatles	Parlophone	44		
2	2	**Please Please Me**	Beatles	Parlophone	63		F
3	3	**How Do You Like It?**	Gerry And The Pacemakers	Columbia	27		FL
4	6	**West Side Story**	Soundtrack	Columbia	154	1	
5	8	**Freddie And The Dreamers**	Freddie And The Dreamers	Columbia	22	19	FL
6	5	**Born Free**	Frank Ifield	Columbia	28		
7	-	**Greatest Hits**	Shadows	Columbia	41		
8	-	**On Tour With The George Mitchell Minstrels**	George Mitchell Minstrels	HMV	4		
9	9	**In Dreams**	Roy Orbison	London	20	35	F
10	-	**Kenny Ball's Golden Hits**	Kenny Ball	Pye	18		L

February 1964

This Mnth	Last Mnth	Title	Artist	Label	Wks in 10	US Pos	
1	1	**With The Beatles**	Beatles	Parlophone	44		
2	2	**Please Please Me**	Beatles	Parlophone	63		F
3	3	**How Do You Like It?**	Gerry And The Pacemakers	Columbia	27		FL
4	4	**West Side Story**	Soundtrack	Columbia	154	1	
5	6	**Born Free**	Frank Ifield	Columbia	28		
6	-	**Meet The Searchers**	Searchers	Pye	37	22	F
7	5	**Freddie And The Dreamers**	Freddie And The Dreamers	Columbia	22	19	FL
8	7	**Greatest Hits**	Shadows	Columbia	41		
9	9	**In Dreams**	Roy Orbison	London	20	35	F
10	-	**Fun In Acapulco (Soundtrack)**	Elvis Presley	RCA	5	3	

March 1964

This Mnth	Last Mnth	Title	Artist	Label	Wks in 10	US Pos	
1	1	**With The Beatles**	Beatles	Parlophone	44		
2	2	**Please Please Me**	Beatles	Parlophone	63		F
3	4	**West Side Story**	Soundtrack	Columbia	154	1	
4	-	**Stay With The Hollies**	Hollies	Parlophone	18		F
5	3	**How Do You Like It?**	Gerry And The Pacemakers	Columbia	27		FL
6	6	**Meet The Searchers**	Searchers	Pye	37	22	F
7	8	**Greatest Hits**	Shadows	Columbia	41		
8	7	**Freddie And The Dreamers**	Freddie And The Dreamers	Columbia	22	19	FL
9	5	**Born Free**	Frank Ifield	Columbia	28		
10	-	**South Pacific**	Soundtrack	RCA	179	1	

US 1964 JAN-MAR

January 1964

This Mnth	Last Mnth	Title	Artist	Label	Wks in 10	UK Pos	
1	1	**The Singing Nun**	Singing Nun	Philips	18		FL
2	2	**In The Wind**	Peter, Paul & Mary	Warner	27	11	
3	3	**The Second Barbra Streisand Album**	Barbra Streisand	Columbia	18		
4	9	**West Side Story**	Soundtrack	Columbia	-	1	3P
5	-	**Fun In Acapulco (Soundtrack)**	Elvis Presley	RCA	7	9	
6	6	**Peter, Paul & Mary**	Peter, Paul & Mary	Warner	84	18	F2P
7	-	**Joan Baez In Concert, Part 2**	Joan Baez	Vanguard	9	8	
8	-	**Maria Elena**	Los Indios Tabajaras	RCA	3		FL
9	5	**Elvis' Golden Records, Vol. 3**	Elvis Presley	RCA	13	6	
10	-	**(Moving)**	Peter, Paul & Mary	Warner	50		

February 1964

This Mnth	Last Mnth	Title	Artist	Label	Wks in 10	UK Pos	
1	1	**The Singing Nun**	Singing Nun	Philips	18		FL
2	2	**In The Wind**	Peter, Paul & Mary	Warner	27	11	
3	-	**Meet The Beatles**	Beatles	Capitol	21		F5P
4	-	**Little Deuce Coupe**	Beach Boys	Capitol	9		P
5	6	**Peter, Paul & Mary**	Peter, Paul & Mary	Warner	84	18	F2P
6	5	**Fun In Acapulco**	Elvis Presley	RCA	7	9	
7	-	**Introducing... The Beatles**	Beatles	Vee Jay	15		
8	-	**Honey In The Horn**	Al Hirt	RCA	22		F
9	4	**West Side Story**	Soundtrack	Columbia	-	1	3P
10	7	**Joan Baez In Concert, Part 2**	Joan Baez	Vanguard	9	8	

March 1964

This Mnth	Last Mnth	Title	Artist	Label	Wks in 10	UK Pos	
1	3	**Meet The Beatles**	Beatles	Capitol	21		F5P
2	7	**Introducing... The Beatles**	Beatles	Vee Jay	15		
3	8	**Honey In The Horn**	Al Hirt	RCA	22		F
4	-	**Hello, Dolly!**	Original Cast	RCA	35		
5	-	**Yesterday's Love Songs/ Today's Blues**	Nancy Wilson	Capitol	6		F
6	2	**In The Wind**	Peter, Paul & Mary	Warner	27	11	
7	-	**The Third Album**	Barbra Streisand	Columbia	22		
8	1	**The Singing Nun**	Singing Nun	Philips	18		FL
9	-	**Charade**	Henry Mancini	RCA	8		
10	-	**There! I've Said It Again**	Bobby Vinton	Epic	5		L

• Helped by a costly and carefully planned campaign, The Beatles took America by storm. Their album **Meet The Beatles** hit the top in just three weeks and their previously unsuccessful debut LP, **Introducing The Beatles**, was soon just one place behind. *Billboard*, who had described their music as "The surf on the Thames sound", proclaimed "US rocks and reels from Beatles invasion". The act ended the quarter by equaling a record set by Elvis Presley in his hey-day, when they simultaneously had 10 sides on the Top 100 singles chart. However, they soon bettered the 'King' by holding down the top five slots on that chart! It was estimated that The Beatles accounted for a staggering 60% of all American record sales in this period!

• Soul music was a term now being bandied around in R&B circles and climbing the album chart was a fine example of the music, **Apollo Saturday Night**. This was a live recording featuring greats of the genre such as Ben E. King, Wilson Pickett with The Falcons and the up-and-coming Otis Redding.

UK 1964 APR-JUNE

April 1964

This Mnth	Last Mnth	Title	Artist	Label	Wks in 10	US Pos	
1	1	**With The Beatles**	Beatles	Parlophone	44		
2	2	**Please Please Me**	Beatles	Parlophone	63		F
3	3	**West Side Story**	Soundtrack	Columbia	154	1	
4	4	**Stay With The Hollies**	Hollies	Parlophone	18		F
5	6	**Meet The Searchers**	Searchers	Pye	37	22	F
6	5	**How Do You Like It?**	Gerry And The Pacemakers	Columbia	27		FL
7	-	**Elvis' Golden Records Vol. 3**	Elvis Presley	RCA	8	3	
8	7	**Greatest Hits**	Shadows	Columbia	41		
9	8	**Freddie And The Dreamers**	Freddie And The Dreamers	Columbia	22	19	FL
10	10	**South Pacific**	Soundtrack	RCA	179	1	

• After residing at Number 1 for over a year with **Please Please Me** and then **With The Beatles**, the fab four's place was taken by The Rolling Stones' self-titled debut album.

May 1964

This Mnth	Last Mnth	Title	Artist	Label	Wks in 10	US Pos	
1	-	**Rolling Stones**	Rolling Stones	Decca	42	11	F
2	1	**With The Beatles**	Beatles	Parlophone	44		
3	-	**A Session With The Dave Clark Five**	Dave Clark Five	Columbia	11		F
4	3	**West Side Story**	Soundtrack	Columbia	154	1	
5	4	**Stay With The Hollies**	Hollies	Parlophone	18		F
6	2	**Please Please Me**	Beatles	Parlophone	63		F
7	-	**A Girl Called Dusty**	Dusty Springfield	Philips	10		F
8	-	**Dance With The Shadows**	Shadows	Columbia	15		
9	-	**Blue Gene**	Gene Pitney	UA	6	105	F
10	7	**Elvis' Golden Records Vol. 3**	Elvis Presley	RCA	8	3	

• The line-up at Wembley Arena for the *NME* Poll Winners concert read like a *Who's Who* of Sixties British rock. Alongside The Beatles, The Rolling Stones, Dave Clark Five, Gerry & The Pacemakers (Gerry Marsden pictured above) and Cliff Richard & The Shadows, were The Hollies, Billy J. Kramer & The Dakotas, The Searchers and Freddie & The Dreamers.

June 1964

This Mnth	Last Mnth	Title	Artist	Label	Wks in 10	US Pos	
1	1	**Rolling Stones**	Rolling Stones	Decca	42	11	F
2	2	**With The Beatles**	Beatles	Parlophone	44		
3	8	**Dance With The Shadows**	Shadows	Columbia	15		
4	4	**West Side Story**	Soundtrack	Columbia	154	1	
5	-	**It's The Searchers**	Searchers	Pye	11		
6	5	**Stay With The Hollies**	Hollies	Parlophone	18		F
7	3	**A Session With The Dave Clark Five**	Dave Clark Five	Columbia	11		F
8	-	**Buddy Holly Showcase**	Buddy Holly	Coral	9		
9	-	**His Latest And Greatest**	Chuck Berry	Pye International	5		
10	7	**A Girl Called Dusty**	Dusty Springfield	Philips	10		F

• British acts, which at times held all the places on the Top 10 singles chart, fared slightly less well in the album market. The soundtrack to **West Side Story** seemed un-moveable, and there was still room in the Top 10 for early rockers Chuck Berry, Buddy Holly and Elvis Presley.

• American acts that made auspicious live debuts in the UK included Bob Dylan, Peter, Paul & Mary and country star Jim Reeves, whose sales were said to be second only to The Beatles in Britain in 1964.

US 1964 APR-JUNE

April 1964

This Mnth	Last Mnth	Title	Artist	Label	Wks in 10	UK Pos	
1	1	**Meet The Beatles**	Beatles	Capitol	21		F5P
2	2	**Introducing... The Beatles**	Beatles	Vee Jay	15		
3	3	**Honey In The Horn**	Al Hirt	RCA	22		F
4	4	**Hello, Dolly!**	Original Cast	RCA	35		
5	7	**The Third Album**	Barbra Streisand	Columbia	22		
6	6	**In The Wind**	Peter, Paul & Mary	Warner	27	11	
7	-	**Dawn (Go Away) And 11 Other Great Songs**	Four Seasons	Philips	5		
8	9	**Charade**	Henry Mancini	RCA	8		
9	5	**Yesterday's Love Songs/ Today's Blues**	Nancy Wilson	Capitol	6		F
10	10	**There! I've Said It Again**	Bobby Vinton	Epic	5		L

May 1964

This Mnth	Last Mnth	Title	Artist	Label	Wks in 10	UK Pos	
1	-	**The Beatles' Second Album**	Beatles	Capitol	22		P
2	4	**Hello, Dolly !**	Original Cast	RCA	35		
3	1	**Meet The Beatles**	Beatles	Capitol	21		F5P
4	3	**Honey In The Horn**	Al Hirt	RCA	22		F
5	-	**Glad All Over**	Dave Clark Five	Epic	10		F
6	-	**Funny Girl**	Barbra Streisand	Columbia	22		
7	-	**Kissin' Cousins (Soundtrack)**	Elvis Presley	RCA	5	5	
8	2	**Introducing... The Beatles**	Beatles	Vee Jay	15		
9	-	**Hello, Dolly!**	Louis Armstrong	Kapp	20	11	L
10	5	**The Third Album**	Barbra Streisand	Columbia	22		

June 1964

This Mnth	Last Mnth	Title	Artist	Label	Wks in 10	UK Pos	
1	9	**Hello, Dolly!**	Louis Armstrong	Kapp	20	11	L
2	2	**Hello, Dolly!**	Original Cast	RCA	35		
3	6	**Funny Girl**	Barbra Streisand	Columbia	22		
4	1	**The Beatles' Second Album**	Beatles	Capitol	22		P
5	-	**"Call Me Irresponsible" And Other Hit Songs**	Andy Williams	Columbia	9		
6	4	**Honey In The Horn**	Al Hirt	RCA	22		F
7	3	**Meet The Beatles**	Beatles	Capitol	21		F5P
8	10	**The Third Album**	Barbra Streisand	Columbia	22		
9	-	**Cotton Candy**	Al Hirt	RCA	11		
10	5	**Glad All Over**	Dave Clark Five	Epic	10		F

• As **Meet The Beatles** became the biggest selling full price LP to date, The Beatles' second album replaced it at the summit and at times they had three out of the top four albums. The second British group to crash into the US Top 10 were The Dave Clark Five with **Glad All Over**. Both The Beatles and Clark had very successful US visits, while The Rolling Stones' debut tour attracted only half-full houses in many cities.

• It took Carol Channing and the rest of the cast of **Hello, Dolly!** to finally replace The Beatles at the summit, and they in turn were speedily dethroned by 63-year-old jazz trumpeter and vocalist Louis Armstrong with his own **Hello, Dolly!** album. Armstrong was not the only trumpeter blowing up a storm, as another New Orleans native, Al Hirt, had two albums hit the Top 10 in short succession, **Honey In The Horn** and **Cotton Candy**.

• Future superstars Johnny Rivers, Bill Cosby, The Temptations, Marvin Gaye and Otis Redding were among the artists climbing the US album chart for the first time, as were Britain's Cliff Richard, Dusty Springfield and The Searchers.

UK 1964 JULY-SEPT

July 1964

This Mnth	Last Mnth	Title	Artist	Label	Wks in 10	US Pos	
1	1	**Rolling Stones**	Rolling Stones	Decca	42	11	F
2	-	**The Bachelors And 16 Great Songs**	Bachelors	Decca	40		F
3	2	**With The Beatles**	Beatles	Parlophone	44		
4	4	**West Side Story**	Soundtrack	Columbia	154	1	
5	3	**Dance With The Shadows**	Shadows	Columbia	15		
6	-	**A Hard Day's Night**	Beatles	Parlophone	32	1	
7	8	**Buddy Holly Showcase**	Buddy Holly	Coral	9		
8	-	**Wonderful Life (soundtrack)**	Cliff Richard	Columbia	19		
9	-	**Kissin' Cousins (Soundtrack)**	Elvis Presley	RCA	16	6	
10	5	**It's The Searchers**	Searchers	Pye	11		

August 1964

This Mnth	Last Mnth	Title	Artist	Label	Wks in 10	US Pos	
1	6	**A Hard Day's Night**	Beatles	Parlophone	32	1	
2	1	**Rolling Stones**	Rolling Stones	Decca	42	11	F
3	8	**Wonderful Life (Soundtrack)**	Cliff Richard	Columbia	19		
4	4	**West Side Story**	Soundtrack	Columbia	154	1	
5	2	**The Bachelors And 16 Great Songs**	Bachelors	Decca	40		F
6	3	**With The Beatles**	Beatles	Parlophone	44		
7	9	**Kissin' Cousins (Soundtrack)**	Elvis Presley	RCA	16	6	
8	5	**Dance With The Shadows**	Shadows	Columbia	15		
9	10	**It's The Searchers**	Searchers	Pye	11		
10	-	**Gentleman Jim**	Jim Reeves	RCA	14		

September 1964

This Mnth	Last Mnth	Title	Artist	Label	Wks in 10	US Pos	
1	1	**A Hard Day's Night**	Beatles	Parlophone	32	1	
2	2	**Rolling Stones**	Rolling Stones	Decca	42	11	F
3	3	**Wonderful Life (Soundtrack)**	Cliff Richard	Columbia	19		
4	10	**Gentleman Jim**	Jim Reeves	RCA	14		
5	5	**The Bachelors And 16 Great Songs**	Bachelors	Decca	40		F
6	-	**Moonlight And Roses**	Jim Reeves	RCA	16	30	
7	4	**West Side Story**	Soundtrack	Columbia	154	1	
8	-	**Five Faces Of Manfred Mann**	Manfred Mann	HMV	13	141	F
9	7	**Kissin' Cousins (Soundtrack)**	Elvis Presley	RCA	16	6	
10	6	**With The Beatles**	Beatles	Parlophone	44		

• A trio of big name soundtrack albums fought it out on the UK chart. As expected, The Beatles' **A Hard Day's Night** led Cliff Richard's **Wonderful Life** and Elvis Presley's **Kissin' Cousins**. For the record, **A Hard Day's Night** amassed unprecedented British advance orders of over 250,000, whilst in the USA it smashed sales records by selling a million copies in four days.

• The death of American country singer Jim Reeves caused a demand for his recordings, the like of which would not be seen again until his label-mate Elvis Presley died in 1977. **Gentleman Jim**, **A Touch Of Velvet** and **Moonlight & Roses** were among his eight albums simultaneously situated in the Top 20!

• British TV producer Jack Good launched his first US TV show *Shindig* it was one of the most successful pop series of the decade.

• Making their recording debuts this quarter were future gold album artists The Who, Tom Jones, Herman's Hermits, Joe Cocker and Rod Stewart.

US 1964 JULY-SEPT

July 1964

This Mnth	Last Mnth	Title	Artist	Label	Wks in 10	UK Pos	
1	1	**Hello, Dolly!**	Louis Armstrong	Kapp	20	11	L
2	2	**Hello, Dolly!**	Original Cast	RCA	35		
3	3	**Funny Girl**	Barbra Streisand	Columbia	22		
4	-	**Getz/Gilberto**	Stan Getz/Joao Gilberto	Verve	16		L
5	4	**The Beatles' Second Album**	Beatles	Capitol	22		P
6	8	**The Third Album**	Barbra Streisand	Columbia	22		
7	-	**The Dave Clark Five Return!**	Dave Clark Five	Epic	7		
8	9	**Cotton Candy**	Al Hirt	RCA	11		
9	-	**A Hard Day's Night**	Beatles	UA	28	1	
10	5	**"Call Me Irresponsible" And Other Hit Songs**	Andy Williams	Columbia	9		

August 1964

This Mnth	Last Mnth	Title	Artist	Label	Wks in 10	UK Pos	
1	9	**A Hard Day's Night**	Beatles	UA	28	1	
2	4	**Getz/Gilberto**	Stan Getz/Joao Gilberto	Verve	16		L
3	1	**Hello, Dolly!**	Louis Armstrong	Kapp	20	11	L
4	2	**Hello, Dolly!**	Original Cast	RCA	35		
5	3	**Funny Girl**	Barbra Streisand	Columbia	22		
6	-	**Something New**	Beatles	Capitol	18		P
7	-	**All Summer Long**	Beach Boys	Capitol	16		
8	7	**The Dave Clark Five Return!**	Dave Clark Five	Epic	7		
9	8	**Cotton Candy**	Al Hirt	RCA	11		
10	6	**The Third Album**	Barbra Streisand	Columbia	22		

September 1964

This Mnth	Last Mnth	Title	Artist	Label	Wks in 10	UK Pos	
1	1	**A Hard Day's Night**	Beatles	UA	28	1	
2	6	**Something New**	Beatles	Capitol	18		P
3	-	**Everybody Loves Somebody**	Dean Martin	Reprise	16		F
4	7	**All Summer Long**	Beach Boys	Capitol	16		
5	2	**Getz/Gilberto**	Stan Getz/Joao Gilberto	Verve	16		L
6	-	**Peter, Paul And Mary In Concert**	Peter, Paul & Mary	Warner	8	20	
7	3	**Hello, Dolly!**	Louis Armstrong	Kapp	20	11	L
8	5	**Funny Girl**	Barbra Streisand	Columbia	22		
9	-	**Rag Doll**	Four Seasons	Philips	5		
10	4	**Hello, Dolly!**	Original Cast	RCA	35		

• As The Beatles embarked on another sell-out stadium tour, their albums continued to monopolize the American chart. Two weeks after entering the Top 200 **A Hard Day's Night** stood at Number 1, and a month later **Something New** – a US compilation that included tracks from the UK version of **A Hard Day's Night** – stood behind it in the runner-up spot. Other Beatle-related Top 20 entries were **The Beatles Song Book** by the Hollyridge Strings, and a spoken word album, **The Beatles American Tour** with Ed Rudy on the News Documentary label. Also climbing fast was the novelty LP **The Chipmunks Sing The Beatles Hits**.

• The Dave Clark Five quickly placed two more LPs in The Top 20, **The Dave Clark Five Return!** and **American Tour.** Hot on their heels were another UK band, The Rolling Stones, with their re-named debut LP, **England's Newest Hitmakers/The Rolling Stones**, which only missed the Top 10 by a whisker.

• Barbra Streisand was featured on two Top 10 LPs; her own **The Third Album** and the original cast of **Funny Girl**, which contained her Grammy winning rendition of 'People'. Another major MOR hit was **Getz/Gilberto** by saxophonist Stan Getz and Brazilian vocalist Joao Gilberto. It went on to take the Grammy Award for Album Of The Year.

UK 1964 OCT-DEC

October 1964

This Mnth	Last Mnth	Title	Artist	Label	Wks in 10	US Pos	
1	1	**A Hard Day's Night**	Beatles	Parlophone	32	1	
2	2	**Rolling Stones**	Rolling Stones	Decca	42	11	F
3	6	**Moonlight And Roses**	Jim Reeves	RCA	16	30	
4	8	**Five Faces Of Manfred Mann**	Manfred Mann	HMV	13	141	F
5	5	**The Bachelors And 16 Great Songs**	Bachelors	Decca	40		F
6	7	**West Side Story**	Soundtrack	Columbia	154	1	
7	3	**Wonderful Life (Soundtrack)**	Cliff Richard	Columbia	19		
8	4	**Gentleman Jim**	Jim Reeves	RCA	14		
9	-	**Kinks**	Kinks	Pye	22		F
10	9	**Kissin' Cousins (Soundtrack)**	Elvis Presley	RCA	16	6	

November 1964

This Mnth	Last Mnth	Title	Artist	Label	Wks in 10	US Pos	
1	1	**A Hard Day's Night**	Beatles	Parlophone	32	1	
2	2	**Rolling Stones**	Rolling Stones	Decca	42	11	F
3	3	**Moonlight And Roses**	Jim Reeves	RCA	16	30	
4	4	**Five Faces Of Manfred Mann**	Manfred Mann	HMV	13	141	F
5	9	**Kinks**	Kinks	Pye	22		F
6	5	**The Bachelors And 16 Great Songs**	Bachelors	Decca	40		F
7	6	**West Side Story**	Soundtrack	Columbia	154	1	
8	-	**In Dreams**	Roy Orbison	London	20	35	F
9	-	**The Animals**	Animals	Columbia	13	7	F
10	8	**Gentleman Jim**	Jim Reeves	RCA	14		

December 1964

This Mnth	Last Mnth	Title	Artist	Label	Wks in 10	US Pos	
1	2	**Rolling Stones**	Rolling Stones	Decca	42	11	F
2	1	**A Hard Day's Night**	Beatles	Parlophone	32	1	
3	6	**The Bachelors And 16 Great Songs**	Bachelors	Decca	40		F
4	-	**Beatles For Sale**	Beatles	Parlophone	37		
5	3	**Moonlight And Roses**	Jim Reeves	RCA	16	30	
6	-	**Twelve Songs Of Christmas**	Jim Reeves	RCA	9		
7	5	**Kinks**	Kinks	Pye	22		F
8	9	**The Animals**	Animals	Columbia	13	7	F
9	4	**Five Faces Of Manfred Mann**	Manfred Mann	HMV	13	141	F
10	7	**West Side Story**	Soundtrack	Columbia	154	1	

• It had been a staggeringly successful year for British acts, who had more American hits in that year than they had achieved in all the previous post-war years combined. On the home front too, things were rosy with total record sales up 18% on 1963.

• One of the most successful American performers in the UK was Roy Orbison, whose year-old **In Dreams** set was quickly followed into the Top 10 by **Oh Pretty Woman**. The title track to the latter album was the first Number 1 single by a US act in Britain for two years.

• One of the most acclaimed new British groups of 1964 were The Animals, whose self-titled debut album reached the Top 10 on both sides of the Atlantic. In America they followed in The Beatles' footsteps by appearing on Ed Sullivan's US TV show, as did fellow British R&B band The Rolling Stones. The Stones' appearance shocked Sullivan and he vowed they would never return to his show. However, their growing popularity later forced him to relent. The Stones also appeared alongside such notables as James Brown, The Beach Boys, Marvin Gaye, Gerry & The Pacemakers, The Supremes and The Miracles in the film *The Tami Show* .

US 1964 OCT-DEC

October 1964

This Mnth	Last Mnth	Title	Artist	Label	Wks in 10	UK Pos	
1	1	**A Hard Day's Night**	Beatles	UA	28	1	
2	3	**Everybody Loves Somebody**	Dean Martin	Reprise	16		F
3	2	**Something New**	Beatles	Capitol	18		P
4	-	**How Glad I Am**	Nancy Wilson	Capitol	10		
5	-	**People**	Barbra Streisand	Columbia	21		
6	4	**All Summer Long**	Beach Boys	Capitol	16		
7	6	**Peter, Paul And Mary In Concert**	Peter, Paul & Mary	Warner	8	20	
8	10	**Hello, Dolly!**	Original Cast	RCA	35		
9	-	**The Impressions Keep On Pushing**	Impressions	ABC Paramount	6		FL
10	5	**Getz/Gilberto**	Stan Getz/Joao Gilberto	Verve	16		L

November 1964

This Mnth	Last Mnth	Title	Artist	Label	Wks in 10	UK Pos	
1	5	**People**	Barbra Streisand	Columbia	21		
2	2	**Everybody Loves Somebody**	Dean Martin	Reprise	16		F
3	1	**A Hard Day's Night**	Beatles	UA	28	1	
4	4	**How Glad I Am**	Nancy Wilson	Capitol	10		
5	3	**Something New**	Beatles	Capitol	18		P
6	6	**All Summer Long**	Beach Boys	Capitol	16		
7	-	**Beach Boys Concert**	Beach Boys	Capitol	20		
8	-	**The Great Songs From 'My Fair Lady' And Other Broadway Hits**	Andy Williams	Columbia	8		
9	-	**The Animals**	Animals	MGM	4	6	F
10	-	**Sugar Lips**	Al Hirt	RCA	3		L

December 1964

This Mnth	Last Mnth	Title	Artist	Label	Wks in 10	UK Pos	
1	7	**Beach Boys Concert**	Beach Boys	Capitol	20		
2	1	**People**	Barbra Streisand	Columbia	21		
3	-	**Roustabout (Soundtrack)**	Elvis Presley	RCA	12	12	
4	-	**12 X 5**	Rolling Stones	London	8		F
5	-	**Where Did Our Love Go**	Supremes	Motown	19		F
6	8	**The Great Songs From 'My Fair Lady' And Other Broadway Hits**	Andy Williams	Columbia	8		
7	3	**A Hard Day's Night**	Beatles	UA	28	1	
8	-	**My Fair Lady**	Soundtrack	Columbia	30	9	
9	2	**Everybody Loves Somebody**	Dean Martin	Reprise	16		F
10	-	**Mary Poppins**	Soundtrack	Buena Vista	48	2	

• When 1964 opened few Americans had heard of The Beatles. When it closed the British group had put 30 tracks in the singles chart and spent 30 weeks at the top of the LP lists – a record never bettered before or since.

• The Grammy for Best Soundtrack Album went to **Mary Poppins**, a Disney musical starring England's Julie Andrews. The LP topped the charts for 14 weeks, one week shy of the period Andrews spent at Number 1 as star of the original cast album of **My Fair Lady**.

• Although The Beatles overshadowed Elvis in 1964 he ended the year with his first Number 1 since 1961, **Roustabout**. It was also the year that his total sales passed 100 million.

• One of the American acts least affected by the British Invasion were The Beach Boys, who notched up four more Top 10 singles in 1964. They also ended the year with two albums in the Top 10. **The Beach Boys Concert** was the first LP by an American rock group to reach Number 1.

UK 1965 JAN-MAR

• There was no sign of waning interest in The Beatles on either side of the Atlantic. **Beatles For Sale** followed **A Hard Day's Night** at the top in Britain. In the USA, the Liverpool lads had three albums in the Top 10; **Beatles '65** – which sold three million copies in its first month, **A Hard Day's Night** and the largely narrative, **The Beatles Story**.

• It was not just British groups that were selling well, several female artists were also hitting the heights. In the UK, 18-year-old barefoot singer Sandie Shaw put her debut LP, **Sandie**, in the Top 10, as did the only female artist managed by Brian Epstein, Cilla Black, with **Cilla**. In America, thanks to the title track from the James Bond film **Goldfinger**, Shirley Bassey found herself in The Top 10 singles and albums listings. Also making her mark Stateside was Petula Clark, whose 'Downtown' picked up the Grammy for Best Rock'n'roll Record. Ironically, the award was presented days after the death of DJ Alan Freed, the person credited with coining the term 'rock'n'roll'. It's unlikely that Freed recognized much similarity between the music he named and Pet's perky pop hit.

January 1965

This Mnth	Last Mnth	Title	Artist	Label	Wks in 10	US Pos	
1	4	**Beatles For Sale**	Beatles	Parlophone	37		
2	3	**The Bachelors And 16 Great Songs**	Bachelors	Decca	40		F
3	-	**Lucky 13 Shades Of Val Doonican**	Val Doonican	Decca	20		F
4	1	**Rolling Stones**	Rolling Stones	Decca	42	11	F
5	2	**A Hard Day's Night**	Beatles	Parlophone	32	1	
6	7	**Kinks**	Kinks	Pye	22		F
7	-	**Oh Pretty Woman**	Roy Orbison	London	10		
8	8	**The Animals**	Animals	Columbia	13	7	F
9	-	**Rolling Stones No. 2**	Rolling Stones	Decca	24		
10	6	**Twelve Songs Of Christmas**	Jim Reeves	RCA	9		

February 1965

This Mnth	Last Mnth	Title	Artist	Label	Wks in 10	US Pos	
1	9	**Rolling Stones No. 2**	Rolling Stones	Decca	24		
2	1	**Beatles For Sale**	Beatles	Parlophone	37		
3	3	**Lucky 13 Shades Of Val Doonican**	Val Doonican	Decca	20		F
4	6	**Kinks**	Kinks	Pye	22		F
5	-	**Best Of Jim Reeves**	Jim Reeves	RCA	16	9	
6	2	**The Bachelors And 16 Great Songs**	Bachelors	Decca	40		F
7	5	**A Hard Day's Night**	Beatles	Parlophone	32	1	
8	-	**Cilla**	Cilla Black	Parlophone	6		F
9	-	**West Side Story**	Soundtrack	Columbia	154	1	
10	7	**Oh Pretty Woman**	Roy Orbison	London	10		

March 1965

This Mnth	Last Mnth	Title	Artist	Label	Wks in 10	US Pos	
1	1	**Rolling Stones No. 2**	Rolling Stones	Decca	24		
2	2	**Beatles For Sale**	Beatles	Parlophone	37		
3	5	**Best Of Jim Reeves**	Jim Reeves	RCA	16	9	
4	3	**Lucky 13 Shades Of Val Doonican**	Val Doonican	Decca	20		F
5	-	**Sandie**	Sandie Shaw	Pye	8		FL
6	8	**Cilla**	Cilla Black	Parlophone	6		F
7	6	**The Bachelors And 16 Great Songs**	Bachelors	Decca	40		F
8	-	**Kinda Kinks**	Kinks	Pye	9	60	
9	-	**The Voice Of Churchill**	Sir Winston Churchill	Decca	6		FL
10	4	**Kinks**	Kinks	Pye	22		F

US 1965 JAN-MAR

January 1965

This Mnth	Last Mnth	Title	Artist	Label	Wks in 10	UK Pos	
1	5	**Where Did Our Love Go**	Supremes	Motown	19		F
2	-	**Beatles '65**	Beatles	Capitol	16		2P
3	10	**Mary Poppins**	Soundtrack	Buena Vista	48	2	
4	1	**Beach Boys Concert**	Beach Boys	Capitol	20		
5	3	**Roustabout (Soundtrack)**	Elvis Presley	RCA	12	12	
6	7	**A Hard Day's Night**	Beatles	UA	28	1	
7	8	**My Fair Lady**	Soundtrack	Columbia	30	9	
8	-	**The Beatles' Story**	Beatles	Capitol	5		
9	4	**12 X 5**	Rolling Stones	London	8		F
10	2	**People**	Barbra Streisand	Columbia	21		

February 1965

This Mnth	Last Mnth	Title	Artist	Label	Wks in 10	UK Pos	
1	2	**Beatles '65**	Beatles	Capitol	16		2P
2	3	**Mary Poppins**	Soundtrack	Buena Vista	48	2	
3	1	**Where Did Our Love Go**	Supremes	Motown	19		F
4	-	**My Love Forgive Me**	Robert Goulet	Columbia	8		L
5	-	**Goldfinger**	Soundtrack	UA	22	14	
6	7	**My Fair Lady**	Soundtrack	Columbia	30	9	
7	4	**Beach Boys Concert**	Beach Boys	Capitol	20		
8	-	**Coast To Coast**	Dave Clark Five	Epic	6		
9	-	**You've Lost That Lovin' Feelin'**	Righteous Brothers	Philles	10		FP
10	-	**Fiddler On The Roof**	Original Cast	RCA	3		2P

March 1965

This Mnth	Last Mnth	Title	Artist	Label	Wks in 10	UK Pos	
1	5	**Goldfinger**	Soundtrack	UA	22	14	
2	2	**Mary Poppins**	Soundtrack	Buena Vista	48	2	
3	1	**Beatles '65**	Beatles	Capitol	16		2P
4	9	**You've Lost That Lovin' Feelin'**	Righteous Brothers	Philles	10		FP
5	3	**Where Did Our Love Go**	Supremes	Motown	19		F
6	6	**My Fair Lady**	Soundtrack	Columbia	30	9	
7	-	**L-O-V-E**	Nat 'King' Cole	Capitol	5		L
8	4	**My Love Forgive Me**	Robert Goulet	Columbia	8		L
9	7	**Beach Boys Concert**	Beach Boys	Capitol	20		
10	-	**People**	Barbra Streisand	Columbia	21		

• The most successful American singles act of the Sixties were The Supremes, fronted by Diana Ross. The trio's first hit album, **Where Did Our Love Go**, contained their three successive Number 1 singles from 1964, 'Where Did Our Love Go', 'Baby Love' and 'Come See About Me'. The R&B-based group were also scoring with a brown-eyed pop album, **A Bit Of Liverpool**, which peaked just outside the Top 20.

• The Righteous Brothers were 'flavor of the month'. The duo's **You've Lost That Lovin' Feelin'** was riding high and two albums they had recorded prior to their liaison with producer Phil Spector called **Some Blue-Eyed Soul** and **Right Now**, were also on the Top 20. The Brothers, who were not related, had built up a vast following through their appearances on *Shindig* and their tour dates with The Beatles.

• The successful pop TV show *Hullabaloo* was launched. Among the acts it helped to American fame were extrovert British band, Freddie & The Dreamers.

UK 1965 APR-JUNE

April 1965

This Mnth	Last Mnth	Title	Artist	Label	Wks in 10	US Pos	
1	1	**Rolling Stones No. 2**	Rolling Stones	Decca	24		
2	2	**Beatles For Sale**	Beatles	Parlophone	37		
3	8	**Kinda Kinks**	Kinks	Pye	9	60	
4	-	**The Freewheelin' Bob Dylan**	Bob Dylan	CBS	22	22	F
5	4	**Lucky 13 Shades Of Val Doonican**	Val Doonican	Decca	20		F
6	5	**Sandie**	Sandie Shaw	Pye	8		FL
7	3	**Best Of Jim Reeves**	Jim Reeves	RCA	16	9	
8	-	**The Times They Are A-Changin'**	Bob Dylan	CBS	9	20	
9	-	**Pretty Things**	Pretty Things	Fontana	5		FL
10	-	**Mary Poppins**	Soundtrack	HMV	55	1	

May 1965

This Mnth	Last Mnth	Title	Artist	Label	Wks in 10	US Pos	
1	2	**Beatles For Sale**	Beatles	Parlophone	37		
2	4	**The Freewheelin' Bob Dylan**	Bob Dylan	CBS	22	22	F
3	1	**Rolling Stones No. 2**	Rolling Stones	Decca	24		
4	-	**The Sound Of Music**	Soundtrack	RCA	235	1	2P
5	10	**Mary Poppins**	Soundtrack	HMV	55	1	
6	8	**The Times They Are A-Changin'**	Bob Dylan	CBS	9	20	
7	3	**Kinda Kinks**	Kinks	Pye	9	60	
8	-	**Bringing It All Back Home**	Bob Dylan	CBS	23	6	
9	-	**Girl Happy (Soundtrack)**	Elvis Presley	RCA	8	8	
10	7	**Best Of Jim Reeves**	Jim Reeves	RCA	16	9	

June 1965

This Mnth	Last Mnth	Title	Artist	Label	Wks in 10	US Pos	
1	4	**The Sound Of Music**	Soundtrack	RCA	235	1	2P
2	8	**Bringing It All Back Home**	Bob Dylan	CBS	23	6	
3	1	**Beatles For Sale**	Beatles	Parlophone	37		
4	5	**Mary Poppins**	Soundtrack	HMV	55	1	
5	-	**Hit Maker - Burt Bacharach**	Burt Bacharach	London	9		F
6	2	**The Freewheelin' Bob Dylan**	Bob Dylan	CBS	22	22	F
7	-	**Animal Tracks**	Animals	Columbia	14	57	
8	-	**What's Bin Did And What's Bin Hid**	Donovan	Pye	9		F
9	9	**Girl Happy (Soundtrack)**	Elvis Presley	RCA	8	8	
10	3	**Rolling Stones No. 2**	Rolling Stones	Decca	24		

• **Rolling Stones No. 2**, which was similar to the US hit, **The Rolling Stones, Now!**, replaced **Beatles For Sale** at the top. Between them, the two groups shared the Number 1 spot from early February 1963 to late May 1965. They finally relinquished that position to Bob Dylan who, thanks to a very successful UK tour, had become the most talked about artist in Britain. After spending 48 weeks on the chart **The Freewheelin' Bob Dylan** hit the top, before being displaced by his **Bringing It All Back Home**. Dylan also cracked the Top 10 this quarter with **The Times They Are A-Changin'** and **Another Side Of Bob Dylan**. Charting alongside him was Donovan – who was tagged Britain's answer to Dylan – with his debut LP **What's Bin Did And What's Bin Hid**.

• The Beatles may have been the most successful album act of the Swinging Sixties but the album that spent the most time at the top of the UK chart was **The Sound Of Music**. The soundtrack to the Julie Andrews film was Number 1 for 70 weeks! Oddly, **The Sound Of Music** album only managed a two week stay at the top in the USA where the **Mary Poppins** soundtrack, Andrews' current film, was far more successful.

US 1965

APR-JUNE

April 1965

This Mnth	Last Mnth	Title	Artist	Label	Wks in 10	UK Pos	
1	2	**Mary Poppins**	Soundtrack	Buena Vista	48	2	
2	1	**Goldfinger**	Soundtrack	UA	22	14	
3	-	**Introducing Herman's Hermits**	Herman's Hermits	MGM	17		F
4	3	**Beatles '65**	Beatles	Capitol	16		2P
5	-	**Blue Midnight**	Bert Kaempfert	Decca	5		L
6	7	**L-O-V-E**	Nat 'King' Cole	Capitol	5		L
7	-	**The Return Of Roger Miller**	Roger Miller	Smash	7		F
8	6	**My Fair Lady**	Soundtrack	Columbia	30	9	
9	-	**The Rolling Stones, Now!**	Rolling Stones	London	9		
10	5	**Where Did Our Love Go**	Supremes	Motown	19		F

May 1965

This Mnth	Last Mnth	Title	Artist	Label	Wks in 10	UK Pos	
1	1	**Mary Poppins**	Soundtrack	Buena Vista	48	2	
2	3	**Introducing Herman's Hermits**	Herman's Hermits	MGM	17		F
3	-	**The Sound Of Music**	Soundtrack	RCA	108	1	
4	-	**The Beach Boys Today!**	Beach Boys	Capitol	14	6	
5	2	**Goldfinger**	Soundtrack	UA	22	14	
6	-	**Dear Heart**	Andy Williams	Columbia	15		
7	8	**My Fair Lady**	Soundtrack	Columbia	30	9	
8	9	**The Rolling Stones, Now!**	Rolling Stones	London	9		
9	7	**The Return Of Roger Miller**	Roger Miller	Smash	7		F
10	-	**A Song Will Rise**	Peter, Paul & Mary	Warner	5		L

June 1965

This Mnth	Last Mnth	Title	Artist	Label	Wks in 10	UK Pos	
1	1	**Mary Poppins**	Soundtrack	Buena Vista	48	2	
2	3	**The Sound Of Music**	Soundtrack	RCA	108	1	
3	-	**My Name Is Barbra**	Barbra Streisand	Columbia	17		
4	6	**Dear Heart**	Andy Williams	Columbia	15		
5	4	**The Beach Boys Today!**	Beach Boys	Capitol	14	6	
6	2	**Introducing Herman's Hermits**	Herman's Hermits	MGM	17		F
7	5	**Goldfinger**	Soundtrack	UA	22	14	
8	-	**Girl Happy (Soundtrack)**	Elvis Presley	RCA	6	8	
9	-	**Bringing It All Back Home**	Bob Dylan	Columbia	14	1	F
10	7	**My Fair Lady**	Soundtrack	Columbia	30	9	

• Bob Dylan finally cracked the Top 10 thanks to his rock-oriented album **Bringing It All Back Home**. Co-incidentally, as Dylan debuted in the Top 10, Peter, Paul & Mary, who had first introduced his songs to the US pop public, visited that chart for the last time with **A Song Will Rise**.

• A second generation of British groups rocketed into the Top 20 chart. Leading the charge were Herman's Hermits from Manchester, fronted by 17-year-old Peter Noone, with **Introducing Herman's Hermits**. Close behind were The Kinks with **Kinks-Size** and Freddie & The Dreamers self-titled American debut album. Herman's Hermits were the only group to really challenge The Beatles' supremacy in 1965.

• The British Invasion reached its peak as nine UK recorded singles were simultaneously situated in the US Top 10. It would be another 18 years before British acts again dominated the US singles chart to such an extent.

UK 1965

JULY-SEPT

• British acts were losing their grip on the UK chart, and often accounted for only 30% of the Top 10 albums and sometimes less than half of the Top 20 singles. *Melody Maker* readers voted Americans Elvis Presley and Brenda Lee Top Male and Female artist.

• Sonny & Cher were the sensation of the summer. The hippie dressers hit with both duets and solo records. Their UK visit was a great success, in stark contrast to the relative failure of the first British dates by The Byrds. Another American riding the crest of a wave was rock-free folk singer Joan Baez, whose **Joan Baez, Joan Baez In Concert Vol. 2** and **Joan Baez No. 5** all spent time in the Top 10.

• The two acts that started the British Invasion, The Beatles and The Dave Clark Five (above), both had hot soundtrack albums. **Help** continued the fab four's run of transatlantic Number 1s, and **Catch Us If You Can** – US title **Having A Wild Weekend** – was a Top 20 record on both sides of the Atlantic.

July 1965

This Mnth	Last Mnth	Title	Artist	Label	Wks in 10	US Pos	
1	1	**The Sound Of Music**	Soundtrack	RCA	235	1	2P
2	2	**Bringing It All Back Home**	Bob Dylan	CBS	23	6	
3	4	**Mary Poppins**	Soundtrack	HMV	55	1	
4	8	**What's Bin Did And What's Bin Hid**	Donovan	Pye	9		F
5	-	**Joan Baez No. 5**	Joan Baez	Fontana	15	12	
6	5	**Hit Maker - Burt Bacharach**	Burt Bacharach	London	9		F
7	3	**Beatles For Sale**	Beatles	Parlophone	37		
8	-	**A World Of Our Own**	Seekers	Columbia	8	123	F
9	6	**The Freewheelin' Bob Dylan**	Bob Dylan	CBS	22	22	F
10	7	**Animal Tracks**	Animals	Columbia	14	57	

August 1965

This Mnth	Last Mnth	Title	Artist	Label	Wks in 10	US Pos	
1	1	**The Sound Of Music**	Soundtrack	RCA	235	1	2P
2	-	**Help**	Beatles	Parlophone	30	1	
3	3	**Mary Poppins**	Soundtrack	HMV	55	1	
4	2	**Bringing It All Back Home**	Bob Dylan	CBS	23	6	
5	5	**Joan Baez No. 5**	Joan Baez	Fontana	15	12	
6	-	**Sound Of The Shadows**	Shadows	Columbia	11		
7	-	**Almost There**	Andy Williams	CBS	24		F
8	7	**Beatles For Sale**	Beatles	Parlophone	37		
9	-	**Joan Baez In Concert Vol. 2**	Joan Baez	Fontana	3	7	F
10	-	**Catch Us If You Can**	Dave Clark Five	Columbia	3	15	

September 1965

This Mnth	Last Mnth	Title	Artist	Label	Wks in 10	US Pos	
1	2	**Help**	Beatles	Parlophone	30	1	
2	1	**The Sound Of Music**	Soundtrack	RCA	235	1	2P
3	3	**Mary Poppins**	Soundtrack	HMV	55	1	
4	4	**Bringing It All Back Home**	Bob Dylan	CBS	23	6	
5	7	**Almost There**	Andy Williams	CBS	24		F
6	5	**Joan Baez No. 5**	Joan Baez	Fontana	15	12	
7	6	**Sound Of The Shadows**	Shadows	Columbia	11		
8	-	**Mr. Tambourine Man**	Byrds	CBS	5	6	FL
9	-	**Animal Tracks**	Animals	Columbia	14	57	
10	9	**Joan Baez In Concert Vol. 2**	Joan Baez	Fontana	3	7	F

US 1965 JULY-SEPT

July 1965

This Mnth	Last Mnth	Title	Artist	Label	Wks in 10	UK Pos	
1	-	**Herman's Hermits On Tour**	Herman's Hermits	MGM	18		
2	1	**Mary Poppins**	Soundtrack	Buena Vista	48	2	
3	-	**Beatles VI**	Beatles	Capitol	13		**P**
4	3	**My Name Is Barbra**	Barbra Streisand	Columbia	17		
5	2	**The Sound Of Music**	Soundtrack	RCA	108	1	
6	4	**Dear Heart**	Andy Williams	Columbia	15		
7	6	**Introducing Herman's Hermits**	Herman's Hermits	MGM	17		**F**
8	-	**The Rolling Stones, Now!**	Rolling Stones	London	9		
9	5	**The Beach Boys Today!**	Beach Boys	Capitol	14	6	
10	-	**Whipped Cream & Other Delights**	Herb Alpert & The Tijuana Brass	A&M	61	2	

August 1965

This Mnth	Last Mnth	Title	Artist	Label	Wks in 10	UK Pos	
1	3	**Beatles VI**	Beatles	Capitol	13		**P**
2	1	**Herman's Hermits On Tour**	Herman's Hermits	MGM	18		
3	-	**Out Of Our Heads**	Rolling Stones	London	16	2	**P**
4	5	**The Sound Of Music**	Soundtrack	RCA	108	1	
5	-	**Summer Days (And Summer Nights!!)**	Beach Boys	Capitol	10	4	
6	4	**My Name Is Barbra**	Barbra Streisand	Columbia	17		
7	2	**Mary Poppins**	Soundtrack	Buena Vista	48	2	
8	-	**Mr. Tambourine Man**	Byrds	Columbia	3	7	**F**
9	-	**Bringing It All Back Home**	Bob Dylan	Columbia	14	1	**F**
10	-	**Just Once In My Life...**	Righteous Brothers	Philles	3		

September 1965

This Mnth	Last Mnth	Title	Artist	Label	Wks in 10	UK Pos	
1	-	**Look At Us**	Sonny & Cher	Atco	14	7	**FL**
2	3	**Out Of Our Heads**	Rolling Stones	London	16	2	**P**
3	-	**Help**	Beatles	Capitol	15	1	
4	4	**The Sound Of Music**	Soundtrack	RCA	108	1	
5	5	**Summer Days (And Summer Nights!!)**	Beach Boys	Capitol	10	4	
6	2	**Herman's Hermits On Tour**	Herman's Hermits	MGM	18		
7	1	**Beatles VI**	Beatles	Capitol	13		**P**
8	7	**Mary Poppins**	Soundtrack	Buena Vista	48	2	
9	-	**The In Crowd**	Ramsey Lewis	Argo	15		**FL**
10	9	**Bringing It All Back Home**	Bob Dylan	Columbia	14	1	**F**

- Folk/rock really took off in the summer of 1967. Bob Dylan's 'Like A Rolling Stone', Barry McGuire's 'Eve Of Destruction' and 'Mr. Tambourine Man' by The Byrds were heard everywhere; as were smash hits from Sonny & Cher and The Turtles. The influence of this genre also spread to the album market where Dylan, The Byrds and Sonny & Cher flew the folk/rock flag.

- There was renewed interest in instrumental albums in the USA, with Herb Alpert & The Tijuana Brass and jazz pianist Ramsey Lewis leading the way. Also sitting in the Top 20 were LPs by German pianist Horst Jankowski and Britain's Sounds Orchestra

- Despite the transatlantic resurgence of interest in American acts, British artists continued to hold their own in the USA. Among the UK acts working successfully in the States were Herman's Hermits, The Dave Clark Five, Donovan, Tom Jones, The Hollies and Liverpool acts The Searchers and Cilla Black. The UK act grabbing most headlines was, of course, The Beatles, their third American stadium tour, which included playing to a record 56,000 fans at New York's Shea Stadium, was amazingly successful.

- Adding to the British acts on the US album chart were first time hitmakers Tom Jones, Them, featuring Van Morrison, Donovan, Marianne Faithfull and The Yardbirds.

UK 1965 OCT-DEC

• The Beatles received their prestigious MBE (Members of the British Empire) Awards from The Queen before they embarked on their last ever British tour – The Moody Blues were among their support acts. It came as no surprise when their album **Rubber Soul** hurriedly headed to the top of the transatlantic charts. In Britain, it even managed to hold **The Sound Of Music** at bay for nine weeks.

• Panic was setting in amongst British pop TV show producers. After several years at the top *Thank Your Lucky Stars* announced that, in an effort to halt its declining ratings, it would include "no more long-haired groups". *Ready Steady Go* was also suffering and was almost discontinued. The most popular music show on the small screen, according to pop paper polls, was relative newcomer *Top Of The Pops*.

• As the old year faded away several new acts started their journeys to fame in Britain. Among them were Van Morrison, the leader of the recently disbanded Them, Marc Bolan, who released his first single, and David Jones who later became David Bowie, who appeared with the Lower Third at London's noted rock venue, the Marquee club.

October 1965

This Mnth	Last Mnth	Title	Artist	Label	Wks in 10	US Pos	
1	2	**The Sound Of Music**	Soundtrack	RCA	235	1	**2P**
2	1	**Help**	Beatles	Parlophone	30	1	
3	3	**Mary Poppins**	Soundtrack	HMV	55	1	
4	-	**Out Of Our Heads**	Rolling Stones	Decca	16	1	
5	5	**Almost There**	Andy Williams	CBS	24		**F**
6	4	**Bringing It All Back Home**	Bob Dylan	CBS	23	6	
7	-	**Highway 61 Revisited**	Bob Dylan	CBS	12	3	
8	6	**Joan Baez No. 5**	Joan Baez	Fontana	15	12	
9	-	**Hollies**	Hollies	Parlophone	8		
10	-	**Look At Us**	Sonny & Cher	Atlantic	6	2	**FL**

November 1965

This Mnth	Last Mnth	Title	Artist	Label	Wks in 10	US Pos	
1	1	**The Sound Of Music**	Soundtrack	RCA	235	1	**2P**
2	2	**Help**	Beatles	Parlophone	30	1	
3	4	**Out Of Our Heads**	Rolling Stones	Decca	16	1	
4	3	**Mary Poppins**	Soundtrack	HMV	55	1	
5	7	**Highway 61 Revisited**	Bob Dylan	CBS	12	3	
6	5	**Almost There**	Andy Williams	CBS	24		**F**
7	-	**Mann Made**	Manfred Mann	HMV	7		
8	-	**Everything Comes Up Dusty**	Dusty Springfield	Philips	8		
9	10	**Look At Us**	Sonny & Cher	Atlantic	6	2	**FL**
10	9	**Hollies**	Hollies	Parlophone	8		

December 1965

This Mnth	Last Mnth	Title	Artist	Label	Wks in 10	US Pos	
1	1	**The Sound Of Music**	Soundtrack	RCA	235	1	**2P**
2	4	**Mary Poppins**	Soundtrack	HMV	55	1	
3	2	**Help**	Beatles	Parlophone	30	1	
4	-	**Farewell Angelina**	Joan Baez	Fontana	7	10	**L**
5	3	**Out Of Our Heads**	Rolling Stones	Decca	16	1	
6	-	**Rubber Soul**	Beatles	Parlophone	30	1	
7	5	**Highway 61 Revisited**	Bob Dylan	CBS	12	3	
8	6	**Almost There**	Andy Williams	CBS	24		**F**
9	7	**Mann Made**	Manfred Mann	HMV	7		
10	-	**Elvis For Everybody**	Elvis Presley	RCA	3	10	

US 1965 OCT-DEC

October 1965

This Mnth	Last Mnth	Title	Artist	Label	Wks in 10	UK Pos	
1	3	**Help**	Beatles	Capitol	15	1	
2	1	**Look At Us**	Sonny & Cher	Atco	14	7	FL
3	4	**The Sound Of Music**	Soundtrack	RCA	108	1	
4	9	**The In Crowd**	Ramsey Lewis	Argo	15		FL
5	2	**Out Of Our Heads**	Rolling Stones	London	16	2	P
6	-	**Highway 61 Revisited**	Bob Dylan	Columbia	8	4	
7	-	**More Hits By The Supremes**	Supremes	Motown	4		
8	7	**Mary Poppins**	Soundtrack	Buena Vista	48	2	
9	-	**Whipped Cream & Other Delights**	Herb Alpert &				
			The Tijuana Brass	A&M	61	2	
10	10	**Bringing It All Back Home**	Bob Dylan	Columbia	14	1	F

November 1965

This Mnth	Last Mnth	Title	Artist	Label	Wks in 10	UK Pos	
1	3	**The Sound Of Music**	Soundtrack	RCA	108	1	
2	1	**Help**	Beatles	Capitol	15	1	
3	9	**Whipped Cream & Other Delights**	Herb Alpert &				
			The Tijuana Brass	A&M	61	2	
4	4	**The In Crowd**	Ramsey Lewis	Argo	15		FL
5	6	**Highway 61 Revisited**	Bob Dylan	Columbia	8	4	
6	2	**Look At Us**	Sonny & Cher	Atco	14	7	FL
7	-	**My Name Is Barbra, Two...**	Barbra Streisand	Columbia	19	6	P
8	5	**Out Of Our Heads**	Rolling Stones	London	16	2	P
9	-	**Going Places**	Herb Alpert &				
			The Tijuana Brass	A&M	48	4	
10	8	**Mary Poppins**	Soundtrack	Buena Vista	48	2	

December 1965

This Mnth	Last Mnth	Title	Artist	Label	Wks in 10	UK Pos	
1	3	**Whipped Cream & Other Delights**	Herb Alpert &				
			The Tijuana Brass	A&M	61	2	
2	1	**The Sound Of Music**	Soundtrack	RCA	108	1	
3	7	**My Name Is Barbra, Two...**	Barbra Streisand	Columbia	19	6	P
4	9	**Going Places**	Herb Alpert &				
			The Tijuana Brass	A&M	48	4	
5	-	**Welcome To The LBJ Ranch!**	Various	Capitol	6		FL
6	-	**The Best Of Herman's Hermits**	Herman's Hermits	MGM	16		L
7	2	**Help**	Beatles	Capitol	15	1	
8	4	**The In Crowd**	Ramsey Lewis	Argo	15		FL
9	-	**Beach Boys Party!**	Beach Boys	Capitol	4	3	
10	6	**Look At Us**	Sonny & Cher	Atco	14	7	FL

- The sales of Barbra Streisand albums seemed unaffected by any musical revolutions that might be going on around her. Both **My Name Is Barbra** and **My Name Is Barbra, Two** reached the uppermost chart rungs.

- The Supremes were another female act that added to their tally of top albums. A collection of their hits reached the Top 10 and a live recording of the trio's show at New York's famed Copacabana Club almost emulated its achievement. On the latter album the Detroit divas sang a handful of their hits, a selection of standards and a Sam Cooke tribute medley.

- After being overshadowed by British bands for two years, American groups were starting to make their presence felt again on the album chart. **A Session With Gary Lewis & The Playboys** put that West coast band in the Top 20. Also, the good time East Coast combo, The Lovin' Spoonful, headed that way with **Do You Believe In Magic**. Among the other new groups starting to attract attention were San Francisco's Grateful Dead and Jefferson Airplane.

UK 1966 JAN-MAR

• Noteworthy new groups enjoying their first major hit albums included mod band The Who with **My Generation**, and R&B band Spencer Davis, which featured soulful teenage vocalist Steve Winwood, whose first two albums, aptly titled **Their 1st LP** and **The 2nd LP** both entered the Top 10. Incidentally, The Who were among the guests on the last *Shindig* TV show seen in the States.

• Soul music was making a big impact in the UK. American headliners James Brown, Wilson Pickett and Stevie Wonder were to the fore, while Otis Redding's soulful **Otis Blue** album was making a name for him.

• It was another interesting period for The Beatles. Their launch pad, the Cavern Club in Liverpool, closed down for the first time, and John Lennon made a casual remark about the group currently being more popular with teenagers than Jesus. This controversial statement was to cause the group much adverse publicity over the next few months.

January 1966

This Mnth	Last Mnth	Title	Artist	Label	Wks in 10	US Pos	
1	6	**Rubber Soul**	Beatles	Parlophone	30	1	
2	1	**The Sound Of Music**	Soundtrack	RCA	235	1	**2P**
3	2	**Mary Poppins**	Soundtrack	HMV	55	1	
4	3	**Help**	Beatles	Parlophone	30	1	
5	-	**A World Of Our Own**	Seekers	Columbia	8	123	**F**
6	-	**Tears Of Happiness**	Ken Dodd	Columbia	3		**F**
7	4	**Farewell Angelina**	Joan Baez	Fontana	7	10	**L**
8	-	**My Generation**	Who	Brunswick	5		**F**
9	-	**Take It Easy**	Walker Brothers	Philips	24		**F**
10	5	**Out Of Our Heads**	Rolling Stones	Decca	16	1	

February 1966

This Mnth	Last Mnth	Title	Artist	Label	Wks in 10	US Pos	
1	2	**The Sound Of Music**	Soundtrack	RCA	235	1	**2P**
2	1	**Rubber Soul**	Beatles	Parlophone	30	1	
3	3	**Mary Poppins**	Soundtrack	HMV	55	1	
4	-	**The 2nd LP**	Spencer Davis Group	Fontana	13		
5	9	**Take It Easy**	Walker Brothers	Philips	24		**F**
6	4	**Help**	Beatles	Parlophone	30	1	
7	-	**My Name Is Barbra, Two**	Barbra Streisand	CBS	11	2	**F**
8	-	**Going Places**	Herb Alpert & The Tijuana Brass	Pye	42	1	**F**
9	-	**Their 1st LP**	Spencer Davis Group	Fontana	5		**F**
10	-	**Beach Boys Party**	Beach Boys	Capitol	9	6	**F**

March 1966

This Mnth	Last Mnth	Title	Artist	Label	Wks in 10	US Pos	
1	1	**The Sound Of Music**	Soundtrack	RCA	235	1	**2P**
2	2	**Rubber Soul**	Beatles	Parlophone	30	1	
3	3	**Mary Poppins**	Soundtrack	HMV	55	1	
4	10	**Beach Boys Party**	Beach Boys	Capitol	9	6	**F**
5	5	**Take It Easy**	Walker Brothers	Philips	24		**F**
6	8	**Going Places**	Herb Alpert & The Tijuana Brass	Pye	42	1	**F**
7	4	**The 2nd LP**	Spencer Davis Group	Fontana	13		
8	-	**Bye Bye Blues**	Bert Kaempfert	Polydor	10	46	**FL**
9	-	**Otis Blue**	Otis Redding	Atlantic	14		**F**
10	-	**A Man And His Music**	Frank Sinatra	Reprise	6	9	

US 1966

JAN-MAR

January 1966

This Mnth	Last Mnth	Title	Artist	Label	Wks in 10	UK Pos	
1	1	**Whipped Cream & Other Delights**	Herb Alpert & The Tijuana Brass	A&M	61	2	
2	2	**The Sound Of Music**	Soundtrack	RCA	108	1	
3	-	**Rubber Soul**	Beatles	Capitol	14	1	**4P**
4	4	**Going Places**	Herb Alpert & The Tijuana Brass	A&M	48	4	
5	-	**December's Children (And Everbody's)**	Rolling Stones	London	8		
6	6	**The Best Of Herman's Hermits**	Herman's Hermits	MGM	16		**L**
7	-	**My World**	Eddy Arnold	RCA	7		**FL**
8	-	**September Of My Years**	Frank Sinatra	Reprise	11		
9	5	**Welcome To The LBJ Ranch!**	Various	Capitol	6		**FL**
10	3	**My Name Is Barbra, Two...**	Barbra Streisand	Columbia	19	6	**P**

February 1966

This Mnth	Last Mnth	Title	Artist	Label	Wks in 10	UK Pos	
1	1	**Whipped Cream & Other Delights**	Herb Alpert & The Tijuana Brass	A&M	61	2	
2	3	**Rubber Soul**	Beatles	Capitol	14	1	**4P**
3	4	**Going Places**	Herb Alpert & The Tijuana Brass	A&M	48	4	
4	2	**The Sound Of Music**	Soundtrack	RCA	108	1	
5	10	**My Name Is Barbra, Two...**	Barbra Streisand	Columbia	19	6	**P**
6	8	**September Of My Years**	Frank Sinatra	Reprise	11		
7	-	**Golden Hits**	Roger Miller	Smash	10		**L**
8	6	**The Best Of Herman's Hermits**	Herman's Hermits	MGM	16		**L**
9	-	**A Man And His Music**	Frank Sinatra	Reprise	3	9	
10	5	**December's Children (And Everbody's)**	Rolling Stones	London	8		

March 1966

This Mnth	Last Mnth	Title	Artist	Label	Wks in 10	UK Pos	
1	1	**Whipped Cream & Other Delights**	Herb Alpert & The Tijuana Brass	A&M	61	2	
2	3	**Going Places**	Herb Alpert & The Tijuana Brass	A&M	48	4	
3	-	**Ballads Of The Green Berets**	Ssgt Barry Sadler	RCA	10		**FL**
4	2	**Rubber Soul**	Beatles	Capitol	14	1	**4P**
5	4	**The Sound Of Music**	Soundtrack	RCA	108	1	
6	6	**September Of My Years**	Frank Sinatra	Reprise	11		
7	7	**Golden Hits**	Roger Miller	Smash	10		**L**
8	8	**The Best Of Herman's Hermits**	Herman's Hermits	MGM	16		**L**
9	5	**My Name Is Barbra, Two...**	Barbra Streisand	Columbia	19	6	**P**
10	-	**The Best Of The Animals**	Animals	MGM	7		**L**

• Among the acts debuting in the Top 20 album charts were Motown groups The Temptations, The Miracles and The Four Tops with **Temptin'-Temptations**, The Miracles' **Going To A Go-Go** and The Four Tops' **Second Album** respectively.

• CBS announced that they were developing a video disk system that would enable people to see and hear artists on their own TVs.

• The biggest selling album inspired by the Vietnam war was **Ballads Of The Green Berets** sung and composed by Staff Sergeant Barry Sadler. Both the LP and the single 'Ballad Of The Green Berets' topped the US charts, with the album leaping from Number 53 directly to the top spot.

• Brian Wilson and The Beach Boys started work on the most ambitious rock album project to date, **Pet Sounds**. Other news from the West Coast included the formation of rock band Buffalo Springfield which included Stephen Stills, Neil Young and Richie Furay.

• Country music was again enjoying good crossover sales. Veteran performer Eddy Arnold scored with **My World**, and Roger Miller clocked up his third Top 20 album of the year with his collection of **Golden Hits**.

UK 1966

APR-JUNE

• The British album chart was extended from a Top 20 to a Top 30.

• Just before Frank Sinatra notched up his only solo transatlantic number 1 hit single with 'Strangers In The Night', his daughter, Nancy – who had accomplished that feat with her first hit, 'These Boots Are Made For Walkin' – reached the transatlantic Top 20 albums chart with **Boots**. For the record, Nancy's album included tracks made famous by The Beatles, The Rolling Stones and The Beach Boys.

• Highly touted new London band The Small Faces, which included Steve Marriott, Ronnie Lane and Kenny Jones, hit the heights with their eponymous debut LP. Another noteworthy act scoring their first Top 10 entry was singer/pianist Georgie Fame with a collection of R&B songs entitled **Sweet Things**.

• The Beatles' final live appearance in Britain was at the *NME* Poll Winners Concert. Among the other acts appearing were their biggest rivals, The Rolling Stones, whose then current album **Aftermath** had given them their third UK chart topper. Before setting out on their World tours, both groups were seen at Bob Dylan's Royal Albert Hall show.

• It was announced that the global sales of the 1961 transatlantic chart topping soundtrack album **West Side Story** had now passed five million.

April 1966

This Mnth	Last Mnth	Title	Artist	Label	Wks in 10	US Pos	
1	1	**The Sound Of Music**	Soundtrack	RCA	235	1	2P
2	2	**Rubber Soul**	Beatles	Parlophone	30	1	
3	5	**Take It Easy**	Walker Brothers	Philips	24		F
4	3	**Mary Poppins**	Soundtrack	HMV	55	1	
5	8	**Bye Bye Blues**	Bert Kaempfert	Polydor	10	46	FL
6	6	**Going Places**	Herb Alpert & The Tijuana Brass	Pye	42	1	F
7	-	**Aftermath**	Rolling Stones	Decca	22	2	
8	9	**Otis Blue**	Otis Redding	Atlantic	14		F
9	4	**Beach Boys Party**	Beach Boys	Capitol	9	6	F
10	7	**The 2nd LP**	Spencer Davis Group	Fontana	13		

May 1966

This Mnth	Last Mnth	Title	Artist	Label	Wks in 10	US Pos	
1	7	**Aftermath**	Rolling Stones	Decca	22	2	
2	1	**The Sound Of Music**	Soundtrack	RCA	235	1	2P
3	2	**Rubber Soul**	Beatles	Parlophone	30	1	
4	-	**Mantovani Magic**	Mantovani	Decca	7	23	
5	-	**Most Of The Animals**	Animals	Columbia	10		
6	3	**Take It Easy**	Walker Brothers	Philips	24		F
7	-	**Beach Boys Today!**	Beach Boys	Capitol	5	4	
8	-	**Cilla Sings A Rainbow**	Cilla Black	Parlophone	11		
9	-	**Small Faces**	Small Faces	Decca	12		F
10	-	**My Name Is Barbra, Two**	Barbra Streisand	CBS	11	2	F

June 1966

This Mnth	Last Mnth	Title	Artist	Label	Wks in 10	US Pos	
1	1	**Aftermath**	Rolling Stones	Decca	22	2	
2	2	**The Sound Of Music**	Soundtrack	RCA	235	1	2P
3	9	**Small Faces**	Small Faces	Decca	12		F
4	8	**Cilla Sings A Rainbow**	Cilla Black	Parlophone	11		
5	-	**Animalisms**	Animals	Decca	8	33	L
6	-	**Shadow Music**	Shadows	Columbia	8		
7	3	**Rubber Soul**	Beatles	Parlophone	30	1	
8	-	**Sweet Things**	Georgie Fame	Columbia	10		F
9	5	**Most Of The Animals**	Animals	Columbia	10		
10	6	**Take It Easy**	Walker Brothers	Philips	24		F

US 1966 APR-JUNE

April 1966

This Mnth	Last Mnth	Title	Artist	Label	Wks in 10	UK Pos	
1	2	**Going Places**	Herb Alpert & The Tijuana Brass	A&M	48	4	
2	3	**Ballads Of The Green Berets**	Ssgt Barry Sadler	RCA	10		FL
3	1	**Whipped Cream & Other Delights**	Herb Alpert & The Tijuana Brass	A&M	61	2	
4	5	**The Sound Of Music**	Soundtrack	RCA	108	1	
5	-	**Boots**	Nancy Sinatra	Reprise	8	12	FL
6	10	**The Best Of The Animals**	Animals	MGM	7		L
7	-	**Color Me Barbra**	Barbra Streisand	Columbia	9		
8	-	**Just Like Us!**	Paul Revere & The Raiders	Columbia	4		F
9	-	**South Of The Border**	Herb Alpert & The Tijuana Brass	A&M	3		
10	4	**Rubber Soul**	Beatles	Capitol	14	1	4P

May 1966

This Mnth	Last Mnth	Title	Artist	Label	Wks in 10	UK Pos	
1	1	**Going Places**	Herb Alpert & The Tijuana Brass	A&M	48	4	
2	-	**Big Hits (High Tide And Green Grass)**	Rolling Stones	London	9	4	2P
3	-	**If You Can Believe Your Eyes And Ears**	Mamas & The Papas	Dunhill	20		F
4	7	**Color Me Barbra**	Barbra Streisand	Columbia	9		
5	3	**Whipped Cream & Other Delights**	Herb Alpert & Tijuana Brass	A&M	61	2	
6	4	**The Sound Of Music**	Soundtrack	RCA	108	1	
7	-	**What Now My Love**	Herb Alpert & Tijuana Brass	A&M	32	18	
8	2	**Ballads Of The Green Berets**	Ssgt Barry Sadler	RCA	10		FL
9	-	**Soul & Inspiration**	Righteous Brothers	Verve	5		L
10	-	**I Hear A Symphony**	Supremes	Motown	6		

June 1966

This Mnth	Last Mnth	Title	Artist	Label	Wks in 10	UK Pos	
1	7	**What Now My Love**	Herb Alpert & The Tijuana Brass	A&M	32	18	
2	3	**If You Can Believe Your Eyes And Ears**	Mamas & The Papas	Dunhill	20		F
3	6	**The Sound Of Music**	Soundtrack	RCA	108	1	
4	5	**Whipped Cream & Other Delights**	Herb Alpert & Tijuana Brass	A&M	61	2	
5	1	**Going Places**	Herb Alpert & Tijuana Brass	A&M	48	4	
6	2	**Big Hits (High Tide And Green Grass)**	Rolling Stones	London	9	4	2P
7	-	**Doctor Zhivago**	Soundtrack	MGM	71	3	
8	4	**Color Me Barbra**	Barbra Streisand	Columbia	9		
9	-	**The Shadow Of Your Smile**	Andy Williams	Columbia	4	24	
10	9	**Soul & Inspiration**	Righteous Brothers	Verve	5		L

• Herb Alpert proved to be a very talented alchemist by turning brass into gold time and time again. Alpert & The Tijuana Brass' first six albums, **The Lonely Bull**, **Herb Alpert & The Tijuana Brass, Volume 2**, **South Of The Border**, **Whipped Cream & Other Delights** and **Going Places** all earned gold discs. Three of them reached Number 1 and all of them resided in this quarter's Top 20. Adding to Alpert's achievements was the fact that they all appeared on his own A&M label.

• As some of Britain's Class Of '64, The Dave Clark Five, The Rolling Stones and The Animals, scored with **'Greatest Hits'** packages, a new generation of American groups joined them on the charts. **If You Can Believe Your Eyes And Ears**, made the hippie West Coast-based Mamas & Papas the first group to top the chart with their debut LP since The Beatles. At the same time, The Lovin' Spoonful were selling a lot of albums on both sides of the Atlantic, and both The Young Rascals and Love were grabbing attention in the US with self-titled debut LPs.

UK 1966

JULY-SEPT

• As guitarist Eric Clapton announced the formation of his new group, Cream (above), an album he recorded with John Mayall, **Blues Breakers**, hit the Top 10, and simultaneously his old group, The Yardbirds, climbed into the Top 20 with their self-titled album. Cream were one of the hits of the National Jazz and Blues Festival, where they appeared alongside The Who, The Move, Georgie Fame and The Small Faces.

• Apart from The Beatles, other British acts touring in the USA were Herman's Hermits, The Animals, Freddie & The Dreamers and The Yardbirds. Meanwhile, American acts Simon & Garfunkel and Sonny & Cher were feted by British audiences.

• The end of summer 1966 was a musical milestone. Just weeks after The Beatles had played their last ever live gig, American singer/guitarist Jimi Hendrix arrived in Britain to launch his solo career, and a new American TV show *The Monkees* was screened Stateside for the first time.

July 1966

This Mnth	Last Mnth	Title	Artist	Label	Wks in 10	US Pos	
1	2	**The Sound Of Music**	Soundtrack	RCA	235	1	2P
2	1	**Aftermath**	Rolling Stones	Decca	22	2	
3	3	**Small Faces**	Small Faces	Decca	12		F
4	-	**Pet Sounds**	Beach Boys	Capitol	26	10	
5	-	**The Mamas And Papas**	Mamas & The Papas	RCA	11	4	F
6	5	**Animalisms**	Animals	Decca	8	33	L
7	-	**Strangers In The Night**	Frank Sinatra	Reprise	8	1	
8	4	**Cilla Sings A Rainbow**	Cilla Black	Parlophone	11		
9	8	**Sweet Things**	Georgie Fame	Columbia	10		F
10	-	**Summer Days**	Beach Boys	Capitol	10	2	

August 1966

This Mnth	Last Mnth	Title	Artist	Label	Wks in 10	US Pos	
1	1	**The Sound Of Music**	Soundtrack	RCA	235	1	2P
2	4	**Pet Sounds**	Beach Boys	Capitol	26	10	
3	-	**Revolver**	Beatles	Parlophone	21	1	
4	10	**Summer Days**	Beach Boys	Capitol	10	2	
5	2	**Aftermath**	Rolling Stones	Decca	22	2	
6	7	**Strangers In The Night**	Frank Sinatra	Reprise	8	1	
7	5	**The Mamas And Papas**	Mamas & The Papas	RCA	11	4	F
8	-	**From Nowhere...The Troggs**	Troggs	Fontana	6		F
9	-	**Paradise Hawaiian Style (Soundtrack)**	Elvis Presley	RCA	2	15	
10	-	**Blonde On Blonde**	Bob Dylan	CBS	8	9	

September 1966

This Mnth	Last Mnth	Title	Artist	Label	Wks in 10	US Pos	
1	3	**Revolver**	Beatles	Parlophone	21	1	
2	1	**The Sound Of Music**	Soundtrack	RCA	235	1	2P
3	2	**Pet Sounds**	Beach Boys	Capitol	26	10	
4	10	**Blonde On Blonde**	Bob Dylan	CBS	8	9	
5	-	**Portrait**	Walker Brothers	Philips	11		
6	5	**Aftermath**	Rolling Stones	Decca	22	2	
7	4	**Summer Days**	Beach Boys	Capitol	10	2	
8	7	**The Mamas And Papas**	Mamas & The Papas	RCA	11	4	F
9	-	**Blues Breakers**	John Mayall & Eric Clapton	Decca	7		F
10	-	**Going Places**	Herb Alpert & The Tijuana Brass	Pye	42	1	F

US 1966

JULY-SEPT

July 1966

This Mnth	Last Mnth	Title	Artist	Label	Wks in 10	UK Pos	
1	1	**What Now My Love**	Herb Alpert & The Tijuana Brass	A&M	32	18	
2	-	**Strangers In The Night**	Frank Sinatra	Reprise	14	4	P
3	2	**If You Can Believe Your Eyes And Ears**	Mamas & The Papas	Dunhill	20		F
4	-	**Lou Rawls Live!**	Lou Rawls	Capitol	6		F
5	7	**Doctor Zhivago**	Soundtrack	MGM	71	3	
6	4	**Whipped Cream & Other Delights**	Herb Alpert & The Tijuana Brass	A&M	61	2	
7	-	**'Yesterday'... And Today**	Beatles	Capitol	9		
8	5	**Going Places**	Herb Alpert & Tijuana Brass	A&M	48	4	
9	3	**The Sound Of Music**	Soundtrack	RCA	108	1	
10	-	**Wonderfulness**	Bill Cosby	Warner	5		FP

August 1966

This Mnth	Last Mnth	Title	Artist	Label	Wks in 10	UK Pos	
1	7	**'Yesterday'... And Today**	Beatles	Capitol	9		
2	1	**What Now My Love**	Herb Alpert & The Tijuana Brass	A&M	32	18	
3	2	**Strangers In The Night**	Frank Sinatra	Reprise	14	4	P
4	-	**Aftermath**	Rolling Stones	London	11	1	P
5	5	**Doctor Zhivago**	Soundtrack	MGM	71	3	
6	-	**Somewhere My Love**	Ray Conniff	Columbia	17	34	PL
7	8	**Going Places**	Herb Alpert & The Tijuana Brass	A&M	48	4	
8	6	**Whipped Cream & Other Delights**	Herb Alpert & Tijuana Brass	A&M	61	2	
9	9	**The Sound Of Music**	Soundtrack	RCA	108	1	
10	3	**If You Can Believe Your Eyes And Ears**	Mamas & The Papas	Dunhill	20		F

September 1966

This Mnth	Last Mnth	Title	Artist	Label	Wks in 10	UK Pos	
1	5	**Doctor Zhivago**	Soundtrack	MGM	71	3	
2	2	**What Now My Love**	Herb Alpert & The Tijuana Brass	A&M	32	18	
3	-	**Revolver**	Beatles	Capitol	14	1	3P
4	6	**Somewhere My Love**	Ray Conniff	Columbia	17	34	PL
5	9	**The Sound Of Music**	Soundtrack	RCA	108	1	
6	3	**Strangers In The Night**	Frank Sinatra	Reprise	14	4	P
7	1	**'Yesterday'... And Today**	Beatles	Capitol	9		
8	8	**Whipped Cream & Other Delights**	Herb Alpert & The Tijuana Brass	A&M	61	2	
9	4	**Aftermath**	Rolling Stones	London	11	1	P
10	-	**Best Of The Beach Boys**	Beach Boys	Capitol	6	2	2P

• Throughout their third and last American tour, The Beatles headed the US album chart, firstly with their special US compilation, **Yesterday...And Today**, and then their British Number 1, **Revolver**, shot past it. They were not the only act with two albums in the higher reaches of the chart. Frank Sinatra had **Strangers In The Night** and **Sinatra At The Sands**, the latter with Count Basie. The Beach Boys did the double with **Pet Sounds** and **Best Of The Beach Boys**. Incidentally, in the UK The Beach Boys had a chart hat-trick with **Pet Sounds, Summer Days** and **Beach Boys Today**.

• The most popular MOR film theme of the period was 'Somewhere My Love' from *Doctor Zhivago*. The song was heard on the chart topping soundtrack album and on the Ray Conniff album of the same name. The Grammy winning song soon appeared on hit albums by several other acts, including Frank Sinatra, Johnny Mathis and Jack Jones.

• Bill Cosby was the latest comedian to tickle America's funny bone. His three albums **Wonderfulness**, **Why Is There Air?** and **I Started Out As A Child** were all successful.

UK 1966 OCT-DEC

• The UK album chart was extended to a Top 40 only to be cut back to a Top 15 two months later.

• British acts played a less significant role on the US scene in 1966, and the year ended with no UK albums in the Top 10. Pundits on both sides of the Atlantic who had said "The British beat boom was over" were proved right.

• The Beach Boys replaced The Beatles as the World's Top Group in the *NME* Poll, and the Californian act were mobbed when they arrived in the UK for a tour. The Beatles, meanwhile, were in the recording studio working on their 'answer' to the Beach Boys' classic **Pet Sounds** album. The result was released the following summer as **Sergeant Pepper's Lonely Hearts Club Band**.

• The last *Ready Steady Go* was seen on British TV – its stars included The Who and early UK rocker Billy Fury. Other TV highlights were the series *This Is Tom Jones* and *I*, whose star Dusty Springfield was enjoying her most successful album, **Golden Hits**.

• American headliners Sammy Davis Jr., Gene Pitney, Henry Mancini, Las Vegas veteran Wayne Newton and Jerry Lee Lewis joined Britain's Bachelors, Matt Monro and Tommy Steele at the *Royal Variety Show*.

October 1966

This Mnth	Last Mnth	Title	Artist	Label	Wks in 10	US Pos	
1	2	**The Sound Of Music**	Soundtrack	RCA	235	1	2P
2	1	**Revolver**	Beatles	Parlophone	21	1	
3	3	**Pet Sounds**	Beach Boys	Capitol	26	10	
4	5	**Portrait**	Walker Brothers	Philips	11		
5	10	**Going Places**	Herb Alpert & The Tijuana Brass	Pye	42	1	F
6	-	**Autumn '66**	Spencer Davis Group	Fontana	8		L
7	-	**Well Respected Kinks**	Kinks	Marble Arch	9		
8	9	**Blues Breakers**	John Mayall & Eric Clapton	Decca	7		F
9	-	**Stars Charity Fantasia Save The Children**	Various	SCF	5		
10	4	**Blonde On Blonde**	Bob Dylan	CBS	8	9	

November 1966

This Mnth	Last Mnth	Title	Artist	Label	Wks in 10	US Pos	
1	1	**The Sound Of Music**	Soundtrack	RCA	235	1	2P
2	-	**Golden Hits**	Dusty Springfield	Philips	10	137	
3	2	**Revolver**	Beatles	Parlophone	21	1	
4	-	**Distant Drums**	Jim Reeves	RCA	14	21	
5	3	**Pet Sounds**	Beach Boys	Capitol	26	10	
6	-	**Best Of The Beach Boys**	Beach Boys	Capitol	55	8	
7	5	**Going Places**	Herb Alpert & The Tijuana Brass	Pye	42	1	F
8	7	**Well Respected Kinks**	Kinks	Marble Arch	9		
9	-	**Big Hits (High Tide And Green Grass)**	Rolling Stones	Decca	10	3	
10	4	**Portrait**	Walker Brothers	Philips	11		

December 1966

This Mnth	Last Mnth	Title	Artist	Label	Wks in 10	US Pos	
1	1	**The Sound Of Music**	Soundtrack	RCA	235	1	2P
2	6	**Best Of The Beach Boys**	Beach Boys	Capitol	55	8	
3	4	**Distant Drums**	Jim Reeves	RCA	14	21	
4	9	**Big Hits (High Tide And Green Grass)**	Rolling Stones	Decca	10	3	
5	-	**Come The Day**	Seekers	Columbia	23		
6	3	**Revolver**	Beatles	Parlophone	21	1	
7	-	**Gentle Shades Of Val Doonican**	Val Doonican	Decca	8		
8	2	**Golden Hits**	Dusty Springfield	Philips	10	137	
9	7	**Going Places**	Herb Alpert & The Tijuana Brass	Pye	42	1	F
10	5	**Pet Sounds**	Beach Boys	Capitol	26	10	

US 1966 OCT-DEC

October 1966

This Mnth	Last Mnth	Title	Artist	Label	Wks in 10	UK Pos	
1	3	**Revolver**	Beatles	Capitol	14	1	3P
2	1	**Doctor Zhivago**	Soundtrack	MGM	71	3	
3	2	**What Now My Love**	Herb Alpert & The Tijuana Brass	A&M	32	18	
4	4	**Somewhere My Love**	Ray Conniff	Columbia	17	34	PL
5	-	**The Supremes A Go-Go**	Supremes	Motown	15	15	
6	5	**The Sound Of Music**	Soundtrack	RCA	108	1	
7	8	**Whipped Cream & Other Delights**	Herb Alpert & The Tijuana Brass	A&M	61	2	
8	-	**The Mamas And The Papas**	Mamas & The Papas	Dunhill	13	3	
9	9	**Aftermath**	Rolling Stones	London	11	1	P
10	-	**And Then...Along Comes The Association**	Association	Valiant	7		F

November 1966

This Mnth	Last Mnth	Title	Artist	Label	Wks in 10	UK Pos	
1	-	**The Monkees**	Monkees	Colgems	32	1	F
2	2	**Doctor Zhivago**	Soundtrack	MGM	71	3	
3	5	**The Supremes A Go-Go**	Supremes	Motown	15	15	
4	8	**The Mamas And The Papas**	Mamas & The Papas	Dunhill	13	3	
5	3	**What Now My Love**	Herb Alpert & The Tijuana Brass	A&M	32	18	
6	10	**And Then...Along Comes The Association**	Association	Valiant	7		F
7	1	**Revolver**	Beatles	Capitol	14	1	3P
8	4	**Somewhere My Love**	Ray Conniff	Columbia	17	34	PL
9	-	**Lou Rawls Soulin'**	Lou Rawls	Capitol	6		
10	6	**The Sound Of Music**	Soundtrack	RCA	108	1	

December 1966

This Mnth	Last Mnth	Title	Artist	Label	Wks in 10	UK Pos	
1	1	**The Monkees**	Monkees	Colgems	32	1	F
2	2	**Doctor Zhivago**	Soundtrack	MGM	71	3	
3	10	**The Sound Of Music**	Soundtrack	RCA	108	1	
4	3	**The Supremes A Go-Go**	Supremes	Motown	15	15	
5	4	**The Mamas And The Papas**	Mamas & The Papas	Dunhill	13	3	
6	-	**Parsley Sage Rosemary And Thyme**	Simon & Garfunkel	Columbia	17	13	F3P
7	-	**S.R.O.**	Herb Alpert & The Tijuana Brass	A&M	19	5	
8	5	**What Now My Love**	Herb Alpert & The Tijuana Brass	A&M	32	18	
9	-	**Going Places**	Herb Alpert & The Tijuana Brass	A&M	48	4	
10	-	**Je M'appelle Barbra**	Barbra Streisand	Columbia	6		

• Tape cassettes and tape cartridges were first introduced commercially in 1966, and sales of albums that year increased by 6%, following a 13% rise in 1965. Albums now accounted for one third of all records sold in the USA. For the first time it was not essential to have a hit single to make money and record labels actively sought acts with album potential, even if their chances of hit singles were slim.

• The Beatles-based TV group *The Monkees* were an instant success and soon headed the singles and album chart. Their eponymous debut LP topped the chart for three months.

• The Supremes became the first female group to head the US album charts when **Supremes A Go-Go** filled the gap between Number 1s by The Beatles and The Monkees.

• As 1966 closed, Grace Slick joined the burgeoning West Coast group Jefferson Airplane, The Jimi Hendrix Experience was formed and, after a couple of US dates with The Yardbirds, Jeff Beck left to form his own group with Rod Stewart and Ron Wood.

UK 1967 JAN-MAR

• The Monkees repeated their American feat by topping the UK lists with their self-titled debut album. Among the other US acts hitting the heights was soul singer Geno Washington, who had moved to the UK when he found it impossible to make a name for himself in his homeland. He became a top attraction on the British club scene and, although he never had a hit single, **Hand Clappin' – Foot Stompin' – Funky Butt – Live**! was one of two albums of his to crack the Top 10.

• UK acts were losing their grip on the British album chart. In March, The Rolling Stones were the only one in the Top 10. In the States, The Stones bowed to pressure and changed the lyric of 'Let's Spend The Night Together' to 'Let's Spend Some Time Together' on Ed Sullivan's US TV show. Back in Britain, The Stones upset the powers-that-be when they broke with tradition by refusing to join other guests on the revolving stage at the finale of the top rated TV show *Sunday Night At The London Palladium*.

• The Beatles, who picked up Grammy Awards for 'Michelle' and 'Eleanor Rigby', re-signed for nine years with EMI. The group also reportedly turned down an unprecedented $1 million to re-appear at New York's Shea Stadium.

January 1967

This Mnth	Last Mnth	Title	Artist	Label	Wks in 10	US Pos	
1	1	**The Sound Of Music**	Soundtrack	RCA	235	1	2P
2	2	**Best Of The Beach Boys**	Beach Boys	Capitol	55	8	
3	5	**Come The Day**	Seekers	Columbia	23		
4	3	**Distant Drums**	Jim Reeves	RCA	14	21	
5	-	**A Quick One**	Who	Reaction	6	67	
6	7	**Gentle Shades Of Val Doonican**	Val Doonican	Decca	8		
7	-	**Finders Keepers (Soundtrack)**	Cliff Richard	Columbia	5		
8	4	**Big Hits (High Tide And Green Grass)**	Rolling Stones	Decca	10	3	
9	-	**Hand Clappin' - Foot Stompin' - Funky Butt - Live!**	Geno Washington	Piccadilly	12		F
10	-	**The Monkees**	Monkees	RCA	26	1	F

February 1967

This Mnth	Last Mnth	Title	Artist	Label	Wks in 10	US Pos	
1	10	**The Monkees**	Monkees	RCA	26	1	F
2	1	**The Sound Of Music**	Soundtrack	RCA	235	1	2P
3	2	**Best Of The Beach Boys**	Beach Boys	Capitol	55	8	
4	-	**Between The Buttons**	Rolling Stones	Decca	12	2	
5	3	**Come The Day**	Seekers	Columbia	23		
6	9	**Hand Clappin' - Foot Stompin' - Funky Butt - Live!**	Geno Washington	Piccadilly	12		F
7	-	**Fresh Cream**	Cream	Reaction	6		F
8	5	**A Quick One**	Who	Reaction	6	67	
9	-	**Going Places**	Herb Alpert & The Tijuana Brass	Pye	42	1	F
10	-	**Greatest Hits**	Bob Dylan	CBS	6	10	

March 1967

This Mnth	Last Mnth	Title	Artist	Label	Wks in 10	US Pos	
1	1	**The Monkees**	Monkees	RCA	26	1	F
2	2	**The Sound Of Music**	Soundtrack	RCA	235	1	2P
3	4	**Between The Buttons**	Rolling Stones	Decca	12	2	
4	3	**Best Of The Beach Boys**	Beach Boys	Capitol	55	8	
5	-	**Four Tops Live!**	Four Tops	Tamla-Motown	12	17	
6	-	**S.R.O.**	Herb Alpert & The Tijuana Brass	Pye	6	2	
7	5	**Come The Day**	Seekers	Columbia	23		
8	9	**Going Places**	Herb Alpert & The Tijuana Brass	Pye	42	1	F
9	6	**Hand Clappin' - Foot Stompin' - Funky Butt - Live!**	Geno Washington	Piccadilly	12		F
10	10	**Greatest Hits**	Bob Dylan	CBS	6	10	

US 1967 JAN-MAR

January 1967

This Mnth	Last Mnth	Title	Artist	Label	Wks in 10	UK Pos	
1	1	The Monkees	Monkees	Colgems	32	1	F
2	7	S.R.O.	Herb Alpert &				
			The Tijuana Brass	A&M	19	5	
3	2	Doctor Zhivago	Soundtrack	MGM	71	3	
4	3	The Sound Of Music	Soundtrack	RCA	108	1	
5	-	Winchester Cathedral	New Vaudeville Band	Fontana	7		FL
6	10	Je M'appelle Barbra	Barbra Streisand	Columbia	6		
7	-	Born Free	Roger Williams	Kapp	4		L
8	9	Going Places	Herb Alpert &				
			The Tijuana Brass	A&M	48	4	
9	-	Got Live If You Want It!	Rolling Stones	London	5		
10	4	The Supremes A Go-Go	Supremes	Motown	15	15	

February 1967

This Mnth	Last Mnth	Title	Artist	Label	Wks in 10	UK Pos	
1	1	The Monkees	Monkees	Colgems	32	1	F
2	2	S.R.O.	Herb Alpert &				
			The Tijuana Brass	A&M	19	5	
3	-	More Of The Monkees	Monkees	Colgems	25	1	
4	3	Doctor Zhivago	Soundtrack	MGM	71	3	
5	4	The Sound Of Music	Soundtrack	RCA	108	1	
6	-	The Temptations Greatest Hits	Temptations	Gordy	14	26	F
7	-	That's Life	Frank Sinatra	Reprise	9	22	
8	5	Winchester Cathedral	New Vaudeville Band	Fontana	7		FL
9	-	The Spirit Of '67	Paul Revere & The Raiders	Columbia	7		
10	9	Got Live If You Want It!	Rolling Stones	London	5		

March 1967

This Mnth	Last Mnth	Title	Artist	Label	Wks in 10	UK Pos	
1	3	More Of The Monkees	Monkees	Colgems	25	1	
2	-	Between The Buttons	Rolling Stones	London	10	3	
3	1	The Monkees	Monkees	Colgems	32	1	F
4	4	Doctor Zhivago	Soundtrack	MGM	71	3	
5	2	S.R.O.	Herb Alpert &				
			The Tijuana Brass	A&M	19	5	
6	7	That's Life	Frank Sinatra	Reprise	9	22	
7	5	The Sound Of Music	Soundtrack	RCA	108	1	
8	6	The Temptations Greatest Hits	Temptations	Gordy	14	26	F
9	-	The Supremes Sing					
		Holland-Dozier-Holland	Supremes	Motown	5		
10	9	The Spirit Of '67	Paul Revere & The Raiders	Columbia	7		

• Underground music now surfaced and the musical seeds for the 'Summer of Love' were sown. San Francisco, the home of psychedelia, hosted a 'Human Be-In', whose headliners included Jefferson Airplane, Grateful Dead and Quicksilver Messenger Service. Donovan's **Mellow Yellow** climbed into the Top 20, and Jefferson Airplane cracked the Top 40 with **After Bathing At Baxter's**. Newcomers on the LP chart included Frank Zappa's group, The Mothers Of Invention, with **Freak Out** as well as self-titled debut albums from Buffalo Springfield, The Doors, The Youngbloods and The Seeds. Cream and The Who made their US live debuts, and Reprise paid a record $50,000 advance for the British-based Jimi Hendrix Experience.

• **The Monkees** was pushed into runner-up spot by **More Of The Monkees** which jumped from Number 122 to Number 1.

• Among the 'Best Of' albums scoring in the States were sets from Gary Lewis & The Playboys, The Temptations, smooth MOR/pop trio The Lettermen and a second volume from Herman's Hermits (above).

UK 1967 APR-JUNE

• Drug taking and rock music were, for the first time, becoming closely linked. The press intimated that many stars including members of The Rolling Stones, The Moody Blues, The Who and Cream often attended parties where drugs were used. The arrest of Stones Mick Jagger and Keith Richards for drug possession, and Paul McCartney's admitted use of LSD, attracted maximum media coverage. Incidentally, the BBC banned The Beatles' single 'A Day In The Life' which they felt might encourage drug taking.

• Decca's new subsidiary Deram released albums by singer/songwriters Cat Stevens, **Matthew And Son**, and David Bowie, **Love You 'Till Tuesday**. The former was the first of many hit albums for Stevens but Bowie still had a while to wait before he found fame.

• James Last hit the Top 10 for the first time with **This Is James Last**. The German orchestra leader has since amassed a total of British chart entries surpassed only by Elvis Presley.

• There was a lot of interest on both sides of the Atlantic in the British-born and Australian-raised Bee Gees. The group who were compared favorably with The Beatles, joined Polydor in the UK and signed a $250,000 deal with Atlantic in the USA.

April 1967

This Mnth	Last Mnth	Title	Artist	Label	Wks in 10	US Pos	
1	2	**The Sound Of Music**	Soundtrack	RCA	235	1	**2P**
2	1	**The Monkees**	Monkees	RCA	26	1	**F**
3	4	**Best Of The Beach Boys**	Beach Boys	Capitol	55	8	
4	-	**More Of The Monkees**	Monkees	RCA	19	1	
5	7	**Come The Day**	Seekers	Columbia	23		
6	5	**Four Tops Live!**	Four Tops	Tamla-Motown	12	17	
7	-	**Images**	Walker Brothers	Philips	6		
8	3	**Between The Buttons**	Rolling Stones	Decca	12	2	
9	-	**Green Green Grass Of Home**	Tom Jones	Decca	11	65	**F**
10	-	**Trini Lopez In London**	Trini Lopez	Reprise	3	114	**L**

May 1967

This Mnth	Last Mnth	Title	Artist	Label	Wks in 10	US Pos	
1	1	**The Sound Of Music**	Soundtrack	RCA	235	1	**2P**
2	4	**More Of The Monkees**	Monkees	RCA	19	1	
3	9	**Green Green Grass Of Home**	Tom Jones	Decca	11	65	**F**
4	2	**The Monkees**	Monkees	RCA	26	1	**F**
5	3	**Best Of The Beach Boys**	Beach Boys	Capitol	55	8	
6	-	**This Is James Last**	James Last	Polydor	6		**F**
7	-	**Fiddler On The Roof**	Original London Cast	CBS	20		
8	-	**Matthew And Son**	Cat Stevens	Deram	4		**F**
9	-	**Secombe's Personal Choice**	Harry Secombe	Philips	3		**F**
10	7	**Images**	Walker Brothers	Philips	6		

June 1967

This Mnth	Last Mnth	Title	Artist	Label	Wks in 10	US Pos	
1	1	**The Sound Of Music**	Soundtrack	RCA	235	1	**2P**
2	-	**Sergeant Pepper's Lonely Hearts Club Band**	Beatles	Parlophone	51	1	**4P**
3	2	**More Of The Monkees**	Monkees	RCA	19	1	
4	-	**Are You Experienced**	Jimi Hendrix Experience	Track	19	5	**F**
5	-	**A Drop Of The Hard Stuff**	Dubliners	Major Minor	10		**F**
6	3	**Green Green Grass Of Home**	Tom Jones	Decca	11	65	**F**
7	5	**Best Of The Beach Boys**	Beach Boys	Capitol	55	8	
8	4	**The Monkees**	Monkees	RCA	26	1	**F**
9	7	**Fiddler On The Roof**	Original London Cast	CBS	20		
10	-	**Release Me**	Engelbert Humperdinck	Decca	14	7	**F**

US 1967

APR-JUNE

April 1967

This Mnth	Last Mnth	Title	Artist	Label	Wks in 10	UK Pos	
1	1	**More Of The Monkees**	Monkees	Colgems	25	1	
2	-	**The Mamas & The Papas Deliver**	Mamas & The Papas	Dunhill	15	4	
3	4	**Doctor Zhivago**	Soundtrack	MGM	71	3	
4	3	**The Monkees**	Monkees	Colgems	32	1	F
5	-	**My Cup Runneth Over**	Ed Ames	RCA	10		FL
6	2	**Between The Buttons**	Rolling Stones	London	10	3	
7	-	**The Best Of The Lovin' Spoonful**	Lovin' Spoonful	Kama Sutra	9		L
8	5	**S.R.O.**	Herb Alpert & The Tijuana Brass	A&M	19	5	
9	7	**The Sound Of Music**	Soundtrack	RCA	108	1	
10	9	**The Supremes Sing Holland-Dozier-Holland**	Supremes	Motown	5		

May 1967

This Mnth	Last Mnth	Title	Artist	Label	Wks in 10	UK Pos	
1	1	**More Of The Monkees**	Monkees	Colgems	25	1	
2	2	**The Mamas & The Papas Deliver**	Mamas & The Papas	Dunhill	15	4	
3	3	**Doctor Zhivago**	Soundtrack	MGM	71	3	
4	7	**The Best Of The Lovin' Spoonful**	Lovin' Spoonful	Kama Sutra	9		L
5	5	**My Cup Runneth Over**	Ed Ames	RCA	10		FL
6	9	**The Sound Of Music**	Soundtrack	RCA	108	1	
7	-	**I Never Loved A Man The Way I Love You**	Aretha Franklin	Atlantic	17	36	F
8	4	**The Monkees**	Monkees	Colgems	32	1	F
9	-	**Revenge**	Bill Cosby	Warner	12		
10	-	**The Temptations Greatest Hits**	Temptations	Gordy	14	26	F

June 1967

This Mnth	Last Mnth	Title	Artist	Label	Wks in 10	UK Pos	
1	7	**I Never Loved A Man The Way I Love You**	Aretha Franklin	Atlantic	17	36	F
2	9	**Revenge**	Bill Cosby	Warner	12		
3	1	**More Of The Monkees**	Monkees	Colgems	25	1	
4	-	**Sounds Like**	Herb Alpert & The Tijuana Brass	A&M	12	21	
5	2	**The Mamas & The Papas Deliver**	Mamas & The Papas	Dunhill	15	4	
6	-	**Born Free**	Andy Williams	Columbia	12	22	
7	-	**Surrealistic Pillow**	Jefferson Airplane	RCA	20		F
8	-	**Headquarters**	Monkees	Colgems	21	2	
9	3	**Doctor Zhivago**	Soundtrack	MGM	71	3	
10	6	**The Sound Of Music**	Soundtrack	RCA	108	1	

• Aretha Franklin's debut Atlantic album, I **Never Loved A Man The Way That I Love You**, was her first major hit. Aretha went on to win the female Grammy Award for R&B Recordings every year from 1967 to 1974, and became one of the biggest selling female artists of all time.

• Among the American underground acts debuting on the extended Top 200 album chart were Grateful Dead, The Velvet Underground & Nico, The Electric Prunes and Country Joe & The Fish. Also joining them were highly touted British acts, Cream and The Who.

• Herb Alpert's fourth Number 1 in 18 months, **Sounds Like**, briefly dethroned The Monkees at the top. However, the group's third album, **Headquarters,** which had amassed over 1 million advance orders, quickly returned them to the summit. The Monkees also picked up an Emmy Award for Outstanding Comedy TV Series, and caused pandemonium on both sides of the Atlantic with appearances at the Hollywood Bowl and London's Wembley Pool.

UK 1967 JULY-SEPT

• Among the acts appearing at the Copacabana in New York were Britain's Dusty Springfield and Motown hitmakers The Temptations, who took over after her three week run at the prestigious club.

• Despite the fact that he had died over eight years earlier, Buddy Holly was voted into the Top 20 Male Artists in the *Record Mirror* poll and a **Greatest Hits** package cracked the Top 10.

• Ray and D.W. Dolby perfected a new noise reduction system for album and tape recording, which made their name world-famous.

• Among the interesting acts making their National Jazz & Blues Festival debuts were ex-John Mayall sideman Peter Green's new group, Fleetwood Mac, and the Jeff Beck Group, with vocalist Rod Stewart.

• The BBC finally realized the need for legal, all-music radio stations in Britain and launched Radio 1 for pop and Radio 2 for MOR. Many of the DJs on Radio 1 had previously broadcast on the recently outlawed pirate radio stations.

July 1967

This Mnth	Last Mnth	Title	Artist	Label	Wks in 10	US Pos	
1	2	**Sergeant Pepper's Lonely Hearts Club Band**	Beatles	Parlophone	51	1	**4P**
2	1	**The Sound Of Music**	Soundtrack	RCA	235	1	**2P**
3	4	**Are You Experienced**	Jimi Hendrix Experience	Track	19	5	**F**
4	9	**Fiddler On The Roof**	Original London Cast	CBS	20		
5	-	**Headquarters**	Monkees	RCA	13	1	
6	3	**More Of The Monkees**	Monkees	RCA	19	1	
7	7	**Best Of The Beach Boys**	Beach Boys	Capitol	55	8	
8	8	**The Monkees**	Monkees	RCA	26	1	**F**
9	-	**Going Places**	Herb Alpert & The Tijuana Brass	Pye	42	1	**F**
10	-	**This Is James Last**	James Last	Polydor	6		**F**

August 1967

This Mnth	Last Mnth	Title	Artist	Label	Wks in 10	US Pos	
1	1	**Sergeant Pepper's Lonely Hearts Club Band**	Beatles	Parlophone	51	1	**4P**
2	5	**Headquarters**	Monkees	RCA	13	1	
3	2	**The Sound Of Music**	Soundtrack	RCA	235	1	**2P**
4	3	**Are You Experienced**	Jimi Hendrix Experience	Track	19	5	**F**
5	-	**The Mamas & The Papas Deliver**	Mamas & The Papas	RCA	9	2	
6	7	**Best Of The Beach Boys**	Beach Boys	Capitol	55	8	
7	4	**Fiddler On The Roof**	Original London Cast	CBS	20		
8	6	**More Of The Monkees**	Monkees	RCA	19	1	
9	-	**Jigsaw**	Shadows	Columbia	4		
10	-	**Doctor Zhivago**	Soundtrack	MGM	14	1	

September 1967

This Mnth	Last Mnth	Title	Artist	Label	Wks in 10	US Pos	
1	1	**Sergeant Pepper's Lonely Hearts Club Band**	Beatles	Parlophone	51	1	**4P**
2	3	**The Sound Of Music**	Soundtrack	RCA	235	1	**2P**
3	6	**Best Of The Beach Boys**	Beach Boys	Capitol	55	8	
4	2	**Headquarters**	Monkees	RCA	13	1	
5	4	**Are You Experienced**	Jimi Hendrix Experience	Track	19	5	**F**
6	10	**Doctor Zhivago**	Soundtrack	MGM	14	1	
7	-	**Piper At The Gates Of Dawn**	Pink Floyd	Columbia	7		**F**
8	-	**Scott**	Scott Walker	Philips	8		**F**
9	5	**The Mamas & The Papas Deliver**	Mamas & The Papas	RCA	9	2	
10	-	**Live At The Talk Of The Town**	Tom Jones	Decca	22	13	

US 1967 JULY-SEPT

July 1967

This Mnth	Last Mnth	Title	Artist	Label	Wks in 10	UK Pos	
1	-	Sergeant Pepper's Lonely Hearts Club Band	Beatles	Capitol	33	1	8P
2	8	Headquarters	Monkees	Colgems	21	2	
3	4	Sounds Like	Herb Alpert & The Tijuana Brass	A&M	12	21	
4	1	I Never Loved A Man The Way I Love You	Aretha Franklin	Atlantic	17	36	F
5	7	Surrealistic Pillow	Jefferson Airplane	RCA	20		F
6	2	Revenge	Bill Cosby	Warner	12		
7	6	Born Free	Andy Williams	Columbia	12	22	
8	9	Doctor Zhivago	Soundtrack	MGM	71	3	
9	3	More Of The Monkees	Monkees	Colgems	25	1	
10	-	The Doors	Doors	Elektra	22		F2P

August 1967

This Mnth	Last Mnth	Title	Artist	Label	Wks in 10	UK Pos	
1	1	Sergeant Pepper's Lonely Hearts Club Band	Beatles	Capitol	33	1	8P
2	2	Headquarters	Monkees	Colgems	21	2	
3	-	Flowers	Rolling Stones	London	10		
4	5	Surrealistic Pillow	Jefferson Airplane	RCA	20		F
5	10	The Doors	Doors	Elektra	22		F2P
6	3	Sounds Like	Herb Alpert & The Tijuana Brass	A&M	12	21	
7	4	I Never Loved A Man The Way I Love You	Aretha Franklin	Atlantic	17	36	F
8	-	Up, Up And Away	5th Dimension	Soul City	3		F
9	7	Born Free	Andy Williams	Columbia	12	22	
10	-	Release Me	Engelbert Humperdinck	Parrot	7	6	F

September 1967

This Mnth	Last Mnth	Title	Artist	Label	Wks in 10	UK Pos	
1	1	Sergeant Pepper's Lonely Hearts Hearts Club Band	Beatles	Capitol	33	1	8P
2	5	The Doors	Doors	Elektra	22		F2P
3	2	Headquarters	Monkees	Colgems	21	2	
4	3	Flowers	Rolling Stones	London	10		
5	4	Surrealistic Pillow	Jefferson Airplane	RCA	20		F
6	-	Groovin'	Young Rascals	Atlantic	13		F
7	10	Release Me	Engelbert Humperdinck	Parrot	7	6	F
8	-	With A Lot O' Soul	Temptations	Gordy	5	19	
9	-	Aretha Arrives	Aretha Franklin	Atlantic	10		
10	-	Ode To Billie Joe	Bobbie Gentry	Capitol	10		FL

• The most successful album in the 'Summer of Love' was **Sergeant Pepper's Lonely Hearts Club Band** by The Beatles. The innovative and much imitated LP, which had taken five months to record, headed the US chart for four months and remained top in Britain for almost six. The album's release coincided with EMI's announcement that the group had sold over 200 million records worldwide in less than five years. **Sergeant Pepper** won four Grammy Awards, and with sales of over four million is still Britain's biggest selling LP ever.

• By September, there was no room in the Top 10 for any of the veteran MOR merchants who had previously been regular visitors. In their place were such first time entrants as The Doors, The Young Rascals and Jefferson Airplane. Among the new acts debuting lower on the chart were Moby Grape, Big Brother & The Holding Company, 16-year-old singer/songwriter Janis Ian, Canned Heat, Procol Harum and Indian sitar star Ravi Shankar.

• Motown, who had recently tagged their music 'The sound of young America', kept the hits coming with albums like **With A Lot O' Soul** from The Temptations, **Reach Out** by The Four Tops and The Supremes' MOR-slanted **Sing Rodgers & Hart**. Florence Ballard left the latter group during a stint in Las Vegas.

UK 1967 OCT-DEC

• A mixed bag of acts was represented on the Top 20 with two albums each. Among these were balladeer Engelbert Humperdinck, folky Irish band The Dubliners and The Beach Boys who had two 'Best Of' compilations plus **Smiley Smile** all selling well. Despite this success, The Beatles regained their title of World's Number 1 group in the *NME* survey from The Beach Boys. The Californian combo followed in the Beatles' footsteps when they were introduced to transcendental meditation by Maharishi Mahesh Yogi.

• Top selling soul singer Otis Redding and members of funk band The Bar-Kays were killed in a plane crash. Redding had just replaced the recently-married Elvis Presley as Top Male Singer in the *Melody Maker* poll.

• The highly touted Bee Gees' debut LP reached the top 10 on both sides of the Atlantic. The group, who turned on the Christmas lights in Carnaby Street, headlined at London's prestigious Saville Theatre, where previously they had been booed off as support act to Fats Domino.

• Announcements from The Beatles camp included the opening of their Apple Boutique and the fact that Paul McCartney was engaged to actress Jane Asher.

October 1967

This Mnth	Last Mnth	Title	Artist	Label	Wks in 10	US Pos	
1	1	**Sergeant Pepper's Lonely Hearts Club Band**	Beatles	Parlophone	51	1	**4P**
2	2	**The Sound Of Music**	Soundtrack	RCA	235	1	**2P**
3	6	**Doctor Zhivago**	Soundtrack	MGM	14	1	
4	8	**Scott**	Scott Walker	Philips	8		**F**
5	3	**Best Of The Beach Boys**	Beach Boys	Capitol	55	8	
6	-	**Release Me**	Engelbert Humperdinck	Decca	14	7	**F**
7	-	**Breakthrough**	Various	Studio Two	15		
8	-	**A Drop Of The Hard Stuff**	Dubliners	Major Minor	10		**F**
9	7	**Piper At The Gates Of Dawn**	Pink Floyd	Columbia	7		**F**
10	-	**Best Of The Beach Boys Vol. 2**	Beach Boys	Capitol	10	50	

November 1967

This Mnth	Last Mnth	Title	Artist	Label	Wks in 10	US Pos	
1	1	**Sergeant Pepper's Lonely Hearts Club Band**	Beatles	Parlophone	51	1	**4P**
2	2	**The Sound Of Music**	Soundtrack	RCA	235	1	**2P**
3	7	**Breakthrough**	Various	Studio Two	15		
4	10	**Best Of The Beach Boys Vol. 2**	Beach Boys	Capitol	10	50	
5	-	**British Motown Chartbusters**	Various	Tamla-Motown	23		
6	-	**Universal Soldier**	Donovan	Marble Arch	9		**L**
7	3	**Doctor Zhivago**	Soundtrack	MGM	14	1	
8	4	**Scott**	Scott Walker	Philips	8		**F**
9	-	**Disraeli Gears**	Cream	Reaction	8	4	
10	5	**Best Of The Beach Boys**	Beach Boys	Capitol	55	8	

December 1967

This Mnth	Last Mnth	Title	Artist	Label	Wks in 10	US Pos	
1	2	**The Sound Of Music**	Soundtrack	RCA	235	1	**2P**
2	1	**Sergeant Pepper's Lonely Hearts Club Band**	Beatles	Parlophone	51	1	**4P**
3	3	**Breakthrough**	Various	Studio Two	15		
4	5	**British Motown Chartbusters**	Various	Tamla-Motown	23		
5	-	**The Last Waltz**	Engelbert Humperdinck	Decca	10	10	
6	9	**Disraeli Gears**	Cream	Reaction	8	4	
7	-	**Val Doonican Rocks But Gently**	Val Doonican	Pye	13		
8	4	**Best Of The Beach Boys Vol. 2**	Beach Boys	Capitol	10	50	
9	6	**Universal Soldier**	Donovan	Marble Arch	9		**L**
10	-	**Axis: Bold As Love**	Jimi Hendrix Experience	Track	5	3	

US 1967 OCT-DEC

October 1967

This Mnth	Last Mnth	Title	Artist	Label	Wks in 10	UK Pos	
1	1	Sergeant Pepper's Lonely Hearts Club Band	Beatles	Capitol	33	1	8P
2	10	Ode To Billie Joe	Bobbie Gentry	Capitol	10		FL
3	2	The Doors	Doors	Elektra	22		F2P
4	-	Diana Ross & The Supremes Greatest Hits	Diana Ross & The Supremes	Motown	24	1	
5	9	Aretha Arrives	Aretha Franklin	Atlantic	10		
6	-	The Byrds' Greatest Hits	Byrds	Columbia	5		PL
7	3	Headquarters	Monkees	Colgems	21	2	
8	6	Groovin'	Young Rascals	Atlantic	13		F
9	4	Flowers	Rolling Stones	London	10		
10	-	Vanilla Fudge	Vanilla Fudge	Atco	11	31	FL

November 1967

This Mnth	Last Mnth	Title	Artist	Label	Wks in 10	UK Pos	
1	4	Diana Ross & The Supremes Greatest Hits	Diana Ross & The Supremes	Motown	24	1	
2	1	Sergeant Pepper's Lonely Hearts Club Band	Beatles	Capitol	33	1	8P
3	3	The Doors	Doors	Elektra	22		F2P
4	-	The Four Tops Greatest Hits	Four Tops	Motown	7	1	FL
5	-	Strange Days	Doors	Elektra	9		
6	2	Ode To Billie Joe	Bobbie Gentry	Capitol	10		FL
7	10	Vanilla Fudge	Vanilla Fudge	Atco	11	31	FL
8	5	Aretha Arrives	Aretha Franklin	Atlantic	10		
9	8	Groovin'	Young Rascals	Atlantic	13		F
10	-	Bee Gees First	Bee Gees	Atco	5	8	F

December 1967

This Mnth	Last Mnth	Title	Artist	Label	Wks in 10	UK Pos	
1	-	Pisces, Aquarius, Capricorn & Jones Ltd	Monkees	Colgems	12	5	
2	1	Diana Ross & The Supremes Greatest Hits	Diana Ross & The Supremes	Motown	24	1	
3	2	Sergeant Pepper's Lonely Hearts Club Band	Beatles	Capitol	33	1	8P
4	5	Strange Days	Doors	Elektra	9		
5	-	Farewell To The First Golden Era	Mamas & The Papas	Dunhill	11		L
6	-	Doctor Zhivago	Soundtrack	MGM	71	3	
7	7	Vanilla Fudge	Vanilla Fudge	Atco	11	31	FL
8	3	The Doors	Doors	Elektra	22		F2P
9	-	The Sound Of Music	Soundtrack	RCA	108	1	
10	-	Are You Experienced?	Jimi Hendrix Experience	Reprise	32	2	F2P

• Singer/songwriter Bobbie Gentry dethroned **Sergeant Pepper** with her debut album, **Ode To Billie Joe**, which helped earn the Mississippi miss the Grammy for Best New Artist.

• 1967 was the first year that American record sales topped the $1 billion mark, and the first year that albums outsold singles. The year ended with The Monkees scoring a still unbeaten record having a fourth Number 1 album in a calendar year with **Pisces, Aquarius, Capricorn & Jones Ltd**. It had been an amazing year for the group, who replaced The Beatles as the world's top selling recording act.

• While many original hippies bemoaned the fact that media over exposure had caused the premature death of their 'Love & Peace' life-style, *Rolling Stone* magazine was launched and the hippie musical *Hair* opened off-Broadway,

• *Billboard* defined 'underground' albums as those that "make it without the impetus of a hit single and contain material and arrangements that are unconventional". That description ideally suited new Top 10 entrant **Are You Experienced?** from the Jimi Hendrix Experience, which was on the charts for over a year before it peaked at Number 5.

UK 1968 JAN-MAR

• Bob Dylan's **John Wesley Harding**, which included 'All Along The Watchtower' and 'I'll Be Your Baby Tonight', was one of the most successful albums of his long career. It topped the British chart for three months and was voted Album Of The Year by *Melody Maker* readers. In his homeland, Dylan's album was unable to pass, firstly, The Beatles and then Paul Mauriat at the summit.

• Often an artist's premature death increases the interest in their recordings. Otis Redding was such a case, and his albums **Otis Blue**, **Dictionary Of Soul** and **History Of Otis Redding** all climbed the chart.

• Future album superstars Genesis and Elton John released their first singles. John was described by his label as "1968's greatest new talent".

• The first R&B album to head the chart, **Greatest Hits** by the Four Tops, was superseded by the first Number 1 from a female group, **Greatest Hits** by Diana Ross & The Supremes.

January 1968

This Mnth	Last Mnth	Title	Artist	Label	Wks in 10	US Pos	
1	7	**Val Doonican Rocks But Gently**	Val Doonican	Pye	13		
2	2	**Sergeant Pepper's Lonely Hearts Club Band**	Beatles	Parlophone	51	1	**4P**
3	1	**The Sound Of Music**	Soundtrack	RCA	235	1	**2P**
4	4	**British Motown Chartbusters**	Various	Tamla-Motown	23		
5	-	**Reach Out**	Four Tops	Tamla-Motown	12	11	
6	-	**Their Satanic Majesties Request**	Rolling Stones	Decca	5	2	
7	5	**The Last Waltz**	Engelbert Humperdinck	Decca	10	10	
8	10	**Axis: Bold As Love**	Jimi Hendrix Experience	Track	5	3	
9	-	**13 Smash Hits**	Tom Jones	Decca	14		
10	3	**Breakthrough**	Various	Studio Two	15		

February 1968

This Mnth	Last Mnth	Title	Artist	Label	Wks in 10	US Pos	
1	3	**The Sound Of Music**	Soundtrack	RCA	235	1	**2P**
2	-	**Greatest Hits**	Four Tops	Tamla-Motown	18	4	
3	-	**Greatest Hits**	Diana Ross & The Supremes	Tamla-Motown	23	1	
4	2	**Sergeant Pepper's Lonely Hearts Club Band**	Beatles	Parlophone	51	1	**4P**
5	4	**British Motown Chartbusters**	Various	Tamla-Motown	23		
6	9	**13 Smash Hits**	Tom Jones	Decca	14		
7	1	**Val Doonican Rocks But Gently**	Val Doonican	Pye	13		
8	-	**Pisces, Aquarius, Capricorn & Jones Ltd.**	Monkees	RCA	8	1	**L**
9	5	**Reach Out**	Four Tops	Tamla-Motown	12	11	
10	10	**Breakthrough**	Various	Studio Two	15		

March 1968

This Mnth	Last Mnth	Title	Artist	Label	Wks in 10	US Pos	
1	3	**Greatest Hits**	Diana Ross & The Supremes	Tamla-Motown	23	1	
2	-	**John Wesley Harding**	Bob Dylan	CBS	21	2	
3	1	**The Sound Of Music**	Soundtrack	RCA	235	1	**2P**
4	2	**Greatest Hits**	Four Tops	Tamla-Motown	18	4	
5	5	**British Motown Chartbusters**	Various	Tamla-Motown	23		
6	-	**History Of Otis Redding**	Otis Redding	Volt	16	9	
7	4	**Sergeant Pepper's Lonely Hearts Club Band**	Beatles	Parlophone	51	1	**4P**
8	6	**13 Smash Hits**	Tom Jones	Decca	14		
9	7	**Val Doonican Rocks But Gently**	Val Doonican	Pye	13		
10	-	**Otis Blue**	Otis Redding	Atlantic	14		**F**

US 1968

JAN-MAR

January 1968

This Mnth	Last Mnth	Title	Artist	Label	Wks in 10	UK Pos	
1	-	Magical Mystery Tour	Beatles	Capitol	14	31	5P
2	-	Their Satanic Majesties Request	Rolling Stones	London	10	3	
3	1	Pisces, Aquarius, Capricorn & Jones Ltd	Monkees	Colgems	12	5	
4	2	Diana Ross & The Supremes Greatest Hits	Diana Ross & The Supremes	Motown	24	1	
5	3	Sergeant Pepper's Lonely Hearts Club Band	Beatles	Capitol	33	1	8P
6	-	Herb Alpert's Ninth	Herb Alpert & Tijuana Brass	A&M	10	26	
7	6	Doctor Zhivago	Soundtrack	MGM	71	3	
8	5	Farewell To The First Golden Era	Mamas & The Papas	Dunhill	11		L
9	9	The Sound Of Music	Soundtrack	RCA	108	1	
10	-	Disraeli Gears	Cream	Atco	30	5	FP

February 1968

This Mnth	Last Mnth	Title	Artist	Label	Wks in 10	UK Pos	
1	1	Magical Mystery Tour	Beatles	Capitol	14	31	5P
2	2	Their Satanic Majesties Request	Rolling Stones	London	10	3	
3	4	Diana Ross & The Supremes Greatest Hits	Diana Ross & The Supremes	Motown	24	1	
4	-	John Wesley Harding	Bob Dylan	Columbia	10	1	
5	6	Herb Alpert's Ninth	Herb Alpert & The Tijuana Brass	A&M	10	26	
6	3	Pisces, Aquarius, Capricorn & Jones Ltd	Monkees	Colgems	12	5	
7	-	The Turtles! Golden Hits	Turtles	White Whale	6		FL
8	-	Blooming Hits	Paul Mauriat	Philips	14		FL
9	10	Disraeli Gears	Cream	Atco	30	5	FP
10	-	Axis: Bold As Love	Jimi Hendrix Experience	Reprise	8	5	P

March 1968

This Mnth	Last Mnth	Title	Artist	Label	Wks in 10	UK Pos	
1	8	Blooming Hits	Paul Mauriat	Philips	14		FL
2	-	Aretha: Lady Soul	Aretha Franklin	Atlantic	16	25	
3	10	Axis: Bold As Love	Jimi Hendrix Experience	Reprise	8	5	P
4	4	John Wesley Harding	Bob Dylan	Columbia	10	1	
5	1	Magical Mystery Tour	Beatles	Capitol	14	31	5P
6	-	The Graduate (Soundtrack)	Simon & Garfunkel	Columbia	26	3	
7	5	Herb Alpert's Ninth	Herb Alpert & The Tijuana Brass	A&M	10	26	
8	3	Diana Ross & The Supremes Greatest Hits	Diana Ross & The Supremes	Motown	24	1	
9	9	Disraeli Gears	Cream	Atco	30	5	FP
10	-	Greatest Hits Vol. 2	Smokey Robinson & The Miracles	Tamla	2		L

• The TV film *Magical Mystery Tour* may have been The Beatles' first artistic and commercial disappointment, but its music sold as well as ever. In the USA, the soundtrack spent two months at the summit while in Britain, where it was a double EP, it reached Number 2, stopped only by the group's single 'Hello Goodbye'. The Beatles flew to India to continue their studies with Maharishi Mahesh Yogi who, shortly after, announced that he would be touring the USA as support to The Beach Boys.

• Early American heavy metal merchants, Iron Butterfly and Blue Cheer, debuted on the album chart with **Heavy** and **Vincebus Eruptum** respectively. Other noteworthy chart debuts included singer/songwriter Leonard Cohen, Kenny Rogers' group The First Edition, Britain's Small Faces and heavily hyped Boston band, The Beacon Street Union.

• French orchestra leader Paul Mauriat, who had co-written the 1963 US Number 1, 'I Will Follow Him' for Little Peggy March, had a chart topper with **Blooming Hits**, which included the Number 1 single 'Love Is Blue'.

• Rock musicians were now taking themselves and their 'art' seriously. Many record buyers found the 'bubble gum' music of comparatively unpretentious acts like The Lemon Pipers and 1910 Fruitgum Co. a much needed relief.

UK 1968 APR-JUNE

• Bill Haley & The Comets, the act most responsible for launching rock'n'roll music around the globe, cracked the British album chart with a collection of their mid-Fifties hits. It was titled after the biggest selling rock single of all time, **Rock Around The Clock**. The title track itself returned to the Top 20 and spearheaded a short-lived UK rock'n'roll revival.

• London's swanky niterie, The Talk Of The Town, was the recording venue for chart albums by both America's top trio, The Supremes, and Britain's Number 1 male soloist Tom Jones. Jones' album bounced up and down the chart for some time alongside his **13 Smash Hits** LP.

• Many of the UK acts that now debuted on the album chart sold few records across the Atlantic. Numbered among these were talented acts like The Move, Julie 'The Face of 68' Driscoll, The Incredible String Band, blues outfit Chicken Shack featuring future Fleetwood Mac vocalist, Christine McVie and top teen idols Amen Corner.

April 1968

This Mnth	Last Mnth	Title	Artist	Label	Wks in 10	US Pos	
1	2	**John Wesley Harding**	Bob Dylan	CBS	21	2	
2	1	**Greatest Hits**	Diana Ross &				
			The Supremes	Tamla-Motown	23	1	
3	6	**History Of Otis Redding**	Otis Redding	Volt	16	9	
4	4	**Greatest Hits**	Four Tops	Tamla-Motown	18	4	
5	3	**The Sound Of Music**	Soundtrack	RCA	235	1	**2P**
6	-	**Fleetwood Mac**	Fleetwood Mac	Blue Horizon	17	1	**F**
7	-	**2 In 3**	Esther & Abi Ofarim	Philips	5		**FL**
8	-	**Live At The Talk Of The Town**	Supremes	Tamla-Motown	8	57	
9	-	**Wild Honey**	Beach Boys	Capitol	5	24	
10	-	**Hangman's Beautiful Daughter**	Incredible String Band	Elektra	10	161	**FL**

May 1968

This Mnth	Last Mnth	Title	Artist	Label	Wks in 10	US Pos	
1	1	**John Wesley Harding**	Bob Dylan	CBS	21	2	
2	3	**History Of Otis Redding**	Otis Redding	Volt	16	9	
3	2	**Greatest Hits**	Diana Ross &				
			The Supremes	Tamla-Motown	23	1	
4	5	**The Sound Of Music**	Soundtrack	RCA	235	1	**2P**
5	-	**Scott 2**	Scott Walker	Philips	12		
6	4	**Greatest Hits**	Four Tops	Tamla-Motown	18	4	
7	6	**Fleetwood Mac**	Fleetwood Mac	Blue Horizon	17	1	**F**
8	10	**Hangman's Beautiful Daughter**	Incredible String Band	Elektra	10	161	**FL**
9	8	**Live At The Talk Of The Town**	Supremes	Tamla-Motown	8	57	
10	-	**Smash Hits**	Jimi Hendrix	Track	10	6	

June 1968

This Mnth	Last Mnth	Title	Artist	Label	Wks in 10	US Pos	
1	1	**John Wesley Harding**	Bob Dylan	CBS	21	2	
2	5	**Scott 2**	Scott Walker	Philips	12		
3	-	**Love Andy**	Andy Williams	CBS	9	8	
4	4	**The Sound Of Music**	Soundtrack	RCA	235	1	**2P**
5	2	**History Of Otis Redding**	Otis Redding	Volt	16	9	
6	7	**Fleetwood Mac**	Fleetwood Mac	Blue Horizon	17	1	**F**
7	-	**Dock Of The Bay**	Otis Redding	Stax	7	4	
8	-	**The Jungle Book**	Soundtrack	Disney	17	19	
9	8	**Hangman's Beautiful Daughter**	Incredible String Band	Elektra	10	161	**FL**
10	-	**Ogden's Nut Gone Flake**	Small Faces	Immediate	9	159	**L**

US 1968

APR-JUNE

April 1968

This Mnth	Last Mnth	Title	Artist	Label	Wks in 10	UK Pos	
1	6	**The Graduate (Soundtrack)**	Simon & Garfunkel	Columbia	26	3	
2	1	**Blooming Hits**	Paul Mauriat	Philips	14		FL
3	2	**Aretha: Lady Soul**	Aretha Franklin	Atlantic	16	25	
4	-	**The Dock Of The Bay**	Otis Redding	Volt	7	1	L
5	-	**Parsley Sage Rosemary And Thyme**	Simon & Garfunkel	Columbia	17	13	F3P
6	-	**Valley Of The Dolls**	Dionne Warwick	Scepter	5	10	L
7	4	**John Wesley Harding**	Bob Dylan	Columbia	10	1	
8	-	**The Good, The Bad And The Ugly**	Soundtrack	UA	10	2	
9	9	**Disraeli Gears**	Cream	Atco	30	5	FP
10	3	**Axis: Bold As Love**	Jimi Hendrix Experience	Reprise	8	5	P

May 1968

This Mnth	Last Mnth	Title	Artist	Label	Wks in 10	UK Pos	
1	1	**The Graduate (Soundtrack)**	Simon & Garfunkel	Columbia	26	3	
2	-	**Bookends**	Simon & Garfunkel	Columbia	20	1	2P
3	3	**Aretha: Lady Soul**	Aretha Franklin	Atlantic	16	25	
4	8	**The Good, The Bad And The Ugly**	Soundtrack	UA	10	2	
5	2	**Blooming Hits**	Paul Mauriat	Philips	14		FL
6	-	**The Birds, The Bees & The Monkees**	Monkees	Colgems	9		L
7	5	**Parsley Sage Rosemary And Thyme**	Simon & Garfunkel	Columbia	17	13	F3P
8	-	**The Beat Of The Brass**	Herb Alpert & The Tijuana Brass	A&M	16	4	
9	4	**The Dock Of The Bay**	Otis Redding	Volt	7	1	L
10	-	**To Russell, My Brother, Whom I Slept With**	Bill Cosby	Warner	4		L

June 1968

This Mnth	Last Mnth	Title	Artist	Label	Wks in 10	UK Pos	
1	2	**Bookends**	Simon & Garfunkel	Columbia	20	1	2P
2	1	**The Graduate (Soundtrack)**	Simon & Garfunkel	Columbia	26	3	
3	8	**The Beat Of The Brass**	Herb Alpert & The Tijuana Brass	A&M	16	4	
4	6	**The Birds, The Bees & The Monkees**	Monkees	Colgems	9		L
5	-	**Honey**	Bobby Goldsboro	UA	9		FL
6	7	**Parsley Sage Rosemary And Thyme**	Simon & Garfunkel	Columbia	17	13	F3P
7	-	**Look Around**	Sergio Mendes & Brasil '66	A&M	9		
8	-	**Disraeli Gears**	Cream	Atco	30	5	FP
9	3	**Aretha: Lady Soul**	Aretha Franklin	Atlantic	16	25	
10	-	**Are You Experienced?**	Jimi Hendrix Experience	Reprise	32	2	F2P

• As Herb Alpert headed the American singles chart for the first time with 'This Guy's In Love With You', its parent album, **The Beat Of The Brass**, gave the trumpeter-turned-vocalist the last of eight consecutive Top 10 albums. Incidentally, Alpert had been the last act to monopolize the Top 10 in the way that Simon & Garfunkel were now doing. The folk-rock duo at times had three of the top five albums with **The Graduate**, **Bookends** and **Parsley, Sage, Rosemary and Thyme**. The first two actually followed each other in the Number 1 slot.

• Boundary stretching funk band Sly & The Family Stone, Blood, Sweat & Tears and Traffic joined the list of late Sixties album chart entrants who would make indelible marks in musical history. There was also Canadian singer/songwriter Joni Mitchell and Capitol's big signing The Steve Miller Band.

• Two veteran black vocal groups, whose music was poles apart, scored the biggest albums of their long careers: doo-wop/soul quintet The Dells hit the Top 40 with **There Is**, and The Mills Brothers, who had first come to prominence in the Thirties, narrowly missed the Top 20 with **Fortuosity**.

UK 1968 JULY-SEPT

• Top selling singles act The Small Faces had their biggest and last chart album with **Ogden's Nut Gone Flake**, which had a round sleeve – thus resembling the tinned tobacco it was named after. It was followed into the top spot by the first chart topping album from Tom Jones, **Delilah**, and then Simon & Garfunkel's first UK chart topper, **Bookends**.

• There was no shortage of British rock festivals in the summer of 1968. Headliners at the Woburn Music Festival included Jimi Hendrix, Donovan, Fleetwood Mac and John Mayall. The all-star Isle Of Wight Festival featured Jefferson Airplane, The Move, The Crazy World of Arthur Brown, The Pretty Things and newcomers Tyrannosaurus Rex.

• Two major British bands, Cream and The Yardbirds, announced that they would be splitting up. Cream called it a day soon after topping the US album chart. When the former group disbanded, Jimmy Page recruited vocalist Robert Plant to front the New Yardbirds, who were soon rechristened Led Zeppelin – the rest, as they say, is rock history.

• Beatle news included John Lennon's divorce from Cynthia and the end of Paul McCartney's engagement to Jane Asher. Despite the group's Apple boutique's ignominious closure, their Apple label was launched successfully.

July 1968

This Mnth	Last Mnth	Title	Artist	Label	Wks in 10	US Pos	
1	10	**Ogden's Nut Gone Flake**	Small Faces	Immediate	9	159	L
2	7	**Dock Of The Bay**	Otis Redding	Stax	7	4	
3	3	**Love Andy**	Andy Williams	CBS	9	8	
4	1	**John Wesley Harding**	Bob Dylan	CBS	21	2	
5	6	**Fleetwood Mac**	Fleetwood Mac	Blue Horizon	17	1	F
6	4	**The Sound Of Music**	Soundtrack	RCA	235	1	2P
7	-	**Smash Hits**	Jimi Hendrix	Track	10	6	
8	2	**Scott 2**	Scott Walker	Philips	12		
9	-	**Crazy World Of Arthur Brown**	Crazy World Of Arthur Brown	Track	8	7	FL
10	-	**Bare Wires**	John Mayall	Decca	7	59	

August 1968

This Mnth	Last Mnth	Title	Artist	Label	Wks in 10	US Pos	
1	-	**Bookends**	Simon & Garfunkel	CBS	21	1	F
2	-	**Delilah**	Tom Jones	Decca	16		
3	9	**Crazy World Of Arthur Brown**	Crazy World Of Arthur Brown	Track	8	7	FL
4	10	**Bare Wires**	John Mayall	Decca	7	59	
5	-	**A Man Without Love**	Engelbert Humperdinck	Decca	15	12	
6	1	**Ogden's Nut Gone Flake**	Small Faces	Immediate	9	159	L
7	6	**The Sound Of Music**	Soundtrack	RCA	235	1	2P
8	-	**Greatest Hits**	Hollies	Parlophone	22	11	
9	-	**The Jungle Book**	Soundtrack	Disney	17	19	
10	2	**Dock Of The Bay**	Otis Redding	Stax	7	4	

September 1968

This Mnth	Last Mnth	Title	Artist	Label	Wks in 10	US Pos	
1	1	**Bookends**	Simon & Garfunkel	CBS	21	1	F
2	8	**Greatest Hits**	Hollies	Parlophone	22	11	
3	2	**Delilah**	Tom Jones	Decca	16		
4	-	**Wheels Of Fire (Double)**	Cream	Polydor	9	1	
5	5	**A Man Without Love**	Engelbert Humperdinck	Decca	15	12	
6	-	**In Search Of The Lost Chord**	Moody Blues	Deram	8	23	F
7	-	**Best Of The Beach Boys**	Beach Boys	Capitol	55	8	
8	7	**The Sound Of Music**	Soundtrack	RCA	235	1	2P
9	3	**Crazy World Of Arthur Brown**	Crazy World Of Arthur Brown	Track	8	7	FL
10	-	**Boogie With Canned Heat**	Canned Heat	Liberty	6	16	F

US 1968 JULY-SEPT

July 1968

This Mnth	Last Mnth	Title	Artist	Label	Wks in 10	UK Pos	
1	1	**Bookends**	Simon & Garfunkel	Columbia	20	1	2P
2	3	**The Beat Of The Brass**	Herb Alpert & The Tijuana Brass	A&M	16	4	
3	2	**The Graduate (Soundtrack)**	Simon & Garfunkel	Columbia	26	3	
4	-	**A Tramp Shining**	Richard Harris	Dunhill	5		FL
5	7	**Look Around**	Sergio Mendes & Brasil '66	A&M	9		
6	8	**Disraeli Gears**	Cream	Atco	30	5	FP
7	10	**Are You Experienced?**	Jimi Hendrix Experience	Reprise	32	2	F2P
8	-	**Wheels Of Fire**	Cream	Atco	20	3	
9	-	**God Bless Tiny Tim**	Tiny Tim	Reprise	2		FL
10	5	**Honey**	Bobby Goldsboro	UA	9		FL

August 1968

This Mnth	Last Mnth	Title	Artist	Label	Wks in 10	UK Pos	
1	8	**Wheels Of Fire**	Cream	Atco	20	3	
2	-	**Time Peace/The Rascals' Greatest Hits**	Rascals	Atlantic	25		L
3	-	**Aretha Now**	Aretha Franklin	Atlantic	8	6	
4	2	**The Beat Of The Brass**	Herb Alpert & The Tijuana Brass	A&M	16	4	
5	3	**The Graduate (Soundtrack)**	Simon & Garfunkel	Columbia	26	3	
6	1	**Bookends**	Simon & Garfunkel	Columbia	20	1	2P
7	6	**Disraeli Gears**	Cream	Atco	30	5	FP
8	-	**Waiting For The Sun**	Doors	Elektra	8	16	P
9	-	**Realization**	Johnny Rivers	Imperial	8		FL
10	7	**Are You Experienced?**	Jimi Hendrix Experience	Reprise	32	2	F2P

September 1968

This Mnth	Last Mnth	Title	Artist	Label	Wks in 10	UK Pos	
1	8	**Waiting For The Sun**	Doors	Elektra	8	16	P
2	2	**Time Peace/The Rascals' Greatest Hits**	Rascals	Atlantic	25		L
3	-	**Feliciano!**	Jose Feliciano	RCA	18	6	FL
4	1	**Wheels Of Fire**	Cream	Atco	20	3	
5	9	**Realization**	Johnny Rivers	Imperial	8		FL
6	-	**Steppenwolf**	Steppenwolf	Dunhill	7	59	F
7	10	**Are You Experienced?**	Jimi Hendrix Experience	Reprise	32	2	F2P
8	7	**Disraeli Gears**	Cream	Atco	30	5	FP
9	-	**Cheap Thrills**	Big Brother & The Holding Company	Columbia	19		FPL
10	3	**Aretha Now**	Aretha Franklin	Atlantic	8	6	

• Underground music now outsold all other musical styles on the album charts. Cream's **Wheels Of Fire**, was followed at the top by **Waiting For The Sun** from The Doors, and albums from Big Brother & The Holding Company and Jimi Hendrix.

• Sonny & Cher, The Byrds, Jefferson Airplane and Grateful Dead were among the acts who played to 100,000 fans at the Newport Pop Festival. In Cleveland, a similar sized crowd watched Gene Pitney, The Box Tops, 1910 Fruitgum Company and The Amboy Dukes. The

Doors (above) wowed the crowd at the Hollywood Bowl, The Bee Gees were a smash at the Forest Hills Stadium and The Rascals attracted throngs of screamagers to the New York Rock & Roll Festival.

• Joining the noteworthy acts who opened their chart accounts in 1968 were retro-rockers Creedence Clearwater Revival, Spirit and prolific singer/songwriter Laura Nyro. Also debuting were British acts Fleetwood Mac, Jeff Beck and Ten Years After.

UK 1968 OCT-DEC

• In 1968, for the first time, more albums were sold in Britain than singles. It was also announced that the biggest-selling album to date, **The Sound Of Music** which again returned to the top spot, had now topped the two million sales mark.

• As **The Beatles (White Album)** became the first double album to head the UK charts, solo albums were released by George Harrison, **Wonderwall Music**, and John Lennon, **Two Virgins**. The latter, which Lennon recorded with Yoko Ono, ran into trouble because the sleeve pictured the couple naked.

• One of Diana Ross' last performances with The Supremes was in front of the Queen at a Royal Variety Show in London. Diana's mid-act plea for racial tolerance made front page news. Another live show that attracted much media coverage was Cream's farewell show at London's Albert Hall, which was released on film as *Goodbye Cream*. Also saying goodbye was Graham Nash, who left the chart topping Hollies, to form Crosby, Stills & Nash.

• Jethro Tull, who were voted best new Group in the *NME* poll, briefly visited the Top 10 with their distinctive debut album, **This Was**.

October 1968

This Mnth	Last Mnth	Title	Artist	Label	Wks in 10	US Pos	
1	2	**Greatest Hits**	Hollies	Parlophone	22	11	
2	1	**Bookends**	Simon & Garfunkel	CBS	21	1	F
3	-	**Live At The Talk Of The Town**	Seekers	Columbia	19		
4	3	**Delilah**	Tom Jones	Decca	16		
5	8	**The Sound Of Music**	Soundtrack	RCA	235	1	2P
6	4	**Wheels Of Fire (Double)**	Cream	Polydor	9	1	
7	-	**Aretha Now**	Aretha Franklin	Atlantic	3	3	FL
8	-	**Idea**	Bee Gees	Polydor	6	17	
9	10	**Boogie With Canned Heat**	Canned Heat	Liberty	6	16	F
10	5	**A Man Without Love**	Engelbert Humperdinck	Decca	15	12	

November 1968

This Mnth	Last Mnth	Title	Artist	Label	Wks in 10	US Pos	
1	1	**Greatest Hits**	Hollies	Parlophone	22	11	
2	3	**Live At The Talk Of The Town**	Seekers	Columbia	19		
3	5	**The Sound Of Music**	Soundtrack	RCA	235	1	2P
4	-	**The Good, The Bad And The Ugly**	Soundtrack	UA	12	4	
5	2	**Bookends**	Simon & Garfunkel	CBS	21	1	F
6	8	**Idea**	Bee Gees	Polydor	6	17	
7	-	**The Graduate (Soundtrack)**	Simon & Garfunkel	CBS	10	1	
8	-	**The Best Of The Seekers**	Seekers	Columbia	47	97	
9	4	**Delilah**	Tom Jones	Decca	16		
10	-	**The Jungle Book**	Soundtrack	Disney	17	19	

December 1968

This Mnth	Last Mnth	Title	Artist	Label	Wks in 10	US Pos	
1	-	**The Beatles (White Album)**	Beatles	Apple	14	1	
2	8	**The Best Of The Seekers**	Seekers	Columbia	47	97	
3	4	**The Good, The Bad And The Ugly**	Soundtrack	UA	12	4	
4	3	**The Sound Of Music**	Soundtrack	RCA	235	1	2P
5	7	**The Graduate (Soundtrack)**	Simon & Garfunkel	CBS	10	1	
6	1	**Greatest Hits**	Hollies	Parlophone	22	11	
7	-	**Electric Ladyland**	Jimi Hendrix Experience	Track	5	1	
8	-	**Val**	Val Doonican	Pye	5		
9	-	**Live At The Talk Of The Town**	Tom Jones	Decca	22	13	
10	2	**Live At The Talk Of The Town**	Seekers	Columbia	19		

US 1968 OCT-DEC

October 1968

This Mnth	Last Mnth	Title	Artist	Label	Wks in 10	UK Pos	
1	9	**Cheap Thrills**	Big Brother & The Holding Company	Columbia	19		FPL
2	2	**Time Peace/The Rascals' Greatest Hits**	Rascals	Atlantic	25		L
3	3	**Feliciano!**	Jose Feliciano	RCA	18	6	FL
4	1	**Waiting For The Sun**	Doors	Elektra	8	16	P
5	-	**Gentle On My Mind**	Glen Campbell	Capitol	14		FP
6	-	**In-A-Gadda-Da-Vida**	Iron Butterfly	Atco	49		F4P
7	-	**The Time Has Come**	Chambers Brothers	Columbia	10		FL
8	-	**Crown Of Creation**	Jefferson Airplane	RCA	5		
9	5	**Realization**	Johnny Rivers	Imperial	8		FL
10	4	**Wheels Of Fire**	Cream	Atco	20	3	

November 1968

This Mnth	Last Mnth	Title	Artist	Label	Wks in 10	UK Pos	
1	1	**Cheap Thrills**	Big Brother & The Holding Company	Columbia	19		FPL
2	3	**Feliciano!**	Jose Feliciano	RCA	18	6	FL
3	-	**Electric Ladyland**	Jimi Hendrix Experience	Reprise	10	6	P
4	2	**Time Peace/The Rascals' Greatest Hits**	Rascals	Atlantic	25		L
5	7	**The Time Has Come**	Chambers Brothers	Columbia	10		FL
6	-	**The Second**	Steppenwolf	Dunhill	16		
7	-	**The Crazy World Of Arthur Brown**	Crazy World Of Arthur Brown	Track	7	2	FL
8	-	**Are You Experienced?**	Jimi Hendrix Experience	Reprise	32	2	F2P
9	10	**Wheels Of Fire**	Cream	Atco	20	3	
10	8	**Crown Of Creation**	Jefferson Airplane	RCA	5		

December 1968

This Mnth	Last Mnth	Title	Artist	Label	Wks in 10	UK Pos	
1	1	**Cheap Thrills**	Big Brother & The Holding Company	Columbia	19		FPL
2	2	**Feliciano!**	Jose Feliciano	RCA	18	6	FL
3	-	**Wichita Lineman**	Glen Campbell	Capitol	22		2P
4	6	**The Second**	Steppenwolf	Dunhill	16		
5	3	**Electric Ladyland**	Jimi Hendrix Experience	Reprise	10	6	P
6	-	**The Beatles (White Album)**	Beatles	Apple	15	1	7P
7	-	**In-A-Gadda-Da-Vida**	Iron Butterfly	Atco	49		F4P
8	4	**Time Peace/The Rascals' Greatest Hits**	Rascals	Atlantic	25		L
9	-	**Wild Flowers**	Judy Collins	Elektra	6		FL
10	9	**Wheels Of Fire**	Cream	Atco	20	3	

• In the early years of the Sixties, MOR music ruled the album chart and rock records were rare visitors. This situation had now been completely reversed. Also interesting to note was the fact that the vast majority of the current best selling album acts were unknown when The Beatles had rewritten musical history just four years earlier.

• Hottest new artist on the album scene was country-oriented vocalist Glen Campbell. He not only had two solo albums riding high, **Gentle On My Mind** and the first country record to reach the top, **Wichita Lineman**, he also had a Top 20 duet album with Bobbie Gentry.

• Several albums now regarded as milestones in rock were climbing the album chart. Numbered among these were **In-A-Gadda-Da-Vida** by Iron Butterfly, **Music From Big Pink** by The Band and Mike Bloomfield, Al Kooper & Stephen Stills' **Super Session**.

UK 1969 JAN-MAR

• Once again, The Beatles managed to grab both of the top two chart positions in the USA with **The Beatles (White Album)** and the soundtrack to the animated film *Yellow Submarine*. Band news this quarter included: Paul and John getting married to Linda and Yoko, Ringo starring in the film *Candy* and George being arrested for drug possession. Their long time rivals, The Rolling Stones, also added to their portfolio of transatlantic Top 10 hits with the long-awaited **Beggar's Banquet**, and completed shooting their *Rock'n'Roll Circus*. The film which also included The Who, Marianne Faithfull, Jethro Tull, John Lennon and Eric Clapton has still not gone on general release.

• Australian folk/pop group, The Seekers, became the first non-American and non-British act to top the UK album chart. Apart from the Number 1 hit **The Best Of The Seekers**, they also were selling stacks of their **Live At The Talk Of The Town** and their budget-priced album, **The Four And Only**.

• Only country singer Glen Campbell's **Wichita Lineman** prevented **Goodbye Cream** from topping the transatlantic chart. Ex-Cream members Eric Clapton and Ginger Baker announced that they were teaming up with ex-Traffic vocalist Steve Winwood to form **Blind Faith**.

January 1969

This Mnth	Last Mnth	Title	Artist	Label	Wks in 10	US Pos	
1	1	The Beatles (White Album)	Beatles	Apple	14	1	
2	2	The Best Of The Seekers	Seekers	Columbia	47	97	
3	-	Beggars Banquet	Rolling Stones	Decca	8	5	
4	4	The Sound Of Music	Soundtrack	RCA	235	1	2P
5	5	The Graduate (Soundtrack)	Simon & Garfunkel	CBS	10	1	
6	-	Help Yourself	Tom Jones	Decca	3	5	
7	8	Val	Val Doonican	Pye	5		
8	-	Greatest Hits	Diana Ross & The Supremes	Tamla-Motown	23	1	
9	6	Greatest Hits	Hollies	Parlophone	22	11	
10	9	Live At The Talk Of The Town	Tom Jones	Decca	22	13	

February 1969

This Mnth	Last Mnth	Title	Artist	Label	Wks in 10	US Pos	
1	2	The Best Of The Seekers	Seekers	Columbia	47	97	
2	1	The Beatles (White Album)	Beatles	Apple	14	1	
3	4	The Sound Of Music	Soundtrack	RCA	235	1	2P
4	-	Diana Ross & The Supremes Join The Temptations	Diana Ross & The Supremes/Temptations	Tamla-Motown	11	2	
5	-	Yellow Submarine	Beatles	Apple	7	2	
6	5	The Graduate (Soundtrack)	Simon & Garfunkel	CBS	10	1	
7	3	Beggars Banquet	Rolling Stones	Decca	8	5	
8	-	Feliciano	Jose Feliciano	RCA	4	2	FL
9	-	Stonedhenge	Ten Years After	Deram	4	61	F
10	-	Hair	Original London Cast	Polydor	14		

March 1969

This Mnth	Last Mnth	Title	Artist	Label	Wks in 10	US Pos	
1	4	Diana Ross & The Supremes Join The Temptations	Diana Ross & The Supremes/Temptations	Tamla-Motown	11	2	
2	-	Engelbert	Engelbert Humperdinck	Decca	6	12	
3	1	The Best Of The Seekers	Seekers	Columbia	47	97	
4	3	The Sound Of Music	Soundtrack	RCA	235	1	2P
5	-	Goodbye	Cream	Polydor	13	2	
6	-	Postcard	Mary Hopkin	Apple	5	28	FL
7	9	Stonedhenge	Ten Years After	Deram	4	61	F
8	-	Oliver	Soundtrack	RCA	26	20	
9	5	Yellow Submarine	Beatles	Apple	7	2	
10	-	Live At The Talk Of The Town	Seekers	Columbia	19		

US 1969

JAN-MAR

January 1969

This Mnth	Last Mnth	Title	Artist	Label	Wks in 10	UK Pos	
1	6	**The Beatles (White Album)**	Beatles	Apple	15	1	7P
2	3	**Wichita Lineman**	Glen Campbell	Capitol	22		2P
3	-	**Fool On The Hill**	Sergio Mendes & Brasil '66	A&M	5		L
4	-	**Diana Ross & The Supremes Join The Temptations**	Diana Ross & The Supremes	Motown	8	1	
5	-	**TCB**	Diana Ross & The Supremes/Temptations	Motown	11	11	L
6	-	**Beggars Banquet**	Rolling Stones	London	4	3	P
7	4	**The Second**	Steppenwolf	Dunhill	16		
8	1	**Cheap Thrills**	Big Brother & The Holding Company	Columbia	19		FPL
9	9	**Wild Flowers**	Judy Collins	Elektra	6		FL
10	7	**In-A-Gadda-Da-Vida**	Iron Butterfly	Atco	49		F4P

February 1969

This Mnth	Last Mnth	Title	Artist	Label	Wks in 10	UK Pos	
1	1	**The Beatles (White Album)**	Beatles	Apple	15	1	7P
2	5	**TCB**	Diana Ross & The Supremes/Temptations	Motown	11	11	L
3	2	**Wichita Lineman**	Glen Campbell	Capitol	22		2P
4	-	**Greatest Hits, Vol. 1**	Association	Warner	10		2PL
5	4	**Diana Ross & The Supremes Join The Temptations**	Diana Ross & The Supremes/Temptations	Motown	8	1	
6	10	**In-A-Gadda-Da-Vida**	Iron Butterfly	Atco	49		F4P
7	-	**Yellow Submarine**	Beatles	Apple	6	3	P
8	-	**Elvis**	Elvis Presley	RCA	3	2	
9	-	**Blood Sweat & Tears**	Blood, Sweat & Tears	Columbia	50	15	3P
10	7	**The Second**	Steppenwolf	Dunhill	16		

March 1969

This Mnth	Last Mnth	Title	Artist	Label	Wks in 10	UK Pos	
1	3	**Wichita Lineman**	Glen Campbell	Capitol	22		2P
2	1	**The Beatles (White Album)**	Beatles	Apple	15	1	7P
3	-	**Goodbye**	Cream	Atco	8	1	
4	-	**Ball**	Iron Butterfly	Atco	8		L
5	7	**Yellow Submarine**	Beatles	Apple	6	3	P
6	4	**Greatest Hits, Vol. 1**	Association	Warner	10		2PL
7	9	**Blood Sweat & Tears**	Blood, Sweat & Tears	Columbia	50	15	3P
8	2	**TCB**	Diana Ross & The Supremes/Temptations	Motown	11	11	L
9	-	**Crimson & Clover**	Tommy James & The Shondells	Roulette	5		FL
10	6	**In-A-Gadda-Da-Vida**	Iron Butterfly	Atco	49		F4P

• Motown's idea of teaming The Supremes and The Temptations proved to be a stroke of genius. The octet at times held two of the top three slots on the chart with the aptly named **Diana Ross & The Supremes Join The Temptations** and **TCB,** back in the days when The Temptations were called The Primes, The Supremes were their sister group, The Primettes. Incidentally, The Temptations' albums **Cloud Nine** and **Live At The Copa** were simultaneously in the Top 20.

• Two of America's most successful singles artists, Tommy James & The Shondells and Gary Puckett & The Union Gap, had their only Top 20 album entries with **Crimson & Clover** and **Incredible** respectively.

• Three of the early Seventies biggest selling acts, scaled the album best sellers for the first time. Three Dog Night's eponymous LP cracked the Top 20 while Bob Seger's **Ramblin' Gamblin' Man** and Jethro Tull's **This Was** peaked outside the Top 40.

• One of the more unusual hits of the period was **Switched-On Bach**, a collection of classical pieces played on the moog synthesizer by Walter Carlos. Another unusual Top 40 entry was **Themes Like Old Times**, a collection of 180 original radio themes.

UK 1969 APR-JUNE

• 150,000 attended Blind Faith's first gig at London's Hyde Park, and down the road, Janis Joplin appeared at the Royal Albert Hall.

• Britain's Procol Harum starred at the first Toronto rock festival alongside The Band, Chuck Berry, Blood Sweat & Tears and Steppenwolf. Joe Cocker lined up with top American acts Creedence Clearwater Revival, Jimi Hendrix, Iron Butterfly and The Mothers Of Invention at the Denver Pop Festival.

• Brian Jones left The Rolling Stones and was found drowned in his swimming pool just a few weeks later.

• The transatlantic blues boom, created by acts like Britain's Cream and John Mayall and America's Janis Joplin and Canned Heat, renewed interest in many of the original blues artists. Performers like B.B. King, Albert King, Muddy Waters, Howlin' Wolf and Buddy Guy benefited and found themselves playing to more people than ever.

April 1969

This Mnth	Last Mnth	Title	Artist	Label	Wks in 10	US Pos	
1	3	**The Best Of The Seekers**	Seekers	Columbia	47	97	
2	5	**Goodbye**	Cream	Polydor	13	2	
3	-	**20/20**	Beach Boys	Capitol	5	68	
4	4	**The Sound Of Music**	Soundtrack	RCA	235	1	2P
5	-	**Hair**	Original London Cast	Polydor	14		
6	-	**Scott 3**	Scott Walker	Philips	3		
7	-	**Beat Of The Brass**	Herb Alpert & The Tijuana Brass	A&M	2	1	
8	1	**Diana Ross & The Supremes Join The Temptations**	Diana Ross & The Supremes/Temptations	Tamla-Motown	11	2	
9	10	**Live At The Talk Of The Town**	Seekers	Columbia	19		
10	-	**Gentle On My Mind**	Dean Martin	Reprise	3	14	F

May 1969

This Mnth	Last Mnth	Title	Artist	Label	Wks in 10	US Pos	
1	-	**On The Threshold Of A Dream**	Moody Blues	Deram	10	20	
2	1	**The Best Of The Seekers**	Seekers	Columbia	47	97	
3	-	**Elvis - NBC TV Special**	Elvis Presley	RCA	6	8	
4	-	**Songs From A Room**	Leonard Cohen	CBS	6		F
5	2	**Goodbye**	Cream	Polydor	13	2	
6	-	**Nashville Skyline**	Bob Dylan	CBS	16	3	
7	5	**Hair**	Original London Cast	Polydor	14		
8	-	**Hollies Sing Dylan**	Hollies	Parlophone	3		
9	-	**Oliver**	Soundtrack	RCA	26	20	
10	-	**Led Zeppelin**	Led Zeppelin	Atlantic	5	10	F

June 1969

This Mnth	Last Mnth	Title	Artist	Label	Wks in 10	US Pos	
1	6	**Nashville Skyline**	Bob Dylan	CBS	16	3	
2	-	**My Way**	Frank Sinatra	Reprise	8	11	
3	1	**On The Threshold Of A Dream**	Moody Blues	Deram	10	20	
4	-	**Tommy**	Who	Track	4	4	
5	2	**The Best Of The Seekers**	Seekers	Columbia	47	97	
6	-	**His Orchestra, His Chorus, His Singers, His Sound**	Ray Conniff	CBS	16		L
7	-	**World Of Val Doonican**	Val Doonican	Decca	18		L
8	-	**World Of Mantovani**	Mantovani	Decca	9	92	
9	-	**This Is Tom Jones**	Tom Jones	Decca	9	4	
10	8	**Hollies Sing Dylan**	Hollies	Parlophone	3		

US 1969

APR-JUNE

April 1969

This Mnth	Last Mnth	Title	Artist	Label	Wks in 10	UK Pos	
1	7	**Blood Sweat & Tears**	Blood, Sweat & Tears	Columbia	50	15	**F3P**
2	-	**Hair**	Original Cast	RCA	28	29	
3	-	**Donovan's Greatest Hits**	Donovan	Epic	14		**FPL**
4	1	**Wichita Lineman**	Glen Campbell	Capitol	22		**2P**
5	10	**In-A-Gadda-Da-Vida**	Iron Butterfly	Atco	49		**F4P**
6	-	**Help Yourself**	Tom Jones	Parrot	13	4	**F**
7	-	**Galveston**	Glen Campbell	Capitol	10		**PL**
8	-	**Cloud Nine**	Temptations	Gordy	9	32	
9	4	**Ball**	Iron Butterfly	Atco	8		**L**
10	3	**Goodbye**	Cream	Atco	8	1	

May 1969

This Mnth	Last Mnth	Title	Artist	Label	Wks in 10	UK Pos	
1	2	**Hair**	Original Cast	RCA	28	29	
2	1	**Blood Sweat & Tears**	Blood, Sweat & Tears	Columbia	50	15	**F3P**
3	7	**Galveston**	Glen Campbell	Capitol	10		**PL**
4	3	**Donovan's Greatest Hits**	Donovan	Epic	14		**FPL**
5	-	**Nashville Skyline**	Bob Dylan	Columbia	13	1	**P**
6	8	**Cloud Nine**	Temptations	Gordy	9	32	
7	5	**In-A-Gadda-Da-Vida**	Iron Butterfly	Atco	49		**F4P**
8	6	**Help Yourself**	Tom Jones	Parrot	13	4	**F**
9	-	**Bayou Country**	Creedence Clearwater Revival	Fantasy	12	62	**F2P**
10	-	**Romeo & Juliet**	Soundtrack	Capitol	17		**P**

June 1969

This Mnth	Last Mnth	Title	Artist	Label	Wks in 10	UK Pos	
1	1	**Hair**	Original Cast	RCA	28	29	
2	2	**Blood Sweat & Tears**	Blood, Sweat & Tears	Columbia	50	15	**F3P**
3	-	**The Age Of Aquarius**	5th Dimension	Soul City	9		
4	5	**Nashville Skyline**	Bob Dylan	Columbia	13	1	**P**
5	10	**Romeo & Juliet**	Soundtrack	Capitol	17		**P**
6	7	**In-A-Gadda-Da-Vida**	Iron Butterfly	Atco	49		**F4P**
7	3	**Galveston**	Glen Campbell	Capitol	10		**PL**
8	9	**Bayou Country**	Creedence Clearwater Revival	Fantasy	12	62	**F2P**
9	4	**Donovan's Greatest Hits**	Donovan	Epic	14		**FPL**
10	-	**Happy Heart**	Andy Williams	Columbia	3	22	

• The first successful rock musical, *Hair*, was a big success on both sides of the Atlantic. The original cast album topped the US chart for three months, and the hit singles from it, 'Aquarius/Let The Sunshine In' and 'Hair', were included on Top 20 LPs by The Fifth Dimension and The Cowsills respectively.

• Major musical figures who took their first steps on the album chart included Neil Young & Crazy Horse, **Everybody Knows This Is Nowhere**, Alice Cooper, **Pretties For You**, Poco, **Pickin' Up The Pieces**, Flying Burrito Brothers, **The Gilded Palace Of Sin**, Columbia's $300,000 signing Johnny Winter, **The Progressive Blues Experiment** and Guess Who, **Wheatfield Soul**. At the same time Chicago, Sly & The Family Stone, Canadian singer/songwriter Joni Mitchell and The Isley Brothers paid the first of many visits to the Top 40.

• Metal-merchants Iron Butterfly started this quarter with their first two albums in the Top 5. Tom Jones fared equally well. At times, three of his albums, **Help Yourself**, **Fever Zone** and the two-year- old **Tom Jones Live!**, were simultaneously in the Top 20. Before the quarter ended they were joined on the chart by **This Is Tom Jones**.

UK 1969 JULY-SEPT

• British group Blind Faith had a short but spectacular career. They opened a sell-out US stadium tour at Madison Square Garden, and their only album, **Blind Faith**, topped the transatlantic charts. At one time they and their predecessor, Cream, held two of the top three album rungs in America.

• There was a resurgence of interest in country music in Britain and America. In the UK, Jim Reeves' **According To My Heart** became the first country album to top the chart, and in the USA **Johnny Cash At San Quentin** reached the top. The latter was the last country album to reach Number 1 until Garth Brooks arrived in 1991.

• As the swinging Sixties drew to an end, there was still room on the UK LP chart for many acts who had started their careers in earlier decades: Ray Conniff, Frank Sinatra, Jim Reeves, Mantovani, Johnny Cash, Elvis Presley, Cliff Richard and The Glenn Miller Orchestra all added to their British hit tallies.

• Also grabbing headlines were Bob Dylan's appearance at the Isle Of Wight festival, the sale of The Beatles song catalog to ATV (which Michael Jackson later purchased) and The Rolling Stones' free concert in Hyde Park, which attracted 250,000 fans.

July 1969

This Mnth	Last Mnth	Title	Artist	Label	Wks in 10	US Pos	
1	-	**According To My Heart**	Jim Reeves	RCA Int.	13		
2	6	**His Orchestra, His Chorus, His Singers, His Sound**	Ray Conniff	CBS	16		L
3	-	**Flaming Star**	Elvis Presley	RCA Int.	11	96	
4	9	**This Is Tom Jones**	Tom Jones	Decca	9	4	
5	7	**World Of Val Doonican**	Val Doonican	Decca	18		L
6	2	**My Way**	Frank Sinatra	Reprise	8	11	
7	1	**Nashville Skyline**	Bob Dylan	CBS	16	3	
8	-	**Best Of Cliff**	Cliff Richard	Columbia	2		
9	-	**The Best Of Glenn Miller**	Glenn Miller	RCA Int.	4		
10	-	**World Of The Bachelors**	Bachelors	Decca	5		L

August 1969

This Mnth	Last Mnth	Title	Artist	Label	Wks in 10	US Pos	
1	1	**According To My Heart**	Jim Reeves	RCA Int.	13		
2	-	**Stand Up**	Jethro Tull	Island	8	20	
3	2	**His Orchestra, His Chorus, His Singers, His Sound**	Ray Conniff	CBS	16		L
4	3	**Flaming Star**	Elvis Presley	RCA Int.	11	96	
5	5	**World Of Val Doonican**	Val Doonican	Decca	18		L
6	-	**From Elvis In Memphis**	Elvis Presley	RCA	5	13	
7	-	**2001 - A Space Odyssey**	Soundtrack	MGM	4	24	
8	-	**Cymansa Gann**	Massed Welsh Choirs	BBC	3		FL
9	4	**This Is Tom Jones**	Tom Jones	Decca	9	4	
10	-	**World Of Mantovani**	Mantovani	Decca	9	92	

September 1969

This Mnth	Last Mnth	Title	Artist	Label	Wks in 10	US Pos	
1	2	**Stand Up**	Jethro Tull	Island	8	20	
2	-	**Johnny Cash At San Quentin**	Johnny Cash	CBS	32	1	
3	1	**According To My Heart**	Jim Reeves	RCA Int.	13		
4	3	**His Orchestra, His Chorus, His Singers, His Sound**	Ray Conniff	CBS	16		L
5	-	**Blind Faith**	Blind Faith	Polydor	5	1	FL
6	6	**From Elvis In Memphis**	Elvis Presley	RCA	5	13	
7	5	**World Of Val Doonican**	Val Doonican	Decca	18		L
8	-	**Nashville Skyline**	Bob Dylan	CBS	16	3	
9	-	**Oliver**	Soundtrack	RCA	26	20	
10	10	**World Of Mantovani**	Mantovani	Decca	9	92	

US 1969

JULY-SEPT

July 1969

This Mnth	Last Mnth	Title	Artist	Label	Wks in 10	UK Pos	
1	1	**Hair**	Original Cast	RCA	28	29	
2	2	**Blood Sweat & Tears**	Blood, Sweat & Tears	Columbia	50	15	F3P
3	5	**Romeo & Juliet**	Soundtrack	Capitol	17		P
4	3	**The Age Of Aquarius**	5th Dimension	Soul City	9		
5	-	**This Is Tom Jones**	Tom Jones	Parrot	11	2	
6	6	**In-A-Gadda-Da-Vida**	Iron Butterfly	Atco	49		F4P
7	-	**Tommy**	Who	Decca	14	2	F2P
8	-	**A Warm Shade Of Ivory**	Henry Mancini	RCA	6		L
9	4	**Nashville Skyline**	Bob Dylan	Columbia	13	1	P
10	-	**Crosby, Stills & Nash**	Crosby, Stills & Nash	Atlantic	17	25	F

August 1969

This Mnth	Last Mnth	Title	Artist	Label	Wks in 10	UK Pos	
1	2	**Blood Sweat & Tears**	Blood, Sweat & Tears	Columbia	50	15	3P
2	1	**Hair**	Original Cast	RCA	28	29	
3	-	**Johnny Cash At San Quentin**	Johnny Cash	Columbia	20	2	F2P
4	3	**Romeo & Juliet**	Soundtrack	Capitol	17		P
5	-	**Best Of Cream**	Cream	Atco	13	6	L
6	5	**This Is Tom Jones**	Tom Jones	Parrot	11	2	
7	6	**In-A-Gadda-Da-Vida**	Iron Butterfly	Atco	49	F	4P
8	-	**Blind Faith**	Blind Faith	Atco	14	1	FPL
9	-	**The Soft Parade**	Doors	Elektra	9		P
10	10	**Crosby, Stills & Nash**	Crosby, Stills & Nash	Atlantic	17	25	F

September 1969

This Mnth	Last Mnth	Title	Artist	Label	Wks in 10	UK Pos	
1	3	**Johnny Cash At San Quentin**	Johnny Cash	Columbia	20	2	F2P
2	8	**Blind Faith**	Blind Faith	Atco	14	1	FPL
3	1	**Blood Sweat & Tears**	Blood, Sweat & Tears	Columbia	50	15	3P
4	5	**Best Of Cream**	Cream	Atco	13	6	L
5	2	**Hair**	Original Cast	RCA	28	29	
6	-	**Smash Hits**	Jimi Hendrix	Reprise	6	4	2P
7	-	**Green River**	Creedence Clearwater Revival	Fantasy	15	20	3P
8	9	**The Soft Parade**	Doors	Elektra	9		P
9	7	**In-A-Gadda-Da-Vida**	Iron Butterfly	Atco	49		4P
10	4	**Romeo & Juliet**	Soundtrack	Capitol	17		P

• Woodstock, the most famous rock festival of all, took place in New York State. Many top album acts appeared during the three day event including Blood, Sweat & Tears, Canned Heat, Joe Cocker, Creedence Clearwater Revival, Crosby, Stills, Nash & Young and Grateful Dead. Other headliners were Jimi Hendrix, Jefferson Airplane, Janis Joplin, Santana, Sly & The Family Stone, Ten Years After and The Who.

• After eight years of solid film work, Elvis Presley returned to the live stage. His first shows were in Las Vegas, the town that had virtually ignored him when he appeared there in 1956.

• Among the ground-breaking albums currently on the chart were the rock opera **Tommy** by The Who, the self-titled debut album from Led Zeppelin, and an album that re-shaped soul/R&B music, **Hot Buttered Soul** by Memphis singer/song-writer Isaac Hayes.

• Chart debuting super-group Crosby, Stills & Nash took the Grammy for Best New Artist of 1969. However, groups were no longer having it all their own way as a handful of noteworthy male solo artists were enjoying their first album action. Among them were singer/songwriters Tony Joe White and Nilsson, jazz/soul singer/guitarist George Benson and Britain's Joe Cocker.

UK 1969

OCT-DEC

October 1969

This Mnth	Last Mnth	Title	Artist	Label	Wks in 10	US Pos	
1	-	**Abbey Road**	Beatles	Apple	31	1	
2	2	**Johnny Cash At San Quentin**	Johnny Cash	CBS	32	1	
3	-	**Through The Past Darkly (Big Hits Vol. 2)**	Rolling Stones	Decca	13	2	
4	5	**Blind Faith**	Blind Faith	Polydor	5	1	FL
5	8	**Nashville Skyline**	Bob Dylan	CBS	16	3	
6	-	**Ssssh**	Ten Years After	Deram	4	20	
7	-	**The Sound Of Music**	Soundtrack	RCA	235	1	2P
8	-	**British Motown Chartbusters Vol. 3**	Various	Tamla-Motown	30		
9	-	**World Of Mantovani Vol. 2**	Mantovani	Decca	1		
10	-	**Then Play On**	Fleetwood Mac	Reprise	5	109	

• **Through The Past Darkly** and **Let It Bleed** added to the Rolling Stones' already very impressive tally of top hits. Also completing transatlantic Top 10 doubles were the albums **Best Of Cream**, **Best Of The Bee Gees**, **Tom Jones Live In Las Vegas** and **Engelbert Humperdinck**.

• Jimi Hendrix's new group, The Band of Gypsys played their first gig. However, it was amen to top teen-appeal band Amen Corner, and Barry Gibb followed brother Robin's example and quit The Bee Gees.

• John Lennon, who played his first gigs in the Plastic Ono Band, returned his MBE to the Queen – he was unhappy about Britain's position over Vietnam. Meanwhile fellow-Beatle Paul McCartney was kept busy denying an American rumour that he had recently died.

• The decade ended on a sour note when a member of the audience was murdered as The Rolling Stones entertained 300,000 rock fans at the Altamont Festival in California.

November 1969

This Mnth	Last Mnth	Title	Artist	Label	Wks in 10	US Pos	
1	1	**Abbey Road**	Beatles	Apple	31	1	
2	8	**British Motown Chartbusters Vol. 3**	Various	Tamla-Motown	30		
3	2	**Johnny Cash At San Quentin**	Johnny Cash	CBS	32	1	
4	-	**Led Zeppelin 2**	Led Zeppelin	Atlantic	56	1	
5	3	**Through The Past Darkly (Big Hits Vol. 2)**	Rolling Stones	Decca	13	2	
6	-	**In The Court Of The Crimson King**	King Crimson	Island	5	28	F
7	-	**Best Of Cream**	Cream	Polydor	5	3	
8	-	**Best Of The Bee Gees**	Bee Gees	Polydor	5	9	
9	-	**Tom Jones Live In Las Vegas**	Tom Jones	Decca	17	3	
10	-	**Ummagumma**	Pink Floyd	Harvest	2	74	

December 1969

This Mnth	Last Mnth	Title	Artist	Label	Wks in 10	US Pos	
1	1	**Abbey Road**	Beatles	Apple	31	1	
2	2	**British Motown Chartbusters Vol. 3**	Various	Tamla-Motown	30		
3	9	**Tom Jones Live In Las Vegas**	Tom Jones	Decca	17	3	
4	-	**To Our Children's Children's Children**	Moody Blues	Deram	8	14	
5	3	**Johnny Cash At San Quentin**	Johnny Cash	CBS	32	1	
6	-	**Let It Bleed**	Rolling Stones	Decca	9	3	
7	-	**Engelbert Humperdinck**	Engelbert Humperdinck	Decca	7	5	
8	-	**The Sound Of Music**	Soundtrack	RCA	235	1	2P
9	4	**Led Zeppelin 2**	Led Zeppelin	Atlantic	56	1	
10	-	**The Best Of The Seekers**	Seekers	Columbia	47	97	

US 1969

OCT-DEC

October 1969

This Mnth	Last Mnth	Title	Artist	Label	Wks in 10	UK Pos	
1	7	**Green River**	Creedence Clearwater Revival	Fantasy	15	20	**3P**
2	1	**Johnny Cash At San Quentin**	Johnny Cash	Columbia	20	2	**F2P**
3	-	**Through The Past Darkly (Big Hits Vol. 2)**	Rolling Stones	London	9	2	**P**
4	2	**Blind Faith**	Blind Faith	Atco	14	1	**FPL**
5	3	**Blood Sweat & Tears**	Blood, Sweat & Tears	Columbia	50	15	**3P**
6	9	**In-A-Gadda-Da-Vida**	Iron Butterfly	Atco	49	F	**4P**
7	4	**Best Of Cream**	Cream	Atco	13	6	**L**
8	5	**Hair**	Original Cast	RCA	28	29	
9	-	**Abbey Road**	Beatles	Apple	27	1	**9P**
10	6	**Smash Hits**	Jimi Hendrix	Reprise	6	4	**2P**

November 1969

This Mnth	Last Mnth	Title	Artist	Label	Wks in 10	UK Pos	
1	9	**Abbey Road**	Beatles	Apple	27	1	**9P**
2	1	**Green River**	Creedence Clearwater Revival	Fantasy	15	20	**3P**
3	2	**Johnny Cash At San Quentin**	Johnny Cash	Columbia	20	2	**F2P**
4	-	**I Got Dem Ol' Kozmic Blues Again Mama**	Janis Joplin	Columbia	5		**F**
5	-	**Crosby, Stills & Nash**	Crosby, Stills & Nash	Atlantic	17	25	**F**
6	-	**Santana**	Santana	Columbia	28	26	**F2P**
7	-	**Led Zeppelin II**	Led Zeppelin	Atlantic	24	1	**6P**
8	3	**Through The Past Darkly (Big Hits Vol. 2)**	Rolling Stones	London	9	2	**P**
9	4	**Blind Faith**	Blind Faith	Atco	14	1	**FPL**
10	-	**Puzzle People**	Temptations	Gordy	11	20	

December 1969

This Mnth	Last Mnth	Title	Artist	Label	Wks in 10	UK Pos	
1	1	**Abbey Road**	Beatles	Apple	27	1	**9P**
2	7	**Led Zeppelin II**	Led Zeppelin	Atlantic	24	1	**6P**
3	-	**Tom Jones Live In Las Vegas**	Tom Jones	Parrot	18	3	
4	2	**Green River**	Creedence Clearwater Revival	Fantasy	15	20	**3P**
5	10	**Puzzle People**	Temptations	Gordy	11	20	
6	-	**Let It Bleed**	Rolling Stones	London	10	1	**2P**
7	6	**Santana**	Santana	Columbia	28	26	**F2P**
8	-	**Blood Sweat & Tears**	Blood, Sweat & Tears	Columbia	50	15	**3P**
9	5	**Crosby, Stills & Nash**	Crosby, Stills & Nash	Atlantic	17	25	**F**
10	-	**Willy And The Poor Boys**	Creedence Clearwater Revival	Fantasy	16	10	**2P**

• In 1969 gold tape awards were introduced for sales over a million and cassette sales accounted for 40% of the $1 billion spent on recorded music. It was also announced that under-25s accounted for 75% of record and tape sales.

• **Abbey Road** proved to be one of The Beatles' biggest selling albums. It topped the American charts for 11 weeks and headed the UK lists for four months. The album included their double sided smash 'Come Together' and 'Something'. The latter, written by George Harrison, was the group' first non-Lennon & McCartney composed single.

• In the last quarter of the Sixties noted artists Santana, Janis Joplin, Crosby, Stills & Nash earned their first Top 10 hits. Making lower chart debuts were Seventies stalwarts Bread, **Bread**, John Denver, **Rhymes & Reasons**, Grand Funk Railroad, **On Time**, Canadian singer/songwriter Gordon Lightfoot, **Sunday Concert**, and Rod Stewart, **The Rod Stewart Album**.

• Herb Alpert announced that his band, The Tijuana Brass, who had sold over 40 million albums in the decade, would not perform live again. He also raved about The Carpenters, whom he had signed to his label, A&M. At the same time, Diana Ross announced she was leaving The Supremes and raved about her newly signed label-mates The Jackson Five.

Rod Stewart

the 1970s

Abba

The Carpenters

David Cassidy

With rock music entering its adolescent years as the new decade began, sales of recorded music increased, now with the added impetus of a new format, the pre-recorded cassette. Sales of albums reached an all time high with British artists like Elton John, Paul McCartney and Rod Stewart, and US acts such as Chicago, John Denver and Bob Dylan selling vast quantities of albums on both sides of the Atlantic. Longevity on the LP chart was no longer a prerogative of easy listening acts and soundtracks; albums by performers like Pink Floyd, Carole King, Simon & Garfunkel and Mike Oldfield started chart runs that would have been the envy of earlier rock acts.

TOP UK ACTS ON THE US CHARTS IN THE 1970s

1	Elton John
2	Paul McCartney
3	Fleetwod Mac
4	The Rolling Stones
5	Led Zeppelin
6	Pink Floyd
7	The Bee Gees
8	Rod Stewart
9	Peter Frampton
10	The Beatles

TOP US ACTS ON THE UK CHARTS IN THE 1970s

1	Simon & Garfunkel
2	The Carpenters
3	Andy Williams
4	Perry Como
5	The Stylistics
6	Bob Dylan
7	Diana Ross
8	Blondie
9	Elvis Presley
10	The Eagles

the 1970s

The inevitable diversification which comes with maturity resulted in several acts who were superstars on one side of the Atlantic failing to make any noticeable impression on the other side. Glam rock dominated the UK charts in the first half of the decade but many of its leading exponents including T. Rex, Slade, Gary Glitter and Mud sold relatively few records in the US. The same can also be said about the British punk rock bands who brought a welcome breath of fresh air to the UK charts at the end of the decade. Similarly American superstars such as Grand Funk Railroad, Three Dog Night, the Allman Brothers and Bob Seger left the UK utterly unmoved.

Heavy metal grew in stature everywhere, and transatlantic teenybop pandemonium greeted the Osmonds, the Jackson Five, David Cassidy and the Bay City Rollers. At the same time, the era of the singer/songwriter virtually wiped out the previous decade's concept of the cover version. Music became more adventurous and diverse, in some measure due to the celebrity achieved by certain record producers, especially during the disco period of the latter half of the decade, when the sound sometimes became more important than the performer. While still often ignored by white record buyers, black music expanded its influence, the period's biggest international black star being Stevie Wonder. Superior pop music from the Carpenters in the US and Abba in Sweden battled for supremacy with country/rock from the Eagles, metal thunder from Led Zeppelin and early AOR from Fleetwood Mac.

America and Europe were not alone in spawning international superstars, as Australian-bred acts spearheaded by Olivia Newton-John and the Bee Gees became a significant chart force. The decade ended with electropop, Eurodisco and synth rock starting to make an impression, along with a second generation of hard rock bands and the earliest appearance of rap – a force for the next two decades.

TOP UK ALBUM ACTS OF THE 1970s

1. Simon & Garfunkel
2. Abba
3. Paul McCartney
4. Rod Stewart
5. Elton John
6. The Carpenters
7. David Bowie
8. Mike Oldfield
9. Andy Williams
10. The Rolling Stones
11. Bay City Rollers
12. The Beatles
13. Led Zeppelin
14. Pink Floyd
15. Slade
16. Perry Como
17. The Stylistics
18. Bob Dylan
19. Queen
20. The Electric Light Orchestra

TOP US ALBUM ACTS OF THE 1970s

1. Elton John
2. Paul McCartney
3. Chicago
4. Fleetwood Mac
5. The Rolling Stones
6. The Eagles
7. Led Zeppelin
8. Carole King
9. John Denver
10. Earth, Wind & Fire
11. Stevie Wonder
12. Pink Floyd
13. The Bee Gees
14. Rod Stewart
15. Peter Frampton
16. Linda Ronstadt
17. The Beatles
18. Olivia Newton-John
19. Barbra Streisand
20. Cat Stevens

Marc Bolan, T.Rex

Olivia Newton John

TOP BRITISH ALBUMS OF THE 1970s

1	**Bridge Over Troubled Water**	Simon & Garfunkel
2	**The Singles 1969-1973**	The Carpenters
3	**Tubular Bells**	Mike Oldfield
4	**Band On The Run**	Wings
5	**Greatest Hits**	Simon & Garfunkel
6	**Greatest Hits**	Abba
7	**Arrival**	Abba
8	**The Best Of The Stylistics**	The Stylistics
9	**Saturday Night Fever**	Soundtrack
10	**Greatest Hits**	Andy Williams
11	**And I Love You So**	Perry Como
12	**Grease**	Soundtrack
13	**Electric Warrior**	T. Rex
14	**Parallel Lines**	Blondie
15	**Rumours**	Fleetwood Mac
16	**The Album**	Abba
17	**Aladdin Sane**	David Bowie
18	**Night Flight To Venus**	Boney M
19	**Rollin'**	Bay City Rollers
20	**Goodbye Yellow Brick Road**	Elton John

TOP AMERICAN ALBUMS OF THE 1970s

1	**Rumours**	Fleetwood Mac
2	**Frampton Comes Alive**	Peter Frampton
3	**Tapestry**	Carole King
4	**Songs In The Key Of Life**	Stevie Wonder
5	**Saturday Night Fever**	Soundtrack
6	**Jesus Christ Superstar**	Various
7	**Hotel California**	The Eagles
8	**Grease**	Soundtrack
9	**Abraxas**	Santana
10	**Breakfast In America**	Supertramp
11	**Goodbye Yellow Brick Road**	Elton John
12	**John Denver's Greatest Hits**	John Denver
13	**Fleetwood Mac**	Fleetwood Mac
14	**Woodstock**	Various
15	**The Long Run**	The Eagles
16	**Band On The Run**	Wings
17	**Wings At The Speed Of Sound**	Wings
18	**Boston**	Boston
19	**Double Vision**	Foreigner
20	**Red Octopus**	Jefferson Starship

Pink Floyd

Stevie Wonder

The Eagles

UK 1970 JAN-MAR

January 1970

This Mnth	Last Mnth	Title	Artist	Label	Wks in 10	US Pos	
1	1	**Abbey Road**	Beatles	Apple	31	1	
2	2	**British Motown Chartbusters Vol. 3**	Various	Tamla-Motown	30		
3	6	**Let It Bleed**	Rolling Stones	Decca	9	3	
4	3	**Tom Jones Live In Las Vegas**	Tom Jones	Decca	17	3	
5	9	**Led Zeppelin 2**	Led Zeppelin	Atlantic	56	1	
6	4	**To Our Children's Children's Children**	Moody Blues	Deram	8	14	
7	8	**The Sound Of Music**	Soundtrack	RCA	235	1	**2P**
8	5	**Johnny Cash At San Quentin**	Johnny Cash	CBS	32	1	
9	7	**Engelbert Humperdinck**	Engelbert Humperdinck	Decca	7	5	
10	-	**Easy Rider**	Soundtrack	Stateside	32	10	

• Simon & Garfunkel's **Bridge Over Troubled Water** has often been voted the Top Album Of The Rock Era. It won the Grammy for Best Album of 1970 and was, remarkably, the Number 1 album in Britain in both 1970 and 1971. The album spent over 300 weeks on the British chart, 135 of them in the Top 10 and 41 of those at the top spot.

• In Britain, singles that enter the chart first week at Number 1 are commonplace. However, in America the highest entry ever was The Beatles' 'Let It Be' which came in the Hot 100 at Number 6. Soon after, the album of the same name also made the highest position on both sides of the Atlantic.

• **Hot Rats** by Frank Zappa, **In The Court Of The Crimson King** by King Crimson, **On The Boards** by Taste and Black Sabbath's eponymous debut album were among the well-rated rock LPs that narrowly missed the month's Top 10 lists.

February 1970

This Mnth	Last Mnth	Title	Artist	Label	Wks in 10	US Pos	
1	2	**British Motown Chartbusters Vol. 3**	Various	Tamla-Motown	30		
2	5	**Led Zeppelin 2**	Led Zeppelin	Atlantic	56	1	
3	1	**Abbey Road**	Beatles	Apple	31	1	
4	-	**A Song For Me**	Family	Reprise	4		
5	-	**Bridge Over Troubled Water**	Simon & Garfunkel	CBS	135	1	**2P**
6	8	**Johnny Cash At San Quentin**	Johnny Cash	CBS	32	1	
7	4	**Tom Jones Live In Las Vegas**	Tom Jones	Decca	17	3	
8	10	**Easy Rider**	Soundtrack	Stateside	32	10	
9	-	**Basket Of Light**	Pentangle	Transatlantic	5	200	**FL**
10	3	**Let It Bleed**	Rolling Stones	Decca	9	3	

March 1970

This Mnth	Last Mnth	Title	Artist	Label	Wks in 10	US Pos	
1	5	**Bridge Over Troubled Water**	Simon & Garfunkel	CBS	135	1	**2P**
2	-	**Paint Your Wagon**	Soundtrack	Paramount	25	28	
3	2	**Led Zeppelin 2**	Led Zeppelin	Atlantic	56	1	
4	1	**British Motown Chartbusters Vol. 3**	Various	Tamla-Motown	30		
5	8	**Easy Rider**	Soundtrack	Stateside	32	10	
6	-	**From Memphis To Vegas - From Vegas To Memphis**	Elvis Presley	RCA	4	12	
7	3	**Abbey Road**	Beatles	Apple	31	1	
8	-	**Hello I'm Johnny Cash**	Johnny Cash	CBS	4	6	
9	6	**Johnny Cash At San Quentin**	Johnny Cash	CBS	32	1	
10	9	**Basket Of Light**	Pentangle	Transatlantic	5	200	**FL**

US 1970

JAN-MAR

January 1970

This Mnth	Last Mnth	Title	Artist	Label	Wks in 10	UK Pos	
1	1	**Abbey Road**	Beatles	Apple	27	1	**9P**
2	2	**Led Zeppelin II**	Led Zeppelin	Atlantic	24	1	**6P**
3	10	**Willy And The Poor Boys**	Creedence Clearwater Revival	Fantasy	16	10	**2P**
4	3	**Tom Jones Live In Las Vegas**	Tom Jones	Parrot	18	3	
5	6	**Let It Bleed**	Rolling Stones	London	10	1	**2P**
6	-	**Captured Live At The Forum**	Three Dog Night	Dunhill	11		**F**
7	8	**Blood Sweat & Tears**	Blood, Sweat & Tears	Columbia	50	15	**3P**
8	-	**Engelbert Humperdinck**	Engelbert Humperdinck	Parrot	9	5	**L**
9	7	**Santana**	Santana	Columbia	28	26	**F2P**
10	9	**Crosby, Stills & Nash**	Crosby, Stills & Nash	Atlantic	17	25	**F**

February 1970

This Mnth	Last Mnth	Title	Artist	Label	Wks in 10	UK Pos	
1	2	**Led Zeppelin II**	Led Zeppelin	Atlantic	24	1	**6P**
2	1	**Abbey Road**	Beatles	Apple	27	1	**9P**
3	3	**Willy And The Poor Boys**	Creedence Clearwater Revival	Fantasy	16	10	**2P**
4	4	**Tom Jones Live In Las Vegas**	Tom Jones	Parrot	18	3	
5	8	**Engelbert Humperdinck**	Engelbert Humperdinck	Parrot	9	5	**L**
6	5	**Let It Bleed**	Rolling Stones	London	10	1	**2P**
7	6	**Captured Live At The Forum**	Three Dog Night	Dunhill	11		**F**
8	9	**Santana**	Santana	Columbia	28	26	**F2P**
9	-	**Diana Ross Presents The Jackson 5**	Jackson 5	Motown	11	16	**F**
10	-	**Bridge Over Troubled Water**	Simon & Garfunkel	Columbia	17	1	**5P**

March 1970

This Mnth	Last Mnth	Title	Artist	Label	Wks in 10	UK Pos	
1	10	**Bridge Over Troubled Water**	Simon & Garfunkel	Columbia	17	1	**5P**
2	1	**Led Zeppelin II**	Led Zeppelin	Atlantic	24	1	**6P**
3	2	**Abbey Road**	Beatles	Apple	27	1	**9P**
4	3	**Willy And The Poor Boys**	Creedence Clearwater Revival	Fantasy	16	10	**2P**
5	-	**Chicago II**	Chicago	Columbia	33	6	**F**
6	-	**Hey Jude**	Beatles	Apple	11		**3P**
7	8	**Santana**	Santana	Columbia	28	26	**F2P**
8	-	**Morrison Hotel/Hard Rock Cafe**	Doors	Elektra	6	12	
9	-	**Hello I'm Johnny Cash**	Johnny Cash	Columbia	4	6	**L**
10	4	**Tom Jones Live In Las Vegas**	Tom Jones	Parrot	18		

• Three Dog Night, The Jackson Five – fronted by 11-year-old Michael Jackson, Chicago, The Plastic Ono Band – fronted by John Lennon, and The Band all made their Top 10 debuts as the new decade dawned.

• Artists who reached the Top 20 for the first time in the early months of the Seventies included heavy rockers Grand Funk Railroad, Britain's Frijid Pink and Mountain, who included Cream producer Felix Pappalardi. Teen idol Bobby Sherman also debuted in the Top 20 as did comedian David Frye. The latter had the biggest of his four President Nixon spoof hit albums with **I Am The President**.

• One of the hottest singles of the period was the Burt Bacharach song 'Raindrops Keep Falling On My Head' by B. J. Thomas. It was featured on two high-flying LPs; Thomas' album of the same name and the soundtrack album of **Butch Cassidy And The Sundance Kid**.

• As Elvis Presley climbed into the transatlantic Top 10s with **From Memphis To Vegas**, he co-starred with Mary Tyler Moore in his last acting movie, *Change Of Habit*.

• Southern rock pioneers, The Allman Brothers, funk master George Clinton's band Funkadelic and ex Lovin' Spoonful front-man, John B. Sebastian; all took their first steps on the LP chart with self-titled albums.

UK 1970 APR-JUNE

• Compilation albums were now becoming frequent visitors to the British Top 20. Numbered among the latest crop to crack the charts were **Fill Your Head With Rock** from CBS, **Bumpers** from Island and two albums from the Trojan label, **Reggae Chartbusters** and **Tighten Up Volume 2**.

• Nana Mouskouri, the most popular female artist in Greece, paid her second visit in a year to the Top 10 with **The Exquisite Nana Mouskouri**, and French heart-throb Sacha Distel's self titled album doubled the number of continental European albums on the chart.

• Hopes were high for the English soccer team as they headed to South America to defend the World Cup that they had won in 1966. As it turned out they were less successful on the pitch than on the album chart where **The World Beaters Sing The World Beaters** reached the Top 5.

• British blues pioneer John Mayall and talent-packed progressive rock band King Crimson spent their last weeks in the Top 20 with **Empty Rooms** and **In The Wake Of Poseidon** respectively.

• Canadian singer/songwriter Joni Mitchell's **Ladies Of The Canyon** introduced her to the UK Top 10. Also saying hello were future rock giants Deep Purple with **Deep Purple In Rock** and The Groundhogs with **Thank Christ For The Bomb**.

April 1970

This Mnth	Last Mnth	Title	Artist	Label	Wks in 10	US Pos	
1	1	**Bridge Over Troubled Water**	Simon & Garfunkel	CBS	135	1	2P
2	5	**Easy Rider**	Soundtrack	Stateside	32	10	
3	-	**Greatest Hits**	Andy Williams	CBS	37	42	
4	3	**Led Zeppelin 2**	Led Zeppelin	Atlantic	56	1	
5	2	**Paint Your Wagon**	Soundtrack	Paramount	25	28	
6	7	**Abbey Road**	Beatles	Apple	31	1	
7	4	**British Motown Chartbusters Vol. 3**	Various	Tamla-Motown	30		
8	-	**Chicago**	Chicago	CBS	4	4	
9	-	**Sentimental Journey**	Ringo Starr	Apple	1	22	F
10	6	**From Memphis To Vegas - From Vegas To Memphis**	Elvis Presley	RCA	4	12	

May 1970

This Mnth	Last Mnth	Title	Artist	Label	Wks in 10	US Pos	
1	1	**Bridge Over Troubled Water**	Simon & Garfunkel	CBS	135	1	2P
2	-	**McCartney**	Paul McCartney	Apple	18	1	F
3	3	**Greatest Hits**	Andy Williams	CBS	37	42	
4	-	**Benefit**	Jethro Tull	Island	4	11	
5	2	**Easy Rider**	Soundtrack	Stateside	32	10	
6	-	**Tom**	Tom Jones	Decca	5	6	
7	-	**Let It Be**	Beatles	Apple	18	1	
8	-	**Cricklewood Green**	Ten Years After	Deram	4	14	
9	-	**The World Beaters Sing The World Beaters**	England Football World Cup Squad	Pye	5		FL
10	4	**Led Zeppelin 2**	Led Zeppelin	Atlantic	56	1	

June 1970

This Mnth	Last Mnth	Title	Artist	Label	Wks in 10	US Pos	
1	1	**Bridge Over Troubled Water**	Simon & Garfunkel	CBS	135	1	2P
2	7	**Let It Be**	Beatles	Apple	18	1	
3	2	**McCartney**	Paul McCartney	Apple	18	1	F
4	-	**Deja Vu**	Crosby, Stills, Nash & Young	Atlantic	5	1	F
5	-	**Live At Leeds**	Who	Track	5	4	
6	5	**Easy Rider**	Soundtrack	Stateside	32	10	
7	-	**Deep Purple In Rock**	Deep Purple	Harvest	32	143	F
8	10	**Led Zeppelin 2**	Led Zeppelin	Atlantic	56	1	
9	-	**In The Wake Of Poseidon**	King Crimson	Island	3	31	L
10	9	**The World Beaters Sing The World Beaters**	England Football World Cup Squad	Pye	5		FL

US 1970 APR-JUNE

April 1970

This Mnth	Last Mnth	Title	Artist	Label	Wks in 10	UK Pos	
1	1	**Bridge Over Troubled Water**	Simon & Garfunkel	Columbia	17	1	5P
2	6	**Hey Jude**	Beatles	Apple	11		3P
3	-	**Deja Vu**	Crosby, Stills, Nash & Young	Atlantic	23	5	F7P
4	7	**Santana**	Santana	Columbia	28	26	F2P
5	2	**Led Zeppelin II**	Led Zeppelin	Atlantic	24	1	6P
6	8	**Morrison Hotel/Hard Rock Cafe**	Doors	Elektra	6	12	
7	-	**Diana Ross Presents The Jackson 5**	Jackson 5	Motown	11	16	F
8	5	**Chicago II**	Chicago	Columbia	33	6	F
9	3	**Abbey Road**	Beatles	Apple	27	1	9P
10	4	**Willy And The Poor Boys**	Creedence Clearwater Revival	Fantasy	16	10	2P

May 1970

This Mnth	Last Mnth	Title	Artist	Label	Wks in 10	UK Pos	
1	1	**Bridge Over Troubled Water**	Simon & Garfunkel	Columbia	17	1	5P
2	3	**Deja Vu**	Crosby, Stills, Nash & Young	Atlantic	23	5	F7P
3	2	**Hey Jude**	Beatles	Apple	11		3P
4	8	**Chicago II**	Chicago	Columbia	33	6	F
5	-	**McCartney**	Paul McCartney	Apple	13	2	F2P
6	-	**Band Of Gypsys**	Jimi Hendrix	Reprise	7	10	P
7	4	**Santana**	Santana	Columbia	28	26	F2P
8	-	**Steppenwolf 'Live'**	Steppenwolf	Dunhill	5	16	L
9	7	**Diana Ross Presents The Jackson 5**	Jackson 5	Motown	11	16	F
10	-	**American Woman**	Guess Who	RCA	7		FL

June 1970

This Mnth	Last Mnth	Title	Artist	Label	Wks in 10	UK Pos	
1	-	**Let It Be**	Beatles	Apple	10	1	
2	5	**McCartney**	Paul McCartney	Apple	13	2	F2P
3	-	**Woodstock**	Various	Cotillion	24	35	2P
4	2	**Deja Vu**	Crosby, Stills, Nash & Young	Atlantic	23	5	F7P
5	6	**Band Of Gypsys**	Jimi Hendrix	Reprise	7	10	P
6	4	**Chicago II**	Chicago	Columbia	33	6	F
7	-	**The 5th Dimension/Greatest Hits**	5th Dimension	Soul City	5		L
8	1	**Bridge Over Troubled Water**	Simon & Garfunkel	Columbia	17	1	5P
9	-	**Live At Leeds**	Who	Decca	14	3	2P
10	-	**The Isaac Hayes Movement**	Isaac Hayes	Enterprise	6		

• Even though all was not well within The Beatles, the group continued to dominate the charts. An American-only compilation **Hey Jude** was soon followed on to the Top 10 by the group's last official release before splitting, **Let It Be**. Also climbing were the first solo albums by members Ringo Starr and Paul McCartney with **Sentimental Journey** and **McCartney** respectively. The latter becoming the first solo Number 1 album from a Beatle in the USA. Incidentally, the only Grammy the group picked up was Best Engineered Recording for **Abbey Road**.

• Woodstock was back in the news. The film of the festival was now on general release and the soundtrack album was selling well. Several of the acts who appeared at the festival were also enjoying hit albums including Crosby, Stills, Nash & Young, **Deja Vu**, Santana, **Santana**, Creedence Clearwater Revival, **Willy And The Poor Boys**, and Jimi Hendrix **Band Of Gypsys**.

UK 1970

JULY-SEPT

• It was a busy period for The Rolling Stones, whose **Get Your Ya-Ya's Out!** gave the quintet their fifth British chart topper. Lead vocalist, Mick Jagger, had two films released, *Ned Kelly* and *Performance*, and the group's contract with Decca expired. Incidentally, it was also the quarter when Stone Bill Wyman's future wife Mandy Smith was born.

• Foremost rock'n'roll duo, The Everly Brothers, whose **Original Greatest Hits** briefly breached the UK Top 10, hosted their own American TV series as a summer replacement to the successful *Johnny Cash Show*.

• Among the major British live shows were the last ever gig of Jimi Hendrix at the Isle Of Wight Festival and Pink Floyd's free concert in London's Hyde Park. Other noteworthy gig news included Emerson, Lake & Palmer's live debut and Lou Reed's final show with The Velvet Underground.

• The first ever gig by members of Abba was hardly noticed. The same was true of Oliva Newton-John's film debut in the musical *Tomorrow* and the addition of drummer Phil Collins to Genesis.

• Led Zeppelin were voted Top Group in the *Melody Maker* poll, replacing The Beatles who had been winners for the previous eight years.

July 1970

This Mnth	Last Mnth	Title	Artist	Label	Wks in 10	US Pos	
1	1	**Bridge Over Troubled Water**	Simon & Garfunkel	CBS	135	1	2P
2	2	**Let It Be**	Beatles	Apple	18	1	
3	-	**Self Portrait**	Bob Dylan	CBS	6	4	
4	3	**McCartney**	Paul McCartney	Apple	18	1	F
5	-	**Fire And Water**	Free	Island	7	17	F
6	6	**Easy Rider**	Soundtrack	Stateside	32	10	
7	-	**Five Bridges**	Nice	Charisma	3	197	
8	-	**Live Cream**	Cream	Polydor	3	15	
9	7	**Deep Purple In Rock**	Deep Purple	Harvest	32	143	F
10	-	**Band Of Gypsys**	Jimi Hendrix	Track	2	5	

August 1970

This Mnth	Last Mnth	Title	Artist	Label	Wks in 10	US Pos	
1	1	**Bridge Over Troubled Water**	Simon & Garfunkel	CBS	135	1	2P
2	-	**On Stage**	Elvis Presley	RCA	8	13	
3	5	**Fire And Water**	Free	Island	7	17	F
4	-	**Paint Your Wagon**	Soundtrack	Paramount	25	28	
5	-	**A Question Of Balance**	Moody Blues	Threshold	10	3	
6	2	**Let It Be**	Beatles	Apple	18	1	
7	3	**Self Portrait**	Bob Dylan	CBS	6	4	
8	6	**Easy Rider**	Soundtrack	Stateside	32	10	
9	4	**McCartney**	Paul McCartney	Apple	18	1	F
10	9	**Deep Purple In Rock**	Deep Purple	Harvest	32	143	F

September 1970

This Mnth	Last Mnth	Title	Artist	Label	Wks in 10	US Pos	
1	1	**Bridge Over Troubled Water**	Simon & Garfunkel	CBS	135	1	2P
2	5	**A Question Of Balance**	Moody Blues	Threshold	10	3	
3	-	**Cosmo's Factory**	Creedence Clearwater Revival	Fantasy	9	1	L
4	4	**Paint Your Wagon**	Soundtrack	Paramount	25	28	
5	-	**Get Your Ya-Ya's Out!**	Rolling Stones	Decca	7	6	
6	6	**Let It Be**	Beatles	Apple	18	1	
7	2	**On Stage**	Elvis Presley	RCA	8	13	
8	-	**Led Zeppelin 2**	Led Zeppelin	Atlantic	56	1	
9	10	**Deep Purple In Rock**	Deep Purple	Harvest	32	143	F
10	-	**Something**	Shirley Bassey	UA	4	105	

US 1970 JULY-SEPT

July 1970

This Mnth	Last Mnth	Title	Artist	Label	Wks in 10	UK Pos	
1	3	**Woodstock**	Various	Cotillion	24	35	2P
2	1	**Let It Be**	Beatles	Apple	10	1	
3	2	**McCartney**	Paul McCartney	Apple	13	2	F2P
4	-	**ABC**	Jackson 5	Motown	9	22	
5	9	**Live At Leeds**	Who	Decca	14	3	2P
6	-	**Self Portrait**	Bob Dylan	Columbia	6	1	
7	4	**Deja Vu**	Crosby, Stills, Nash & Young	Atlantic	23	5	F7P
8	6	**Chicago II**	Chicago	Columbia	33	6	F
9	7	**The 5th Dimension/Greatest Hits**	5th Dimension	Soul City	5		L
10	-	**Blood, Sweat & Tears 3**	Blood, Sweat & Tears	Columbia	11	14	

August 1970

This Mnth	Last Mnth	Title	Artist	Label	Wks in 10	UK Pos	
1	-	**Cosmo's Factory**	Creedence Clearwater Revival	Fantasy	19	1	4P
2	10	**Blood, Sweat & Tears 3**	Blood, Sweat & Tears	Columbia	11	14	
3	1	**Woodstock**	Various	Cotillion	24	35	2P
4	5	**Live At Leeds**	Who	Decca	14	3	2P
5	7	**Deja Vu**	Crosby, Stills, Nash & Young	Atlantic	23	5	F7P
6	8	**Chicago II**	Chicago	Columbia	33	6	F
7	4	**ABC**	Jackson 5	Motown	9	22	
8	-	**John Barleycorn Must Die**	Traffic	UA	5	11	F
9	2	**Let It Be**	Beatles	Apple	10	1	
10	6	**Self Portrait**	Bob Dylan	Columbia	6	1	

September 1970

This Mnth	Last Mnth	Title	Artist	Label	Wks in 10	UK Pos	
1	1	**Cosmo's Factory**	Creedence Clearwater Revival	Fantasy	19	1	4P
2	3	**Woodstock**	Various	Cotillion	24	35	2P
3	6	**Chicago II**	Chicago	Columbia	33	6	F
4	2	**Blood, Sweat & Tears 3**	Blood, Sweat & Tears	Columbia	11	14	
5	-	**Mad Dogs & Englishmen**	Joe Cocker	A&M	8	16	FL
6	-	**Tommy**	Who	Decca	14	2	F2P
7	-	**Closer To Home**	Grand Funk Railroad	Capitol	12		F2P
8	-	**Stage Fright**	Band	Capitol	4	15	
9	4	**Live At Leeds**	Who	Decca	14	3	2P
10	5	**Deja Vu**	Crosby, Stills, Nash & Young	Atlantic	23	5	F7P

• It was another good summer for rock festivals. The Atlanta Pop Festival featured Jimi Hendrix, The Allman Brothers, blues singer and guitar virtuoso B.B. King, Motown's rock band Rare Earth, and British acts, Jethro Tull and Procol Harum. A poorly attended Anti-War Rock Festival at New York's Shea Stadium was headlined by Janis Joplin, Paul Simon and John Sebastian, and The Randall Island Festival featured Hendrix, Grand Funk, Steppenwolf, Jethro Tull and early rock great, Little Richard.

• The Jackson 5, who had sold 10 million singles in nine months, scored their second Top 10 album of the year, **ABC**. Also flying high were another ultra-successful singles act, Creedence Clearwater Revival, who hit the top on both sides of the Atlantic with **Cosmo's Factory**.

• Elvis Presley announced he would be touring the USA for the first time since the mid-Fifties, and newcomer Elton John played his first American gig at the Troubador Club in Los Angeles.

• Jim Morrison, the leader of The Doors, was arrested for being drunk in public and was found guilty of separate charges of indecent exposure and profanity. Also in trouble with the law was Stephen Stills, of Crosby, Stills & Nash who was arrested on suspected drug charges.

UK 1970 OCT-DEC

• The biggest news of the year was that Paul McCartney was seeking the legal dissolution of The Beatles partnership.

• One of the earliest rock memorabilia auction sales was staged by entrepreneur Bill Graham at New York's Fillmore East. Among the items that went under the hammer were bits of a broken Pete Townshend guitar, a notebook of Joni Mitchell's and a flute that had belonged to Jethro Tull's charismatic front man, Ian Anderson.

• Relaxed American MOR-merchant Andy Williams had three hot albums in the winter of 1970; the chart topping **Greatest Hits**, **Andy Williams Show** and **Can't Help Falling In Love**, which returned to the upper reaches.

• The year's biggest selling album **Bridge Over Troubled Waters** did allow a few other records to occupy the Number 1 position. Among these were two classic heavy metal sets, **Led Zeppelin III** and Black Sabbath's **Paranoid**. Also spending a little time at the top were Pink Floyd's **Atom Heart Mother**, Bob Dylan's **New Morning** and the latest in the very successful **Motown Chartbusters** series.

• Rod Stewart had his first UK chart album with **Gasoline Alley**, and fellow-future superstars of the decade Diana Ross and Emerson, Lake & Palmer debuted with self-titled LPs.

October 1970

This Mnth	Last Mnth	Title	Artist	Label	Wks in 10	US Pos	
1	-	**Paranoid**	Black Sabbath	Vertigo	9	12	
2	1	**Bridge Over Troubled Water**	Simon & Garfunkel	CBS	135	1	2P
3	5	**Get Your Ya-Ya's Out!**	Rolling Stones	Decca	7	6	
4	8	**Led Zeppelin 2**	Led Zeppelin	Atlantic	56	1	
5	3	**Cosmo's Factory**	Creedence Clearwater Revival	Liberty	9	1	L
6	-	**Atom Heart Mother**	Pink Floyd	Harvest	5	55	
7	9	**Deep Purple In Rock**	Deep Purple	Harvest	32	143	F
8	-	**Motown Chartbusters Vol. 4**	Various	Tamla-Motown	20		
9	2	**A Question Of Balance**	Moody Blues	Threshold	10	3	
10	-	**Greatest Hits**	Beach Boys	Capitol	5		

November 1970

This Mnth	Last Mnth	Title	Artist	Label	Wks in 10	US Pos	
1	-	**Led Zeppelin 3**	Led Zeppelin	Atlantic	21	1	
2	8	**Motown Chartbusters Vol. 4**	Various	Tamla-Motown	20		
3	2	**Bridge Over Troubled Water**	Simon & Garfunkel	CBS	135	1	2P
4	1	**Paranoid**	Black Sabbath	Vertigo	9	12	
5	7	**Deep Purple In Rock**	Deep Purple	Harvest	32	143	F
6	6	**Atom Heart Mother**	Pink Floyd	Harvest	5	55	
7	-	**Candles In The Rain**	Melanie	Buddah	10	17	F
8	4	**Led Zeppelin 2**	Led Zeppelin	Atlantic	56	1	
9	-	**New Morning**	Bob Dylan	CBS	3	7	
10	-	**Original Greatest Hits**	Everly Brothers	CBS	4	180	

December 1970

This Mnth	Last Mnth	Title	Artist	Label	Wks in 10	US Pos	
1	-	**Greatest Hits**	Andy Williams	CBS	37	42	
2	1	**Led Zeppelin 3**	Led Zeppelin	Atlantic	21	1	
3	3	**Bridge Over Troubled Water**	Simon & Garfunkel	CBS	135	1	2P
4	2	**Motown Chartbusters Vol. 4**	Various	Tamla-Motown	20		
5	-	**Emerson, Lake And Palmer**	Emerson, Lake & Palmer	Island	10	18	F
6	8	**Led Zeppelin 2**	Led Zeppelin	Atlantic	56	1	
7	9	**New Morning**	Bob Dylan	CBS	3	7	
8	-	**The Sound Of Music**	Soundtrack	RCA	235	1	2P
9	-	**Johnny Cash At San Quentin**	Johnny Cash	CBS	32	1	
10	-	**Abraxas**	Santana	CBS	1	1	F

US 1970 OCT-DEC

October 1970

This Mnth	Last Mnth	Title	Artist	Label	Wks in 10	UK Pos	
1	1	**Cosmo's Factory**	Creedence Clearwater Revival	Fantasy	19	1	**4P**
2	-	**Abraxas**	Santana	Columbia	30	7	**4P**
3	5	**Mad Dogs & Englishmen**	Joe Cocker	A&M	8	16	**FL**
4	2	**Woodstock**	Various	Cotillion	24	35	**2P**
5	-	**Third Album**	Jackson 5	Motown	11		
6	-	**A Question Of Balance**	Moody Blues	Threshold	5	1	**P**
7	-	**Led Zeppelin III**	Led Zeppelin	Atlantic	14	1	**3P**
8	-	**Sweet Baby James**	James Taylor	Warner	12	7	**F3P**
9	3	**Chicago II**	Chicago	Columbia	33	6	**F**
10	-	**Get Yer Ya-Ya's Out!**	Rolling Stones	London	7	1	**P**

November 1970

This Mnth	Last Mnth	Title	Artist	Label	Wks in 10	UK Pos	
1	7	**Led Zeppelin III**	Led Zeppelin	Atlantic	14	1	**3P**
2	2	**Abraxas**	Santana	Columbia	30	7	**4P**
3	8	**Sweet Baby James**	James Taylor	Warner	12	7	**F3P**
4	-	**Close To You**	Carpenters	A&M	15	23	**F**
5	5	**Third Album**	Jackson 5	Motown	11		
6	1	**Cosmo's Factory**	Creedence Clearwater Revival	Fantasy	19	1	**4P**
7	10	**Get Yer Ya-Ya's Out!**	Rolling Stones	London	7	1	**P**
8	-	**After The Gold Rush**	Neil Young	Reprise	9	7	**F2P**
9	-	**Greatest Hits**	Sly & The Family Stone	Epic	15		**F3P**
10	4	**Woodstock**	Various	Cotillion	24	35	**2P**

December 1970

This Mnth	Last Mnth	Title	Artist	Label	Wks in 10	UK Pos	
1	2	**Abraxas**	Santana	Columbia	30	7	**4P**
2	1	**Led Zeppelin III**	Led Zeppelin	Atlantic	14	1	**3P**
3	9	**Greatest Hits**	Sly & The Family Stone	Epic	15		**F3P**
4	4	**Close To You**	Carpenters	A&M	15	23	**F**
5	-	**Stephen Stills**	Stephen Stills	Atlantic	10	30	**F**
6	3	**Sweet Baby James**	James Taylor	Warner	12	7	**F3P**
7	-	**All Things Must Pass**	George Harrison	Apple	14	4	**F2P**
8	5	**Third Album**	Jackson 5	Motown	11		
9	-	**Live Album**	Grand Funk Railroad	Capitol	8		**2P**
10	-	**Jesus Christ Superstar**	Various	Decca	41	6	

• In 1970, a record breaking eight and a half million cassette tape players were sold in America. Bing Crosby was presented with an award for selling a record 300 million units, and it was rumoured that Bob Dylan's bootleg album **Great White Wonder** had sold an unprecedented 350,000 copies.

• Not long after Vice President Spiro Agnew had claimed that some rock music promoted drug use, Janis Joplin died from a heroin overdose. President Nixon appealed for the screening of rock lyrics and for drug-oriented records to be banned. Nixon commended youthful MGM head Mike Curb for dropping several acts whom he felt exploited and promoted hard drugs through their music.

• Male singer/songwriters were fast becoming the vogue. Joining veteran exponent Bob Dylan on the chart were such talents as James Taylor (above), Elton John, Beatle George Harrison, ex-Impressions leader Curtis Mayfield, Stephen Stills and Neil Young.

UK 1971 JAN-MAR

January 1971

This Mnth	Last Mnth	Title	Artist	Label	Wks in 10	US Pos	
1	3	**Bridge Over Troubled Water**	Simon & Garfunkel	CBS	135	1	2P
2	1	**Greatest Hits**	Andy Williams	CBS	37	42	
3	4	**Motown Chartbusters Vol. 4**	Various	Tamla-Motown	20		
4	2	**Led Zeppelin 3**	Led Zeppelin	Atlantic	21	1	
5	-	**All Things Must Pass**	George Harrison	Apple	10	1	F
6	5	**Emerson, Lake And Palmer**	Emerson, Lake & Palmer	Island	10	18	F
7	8	**The Sound Of Music**	Soundtrack	RCA	235	1	2P
8	-	**Can't Help Falling In Love**	Andy Williams	CBS	6		
9	-	**Greatest Hits Vol. 2**	Frank Sinatra	Reprise	13	88	
10	-	**Deep Purple In Rock**	Deep Purple	Harvest	32	143	F

• George Harrison's (above) first solo album, **All Things Must Pass**, was an international chart topper, and proved far more successful than **John Lennon/Plastic Ono Band Live** by that more prominent member of The Beatles.

• Singer/songwriter Elton John was the hottest new act on both sides of the Atlantic with his eponymous album and **Tumbleweed Connection** hitting the Top 10 in both territories. He was hailed by the Los Angeles Times as 'The first superstar of the Seventies'.

• **Bridge Over Troubled Water** added another 11 weeks to its chart topping tally in the UK. In America, Simon & Garfunkel grabbed six Grammy Awards for the album and its title track.

• Progressive rock band Yes debuted in the Top 10 with **The Yes Album** and the heavily hyped Curved Air, featuring Sonja Kristina, scored with **Air Conditioning**, the first album picture disc in Britain.

February 1971

This Mnth	Last Mnth	Title	Artist	Label	Wks in 10	US Pos	
1	5	**All Things Must Pass**	George Harrison	Apple	10	1	F
2	1	**Bridge Over Troubled Water**	Simon & Garfunkel	CBS	135	1	2P
3	-	**Tumbleweed Connection**	Elton John	DJM	11	5	F
4	2	**Greatest Hits**	Andy Williams	CBS	37	42	
5	3	**Motown Chartbusters Vol. 4**	Various	Tamla-Motown	20		
6	4	**Led Zeppelin 3**	Led Zeppelin	Atlantic	21	1	
7	-	**Sweet Baby James**	James Taylor	Warner	11	3	F
8	-	**Air Conditioning**	Curved Air	Warner	5		FL
9	9	**Greatest Hits Vol. 2**	Frank Sinatra	Reprise	13	88	
10	6	**Emerson, Lake And Palmer**	Emerson, Lake & Palmer	Island	10	18	F

March 1971

This Mnth	Last Mnth	Title	Artist	Label	Wks in 10	US Pos	
1	2	**Bridge Over Troubled Water**	Simon & Garfunkel	CBS	135	1	2P
2	1	**All Things Must Pass**	George Harrison	Apple	10	1	F
3	3	**Tumbleweed Connection**	Elton John	DJM	11	5	F
4	4	**Greatest Hits**	Andy Williams	CBS	37	42	
5	-	**Home Loving Man**	Andy Williams	CBS	17		
6	6	**Led Zeppelin 3**	Led Zeppelin	Atlantic	21	1	
7	7	**Sweet Baby James**	James Taylor	Warner	11	3	F
8	9	**Greatest Hits Vol. 2**	Frank Sinatra	Reprise	13	88	
9	-	**Cry Of Love**	Jimi Hendrix	Track	8	3	
10	-	**The Yes Album**	Yes	Atlantic	8	40	F

US 1971

JAN-MAR

January 1971

This Mnth	Last Mnth	Title	Artist	Label	Wks in 10	UK Pos	
1	7	**All Things Must Pass**	George Harrison	Apple	14	4	**F2P**
2	1	**Abraxas**	Santana	Columbia	30	7	**4P**
3	3	**Greatest Hits**	Sly & The Family Stone	Epic	15		**F3P**
4	10	**Jesus Christ Superstar**	Various	Decca	41	6	
5	5	**Stephen Stills**	Stephen Stills	Atlantic	10	30	**F**
6	-	**The Partridge Family Album**	Partridge Family	Bell	8		**F**
7	-	**Pendulum**	Creedence Clearwater Revival	Fantasy	11	23	**PL**
8	9	**Live Album**	Grand Funk Railroad	Capitol	8		**2P**
9	-	**John Lennon/Plastic Ono Band**	John Lennon	Apple	4	11	
10	2	**Led Zeppelin III**	Led Zeppelin	Atlantic	14	1	**3P**

February 1971

This Mnth	Last Mnth	Title	Artist	Label	Wks in 10	UK Pos	
1	4	**Jesus Christ Superstar**	Various	Decca	41	6	
2	1	**All Things Must Pass**	George Harrison	Apple	14	4	**F2P**
3	-	**Chicago III**	Chicago	Columbia	10	31	**P**
4	2	**Abraxas**	Santana	Columbia	30	7	**4P**
5	-	**Tumbleweed Connection**	Elton John	Uni	9	6	
6	-	**Pearl**	Janis Joplin	Columbia	15	50	**3P**
7	-	**Love Story**	Soundtrack	Paramount	13	10	
8	-	**Elton John**	Elton John	Uni	6		**F**
9	3	**Greatest Hits**	Sly & The Family Stone	Epic	15		**F3P**
10	7	**Pendulum**	Creedence Clearwater Revival	Fantasy	11	23	**L**

March 1971

This Mnth	Last Mnth	Title	Artist	Label	Wks in 10	UK Pos	
1	6	**Pearl**	Janis Joplin	Columbia	15	50	**3P**
2	7	**Love Story**	Soundtrack	Paramount	13	10	
3	3	**Chicago III**	Chicago	Columbia	10	31	**P**
4	1	**Jesus Christ Superstar**	Various	Decca	41	6	
5	4	**Abraxas**	Santana	Columbia	30	7	**4P**
6	5	**Tumbleweed Connection**	Elton John	Uni	9	6	
7	-	**The Cry Of Love**	Jimi Hendrix	Reprise	7	2	
8	-	**Love Story**	Andy Williams	Columbia	9	11	**PL**
9	2	**All Things Must Pass**	George Harrison	Apple	14	4	**F2P**
10	10	**Pendulum**	Creedence Clearwater Revival	Fantasy	11	23	**L**

• The cast album of British composers Andrew Lloyd Webber and Tim Rice's first major hit musical, **Jesus Christ Superstar**, was followed at the summit by Janis Joplin's **Pearl** – the first by a female rock artist to reach the top. The latter contained Joplin's Number 1 single, 'Me And Bobby McGee', which was penned by Kris Kristofferson, recently voted Songwriter Of The Year by the Nashville Songwriters Association.

• It was teen idol time again, and fighting it out in the pin-up popularity stakes were The Partridge Family, featuring photogenic David Cassidy, and The Osmonds, who included good looking 13-year-old Donny Osmond. The former group were scoring with **The Partridge Family Album** while the latter's self-titled album peaked just outside the Top 10.

• Hottest MOR song of the season was the movie theme '(Where Do I Begin) Love Story'. Both the **Love Story** soundtrack album and an Andy Williams album of the same name were top sellers.

• Making lowly chart entries were two of the most influential R&B acts of the Seventies, Kool & The Gang and The Last Poets. The former went on to have a string of highly-successful transatlantic hits and the latter were the forefathers of rap.

UK 1971 APR-JUNE

• The Rolling Stones topped the transatlantic charts with the first album on their own label, **Sticky Fingers**. The album, which featured a real trouser zip on the sleeve, included new guitarist Mick Taylor. Also in this quarter, front man Mick Jagger married Bianca Perez Morena De Macias. Among the wedding guests were Paul McCartney, Ringo Starr, Stephen Stills and Eric Clapton.

• Six months after his death, Jimi Hendrix's last official album, **Cry Of Love**, cracked the Top 3 in both the US and UK and earned a gold disk. Among the other albums that clicked on both sides of the Atlantic were **Aqualung** by Jethro Tull, **Tarkus** by progressive rock purveyors Emerson, Lake & Palmer and **4 Way Street** by Crosby, Stills, Nash & Young. The latter, a half acoustic/half electric double album was the last album recorded by the quartet in the Seventies.

• The first Glastonbury Festival took place. Among the artists appearing was David Bowie, who played an acoustic set to the mainly hippie crowd.

• Only Carole King's unstoppable **Tapestry** prevented Paul McCartney's second album, **Ram**, from giving him two successive US chart toppers. However, in Britain, the album, which also featured his wife Linda, hit the top spot.

April 1971

This Mnth	Last Mnth	Title	Artist	Label	Wks in 10	US Pos	
1	5	**Home Loving Man**	Andy Williams	CBS	17		
2	1	**Bridge Over Troubled Water**	Simon & Garfunkel	CBS	135	1	2P
3	9	**Cry Of Love**	Jimi Hendrix	Track	8	3	
4	-	**Aqualung**	Jethro Tull	Island	8	7	
5	-	**Motown Chartbusters Vol. 5**	Various	Tamla-Motown	19		
6	4	**Greatest Hits**	Andy Williams	CBS	37	42	
7	-	**Portrait In Music**	Burt Bacharach	A&M	3		L
8	-	**Elegy**	Nice	Charisma	2		L
9	-	**Elvis Country**	Elvis Presley	RCA	3	12	
10	-	**Stone Age**	Rolling Stones	Decca	2		

May 1971

This Mnth	Last Mnth	Title	Artist	Label	Wks in 10	US Pos	
1	5	**Motown Chartbusters Vol. 5**	Various	Tamla-Motown	19		
2	-	**Sticky Fingers**	Rolling Stones	Rolling Stones	15	1	
3	2	**Bridge Over Troubled Water**	Simon & Garfunkel	CBS	135	1	2P
4	1	**Home Loving Man**	Andy Williams	CBS	17		
5	-	**Songs Of Love And Hate**	Leonard Cohen	CBS	6		L
6	-	**Symphonies For The Sevenites**	Waldo De Los Rios	A&M	9		FL
7	-	**Split**	Groundhogs	Liberty	9		
8	4	**Aqualung**	Jethro Tull	Island	8	7	
9	-	**Four-Way Street**	Crosby, Stills, Nash & Young	Atlantic	2	1	L
10	3	**Cry Of Love**	Jimi Hendrix	Track	8	3	

June 1971

This Mnth	Last Mnth	Title	Artist	Label	Wks in 10	US Pos	
1	2	**Sticky Fingers**	Rolling Stones	Rolling Stones	15	1	
2	-	**Ram**	Paul & Linda McCartney	Apple	15	2	
3	3	**Bridge Over Troubled Water**	Simon & Garfunkel	CBS	135	1	2P
4	1	**Motown Chartbusters Vol. 5**	Various	Tamla-Motown	19		
5	4	**Home Loving Man**	Andy Williams	CBS	17		
6	-	**Tarkus**	Emerson, Lake & Palmer	Island	10	9	
7	-	**Mud Slide Slim And The Blue Horizon**	James Taylor	Warner	17	2	L
8	7	**Split**	Groundhogs	Liberty	9		
9	6	**Symphonies For The Sevenites**	Waldo De Los Rios	A&M	9		FL
10	-	**Free Live!**	Free	Island	6	89	

US 1971 APR-JUNE

April 1971

This Mnth	Last Mnth	Title	Artist	Label	Wks in 10	UK Pos	
1	1	**Pearl**	Janis Joplin	Columbia	15	50	**3P**
2	4	**Jesus Christ Superstar**	Various	Decca	41	6	
3	2	**Love Story**	Soundtrack	Paramount	13	10	
4	8	**Love Story**	Andy Williams	Columbia	9	11	**PL**
5	7	**The Cry Of Love**	Jimi Hendrix	Reprise	7	2	
6	-	**Golden Bisquits**	Three Dog Night	Dunhill	9		
7	-	**Up To Date**	Partridge Family	Bell	12	46	
8	5	**Abraxas**	Santana	Columbia	30	7	**4P**
9	3	**Chicago III**	Chicago	Columbia	10	31	**P**
10	-	**Tea For The Tillerman**	Cat Stevens	A&M	6	20	**F**

May 1971

This Mnth	Last Mnth	Title	Artist	Label	Wks in 10	UK Pos	
1	2	**Jesus Christ Superstar**	Various	Decca	41	6	
2	-	**4 Way Street**	Crosby, Stills, Nash & Young	Atlantic	13	5	**4P**
3	7	**Up To Date**	Partridge Family	Bell	12	46	
4	1	**Pearl**	Janis Joplin	Columbia	15	50	**3P**
5	6	**Golden Bisquits**	Three Dog Night	Dunhill	9		
6	-	**Sticky Fingers**	Rolling Stones	Rolling Stones	15	1	
7	-	**Mud Slide Slim And The Blue Horizon**	James Taylor	Warner	20	4	**2P**
8	-	**Tapestry**	Carole King	Ode	46	4	**F2P**
9	-	**Survival**	Grand Funk Railroad	Capitol	6		**P**
10	3	**Love Story**	Soundtrack	Paramount	13	10	

June 1971

This Mnth	Last Mnth	Title	Artist	Label	Wks in 10	UK Pos	
1	6	**Sticky Fingers**	Rolling Stones	Rolling Stones	15	1	
2	8	**Tapestry**	Carole King	Ode	46	4	**F2P**
3	1	**Jesus Christ Superstar**	Various	Decca	41	6	
4	-	**Ram**	Paul & Linda McCartney	Apple	24	1	**P**
5	7	**Mud Slide Slim And The Blue Horizon**	James Taylor	Warner	20	4	**2P**
6	-	**Carpenters**	Carpenters	A&M	24	12	
7	2	**4 Way Street**	Crosby, Stills, Nash & Young	Atlantic	13	5	**4P**
8	-	**Aqualung**	Jethro Tull	Reprise	16	4	**F3P**
9	3	**Up To Date**	Partridge Family	Bell	12	46	
10	-	**Aretha Live At Fillmore West**	Aretha Franklin	Atlantic	5		

• After many years as a top songwriter, Carole King was accepted as a major recording artist in her own right. Her album **Tapestry** held the top spot for over three months and remained on the LP chart for more than 300 weeks, a record at the time for rock music. It picked up the Grammy for Top Album of 1971 and went on to become the most successful album by a female artist in the decade. One of the songs on **Tapestry**, 'You've Got A Friend', was also the most played track from James Taylor's **Mud Slide Slim And The Blue Horizon**. The latter album was only kept off the top spot by King's classic recording.

• Among the talented acts debuting in the Top 200 album chart were British bands T. Rex, Humble Pie and Yes, future solo stars Steve Winwood, Carly Simon, Boz Scaggs and Helen Reddy, and critically acclaimed West Coast combos Earth, Wind & Fire and Tower Of Power.

UK 1971 JULY-SEPT

• During the last five months of 1971, the full price UK album chart was combined with the previously separate budget priced chart and therefore many low-priced records charted. Among these were cover version hit collections, **Hot Hits 6** and **Top Of The Pops Vol. 18**. Also reaching the Top 10 were budget albums from such notable acts as Jim Reeves and Elvis Presley.

• Cliff Richard was presented with a special Ivor Novello Award for Outstanding Services to British Music, and in the USA his first inspiration, Elvis Presley, received the Bing Crosby Award. The latter coveted trophy had previously been given to MOR and jazz stalwarts such as Frank Sinatra, Duke Ellington, Ella Fitzgerald and Irving Berlin.

• Despite the fact that Andy Williams' TV series was one of the most popular shows on British television, it was dropped in the USA where its ratings were decreasing. Among the TV shows that first aired Stateside were *The Sonny & Cher Comedy Hour* and the short-lived *Make Your Own Kind Of Music* hosted by The Carpenters. Incidentally, the sibling duo appeared at London's prestigious Royal Albert Hall during their first UK visit.

July 1971

This Mnth	Last Mnth	Title	Artist	Label	Wks in 10	US Pos	
1	3	**Bridge Over Troubled Water**	Simon & Garfunkel	CBS	135	1	2P
2	2	**Ram**	Paul & Linda McCartney	Apple	15	2	
3	1	**Sticky Fingers**	Rolling Stones	Rolling Stones	15	1	
4	6	**Tarkus**	Emerson, Lake & Palmer	Island	10	9	
5	4	**Motown Chartbusters Vol. 5**	Various	Tamla-Motown	19		
6	10	**Free Live!**	Free	Island	6	89	
7	-	**Magnificent Seven**	Supremes & Four Tops	Tamla-Motown	3	113	L
8	-	**Blue**	Joni Mitchell	Reprise	2	15	L
9	-	**Every Picture Tells A Story**	Rod Stewart	Mercury	27	1	F
10	-	**Greatest Hits**	Andy Williams	CBS	37	42	

August 1971

This Mnth	Last Mnth	Title	Artist	Label	Wks in 10	US Pos	
1	-	**Hot Hits 6**	Various	MFP	5		
2	-	**Every Good Boy Deserves Favour**	Moody Blues	Threshold	9	2	
3	-	**Top Of The Pops Vol. 18**	Various	Hallmark	8		
4	1	**Bridge Over Troubled Water**	Simon & Garfunkel	CBS	135	1	2P
5	2	**Ram**	Paul & Linda McCartney	Apple	15	2	
6	-	**C'mon Everybody**	Elvis Presley	RCA International	5	70	
7	3	**Sticky Fingers**	Rolling Stones	Rolling Stones	15	1	
8	-	**Mud Slide Slim And The Blue Horizon**	James Taylor	Warner	17	2	L
9	5	**Motown Chartbusters Vol. 5**	Various	Tamla-Motown	19		
10	-	**Master Of Reality**	Black Sabbath	Vertigo	3	8	

September 1971

This Mnth	Last Mnth	Title	Artist	Label	Wks in 10	US Pos	
1	4	**Bridge Over Troubled Water**	Simon & Garfunkel	CBS	135	1	2P
2	2	**Every Good Boy Deserves Favour**	Moody Blues	Threshold	9	2	
3	-	**Who's Next**	Who	Track	7	4	
4	3	**Top Of The Pops Vol. 18**	Various	Hallmark	8		
5	-	**Every Picture Tells A Story**	Rod Stewart	Mercury	27	1	F
6	-	**Tapestry**	Carole King	A&M	18	1	FL
7	-	**Fireball**	Deep Purple	Harvest	7	32	
8	10	**Master Of Reality**	Black Sabbath	Vertigo	3	8	
9	1	**Hot Hits 6**	Various	MFP	5		
10	5	**Ram**	Paul & Linda McCartney	Apple	15	2	

US 1971 JULY-SEPT

July 1971

This Mnth	Last Mnth	Title	Artist	Label	Wks in 10	UK Pos	
1	2	**Tapestry**	Carole King	Ode	46	4	F2P
2	1	**Sticky Fingers**	Rolling Stones	Rolling Stones	15	1	
3	4	**Ram**	Paul & Linda McCartney	Apple	24	1	P
4	6	**Carpenters**	Carpenters	A&M	24	12	
5	5	**Mud Slide Slim And The Blue Horizon**	James Taylor	Warner	20	4	2P
6	3	**Jesus Christ Superstar**	Various	Decca	41	6	
7	8	**Aqualung**	Jethro Tull	Reprise	16	4	F3P
8	-	**What's Going On**	Marvin Gaye	Tamla	10		F
9	10	**Aretha Live At Fillmore West**	Aretha Franklin	Atlantic	5		
10	7	**4 Way Street**	Crosby, Stills, Nash & Young	Atlantic	13	5	4P

August 1971

This Mnth	Last Mnth	Title	Artist	Label	Wks in 10	UK Pos	
1	1	**Tapestry**	Carole King	Ode	46	4	F2P
2	5	**Mud Slide Slim And The Blue Horizon**	James Taylor	Warner	20	4	2P
3	3	**Ram**	Paul & Linda McCartney	Apple	24	1	P
4	6	**Jesus Christ Superstar**	Various	Decca	41	6	
5	4	**Carpenters**	Carpenters	A&M	24	12	
6	2	**Sticky Fingers**	Rolling Stones	Rolling Stones	15	1	
7	8	**What's Going On**	Marvin Gaye	Tamla	10		F
8	7	**Aqualung**	Jethro Tull	Reprise	16	4	F3P
9	-	**Every Picture Tells A Story**	Rod Stewart	Mercury	20	1	F
10	-	**Stephen Stills 2**	Stephen Stills	Atlantic	3	22	

September 1971

This Mnth	Last Mnth	Title	Artist	Label	Wks in 10	UK Pos	
1	1	**Tapestry**	Carole King	Ode	46	4	F2P
2	-	**Every Good Boy Deserves Favour**	Moody Blues	Threshold	13	1	
3	9	**Every Picture Tells A Story**	Rod Stewart	Mercury	20	1	F
4	3	**Ram**	Paul & Linda McCartney	Apple	24	1	P
5	-	**Who's Next**	Who	Decca	11	1	3P
6	5	**Carpenters**	Carpenters	A&M	24	12	
7	2	**Mud Slide Slim And The Blue Horizon**	James Taylor	Warner	20	4	2P
8	-	**Shaft (Soundtrack)**	Isaac Hayes	Enterprise	15	17	
9	8	**Aqualung**	Jethro Tull	Reprise	16	4	3P
10	4	**Jesus Christ Superstar**	Various	Decca	41	6	

• Jim Morrison, the controversial lead singer of The Doors died in Paris just days before the group's latest album, **L.A. Woman**, was certified gold. It was the group's last Top 10 album for twenty years, when the film *The Doors* re-kindled interest in them. Another star who died was 70-year-old Louis Armstrong, the first artist to dethrone The Beatles at the top of the US singles chart in 1964.

• Soul superstar Marvin Gaye's 15th chart entry, **What's Going On**, not only gave the talented performer his first Top 20 entry but it also earned him kudos from rock critics and fans alike. Another gold-plated R&B singer/songwriter, Isaac Hayes clocked up the biggest hit of his career with music from the movie *Shaft*. The chart topping album went on to grab the Grammy Award for Best Soundtrack of 1971.

• The latest singer/songwriters to reach the Top 20 were John Denver with **Poems, Prayers & Promises,** Joni Mitchell with **Blue**, and close behind was Kris Kristofferson's **The Silver Tongued Devil & I**.

UK 1971 OCT-DEC

• **Led Zeppelin IV (Four Symbols)** which included the classic 'Stairway To Heaven', gave the group the third of eight successive British Number 1 albums – five of which entered in top spot. In America, although it narrowly failed to reach the summit, it went on to spend five years on the chart and sold over eleven million copies.

• British rock stars Rod Stewart (above) and John Lennon scored transatlantic Number 1 hits with **Every Picture Tells A Story** and **Imagine** respectively. The former contained the chart topping single 'Maggie May' and the title track of the latter was also a major hit on both sides of the Atlantic. Stewart's set was the first of six consecutive British chart toppers for the lead singer of The Faces. As his solo album was flying high, The Faces broke a record set by countrymen Led Zeppelin when they sold out New York's Madison Square Garden in record time.

October 1971

This Mnth	Last Mnth	Title	Artist	Label	Wks in 10	US Pos	
1	5	**Every Picture Tells A Story**	Rod Stewart	Mercury	27	1	**F**
2	-	**Electric Warrior**	T. Rex	Fly	29	32	**F**
3	-	**Top Of The Pops Vol. 19**	Various	Hallmark	4		
4	7	**Fireball**	Deep Purple	Harvest	7	32	
5	-	**Bridge Over Troubled Water**	Simon & Garfunkel	CBS	135	1	**2P**
6	-	**Mud Slide Slim And The Blue Horizon**	James Taylor	Warner	17	2	**L**
7	6	**Tapestry**	Carole King	A&M	18	1	**FL**
8	-	**Motown Chartbusters Vol. 6**	Various	Tamla-Motown	13		
9	-	**Hot Hits 7**	Various	MFP	5		
10	-	**Teaser And The Firecat**	Cat Stevens	Island	18	2	

November 1971

This Mnth	Last Mnth	Title	Artist	Label	Wks in 10	US Pos	
1	1	**Every Picture Tells A Story**	Rod Stewart	Mercury	27	1	**F**
2	-	**Imagine**	John Lennon	Apple	23	1	**F**
3	8	**Motown Chartbusters Vol. 6**	Various	Tamla-Motown	13		
4	2	**Electric Warrior**	T. Rex	Fly	29	32	**F**
5	-	**Top Of The Pops Vol. 20**	Various	Hallmark	6		
6	7	**Tapestry**	Carole King	A&M	18	1	**FL**
7	9	**Hot Hits 7**	Various	MFP	5		
8	5	**Bridge Over Troubled Water**	Simon & Garfunkel	CBS	135	1	**2P**
9	-	**Meddle**	Pink Floyd	Harvest	2	70	
10	-	**Santana 3**	Santana	CBS	2	1	

December 1971

This Mnth	Last Mnth	Title	Artist	Label	Wks in 10	US Pos	
1	-	**Four Symbols (Led Zeppelin IV)**	Led Zeppelin	Atlantic	12	2	
2	4	**Electric Warrior**	T. Rex	Fly	29	32	**F**
3	-	**Pictures At An Exhibition**	Emerson, Lake & Palmer	Island	5	10	
4	5	**Top Of The Pops Vol. 20**	Various	Hallmark	6		
5	-	**Hot Hits 8**	Various	MFP	3		
6	-	**Twelve Songs Of Christmas**	Jim Reeves	RCA	9		
7	2	**Imagine**	John Lennon	Apple	23	1	**F**
8	8	**Bridge Over Troubled Water**	Simon & Garfunkel	CBS	135	1	**2P**
9	1	**Every Picture Tells A Story**	Rod Stewart	Mercury	27	1	**F**
10	3	**Motown Chartbusters Vol. 6**	Various	Tamla-Motown	13		

US 1971 OCT-DEC

October 1971

This Mnth	Last Mnth	Title	Artist	Label	Wks in 10	UK Pos	
1	3	**Every Picture Tells A Story**	Rod Stewart	Mercury	20	1	F
2	1	**Tapestry**	Carole King	Ode	46	4	F2P
3	-	**Imagine**	John Lennon	Apple	13	1	
4	8	**Shaft (Soundtrack)**	Isaac Hayes	Enterprise	15	17	
5	2	**Every Good Boy Deserves Favour**	Moody Blues	Threshold	13	1	
6	6	**Carpenters**	Carpenters	A&M	24	12	
7	4	**Ram**	Paul & Linda McCartney	Apple	24	1	P
8	-	**Santana III**	Santana	Columbia	11	6	2P
9	5	**Who's Next**	Who	Decca	11	1	3P
10	-	**Teaser And The Firecat**	Cat Stevens	A&M	17	3	

November 1971

This Mnth	Last Mnth	Title	Artist	Label	Wks in 10	UK Pos	
1	8	**Santana III**	Santana	Columbia	11	6	2P
2	4	**Shaft (Soundtrack)**	Isaac Hayes	Enterprise	15	17	
3	3	**Imagine**	John Lennon	Apple	13	1	
4	10	**Teaser And The Firecat**	Cat Stevens	A&M	17	3	
5	1	**Every Picture Tells A Story**	Rod Stewart	Mercury	20	1	F
6	2	**Tapestry**	Carole King	Ode	46	4	F2P
7	-	**There's A Riot Goin' On**	Sly & The Family Stone	Epic	10	31	
8	6	**Carpenters**	Carpenters	A&M	24	12	
9	5	**Every Good Boy Deserves Favour**	Moody Blues	Threshold	13	1	
10	-	**Harmony**	Three Dog Night	Dunhill	4		

December 1971

This Mnth	Last Mnth	Title	Artist	Label	Wks in 10	UK Pos	
1	7	**There's A Riot Goin' On**	Sly & The Family Stone	Epic	10	31	
2	1	**Santana III**	Santana	Columbia	11	6	2P
3	4	**Teaser And The Firecat**	Cat Stevens	A&M	17	3	
4	-	**Led Zeppelin IV (Four Symbols)**	Led Zeppelin	Atlantic	14	1	11P
5	2	**Shaft (Soundtrack)**	Isaac Hayes	Enterprise	15	17	
6	-	**At Carnegie Hall**	Chicago	Columbia	13		P
7	-	**Music**	Carole King	Ode	16	18	
8	6	**Tapestry**	Carole King	Ode	46	4	F2P
9	3	**Imagine**	John Lennon	Apple	13	1	
10	-	**E Pluribus Funk**	Grand Funk Railroad	Capitol	5		P

• The sales of records and tapes in America in 1972 increased to $1.7 billion, and a survey showed 60% of these purchases were made by people under 30.

• Guitar virtuoso Duane Allman of The Allman Brothers died in a motorcycle accident, just a few days after the pioneering southern rock band's album **At Fillmore East** was certified gold.

• **Santana III** gave the latin/jazz/rock outfit their second successive Number 1. Carole King also returned to the top with **Music**, while **There's A Riot Goin' On** became funk rock band Sly & The Family Stone's only chart topper. The latter group's reputation for non-appearances at gigs equalled that for causing riots when they did show up.

• Adding to their tallies of major American hit albums were Three Dog Night with **Harmony**, Chicago with the 4-album boxed set, **At Carnegie Hall**, and Grand Funk Railroad with **E Pluribus Funk**. Despite their continued success, Grand Funk Railroad were still receiving bad press from rock critics and little support from the top US radio stations.

• Two television soundtrack albums scored in the Top 20: **Goin' Back To Indiana** from the Jackson 5 and **All In The Family** which contained excerpts from the popular situation comedy.

UK 1972 JAN-MAR

• It was back to normal again on the British album chart with all budget albums excluded.

• T. Rex, the most talked about act in Britain, scored the first of three successive Number 1s with **Electric Warrior**. The duo's sell-out Wembley shows were filmed by ex-Beatle Ringo Starr for the film *Born To Boogie*.

• Neil Reid became the youngest artist to top the UK chart when his eponymous debut gave the 11-year-old his only hit. Neil, like several other one-hit wonders,was a winner on TV's top talent discovery show *Opportunity Knocks*.

• As the first official Beatles fan club closed due to lack of interest from the group, Paul McCartney took his new group, Wings, out on tour in the UK, and despite being slated by the critics their album **Wild Life** was a Top 20 entry on both sides of the Atlantic. Meanwhile, his ex-songwriting partner John Lennon was served a deportation order by the American Immigration & Naturalization office.

• British acts were riding high in the USA with The Rolling Stones, The Faces, Yes, Traffic and Elton John joining George Harrison and Led Zeppelin on February's Top 10.

January 1972

This Mnth	Last Mnth	Title	Artist	Label	Wks in 10	US Pos	
1	2	**Electric Warrior**	T. Rex	Fly	29	32	**F**
2	8	**Bridge Over Troubled Water**	Simon & Garfunkel	CBS	135	1	**2P**
3	-	**Teaser And The Firecat**	Cat Stevens	Island	18	2	
4	-	**A Nod's As Good As A Wink... To A Blind Horse**	Faces	Warner	11	6	**F**
5	7	**Imagine**	John Lennon	Apple	23	1	**F**
6	1	**Four Symbols (Led Zeppelin IV)**	Led Zeppelin	Atlantic	12	2	
7	9	**Every Picture Tells A Story**	Rod Stewart	Mercury	27	1	**F**
8	-	**Concert For Bangladesh**	George Harrison & Friends	Apple	5	2	
9	10	**Motown Chartbusters Vol. 6**	Various	Tamla-Motown	13		
10	5	**Hot Hits 8**	Various	MFP	3		

February 1972

This Mnth	Last Mnth	Title	Artist	Label	Wks in 10	US Pos	
1	1	**Electric Warrior**	T. Rex	Fly	29	32	**F**
2	-	**Neil Reid**	Neil Reid	Decca	10		**FL**
3	3	**Teaser And The Firecat**	Cat Stevens	Island	18	2	
4	4	**A Nod's As Good As A Wink... To A Blind Horse**	Faces	Warner	11	6	**F**
5	2	**Bridge Over Troubled Water**	Simon & Garfunkel	CBS	135	1	**2P**
6	8	**Concert For Bangladesh**	George Harrison & Friends	Apple	5	2	
7	5	**Imagine**	John Lennon	Apple	23	1	**F**
8	-	**Hendrix In The West**	Jimi Hendrix	Polydor	4	12	
9	6	**Four Symbols (Led Zeppelin IV)**	Led Zeppelin	Atlantic	12	2	
10	-	**Paul Simon**	Paul Simon	CBS	14	4	**F**

March 1972

This Mnth	Last Mnth	Title	Artist	Label	Wks in 10	US Pos	
1	-	**Harvest**	Neil Young	Reprise	12	1	
2	2	**Neil Reid**	Neil Reid	Decca	10		**FL**
3	10	**Paul Simon**	Paul Simon	CBS	14	4	**F**
4	-	**Fog On The Tyne**	Lindisfarne	Charisma	21		**F**
5	1	**Electric Warrior**	T. Rex	Fly	29	32	**F**
6	5	**Bridge Over Troubled Water**	Simon & Garfunkel	CBS	135	1	**2P**
7	-	**Nilsson Schmilsson**	Nilsson	RCA	12	3	**FL**
8	3	**Teaser And The Firecat**	Cat Stevens	Island	18	2	
9	-	**Thick As A Brick**	Jethro Tull	Chrysalis	4	1	
10	4	**A Nod's As Good As A Wink... To A Blind Horse**	Faces	Warner	11	6	**F**

US 1972 JAN-MAR

January 1972

This Mnth	Last Mnth	Title	Artist	Label	Wks in 10	UK Pos	
1	7	**Music**	Carole King	Ode	16	18	
2	-	**American Pie**	Don McLean	UA	17	3	**FL**
3	4	**Led Zeppelin IV (Four Symbols)**	Led Zeppelin	Atlantic	14	1	**11P**
4	6	**At Carnegie Hall**	Chicago	Columbia	13		**P**
5	-	**The Concert For Bangla Desh**	George Harrison & Friends	Apple	10	1	
6	3	**Teaser And The Firecat**	Cat Stevens	A&M	17	3	
7	8	**Tapestry**	Carole King	Ode	46	4	**F2P**
8	1	**There's A Riot Goin' On**	Sly & The Family Stone	Epic	10	31	
9	10	**E Pluribus Funk**	Grand Funk Railroad	Capitol	5		**P**
10	-	**All In The Family**	TV Soundtrack	Atlantic	6		

February 1972

This Mnth	Last Mnth	Title	Artist	Label	Wks in 10	UK Pos	
1	2	**American Pie**	Don McLean	UA	17	3	**FL**
2	5	**The Concert For Bangla Desh**	George Harrison & Friends	Apple	10	1	
3	1	**Music**	Carole King	Ode	16	18	
4	-	**Hot Rocks 1964-1971**	Rolling Stones	London	8	3	**6P**
5	3	**Led Zeppelin IV (Four Symbols)**	Led Zeppelin	Atlantic	14	1	**11P**
6	-	**A Nod Is As Good As A Wink... To A Blind Horse**	Faces	Warner	6	2	**FL**
7	-	**Fragile**	Yes	Atlantic	15	7	**F**
8	7	**Tapestry**	Carole King	Ode	46	4	**F2P**
9	-	**The Low Spark Of High Heeled Boys**	Traffic	Island	2		
10	-	**Madman Across The Water**	Elton John	Uni	4	41	**P**

March 1972

This Mnth	Last Mnth	Title	Artist	Label	Wks in 10	UK Pos	
1	1	**American Pie**	Don McLean	UA	17	3	**FL**
2	-	**Harvest**	Neil Young	Reprise	16	1	**4P**
3	7	**Fragile**	Yes	Atlantic	15	7	**F**
4	-	**Nilsson Schmilsson**	Nilsson	RCA	12	4	**FL**
5	-	**America**	America	Warner	13	14	**FP**
6	3	**Music**	Carole King	Ode	16	18	
7	2	**The Concert For Bangla Desh**	George Harrison & Friends	Apple	10	1	
8	-	**Baby I'm-A Want You**	Bread	Elektra	10	9	**F**
9	-	**Paul Simon**	Paul Simon	Columbia	11	1	**FP**
10	4	**Hot Rocks 1964-1971**	Rolling Stones	London	8	3	**6P**

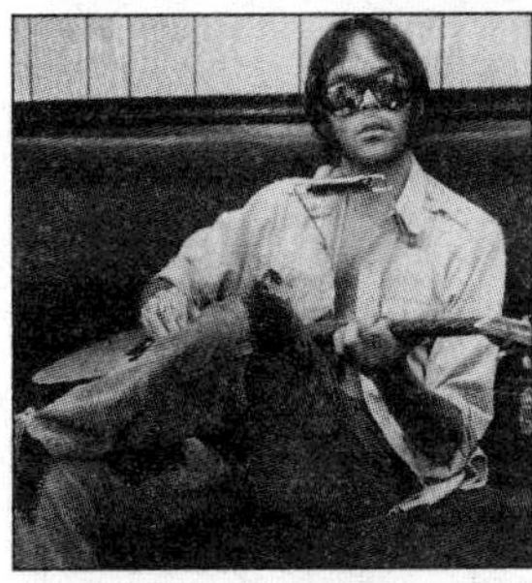

• Singer/songwriters Neil Young and Don McLean topped both the album and singles chart. Young achieved the feat with **Harvest**, which took only two weeks on the Top 200 to hit Number 1, and 'Heart Of Gold' respectively. Newcomer McLean reached the summits with **American Pie** and its title song.

• As The Osmonds clocked up their sole Top 10 album, **Phase III**, fellow teen idols Michael Jackson and David Cassidy scored their first Top 20 solo entries with **Got To Be There** and **Cherish** respectively.

• George Harrison's charity raising triple album **The Concert For Bangladesh** was a major transatlantic success. The album included guest appearances by such notables as Bob Dylan, Ringo Starr and Eric Clapton. The set went on to win the Grammy for Best Album of 1972, and after numerous legal problems Harrison was able to present a cheque for $8.8 million to UNICEF in 1982.

UK 1972 APR-JUNE

• The chart topping exploits of K-Tel Records' **20 Dynamic Hits** heralded the dawn of the TV-advertised compilation. Over the next 16 years – until such albums were given a separate chart – scores of similar albums would reach the top rungs of the UK chart.

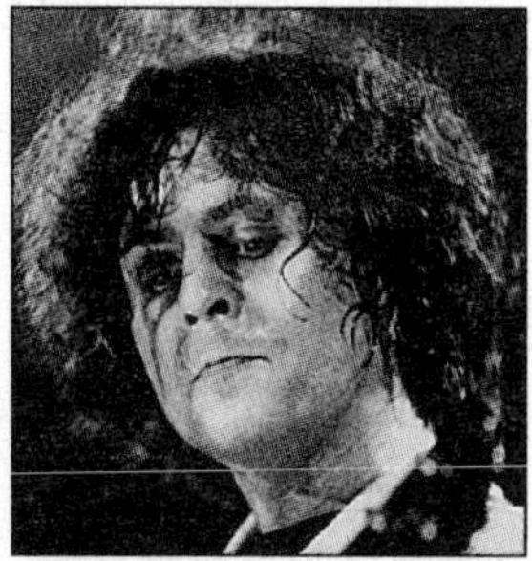

• The UK's top selling singles acts, T. Rex and Slade, were also selling vast quantities of albums. T. Rex achieved three Number 1s in six months when **Bolan Boogie** followed their four-year-old **My People Were Fair And Had Sky In Their Hair But Now They're Content To Wear Stars On Their Brows** into the top slot. Slade's Noddy Holder may have been charged with using bad language and behaving obscenely during their first major UK tour, but this did not stop the progress of their debut album **Slade Alive.**

• The Rolling Stones, whose first US tour since 1969 was a complete sell out, scored their second successive transatlantic Number 1 with the double album, **Exile On Main Street**.

April 1972

This Mnth	Last Mnth	Title	Artist	Label	Wks in 10	US Pos	
1	4	**Fog On The Tyne**	Lindisfarne	Charisma	21		F
2	1	**Harvest**	Neil Young	Reprise	12	1	
3	-	**We'd Like To Teach The World To Sing**	New Seekers	Polydor	7	37	FL
4	-	**Machine Head**	Deep Purple	Purple	8	7	
5	6	**Bridge Over Troubled Water**	Simon & Garfunkel	CBS	135	1	2P
6	7	**Nilsson Schmilsson**	Nilsson	RCA	12	3	FL
7	-	**Himself**	Gilbert O'Sullivan	MAM	8	9	F
8	3	**Paul Simon**	Paul Simon	CBS	14	4	F
9	-	**Slade Alive**	Slade	Polydor	22	158	F
10	-	**Prophets, Seers & Sages The Angels Of The Ages/My People Were Fair & Had Sky In Their Hair But Now...**	T. Rex	Fly	5		

May 1972

This Mnth	Last Mnth	Title	Artist	Label	Wks in 10	US Pos	
1	4	**Machine Head**	Deep Purple	Purple	8	7	
2	5	**Bridge Over Troubled Water**	Simon & Garfunkel	CBS	135	1	2P
3	10	**Prophets, Seers & Sages The Angels Of The Ages/My People Were Fair & Had Sky In Their Hair But Now...**	T. Rex	Fly	5		
4	1	**Fog On The Tyne**	Lindisfarne	Charisma	21		F
5	-	**Bolan Boogie**	T. Rex	Fly	9		
6	2	**Harvest**	Neil Young	Reprise	12	1	
7	8	**Paul Simon**	Paul Simon	CBS	14	4	F
8	-	**Argus**	Wishbone Ash	MCA	4		FL
9	3	**We'd Like To Teach The World To Sing**	New Seekers	Polydor	7	37	FL
10	-	**Cherish**	David Cassidy	Bell	10	15	F

June 1972

This Mnth	Last Mnth	Title	Artist	Label	Wks in 10	US Pos	
1	5	**Bolan Boogie**	T. Rex	Fly	9		
2	-	**Honky Chateau**	Elton John	DJM	7	1	
3	-	**20 Dynamic Hits**	Various	K-Tel	15		
4	-	**Exile On Main Street**	Rolling Stones	Rolling Stones	5	1	
5	2	**Bridge Over Troubled Water**	Simon & Garfunkel	CBS	135	1	2P
6	4	**Fog On The Tyne**	Lindisfarne	Charisma	21		F
7	-	**American Pie**	Don McLean	UA	16	1	F
8	10	**Cherish**	David Cassidy	Bell	10	15	F
9	-	**Bread Winners**	Jack Jones	RCA	4		
10	8	**Argus**	Wishbone Ash	MCA	4		FL

US 1972

APR-JUN

April 1972

This Mnth	Last Mnth	Title	Artist	Label	Wks in 10	UK Pos	
1	5	**America**	America	Warner	13	14	**FP**
2	2	**Harvest**	Neil Young	Reprise	16	1	**4P**
3	4	**Nilsson Schmilsson**	Nilsson	RCA	12	4	**FL**
4	3	**Fragile**	Yes	Atlantic	15	7	**F**
5	-	**First Take**	Roberta Flack	Atlantic	14	47	**F**
6	9	**Paul Simon**	Paul Simon	Columbia	11	1	**FP**
7	-	**Eat A Peach**	Allman Brothers Band	Capricorn	10		**F**
8	8	**Baby I'm-A Want You**	Bread	Elektra	10	9	**F**
9	-	**Let's Stay Together**	Al Green	Hi	6		**F**
10	1	**American Pie**	Don McLean	UA	17	3	**FL**

May 1972

This Mnth	Last Mnth	Title	Artist	Label	Wks in 10	UK Pos	
1	5	**First Take**	Roberta Flack	Atlantic	14	47	**F**
2	2	**Harvest**	Neil Young	Reprise	16	1	**4P**
3	1	**America**	America	Warner	13	14	**FP**
4	7	**Eat A Peach**	Allman Brothers Band	Capricorn	10		**F**
5	4	**Fragile**	Yes	Atlantic	15	7	**F**
6	-	**Graham Nash/David Crosby**	David Crosby/Graham Nash	Atlantic	7		**F**
7	-	**Manassas**	Stephen Stills	Atlantic	7		**L**
8	-	**Smokin'**	Humble Pie	A&M	4	28	**FL**
9	-	**Thick As A Brick**	Jethro Tull	Reprise	10	5	
10	-	**Tapestry**	Carole King	Ode	46	4	**F2P**

June 1972

This Mnth	Last Mnth	Title	Artist	Label	Wks in 10	UK Pos	
1	9	**Thick As A Brick**	Jethro Tull	Reprise	10	5	
2	1	**First Take**	Roberta Flack	Atlantic	14	47	**F**
3	-	**Joplin In Concert**	Janis Joplin	Columbia	8	30	**L**
4	7	**Manassas**	Stephen Stills	Atlantic	7		**L**
5	-	**Exile On Main Street**	Rolling Stones	Rolling Stones	11	1	
6	2	**Harvest**	Neil Young	Reprise	16	1	**4P**
7	-	**A Lonely Man**	Chi-Lites	Brunswick	6		**FL**
8	6	**Graham Nash/David Crosby**	David Crosby/Graham Nash	Atlantic	7		**F**
9	-	**History Of Eric Clapton**	Eric Clapton	Atco	6		**F**
10	-	**Roberta Flack & Donny Hathaway**	Roberta Flack	Atlantic	8	31	

• Amazingly, nine of April's Top 10 albums were by artists debuting in that chart: America, Nilsson, Yes, Roberta Flack, Paul Simon (his first solo entry), The Allman Brothers, Bread, Al Green and Don McLean. Incidentally, America, whose eponymous LP led the field, grabbed the Grammy for Best New Act of 1972.

• **First Take**, which had first entered the Top 200 in January 1970, made singer/songwriter/pianist Roberta Flack the first black female soloist to reach the top. It was soon joined in the Top 5 by her duet album with Donny Hathaway. Among the other R&B acts situated in the Top 20 were Joe Tex with **I Gotcha**, War's **All Day Music**, Al Green's **Let's Stay Together**, The Chi-Lites' **A Lonely Man** and The Staple Singers' **Bealtitude/Respect Yourself**.

• Taking their first steps on the Top 200 album chart were Britain's David Bowie, ELO, and US rock bands ZZ Top and Blue Oyster Cult. Also collecting their first chart entries were The Eagles, Dr. Hook, The Raspberries – with Eric Carmen and ex-Velvet Underground front man Lou Reed.

• Columbia's A&R super-scout John Hammond, who had helped the careers of Bob Dylan, Billie Holiday and Aretha Franklin, signed his latest discovery, Bruce Springsteen, to the label.

UK 1972

JULY-SEPT

• The successful TV show, *The Old Grey Whistle Test* was first seen in Britain. One of the many album-oriented acts it helped was David Bowie, whose **The Rise And Fall Of Ziggy Stardust And The Spiders From Mars** gave the multi-talented artist his first hit album. However, Bowie's US debut at New York's famous Carnegie Hall was only coolly received.

• John Lennon made his first real solo performance at New York's Madison Square Garden in a concert for the One To One charity. Other headliners included Stevie Wonder, who had been touring the States with The Rolling Stones and US album chart queen, Roberta Flack.

• Among the albums scoring on both sides of the Atlantic were Neil Diamond's first UK success, **Moods**, Rod Stewart's **Never A Dull Moment**, the only solo artist album to top the UK chart this quarter, and horror rocker Alice Cooper's **School's Out**.

• The first of numerous pop concerts took place in London's Wembley Stadium. 45,000 oldies fans turned out to see Chuck Berry, Bo Diddley, Bill Haley & The Comets, Jerry Lee Lewis and Little Richard.

July 1972

This Mnth	Last Mnth	Title	Artist	Label	Wks in 10	US Pos	
1	3	**20 Dynamic Hits**	Various	K-Tel	15		
2	7	**American Pie**	Don McLean	UA	16	1	F
3	-	**Slade Alive**	Slade	Polydor	22	158	F
4	5	**Bridge Over Troubled Water**	Simon & Garfunkel	CBS	135	1	2P
5	1	**Bolan Boogie**	T. Rex	Fly	9		
6	2	**Honky Chateau**	Elton John	DJM	7	1	
7	-	**Greatest Hits**	Simon & Garfunkel	CBS	59	5	2P
8	-	**Trilogy**	Emerson, Lake & Palmer	Island	5	5	
9	-	**Elvis At Madison Square Garden**	Elvis Presley	RCA	3	11	
10	4	**Exile On Main Street**	Rolling Stones	Rolling Stones	5	1	

August 1972

This Mnth	Last Mnth	Title	Artist	Label	Wks in 10	US Pos	
1	-	**20 Fantastic Hits**	Various	Arcade	15		
2	1	**20 Dynamic Hits**	Various	K-Tel	15		
3	-	**Never A Dull Moment**	Rod Stewart	Philips	20	2	
4	7	**Greatest Hits**	Simon & Garfunkel	CBS	59	5	2P
5	-	**The Slider**	T. Rex	EMI	7	17	
6	-	**School's Out**	Alice Cooper	Warner	10	2	F
7	2	**American Pie**	Don McLean	UA	16	1	F
8	3	**Slade Alive**	Slade	Polydor	22	158	F
9	-	**The Rise & Fall Of Ziggy Stardust & The Spiders From Mars**	David Bowie	RCA	20	75	F
10	4	**Bridge Over Troubled Water**	Simon & Garfunkel	CBS	135	1	2P

September 1972

This Mnth	Last Mnth	Title	Artist	Label	Wks in 10	US Pos	
1	1	**20 Fantastic Hits**	Various	Arcade	15		
2	3	**Never A Dull Moment**	Rod Stewart	Philips	20	2	
3	4	**Greatest Hits**	Simon & Garfunkel	CBS	59	5	2P
4	8	**Slade Alive**	Slade	Polydor	22	158	F
5	6	**School's Out**	Alice Cooper	Warner	10	2	F
6	5	**The Slider**	T. Rex	EMI	7	17	
7	2	**20 Dynamic Hits**	Various	K-Tel	15		
8	10	**Bridge Over Troubled Water**	Simon & Garfunkel	CBS	135	1	2P
9	9	**The Rise & Fall Of Ziggy Stardust & The Spiders From Mars**	David Bowie	RCA	20	75	F
10	-	**Moods**	Neil Diamond	Uni	5	5	F

US 1972 JULY-SEPT

July 1972

This Mnth	Last Mnth	Title	Artist	Label	Wks in 10	UK Pos	
1	5	**Exile On Main Street**	Rolling Stones	Rolling Stones	11	1	
2	-	**Honky Chateau**	Elton John	Uni	18	2	
3	10	**Roberta Flack & Donny Hathaway**	Roberta Flack	Atlantic	8	31	
4	1	**Thick As A Brick**	Jethro Tull	Reprise	10	5	
5	3	**Joplin In Concert**	Janis Joplin	Columbia	8	30	L
6	-	**Still Bill**	Bill Withers	Sussex	4		FL
7	-	**Live In Concert With The Edmonton Symphony Orchestra**	Procol Harum	A&M	5	48	FL
8	-	**Portrait Of Donny**	Donny Osmond	MGM	4	5	FL
9	2	**First Take**	Roberta Flack	Atlantic	14	47	F
10	9	**History Of Eric Clapton**	Eric Clapton	Atco	6		F

August 1972

This Mnth	Last Mnth	Title	Artist	Label	Wks in 10	UK Pos	
1	2	**Honky Chateau**	Elton John	Uni	18	2	
2	-	**School's Out**	Alice Cooper	Warner	6	4	FP
3	-	**Chicago V**	Chicago	Columbia	13	24	2P
4	-	**A Song For You**	Carpenters	A&M	5	13	
5	-	**Simon & Garfunkel's Greatest Hits**	Simon & Garfunkel	Columbia	7	2	6P
6	-	**Big Bambu**	Cheech & Chong	Ode	12		F
7	1	**Exile On Main Street**	Rolling Stones	Rolling Stones	11	1	
8	-	**Moods**	Neil Diamond	Uni	11	7	P
9	6	**Still Bill**	Bill Withers	Sussex	4		FL
10	-	**Lookin' Through The Windows**	Jackson 5	Motown	5	16	

September 1972

This Mnth	Last Mnth	Title	Artist	Label	Wks in 10	UK Pos	
1	3	**Chicago V**	Chicago	Columbia	13	24	2P
2	-	**Never A Dull Moment**	Rod Stewart	Mercury	14	1	
3	6	**Big Bambu**	Cheech & Chong	Ode	12		F
4	-	**Carney**	Leon Russell	Shelter	10		F
5	8	**Moods**	Neil Diamond	Uni	11	7	P
6	1	**Honky Chateau**	Elton John	Uni	18	2	
7	-	**Trilogy**	Emerson, Lake & Palmer	Cotillion	7	2	
8	-	**Seven Separate Fools**	Three Dog Night	Dunhill	6		L
9	-	**Carlos Santana & Buddy Miles! Live!**	Carlos Santana	Columbia	8	29	FL
10	2	**School's Out**	Alice Cooper	Warner	6	4	FP

• Critically acclaimed R&B-based singer/songwriter Bill Withers visited the Top 10 pop albums for the only time with **Still Bill**. Among the other noted acts who had their only spell in the Top 10 were teen idol Donny Osmond, distinctive Irish singer/songwriter Gilbert O'Sullivan with **Himself** and British art rock band, **Procol Harum**. The latter hit with an album recorded live in Canada with the Edmonton Symphony Orchestra.

• Both Chicago (above) and Elton John started runs of five successive chart topping American albums. The jazz rock combo, who in their career have amassed more platinum albums than any other group, reached the summit with **Chicago V**, while Elton collected his first Stateside Number 1 with **Honky Chateau**.

• Live albums were proving very popular in the USA with Top 20 sets coming from Janis Joplin, The Osmonds, Elvis Presley, Procol Harum and the super-duo of Carlos Santana & Buddy Miles.

UK 1972 OCT-DEC

• Nostalgia was big business in Britain in 1972. There was a record number of reissues on the singles chart, and compilation albums of 'oldies' cluttered the December chart hogging the Top 4 rungs. In fact, albums containing old rock'n'roll hits held the top spot for 14 consecutive weeks.

• As the T. Rex movie *Born To Boogie* opened, **The Slider** gave Britain's top group of 1972 their only American Top 20 entry. Simultaneously, fellow US glitter rock superstars Slade's **Slade Alive!** and Gary Glitter's **Glitter** took their first steps on the US Top 200. Other noteworthy performers debuting on the American LP chart included Peter Frampton with **Winds Of Change**, and later US superstars Bonnie Raitt with **Give It Up** and Steely Dan with **Can't Buy A Thrill**.

• The Rainbow, which claimed to be London's first major all-rock venue, was opened. The Who were the first act to perform and several members of the group appeared in an all-star version of *Tommy* staged there soon after. Elton John was also a success on the London stage, when he became the first rock act since The Beatles in 1963 to appear in front of the Queen at a Royal Variety Show.

October 1972

This Mnth	Last Mnth	Title	Artist	Label	Wks in 10	US Pos	
1	-	**20 All Time Hits Of The Fifties**	Various	K-Tel	15		
2	-	**Catch Bull At Four**	Cat Stevens	Island	10	1	
3	3	**Greatest Hits**	Simon & Garfunkel	CBS	59	5	2P
4	2	**Never A Dull Moment**	Rod Stewart	Philips	20	2	
5	1	**20 Fantastic Hits**	Various	Arcade	15		
6	-	**Dingly Dell**	Lindisfarne	Charisma	5		L
7	-	**20 Star Tracks**	Various	Ronco	9		
8	4	**Slade Alive**	Slade	Polydor	22	158	F
9	-	**Close To The Edge**	Yes	Atlantic	4	3	
10	-	**Black Sabbath Vol. 4**	Black Sabbath	Vertigo	5	13	

November 1972

This Mnth	Last Mnth	Title	Artist	Label	Wks in 10	US Pos	
1	1	**20 All Time Hits Of The Fifties**	Various	K-Tel	15		
2	7	**20 Star Tracks**	Various	Ronco	9		
3	3	**Greatest Hits**	Simon & Garfunkel	CBS	59	5	2P
4	2	**Catch Bull At Four**	Cat Stevens	Island	10	1	
5	-	**Sing Along With Max**	Max Bygraves	Pye	7		F
6	-	**Back To Front**	Gilbert O'Sullivan	MAM	19	48	
7	4	**Never A Dull Moment**	Rod Stewart	Philips	20	2	
8	-	**25 Dynamic Hits Vol. 2**	Various	K-Tel	9		
9	-	**20 Fantastic Hits Vol. 2**	Various	Arcade	10		
10	-	**The Best Of Bread**	Bread	Elektra	3	2	

December 1972

This Mnth	Last Mnth	Title	Artist	Label	Wks in 10	US Pos	
1	-	**25 Rockin' & Rollin' Greats**	Various	K-Tel	10		
2	1	**20 All Time Hits Of The Fifties**	Various	K-Tel	15		
3	8	**25 Dynamic Hits Vol. 2**	Various	K-Tel	9		
4	9	**20 Fantastic Hits Vol. 2**	Various	Arcade	10		
5	6	**Back To Front**	Gilbert O'Sullivan	MAM	19	48	
6	-	**Slayed**	Slade	Polydor	16	69	
7	-	**Seventh Sojourn**	Moody Blues	Threshold	3	1	
8	-	**Portrait Of Donny**	Donny Osmond	MGM	11	6	F
9	-	**Too Young**	Donny Osmond	MGM	8	11	
10	2	**20 Star Tracks**	Various	Ronco	9		

US 1972 OCT-DEC

October 1972

This Mnth	Last Mnth	Title	Artist	Label	Wks in 10	UK Pos	
1	4	**Carney**	Leon Russell	Shelter	10		F
2	1	**Chicago V**	Chicago	Columbia	13	24	2P
3	2	**Never A Dull Moment**	Rod Stewart	Mercury	14	1	
4	-	**Superfly (Soundtrack)**	Curtis Mayfield	Curtom	11	26	FL
5	-	**Days Of Future Passed**	Moody Blues	Deram	6	27	FP
6	6	**Honky Chateau**	Elton John	Uni	18	2	
7	3	**Big Bambu**	Cheech & Chong	Ode	12		F
8	-	**All Directions**	Temptations	Gordy	11	19	
9	8	**Seven Separate Fools**	Three Dog Night	Dunhill	6		L
10	-	**The London Chuck Berry Sessions**	Chuck Berry	Chess	7		FL

November 1972

This Mnth	Last Mnth	Title	Artist	Label	Wks in 10	UK Pos	
1	-	**Catch Bull At Four**	Cat Stevens	A&M	12	2	
2	4	**Superfly (Soundtrack)**	Curtis Mayfield	Curtom	11	26	FL
3	8	**All Directions**	Temptations	Gordy	11	19	
4	5	**Days Of Future Passed**	Moody Blues	Deram	6	27	FP
5	-	**Ben**	Michael Jackson	Motown	6	17	F
6	-	**Rock Of Ages**	Band	Capitol	7		L
7	-	**Close To The Edge**	Yes	Atlantic	7	4	
8	3	**Never A Dull Moment**	Rod Stewart	Mercury	14	1	
9	-	**Rhymes & Reasons**	Carole King	Ode	16	40	
10	10	**The London Chuck Berry Sessions**	Chuck Berry	Chess	7		FL

December 1972

This Mnth	Last Mnth	Title	Artist	Label	Wks in 10	UK Pos	
1	-	**Seventh Sojourn**	Moody Blues	Threshold	12	5	
2	9	**Rhymes & Reasons**	Carole King	Ode	16	40	
3	1	**Catch Bull At Four**	Cat Stevens	A&M	12	2	
4	3	**All Directions**	Temptations	Gordy	11	19	
5	-	**Living In The Past**	Jethro Tull	Chrysalis	10	8	
6	7	**Close To The Edge**	Yes	Atlantic	7	4	
7	-	**I'm Still In Love With You**	Al Green	Hi	6		
8	2	**Superfly (Soundtrack)**	Curtis Mayfield	Curtom	11	26	FL
9	-	**Summer Breeze**	Seals & Crofts	Warner	5		F
10	-	**Caravanserai**	Santana	Columbia	6	6	P

• In 1972 sales of records and tapes passed the $2 billion mark for the first time.

• Producer Don Kirshner, who had given the world The Monkees, launched the TV series *In Concert*. Initial guests included Alice Cooper, Blood, Sweat & Tears, Chuck Berry and The Allman Brothers. Berry was enjoying the biggest album of his long career with **The London Chuck Berry Sessions**. It was the last appearance for Berry Oakley of The Allman Brothers who died in a motorcycle accident soon after the group filmed their spot.

• The Moody Blues' four-year-old album, **Days Of Future Passed**, returned to the heights, thanks in part to the success of its track 'Nights In White Satin' on the singles chart. It was joined in The Top 10 by their latest LP, **Seventh Sojourn**, which was their first Number 1 and their first newly recorded album for five years.

UK 1973 JAN-MAR

• The London Symphony Orchestra's album of music from the TV series **The Strauss Family** and ex-Yes man Rick Wakeman's **The Six Wives of Henry VIII** were among Britain's biggest selling instrumental albums of the year. In America, a handful of instrumental albums made their presence felt in the Top 20 by such varied acts as banjo picker Eric Weissberg, Brazilian pianist Eumir Deodata, Dutch progressive rockers Focus and British jazz guitarist John McLaughlin's Mahavishnu Orchestra.

• British acts on the road included David Bowie and The Rolling Stones. Bowie started a 100-day world tour and The Stones gig at The Forum in Los Angeles, with Santana (above) and Cheech and Chong raised over half a million dollars for the victims of the recent earthquake in Nicaragua. Mick Jagger also added $150,000 of his own money to that total.

• Shortly after their wedding, both Carly Simon and her husband James Taylor had transatlantic chart entries. with **No Secrets** and **One Man Dog** respectively.

January 1973

This Mnth	Last Mnth	Title	Artist	Label	Wks in 10	US Pos	
1	6	**Slayed**	Slade	Polydor	16	69	
2	5	**Back To Front**	Gilbert O'Sullivan	MAM	19	48	
3	1	**25 Rockin' & Rollin' Greats**	Various	K-Tel	10		
4	4	**20 Fantastic Hits Vol. 2**	Various	Arcade	10		
5	-	**Greatest Hits**	Simon & Garfunkel	CBS	59	5	**2P**
6	3	**25 Dynamic Hits Vol. 2**	Various	K-Tel	9		
7	8	**Portrait Of Donny**	Donny Osmond	MGM	11	6	**F**
8	2	**20 All Time Hits Of The Fifties**	Various	K-Tel	15		
9	-	**No Secrets**	Carly Simon	Elektra	4	1	**FL**
10	-	**The Strauss Family**	London Symphony Orchestra	Polydor	7		**F**

February 1973

This Mnth	Last Mnth	Title	Artist	Label	Wks in 10	US Pos	
1	10	**The Strauss Family**	London Symphony Orchestra	Polydor	7		**F**
2	-	**Don't Shoot Me I'm Only The Piano Player**	Elton John	DJM	11	1	
3	5	**Greatest Hits**	Simon & Garfunkel	CBS	59	5	**2P**
4	1	**Slayed**	Slade	Polydor	16	69	
5	9	**No Secrets**	Carly Simon	Elektra	4	1	**FL**
6	2	**Back To Front**	Gilbert O'Sullivan	MAM	19	48	
7	-	**Moving Waves**	Focus	Polydor	6	8	**F**
8	-	**Too Young**	Donny Osmond	MGM	8	11	
9	-	**Rock Me Baby**	David Cassidy	Bell	8	41	
10	-	**The Rise & Fall Of Ziggy Stardust & The Spiders From Mars**	David Bowie	RCA	20	75	**F**

March 1973

This Mnth	Last Mnth	Title	Artist	Label	Wks in 10	US Pos	
1	2	**Don't Shoot Me I'm Only The Piano Player**	Elton John	DJM	11	1	
2	-	**Bursting At The Seams**	Strawbs	A&M	5	121	**FL**
3	3	**Greatest Hits**	Simon & Garfunkel	CBS	59	5	**2P**
4	7	**Moving Waves**	Focus	Polydor	6	8	**F**
5	9	**Rock Me Baby**	David Cassidy	Bell	8	41	
6	-	**Clockwork Orange**	Soundtrack	Warner	8	34	
7	-	**Billion Dollar Babies**	Alice Cooper	Warner	9	1	
8	4	**Slayed**	Slade	Polydor	16	69	
9	-	**20 Flashback Greats Of The Sixties**	Various	K-Tel	6		
10	-	**Dark Side Of The Moon**	Pink Floyd	Harvest	43	1	**2P**

US 1973

JAN-MAR

January 1973

This Mnth	Last Mnth	Title	Artist	Label	Wks in 10	UK Pos	
1	-	No Secrets	Carly Simon	Elektra	14	3	F
2	2	Rhymes & Reasons	Carole King	Ode	16	40	
3	1	Seventh Sojourn	Moody Blues	Threshold	12	5	
4	5	Living In The Past	Jethro Tull	Chrysalis	10	8	
5	-	One Man Dog	James Taylor	Warner	7	27	
6	-	The World Is A Ghetto	War	UA	16		F
7	7	I'm Still In Love With You	Al Green	Hi	6		
8	-	Tommy	Various	Ode	6		
9	3	Catch Bull At Four	Cat Stevens	A&M	12	2	
10	-	Homecoming	America	Warner	4	21	

February 1973

This Mnth	Last Mnth	Title	Artist	Label	Wks in 10	UK Pos	
1	1	No Secrets	Carly Simon	Elektra	14	3	F
2	6	The World Is A Ghetto	War	UA	16		F
3	-	Talking Book	Stevie Wonder	Tamla	9	16	
4	2	Rhymes & Reasons	Carole King	Ode	16	40	
5	-	Hot August Night	Neil Diamond	MCA	9	32	2P
6	8	Tommy	Various	Ode	6		
7	4	Living In The Past	Jethro Tull	Chrysalis	10	8	
8	-	Lady Sings The Blues (Soundtrack)	Diana Ross	Motown	13	50	
9	-	Don't Shoot Me I'm Only The Piano Player	Elton John	MCA	9	1	2P
10	3	Seventh Sojourn	Moody Blues	Threshold	12	5	

March 1973

This Mnth	Last Mnth	Title	Artist	Label	Wks in 10	UK Pos	
1	9	Don't Shoot Me I'm Only The Piano Player	Elton John	MCA	9	1	2P
2	-	Dueling Banjos/Deliverance (Soundtrack)	Eric Weissberg	Warner	9		FL
3	8	Lady Sings The Blues (Soundtrack)	Diana Ross	Motown	13	50	
4	-	Rocky Mountain High	John Denver	RCA	9		F
5	1	No Secrets	Carly Simon	Elektra	14	3	F
6	2	The World Is A Ghetto	War	UA	16		F
7	-	Prelude	Deodato	CTI	5		FL
8	-	Shoot Out At The Fantasy Factory	Traffic	Island	6		
9	5	Hot August Night	Neil Diamond	MCA	9	32	2P
10	3	Talking Book	Stevie Wonder	Tamla	9	16	

• Bruce Springsteen, who was given a showcase at the trendy New York club, Max's Kansas City, released his debut album **Greetings From Asbury Park, N.J.**

• Diana Ross clicked with the soundtrack album to her first film **Lady Sings The Blues**, in which she played the late blues singer Billie Holiday. The success of the film was also responsible for three reissued albums by Miss Holiday climbing the chart.

• As a ceasefire was declared in Vietnam, legendary actor John Wayne headed up the Top 100 with a collection of patriotic tunes entitled **America, Why I Love Her**.

• Several critically acclaimed rock albums narrowly missed the Top 10; **Can't Buy A Thrill** by Steely Dan, the five-year-old **Space Oddity** from David Bowie, the double LP **Derek & The Dominos In Concert** and Loggins & Messina's self-titled album. Eric Clapton, the leader of Derek & The Dominos, returned to the stage after a two year lay-off with a show at the Rainbow in London.

• The most talked about new MOR entertainer, Bette Midler, hit the Top 10 with her debut album **The Divine Miss M** – co-produced by newcomer Barry Manilow. Miss Midler went on to earn the Grammy for Best New Artist of 1973.

UK 1973 APR-JUNE

• Led Zeppelin, whose latest album **Houses Of The Holy** had given them their third transatlantic chart topper, embarked on their latest US tour. It was rightfully tagged, "The biggest and most profitable rock'n'roll tour in the history of the United States".

• There was still room for MOR albums on the Top 20. American balladeer Jack Jones reached the Top 10 for the third time with **Together**. Veteran British entertainer Max Bygraves put another of his singalong series of albums in the charts. US song stylist Liza Minnelli hit the Top 10 with **Liza With A Z** and Shirley Bassey's **Never Never Never** became her tenth British Top 10 entry and also her biggest US solo album.

• Rod Stewart's group The Faces clocked up their only chart topping album with **Ooh-La-La** and David Bowie scored the first of three successive Number 1s with **Aladdin Sane,** which went on to become the top album of the year in the UK.

April 1973

This Mnth	Last Mnth	Title	Artist	Label	Wks in 10	US Pos	
1	-	**40 Fantastic Hits From The 50s And 60s**	Various	Arcade	7		
2	9	**20 Flashback Greats Of The Sixties**	Various	K-Tel	6		
3	-	**Houses Of The Holy**	Led Zeppelin	Atlantic	5	1	
4	-	**For Your Pleasure**	Roxy Music	Island	6	193	
5	7	**Billion Dollar Babies**	Alice Cooper	Warner	9	1	
6	10	**Dark Side Of The Moon**	Pink Floyd	Harvest	43	1	**2P**
7	-	**Ooh-La-La**	Faces	Warner	4	21	
8	-	**Tanx**	T. Rex	EMI	4	102	
9	-	**Believe In Music**	Various	K-Tel	4		
10	1	**Don't Shoot Me I'm Only The Piano Player**	Elton John	DJM	11	1	

May 1973

This Mnth	Last Mnth	Title	Artist	Label	Wks in 10	US Pos
1	-	**Aladdin Sane**	David Bowie	RCA	27	17
2	-	**The Beatles 1967-1970**	Beatles	Apple	19	1
3	-	**The Beatles 1962-1966**	Beatles	Apple	16	3
4	9	**Believe In Music**	Various	K-Tel	4	
5	1	**40 Fantastic Hits From The 50s And 60s**	Various	Arcade	7	
6	7	**Ooh-La-La**	Faces	Warner	4	21
7	5	**Billion Dollar Babies**	Alice Cooper	Warner	9	1
8	-	**Red Rose Speedway**	Paul McCartney & Wings	Apple	6	1
9	-	**20 Fantastic Hits Vol. 3**	Various	Arcade	5	
10	-	**Singalongamax Vol. 3**	Max Bygraves	Pye	1	

June 1973

This Mnth	Last Mnth	Title	Artist	Label	Wks in 10	US Pos
1	-	**Pure Gold**	Various	EMI	5	
2	1	**Aladdin Sane**	David Bowie	RCA	27	17
3	2	**The Beatles 1967-1970**	Beatles	Apple	19	1
4	3	**The Beatles 1962-1966**	Beatles	Apple	16	3
5	9	**20 Fantastic Hits Vol. 3**	Various	Arcade	5	
6	-	**Touch Me**	Gary Glitter	Bell	6	
7	-	**That'll Be The Day**	Various	Ronco	8	
8	-	**There Goes Rhymin' Simon**	Paul Simon	CBS	7	2
9	8	**Red Rose Speedway**	Paul McCartney & Wings	Apple	6	1
10	-	**Alone Together**	Donny Osmond	MGM	4	26

US 1973 APR-JUNE

April 1973

This Mnth	Last Mnth	Title	Artist	Label	Wks in 10	UK Pos	
1	3	**Lady Sings The Blues (Soundtrack)**	Diana Ross	Motown	13	50	
2	-	**Billion Dollar Babies**	Alice Cooper	Warner	10	1	P
3	-	**Dark Side Of The Moon**	Pink Floyd	Harvest	27	2	F13P
4	6	**The World Is A Ghetto**	War	UA	16	F	
5	1	**Don't Shoot Me I'm Only The Piano Player**	Elton John	MCA	9	1	2P
6	-	**Aloha From Hawaii Via Satellite**	Elvis Presley	RCA	7	11	2P
7	7	**Prelude**	Deodato	CTI	5		FL
8	2	**Dueling Banjos/Deliverance (Soundtrack)**	Eric Weissberg	Warner	9		FL
9	-	**The Best Of Bread**	Bread	Elektra	8	7	L
10	-	**Masterpiece**	Temptations	Gordy	5	28	L

May 1973

This Mnth	Last Mnth	Title	Artist	Label	Wks in 10	UK Pos	
1	-	**Houses Of The Holy**	Led Zeppelin	Atlantic	14	1	6P
2	9	**The Best Of Bread**	Bread	Elektra	8	7	L
3	-	**The Beatles/1967-1970**	Beatles	Apple	11	2	5P
4	-	**The Beatles/1962-1966**	Beatles	Apple	8	3	5P
5	6	**Aloha From Hawaii Via Satellite**	Elvis Presley	RCA	7	11	2P
6	3	**Dark Side Of The Moon**	Pink Floyd	Harvest	27	2	F13P
7	-	**They Only Come Out At Night**	Edgar Winter Group	Epic	9		F2PL
8	2	**Billion Dollar Babies**	Alice Cooper	Warner	10	1	P
9	10	**Masterpiece**	Temptations	Gordy	5	28	L
10	-	**Neither One Of Us**	Gladys Knight & The Pips	Soul	4	F	

June 1973

This Mnth	Last Mnth	Title	Artist	Label	Wks in 10	UK Pos	
1	-	**Red Rose Speedway**	Wings	Apple	9	5	
2	1	**Houses Of The Holy**	Led Zeppelin	Atlantic	14	1	6P
3	3	**The Beatles/1967-1970**	Beatles	Apple	11	2	5P
4	7	**They Only Come Out At Night**	Edgar Winter Group	Epic	9		F2PL
5	-	**Living In The Material World**	George Harrison	Apple	7	2	
6	6	**Dark Side Of The Moon**	Pink Floyd	Harvest	27	2	F13P
7	-	**There Goes Rhymin' Simon**	Paul Simon	Columbia	8	4	P
8	4	**The Beatles/1962-1966**	Beatles	Apple	8	3	5P
9	-	**Diamond Girl**	Seals & Crofts	Warner	12		L
10	2	**The Best Of Bread**	Bread	Elektra	8	7	L

• Once again, The Beatles had two albums in the transatlantic charts: the compilations **The Beatles 1962-1966** and **The Beatles 1967-1970**. The latter topped the US list until it was dethroned by **Red Rose Speedway** from Paul McCartney & Wings. This in turn was replaced by **Living In The Material World** by another ex-Beatle, George Harrison.

• Elvis Presley had his first Number 1 for nine years with the quadrophonically recorded soundtrack album to his TV show **Aloha From Hawaii**, which was seen by the biggest world-wide TV audience to date. The album reportedly amassed over a million advance orders in the USA, and in the UK, where the show was not seen, it became his 11th Top 20 album of the decade.

• The Temptations' aptly titled **Masterpiece** returned them to the top end of the chart where it was joined by other Motown releases such as Gladys Knight & The Pips' biggest album, **Neither One Of Us** and the eponymous chart debuting album by The Spinners. Other noteworthy R&B releases in the Top 20 included **Call Me** by Al Green, Isaac Hayes' **Live At The Sahara Tahoe** and Barry White's debut, **I've Got So Much To Give**.

UK 1973

JULY-SEPT

• Lindisfarne joined American headliners Sly & The Family Stone, Canned Heat and Edgar Winter at a major rock gig at London's White City. Winter's latest album offering, **They Only Come Out At Night** – which included new group members Ronnie Montrose and Dan Hartman – had just given him the biggest hit of his career. Interestingly, Edgar's better known – though less successful chartwise – older brother Johnny had also just had his biggest hit with **Still Alive And Well**.

• There were many British acts on the road in the USA. Elton John was playing to sell-out stadium audiences while T. Rex gained themselves many new fans on a smaller-scale tour. Led Zeppelin's concert at Madison Square Garden was filmed and seen later as **The Song Remains The Same**. The Rolling Stones were seen on US television for the first time in six years. They sang three songs from their new album **Goat's Head Soup** on the recently launched series *In Concert*.

• At the end of a long and arduous tour, David Bowie announced to a shocked audience in London that he would never play live again. However, Bowie, who was the hottest album act in the UK, with three albums simultaneously in the Top 10, returned to the stage after a year off.

July 1973

This Mnth	Last Mnth	Title	Artist	Label	Wks in 10	US Pos	
1	7	**That'll Be The Day**	Various	Ronco	8		
2	-	**We Can Make It**	Peters & Lee	Philips	15		F
3	-	**And I Love You So**	Perry Como	RCA	44	34	
4	-	**Living In The Material World**	George Harrison	Apple	5	1	
5	2	**Aladdin Sane**	David Bowie	RCA	27	17	
6	8	**There Goes Rhymin' Simon**	Paul Simon	CBS	7	2	
7	3	**The Beatles 1967-1970**	Beatles	Apple	19	1	
8	-	**Foreigner**	Cat Stevens	Island	6	3	
9	4	**The Beatles 1962-1966**	Beatles	Apple	16	3	
10	-	**Now & Then**	Carpenters	A&M	22	2	F

August 1973

This Mnth	Last Mnth	Title	Artist	Label	Wks in 10	US Pos	
1	2	**We Can Make It**	Peters & Lee	Philips	15		F
2	5	**Aladdin Sane**	David Bowie	RCA	27	17	
3	-	**Hunky Dory**	David Bowie	RCA	12	93	
4	10	**Now & Then**	Carpenters	A&M	22	2	F
5	1	**That'll Be The Day**	Various	Ronco	8		
6	3	**And I Love You So**	Perry Como	RCA	44	34	
7	8	**Foreigner**	Cat Stevens	Island	6	3	
8	-	**Sing It Again Rod**	Rod Stewart	Mercury	9	31	
9	-	**The Rise & Fall Of Ziggy Stardust & The Spiders From Mars**	David Bowie	RCA	20	75	F
10	7	**The Beatles 1967-1970**	Beatles	Apple	19	1	

September 1973

This Mnth	Last Mnth	Title	Artist	Label	Wks in 10	US Pos	
1	8	**Sing It Again Rod**	Rod Stewart	Mercury	9	31	
2	1	**We Can Make It**	Peters & Lee	Philips	15		F
3	4	**Now & Then**	Carpenters	A&M	22	2	F
4	2	**Aladdin Sane**	David Bowie	RCA	27	17	
5	3	**Hunky Dory**	David Bowie	RCA	12	93	
6	-	**Goat's Head Soup**	Rolling Stones	Rolling Stones	6	1	
7	-	**The Plan**	Osmonds	MGM	5	58	
8	9	**The Rise & Fall Of Ziggy Stardust & The Spiders From Mars**	David Bowie	RCA	20	75	F
9	-	**Greatest Hits**	Simon & Garfunkel	CBS	59	5	2P
10	-	**Tubular Bells**	Mike Oldfield	Virgin	74	3	FP

US 1973 JULY-SEPT

July 1973

This Mnth	Last Mnth	Title	Artist	Label	Wks in 10	UK Pos	
1	5	**Living In The Material World**	George Harrison	Apple	7	2	
2	6	**Dark Side Of The Moon**	Pink Floyd	Harvest	27	2	F13P
3	7	**There Goes Rhymin' Simon**	Paul Simon	Columbia	8	4	P
4	-	**Now & Then**	Carpenters	A&M	8	2	
5	1	**Red Rose Speedway**	Wings	Apple	9	5	
6	-	**Fantasy**	Carole King	Ode	5		
7	2	**Houses Of The Holy**	Led Zeppelin	Atlantic	14	1	6P
8	-	**Chicago VI**	Chicago	Columbia	10		2P
9	-	**Made In Japan**	Deep Purple	Warner	12	16	P
10	-	**The Captain And Me**	Doobie Brothers	Warner	3		F2P

August 1973

This Mnth	Last Mnth	Title	Artist	Label	Wks in 10	UK Pos	
1	8	**Chicago VI**	Chicago	Columbia	10		2P
2	2	**Dark Side Of The Moon**	Pink Floyd	Harvest	27	2	F13P
3	-	**A Passion Play**	Jethro Tull	Chrysalis	6	13	
4	-	**Diamond Girl**	Seals & Crofts	Warner	12		L
5	4	**Now & Then**	Carpenters	A&M	8	2	
6	-	**Foreigner**	Cat Stevens	A&M	6	3	
7	9	**Made In Japan**	Deep Purple	Warner	12	16	P
8	-	**Fresh**	Sly & The Family Stone	Epic	6		L
9	-	**Machine Head**	Deep Purple	Warner	6	1	F2P
10	-	**Touch Me In The Morning**	Diana Ross	Motown	6	7	

September 1973

This Mnth	Last Mnth	Title	Artist	Label	Wks in 10	UK Pos	
1	-	**Brothers And Sisters**	Allman Brothers Band	Capricorn	15	42	
2	1	**Chicago VI**	Chicago	Columbia	10		2P
3	-	**We're An American Band**	Grand Funk	Capitol	8		P
4	-	**Killing Me Softly**	Roberta Flack	Atlantic	7	40	
5	2	**Dark Side Of The Moon**	Pink Floyd	Harvest	27	2	F13P
6	10	**Touch Me In The Morning**	Diana Ross	Motown	6	7	
7	-	**Innervisions**	Stevie Wonder	Tamla	10	8	
8	6	**Foreigner**	Cat Stevens	A&M	6	3	
9	-	**Los Cochinos**	Cheech & Chong	Ode	12		
10	3	**A Passion Play**	Jethro Tull	Chrysalis	6	13	

• Pink Floyd's **Dark Side Of The Moon** may have only spent one week at the summit but it went on to disintegrate the record for longevity on the US album chart. It sold approximately 20 million copies worldwide, remained on the US Top 200 for an amazing 17 years and was still riding high on the US catalog album chart in the mid-Nineties.

• Over half a million people attended the Summer Jam Festival at Watkins Glen, New York. Among the headliners were The Grateful Dead, The Band and The Allman Brothers.

• Among the acclaimed acts opening their chart account in the States were Canada's Bachman-Turner Overdrive and southern rockers Lynyrd Skynyrd, who both debuted with eponymous albums, and Roxy Music who hit with **For You Pleasure**. Noted acts who cracked the Top 20 for the first time included The Doobie Brothers with **The Captain & Me**, Deep Purple with **Made In Japan** and The Pointer Sisters with a self-titled album.

UK 1973 OCT-DEC

• The chart topping **Pin Ups**, which was a collection of David Bowie's favourite Sixties songs, pushed his British album sales in 1973 over the million mark. Another oldies-packed album was Roxy Music front man Bryan Ferry's debut solo set, **These Foolish Things**, which charted alongside his group's first Number 1, **Stranded**.

• The Who's American tour was a great success even though drummer Keith Moon collapsed on stage in San Francisco, and the whole group were jailed overnight after a hotel wrecking incident in Montreal. Their double album **Quadrophenia** narrowly missed the top spot on both sides of the Atlantic, and their previous rock opera *Tommy* was again seen on stage in London.

• For the second year running teen idols David Cassidy (above) and Donny Osmond reached the Top 10 over the Christmas period. In fact, Cassidy, who had not even graced the Top 200 in his homeland this year, headed the chart with **Dreams Are Nothin' More Than Wishes**.

October 1973

This Mnth	Last Mnth	Title	Artist	Label	Wks in 10	US Pos	
1	-	**Sladest**	Slade	Polydor	13	129	
2	-	**Hello**	Status Quo	Vertigo	9		
3	6	**Goat's Head Soup**	Rolling Stones	Rolling Stones	6	1	
4	-	**I'm A Writer Not A Fighter**	Gilbert O'Sullivan	MAM	16	101	
5	-	**And I Love You So**	Perry Como	RCA	44	34	
6	1	**Sing It Again Rod**	Rod Stewart	Mercury	9	31	
7	-	**Selling England By The Pound**	Genesis	Charisma	4	70	
8	3	**Now & Then**	Carpenters	A&M	22	2	F
9	4	**Aladdin Sane**	David Bowie	RCA	27	17	
10	5	**Hunky Dory**	David Bowie	RCA	12	93	

November 1973

This Mnth	Last Mnth	Title	Artist	Label	Wks in 10	US Pos	
1	-	**Pin Ups**	David Bowie	RCA	13	23	
2	-	**Goodbye Yellow Brick Road**	Elton John	DJM	25	1	
3	5	**And I Love You So**	Perry Como	RCA	44	34	
4	2	**Hello**	Status Quo	Vertigo	9		
5	1	**Sladest**	Slade	Polydor	13	129	
6	-	**These Foolish Things**	Bryan Ferry	Island	4		F
7	-	**Quadrophenia**	Who	Track	5	2	
8	4	**I'm A Writer Not A Fighter**	Gilbert O'Sullivan	MAM	16	101	
9	7	**Selling England By The Pound**	Genesis	Charisma	4	70	
10	-	**Dark Side Of The Moon**	Pink Floyd	Harvest	43	1	2P

December 1973

This Mnth	Last Mnth	Title	Artist	Label	Wks in 10	US Pos	
1	1	**Pin Ups**	David Bowie	RCA	13	23	
2	-	**Stranded**	Roxy Music	Island	8		
3	-	**Dreams Are Nothin' More Than Wishes**	David Cassidy	Bell	7		
4	3	**And I Love You So**	Perry Como	RCA	44	34	
5	2	**Goodbye Yellow Brick Road**	Elton John	DJM	25	1	
6	8	**I'm A Writer Not A Fighter**	Gilbert O'Sullivan	MAM	16	101	
7	-	**Sabbath Bloody Sabbath**	Black Sabbath	WEA	2	11	
8	7	**Quadrophenia**	Who	Track	5	2	
9	-	**A Time For Us**	Donny Osmond	MGM	5	58	L
10	-	**Ringo**	Ringo Starr	Apple	3	2	L

US 1973 OCT-DEC

October 1973

This Mnth	Last Mnth	Title	Artist	Label	Wks in 10	UK Pos	
1	1	**Brothers And Sisters**	Allman Brothers Band	Capricorn	15	42	
2	-	**Let's Get It On**	Marvin Gaye	Tamla	8	39	
3	-	**Goat's Head Soup**	Rolling Stones	Rolling Stones	11	1	
4	9	**Los Cochinos**	Cheech & Chong	Ode	12		
5	7	**Innervisions**	Stevie Wonder	Tamla	10	8	
6	-	**Deliver The Word**	War	UA	7		
7	3	**We're An American Band**	Grand Funk	Capitol	8		**P**
8	4	**Killing Me Softly**	Roberta Flack	Atlantic	7	40	
9	-	**Goodbye Yellow Brick Road**	Elton John	MCA	36	1	**5P**
10	-	**Angel Clare**	Art Garfunkel	Columbia	5	14	**F**

November 1973

This Mnth	Last Mnth	Title	Artist	Label	Wks in 10	UK Pos	
1	9	**Goodbye Yellow Brick Road**	Elton John	MCA	36	1	**5P**
2	3	**Goat's Head Soup**	Rolling Stones	Rolling Stones	11	1	
3	1	**Brothers And Sisters**	Allman Brothers Band	Capricorn	15	42	
4	4	**Los Cochinos**	Cheech & Chong	Ode	12		
5	-	**Quadrophenia**	Who	MCA	9	2	**P**
6	10	**Angel Clare**	Art Garfunkel	Columbia	5	14	**F**
7	-	**The Smoker You Drink, The Player You Get**	Joe Walsh	Dunhill	6		**F**
8	2	**Let's Get It On**	Marvin Gaye	Tamla	8	39	
9	-	**You Don't Mess Around With Jim**	Jim Croce	ABC	19		**F**
10	-	**Ringo**	Ringo Starr	Apple	8	7	**FP**

December 1973

This Mnth	Last Mnth	Title	Artist	Label	Wks in 10	UK Pos	
1	1	**Goodbye Yellow Brick Road**	Elton John	MCA	36	1	**5P**
2	10	**Ringo**	Ringo Starr	Apple	8	7	**FP**
3	-	**Jonathan Livingston Seagull (Soundtrack)**	Neil Diamond	Columbia	10	35	**2P**
4	-	**The Joker**	Steve Miller Band	Capitol	13		**FP**
5	9	**You Don't Mess Around With Jim**	Jim Croce	ABC	19		**F**
6	5	**Quadrophenia**	Who	MCA	9	2	**P**
7	-	**The Singles 1969-1973**	Carpenters	A&M	9	1	**4PL**
8	-	**Life And Times**	Jim Croce	ABC	8		
9	2	**Goat's Head Soup**	Rolling Stones	Rolling Stones	11	1	
10	-	**Mind Games**	John Lennon	Apple	3	13	

• Rock continued to fragment in 1973, progressive FM radio – later tagged AOR – broke fewer new acts and 75% of albums failed to break even. As *Rolling Stone* wondered if "rock had run out of things to say", Aerosmith, Queen and Genesis made their initial chart entries. Genesis' hit, **Selling England By The Pound**, became their 10th US gold album when it finally passed the million mark in the early Nineties.

• Music from the movie *Jonathan Livingston Seagull* gave Neil Diamond the biggest hit of his long career and won the Grammy for Best Soundtrack. Other top selling soundtracks included **American Graffiti** and **Pat Garrett & Billy The Kid**. The former contained early rock'n'roll hits and the latter featured Bob Dylan.

• Funny man Allan Sherman and the multi-talented Bobby Darin died. They had been two of the early Sixties top selling album artists.

• The Steve Miller Band, who had signed to Capitol in 1967, finally reached the Top 10 with **The Joker**. Incidentally, the title track gave Miller his first UK Number 1 in 1990, after it was featured in a jeans commercial. Another American record that fared well in Britain was **The Singles 1969-1973** by The Carpenters, which became the UK's top LP of 1974.

UK 1974 JAN-MAR

• Bob Dylan's first album after leaving Columbia, **Planet Waves**, which failed to give him his seventh UK chart topper, became his first American Number 1. Dylan's first US tour for eight years was enormously successful. His show in Miami caused the biggest traffic jam since Woodstock.

• All was not well with two of the Sixties' best known married couples: Elvis and Priscilla Presley's divorce came through and Cher filed for hers from Sonny.

• Among the new faces on the British album chart were children's TV characters The Wombles, nine-year-old Lena Zavaroni and middle-aged miners Millican and Nesbitt with their self titled debut. The latter two thanks to appearances on TV's *Opportunity Knocks*. In America, new chart entrants included Billy Joel with **Piano Man**, REO Speedwagon with **Ridin' The Storm Out**, Chicago quintet Styx with **The Serpent Is Rising**, Hall & Oates with **Abandoned Luncheonette** and the pride of the Florida Keys, Jimmy Buffet with **Living And Dying In 3/4 Time**.

• Slade notched up their third and last Number 1 with **Old New Borrowed And Blue** and progressive rockers Yes scored their first with **Tales From Topographic Oceans**. Yes also fared well Stateside, where a show at Madison Square Garden quickly sold out by word of mouth alone.

January 1974

This Mnth	Last Mnth	Title	Artist	Label	Wks in 10	US Pos	
1	-	**Brain Salad Surgery**	Emerson, Lake & Palmer	Island	4	11	
2	5	**Goodbye Yellow Brick Road**	Elton John	DJM	25	1	
3	-	**Tales From Topographic Oceans**	Yes	Atlantic	5	6	
4	-	**Sladest**	Slade	Polydor	13	129	
5	1	**Pin Ups**	David Bowie	RCA	13	23	
6	6	**I'm A Writer Not A Fighter**	Gilbert O'Sullivan	MAM	16	101	
7	4	**And I Love You So**	Perry Como	RCA	44	34	
8	9	**A Time For Us**	Donny Osmond	MGM	5	58	L
9	2	**Stranded**	Roxy Music	Island	8		
10	-	**Band On The Run**	Paul McCartney & Wings	Apple	49	1	P

February 1974

This Mnth	Last Mnth	Title	Artist	Label	Wks in 10	US Pos	
1	-	**The Singles 1969-1973**	Carpenters	A&M	64	1	2P
2	7	**And I Love You So**	Perry Como	RCA	44	34	
3	-	**Silver Bird**	Leo Sayer	Chrysalis	7		F
4	10	**Band On The Run**	Paul McCartney & Wings	Apple	49	1	P
5	-	**Overture And Beginners**	Faces	Mercury	3	63	L
6	-	**Solitaire**	Andy Williams	CBS	6	185	
7	-	**Tubular Bells**	Mike Oldfield	Virgin	74	3	FP
8	-	**Greatest Hits**	Simon & Garfunkel	CBS	59	5	2P
9	-	**Dark Side Of The Moon**	Pink Floyd	Harvest	43	1	2P
10	-	**Old New Borrowed And Blue**	Slade	Polydor	9		

March 1974

This Mnth	Last Mnth	Title	Artist	Label	Wks in 10	US Pos	
1	1	**The Singles 1969-1973**	Carpenters	A&M	64	1	2P
2	4	**Band On The Run**	Wings	Apple	49	1	P
3	10	**Old New Borrowed And Blue**	Slade	Polydor	9		
4	-	**Goodbye Yellow Brick Road**	Elton John	DJM	25	1	
5	-	**Burn**	Deep Purple	Purple	4	9	
6	-	**The Free Story**	Free	Island	2		
7	7	**Tubular Bells**	Mike Oldfield	Virgin	74	3	FP
8	2	**And I Love You So**	Perry Como	RCA	44	34	
9	6	**Solitaire**	Andy Williams	CBS	6	185	
10	-	**Planet Waves**	Bob Dylan	Island	2	1	

US 1974 JAN-MAR

January 1974

This Mnth	Last Mnth	Title	Artist	Label	Wks in 10	UK Pos	
1	5	**You Don't Mess Around With Jim**	Jim Croce	ABC	19		**F**
2	7	**The Singles 1969-1973**	Carpenters	A&M	9	1	**4PL**
3	1	**Goodbye Yellow Brick Road**	Elton John	MCA	36	1	**5P**
4	-	**I Got A Name**	Jim Croce	ABC	8		
5	4	**The Joker**	Steve Miller Band	Capitol	13		**FP**
6	3	**Jonathan Livingston Seagull (Soundtrack)**	Neil Diamond	Columbia	10	35	**2P**
7	-	**Bette Midler**	Bette Midler	Atlantic	5		
8	-	**John Denver's Greatest Hits**	John Denver	RCA	28		
9	6	**Quadrophenia**	Who	MCA	9	2	**P**
10	-	**Band On The Run**	Wings	Apple	32	1	**3P**

February 1974

This Mnth	Last Mnth	Title	Artist	Label	Wks in 10	UK Pos	
1	8	**John Denver's Greatest Hits**	John Denver	RCA	28		
2	1	**You Don't Mess Around With Jim**	Jim Croce	ABC	19		**F**
3	-	**Under The Influence Of ...**	Love Unlimited	20th Century	5		**FL**
4	3	**Goodbye Yellow Brick Road**	Elton John	MCA	36	1	**5P**
5	4	**I Got A Name**	Jim Croce	ABC	8		
6	-	**Planet Waves**	Bob Dylan	Asylum	7	7	
7	5	**The Joker**	Steve Miller Band	Capitol	13		**FP**
8	10	**Band On The Run**	Wings	Apple	32	1	**3P**
9	2	**The Singles 1969-1973**	Carpenters	A&M	9	1	**4PL**
10	-	**Behind Closed Doors**	Charlie Rich	Epic	6	4	**FPL**

March 1974

This Mnth	Last Mnth	Title	Artist	Label	Wks in 10	UK Pos	
1	-	**Court And Spark**	Joni Mitchell	Asylum	15	14	**F**
2	1	**John Denver's Greatest Hits**	John Denver	RCA	28		
3	6	**Planet Waves**	Bob Dylan	Asylum	7	7	
4	-	**The Way We Were**	Barbra Streisand	Columbia	6	49	**P**
5	-	**Hotcakes**	Carly Simon	Elektra	7	19	
6	-	**Tubular Bells**	Mike Oldfield	Virgin	12	1	**FL**
7	8	**Band On The Run**	Wings	Apple	32	1	**3P**
8	-	**Tales From Topographic Oceans**	Yes	Atlantic	6	1	
9	2	**You Don't Mess Around With Jim**	Jim Croce	ABC	19		**F**
10	4	**Goodbye Yellow Brick Road**	Elton John	MCA	36	1	**5P**

• Singer/songwriter Jim Croce, who had been killed in a plane crash in September 1973, became the first artist to top the American chart after their death. Not only did **You Don't Mess Around With Jim** reach the top spot, but it was joined in the Top 10 by **I Got A Name**, giving him the top two positions. No other artist including Elvis and John Lennon has ever had such posthumous Stateside success.

• Stevie Wonder was the big winner at the Grammy Awards. He walked away with five trophies including Album of The Year for **Innervisions.** In direct competition to this prestigious event, Dick Clark launched the American Music Awards. The AMA has now attained a status almost equal to the Grammy Awards.

• Three Barry White projects reached the Top 20: Love Unlimited Orchestra's **Rhapsody In White**, Love Unlimited's **Under The Influence Of...** and his own **Stone Gon'**.

UK 1974 APR-JUNE

• **Sergeant Pepper's Lonely Hearts Club Band** by The Beatles, **Blonde On Blonde** by Bob Dylan and **Pet Sounds** by the Beach Boys were selected by the *NME* writing staff as the three greatest albums ever recorded.

• Among the new groups getting their first taste of British chart action were local bands Queen and Bad Company, the American-fronted group Sparks, German synth band Tangerine Dream and Swedish quartet Abba. The latter had recently won the Eurovision song contest with 'Waterloo'.

• After seeing him on stage at Charley's Club in Cambridge, Massachusetts, *Rolling Stone* writer Jon Landau made his famous remark "I saw rock'n-'roll's future – and its name is Bruce Springsteen". The music critic went on to co-produce many of The Boss' hits.

• The Carpenters, who topped the quarter's album listing with **The Singles 1969-1973**, played for President Nixon at the White House.

• Rick Wakeman, who had recently left Yes, scored his biggest transatlantic hit with **Journey To The Centre Of The Earth**. Other British acts who clicked on both sides of the Atlantic included ex-Deram Records label-mates Cat Stevens and David Bowie with **Buddah And The Chocolate Box** and **Diamond Dogs** respectively.

April 1974

This Mnth	Last Mnth	Title	Artist	Label	Wks in 10	US Pos	
1	1	**The Singles 1969-1973**	Carpenters	A&M	64	1	**2P**
2	4	**Goodbye Yellow Brick Road**	Elton John	DJM	25	1	
3	-	**Millican And Nesbit**	Millican And Nesbit	Pye	9		**FL**
4	2	**Band On The Run**	Paul McCartney & Wings	Apple	49	1	**P**
5	-	**Buddah And The Chocolate Box**	Cat Stevens	Island	5	2	
6	3	**Old New Borrowed And Blue**	Slade	Polydor	9		
7	-	**Diana & Marvin**	Diana Ross & Marvin Gaye	Tamla-Motown	7		**F**
8	7	**Tubular Bells**	Mike Oldfield	Virgin	74	3	**FP**
9	-	**Queen 2**	Queen	EMI	4	49	**F**
10	-	**The Sting**	Marvin Hamlisch	MCA	7	1	**FL**

May 1974

This Mnth	Last Mnth	Title	Artist	Label	Wks in 10	US Pos	
1	1	**The Singles 1969-1973**	Carpenters	A&M	64	1	**2P**
2	4	**Band On The Run**	Wings	Apple	49	1	**P**
3	2	**Goodbye Yellow Brick Road**	Elton John	DJM	25	1	
4	8	**Tubular Bells**	Mike Oldfield	Virgin	74	3	**FP**
5	-	**Behind Closed Doors**	Charlie Rich	Epic	6	8	**FL**
6	-	**Quo**	Status Quo	Vertigo	6		
7	5	**Buddah And The Chocolate Box**	Cat Stevens	Island	5	2	
8	7	**Diana & Marvin**	Diana Ross & Marvin Gaye	Tamla-Motown	7		**F**
9	-	**Journey To The Centre Of The Earth**	Rick Wakeman	A&M	12	3	
10	3	**Millican And Nesbit**	Millican And Nesbit	Pye	9		**FL**

June 1974

This Mnth	Last Mnth	Title	Artist	Label	Wks in 10	US Pos	
1	1	**The Singles 1969-1973**	Carpenters	A&M	64	1	**2P**
2	-	**Diamond Dogs**	David Bowie	RCA	9	5	
3	9	**Journey To The Centre Of The Earth**	Rick Wakeman	A&M	12	3	
4	4	**Tubular Bells**	Mike Oldfield	Virgin	74	3	**FP**
5	-	**Kimono My House**	Sparks	Island	11	101	**F**
6	2	**Band On The Run**	Paul McCartney & Wings	Apple	49	1	**P**
7	6	**Quo**	Status Quo	Vertigo	6		
8	-	**Easy Easy**	Scotland Football World Cup Squad	Polydor	4		**FL**
9	-	**Bad Company**	Bad Company	Island	6	1	**F**
10	5	**Behind Closed Doors**	Charlie Rich	Epic	6	8	**FL**

US 1974

APR-JUNE

April 1974

This Mnth	Last Mnth	Title	Artist	Label	Wks in 10	UK Pos	
1	2	**John Denver's Greatest Hits**	John Denver	RCA	28		
2	7	**Band On The Run**	Wings	Apple	32	1	3P
3	6	**Tubular Bells**	Mike Oldfield	Virgin	12	1	FL
4	-	**Love Is The Message**	MFSB	Philly Int.	4		FL
5	1	**Court And Spark**	Joni Mitchell	Asylum	15	14	F
6	-	**Chicago VII**	Chicago	Columbia	14		P
7	-	**The Sting (Soundtrack)**	Marvin Hamlisch	MCA	15	7	FL
8	4	**The Way We Were**	Barbra Streisand	Columbia	6	49	P
9	10	**Goodbye Yellow Brick Road**	Elton John	MCA	36	1	5P
10	-	**What Were Once Vices Are Now Habits**	Doobie Brothers	Warner	10	19	P

May 1974

This Mnth	Last Mnth	Title	Artist	Label	Wks in 10	UK Pos	
1	7	**The Sting (Soundtrack)**	Marvin Hamlisch	MCA	15	7	FL
2	-	**Buddah And The Chocolate Box**	Cat Stevens	A&M	13	3	
3	1	**John Denver's Greatest Hits**	John Denver	RCA	28		
4	-	**Maria Muldaur**	Maria Muldaur	Reprise	11		FL
5	6	**Chicago VII**	Chicago	Columbia	14		P
6	-	**Shinin' On**	Grand Funk	Capitol	10		
7	2	**Band On The Run**	Wings	Apple	32	1	3P
8	9	**Goodbye Yellow Brick Road**	Elton John	MCA	36	1	5P
9	3	**Tubular Bells**	Mike Oldfield	Virgin	12	1	FL
10	5	**Court And Spark**	Joni Mitchell	Asylum	15	14	F

June 1974

This Mnth	Last Mnth	Title	Artist	Label	Wks in 10	UK Pos	
1	7	**Band On The Run**	Wings	Apple	32	1	3P
2	1	**The Sting (Soundtrack)**	Marvin Hamlisch	MCA	15	7	FL
3	-	**Sundown**	Gordon Lightfoot	Reprise	8	45	FP
4	2	**Buddah And The Chocolate Box**	Cat Stevens	A&M	13	3	
5	4	**Maria Muldaur**	Maria Muldaur	Reprise	11		FL
6	3	**John Denver's Greatest Hits**	John Denver	RCA	28		
7	6	**Shinin' On**	Grand Funk	Capitol	10		
8	10	**Court And Spark**	Joni Mitchell	Asylum	15	14	F
9	8	**Goodbye Yellow Brick Road**	Elton John	MCA	36	1	5P
10	5	**Chicago VII**	Chicago	Columbia	14		P

• Black Sabbath, Deep Purple, The Eagles and Emerson, Lake & Palmer were among the headliners at the California Jam Festival. Over in Richmond, Virginia at the Cherry Blossom Music Festival, a four-hour battle occurred between rock fans and police after several drug busts were made. The other entertainment there was provided by acts such as The Steve Miller Band, Boz Scaggs and The Stories. Meanwhile, at a David Cassidy concert in London a fan was tragically killed in the crush while more than 50 were injured in skirmishes after a Jackson 5 show at Washington's RFK stadium.

• The ground-breaking **Ship Ahoy** by The O'Jays was joined at the top end of the chart by several other meritorious R&B releases. Among these were **Skin Tight** by The Ohio Players, **Open Our Eyes** by Earth, Wind & Fire and **Let's Put It All Together** by The Stylistics (above).

• Among the acts making chart debuts were rock bands Kansas and Kiss with self-titled albums.

UK 1974

JULY-SEPT

• American teen idols The Osmonds and David Cassidy, who had run out of steam in their homeland some time before, had their final entries in the UK Top 10 with **Our Best To You** and **David Cassidy Live**. Simultaneously, Britain's king of glitter rock, Gary Glitter, had his last major hit, **Remember Me This Way**, and his group, The Glitter Band, had their most successful album **Hey**.

• The first solo instrumentalist to top the UK chart was Mike Oldfield, whose **Hergest Ridge** was replaced at Number 1 by his critically acclaimed debut album, **Tubular Bells**. The latter had taken 15 months to reach the summit.

• The New York Dolls, who greatly influenced the late Seventies British punk scene, split up after only two albums. Their latest LP, **Too Much Too Soon** was, like their self-titled debut, only a minor US hit. At the same time, two other pioneers of punk made their New York debuts, Blondie and The Ramones.

July 1974

This Mnth	Last Mnth	Title	Artist	Label	Wks in 10	US Pos	
1	6	**Band On The Run**	Paul McCartney & Wings	Apple	49	1	**P**
2	4	**Tubular Bells**	Mike Oldfield	Virgin	74	3	**FP**
3	1	**The Singles 1969-1973**	Carpenters	A&M	64	1	**2P**
4	-	**Caribou**	Elton John	DJM	6	1	
5	2	**Diamond Dogs**	David Bowie	RCA	9	5	
6	-	**Remember Me This Way**	Gary Glitter	Bell	5		**L**
7	-	**Another Time, Another Place**	Bryan Ferry	Island	14		
8	9	**Bad Company**	Bad Company	Island	6	1	**F**
9	3	**Journey To The Centre Of The Earth**	Rick Wakeman	A&M	12	3	
10	5	**Kimono My House**	Sparks	Island	11	101	**F**

August 1974

This Mnth	Last Mnth	Title	Artist	Label	Wks in 10	US Pos	
1	1	**Band On The Run**	Paul McCartney & Wings	Apple	49	1	**P**
2	2	**Tubular Bells**	Mike Oldfield	Virgin	74	3	**FP**
3	3	**The Singles 1969-1973**	Carpenters	A&M	64	1	**2P**
4	10	**Kimono My House**	Sparks	Island	11	101	**F**
5	7	**Another Time, Another Place**	Bryan Ferry	Island	14		
6	-	**Fulfillingness' First Finale**	Stevie Wonder	Tamla-Motown	4	1	
7	-	**461 Ocean Boulevard**	Eric Clapton	RSO	7	1	
8	-	**Dark Side Of The Moon**	Pink Floyd	Harvest	43	1	**2P**
9	4	**Caribou**	Elton John	DJM	6	1	
10	-	**Welcome Back My Friends To The Show That Never Ends - Ladies & Gentlemen I Give You: Emerson Lake & Palmer**	Emerson, Lake & Palmer	Manticore	2	4	

September 1974

This Mnth	Last Mnth	Title	Artist	Label	Wks in 10	US Pos	
1	2	**Tubular Bells**	Mike Oldfield	Virgin	74	3	**FP**
2	1	**Band On The Run**	Paul McCartney & Wings	Apple	49	1	**P**
3	-	**Hergest Ridge**	Mike Oldfield	Virgin	7	87	
4	5	**Another Time, Another Place**	Bryan Ferry	Island	14		
5	3	**The Singles 1969-1973**	Carpenters	A&M	64	1	**2P**
6	7	**461 Ocean Boulevard**	Eric Clapton	RSO	7	1	
7	-	**Back Home Again**	John Denver	RCA	10	1	
8	-	**Our Best To You**	Osmonds	MGM	4		**L**
9	8	**Dark Side Of The Moon**	Pink Floyd	Harvest	43	1	**2P**
10	-	**The Psychomodo**	Cockney Rebel	EMI	3		**F**

US 1974

JULY-SEPT

July 1974

This Mnth	Last Mnth	Title	Artist	Label	Wks in 10	UK Pos	
1	-	**Caribou**	Elton John	MCA	14	1	2P
2	1	**Band On The Run**	Wings	Apple	32	1	3P
3	-	**Back Home Again**	John Denver	RCA	23	3	
4	-	**Journey To The Centre Of The Earth**	Rick Wakeman	A&M	6	1	FL
5	3	**Sundown**	Gordon Lightfoot	Reprise	8	45	FP
6	4	**Buddah And The Chocolate Box**	Cat Stevens	A&M	13	3	
7	-	**Diamond Dogs**	David Bowie	RCA	4	1	F
8	2	**The Sting (Soundtrack)**	Marvin Hamlisch	MCA	15	7	FL
9	6	**John Denver's Greatest Hits**	John Denver	RCA	28		
10	-	**Before The Flood**	Bob Dylan	Asylum	5	8	

August 1974

This Mnth	Last Mnth	Title	Artist	Label	Wks in 10	UK Pos	
1	3	**Back Home Again**	John Denver	RCA	23	3	
2	-	**461 Ocean Boulevard**	Eric Clapton	RSO	9	3	
3	1	**Caribou**	Elton John	MCA	14	1	2P
4	-	**Bachman-Turner Overdrive II**	Bachman-Turner Overdrive	Mercury	11		F
5	10	**Before The Flood**	Bob Dylan	Asylum	5	8	
6	-	**Fulfillingness' First Finale**	Stevie Wonder	Tamla	7	5	
7	-	**On Stage**	Loggins & Messina	Columbia	9		P
8	4	**Journey To The Centre Of The Earth**	Rick Wakeman	A&M	6	1	FL
9	-	**Bad Company**	Bad Company	Swan Song	8	3	F4P
10	-	**Bridge Of Sighs**	Robin Trower	Chrysalis	3		F

September 1974

This Mnth	Last Mnth	Title	Artist	Label	Wks in 10	UK Pos	
1	6	**Fulfillingness' First Finale**	Stevie Wonder	Tamla	7	5	
2	9	**Bad Company**	Bad Company	Swan Song	8	3	F4P
3	-	**Endless Summer**	Beach Boys	Capitol	6		
4	2	**461 Ocean Boulevard**	Eric Clapton	RSO	9	3	
5	-	**If You Love Me, Let Me Know**	Olivia Newton-John	MCA	6		F
6	-	**Rags To Rufus**	Rufus Featuring				
			Chaka Khan	ABC	4		F
7	4	**Bachman-Turner Overdrive II**	Bachman-Turner Overdrive	Mercury	11		F
8	3	**Caribou**	Elton John	MCA	14	1	2P
9	1	**Back Home Again**	John Denver	RCA	23	3	
10	-	**Chicago VII**	Chicago	Columbia	14		P

• Solo male artists held nine of the Top 10 positions in July – and the only other chart act, Wings, was basically Paul McCartney with a backing band.

• Several important and influential acts debuted in the Top 10 including David Bowie, Rufus featuring Chaka Kahn, Texan rockers ZZ Top and Steely Dan. For the record, the latter act had lost its noted guitarist Jeff 'Skunk' Baxter who defected to The Doobie Brothers. Other rock bands denting the chart for the first time were veteran Dutch group Golden Earring with **Moontan**, Little Feat with **Feats Don't Fail Me Now** and Canadian trio Rush with their eponymous LP.

• The Grateful Dead picked up gold albums for both **Workingman's Dead** and **American Beauty**. The act, who amazingly did not crack the Top 10 until 1987, had already notched up half a dozen Top 100 entries.

• Among the live albums doing well were **Marvin Gaye Live** and the double albums **Before The Flood** and **On Stage** from Bob Dylan and Loggins & Messina respectively. For the record, a David Bowie show in Philadelphia was recorded for later release as **David Live**.

UK 1974 OCT-DEC

• In the last few weeks before The Beatles & Co partnership was officially dissolved, ex-member John Lennon scored his first American Number 1 album and single with **Walls and Bridges** and 'Whatever Gets You Thru The Night'. George Harrison became the first ex-Beatle to tour America, and whilst on the road he found time to lunch at the White House with President Ford. As the year ended, Harrison's **Dark Horse** was heading towards the Top 20 where Ringo Starr's **Goodnight Vienna** was already situated.

• Elton John, who had recently re-signed with MCA for a record $8 million, ended 1974 with his first volume of **Greatest Hits** topping the chart on both sides of the Atlantic. In fact, this collection was America's most successful chart album of the year.

• Early Seventies pop giants Slade said goodbye to the Top 10 with **Slade In Flame**, while new teen idols Bay City Rollers with **Rollin'**, Mud with **Mud Rock** and Showaddywaddy with **Showaddywaddy** cracked the Top 10 for the first time.

• Mick Taylor exited The Rolling Stones after a five-year stint and Americans Stevie Nicks and Lindsay Buckingham were the latest additions to British band Fleetwood Mac.

October 1974

This Mnth	Last Mnth	Title	Artist	Label	Wks in 10	US Pos	
1	1	**Tubular Bells**	Mike Oldfield	Virgin	74	3	**FP**
2	-	**Rollin'**	Bay City Rollers	Bell	26		**F**
3	7	**Back Home Again**	John Denver	RCA	10	1	
4	3	**Hergest Ridge**	Mike Oldfield	Virgin	7	87	
5	2	**Band On The Run**	Paul McCartney & Wings	Apple	49	1	**P**
6	-	**Smiler**	Rod Stewart	Mercury	6	13	
7	5	**The Singles 1969-1973**	Carpenters	A&M	64	1	**2P**
8	4	**Another Time, Another Place**	Bryan Ferry	Island	14		
9	-	**Rainbow**	Peters & Lee	Philips	3		
10	-	**Walls And Bridges**	John Lennon	Apple	2	1	

November 1974

This Mnth	Last Mnth	Title	Artist	Label	Wks in 10	US Pos	
1	2	**Rollin'**	Bay City Rollers	Bell	26		**F**
2	1	**Tubular Bells**	Mike Oldfield	Virgin	74	3	**FP**
3	6	**Smiler**	Rod Stewart	Mercury	6	13	
4	-	**It's Only Rock 'n' Roll**	Rolling Stones	Rolling Stones	3	1	
5	-	**Elton John's Greatest Hits**	Elton John	DJM	22	1	
6	-	**David Essex**	David Essex	CBS	15		
7	-	**David Live**	David Bowie	RCA	3	8	
8	-	**Can't Get Enough**	Barry White	20th Century	16	1	**F**
9	-	**Sheer Heart Attack**	Queen	EMI	12	12	
10	-	**Just A Boy**	Leo Sayer	Chrysalis	4	16	

December 1974

This Mnth	Last Mnth	Title	Artist	Label	Wks in 10	US Pos	
1	5	**Elton John's Greatest Hits**	Elton John	DJM	22	1	
2	6	**David Essex**	David Essex	CBS	15		
3	1	**Rollin'**	Bay City Rollers	Bell	26		**F**
4	8	**Can't Get Enough**	Barry White	20th Century	16	1	**F**
5	9	**Sheer Heart Attack**	Queen	EMI	12	12	
6	2	**Tubular Bells**	Mike Oldfield	Virgin	74	3	**FP**
7	-	**Relayer**	Yes	Atlantic	4	5	
8	-	**Country Life**	Roxy Music	Island	3	37	
9	-	**Engelbert Humperdinck - His Greatest Hits**	Engelbert Humperdinck	Decca	14	103	**L**
10	-	**Slade In Flame**	Slade	Polydor	2	93	**L**

US 1974 OCT-DEC

October 1974

This Mnth	Last Mnth	Title	Artist	Label	Wks in 10	UK Pos	
1	-	**Can't Get Enough**	Barry White	20th Century	7	4	F
2	-	**Not Fragile**	Bachman-Turner Overdrive	Mercury	15	12	
3	5	**If You Love Me, Let Me Know**	Olivia Newton-John	MCA	6		F
4	9	**Back Home Again**	John Denver	RCA	23	3	
5	-	**So Far**	Crosby, Stills, Nash & Young	Atlantic	5	25	6PL
6	-	**Welcome Back, My Friends, To The Show**	Emerson, Lake & Palmer	Manticore	5	5	L
7	2	**Bad Company**	Bad Company	Swan Song	8	3	F4P
8	8	**Caribou**	Elton John	MCA	14	1	2P
9	3	**Endless Summer**	Beach Boys	Capitol	6		
10	-	**Wrap Around Joy**	Carole King	Ode	5		

November 1974

This Mnth	Last Mnth	Title	Artist	Label	Wks in 10	UK Pos	
1	-	**Walls And Bridges**	John Lennon	Apple	6	6	
2	-	**Photographs & Memories/ His Greatest Hits**	Jim Croce	ABC	8		PL
3	2	**Not Fragile**	Bachman-Turner Overdrive	Mercury	15	12	
4	-	**It's Only Rock 'n' Roll**	Rolling Stones	Rolling Stones	7	2	
5	-	**Holiday**	America	Warner	7		
6	10	**Wrap Around Joy**	Carole King	Ode	5		
7	5	**So Far**	Crosby, Stills, Nash & Young	Atlantic	5	25	6PL
8	-	**Cheech & Chong's Wedding Album**	Cheech & Chong	Ode	3		L
9	1	**Can't Get Enough**	Barry White	20th Century	7	4	F
10	-	**Elton John - Greatest Hits**	Elton John	MCA	11	1	10P

December 1974

This Mnth	Last Mnth	Title	Artist	Label	Wks in 10	UK Pos	
1	10	**Elton John - Greatest Hits**	Elton John	MCA	11	1	10P
2	4	**It's Only Rock 'n' Roll**	Rolling Stones	Rolling Stones	7	2	
3	-	**War Child**	Jethro Tull	Chrysalis	16	14	
4	-	**Serenade**	Neil Diamond	Columbia	8	11	P
5	3	**Not Fragile**	Bachman-Turner Overdrive	Mercury	15	12	
6	-	**Verities & Balderdash**	Harry Chapin	Elektra	7		FL
7	-	**Back Home Again**	John Denver	RCA	23	3	
8	-	**Fire**	Ohio Players	Mercury	10		F
9	-	**Mother Lode**	Loggins & Messina	Columbia	4		L
10	1	**Walls And Bridges**	John Lennon	Apple	6	6	

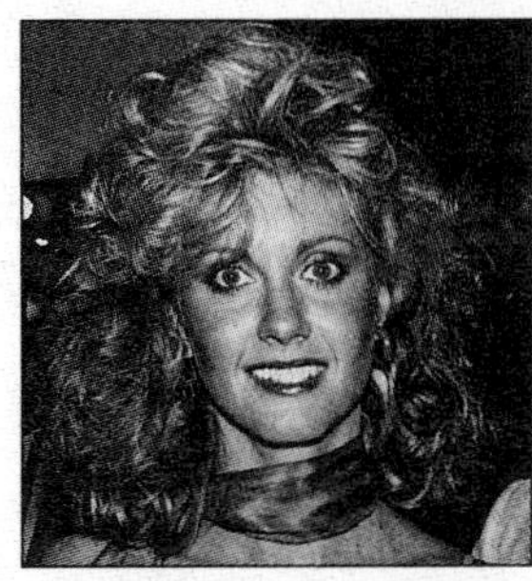

• **Endless Summer** gave The Beach Boys their first chart topper since 1964. It was followed at Number 1 by Olivia Newton-John's **If You Love Me, Let Me Know**, which included the Grammy-winning single 'I Honestly Love You'. British born/Australian raised Olivia shared the *Billboard* Award with Dolly Parton for America's Top Female Country Artist of 1974 – a fact that annoyed many in the country music community.

• Barry White's first solo Top 10 entry, **Can't Get Enough**, was the biggest R&B album of the quarter. The disk, which included his chart topping single 'You're The First, The Last, My Everything', was his first and last Number 1 pop album. Among the other noteworthy R&B records that reached the pop Top 20 were **Fire** from the funky Ohio Players, **Live It Up** by the Isley Brothers, **Do It ('Til You're Satisfied)** from funk/disco band B.T. Express and **Caught Up** by raunchy rapper Millie Jackson.

UK 1975 JAN-MAR

• Critics on both sides of the Atlantic agreed that **Blood On The Tracks**, the first album released by Bob Dylan under his new Columbia contract, was his best recording for some time. *Rolling Stone* devoted the whole review page to it and the *NME* voted it Album of the Year.

• John Lennon released **Rock'n' Roll,** a collection of his favorite early rock songs. It would be his last recording for five years. His ex-songwriting partner, Paul McCartney, had no intention of dropping out of the business. He was recording in New Orleans with legendary R&B producer/composer/pianist Allen Toussaint.

• Paul McCartney & Wings were awarded the Grammy for Best Pop Vocal Group Performance for **Band On The Run**. The year's biggest winner was Stevie Wonder, whose four awards included Album of the Year for **Fullfillingness' First Finale**. Elvis Presley also joined the winners; his LP **How Great Thou Art** walked away with the trophy for Best Inspirational Record.

• The 11-week chart topping run of **Elton John's Greatest Hits** was ended by a similar collection from MOR megastar Engelbert Humperdinck. Soon afterwards the latter's label and managerial stable-mate, Tom Jones, took over the top spot with an album of his biggest hits.

January 1975

This Mnth	Last Mnth	Title	Artist	Label	Wks in 10	US Pos	
1	1	**Elton John's Greatest Hits**	Elton John	DJM	22	1	
2	2	**David Essex**	David Essex	CBS	15		
3	6	**Tubular Bells**	Mike Oldfield	Virgin	74	3	FP
4	9	**Engelbert Humperdinck - His Greatest Hits**	Engelbert Humperdinck	Decca	14	103	L
5	4	**Can't Get Enough**	Barry White	20th Century	16	1	F
6	-	**Greatest Hits**	Simon & Garfunkel	CBS	59	5	2P
7	-	**The Singles 1969-1973**	Carpenters	A&M	64	1	2P
8	3	**Rollin'**	Bay City Rollers	Bell	26		F
9	-	**Band On The Run**	Paul McCartney & Wings	Apple	49	1	P
10	-	**Dark Side Of The Moon**	Pink Floyd	Harvest	43	1	2P

February 1975

This Mnth	Last Mnth	Title	Artist	Label	Wks in 10	US Pos	
1	4	**Engelbert Humperdinck - His Greatest Hits**	Engelbert Humperdinck	Decca	14	103	L
2	1	**Elton John's Greatest Hits**	Elton John	DJM	22	1	
3	3	**Tubular Bells**	Mike Oldfield	Virgin	74	3	FP
4	7	**The Singles 1969-1973**	Carpenters	A&M	64	1	2P
5	-	**Sheer Heart Attack**	Queen	EMI	12	12	
6	6	**Greatest Hits**	Simon & Garfunkel	CBS	59	5	2P
7	2	**David Essex**	David Essex	CBS	15		
8	10	**Dark Side Of The Moon**	Pink Floyd	Harvest	43	1	2P
9	5	**Can't Get Enough**	Barry White	20th Century	16	1	F
10	-	**Blood On The Tracks**	Bob Dylan	CBS	4	1	

March 1975

This Mnth	Last Mnth	Title	Artist	Label	Wks in 10	US Pos	
1	-	**On The Level**	Status Quo	Vertigo	5		
2	-	**Physical Graffiti**	Led Zeppelin	Swan Song	6	1	
3	1	**Engelbert Humperdinck - His Greatest Hits**	Engelbert Humperdinck	Decca	14	103	L
4	2	**Elton John's Greatest Hits**	Elton John	DJM	22	1	
5	4	**The Singles 1969-1973**	Carpenters	A&M	64	1	2P
6	-	**20 Greatest Hits**	Tom Jones	Decca	12		
7	-	**The Shirley Bassey Singles Album**	Shirley Bassey	UA	8		
8	3	**Tubular Bells**	Mike Oldfield	Virgin	74	3	FP
9	6	**Greatest Hits**	Simon & Garfunkel	CBS	59	5	2P
10	-	**The Best Years Of Our Lives**	Steve Harley & Cockney Rebel	EMI	3		L

US 1975

JAN-MAR

January 1975

This Mnth	Last Mnth	Title	Artist	Label	Wks in 10	UK Pos	
1	1	**Elton John - Greatest Hits**	Elton John	MCA	11	1	**10P**
2	8	**Fire**	Ohio Players	Mercury	10		**F**
3	-	**Miles Of Aisles**	Joni Mitchell	Asylum	8	34	
4	7	**Back Home Again**	John Denver	RCA	23	3	
5	3	**War Child**	Jethro Tull	Chrysalis	16	14	
6	-	**Dark Horse**	George Harrison	Apple	5		
7	4	**Serenade**	Neil Diamond	Columbia	8	11	**P**
8	-	**Heart Like A Wheel**	Linda Ronstadt	Capitol	11		**F2P**
9	6	**Verities & Balderdash**	Harry Chapin	Elektra	7		**FL**
10	-	**Relayer**	Yes	Atlantic	4	4	

February 1975

This Mnth	Last Mnth	Title	Artist	Label	Wks in 10	UK Pos	
1	8	**Heart Like A Wheel**	Linda Ronstadt	Capitol	11		**F2P**
2	3	**Miles Of Aisles**	Joni Mitchell	Asylum	8	34	
3	-	**AWB**	Average White Band	Atalantic	9	6	**F**
4	2	**Fire**	Ohio Players	Mercury	10		**F**
5	5	**War Child**	Jethro Tull	Chrysalis	16	14	
6	1	**Elton John - Greatest Hits**	Elton John	MCA	11	1	**10P**
7	-	**Blood On The Tracks**	Bob Dylan	Columbia	9	4	**2P**
8	6	**Dark Horse**	George Harrison	Apple	5		
9	10	**Relayer**	Yes	Atlantic	4	4	
10	-	**Do It ('Til You're Satisfied)**	B.T. Express	Roadshow	5		**FL**

March 1975

This Mnth	Last Mnth	Title	Artist	Label	Wks in 10	UK Pos	
1	7	**Blood On The Tracks**	Bob Dylan	Columbia	9	4	**2P**
2	-	**Have You Never Been Mellow**	Olivia Newton-John	MCA	12	37	
3	-	**Physical Graffiti**	Led Zeppelin	Swan Song	12	1	**4P**
4	-	**What Were Once Vices Are Now Habits**	Doobie Brothers	Warner	10	19	**P**
5	-	**Phoebe Snow**	Phoebe Snow	Shelter	5		**FL**
6	1	**Heart Like A Wheel**	Linda Ronstadt	Capitol	11		**F2P**
7	-	**Perfect Angel**	Minnie Riperton	Epic	6	33	**FL**
8	3	**AWB**	Average White Band	Atalantic	9	6	**F**
9	-	**Nightbirds**	LaBelle	Epic	4		**FL**
10	10	**Do It ('Til You're Satisfied)**	B.T. Express	Roadshow	5		**FL**

• Led Zeppelin-mania gripped America. The 60,000 tickets for their Madison Square Garden gigs sold out in a record four hours. They became the first act in history to have six albums in the chart simultaneously, when their entire back catalog returned to the chart. The group's first release on their own Swan Song label, **Physical Graffiti**, topped the charts on both sides of the Atlantic.

• Female artists were really making their presence felt. Joni Mitchell's **Miles Of Aisles**, Olivia Newton-John's **Have You Never Been Mellow** and ex-Stone Ponys' vocalist Linda Ronstadt's (above) **Heart Like A Wheel** all climbed into the Top 3. In March they were joined in the Top 10 by Phoebe Snow, R&B trio LaBelle, featuring Patti LaBelle and Minnie Riperton. Other ladies making their mark included chart debutante Emmylou Harris with **Pieces Of The Sky** and Melissa Manchester, whose **Melissa** was the biggest hit of her career.

UK 1975 APR-JUNE

• Elton John was riding on the crest of a wave. His album **Captain Fantastic And The Brown Dirt Cowboy**, which became the first album to enter the American chart at Number 1, went on to become America's Top Album of 1975. Elton attracted 80,000 fans to a concert at Wembley Stadium, supported by top-line US acts The Eagles and Rufus. He also brought the house down when he unexpectedly joined The Eagles and The Doobie Brothers on stage at California's Oakland Coliseum.

• The tartan teeny bop idols Bay City Rollers entered the British album chart at Number 1 with **Once Upon A Star** which was joined in the Top 3 by their previous LP, **Rollin'**. The former album was voted Top LP of 1975 by the readers of *Record Mirror*.

• British acts debuting in the American Top 20 included Queen with **Sheer Heart Attack**, Ace, who featured Paul Carrack, with **Five A Side**, Justin Hayward and John Lodge with **Blue Jays** and Leo Sayer with **Just A Boy**.

April 1975

This Mnth	Last Mnth	Title	Artist	Label	Wks in 10	US Pos	
1	6	**20 Greatest Hits**	Tom Jones	Decca	12		
2	7	**The Shirley Bassey Singles Album**	Shirley Bassey	UA	8		
3	-	**The Best Of The Stylistics**	Stylistics	Avco	32	41	F
4	-	**Young Americans**	David Bowie	RCA	3	9	
5	-	**Straight Shooter**	Bad Company	Island	6	3	
6	-	**Rollin'**	Bay City Rollers	Bell	26		F
7	-	**Bluejays**	Justin Hayward & John Lodge	Threshhold	7	16	FL
8	-	**The Myths And Legends Of King Arthur And The Knights Of The Round Table**	Rick Wakeman	A&M	5	21	
9	-	**The Original Soundtrack**	10 C.C.	Mercury	19	15	
10	4	**Elton John's Greatest Hits**	Elton John	DJM	22	1	

May 1975

This Mnth	Last Mnth	Title	Artist	Label	Wks in 10	US Pos	
1	-	**Once Upon A Star**	Bay City Rollers	Bell	23		
2	3	**The Best Of The Stylistics**	Stylistics	Avco	32	41	F
3	6	**Rollin'**	Bay City Rollers	Bell	26		F
4	1	**20 Greatest Hits**	Tom Jones	Decca	12		
5	8	**The Myths And Legends Of King Arthur And The Knights Of The Round Table**	Rick Wakeman	A&M	5	21	
6	5	**Straight Shooter**	Bad Company	Island	6	3	
7	-	**The Singles 1969-1973**	Carpenters	A&M	64	1	2P
8	9	**The Original Soundtrack**	10 C.C.	Mercury	19	15	
9	-	**Tubular Bells**	Mike Oldfield	Virgin	74	3	FP
10	2	**The Shirley Bassey Singles Album**	Shirley Bassey	UA	8		

June 1975

This Mnth	Last Mnth	Title	Artist	Label	Wks in 10	US Pos	
1	2	**The Best Of The Stylistics**	Stylistics	Avco	32	41	F
2	-	**Captain Fantastic And The Brown Dirt Cowboy**	Elton John	DJM	13	1	
3	1	**Once Upon A Star**	Bay City Rollers	Bell	23		
4	-	**The Best Of Tammy Wynette**	Tammy Wynette	Epic	5		F
5	-	**Venus And Mars**	Wings	Apple	14	1	
6	-	**Autobahn**	Kraftwerk	Vertigo	5	5	F
7	8	**The Original Soundtrack**	10 C.C.	Mercury	19	15	
8	-	**Take Good Care Of Yourself**	Three Degrees	Philly Int.	6		F
9	-	**Horizon**	Carpenters	A&M	16	13	
10	7	**The Singles 1969-1973**	Carpenters	A&M	64	1	2P

US 1975

APR-JUNE

April 1975

This Mnth	Last Mnth	Title	Artist	Label	Wks in 10	UK Pos	
1	3	**Physical Graffiti**	Led Zeppelin	Swan Song	12	1	**4P**
2	2	**Have You Never Been Mellow**	Olivia Newton-John	MCA	12	37	
3	-	**An Evening With John Denver**	John Denver	RCA	10		
4	-	**Chicago VIII**	Chicago	Columbia	11		**P**
5	-	**For Earth Below**	Robin Trower	Chrysalis	6	26	
6	1	**Blood On The Tracks**	Bob Dylan	Columbia	9	4	**2P**
7	-	**Autobahn**	Kraftwerk	Vertigo	5	4	**FL**
8	-	**Rock 'n' Roll**	John Lennon	Apple	5	6	
9	-	**That's The Way Of The World (Soundtrack)**	Earth, Wind & Fire	Columbia	21		**F2P**
10	7	**Perfect Angel**	Minnie Riperton	Epic	6	33	**FL**

May 1975

This Mnth	Last Mnth	Title	Artist	Label	Wks in 10	UK Pos	
1	9	**That's The Way Of The World (Soundtrack)**	Earth, Wind & Fire	Columbia	21		**F2P**
2	4	**Chicago VIII**	Chicago	Columbia	11		**P**
3	1	**Physical Graffiti**	Led Zeppelin	Swan Song	12	1	**4P**
4	-	**Tommy**	Soundtrack	Polydor	11	21	
5	-	**Straight Shooter**	Bad Company	Swan Song	5	3	**3P**
6	2	**Have You Never Been Mellow**	Olivia Newton-John	MCA	12	37	
7	-	**Funny Lady (Soundtrack)**	Barbra Streisand	Arista	4		
8	-	**Blow By Blow**	Jeff Beck	Epic	4		**FPL**
9	-	**Crash Landing**	Jimi Hendrix	Reprise	4	35	**L**
10	-	**Welcome To My Nightmare**	Alice Cooper	Warner	10	19	**PL**

June 1975

This Mnth	Last Mnth	Title	Artist	Label	Wks in 10	UK Pos	
1	-	**Captain Fantastic And The Brown Dirt Cowboy**	Elton John	MCA	17	2	**3P**
2	1	**That's The Way Of The World (Soundtrack)**	Earth, Wind & Fire	Columbia	21		**F2P**
3	4	**Tommy**	Soundtrack	Polydor	11	21	
4	10	**Welcome To My Nightmare**	Alice Cooper	Warner	10	19	**PL**
5	-	**Venus And Mars**	Wings	Capitol	8	1	**P**
6	-	**Stampede**	Doobie Brothers	Warner	4	14	
7	2	**Chicago VIII**	Chicago	Columbia	11		**P**
8	-	**Hearts**	America	Warner	6		
9	-	**Four Wheel Drive**	Bachman-Turner Overdrive	Mercury	4		**L**
10	8	**Blow By Blow**	Jeff Beck	Epic	4		**FPL**

• Over 120,000 fans attended a celebration of 'Human Kindness Day' at the Washington Monument – headliner was Stevie Wonder. As part of their US tour, The Rolling Stones played six shows at Madison Square Garden. The tour, which featured the quintet's new guitarist Ron Wood, grossed $13 million. Also earning big bucks on the road was a tour by The Beach Boys and Chicago, whose **Chicago VIII** gave them their third successive chart topper. It was seen by over 700,000 who paid more than $7 million for the privilege.

• Rock giants making their last trip to the Top 10 included the late Jimi Hendrix with **Crash Landing**, Canada's Bachman Turner Overdrive with **Four Wheel Drive** and **Welcome To My Nightmare** by Alice Cooper. Simultaneously, groundbreaking German electronic duo Kraftwerk with **Autobahn** and British guitar virtuoso Jeff Beck with **Blow By Blow**, reached the Top 10 for the only time.

• Album chart debuts were made by the talented Manhattan Transfer, Ambrosia and Journey with self-titled LPs and reggae superstar Bob Marley with **Natty Dread**. British acts making their first US chart dents included comedy team Monty Python with **Matching Tie & Handkerchief** and Robert Palmer with **Sneakin' Sally Through The Alley**.

UK 1975 JULY-SEPT

• Smooth vocal group The Stylistics had two simultaneous Top 5 entries: **Thank You Baby** and **The Best Of The Stylistics**. The latter headed the chart for two months and went on to become Britain's top album of 1975. The Three Degrees were another US R&B group that were now more successful in Britain. The female Philadelphian trio reached the Top 10 with **Take Good Care Of Yourself**.

• The British pop film *Never Too Young To Rock* went on general release. It starred glam/glitter rock acts Mud, The Glitter Band and The Rubettes – who had all passed their sales peak date.

• The album chart in Britain was extended to a Top 60 – it stayed that way until late 1978.

• Pink Floyd, whose **Wish You Were Here** was heading to the top, performed their first British gig of 1975 at the Knebworth Festival. It was one of their most spectacular shows and included real Spitfire aircraft. Another internationally successful British rock band, Black Sabbath, who were scoring with **Sabotage**, made their New York debut at Madison Square Garden.

July 1975

This Mnth	Last Mnth	Title	Artist	Label	Wks in 10	US Pos	
1	9	**Horizon**	Carpenters	A&M	16	13	
2	5	**Venus And Mars**	Wings	Apple	14	1	
3	2	**Captain Fantastic And The Brown Dirt Cowboy**	Elton John	DJM	13	1	
4	1	**The Best Of The Stylistics**	Stylistics	Avco	32	41	**F**
5	3	**Once Upon A Star**	Bay City Rollers	Bell	23		
6	7	**The Original Soundtrack**	10 C.C.	Mercury	19	15	
7	-	**Step Two**	Showaddywaddy	Bell	3		
8	-	**One Of These Nights**	Eagles	Asylum	11	1	**F**
9	-	**Rollin'**	Bay City Rollers	Bell	26		**F**
10	-	**Return To Fantasy**	Uriah Heep	Bronze	1	85	**FL**

August 1975

This Mnth	Last Mnth	Title	Artist	Label	Wks in 10	US Pos	
1	1	**Horizon**	Carpenters	A&M	16	13	
2	4	**The Best Of The Stylistics**	Stylistics	Avco	32	41	**F**
3	2	**Venus And Mars**	Wings	Apple	14	1	
4	5	**Once Upon A Star**	Bay City Rollers	Bell	23		
5	3	**Captain Fantastic And The Brown Dirt Cowboy**	Elton John	DJM	13	1	
6	-	**Ten Years Non-Stop Jubilee**	James Last	Polydor	3		
7	-	**Mud Rock Vol. 2**	Mud	RAK	5		**L**
8	-	**Thank You Baby**	Stylistics	Avco	5	72	
9	-	**Atlantic Crossing**	Rod Stewart	Warner	24	9	
10	8	**One Of These Nights**	Eagles	Asylum	11	1	**F**

September 1975

This Mnth	Last Mnth	Title	Artist	Label	Wks in 10	US Pos	
1	9	**Atlantic Crossing**	Rod Stewart	Warner	24	9	
2	2	**The Best Of The Stylistics**	Stylistics	Avco	32	41	**F**
3	-	**Greatest Hits**	Cat Stevens	Island	10	6	
4	1	**Horizon**	Carpenters	A&M	16	13	
5	4	**Once Upon A Star**	Bay City Rollers	Bell	23		
6	8	**Thank You Baby**	Stylistics	Avco	5	72	
7	-	**The Very Best Of Roger Whittaker**	Roger Whittaker	CBS	10		**FL**
8	-	**Wish You Were Here**	Pink Floyd	Harvest	7	1	
9	10	**One Of These Nights**	Eagles	Asylum	11	1	**F**
10	-	**Tubular Bells**	Mike Oldfield	Virgin	74	3	**FP**

US 1975 JULY-SEPT

July 1975

This Mnth	Last Mnth	Title	Artist	Label	Wks in 10	UK Pos	
1	5	**Venus And Mars**	Wings	Capitol	8	1	P
2	1	**Captain Fantastic And The Brown Dirt Cowboy**	Elton John	MCA	17	2	3P
3	-	**One Of These Nights**	Eagles	Asylum	18	8	F
4	-	**Love Will Keep Us Together**	Captain & Tennille	A&M	9		F
5	2	**That's The Way Of The World (Soundtrack)**	Earth, Wind & Fire	Columbia	21		F2P
6	-	**Cut The Cake**	Average White Band	Atlantic	9	28	
7	-	**Made In The Shade**	Rolling Stones	Rolling Stones	4	14	
8	6	**Stampede**	Doobie Brothers	Warner	4	14	
9	-	**Metamorphosis**	Rolling Stones	Abko	3	45	
10	9	**Four Wheel Drive**	Bachman-Turner Overdrive	Mercury	4		L

August 1975

This Mnth	Last Mnth	Title	Artist	Label	Wks in 10	UK Pos	
1	3	**One Of These Nights**	Eagles	Asylum	18	8	F
2	-	**The Heat Is On**	Isley Brothers	T-Neck	11		P
3	2	**Captain Fantastic And The Brown Dirt Cowboy**	Elton John	MCA	17	2	3P
4	6	**Cut The Cake**	Average White Band	Atlantic	9	28	
5	-	**Red Octopus**	Jefferson Starship	Grunt	21		
6	4	**Love Will Keep Us Together**	Captain & Tennille	A&M	9		F
7	-	**Greatest Hits**	Cat Stevens	A&M	8	2	3P
8	-	**Between The Lines**	Janis Ian	Columbia	9		FPL
9	-	**Gorilla**	James Taylor	Warner	6		
10	1	**Venus And Mars**	Wings	Capitol	8	1	P

September 1975

This Mnth	Last Mnth	Title	Artist	Label	Wks in 10	UK Pos	
1	5	**Red Octopus**	Jefferson Starship	Grunt	21		
2	8	**Between The Lines**	Janis Ian	Columbia	9		FPL
3	2	**The Heat Is On**	Isley Brothers	T-Neck	11		P
4	3	**Captain Fantastic And The Brown Dirt Cowboy**	Elton John	MCA	17	2	3P
5	1	**One Of These Nights**	Eagles	Asylum	18	8	F
6	-	**Honey**	Ohio Players	Mercury	8		L
7	7	**Greatest Hits**	Cat Stevens	A&M	8	2	3P
8	-	**Born To Run**	Bruce Springsteen	Columbia	11	17	F4P
9	-	**The Basement Tapes**	Bob Dylan	Columbia	4	8	
10	-	**That's The Way Of The World (Soundtrack)**	Earth, Wind & Fire	Columbia	21		F2P

• Three of the Seventies most successful album artists made their first Top 10 entrances: The Eagles (above) with **One Of These Nights**, Fleetwood Mac with their eponymous album and Bruce Springsteen with **Born To Run**.

• Disco music, which was selling stacks of singles, was also making its mark on the album charts. Among the most popular disco LPs were **Non Stop** by B.T. Express, KC & The Sunshine Band's self-titled album and **Disco Baby** by Van McCoy. KC's set included two Number 1 singles, 'Get Down Tonight' and 'That's The Way (I Like It)', and McCoy's LP included the chart topper 'The Hustle'.

• The Grand Ole Opry celebrated its 50th birthday in the year that that country music lost two legendary artists; Bob Wills and Lefty Frizzell. Other country news included Glen Campbell's chart topping single 'Rhinestone Cowboy' and Willie Nelson's pop album debut with **Red Headed Stranger**.

UK 1975 OCT-DEC

• Elton John ended his very successful American tour wearing a sequin-bedecked Dodgers outfit for his two sold-out performances at the Dodgers Stadium in Los Angeles. Amazingly, his **Rock Of The Westies** album repeated the record breaking feat of its predecessor, **Captain Fantastic**, when it too entered the US chart at Number 1.

• MOR music made quite a dent on the UK chart as Christmas approached. Perry Como and the late Jim Reeves hit the top with TV-advertised collections of hits, and the Nigel Brooks Singers, James Last's German orchestra and Peters & Lee also climbed into the Top 10.

• Humorous records were going through an upsurge in popularity. Welsh funny man Max Boyce reached Number 1 with **We All Had Doctors Papers**, Jasper Carrot scored with **Rabbits On And On** and Scottish comedian Billy Connolly hit with **Get Right Intae Him**. There was even room at the bottom of the chart for **The New Goodies LP** and a collection of pre-war Laurel & Hardy recordings.

• Both Bruce Springsteen and The Sex Pistols made their London stage debuts. The former artist having recently been featured on the front covers of both *Time* and *Newsweek* in the USA.

October 1975

This Mnth	Last Mnth	Title	Artist	Label	Wks in 10	US Pos	
1	1	**Atlantic Crossing**	Rod Stewart	Warner	24	9	
2	8	**Wish You Were Here**	Pink Floyd	Harvest	7	1	
3	-	**All The Fun Of The Fair**	David Essex	CBS	9		
4	3	**Greatest Hits**	Cat Stevens	Island	10	6	
5	-	**Favourites**	Peters & Lee	Philips	16		**L**
6	-	**40 Golden Greats**	Jim Reeves	Arcade	14		
7	2	**The Best Of The Stylistics**	Stylistics	Avco	32	41	**F**
8	7	**The Very Best Of Roger Whittaker**	Roger Whittaker	CBS	10		**FL**
9	-	**Another Year**	Leo Sayer	Chrysalis	4	125	
10	4	**Horizon**	Carpenters	A&M	16	13	

November 1975

This Mnth	Last Mnth	Title	Artist	Label	Wks in 10	US Pos	
1	6	**40 Golden Greats**	Jim Reeves	Arcade	14		
1	-	**Breakaway**	Art Garfunkel	CBS	3	7	**F**
2	5	**Favourites**	Peters & Lee	Philips	16		**L**
3	-	**40 Greatest Hits**	Perry Como	K-Tel	15		**L**
4	-	**We All Had Doctors' Papers**	Max Boyce	EMI	5		**F**
5	-	**Siren**	Roxy Music	Island	4	50	
6	1	**Atlantic Crossing**	Rod Stewart	Warner	24	9	
7	-	**Rock Of The Westies**	Elton John	DJM	4	1	
8	-	**Ommadawn**	Mike Oldfield	Virgin	9	146	
9	3	**All The Fun Of The Fair**	David Essex	CBS	9		
10	8	**The Very Best Of Roger Whittaker**	Roger Whittaker	CBS	10		**FL**

December 1975

This Mnth	Last Mnth	Title	Artist	Label	Wks in 10	US Pos	
1	3	**40 Greatest Hits**	Perry Como	K-Tel	15		**L**
2	1	**40 Golden Greats**	Jim Reeves	Arcade	14		
3	-	**A Night At The Opera**	Queen	EMI	12	4	
4	-	**Make The Party Last**	James Last	Polydor	9		
5	2	**Favourites**	Peters & Lee	Philips	16		**L**
6	-	**Wouldn't You Like It**	Bay City Rollers	Bell	7		
7	-	**Songs Of Joy**	Nigel Brooks Singers	K-Tel	5		**FL**
8	-	**24 Original Hits**	Drifters	Atlantic	11		**FL**
9	-	**Get Right Intae Him**	Billy Connolly	Polydor	2		**L**
10	-	**Disco Hits '75**	Various	Arcade	2		

US 1975 OCT-DEC

October 1975

This Mnth	Last Mnth	Title	Artist	Label	Wks in 10	UK Pos	
1	-	Windsong	John Denver	RCA	16	14	
2	-	Wish You Were Here	Pink Floyd	Columbia	9	1	4P
3	5	One Of These Nights	Eagles	Asylum	18	8	F
4	8	Born To Run	Bruce Springsteen	Columbia	11	17	F4P
5	1	Red Octopus	Jefferson Starship	Grunt	21		
6	-	Win, Lose Or Draw	Allman Brothers Band	Capricorn	5		
7	-	Prisoner In Disguise	Linda Ronstadt	Asylum	8		P
8	2	Between The Lines	Janis Ian	Columbia	9		FPL
9	-	Pick Of The Litter	Spinners	Atlantic	5		L
10	-	Minstrel In The Gallery	Jethro Tull	Chrysalis	5	20	

November 1975

This Mnth	Last Mnth	Title	Artist	Label	Wks in 10	UK Pos	
1	5	Red Octopus	Jefferson Starship	Grunt	21		
2	1	Windsong	John Denver	RCA	16	14	
3	-	Rock Of The Westies	Elton John	MCA	7	5	P
4	2	Wish You Were Here	Pink Floyd	Columbia	9	1	4P
5	7	Prisoner In Disguise	Linda Ronstadt	Asylum	8		P
6	4	Born To Run	Bruce Springsteen	Columbia	11	17	F4P
7	-	Still Crazy After All These Years	Paul Simon	Columbia	22	6	
8	-	Wind On The Water	David Crosby/Graham Nash	ABC	6		L
9	10	Minstrel In The Gallery	Jethro Tull	Chrysalis	5	20	
10	-	Extra Texture (Read All About It)	George Harrison	Apple	5	16	

December 1975

This Mnth	Last Mnth	Title	Artist	Label	Wks in 10	UK Pos	
1	-	Chicago IX - Chicago's Greatest Hits	Chicago	Columbia	13		5P
2	1	Red Octopus	Jefferson Starship	Grunt	21		
3	7	Still Crazy After All These Years	Paul Simon	Columbia	22	6	
4	-	Gratitude	Earth, Wind & Fire	Columbia	13		2P
5	2	Windsong	John Denver	RCA	16	14	
6	-	KC & The Sunshine Band	KC & The Sunshine Band	TK	7	26	FL
7	3	Rock Of The Westies	Elton John	MCA	7	5	P
8	-	History/America's Greatest Hits	America	Warner	12	60	L
9	-	The Hissing Of Summer Lawns	Joni Mitchell	Asylum	7	14	L
10	8	Wind On The Water	David Crosby/Graham Nash	ABC	6		L

• Sales of records and tapes in America in 1975 were over $2.36 billion.

• Simon & Garfunkel briefly reunited to plug their newly recorded single, 'My Little Town', on NBC's new TV series *Saturday Night Live*. Paul Simon's solo album **Still Crazy After All These Years** headed the chart and went on to win two Grammy Awards including Album of the Year. Art Garfunkel reached Number 7 on both sides of the Atlantic with **Breakaway** and his single, 'I Only Have Eyes For You', topped the UK chart.

• Jazz saxophonist Grover Washington Jr. paid his second trip to the Top 10 with **Feels So Good**. Also briefly visiting were **Alive!**, the first Top 20 hit for fast rising glam rockers Kiss, and **Save Me** by German-based disco trio Silver Convention. Another German recorded disco artist doing well was American born Donna Summer with her debut LP, **Love To Love You Baby**.

• Chicago scored their fifth successive Number 1 with a greatest hits package, **Chicago IX**, and **Gratitude** made it two toppers in a row for Earth, Wind & Fire. Among other acts hitting the peak was singer/songwriter John Denver; not only did his **Windsong** reach Number 1 but a seasonal album, **Rocky Mountain Christmas**, also climbed into the Top 20.

UK 1976 JAN-MAR

• Fleetwood Mac, whose eponymous album had made little impression in the UK, took it into the US Top 10. It finally went on to top the chart over a year after it had first entered. Peter Frampton was another British act whose current recordings sold better on the other side of the Atlantic. His double album, **Frampton Comes Alive**, topped the chart and went on to become the year's top album. With sales of over six million it is the biggest selling live album of all time as well being the first album to earn a platinum cassette.

• The Beatles refused to play together again despite an offer of $30 million. EMI reissued all 22 of the group's singles and, days before his son Sean was born, John Lennon finally won his battle to stay in the USA.

• Three more veteran American acts found themselves in the UK Top 10 with **Greatest Hits** offerings; The Drifters, Roy Orbison and Slim Whitman. The most surprising of these being country singer/yodeller Whitman, who despite his success in Britain in the mid-Fifties had never really made his mark on the US pop scene.

January 1976

This Mnth	Last Mnth	Title	Artist	Label	Wks in 10	US Pos	
1	3	**A Night At The Opera**	Queen	EMI	12	4	
2	1	**40 Greatest Hits**	Perry Como	K-Tel	15		L
3	8	**24 Original Hits**	Drifters	Atlantic	11		FL
4	6	**Wouldn't You Like It**	Bay City Rollers	Bell	7		
5	4	**Make The Party Last**	James Last	Polydor	9		
6	2	**40 Golden Greats**	Jim Reeves	Arcade	14		
7	-	**The Best Of Roy Orbison**	Roy Orbison	Arcade	10		
8	-	**Ommadawn**	Mike Oldfield	Virgin	9	146	
9	-	**Still Crazy After All These Years**	Paul Simon	CBS	3	1	
10	5	**Favourites**	Peters & Lee	Philips	16		L

February 1976

This Mnth	Last Mnth	Title	Artist	Label	Wks in 10	US Pos	
1	-	**The Very Best Of Slim Whitman**	Slim Whitman	UA	10		F
2	7	**The Best Of Roy Orbison**	Roy Orbison	Arcade	10		
3	-	**Desire**	Bob Dylan	CBS	11	1	
4	-	**Music Express**	Various	K-Tel	7		
5	1	**A Night At The Opera**	Queen	EMI	12	4	
6	3	**24 Original Hits**	Drifters	Atlantic	11		FL
7	-	**Run With The Pack**	Bad Company	Island	5	5	
8	-	**Station To Station**	David Bowie	RCA	3	3	
9	-	**How Dare You?**	10 C.C.	Mercury	11	49	
10	-	**The Best Of Helen Reddy**	Helen Reddy	Capitol	6	5	FL

March 1976

This Mnth	Last Mnth	Title	Artist	Label	Wks in 10	US Pos	
1	1	**The Very Best Of Slim Whitman**	Slim Whitman	UA	10		F
2	-	**A Trick Of The Tail**	Genesis	Charisma	6	31	
3	-	**Carnival**	Manuel & His Music Of The Mountains	Studio Two	7		FL
4	-	**Their Greatest Hits 1971-1975**	Eagles	Asylum	11	1	
5	2	**The Best Of Roy Orbison**	Roy Orbison	Arcade	10		
6	-	**Blue For You**	Status Quo	Vertigo	6		
7	10	**The Best Of Helen Reddy**	Helen Reddy	Capitol	6	5	FL
8	3	**Desire**	Bob Dylan	CBS	11	1	
9	4	**Music Express**	Various	K-Tel	7		
10	7	**Run With The Pack**	Bad Company	Island	5	5	

US 1976 JAN-MAR

January 1976

This Mnth	Last Mnth	Title	Artist	Label	Wks in 10	UK Pos	
1	4	**Gratitude**	Earth, Wind & Fire	Columbia	13		2P
2	1	**Chicago IX - Chicago's Greatest Hits**	Chicago	Columbia	13		5P
3	8	**History/America's Greatest Hits**	America	Warner	12	60	L
4	3	**Still Crazy After All These Years**	Paul Simon	Columbia	22	6	
5	9	**The Hissing Of Summer Lawns**	Joni Mitchell	Asylum	7	14	L
6	-	**Helen Reddy's Greatest Hits**	Helen Reddy	Capitol	7	5	2PL
7	5	**Windsong**	John Denver	RCA	16	14	
8	-	**Family Reunion**	O'Jays	Philly Int.	7		P
9	6	**KC & The Sunshine Band**	KC & The Sunshine Band	TK	7	26	FL
10	-	**Tryin' To Get The Feeling**	Barry Manilow	Arista	4		2P

February 1976

This Mnth	Last Mnth	Title	Artist	Label	Wks in 10	UK Pos	
1	-	**Desire**	Bob Dylan	Columbia	13	3	P
2	4	**Still Crazy After All These Years**	Paul Simon	Columbia	22	6	
3	1	**Gratitude**	Earth, Wind & Fire	Columbia	13		2P
4	2	**Chicago IX - Chicago's Greatest Hits**	Chicago	Columbia	13		5P
5	-	**Station To Station**	David Bowie	RCA	9	5	
6	-	**Frampton Comes Alive!**	Peter Frampton	A&M	51	19	F6P
7	10	**Tryin' To Get The Feeling**	Barry Manilow	Arista	4		2P
8	-	**Fleetwood Mac**	Fleetwood Mac	Reprise	37	23	F5P
9	3	**History/America's Greatest Hits**	America	Warner	12	60	L
10	8	**Family Reunion**	O'Jays	Philly Int.	7		P

March 1976

This Mnth	Last Mnth	Title	Artist	Label	Wks in 10	UK Pos	
1	-	**Eagles/Their Greatest Hits 1971-1975**	Eagles	Asylum	12	2	14P
2	6	**Frampton Comes Alive!**	Peter Frampton	A&M	51	19	F6P
3	1	**Desire**	Bob Dylan	Columbia	13	3	P
4	5	**Station To Station**	David Bowie	RCA	9	5	
5	-	**Thoroughbred**	Carole King	Ode	8		L
6	8	**Fleetwood Mac**	Fleetwood Mac	Reprise	37	23	F5P
7	2	**Still Crazy After All These Years**	Paul Simon	Columbia	22	6	
8	-	**Run With The Pack**	Bad Company	Swan Song	6	4	P
9	-	**Rufus Featuring Chaka Khan**	Rufus Featuring Chaka Khan	ABC	5		L
10	-	**A Night At The Opera**	Queen	Elektra	7	1	F

• The platinum album award was introduced for albums that had sold over a million copies. The first album to receive this award was **Eagles/Their Greatest Hits 1971-1974**, which went on to sell over 14 million copies.

• David Bowie started a new world tour soon after the premiere of his film *The Man Who Fell To Earth*. Early in the tour he, and Iggy Popp were arrested in a hotel room for suspected drug possession.

• As **Desire** shot Bob Dylan to the top of the US chart for the third time, he took his Rolling Thunder Revue to Houston to appear in the *Night Of The Hurricane II* show. Also appearing at the gig were Isaac Hayes, Ringo Starr, Stephen Stills, Carlos Santana and Stevie Wonder who had recently re-signed with Motown for a record $13 million.

• Many of the female artists who had been chart regulars in the early Seventies were losing ground. As Carole King, Joni Mitchell and Helen Reddy enjoyed their last Top 10 entries, Janis Ian and Phoebe Snow reached the Top 20 for the final time with **Aftertones** and **Second Childhood** respectively.

UK 1976 APR-JUNE

• The Rolling Stones, whose **Black And Blue** was their sixth US chart topper, went on an eight-week European tour which included six shows at London's Earls Court. Other successful British shows included The Who's performance at the Charlton football ground, and David Bowie's first UK gigs for three years at Wembley.

• British rockers Gary Wright and Robin Trower, who were both better known in the USA, had their sole US Top 10 entries with **The Dream Weaver** and **Robin Trower Live!**.

• Even though compilation albums again took many slots on the Top 10, Swedish group Abba's **Greatest Hits** managed to hold on to the top spot for nine weeks. Incidentally, the quartet played in front of the King and Queen-to-be of Sweden on the eve of their Royal Wedding.

• John Denver, who recorded live albums in many corners of the world, had the biggest British hit of his career with **Live In London**. Only Abba prevented the singer/songwriter from reaching the top.

• Cliff Richard's album **I'm Nearly Famous** was his most successful newly-recorded album for 10 years. In America, it took Cliff into the US Top 100 for the first time and a single from it, 'Devil Woman', gave him his first Top 10 entry there.

April 1976

This Mnth	Last Mnth	Title	Artist	Label	Wks in 10	US Pos	
1	4	**Their Greatest Hits 1971-1975**	Eagles	Asylum	11	1	
2	-	**Rock Follies (TV Soundtrack)**	Various	Island	8		
3	6	**Blue For You**	Status Quo	Vertigo	6		
4	-	**Diana Ross**	Diana Ross	Tamla-Motown	7	5	
5	-	**Juke Box Jive**	Various	K-Tel	7		
6	-	**Wings At The Speed Of Sound**	Wings	Apple	21	1	
7	-	**Greatest Hits**	Abba	Epic	49	48	**FP**
8	-	**Presence**	Led Zeppelin	Swan Song	5	1	
9	8	**Desire**	Bob Dylan	CBS	11	1	
10	1	**The Very Best Of Slim Whitman**	Slim Whitman	UA	10		**F**

May 1976

This Mnth	Last Mnth	Title	Artist	Label	Wks in 10	US Pos	
1	7	**Greatest Hits**	Abba	Epic	49	48	**FP**
2	-	**Instrumental Gold**	Various	Warwick	11		
3	2	**Rock Follies (TV Soundtrack)**	Various	Island	8		
4	6	**Wings At The Speed Of Sound**	Wings	Apple	21	1	
5	-	**Black And Blue**	Rolling Stones	Rolling Stones	8	1	
6	8	**Presence**	Led Zeppelin	Swan Song	5	1	
7	5	**Juke Box Jive**	Various	K-Tel	7		
8	-	**Live In London**	John Denver	RCA	9		
9	-	**Hit Machine**	Various	K-Tel	4		
10	1	**Their Greatest Hits 1971-1975**	Eagles	Asylum	11	1	

June 1976

This Mnth	Last Mnth	Title	Artist	Label	Wks in 10	US Pos	
1	1	**Greatest Hits**	Abba	Epic	49	48	**FP**
2	8	**Live In London**	John Denver	RCA	9		
3	2	**Instrumental Gold**	Various	Warwick	11		
4	4	**Wings At The Speed Of Sound**	Wings	Apple	21	1	
5	-	**Changesonebowie**	David Bowie	RCA	11	10	
6	5	**Black And Blue**	Rolling Stones	Rolling Stones	8	1	
7	-	**I'm Nearly Famous**	Cliff Richard	EMI	4	76	
8	-	**The Best Of Gladys Knight And The Pips**	Gladys Knight & The Pips	Buddah	6	36	**F**
9	-	**Frampton Comes Alive**	Peter Frampton	A&M	6	1	**FL**
10	9	**Hit Machine**	Various	K-Tel	4		

US 1976

APR-JUNE

April 1976

This Mnth	Last Mnth	Title	Artist	Label	Wks in 10	UK Pos	
1	1	Eagles/Their Greatest Hits 1971-1975	Eagles	Asylum	12	2	14P
2	2	Frampton Comes Alive!	Peter Frampton	A&M	51	19	F6P
3	10	A Night At The Opera	Queen	Elektra	7	1	F
4	5	Thoroughbred	Carole King	Ode	8		L
5	-	Wings At The Speed Of Sound	Wings	Capitol	21	2	P
6	8	Run With The Pack	Bad Company	Swan Song	6	4	P
7	3	Desire	Bob Dylan	Columbia	13	3	P
8	-	Eargasm	Johnnie Taylor	Columbia	6		FL
9	-	The Dream Weaver	Gary Wright	Warner	8		FPL
10	-	Presence	Led Zeppelin	Swan Song	9	1	P

May 1976

This Mnth	Last Mnth	Title	Artist	Label	Wks in 10	UK Pos	
1	5	Wings At The Speed Of Sound	Wings	Capitol	21	2	P
2	10	Presence	Led Zeppelin	Swan Song	9	1	P
3	2	Frampton Comes Alive!	Peter Frampton	A&M	51	19	F6P
4	-	Black And Blue	Rolling Stones	Rolling Stones	9	2	P
5	-	I Want You	Marvin Gaye	Tamla	6	22	
6	1	Eagles/Their Greatest Hits 1971-1975	Eagles	Asylum	12	2	14P
7	-	Fleetwood Mac	Fleetwood Mac	Reprise	37	23	F5P
8	8	Eargasm	Johnnie Taylor	Columbia	6		FL
9	3	A Night At The Opera	Queen	Elektra	7	1	F
10	-	Here And There	Elton John	MCA	5	6	

June 1976

This Mnth	Last Mnth	Title	Artist	Label	Wks in 10	UK Pos	
1	1	Wings At The Speed Of Sound	Wings	Capitol	21	2	P
2	4	Black And Blue	Rolling Stones	Rolling Stones	9	2	P
3	3	Frampton Comes Alive!	Peter Frampton	A&M	51	19	F6P
4	10	Here And There	Elton John	MCA	5	6	
5	-	Diana Ross	Diana Ross	Motown	7	4	
6	-	Rocks	Aerosmith	Columbia	10		F3P
7	7	Fleetwood Mac	Fleetwood Mac	Reprise	37	23	F5P
8	2	Presence	Led Zeppelin	Swan Song	9	1	P
9	-	Breezin'	George Benson	Warner	15		F3P
10	5	I Want You	Marvin Gaye	Tamla	6	22	

• Paul McCartney & Wings' Wings Over America tour was a tremendous success with the group breaking the record for an indoor crowd when 67,000 saw them in Seattle. Their latest album **Wings At The Speed Of Sound** topped the chart which prevented his old band The Beatles from getting their 16th Number 1 with **Rock'n'Roll Music**.

• Several R&B acts tasted Top 20 success for the only time: Johnnie Taylor with **Eargasm**, jazzman Donald Byrd's group, The Blackbyrds, with **City Life**, George Clinton's group Parliament with **Mothership Connection** and Brass Construction with a self-titled set, which also graced the British Top 10.

• Three top album artists of the late Seventies made their Top 10 debuts; Queen, Aerosmith and jazz guitarist/vocalist George Benson. The Top 20 welcomed newcomers Daryl Hall & John Oates with their self-titled album, which included the hit single 'Sara Smiles' and Boz Scaggs with his five million seller, **Silk Degrees**. A mixed bag of acts made their first moves up the Top 200 including John Travolta, punk pioneers The Ramones, Thin Lizzy and The Alan Parsons Project.

UK 1976 JULY-SEPT

• Rotund Greek vocalist Demis Roussos was one of biggest acts in Britain with two simultaneous Top 10 entries, **Happy To Be** and **Forever And Ever**. Fellow Greek, Nana Mouskouri's **Passport** also made the Top 10.

• The Beach Boys' first British Number 1 album, **20 Golden Greats**, fought off all challengers for over two months. During a gig in California, they were joined on stage, for the first time in seven years, by their founder Brian Wilson.

• Almost a quarter of a million fans saw The Rolling Stones and Lynyrd Skynyrd at Knebworth. Other noteworthy gigs included Queen at Hyde Park and The Grateful Dead with Santana at Wembley.

• Punk music was breaking in Britain. The Sex Pistols made their TV debut on *So It Goes*, and The Clash, The Buzzcocks, The Damned, The Stranglers and Siouxsie & The Banshees made their first live appearances. Also helping to build interest was the UK visit by The Ramones and the launch of both Stiff Records and the fanzine *Sniffin' Glue*. Interestingly, the magazine's editor Danny Baker was later to become one of Britain's top TV presenters.

July 1976

This Mnth	Last Mnth	Title	Artist	Label	Wks in 10	US Pos	
1	-	**A Night On The Town**	Rod Stewart	Riva	18	2	
2	1	**Greatest Hits**	Abba	Epic	49	48	FP
3	5	**Changesonebowie**	David Bowie	RCA	11	10	
4	-	**20 Golden Greats**	Beach Boys	Capitol	15		
5	-	**Forever And Ever**	Demis Roussos	Philips	14		F
6	-	**A Kind Of Hush**	Carpenters	A&M	5	33	
7	-	**Happy To Be**	Demis Roussos	Philips	5		L
8	-	**Laughter And Tears - The Best Of Neil Sedaka**	Neil Sedaka	Polydor	13		F
9	2	**Live In London**	John Denver	RCA	9		
10	4	**Wings At The Speed Of Sound**	Wings	Apple	21	1	

August 1976

This Mnth	Last Mnth	Title	Artist	Label	Wks in 10	US Pos	
1	4	**20 Golden Greats**	Beach Boys	Capitol	15		
2	8	**Laughter And Tears - The Best Of Neil Sedaka**	Neil Sedaka	Polydor	13	F	
3	5	**Forever And Ever**	Demis Roussos	Philips	14		F
4	-	**Passport**	Nana Mouskouri	Philips	8		L
5	-	**A Little Bit More**	Dr. Hook	Capitol	8	62	F
6	1	**A Night On The Town**	Rod Stewart	Riva	18	2	
7	2	**Greatest Hits**	Abba	Epic	49	48	FP
8	3	**Changesonebowie**	David Bowie	RCA	11	10	
9	-	**Viva Roxy Music**	Roxy Music	Island	3	81	
10	-	**Greatest Hits 2**	Diana Ross	Tamla-Motown	8		

September 1976

This Mnth	Last Mnth	Title	Artist	Label	Wks in 10	US Pos	
1	1	**20 Golden Greats**	Beach Boys	Capitol	15		
2	10	**Greatest Hits 2**	Diana Ross	Tamla-Motown	8		
3	2	**Laughter And Tears - The Best Of Neil Sedaka**	Neil Sedaka	Polydor	13		F
4	6	**A Night On The Town**	Rod Stewart	Riva	18	2	
5	7	**Greatest Hits**	Abba	Epic	49	48	FP
6	3	**Forever And Ever**	Demis Roussos	Philips	14		F
7	-	**Wings At The Speed Of Sound**	Wings	Capitol	21	1	
8	5	**A Little Bit More**	Dr. Hook	Capitol	8	62	F
9	-	**Best Of The Stylistics Vol 2**	Stylistics	H&L	8		
10	4	**Passport**	Nana Mouskouri	Philips	8		L

US 1976

JULY-SEPT

July 1976

This Mnth	Last Mnth	Title	Artist	Label	Wks in 10	UK Pos	
1	1	**Wings At The Speed Of Sound**	Wings	Capitol	21	2	**P**
2	9	**Breezin'**	George Benson	Warner	15		**F3P**
3	3	**Frampton Comes Alive!**	Peter Frampton	A&M	51	19	**F6P**
4	-	**Rock 'n' Roll Music**	Beatles	Capitol	9	11	**P**
5	7	**Fleetwood Mac**	Fleetwood Mac	Reprise	37	23	**F5P**
6	-	**Chicago X**	Chicago	Columbia	17	21	**2P**
7	6	**Rocks**	Aerosmith	Columbia	10		**F3P**
8	-	**Beautiful Noise**	Neil Diamond	Columbia	8	10	**P**
9	-	**Spitfire**	Jefferson Starship	Grunt	13	30	**P**
10	-	**Rastaman Vibration**	Bob Marley & The Wailers	Island	4	15	**FL**

August 1976

This Mnth	Last Mnth	Title	Artist	Label	Wks in 10	UK Pos	
1	3	**Frampton Comes Alive!**	Peter Frampton	A&M	51	19	**F6P**
2	2	**Breezin'**	George Benson	Warner	15		**F3P**
3	9	**Spitfire**	Jefferson Starship	Grunt	13	30	**P**
4	8	**Beautiful Noise**	Neil Diamond	Columbia	8	10	**P**
5	5	**Fleetwood Mac**	Fleetwood Mac	Reprise	37	23	**F5P**
6	1	**Wings At The Speed Of Sound**	Wings	Capitol	21	2	**P**
7	6	**Chicago X**	Chicago	Columbia	17	21	**2P**
8	4	**Rock 'n' Roll Music**	Beatles	Capitol	9	11	**P**
9	-	**Rocks**	Aerosmith	Columbia	10		**F3P**
10	-	**15 Big Ones**	Beach Boys	Brother	3	31	**L**

September 1976

This Mnth	Last Mnth	Title	Artist	Label	Wks in 10	UK Pos	
1	1	**Frampton Comes Alive!**	Peter Frampton	A&M	51	19	**F6P**
2	5	**Fleetwood Mac**	Fleetwood Mac	Reprise	37	23	**F5P**
3	-	**Silk Degrees**	Boz Scaggs	Columbia	10	37	**F5P**
4	3	**Spitfire**	Jefferson Starship	Grunt	13	30	**P**
5	-	**Hasten Down The Wind**	Linda Ronstadt	Asylum	8	32	**P**
6	2	**Breezin'**	George Benson	Warner	15		**F3P**
7	-	**Wild Cherry**	Wild Cherry	Sweet City	8		**FPL**
8	-	**All Things In Time**	Lou Rawls	Philly Int.	4		**L**
9	-	**Spirit**	John Denver	RCA	6	9	**P**
10	-	**Greatest Hits**	War	UA	4		**PL**

• Elton John's record breaking seven nights at Madison Square Garden grossed a staggering $1.25 million. Neil Diamond was another noted singer/songwriter who packed them in. After more than three years away from the stage, Diamond wowed the crowd in Las Vegas.

• Bob Marley & The Wailers reached the US Top 10 for the only time with **Rastaman Vibration** – it was the first reggae album to reach such heights. Marley's most successful US album, the five million selling 1984 release **Legend**, surprisingly failed to reach the Top 40.

• The Grammy for Best Female Performance went to Linda Ronstadt for **Hasten Down The Wind**. The award for Best New Artist was won by Starland Vocal Band, whose self-titled debut LP reached the Top 20.

• Appearing in the Top 20 for the first time were Motown group The Commodores, fronted by Lionel Richie, with **Hot On The Tracks**, and rock band Heart (above), fronted by sisters Ann & Nancy Wilson, with **Dreamboat Annie**.

UK 1976 OCT-DEC

• Guitarist Bert Weedon, whose only previous hit had been a cover of 'Guitar Boogie Shuffle' in 1959, had a surprise chart topper with a collection of well-known instrumentals tagged **22 Golden Guitar Greats**. It managed to keep Stevie Wonder's classic **Songs In The Key Of Life** in runner up position as the TV-advertised compilation LP, **Soul Motion**, had done previously.

• Christmas was the time again for **Greatest Hits** compilations to zoom up the charts. Among the acts earning big money from their past recordings were Americans Glen Campbell, whose **20 Golden Greats** reached Number 1, Dean Martin, Gene Pitney and The Four Seasons. European acts clicking with their old hits included Abba, Hot Chocolate, The Who, Showaddywaddy and Gilbert O'Sullivan.

• The news-oriented London based LBC became Britain's first commercial radio station.

• The music scene was changing fast in Britain. Raw pub-rock band Dr. Feelgood went all the way to Number 1 with **Stupidity**. EMI signed the much hyped punk outfit The Sex Pistols, only to release them weeks later when they found they could not control them, and rejected the mod-looking London trio The Jam.

October 1976

This Mnth	Last Mnth	Title	Artist	Label	Wks in 10	US Pos	
1	5	**Greatest Hits**	Abba	Epic	49	48	**FP**
2	9	**Best Of The Stylistics Vol 2**	Stylistics	H&L	8		
3	-	**Stupidity**	Dr. Feelgood	UA	5		**F**
4	4	**A Night On The Town**	Rod Stewart	Riva	18	2	
5	-	**The Story Of The Who**	Who	Polydor	6		
6	1	**20 Golden Greats**	Beach Boys	Capitol	15		
7	-	**Soul Motion**	Various	K-Tel	7		
8	-	**Songs In The Key Of Life**	Stevie Wonder	Tamla-Motown	19	1	
9	-	**Dedication**	Bay City Rollers	Bell	3	26	**L**
10	2	**Greatest Hits 2**	Diana Ross	Tamla-Motown	8		

November 1976

This Mnth	Last Mnth	Title	Artist	Label	Wks in 10	US Pos	
1	7	**Soul Motion**	Various	K-Tel	7		
2	8	**Songs In The Key Of Life**	Stevie Wonder	Tamla-Motown	19	1	
3	-	**22 Golden Guitar Greats**	Bert Weedon	Warwick	8		**FL**
4	-	**The Song Remains The Same**	Led Zeppelin	Swan Song	4	2	
5	-	**100 Golden Greats**	Max Bygraves	Ronco	9		
6	-	**20 Golden Greats**	Glen Campbell	Capitol	10		**L**
7	5	**The Story Of The Who**	Who	Polydor	6		
8	1	**Greatest Hits**	Abba	Epic	49	48	**FP**
9	-	**Blue Moves**	Elton John	Rocket	2	3	
10	-	**20 Original Dean Martin Hits**	Dean Martin	Reprise	4		**L**

December 1976

This Mnth	Last Mnth	Title	Artist	Label	Wks in 10	US Pos	
1	6	**20 Golden Greats**	Glen Campbell	Capitol	10		**L**
2	-	**Arrival**	Abba	Epic	34	20	**P**
3	5	**100 Golden Greats**	Max Bygraves	Ronco	9		
4	3	**22 Golden Guitar Greats**	Bert Weedon	Warwick	8		**FL**
5	-	**Greatest Hits**	Four Seasons	K-Tel	7		**F**
6	-	**Disco Rocket**	Various	K-Tel	6		
7	2	**Songs In The Key Of Life**	Stevie Wonder	Tamla-Motown	19	1	
8	8	**Greatest Hits**	Abba	Epic	49	48	**FP**
9	-	**Hotel California**	Eagles	Asylum	22	1	
10	10	**20 Original Dean Martin Hits**	Dean Martin	Reprise	4		**L**

US 1976 OCT-DEC

October 1976

This Mnth	Last Mnth	Title	Artist	Label	Wks in 10	UK Pos	
1	1	**Frampton Comes Alive!**	Peter Frampton	A&M	51	19	F6P
2	3	**Silk Degrees**	Boz Scaggs	Columbia	10	37	F5P
3	5	**Hasten Down The Wind**	Linda Ronstadt	Asylum	8	32	P
4	-	**Fly Like An Eagle**	Steve Miller Band	Capitol	30	11	4P
5	-	**Songs In The Key Of Life**	Stevie Wonder	Tamla	35	2	
6	2	**Fleetwood Mac**	Fleetwood Mac	Reprise	37	23	F5P
7	7	**Wild Cherry**	Wild Cherry	Sweet City	8		FPL
8	-	**Spirit**	Earth, Wind & Fire	Columbia	9		2P
9	10	**Greatest Hits**	War	UA	4		PL
10	4	**Spitfire**	Jefferson Starship	Grunt	13	30	P

November 1976

This Mnth	Last Mnth	Title	Artist	Label	Wks in 10	UK Pos	
1	5	**Songs In The Key Of Life**	Stevie Wonder	Tamla	35	2	
2	-	**The Soundtrack From The Film 'The Song Remains The Same'**	Led Zeppelin	Swan Song	7		12P
3	8	**Spirit**	Earth, Wind & Fire	Columbia	9		2P
4	-	**Blue Moves**	Elton John	MCA/Rocket	6	3	P
5	-	**Boston**	Boston	Epic	30	11	F15P
6	1	**Frampton Comes Alive!**	Peter Frampton	A&M	51	19	F6P
7	4	**Fly Like An Eagle**	Steve Miller Band	Capitol	30	11	4P
8	-	**Children Of The World**	Bee Gees	RSO	5		P
9	-	**A Night On The Town**	Rod Stewart	Warner	11	1	2P
10	-	**One More From The Road**	Lynyrd Skynyrd	MCA	4	17	3P

December 1976

This Mnth	Last Mnth	Title	Artist	Label	Wks in 10	UK Pos	
1	1	**Songs In The Key Of Life**	Stevie Wonder	Tamla	35	2	
2	9	**A Night On The Town**	Rod Stewart	Warner	11	1	2P
3	5	**Boston**	Boston	Epic	30	11	F15P
4	3	**Spirit**	Earth, Wind & Fire	Columbia	9		2P
5	-	**The Pretender**	Jackson Browne	Asylum	5	26	FP
6	2	**The Soundtrack From The Film 'The Song Remains The Same'**	Led Zeppelin	Swan Song	7		12P
7	4	**Blue Moves**	Elton John	MCA/Rocket	6	3	P
8	-	**A New World Record**	Electric Light Orchestra	UA	7	6	P
9	6	**Frampton Comes Alive!**	Peter Frampton	A&M	51	19	F6P
10	-	**Hotel California**	Eagles	Asylum	28	2	10P

• American record and tape sales in 1976 reached $2.74 billion. Among the year's biggest earning albums was the self-titled set by studio group Boston. Although it never reached the summit, **Boston** eventually sold over 15 million copies in the US alone.

• Two other top selling albums of the Seventies climbed the charts. **The Best Of The Doobie Brothers** gave the group their fifth Top 10 entry and went on to sell over 7 million copies. The Eagles third successive Number 1, **Hotel California**, fared even better with total sales passing ten million.

• Stevie Wonder's long-awaited **Songs In The Key Of Life** topped the US lists for three months and went on to pick up three Grammy Awards including Album Of The Year. It also stopped Led Zeppelin from making it five successive Number 1 albums with the soundtrack album from their newly released film, **The Song Remains The Same**.

UK 1977 JAN-MAR

• Most music industry people did not understand or appreciate punk music. However, it had caught the record buyers' imagination and therefore most labels quickly jumped aboard the bandwagon. The Stranglers, Elvis Costello and The Jam got themselves record deals and **Damned Damned Damned** by The Damned became the first punk album to chart. London's first all-punk venue, the Roxy, was opened by The Clash. Sid Vicious joined the Sex Pistols, who were signed to A&M for nine days before they too found them impossible to work with and paid them off with £75,000.

• Sweden's Abba were the hottest act in the UK. At times, the quartet held the top two places with **Arrival** and **Greatest Hits**, and their two shows at the prestigious Royal Festival Hall in London were complete sell-outs.

• The Shadows returned to the top for the first time in 15 years with a collection of earlier hits. They had been the first UK act to top the British singles, EP and album charts.

January 1977

This Mnth	Last Mnth	Title	Artist	Label	Wks in 10	US Pos	
1	2	**Arrival**	Abba	Epic	34	20	P
2	-	**A Day At The Races**	Queen	EMI	6	5	
3	8	**Greatest Hits**	Abba	Epic	49	48	FP
4	-	**Red River Valley**	Slim Whitman	UA	7		
5	1	**20 Golden Greats**	Glen Campbell	Capitol	10		L
6	-	**Greatest Hits**	Showaddywaddy	Arista	6		
7	6	**Disco Rocket**	Various	K-Tel	6		
8	7	**Songs In The Key Of Life**	Stevie Wonder	Tamla-Motown	19	1	
9	9	**Hotel California**	Eagles	Asylum	22	1	
10	-	**David Soul**	David Soul	Private Stock	6	40	F

February 1977

This Mnth	Last Mnth	Title	Artist	Label	Wks in 10	US Pos	
1	4	**Red River Valley**	Slim Whitman	UA	7		
2	-	**Evita**	Studio Cast	MCA	7	105	
3	8	**Songs In The Key Of Life**	Stevie Wonder	Tamla-Motown	19	1	
4	10	**David Soul**	David Soul	Private Stock	6	40	F
5	-	**20 Golden Greats**	Shadows	EMI	14		
6	-	**Animals**	Pink Floyd	Harvest	11	3	
7	-	**Low**	David Bowie	RCA	3	11	
8	-	**Endless Flight**	Leo Sayer	Chrysalis	16	10	
9	-	**Heartbreakers**	Various	K-Tel	8		
10	9	**Hotel California**	Eagles	Asylum	22	1	

March 1977

This Mnth	Last Mnth	Title	Artist	Label	Wks in 10	US Pos	
1	5	**20 Golden Greats**	Shadows	EMI	14		
2	9	**Heartbreakers**	Various	K-Tel	8		
3	-	**Animals**	Pink Floyd	Harvest	11	3	
4	8	**Endless Flight**	Leo Sayer	Chrysalis	16	10	
5	-	**Live**	Status Quo	Vertigo	4		
6	-	**In Your Mind**	Bryan Ferry	Polydor	3	126	
7	-	**Arrival**	Abba	Epic	34	20	P
8	2	**Evita**	Studio Cast	MCA	7	105	
9	-	**Portrait Of Sinatra**	Frank Sinatra	Reprise	8		
10	-	**Dance To The Music**	Various	K-Tel	3		

US 1977 JAN-MAR

January 1977

This Mnth	Last Mnth	Title	Artist	Label	Wks in 10	UK Pos	
1	1	**Songs In The Key Of Life**	Stevie Wonder	Tamla	35	2	
2	10	**Hotel California**	Eagles	Asylum	28	2	**10P**
3	-	**Wings Over America**	Wings	Capitol	11	8	**P**
4	3	**Boston**	Boston	Epic	30	11	**F15P**
5	-	**The Best Of The Doobies**	Doobie Brothers	Warner	8		**7P**
6	8	**A New World Record**	Electric Light Orchestra	UA	7	6	**P**
7	2	**A Night On The Town**	Rod Stewart	Warner	11	1	**2P**
8	9	**Frampton Comes Alive!**	Peter Frampton	A&M	51	19	**F6P**
9	-	**Greatest Hits**	Linda Ronstadt	Asylum	7	37	**5P**
10	-	**A Star Is Born (Soundtrack)**	Barbra Streisand	Columbia	18	1	**4P**

February 1977

This Mnth	Last Mnth	Title	Artist	Label	Wks in 10	UK Pos	
1	10	**A Star Is Born (Soundtrack)**	Barbra Streisand	Columbia	18	1	**4P**
2	2	**Hotel California**	Eagles	Asylum	28	2	**10P**
3	1	**Songs In The Key Of Life**	Stevie Wonder	Tamla	35	2	
4	3	**Wings Over America**	Wings	Capitol	11	8	**P**
5	-	**Year Of The Cat**	Al Stewart	Janus	5	38	**FP**
6	4	**Boston**	Boston	Epic	30	11	**F15P**
7	-	**A Day At The Races**	Queen	Elektra	4	1	
8	9	**Greatest Hits**	Linda Ronstadt	Asylum	7	37	**5P**
9	-	**Fly Like An Eagle**	Steve Miller Band	Capitol	30	11	**4P**
10	8	**Frampton Comes Alive!**	Peter Frampton	A&M	51	19	**F6P**

March 1977

This Mnth	Last Mnth	Title	Artist	Label	Wks in 10	UK Pos	
1	1	**A Star Is Born (Soundtrack)**	Barbra Streisand	Columbia	18	1	**4P**
2	2	**Hotel California**	Eagles	Asylum	28	2	**10P**
3	-	**Rumours**	Fleetwood Mac	Warner	52	1	**17P**
4	3	**Songs In The Key Of Life**	Stevie Wonder	Tamla	35	2	
5	-	**Animals**	Pink Floyd	Columbia	5	2	**4P**
6	9	**Fly Like An Eagle**	Steve Miller Band	Capitol	30	11	**4P**
7	6	**Boston**	Boston	Epic	30	11	**F15P**
8	-	**John Denver's Greatest Hits Vol. 2**	John Denver	RCA	4	9	**PL**
9	5	**Year Of The Cat**	Al Stewart	Janus	5	38	**FP**
10	-	**Night Moves**	Bob Seger & The Silver Bullet Band	Capitol	4		**F5P**

• As their highly respected founder member, Peter Green, was admitted into a mental hospital, Fleetwood Mac's **Rumours** climbed the American chart. It was to become one of the biggest sellers of all time. In the USA it passed the 17 million mark, whilst in Britain alone it sold over two million and spent more than 400 weeks on the chart. **Rumours** was America's top album of the decade.

• Respected rockers who reached the Top 20 for the first time included relative veterans Bob Seger and Manfred Mann with **Night Moves** and **The Roaring Silence** respectively.

• Adding to the tally of British groups with albums in the Top 20 on both sides of the Atlantic were Paul McCartney & Wing's **Wings Over America**, Queen's **A Day At The Races** and Pink Floyd's **Animals**. British male soloists with transatlantic smashes included David Bowie with **Low** and Leo Sayer with **Endless Flight**. The latter included two US Number 1 singles, 'You Make Me Feel Like Dancing' and 'When I Need You'.

• At 53, American country singer Slim Whitman became the oldest artist to top the UK charts with newly recorded material. It was the second Number 1 in a year for the performer who had last reached the US Top 20 in 1952!

UK 1977 APR-JUNE

• **Stranglers IV (Rattus Norvegicus)** by The Stranglers was the first punk album to reach the Top 10. Making the Top 20 with debut albums were The Jam with **In The City** and The Clash with their self-titled set. US punk pioneers Blondie, The Ramones, Talking Heads and Television appeared in the UK, and The Damned became the first British punks to play in the USA, at New York's CBGB club. Other punk news included two members of The Clash being jailed for alleged theft, Boomtown Rats' vocalist Bob Geldof being attacked on stage and new band Adam & The Ants making their debut at the Roxy.

• After almost 40 years in the business, Frank Sinatra had his first British Number 1, **Portrait Of Sinatra**. Simultaneously, another headlining act from the same era, The Glenn Miller Orchestra, had their most successful UK album, **The Unforgettable Glenn Miller**.

• For many years reggae records had been frequent visitors to the singles Top 10. Bob Marley & The Wailers' **Exodus** was the first album by a reggae act to crack the Top 10.

• Three noted British females debuted on the chart: Elkie Brooks with **Two Days Away**, Barbara Dickson with **Morning Comes Quickly** and Kiki Dee with a self-titled LP.

April 1977

This Mnth	Last Mnth	Title	Artist	Label	Wks in 10	US Pos	
1	7	**Arrival**	Abba	Epic	34	20	P
2	9	**Portrait Of Sinatra**	Frank Sinatra	Reprise	8		
3	1	**20 Golden Greats**	Shadows	EMI	14		
4	-	**Hollies Live Hits**	Hollies	Parlophone	6		
5	4	**Endless Flight**	Leo Sayer	Chrysalis	16	10	
6	3	**Animals**	Pink Floyd	Harvest	11	3	
7	-	**The Unforgettable Glenn Miller**	Glenn Miller	RCA	3		L
8	2	**Heartbreakers**	Various	K-Tel	8		
9	-	**Greatest Hits**	Abba	Epic	49	48	FP
10	-	**Every Face Tells A Story**	Cliff Richard	EMI	2		

May 1977

This Mnth	Last Mnth	Title	Artist	Label	Wks in 10	US Pos	
1	-	**Arrival**	Abba	Epic	34	20	P
2	-	**Hotel California**	Eagles	Asylum	22	1	
3	-	**A Star Is Born (Soundtrack)**	Barbra Streisand	CBS	23	1	
4	-	**20 Golden Greats**	Shadows	EMI	14		
5	-	**Stranglers IV (Rattus Norvegicus)**	Stranglers	UA	17		F
6	-	**Endless Flight**	Leo Sayer	Chrysalis	16	10	
7	-	**Deceptive Bends**	10 C.C.	Mercury	8	31	
8	-	**Greatest Hits**	Smokie	RAK	5		FL
9	-	**The Beatles At The Hollywood Bowl**	Beatles	Parlophone	9	2	
10	-	**Greatest Hits**	Abba	Epic	49	48	FP

June 1977

This Mnth	Last Mnth	Title	Artist	Label	Wks in 10	US Pos	
1	1	**Arrival**	Abba	Epic	34	20	P
2	9	**The Beatles At The Hollywood Bowl**	Beatles	Parlophone	9	2	
3	2	**Hotel California**	Eagles	Asylum	22	1	
4	-	**The Muppet Show**	Muppets	Pye	8	153	FL
5	3	**A Star Is Born (Soundtrack)**	Barbra Streisand	CBS	23	1	
6	7	**Deceptive Bends**	10 C.C.	Mercury	8	31	
7	-	**Sheer Magic**	Mr. Acker Bilk	Warwick	5		L
8	5	**Stranglers IV (Rattus Norvegicus)**	Stranglers	UA	17		F
9	-	**A New World Record**	Electric Light Orchestra	Jet	16	5	F
10	-	**The Johnny Mathis Collection**	Johnny Mathis	CBS	13		

US 1977 APR-JUNE

April 1977

This Mnth	Last Mnth	Title	Artist	Label	Wks in 10	UK Pos	
1	2	**Hotel California**	Eagles	Asylum	28	2	**10P**
2	3	**Rumours**	Fleetwood Mac	Warner	52	1	**17P**
3	4	**Songs In The Key Of Life**	Stevie Wonder	Tamla	35	2	
4	1	**A Star is Born (Soundtrack)**	Barbra Streisand	Columbia	18	1	**4P**
5	-	**Leftoverture**	Kansas	Kirshner	7		**F3P**
6	7	**Boston**	Boston	Epic	30	11	**F15P**
7	-	**This One's For You**	Barry Manilow	Arista	5		**2P**
8	-	**Unpredictable**	Natalie Cole	Capitol	4		**FP**
9	6	**Fly Like An Eagle**	Steve Miller Band	Capitol	30	11	**4P**
10	-	**Love At The Greek**	Neil Diamond	Columbia	3	3	**2P**

May 1977

This Mnth	Last Mnth	Title	Artist	Label	Wks in 10	UK Pos	
1	2	**Rumours**	Fleetwood Mac	Warner	52	1	**17P**
2	1	**Hotel California**	Eagles	Asylum	28	2	**10P**
3	-	**Marvin Gaye Live At The London Palladium**	Marvin Gaye	Tamla	11		
4	-	**Rocky**	Soundtrack	UA	9		**P**
5	3	**Songs In The Key Of Life**	Stevie Wonder	Tamla	35	2	
6	-	**Go For Your Guns**	Isley Brothers	T-Neck	5	46	**P**
7	6	**Boston**	Boston	Epic	30	11	**F15P**
8	4	**A Star Is Born (Soundtrack)**	Barbra Streisand	Columbia	18	1	**4P**
9	-	**Songs From The Wood**	Jethro Tull	Chrysalis	4	13	**L**
10	-	**Commodores**	Commodores	Motown	19		**F**

June 1977

This Mnth	Last Mnth	Title	Artist	Label	Wks in 10	UK Pos	
1	1	**Rumours**	Fleetwood Mac	Warner	52	1	**17P**
2	2	**Hotel California**	Eagles	Asylum	28	2	**10P**
3	10	**Commodores**	Commodores	Motown	19		**F**
4	-	**The Beatles At The Hollywood Bowl**	Beatles	Capitol	4	1	**P**
5	4	**Rocky**	Soundtrack	UA	9		**P**
6	-	**Book Of Dreams**	Steve Miller Band	Capitol	13	12	**3P**
7	-	**Barry Manilow Live**	Barry Manilow	Arista	11		**3P**
8	3	**Marvin Gaye Live At The London Palladium**	Marvin Gaye	Tamla	11		
9	-	**I'm In You**	Peter Frampton	A&M	12		**PL**
10	5	**Songs In The Key Of Life**	Stevie Wonder	Tamla	35	2	

• Elvis Presley packed in the crowds at the Market Square Arena, Indianapolis, at what was to be his last live performance. Led Zeppelin attracted even more fans to the Silverdrome in Michigan – the 76,000 crowd breaking the attendance record for a single act show.

• The Beatles narrowly failed to notch up another transatlantic Number 1 with **The Beatles At The Hollywood Bowl**, which had been recorded at their 1964 and 1965 shows at that world famous venue. The only record which stopped them hitting the top was Fleetwood Mac's (above) **Rumours** , which led the list for seven months.

• Top R&B sellers were the Motown albums **Marvin Gaye At The London Palladium, Anyway You Like It** by Thelma Houston and a self-titled set by The Commodores. Also in the leading 20 were **Go For Your Guns** by The Isley Brothers, the funky Bootsy's Rubber Band with **Aah...The Name Is Bootsy, Baby!**, and **Right On Time** from the Brothers Johnson.

UK 1977

JULY-SEPT

• Elvis Presley, the King of Rock'n' Roll, died on August 16. He was the most important and influential artist of the rock era. Instantly, there was an unprecedented demand for his albums around the world, and it was estimated that 20 million Elvis records were sold in the 24 hours after his death! His latest album **Moody Blue** became his first transatlantic Top 3 album for 15 years. Soon after his death, he had a record-shattering 27 albums simultaneously in the British Top 100!

• Connie Francis, the Queen of Rock'n' Roll, became the first female soloist to top the UK album chart thanks to her **20 All Time Greats**.

• Marc Bolan, who had fronted the ultra-successful T. Rex, died in a car accident in London on September 16. He was one of Britain's most important and influential recording artists in the Seventies.

• Among interesting new acts selling albums were Elvis Costello with the Nick Lowe-produced **My Aim Is True**, The Vibrators with their self-titled album, and American Jonathan Richman & The Modern Lovers with **Rock'N'Roll With The Modern Lovers**. Among the new acts creating interest were the Tom Robinson Band, Ian Dury, Siouxsie & The Banshees, The Buzzcocks and The Police, who had been trimmed down from a quartet to a trio.

July 1977

This Mnth	Last Mnth	Title	Artist	Label	Wks in 10	US Pos	
1	5	**A Star Is Born (Soundtrack)**	Barbra Streisand	CBS	23	1	
2	10	**The Johnny Mathis Collection**	Johnny Mathis	CBS	13		
3	4	**The Muppet Show**	Muppets	Pye	8	153	FL
4	-	**Love At The Greek**	Neil Diamond	CBS	8	8	
5	2	**The Beatles At The Hollywood Bowl**	Beatles	Parlophone	9	2	
6	1	**Arrival**	Abba	Epic	34	20	P
7	8	**Stranglers IV (Rattus Norvegicus)**	Stranglers	UA	17		F
8	3	**Hotel California**	Eagles	Asylum	22	1	
9	-	**I Remember Yesterday**	Donna Summer	GTO	8	18	F
10	-	**Going For The One**	Yes	Atlantic	13	8	

August 1977

This Mnth	Last Mnth	Title	Artist	Label	Wks in 10	US Pos	
1	10	**Going For The One**	Yes	Atlantic	13	8	
2	2	**The Johnny Mathis Collection**	Johnny Mathis	CBS	13		
3	1	**A Star Is Born (Soundtrack)**	Barbra Streisand	CBS	23	1	
4	-	**20 All Time Greats**	Connie Francis	Polydor	10		FL
5	9	**I Remember Yesterday**	Donna Summer	GTO	8	18	F
6	-	**Rumours**	Fleetwood Mac	Warner	41	1	2P
7	4	**Love At The Greek**	Neil Diamond	CBS	8	8	
8	7	**Stranglers IV (Rattus Norvegicus)**	Stranglers	UA	17		F
9	8	**Hotel California**	Eagles	Asylum	22	1	
10	-	**On Stage**	Rainbow	Polydor	2	65	F

September 1977

This Mnth	Last Mnth	Title	Artist	Label	Wks in 10	US Pos	
1	-	**Oxygene**	Jean-Michel Jarre	Polydor	11	78	F
2	4	**20 All Time Greats**	Connie Francis	Polydor	10		FL
3	-	**Moody Blue**	Elvis Presley	RCA	8	3	
4	-	**40 Greatest Hits**	Elvis Presley	Arcade	4		
5	3	**A Star Is Born (Soundtrack)**	Barbra Streisand	CBS	23	1	
6	6	**Rumours**	Fleetwood Mac	Warner	41	1	2P
7	-	**20 Golden Greats**	Diana Ross & The Supremes	Motown	14		
8	1	**Going For The One**	Yes	Atlantic	13	8	
9	2	**The Johnny Mathis Collection**	Johnny Mathis	CBS	13		
10	8	**Stranglers IV (Rattus Norvegicus)**	Stranglers	UA	17		F

US 1977

JULY-SEPT

July 1977

This Mnth	Last Mnth	Title	Artist	Label	Wks in 10	UK Pos	
1	1	**Rumours**	Fleetwood Mac	Warner	52	1	**17P**
2	9	**I'm In You**	Peter Frampton	A&M	12		**PL**
3	7	**Barry Manilow Live**	Barry Manilow	Arista	11		**3P**
4	6	**Book Of Dreams**	Steve Miller Band	Capitol	13	12	**3P**
5	3	**Commodores**	Commodores	Motown	19		**F**
6	-	**Streisand Superman**	Barbra Streisand	Columbia	7	32	**2P**
7	-	**Love Gun**	Kiss	Casablanca	7		**P**
8	8	**Marvin Gaye Live At The London Palladium**	Marvin Gaye	Tamla	11		
9	-	**Foreigner**	Foreigner	Atlantic	18		**F4P**
10	-	**CSN**	Crosby, Stills & Nash	Atlantic	10	23	**4P**

August 1977

This Mnth	Last Mnth	Title	Artist	Label	Wks in 10	UK Pos	
1	1	**Rumours**	Fleetwood Mac	Warner	52	1	**17P**
2	10	**CSN**	Crosby, Stills & Nash	Atlantic	10	23	**4P**
3	6	**Streisand Superman**	Barbra Streisand	Columbia	7	32	**2P**
4	2	**I'm In You**	Peter Frampton	A&M	12		**PL**
5	-	**JT**	James Taylor	Columbia	12		**2P**
6	-	**Star Wars**	Soundtrack	20th Century	10		**P**
7	4	**Book Of Dreams**	Steve Miller Band	Capitol	13	12	**3P**
8	7	**Love Gun**	Kiss	Casablanca	7		**P**
9	-	**Rejoice**	Emotions	Columbia	7		**FPL**
10	5	**Commodores**	Commodores	Motown	19		**F**

September 1977

This Mnth	Last Mnth	Title	Artist	Label	Wks in 10	UK Pos	
1	1	**Rumours**	Fleetwood Mac	Warner	52	1	**17P**
2	6	**Star Wars**	Soundtrack	20th Century	10		**P**
3	-	**Moody Blue**	Elvis Presley	RCA	8	3	**P**
4	5	**JT**	James Taylor	Columbia	12		**2P**
5	2	**CSN**	Crosby, Stills & Nash	Atlantic	10	23	**4P**
6	10	**Commodores**	Commodores	Motown	19		**F**
7	-	**Shaun Cassidy**	Shaun Cassidy	Warner	11		**FP**
8	9	**Rejoice**	Emotions	Columbia	7		**FPL**
9	-	**Foreigner**	Foreigner	Atlantic	18		**F4P**
10	4	**I'm In You**	Peter Frampton	A&M	12		**PL**

• The Florida Keys' best known singer/songwriter, Jimmy Buffet, debuted in the Top 20 with **Changes In Latitudes, Changes In Attitudes**. Other interesting newcomers in that chart included British rock band Supertramp with **Even In The Quietest Moments** and Detroit's heavy metal hero Ted Nugent with **Cat Scratch Fever**. Controversial country outlaw Waylon Jennings also notched up his first Top 20 pop hit with **Ol' Waylon**. Old Waylon had recently been arrested for suspected cocaine possession. Lower down the chart, Australia's AC/DC with **Let There Be Rock**, funk groundbreakers Cameo with **Cardiac Arrest** and new US rock band Cheap Trick with **In Color** had their first entries, as did Tom Petty & The Heartbreakers with their self-titled debut LP.

• For one week, **Barry Manilow Live** managed to displace Fleetwood Mac at the top. The album failed to chart in Britain, but five years later a Manilow album recorded live in the UK reached Number 1 there.

UK 1977 OCT-DEC

• Bing Crosby died on October 14 – alongside the recently deceased Elvis Presley he was the most successful solo artist of the century. His timeless single 'White Christmas', which had sold over 20 million copies worldwide, returned him to the UK Top 5 as did his album **Live At The London Palladium**. He also had two other chart albums **The Best Of Bing** and **Seasons**. Incidentally, Bing was seen duetting with David Bowie on a TV special made earlier in the year. They sang 'Peace on Earth – Little Drummer Boy' which gave the odd couple a Top 10 hit single in Britain five years later.

• Proof of the acceptance of punk music in Britain came with the entry at Number 1 of **Never Mind The Bollocks Here's The Sex Pistols**. The controversial group's first LP even helped stop Rod Stewart from scoring his seventh successive Number 1 with **Foot Loose And Fancy Free**.

• Acts enjoying chart success with Greatest Hits LPs included Diana Ross, Cliff Richard, Bread, Gladys Knight & The Pips, Paul Simon and George Mitchell's Minstrels.

October 1977

This Mnth	Last Mnth	Title	Artist	Label	Wks in 10	US Pos	
1	7	**20 Golden Greats**	Diana Ross & The Supremes	Motown	14		
2	1	**Oxygene**	Jean-Michel Jarre	Polydor	11	78	F
3	-	**No More Heroes**	Stranglers	UA	6		
4	6	**Rumours**	Fleetwood Mac	Warner	41	1	2P
5	3	**Moody Blue**	Elvis Presley	RCA	8	3	
6	-	**Love You Live**	Rolling Stones	Rolling Stones	3	5	
7	-	**Home On The Range**	Slim Whitman	UA	3		L
8	-	**40 Golden Greats**	Cliff Richard	EMI	8		
9	8	**Going For The One**	Yes	Atlantic	13	8	
10	-	**Aja**	Steely Dan	ABC	3	3	FL

November 1977

This Mnth	Last Mnth	Title	Artist	Label	Wks in 10	US Pos	
1	-	**Never Mind The Bollocks Here's The Sex Pistols**	Sex Pistols	Virgin	10	106	F
2	-	**The Sound Of Bread**	Bread	Elektra	17		L
3	8	**40 Golden Greats**	Cliff Richard	EMI	8		
4	1	**20 Golden Greats**	Diana Ross & The Supremes	Motown	14		
5	-	**Foot Loose And Fancy Free**	Rod Stewart	Riva	16	2	
6	-	**Heroes**	David Bowie	RCA	3	35	
7	-	**Out Of The Blue**	Electric Light Orchestra	Jet	17	4	
8	-	**News Of The World**	Queen	EMI	8	3	
9	-	**Seconds Out**	Genesis	Charisma	3	47	
10	3	**No More Heroes**	Stranglers	UA	6		

December 1977

This Mnth	Last Mnth	Title	Artist	Label	Wks in 10	US Pos	
1	-	**Disco Fever**	Various	K-Tel	13		
2	2	**The Sound Of Bread**	Bread	Elektra	17		L
3	1	**Never Mind The Bollocks Here's The Sex Pistols**	Sex Pistols	Virgin	10	106	F
4	-	**30 Greatest**	Gladys Knight & The Pips	K-Tel	8		L
5	-	**Feelings**	Various	K-Tel	7		
6	5	**Foot Loose And Fancy Free**	Rod Stewart	Riva	16	2	
7	-	**Greatest Hits, Etc.**	Paul Simon	CBS	4	18	
8	8	**News Of The World**	Queen	EMI	8	3	
9	-	**Rockin' All Over The World**	Status Quo	Vertigo	4		
10	-	**Rumours**	Fleetwood Mac	Warner	41	1	2P

US 1977 OCT-DEC

October 1977

This Mnth	Last Mnth	Title	Artist	Label	Wks in 10	UK Pos	
1	1	**Rumours**	Fleetwood Mac	Warner	52	1	**17P**
2	-	**Simple Dreams**	Linda Ronstadt	Asylum	16	15	**3P**
3	7	**Shaun Cassidy**	Shaun Cassidy	Warner	11		**FP**
4	9	**Foreigner**	Foreigner	Atlantic	18		**F4P**
5	3	**Moody Blue**	Elvis Presley	RCA	8	3	**P**
6	-	**Anytime...Anywhere**	Rita Coolidge	A&M	7	6	**FPL**
7	2	**Star Wars**	Soundtrack	20th Century	10		**P**
8	-	**Aja**	Steely Dan	ABC	20	5	**2P**
9	-	**Love You Live**	Rolling Stones	Rolling Stones	4	3	
10	4	**JT**	James Taylor	Columbia	12		**2P**

November 1977

This Mnth	Last Mnth	Title	Artist	Label	Wks in 10	UK Pos	
1	1	**Rumours**	Fleetwood Mac	Warner	52	1	**17P**
2	2	**Simple Dreams**	Linda Ronstadt	Asylum	16	15	**3P**
3	8	**Aja**	Steely Dan	ABC	20	5	**2P**
4	4	**Foreigner**	Foreigner	Atlantic	18		**F4P**
5	-	**Elvis In Concert**	Elvis Presley	RCA	4		**PL**
6	-	**Chicago XI**	Chicago	Columbia	4		**P**
7	9	**Love You Live**	Rolling Stones	Rolling Stones	4	3	
8	-	**Street Survivors**	Lynyrd Skynyrd	MCA	5	13	**2PL**
9	-	**Commodores Live!**	Commodores	Motown	6	60	
10	6	**Anytime...Anywhere**	Rita Coolidge	A&M	7	6	**FPL**

December 1977

This Mnth	Last Mnth	Title	Artist	Label	Wks in 10	UK Pos	
1	2	**Simple Dreams**	Linda Ronstadt	Asylum	16	15	**3P**
2	1	**Rumours**	Fleetwood Mac	Warner	52	1	**17P**
3	-	**Foot Loose & Fancy Free**	Rod Stewart	Warner	15	3	**3P**
4	9	**Commodores Live!**	Commodores	Motown	6	60	
5	-	**All 'n All**	Earth, Wind & Fire	Columbia	15	13	**3P**
6	-	**You Light Up My Life**	Debby Boone	Warner	6		**FPL**
7	3	**Aja**	Steely Dan	ABC	20	5	**2P**
8	-	**Out Of The Blue**	Electric Light Orchestra	Jet	9	4	**P**
9	8	**Street Survivors**	Lynyrd Skynyrd	MCA	5	13	**2PL**
10	-	**Point Of Know Return**	Kansas	Kirshner	13		**3P**

• In the year that the phonograph (record player) and microphone celebrated their 100th birthdays, sales of records and tapes zoomed to over $3.5 billion, with the former still accounting for three quarters of the business.

• The classic **Bat Out Of Hell** gave Meat Loaf his first taste of album success. Other acts debuting on the chart included Talking Heads, The Sex Pistols and Elvis Costello. Incidentally, Costello, whose backing band on **My Aim Is True** included Huey Lewis, became the first of the new wave of British acts to appear on US TV.

• Among the 1977 Grammy winners in the Top 10 were Pat Boone's daughter, Debbie, who was voted Best New Artist, Steve Martin, whose **Let's Get Small** was selected as Best Comedy Performance, and **Star Wars** which earned the trophy for Best Soundtrack.

• Lynyrd Skynyrd's **Street Survivors** was released just three days before several of the group's members, including lead singer Ronnie Van Zant were killed in a plane crash. It went on to become the southern rock band's most successful album on both sides of the Atlantic.

• Fleetwood Mac's **Rumours** was finally dethroned by Linda Ronstadt's first Number 1, **Simple Dreams**. The album contained her revivals of Roy Orbison's 'Blue Bayou' and The Crickets' 'It's So Easy', which at one time were simultaneously in the singles Top 5.

UK 1978 JAN-MAR

January 1978

This Mnth	Last Mnth	Title	Artist	Label	Wks in 10	US Pos	
1	2	**The Sound Of Bread**	Bread	Elektra	17		**L**
2	1	**Disco Fever**	Various	K-Tel	13		
3	10	**Rumours**	Fleetwood Mac	Warner	41	1	**2P**
4	-	**20 Country Classics**	Tammy Wynette	CBS	5		**L**
5	6	**Foot Loose And Fancy Free**	Rod Stewart	Riva	16	2	
6	-	**Greatest Hits**	Donna Summer	GTO	8		
7	4	**30 Greatest**	Gladys Knight & The Pips	K-Tel	8		**L**
8	5	**Feelings**	Various	K-Tel	7		
9	-	**Greatest Hits Vol. 2**	Elton John	DJM	3	21	
10	-	**Love Songs**	Beatles	Parlophone	5	24	

February 1978

This Mnth	Last Mnth	Title	Artist	Label	Wks in 10	US Pos	
1	-	**The Album**	Abba	Epic	25	14	
2	3	**Rumours**	Fleetwood Mac	Warner	41	1	**2P**
3	-	**Reflections**	Andy Williams	CBS	11		**L**
4	6	**Greatest Hits**	Donna Summer	GTO	8		
5	1	**The Sound Of Bread**	Bread	Elektra	17		**L**
6	-	**Variations**	Andrew Lloyd Webber	MCA	6		**F**
7	2	**Disco Fever**	Various	K-Tel	13		
8	-	**Out Of The Blue**	Electric Light Orchestra	Jet	17	4	
9	5	**Foot Loose And Fancy Free**	Rod Stewart	Riva	16	2	
10	10	**Love Songs**	Beatles	Parlophone	5	24	

March 1978

This Mnth	Last Mnth	Title	Artist	Label	Wks in 10	US Pos	
1	1	**The Album**	Abba	Epic	25	14	
2	3	**Reflections**	Andy Williams	CBS	11		**L**
3	-	**20 Golden Greats**	Buddy Holly & Crickets	MCA	8	55	
4	6	**Variations**	Andrew Lloyd Webber	MCA	6		**F**
5	2	**Rumours**	Fleetwood Mac	Warner	41	1	**2P**
6	8	**Out Of The Blue**	Electric Light Orchestra	Jet	17	4	
7	-	**The Kick Inside**	Kate Bush	EMI	14		**F**
8	9	**Foot Loose And Fancy Free**	Rod Stewart	Riva	16	2	
9	-	**Boogie Nights**	Various	Ronco	2		
10	-	**Disco Stars**	Various	K-Tel	2		

• New faces making their first marks on the scene included Adam & The Ants, who debuted on John Peel's celebrated radio show, The Police who signed to A&M and Ireland's U2, who won a record audition with CBS.

• Few Americans noticed that British groups The Stranglers and The Jam played dates there. There was more US media interest in the hyped first US tour by the Sex Pistols, which encountered many problems and which ended with the group disbanding. Fellow punk pioneers, The Damned, also split up reuniting later, and the original punk fanzine *Sniffin' Glue* folded. It appeared that basic raw punk music had reached the end of its road. Many new acts were smoothing punk's rough edges, giving it a gloss coat and calling it new wave.

• Fifties rock'n'roll music was once again popular. Buddy Holly & The Crickets topped the charts with their **Greatest Hits** and a collection of **Fonzie's Favourites** also reached the Top 10. On the subject of old rockers, Neil Sedaka was given a brass star on Hollywood Boulevard and the chronologically incorrect *American Hot Wax* movie was released.

US 1978 JAN-MAR

January 1978

This Mnth	Last Mnth	Title	Artist	Label	Wks in 10	UK Pos	
1	3	**Foot Loose & Fancy Free**	Rod Stewart	Warner	15	3	**3P**
2	5	**All 'n All**	Earth, Wind & Fire	Columbia	15	13	**3P**
3	2	**Rumours**	Fleetwood Mac	Warner	52	1	**17P**
4	8	**Out Of The Blue**	Electric Light Orchestra	Jet	9	4	**P**
5	-	**Saturday Night Fever**	Soundtrack	RSO	35	1	**11P**
6	-	**Born Late**	Shaun Cassidy	Warner	4		**PL**
7	-	**News Of The World**	Queen	Elektra	13	4	**P**
8	1	**Simple Dreams**	Linda Ronstadt	Asylum	16	15	**3P**
9	-	**I'm Glad You're Here With Me Tonight**	Neil Diamond	Columbia	7	16	**2P**
10	-	**Alive II**	Kiss	Casablanca	4	60	**P**

February 1978

This Mnth	Last Mnth	Title	Artist	Label	Wks in 10	UK Pos	
1	5	**Saturday Night Fever**	Soundtrack	RSO	35	1	**11P**
2	1	**Foot Loose & Fancy Free**	Rod Stewart	Warner	15	3	**3P**
3	2	**All 'n All**	Earth, Wind & Fire	Columbia	15	13	**3P**
4	7	**News Of The World**	Queen	Elektra	13	4	**P**
5	-	**The Stranger**	Billy Joel	Columbia	19	25	**F9P**
6	-	**The Grand Illusion**	Styx	A&M	12		**F3P**
7	9	**I'm Glad You're Here With Me Tonight**	Neil Diamond	Columbia	7	16	**2P**
8	3	**Rumours**	Fleetwood Mac	Warner	52	1	**17P**
9	-	**Running On Empty**	Jackson Browne	Asylum	17	28	**P**
10	4	**Out Of The Blue**	Electric Light Orchestra	Jet	9	4	**P**

March 1978

This Mnth	Last Mnth	Title	Artist	Label	Wks in 10	UK Pos	
1	1	**Saturday Night Fever**	Soundtrack	RSO	35	1	**11P**
2	5	**The Stranger**	Billy Joel	Columbia	19	25	**F9P**
3	9	**Running On Empty**	Jackson Browne	Asylum	17	28	**P**
4	-	**Slowhand**	Eric Clapton	RSO	16	23	**3P**
5	4	**News Of The World**	Queen	Elektra	13	4	**P**
6	-	**Aja**	Steely Dan	ABC	20	5	**2P**
7	-	**Weekend In L.A.**	George Benson	Warner	10	47	**P**
8	6	**The Grand Illusion**	Styx	A&M	12		**F3P**
9	3	**All 'n All**	Earth, Wind & Fire	Columbia	15	13	**3P**
10	-	**Even Now**	Barry Manilow	Arista	7	12	**3P**

• Disco music reached its pinnacle when the soundtrack to **Saturday Night Fever** topped the chart for an amazing six months. The album, which heavily featured The Bee Gees, was the biggest record of 1978 on both sides of the Atlantic. It sold 11 million in the US and 25 million globally – a record at the time. Simultaneously, the Bee Gees label, RSO, had a record six successive Number 1 singles, and at one time The Bee Gees composed and produced the entire top four – an unprecedented achievement.

• NBC celebrated 50 years of country music with a TV special. Country acts with crossover pop hits included Dolly Parton's first Top 40 entry, **Here You Come Again**, outlaws Waylon Jennings & Willie Nelson's Top 20 hit **Waylon & Willie** and The Oak Ridge Boys' **Y'All Come Back Saloon**. In Britain, Tammy Wynette's **20 Country Classics** and Crystal Gayle's **We Must Believe In Magic** reached The Top 20.

UK 1978 APR-JUNE

April 1978

This Mnth	Last Mnth	Title	Artist	Label	Wks in 10	US Pos	
1	1	**The Album**	Abba	Epic	25	14	
2	3	**20 Golden Greats**	Buddy Holly & Crickets	MCA	8	55	
3	-	**20 Golden Greats**	Nat 'King' Cole	Capitol	10		
4	7	**The Kick Inside**	Kate Bush	EMI	14		F
5	-	**And Then There Were Three**	Genesis	Charisma	9	14	
6	-	**Saturday Night Fever**	Soundtrack	RSO	29	1	
7	-	**London Town**	Wings	Parlophone	7	2	
8	-	**Kaya**	Bob Marley & The Wailers	Island	4	50	
9	-	**This Year's Model**	Elvis Costello	Radar	3	30	F
10	-	**City To City**	Gerry Rafferty	UA	9	1	F

• As collections of twenty-something-year-old tracks by Frank Sinatra and The Platters climbed into the Top 10, a set of similar vintage from Nat 'King' Cole replaced a collection of Buddy Holly's old hits in the top spot. The Number 1 position was then shanghaied by America's unstoppable chart topper, **Saturday Night Fever**, which held off all competition for four months – a record for the Seventies.

• The times – and music – may have been a-changing but Bob Dylan was still one of the most popular live acts in the UK. All 90,000 tickets for his Wembley concert were sold in less than eight hours.

• Three of the year's most talked about acts debuted in the Top 10: Elvis Costello, Ian Dury & The Blockheads and The Tom Robinson Band. The albums that took them there were **This Year's Model**, **New Boots And Panties!!** and **Power In The Darkness** respectively. Among the interesting new acts whose debut hits did not crack the 10 were America's Patti Smith Group with **Easter**, Sham 69 with **Tell Us The Truth**, Manchester band The Buzzcocks' **Another Music In A Different Kitchen** and eponymous albums from Television and The Beatles-spoof group, The Ruttles

May 1978

This Mnth	Last Mnth	Title	Artist	Label	Wks in 10	US Pos	
1	6	**Saturday Night Fever**	Soundtrack	RSO	29	1	
2	3	**20 Golden Greats**	Nat 'King' Cole	Capitol	10		
3	-	**The Stud**	Soundtrack	Ronco	10		
4	5	**And Then There Were Three**	Genesis	Charisma	9	14	
5	-	**The Album**	Abba	Epic	25	14	
6	-	**You Light Up My Life**	Johnny Mathis	CBS	10	9	
7	7	**London Town**	Wings	Parlophone	7	2	
8	-	**20 Golden Greats**	Frank Sinatra	Capitol	4		
9	-	**Long Live Rock 'n' Roll**	Rainbow	Polydor	3	89	
10	-	**20 Classic Hits**	Platters	Mercury	2		FL

June 1978

This Mnth	Last Mnth	Title	Artist	Label	Wks in 10	US Pos	
1	1	**Saturday Night Fever**	Soundtrack	RSO	29	1	
2	5	**The Album**	Abba	Epic	25	14	
3	3	**The Stud**	Soundtrack	Ronco	10		
4	-	**Black And White**	Stranglers	UA	4		
5	6	**You Light Up My Life**	Johnny Mathis	CBS	10	9	
6	-	**I Know Cos I Was There**	Max Boyce	EMI	5		L
7	-	**Live And Dangerous**	Thin Lizzy	Vertigo	10	84	
8	-	**Power In The Darkness**	Tom Robinson Band	EMI	3	144	FL
9	-	**Anytime Anywhere**	Rita Coolidge	A&M	3	6	F
10	8	**20 Golden Greats**	Frank Sinatra	Capitol	4		

US 1978 APR-JUNE

April 1978

This Mnth	Last Mnth	Title	Artist	Label	Wks in 10	UK Pos	
1	1	**Saturday Night Fever**	Soundtrack	RSO	35	1	**11P**
2	4	**Slowhand**	Eric Clapton	RSO	16	23	**3P**
3	2	**The Stranger**	Billy Joel	Columbia	19	25	**F9P**
4	10	**Even Now**	Barry Manilow	Arista	7	12	**3P**
5	7	**Weekend In L.A.**	George Benson	Warner	10	47	**P**
6	-	**Point Of Know Return**	Kansas	Kirshner	13		**3P**
7	6	**Aja**	Steely Dan	ABC	20	5	**2P**
8	-	**Earth**	Jefferson Starship	Grunt	12		**P**
9	-	**London Town**	Wings	Capitol	10	4	**P**
10	3	**Running On Empty**	Jackson Browne	Asylum	17	28	**P**

May 1978

This Mnth	Last Mnth	Title	Artist	Label	Wks in 10	UK Pos	
1	1	**Saturday Night Fever**	Soundtrack	RSO	35	1	**11P**
2	9	**London Town**	Wings	Capitol	10	4	**P**
3	2	**Slowhand**	Eric Clapton	RSO	16	23	**3P**
4	8	**Earth**	Jefferson Starship	Grunt	12		**P**
5	-	**Feels So Good**	Chuck Mangione	A&M	11		**F2P**
6	6	**Point Of Know Return**	Kansas	Kirshner	13		**3P**
7	10	**Running On Empty**	Jackson Browne	Asylum	17	28	**P**
8	-	**Excitable Boy**	Warren Zevon	Asylum	4		**FL**
9	3	**The Stranger**	Billy Joel	Columbia	19	25	**F9P**
10	-	**Champagne Jam**	Atlanta Rhythm Section	Polydor	5		**FPL**

June 1978

This Mnth	Last Mnth	Title	Artist	Label	Wks in 10	UK Pos	
1	1	**Saturday Night Fever**	Soundtrack	RSO	35	1	**11P**
2	5	**Feels So Good**	Chuck Mangione	A&M	11		**F2P**
3	2	**London Town**	Wings	Capitol	10	4	**P**
4	-	**Showdown**	Isley Brothers	T-Neck	4	50	**P**
5	4	**Earth**	Jefferson Starship	Grunt	12		**P**
6	-	**City To City**	Gerry Rafferty	UA	8	6	**FPL**
7	-	**FM**	Soundtrack	MCA	4	37	**P**
8	3	**Slowhand**	Eric Clapton	RSO	16	23	**3P**
9	-	**So Full Of Love**	O'Jays	Philly Int.	3		**PL**
10	10	**Champagne Jam**	Atlanta Rhythm Section	Polydor	5		**FPL**

• The soundtrack albums to the movies **Thank God It's Friday** and **FM** reached the Top 20. The former featured Donna Summer and The Commodores, while the latter included hit singles from such acts as Tom Petty, Foreigner, Steely Dan, Steve Miller and The Eagles.

• **London Town** by Paul McCartney & Wings was the latest album to be kept out of the top spot by **Saturday Night Fever**. It followed in the footsteps of such noted albums as **Slowhand** by Eric Clapton, **The Stranger** by Billy Joel and **Foot Loose And Fancy Free** by Rod Stewart.

• Clocking up their last Top 10 entries were such notables as Johnny Mathis with **You Light Up My Life**, Roberta Flack with **Blue Lights In The Basement**, and The O'Jays with **So Full Of Love**.

• Among the acts who reached the Top 40 for the first time were: punk funkster Rick James with **Come Get It!** and instrumentalist Chuck Mangione with **Feels So Good**. There was also Van Halen's eponymous debut and the Bee Gees youngest brother, Andy Gibb, with **Flowing Rivers**. The latter album contained two Number 1 singles, 'I Just Want To Be Your Everything' and '(Love Is) Thicker Than Water'.

UK 1978 JULY-SEPT

• The British music media raved about new wave. Acts such as The Rezillos with **Can't Stand The Rezillos**, Magazine with **Real Life** and left-field Ohio band Devo with **Q: Are We Not Men? A: No We Are Devo!** charted. However, old wave still ruled, with artists like The Rolling Stones, Bob Dylan and The Who adding to their hit totals. By the way, in the USA veteran rockers The Stones broke the indoor attendance record when 80,000 people paid over $1 million to see them at the New Orleans Superdome.

• Motorhead and The Cure signed new record deals as did rock revivalist Shakin' Stevens – who played the lead in the musical *Elvis*. Joy Division – who later evolved into New Order – released their debut single, and ex-Sex Pistol Johnny Rotten launched his new outfit, Public Image Ltd.

• Foreigner, who had still to crack the UK market, joined The Jam, Ultravox, Status Quo and American singer Patti Smith at the Reading Festival. Eric Clapton, Graham Parker and Joan Armatrading supported Bob Dylan at a massive gig on a Surrey airfield, it took five hours to clear the car park. Other live news included David Bowie starting the UK leg of his world tour and Fleetwood Mac selling out their American tour.

July 1978

This Mnth	Last Mnth	Title	Artist	Label	Wks in 10	US Pos	
1	1	**Saturday Night Fever**	Soundtrack	RSO	29	1	
2	7	**Live And Dangerous**	Thin Lizzy	Vertigo	10	84	
3	-	**Some Girls**	Rolling Stones	Rolling Stones	6	1	
4	-	**Street Legal**	Bob Dylan	CBS	9	11	
5	-	**The Kick Inside**	Kate Bush	EMI	14		F
6	-	**Octave**	Moody Blues	Threshold	5	13	
7	2	**The Album**	Abba	Epic	25	14	
8	-	**20 Golden Greats**	Hollies	EMI	7		L
9	5	**You Light Up My Life**	Johnny Mathis	CBS	10	9	
10	-	**War Of The Worlds**	Jeff Wayne	CBS	20		FPL

August 1978

This Mnth	Last Mnth	Title	Artist	Label	Wks in 10	US Pos	
1	1	**Saturday Night Fever**	Soundtrack	RSO	29	1	
2	-	**Night Flight To Venus**	Boney M	Atlantic/Hansa	26	134	F
3	8	**20 Golden Greats**	Hollies	EMI	7		L
4	-	**20 Giant Hits**	Nolans	Target	5		F
5	4	**Street Legal**	Bob Dylan	CBS	9	11	
6	-	**Grease**	Soundtrack	RSO	28	1	P
7	2	**Live And Dangerous**	Thin Lizzy	Vertigo	10	84	
8	5	**The Kick Inside**	Kate Bush	EMI	14		F
9	10	**War Of The Worlds**	Jeff Wayne	CBS	20		FPL
10	-	**Star Party**	Various	K-Tel	4		

September 1978

This Mnth	Last Mnth	Title	Artist	Label	Wks in 10	US Pos	
1	2	**Night Flight To Venus**	Boney M	Atlantic/Hansa	26	134	F
2	1	**Saturday Night Fever**	Soundtrack	RSO	29	1	
3	-	**Classic Rock**	London Symphony Orchestra	K-Tel	11	185	
4	6	**Grease**	Soundtrack	RSO	28	1	P
5	-	**Images**	Don Williams	K-Tel	13		FL
6	9	**War Of The Worlds**	Jeff Wayne	CBS	20		FPL
7	-	**Who Are You**	Who	Polydor	5	2	
8	10	**Star Party**	Various	K-Tel	4		
9	-	**James Galway Plays Songs For Annie**	James Galway	RCA Red Seal	4	153	FL
10	4	**20 Giant Hits**	Nolans	Target	5		F

US 1978 JULY-SEPT

July 1978

This Mnth	Last Mnth	Title	Artist	Label	Wks in 10	UK Pos	
1	6	**City To City**	Gerry Rafferty	UA	8	6	**FPL**
2	-	**Natural High**	Commodores	Motown	16	8	**P**
3	-	**Some Girls**	Rolling Stones	Rolling Stones	23	2	**4P**
4	1	**Saturday Night Fever**	Soundtrack	RSO	35	1	**11P**
5	-	**Stranger In Town**	Bob Seger &				
			The Silver Bullet Band	Capitol	12	31	**5P**
6	-	**Grease**	Soundtrack	RSO	29	1	**8P**
7	-	**Darkness On The Edge Of Town**	Bruce Springsteen	Columbia	8	16	**2P**
8	-	**Shadow Dancing**	Andy Gibb	RSO	9	15	**FPL**
9	2	**Feels So Good**	Chuck Mangione	A&M	11		**F2P**
10	7	**FM**	Soundtrack	MCA	4	37	**P**

August 1978

This Mnth	Last Mnth	Title	Artist	Label	Wks in 10	UK Pos	
1	6	**Grease**	Soundtrack	RSO	29	1	**8P**
2	3	**Some Girls**	Rolling Stones	Rolling Stones	23	2	**4P**
3	2	**Natural High**	Commodores	Motown	16	8	**P**
4	-	**Double Vision**	Foreigner	Atlantic	27	32	**5P**
5	5	**Stranger In Town**	Bob Seger &				
			The Silver Bullet Band	Capitol	12	31	**5P**
6	-	**Sergeant Pepper's Lonely Hearts**					
		Club Band	Soundtrack	RSO	9	38	**P**
7	7	**Darkness On The Edge Of Town**	Bruce Springsteen	Columbia	8	16	**2P**
8	8	**Shadow Dancing**	Andy Gibb	RSO	9	15	**FPL**
9	-	**Worlds Away**	Pablo Cruise	A&M	4		**FPL**
10	4	**Saturday Night Fever**	Soundtrack	RSO	35	1	**11P**

September 1978

This Mnth	Last Mnth	Title	Artist	Label	Wks in 10	UK Pos	
1	1	**Grease**	Soundtrack	RSO	29	1	**8P**
2	2	**Some Girls**	Rolling Stones	Rolling Stones	23	2	**4P**
3	4	**Double Vision**	Foreigner	Atlantic	27	32	**5P**
4	-	**Don't Look Back**	Boston	Epic	11	9	**6P**
5	6	**Sergeant Pepper's Lonely Hearts**					
		Club Band	Soundtrack	RSO	9	38	**P**
6	3	**Natural High**	Commodores	Motown	16	8	**P**
7	-	**Who Are You**	Who	MCA	10	6	**P**
8	-	**Blam!**	Brothers Johnson	A&M	5	48	**P**
9	9	**Worlds Away**	Pablo Cruise	A&M	4		**FPL**
10	-	**A Taste Of Honey**	Taste Of Honey	Capitol	5		**FPL**

• The soundtrack from *Saturday Night Fever* star John Travolta's latest movie, **Grease** topped the US and UK charts for three months with combined sales of almost 10 million. It contained 'You're The One That I Want' and 'Summer Nights' by Travolta and Olivia Newton-John, which both sold over a million copies in the UK alone. RSO Records also hit with the soundtrack to **Sergeant Pepper's Lonely Hearts Club Band,** which starred The Bee Gees and Peter Frampton. The film was no classic, but it encouraged enough people to buy The Beatles original, returning that to the Top 20.

• America's top albums achieved impressive sales figures. Boston's first two albums eventually sold over six million copies each, Bob Seger's first two Top 10 entries went on to sell over five million each and Foreigner's (above) first couple both passed the four million mark. Incidentally, Boston's last LP for eight years, **Don't Look Back,** hit the top in just three weeks.

UK 1978 OCT-DEC

October 1978

This Mnth	Last Mnth	Title	Artist	Label	Wks in 10	US Pos	
1	4	**Grease**	Soundtrack	RSO	28	1	P
2	5	**Images**	Don Williams	K-Tel	13		FL
3	-	**Big Wheels Of Motown**	Various	Motown	6		
4	1	**Night Flight To Venus**	Boney M	Atlantic/Hansa	26	134	F
5	3	**Classic Rock**	London Symphony Orchestra	K-Tel	11	185	
6	6	**War Of The Worlds**	Jeff Wayne	CBS	20		FPL
7	-	**Bloody Tourists**	10 C.C.	Mercury	5	69	
8	-	**Strikes Again**	Rose Royce	Whitfield	3	28	F
9	-	**Stage**	David Bowie	RCA	2	44	
10	2	**Saturday Night Fever**	Soundtrack	RSO	29	1	

November 1978

This Mnth	Last Mnth	Title	Artist	Label	Wks in 10	US Pos	
1	1	**Grease**	Soundtrack	RSO	28	1	P
2	4	**Night Flight To Venus**	Boney M	Atlantic/Hansa	26	134	F
3	-	**Emotions**	Various	K-Tel	8		
4	3	**Big Wheels Of Motown**	Various	Motown	6		
5	-	**25th Anniversary Album**	Shirley Bassey	UA	4		L
6	2	**Images**	Don Williams	K-Tel	13		FL
7	-	**Can't Stand The Heat**	Status Quo	Vertigo	2		
8	6	**War Of The Worlds**	Jeff Wayne	CBS	20		FPL
9	-	**Give 'em Enough Rope**	Clash	CBS	2	128	F
10	-	**Brotherhood Of Man**	Brotherhood Of Man	K-Tel	3		FL

December 1978

This Mnth	Last Mnth	Title	Artist	Label	Wks in 10	US Pos	
1	1	**Grease**	Soundtrack	RSO	28	1	P
2	-	**Singles 1974-78**	Carpenters	A&M	8		
3	-	**20 Golden Greats**	Neil Diamond	MCA	8		
4	-	**Blondes Have More Fun**	Rod Stewart	Riva	12	1	
5	-	**Midnight Hustle**	Various	K-Tel	7		
6	-	**Jazz**	Queen	EMI	5	6	
7	2	**Night Flight To Venus**	Boney M	Atlantic/Hansa	26	134	F
8	-	**Greatest Hits**	Showaddywaddy	Arista	6		
9	3	**Emotions**	Various	K-Tel	8		
10	-	**Lionheart**	Kate Bush	EMI	3		

• Sex Pistol Sid Vicious was charged with the murder of his American girlfriend Nancy Spungen in New York. He died from a heroin overdose before the case went to court.

• 1978 was undoubtedly a year of great musical change in Britain. It ended with The Jam, The Clash and Ireland's Boomtown Rats all hitting the Top 10 for the first time with **All Mod Cons, Give 'Em Enough Rope** and **Tonic For The Troops** respectively. Further down the chart, music media darlings X-Ray Spex and Siouxsie & The Banshees debuted with **Germ Free Adolescents** and **The Scream**. Also making their first entries were two Sex Pistols spin-offs, Johnny Rotten's new band Public Image Ltd with **Public Image** and Glen Matlock's band The Rich Kids with **Ghost Of Princes In The Tower**. Also enjoying their first taste of album success was new heavy metal outfit Whitesnake, including ex-Deep Purple members David Coverdale and Jon Lord, with **Trouble**.

• The soundtrack to *Grease* topped the chart for the whole quarter, which stopped the following noteworthy compilation albums from reaching the Number 1 slot: **Images** by country performer Don Williams, **Singles 1974-1978** by The Carpenters and **20 Golden Greats** from Neil Diamond.

US 1978 OCT-DEC

October 1978

This Mnth	Last Mnth	Title	Artist	Label	Wks in 10	UK Pos	
1	1	**Grease**	Soundtrack	RSO	29	1	**8P**
2	4	**Don't Look Back**	Boston	Epic	11	9	**6P**
3	7	**Who Are You**	Who	MCA	10	6	**P**
4	3	**Double Vision**	Foreigner	Atlantic	27	32	**5P**
5	-	**Living In The USA**	Linda Ronstadt	Asylum	9	39	**P**
6	-	**Nightwatch**	Kenny Loggins	Columbia	7		**FPL**
7	2	**Some Girls**	Rolling Stones	Rolling Stones	23	2	**4P**
8	-	**Live And More**	Donna Summer	Casablanca	12	16	**FP**
9	10	**A Taste Of Honey**	Taste Of Honey	Capitol	5		**FPL**
10	-	**Twin Sons Of Different Mothers**	Dan Fogelberg & Tim Weisberg	Full Moon	5		**FP**

November 1978

This Mnth	Last Mnth	Title	Artist	Label	Wks in 10	UK Pos	
1	8	**Live And More**	Donna Summer	Casablanca	12	16	**FP**
2	5	**Living In The USA**	Linda Ronstadt	Asylum	9	39	**P**
3	1	**Grease**	Soundtrack	RSO	29	1	**8P**
4	4	**Double Vision**	Foreigner	Atlantic	27	32	**5P**
5	-	**52nd Street**	Billy Joel	Columbia	22	10	**7P**
6	3	**Who Are You**	Who	MCA	10	6	**P**
7	-	**Pieces Of Eight**	Styx	A&M	8		**3P**
8	-	**A Wild And Crazy Guy**	Steve Martin	Warner	10		**PL**
9	2	**Don't Look Back**	Boston	Epic	11	9	**6P**
10	7	**Some Girls**	Rolling Stones	Rolling Stones	23	2	**4P**

December 1978

This Mnth	Last Mnth	Title	Artist	Label	Wks in 10	UK Pos	
1	5	**52nd Street**	Billy Joel	Columbia	22	10	**7P**
2	8	**A Wild And Crazy Guy**	Steve Martin	Warner	10		**PL**
3	-	**Barbra Streisand's Greatest Hits, Volume 2**	Barbra Streisand	Columbia	11	1	**5P**
4	1	**Live And More**	Donna Summer	Casablanca	12	16	**FP**
5	4	**Double Vision**	Foreigner	Atlantic	27	32	**5P**
6	3	**Grease**	Soundtrack	RSO	29	1	**8P**
7	-	**C'est Chic**	Chic	Atlantic	11	2	**FP**
8	-	**Comes A Time**	Neil Young	Reprise	4	42	
9	-	**Jazz**	Queen	Elektra	5	2	**P**
10	7	**Pieces Of Eight**	Styx	A&M	8		**3P**

• Many musical styles fared well in 1978, helping to push the sales of records and tapes in the USA over $4 billion for the first time. With the aim of grossing even more money in 1979, CBS Records upped the price of albums by a dollar to $8.98.

• Female singers were again riding high with three acts taking their albums all the way to Number 1: Linda Ronstadt's **Living In The USA**, Barbra Streisand's **Greatest Hits Volume 2** and Donna Summer's **Live And More**. Disco diva Summer's first Top 10 entry was a double album that included the Number 1 single 'MacArthur Park'.

• The multi-talented Prince debuted on the chart with **Prince – For You**. Also scoring for the first time was ex-Rufus vocalist Chaka Khan with **Chaka**. Co-incidentally, six years later Khan would have a massive transatlantic hit with the Prince composed song 'I Feel For You'.

UK 1979 JAN-MAR

• On the social side, Eric Clapton married George Harrison's ex-wife Patti and Rod Stewart prepared to wed Alana Hamilton. Cher and Greg Allman's very short marriage ended, as did Beach Boy Brian Wilson's 15 year marriage.

• British acts, whose current UK hits gave them their first taste of US chart success included Elvis Costello, The Clash and The Boomtown Rats. At the same time, two British groups who had yet to make a major mark in their homeland were enjoying American chart success; The Police with **Outlandos d'Amour** and Dire Straits with their eponymous debut LP. Both acts capitolized on the situation by embarking on their first American tours.

• In order to increase the sales of singles, many companies were now releasing 12-inch records pressed on different colored vinyl. They were also using expensive and elaborate sleeves and some labels even die-cut records in different shapes in the hope of catching the public's eye. It was getting more and more expensive to properly launch an act on to the market. *Rolling Stone* reported that it now cost between $350,000-$500,000 to promote, support and produce product for a new album-oriented act.

January 1979

This Mnth	Last Mnth	Title	Artist	Label	Wks in 10	US Pos	
1	8	**Greatest Hits**	Showaddywaddy	Arista	6		
2	-	**Don't Walk Boogie**	Various	EMI	7		
3	2	**Singles 1974-78**	Carpenters	A&M	8		
4	1	**Grease**	Soundtrack	RSO	28	1	P
5	7	**Night Flight To Venus**	Boney M	Atlantic/Hansa	26	134	F
6	-	**Armed Forces**	Elvis Costello	Radar	13	10	
7	5	**Midnight Hustle**	Various	K-Tel	7		
8	-	**Parallel Lines**	Blondie	Chrysalis	37	6	P
9	3	**20 Golden Greats**	Neil Diamond	MCA	8		
10	4	**Blondes Have More Fun**	Rod Stewart	Riva	12	1	

February 1979

This Mnth	Last Mnth	Title	Artist	Label	Wks in 10	US Pos	
1	8	**Parallel Lines**	Blondie	Chrysalis	37	6	P
2	-	**Action Replay**	Various	K-Tel	7		
3	6	**Armed Forces**	Elvis Costello	Radar	13	10	
4	2	**Don't Walk Boogie**	Various	EMI	7		
5	-	**New Boots And Panties!!**	Ian Dury & The Blockheads	Stiff	11	168	F
6	-	**Spirits Having Flown**	Bee Gees	RSO	15	1	
7	-	**The Best Of Earth, Wind & Fire Vol. 1**	Earth, Wind & Fire	CBS	6	6	F
8	-	**Wings Greatest Hits**	Wings	Parlophone	4	29	
9	-	**Marty Robbins Collection**	Marty Robbins	Lotus	4		FL
10	-	**Strangers In The Night**	UFO	Chrysalis	3	42	F

March 1979

This Mnth	Last Mnth	Title	Artist	Label	Wks in 10	US Pos	
1	6	**Spirits Having Flown**	Bee Gees	RSO	15	1	
2	1	**Parallel Lines**	Blondie	Chrysalis	37	6	P
3	3	**Armed Forces**	Elvis Costello	Radar	13	10	
4	-	**Manilow Magic**	Barry Manilow	Arista	32		F
5	-	**C'est Chic**	Chic	Atlantic	9	4	FL
6	-	**Thank You Very Much-Reunion Concert At The London Palladium**	Cliff Richard	EMI	3		
7	-	**Greatest Hits Vol. 2**	Barbra Streisand	CBS	9	1	
8	-	**The Great Rock 'n' Roll Swindle**	Sex Pistols	Virgin	3		
9	2	**Action Replay**	Various	K-Tel	7		
10	5	**New Boots And Panties!!**	Ian Dury & The Blockheads	Stiff	11	168	F

US 1979 JAN-MAR

January 1979

This Mnth	Last Mnth	Title	Artist	Label	Wks in 10	UK Pos	
1	3	**Barbra Streisand's Greatest Hits, Volume 2**	Barbra Streisland	Columbia	11	1	**5p**
2	1	**52nd Street**	Billy Joel	Columbia	22	10	**7P**
3	-	**Briefcase Full Of Blues**	Blues Brothers	Atlantic	13		**F2PL**
4	2	**A Wild And Crazy Guy**	Steve Martin	Warner	10		**PL**
5	7	**C'est Chic**	Chic	Atlantic	11	2	**FP**
6	-	**The Best Of Earth, Wind & Fire Vol. 1**	Earth, Wind & Fire	ARC	8	6	**4P**
7	-	**You Don't Bring Me Flowers**	Neil Diamond	Columbia	6	15	**2P**
8	-	**Backless**	Eric Clapton	RSO	8	18	**P**
9	9	**Jazz**	Queen	Elektra	5	2	**P**
10	6	**Grease**	Soundtrack	RSO	29	1	**8P**

February 1979

This Mnth	Last Mnth	Title	Artist	Label	Wks in 10	UK Pos	
1	-	**Blondes Have More Fun**	Rod Stewart	Warner	14	3	**3P**
2	3	**Briefcase Full Of Blues**	Blues Brothers	Atlantic	13		**F2PL**
3	2	**52nd Street**	Billy Joel	Columbia	22	10	**7P**
4	-	**Cruisin'**	Village People	Casablanca	9	24	**FP**
5	-	**Spirits Having Flown**	Bee Gees	RSO	18	1	**P**
6	5	**C'est Chic**	Chic	Atlantic	11	2	**FP**
7	7	**You Don't Bring Me Flowers**	Neil Diamond	Columbia	6	15	**2P**
8	1	**Barbra Streisand's Greatest Hits, Volume 2**	Barbra Streisand	Columbia	11	1	**5P**
9	-	**Dire Straits**	Dire Straits	Warner	13	5	**F2P**
10	-	**Greatest Hits**	Barry Manilow	Arista	3		**3P**

March 1979

This Mnth	Last Mnth	Title	Artist	Label	Wks in 10	UK Pos	
1	5	**Spirits Having Flown**	Bee Gees	RSO	18	1	**P**
2	1	**Blondes Have More Fun**	Rod Stewart	Warner	14	3	**3P**
3	-	**Minute By Minute**	Doobie Brothers	Warner	16		**3P**
4	9	**Dire Straits**	Dire Straits	Warner	13	5	**F2P**
5	4	**Cruisin'**	Village People	Casablanca	9	24	**FP**
6	-	**Love Tracks**	Gloria Gaynor	Polydor	9	31	**FPL**
7	2	**Briefcase Full Of Blues**	Blues Brothers	Atlantic	13		**F2PL**
8	-	**Totally Hot**	Olivia Newton-John	MCA	6	30	**P**
9	3	**52nd Street**	Billy Joel	Columbia	22	10	**7P**
10	-	**2 Hot!**	Peaches & Herb	Polydor	13		**FPL**

• Digital recording was starting to make news, with many experts considering it the biggest advance since stereo. Unlike analogue recording, it did not involve the use of tapes. Instead sounds were sampled 40-50,000 times a second, and the information stored in binary numbers. Stephen Stills was acknowledged to be the first rock act to record digitally.

• Veteran rock group The Bee Gees, who were riding on the crest of the disco wave, were given their own star on the Hollywood Walk Of Fame. The group, whose **Spirits Having Flown** was a transatlantic Number 1, also grabbed themselves another Grammy – for Best Group Perfomance on 'How Deep Is Your Love'. They were not the only disco act with a top selling album; The Village People scored with **Crusin'** and Chic clicked with **C'est Chic**. At the same time, Gloria Gaynor and Peaches & Herb had their sole Top 10 entries with **Love Tracks** and **2 Hot!** respectively.

• Among the most noteworthy new American rock acts debuting in the Top 20 were ex-New York policeman Eddie Money with **Life For The Taking**, Cheap Trick **At Budokan**, The Cars and West Coast group Toto, the latter two hitting the heights with self-titled sets.

UK 1979 APR-JUNE

• German band leader James Last has had 57 chart entries without ever reaching the Number 1 position. His most successful LP to date is **Last The Whole Night Long** which reached the runner-up position this year.

• Top album sellers of the Eighties who made their chart debuts included Gary Numan & Tubeway Army with **Replicas**, singer/songwriter Chris Rea with **Deltics** and The Cure with **Three Imaginary Boys**. There were also the critically acclaimed bands Squeeze and Simple Minds who charted with **Cool For Cats** and **A Life In The Day** respectively.

• Among the news that made the headlines in the British music press was Elton John's very successful Russian tour, distinctive singer/songwriter Kate Bush's live debut and Abba's second successive chart entry at Number 1 with **Voulez-Vous**. There was also the return of *Juke Box Jury* to the TV screen, first Number 1 albums for Barbra Streisand and The Electric Light Orchestra, and Dire Straits' first Top 10 entry.

• The Boomtown Rats, whose singles 'I Don't Like Mondays' and 'Rat Trap' both hit Number 1 earlier this year, appeared at the California Music Festival. Other acts on the bill included top-line US rockers Van Halen, Cheap Trick, Aerosmith and Ted Nugent.

April 1979

This Mnth	Last Mnth	Title	Artist	Label	Wks in 10	US Pos	
1	7	**Greatest Hits Vol. 2**	Barbra Streisand	CBS	9	1	
2	-	**The Very Best Of Leo Sayer**	Leo Sayer	Chrysalis	10		L
3	5	**C'est Chic**	Chic	Atlantic	9	4	FL
4	1	**Spirits Having Flown**	Bee Gees	RSO	15	1	
5	-	**Breakfast In America**	Supertramp	A&M	20	1	
6	-	**Dire Straits**	Dire Straits	Vertigo	8	2	F
7	4	**Manilow Magic**	Barry Manilow	Arista	32		F
8	2	**Parallel Lines**	Blondie	Chrysalis	37	6	P
9	-	**Country Life**	Various	EMI	5		
10	-	**A Collection Of Their 20 Greatest Hits**	Three Degrees	Ariola	7		

May 1979

This Mnth	Last Mnth	Title	Artist	Label	Wks in 10	US Pos	
1	2	**The Very Best Of Leo Sayer**	Leo Sayer	Chrysalis	10		L
2	5	**Breakfast In America**	Supertramp	A&M	20	1	
3	-	**Black Rose (A Rock Legend)**	Thin Lizzy	Vertigo	4	81	
4	-	**Fate For Breakfast**	Art Garfunkel	CBS	4	67	L
5	-	**Voulez-Vous**	Abba	Epic	18	19	
6	-	**Last The Whole Night Long**	James Last	Polydor	12		
7	9	**Country Life**	Various	EMI	5		
8	4	**Spirits Having Flown**	Bee Gees	RSO	15	1	
9	1	**Greatest Hits Vol. 2**	Barbra Streisand	CBS	9	1	
10	6	**Dire Straits**	Dire Straits	Vertigo	8	2	F

June 1979

This Mnth	Last Mnth	Title	Artist	Label	Wks in 10	US Pos	
1	5	**Voulez-Vous**	Abba	Epic	18	19	
2	-	**Parallel Lines**	Blondie	Chrysalis	37	6	P
3	6	**Last The Whole Night Long**	James Last	Polydor	12		
4	-	**Do It Yourself**	Ian Dury & The Blockheads	Stiff	5	126	L
5	-	**Discovery**	Electric Light Orchestra	Jet	20	5	
6	-	**Lodger**	David Bowie	RCA	4	20	
7	-	**Bob Dylan At Budokan**	Bob Dylan	CBS	4	13	
8	-	**Communique**	Dire Straits	Vertigo	3	11	
9	-	**This Is It**	Various	CBS	3		
10	-	**Manifesto**	Roxy Music	Polydor	5	23	

US 1979 APR-JUNE

April 1979

This Mnth	Last Mnth	Title	Artist	Label	Wks in 10	UK Pos	
1	3	**Minute By Minute**	Doobie Brothers	Warner	16		**3P**
2	1	**Spirits Having Flown**	Bee Gees	RSO	18	1	**P**
3	4	**Dire Straits**	Dire Straits	Warner	13	5	**F2P**
4	10	**2 Hot!**	Peaches & Herb	Polydor	13		**FPL**
5	2	**Blondes Have More Fun**	Rod Stewart	Warner	14	3	**3P**
6	-	**Desolation Angels**	Bad Company	Swan Song	14	10	**2PL**
7	-	**Livin' Inside Your Love**	George Benson	Warner	5	24	
8	6	**Love Tracks**	Gloria Gaynor	Polydor	9	31	**FPL**
9	-	**Parallel Lines**	Blondie	Chrysalis	5	1	**FP**
10	-	**Enlightened Rouges**	Allman Brothers Band	Capricorn	5		**L**

May 1979

This Mnth	Last Mnth	Title	Artist	Label	Wks in 10	UK Pos	
1	4	**2 Hot!**	Peaches & Herb	Polydor	13		**FPL**
2	-	**Breakfast In America**	Supertramp	A&M	26	3	**F4P**
3	1	**Minute By Minute**	Doobie Brothers	Warner	16		**3P**
4	6	**Desolation Angels**	Bad Company	Swan Song	14	10	**2PL**
5	2	**Spirits Having Flown**	Bee Gees	RSO	18	1	**P**
6	-	**Van Halen II**	Van Halen	Warner	9	23	**F3P**
7	9	**Parallel Lines**	Blondie	Chrysalis	5	1	**FP**
8	-	**We Are Family**	Sister Sledge	Cotillion	9	7	**FL**
9	-	**Go West**	Village People	Casablanca	5	14	**PL**
10	-	**Bad Girls**	Donna Summer	Casablanca	16	23	**2P**

June 1979

This Mnth	Last Mnth	Title	Artist	Label	Wks in 10	UK Pos	
1	2	**Breakfast In America**	Supertramp	A&M	26	3	**F4P**
2	10	**Bad Girls**	Donna Summer	Casablanca	16	23	**2P**
3	8	**We Are Family**	Sister Sledge	Cotillion	9	7	**FL**
4	-	**Rickie Lee Jones**	Rickie Lee Jones	Warner	8	18	**FP**
5	1	**2 Hot!**	Peaches & Herb	Polydor	13		**FPL**
6	-	**Cheap Trick At Budokan**	Cheap Trick	Epic	14	29	**FP**
7	6	**Van Halen II**	Van Halen	Warner	9	23	**F3P**
8	4	**Desolation Angels**	Bad Company	Swan Song	14	10	**2PL**
9	3	**Minute By Minute**	Doobie Brothers	Warner	16		**3P**
10	-	**I Am**	Earth, Wind & Fire	ARC	15	5	**2P**

• Female vocalists kept up the pressure at the top end of the chart. Making their first entries were singer/songwriter Rickie Lee Jones with her self-titled debut album, and the Debbie Harry-fronted new wave act Blondie with **Parallel Lines**. There was also no shortage of female disco divas in the Top 10. Sister Sledge made it with **We Are Family** – produced by Chic's Nile Rodgers and Bernard Edwards – and Anita Ward scored with **Songs Of Love**. Donna Summer clocked up her second successive chart topping double album with **Bad Girls**. Ward's album contained her transatlantic chart topper 'Ring My Bell' and Summer's set included the Number 1 singles 'Hot Stuff' and 'Bad Girls'.

• The Doobie Brothers' (above) seventh Top 10 entry, **Minute By Minute**, gave the noted Californian group their one chart topping album. Another rock band who reached the summit for the only time was British band Supertramp with **Breakfast In America**.

UK 1979 JULY-SEPT

July 1979

This Mnth	Last Mnth	Title	Artist	Label	Wks in 10	US Pos	
1	5	**Discovery**	Electric Light Orchestra	Jet	20	5	
2	-	**Replicas**	Tubeway Army	Beggars Banquet	9		F
3	2	**Parallel Lines**	Blondie	Chrysalis	37	6	P
4	-	**The Best Disco Album In The World**	Various	Warner	11		
5	-	**Live Killers**	Queen	EMI	5	16	
6	-	**Bridges**	John Williams	Lotus	5		FL
7	-	**I Am**	Earth, Wind & Fire	CBS	14	3	
8	-	**Breakfast In America**	Supertramp	A&M	20	1	
9	3	**Last The Whole Night Long**	James Last	Polydor	12		
10	1	**Voulez-Vous**	Abba	Epic	18	19	

August 1979

This Mnth	Last Mnth	Title	Artist	Label	Wks in 10	US Pos	
1	4	**The Best Disco Album In The World**	Various	Warner	11		
2	1	**Discovery**	Electric Light Orchestra	Jet	20	5	
3	8	**Breakfast In America**	Supertramp	A&M	20	1	
4	2	**Replicas**	Tubeway Army	Beggars Banquet	9		F
5	10	**Voulez-Vous**	Abba	Epic	18	19	
6	7	**I Am**	Earth, Wind & Fire	CBS	14	3	
7	3	**Parallel Lines**	Blondie	Chrysalis	37	6	P
8	-	**Some Product - Carri On Sex Pistols**	Sex Pistols	Virgin	3		
9	-	**The Best Of The Dooleys**	Dooleys	GTO	2		FL
10	-	**Outlandos D'amour**	Police	A&M	11	23	F

September 1979

This Mnth	Last Mnth	Title	Artist	Label	Wks in 10	US Pos	
1	2	**Discovery**	Electric Light Orchestra	Jet	20	5	
2	-	**In Through The Out Door**	Led Zeppelin	Swan Song	5	1	
3	1	**The Best Disco Album In The World**	Various	Warner	11		
4	-	**Slow Train Coming**	Bob Dylan	Columbia	11	3	
5	6	**I Am**	Earth, Wind & Fire	CBS	14	3	
6	-	**The Pleasure Principal**	Gary Numan	Beggars Banquet	6	16	
7	5	**Voulez-Vous**	Abba	Epic	18	19	
8	3	**Breakfast In America**	Supertramp	A&M	20	1	
9	-	**Rock 'n' Roll Juvenile**	Cliff Richard	EMI	3		
10	7	**Parallel Lines**	Blondie	Chrysalis	37	6	P

• As the first rap hit single 'Rapper's Delight' by the Sugarhill Gang was released Stateside, 2-Tone music first made the British charts courtesy of The Specials and Madness.

• As the decade wound down, *Rolling Stone* noted that videos were beginning to become a very important tool in record promotion. They named David Bowie's 'Boys Keep Swinging' and Queen's 'Bohemian Rhapsody' as good examples.

• Neil Young's concert movie **Rust Never Sleeps** was released and the double album from it took him back into the transatlantic Top 20. Another singer/songwriter adding to his hit score was Bob Dylan whose born-again album **Slow Train Coming** proved to be the last American Top 10 entry to date for this legendary artist.

• Fifties rockers in the news included Chuck Berry, who was jailed for four months for tax evasion, just four months after playing for the President at the White House. Reverend Richard Penniman aka Little Richard warned his congregations about the evils of rock'n'roll music, and Dorsey Burnette of The Johnny Burnette Trio died of a heart attack. In Britain, Fifties rock TV show *Oh Boy!* was relaunched, Cliff Richard clicked with **Rock'n'Roll Juvenile** and his ex-backing band The Shadows whose **String Of Hits** reached Number 1.

US 1979 JULY-SEPT

July 1979

This Mnth	Last Mnth	Title	Artist	Label	Wks in 10	UK Pos	
1	2	**Bad Girls**	Donna Summer	Casablanca	16	23	**2P**
2	1	**Breakfast In America**	Supertramp	A&M	26	3	**F4P**
3	10	**I Am**	Earth, Wind & Fire	ARC	15	5	**2P**
4	6	**Cheap Trick At Budokan**	Cheap Trick	Epic	14	29	**FP**
5	-	**Discovery**	Electric Light Orchestra	Jet	10	1	**P**
6	4	**Rickie Lee Jones**	Rickie Lee Jones	Warner	8	18	**FP**
7	-	**Candy-O**	Cars	Elektra	12	30	**FP**
8	-	**Back To The Egg**	Paul McCartney	Columbia	5	6	**P**
9	-	**Songs Of Love**	Anita Ward	Juana	4		**FL**
10	8	**Desolation Angels**	Bad Company	Swan Song	14	10	**2PL**

August 1979

This Mnth	Last Mnth	Title	Artist	Label	Wks in 10	UK Pos	
1	-	**Get The Knack**	Knack	Capitol	15	65	**F2PL**
2	1	**Bad Girls**	Donna Summer	Casablanca	16	23	**2P**
3	2	**Breakfast In America**	Supertramp	A&M	26	3	**F4P**
4	7	**Candy-O**	Cars	Elektra	12	30	**FP**
5	3	**I Am**	Earth, Wind & Fire	ARC	15	5	**2P**
6	-	**Teddy**	Teddy Pendergrass	Philly Int.	5		**FPL**
7	5	**Discovery**	Electric Light Orchestra	Jet	10	1	**P**
8	4	**Cheap Trick At Budokan**	Cheap Trick	Epic	14	29	**FP**
9	-	**The Kids Are Alright**	Who	MCA	3	26	**P**
10	-	**Million Mile Reflections**	Charlie Daniels Band	Epic	5	74	**F2PL**

September 1979

This Mnth	Last Mnth	Title	Artist	Label	Wks in 10	UK Pos	
1	1	**Get The Knack**	Knack	Capitol	15	65	**F2PL**
2	3	**Breakfast In America**	Supertramp	A&M	26	3	**F4P**
3	-	**In Through The Out Door**	Led Zeppelin	Swan Song	18	1	**5P**
4	4	**Candy-O**	Cars	Elektra	12	30	**FP**
5	-	**Risque**	Chic	Atlantic	7	29	**PL**
6	5	**I Am**	Earth, Wind & Fire	Arc	15	5	**2P**
7	10	**Million Mile Reflections**	Charlie Daniels Band	Epic	5	74	**F2PL**
8	-	**Slow Train Coming**	Bob Dylan	Columbia	6	2	**PL**
9	-	**Midnight Magic**	Commodores	Motown	15		
10	-	**Off The Wall**	Michael Jackson	Epic	29	5	**6P**

• Bruce Springsteen, James Taylor, The Doobie Brothers, Bonnie Raitt, Carly Simon and Crosby, Stills & Nash took part in the *No Nukes* shows at Madison Square Garden. The Cars and James Taylor attracted large crowds at New York's Central Park. Swedish superstars Abba, who scored their third US Top 20 album with **Voulez-Vous**, made their North American concert debut. In Britain, The Who, plus AC/DC and The Stranglers drew big crowds to Wembley, and Led Zeppelin's first UK show for four years drew 120,000 fans to the Knebworth Festival. They scored their eighth and last successive UK Number 1 LP with **In Through The Out Door**.

• A wide variety of artists were enjoying their only Top 10 entries. Numbered among these were soulful Teddy Pendergrass, Beatles-esque group, The Knack, and country/rockers The Charlie Daniels Band. There was also folk/pop singer/songwriter John Stewart, noted actor Robin Williams and Australia's Little River Band.

• The Top 20 welcomed back Michael Jackson, Dionne Warwick and The Kinks. After an eight year absence, Jackson returned with the classic **Off The Wall** and Warwick resurfaced for the first time since 1969 with the Barry Manilow-produced **Dionne**. The Kinks, who had not had reached the 20 for 13 years, made that journey with **Low Budget**.

UK 1979 OCT-DEC

October 1979

This Mnth	Last Mnth	Title	Artist	Label	Wks in 10	US Pos	
1	-	**Reggatta De Blanc**	Police	A&M	26	25	
2	-	**Eat To The Beat**	Blondie	Chrysalis	5	17	
3	6	**The Pleasure Principal**	Gary Numan	Beggars Banquet	6	16	
4	-	**The Long Run**	Eagles	Asylum	4	1	
5	-	**Oceans Of Fantasy**	Boney M	Atlantic/Hansa	4		
6	-	**Whatever You Want**	Status Quo	Vertigo	3		
7	1	**Discovery**	Electric Light Orchestra	Jet	20	5	
8	-	**Off The Wall**	Michael Jackson	Epic	21	3	F
9	-	**String Of Hits**	Shadows	EMI	12		
10	-	**Outlandos D'amour**	Police	A&M	11	23	F

• The Police scored the first of five successive Number 1 albums with **Regatta De Blanc**. Amazingly, each of them entered at Number 1. In America, The Eagles scored their fourth successive Number 1 with **The Long Run** and The Bee Gees scored their third with **Bee Gees Greatest**.

• The last major record deals of the Seventies included Paul McCartney's $20 million deal with Columbia and Paul Simon's $14 million deal with Warners.

• One of the century's greatest composers Richard Rodgers died. Among his many works were the musicals *South Pacific* and *The Sound Of Music*, both of which had spawned amazingly successful albums in the Sixties.

• There was an upsurge of interest in heavy metal music in Britain. Whitesnake charted with **Love Hunter**, Motorhead with **Bomber**, Gillan's **Mr. Universe** reached the Top 20, and Judas Priest scored their first Top 10 entry with **Unleashed In The East**.

• A series of concerts for the people of Kampuchea were held in London. The headliners included Paul McCartney, The Clash, The Who, Elvis Costello, Ian Dury, Anglo-American band The Pretenders, The Specials and Led Zeppelin's Robert Plant.

November 1979

This Mnth	Last Mnth	Title	Artist	Label	Wks in 10	US Pos	
1	1	**Reggatta De Blanc**	Police	A&M	26	25	
2	-	**Tusk**	Fleetwood Mac	Warner	6	4	
3	-	**Greatest Hits Vol. 2**	Abba	Epic	13	46	
4	-	**Greatest Hits**	Rod Stewart	Riva	12	22	
5	-	**Rock 'n' Roller Disco**	Various	Ronco	5		
6	-	**Lena's Music Album**	Lena Martell	Pye	6		F
7	-	**Greatest Hits 1972-1978**	10 C.C.	Mercury	5	188	
8	-	**20 Golden Greats**	Diana Ross	Motown	8		
9	-	**Specials**	Specials	2-Tone	6	84	F
10	2	**Eat To The Beat**	Blondie	Chrysalis	5	17	

December 1979

This Mnth	Last Mnth	Title	Artist	Label	Wks in 10	US Pos
1	4	**Greatest Hits**	Rod Stewart	Riva	12	22
2	3	**Greatest Hits Vol. 2**	Abba	Epic	13	46
3	1	**Reggatta De Blanc**	Police	A&M	26	25
4	-	**The Wall**	Pink Floyd	Harvest	9	1
5	-	**Love Songs**	Elvis Presley	K-Tel	6	
6	8	**20 Golden Greats**	Diana Ross	Motown	8	
7	-	**Peace In The Valley**	Various	Ronco	4	
8	-	**20 Hottest Hits**	Hot Chocolate	RAK	6	
9	-	**ELO's Greatest Hits**	Electric Light Orchestra	Jet	6	30
10	5	**Rock 'n' Roller Disco**	Various	Ronco	5	

US 1979 OCT-DEC

October 1979

This Mnth	Last Mnth	Title	Artist	Label	Wks in 10	UK Pos	
1	3	**In Through The Out Door**	Led Zeppelin	Swan Song	18	1	**5P**
2	1	**Get The Knack**	Knack	Capitol	15	65	**F2PL**
3	9	**Midnight Magic**	Commodores	Motown	15		
4	8	**Slow Train Coming**	Bob Dylan	Columbia	6	2	**PL**
5	10	**Off The Wall**	Michael Jackson	Epic	29	5	**6P**
6	-	**Head Games**	Foreigner	Atlantic	6		**2P**
7	-	**The Long Run**	Eagles	Asylum	21	4	**4P**
8	2	**Breakfast In America**	Supertramp	A&M	26	3	**F4P**
9	-	**Dream Police**	Cheap Trick	Epic	3	41	**PL**
10	-	**Cornerstone**	Styx	A&M	18	36	**2P**

November 1979

This Mnth	Last Mnth	Title	Artist	Label	Wks in 10	UK Pos	
1	7	**The Long Run**	Eagles	Asylum	21	4	**4P**
2	1	**In Through The Out Door**	Led Zeppelin	Swan Song	18	1	**5P**
3	10	**Cornerstone**	Styx	A&M	18	36	**2P**
4	-	**Tusk**	Fleetwood Mac	Warner	16	1	**2P**
5	3	**Midnight Magic**	Commodores	Motown	15		
6	-	**On The Radio-Greatest Hits Volumes I & II**	Donna Summer	Casablanca	18	24	**2P**
7	-	**Rise**	Herb Alpert	A&M	7	37	**PL**
8	6	**Head Games**	Foreigner	Atlantic	6		**2P**
9	-	**Wet**	Barbra Streisand	Columbia	8	25	**P**
10	-	**Journey Through The Secret Life Of Plants**	Stevie Wonder	Tamla	9	8	

December 1979

This Mnth	Last Mnth	Title	Artist	Label	Wks in 10	UK Pos	
1	1	**The Long Run**	Eagles	Asylum	21	4	**4P**
2	6	**On The Radio-Greatest Hits Volumes I & II**	Donna Summer	Casablanca	18	24	**2P**
3	3	**Cornerstone**	Styx	A&M	18	36	**2P**
4	10	**Journey Through The Secret Life Of Plants**	Stevie Wonder	Tamla	9	8	
5	2	**In Through The Out Door**	Led Zeppelin	Swan Song	18	1	**5P**
6	-	**Bee Gees Greatest**	Bee Gees	RSO	13	6	**P**
7	4	**Tusk**	Fleetwood Mac	Warner	16	1	**2P**
8	9	**Wet**	Barbra Streisand	Columbia	8	25	**P**
9	7	**Rise**	Herb Alpert	A&M	7	37	**PL**
10	-	**Damn The Torpedoes**	Tom Petty & The Heartbreakers	Backstreet	20	57	**F2P**

• As the decade closed, the disco boom ended and record sales dropped after being at an all time high. In 1979, record and tape sales decreased 11% to $3.7 billion, albums accounted for 90% of the total, and platinum and gold record awards plummeted by almost 50%.

• Double albums were in vogue with Top 10 entries coming from Stevie Wonder, The Bee Gees, Fleetwood Mac and Donna Summer. The latter artist scoring her third consecutive Number 1 with a double album.

• Operatic superstar Luciano Pavarotti with **O Sole Mio – Favorite Neapolitan Songs** and female rock queen Pat Benatar with **In The Heat Of The Night** made their first Top 200 appearances. Australian AC/DC's **Highway To Hell** and the foremost funk band Kool & The Gang's **Ladies Night** debuted in the Top 20.

• Eleven fans were crushed to death at a Who concert in Cincinnati. Elton John packed Madison Square Garden for eight consecutive nights and yet another British act, Jethro Tull, followed him into that prestigious venue. Also attracting throngs of New Yorkers was Stevie Wonder who performed songs from his new album **Journey Through The Secret Life Of Plants** at the Metropolitan Opera House, backed by the National Afro-American Philharmonic Orchestra.

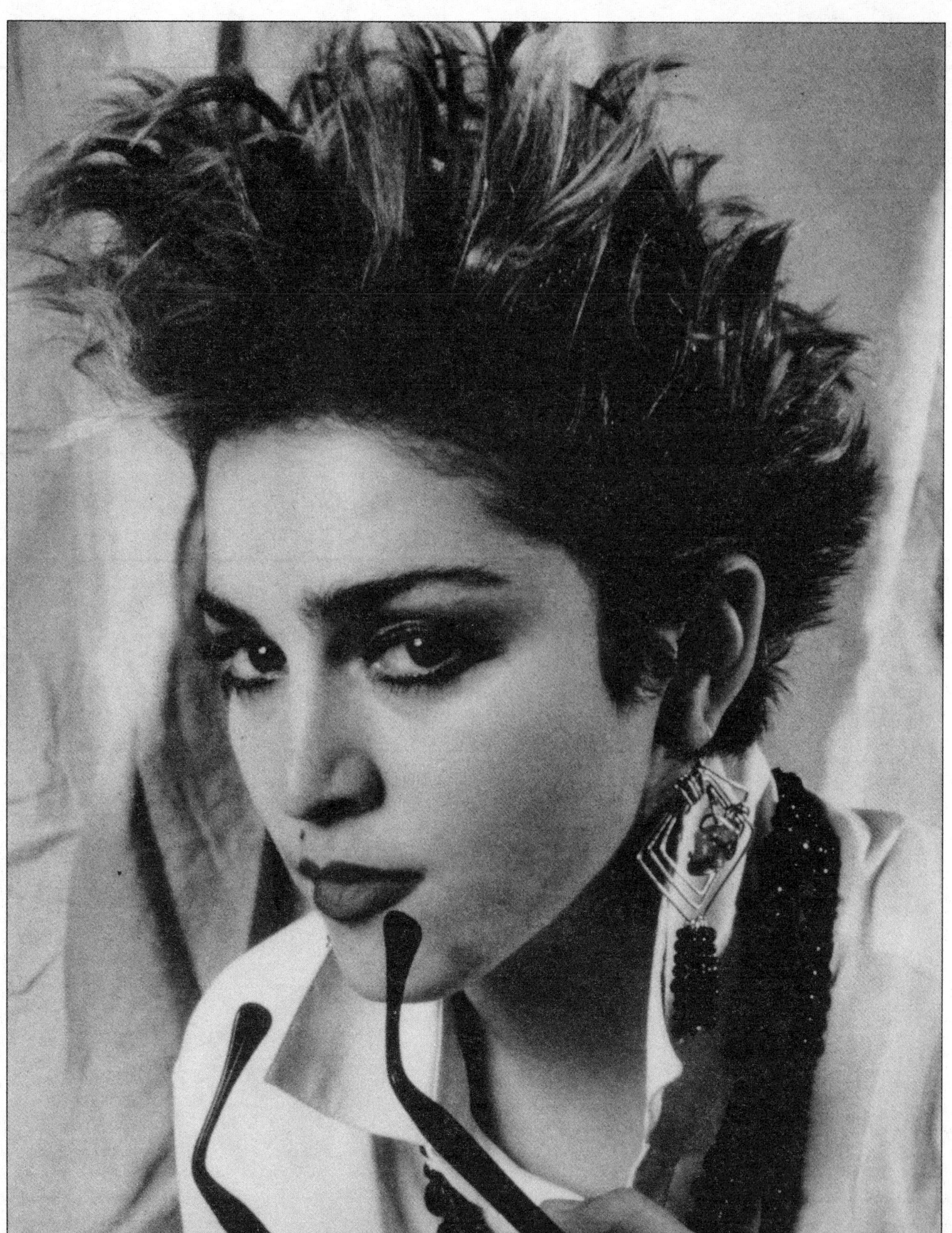

Madonna

the 1980s

Aerosmith

Eurythmics

Adam Ant

TOP UK ACTS ON THE US CHARTS IN THE 1980s	
1	Def Leppard
2	The Police
3	The Rolling Stones
4	Phil Collins
5	George Michael
6	Foreigner
7	Pink Floyd
8	U2
9	Whitesnake
10	Steve Winwood

After twenty years of revolution and change, it was perhaps surprising to see such acts as Johnny Mathis, the Rolling Stones, Barbra Streisand, the Bee Gees and Kenny Rogers scoring Number 1 albums in the first year of the new decade. However, transformation was just around the corner and, unlike earlier decades, it was to be a transformation based on technology as much as musical innovation. As the decade got into its stride, the synthesizer started to dominate the music scene in Britain and, thanks to acts like the Human League and Duran Duran, its popularity spread to the States.

TOP US ACTS ON THE UK CHARTS IN THE 1980s	
1	Michael Jackson
2	Madonna
3	Lionel Richie
4	Barbra Streisand
5	Bruce Springsteen
6	Whitney Houston
7	The Kids From Fame
8	Gloria Estefan/Miami Sound Machine
9	Paul Simon
10	Tina Turner

the 1980s

The synth-led groups played a major role in the second major British Invasion of the US charts (1982-1985): an invasion which made acts such as Culture Club, Tears For Fears and Wham! international superstars. It was a period when an artist's image became as important as their sound and this new breed of group found a very useful ally in MTV – another major musical innovation of the era. Acts with flamboyant images and extravagant videos reaped much MTV exposure, which in turn led to burgeoning sales.

Many records were smash hits in the decade. Michael Jackson shifted a staggering 40 million copies worldwide of *Thriller*, aided by a million dollar video and the unprecedented release of seven singles (six in the UK) from the set. Bruce Springsteen took a five-album box set straight into the Number 1 position on the US chart, and acts like Lionel Richie, Def Leppard, Billy Joel, Guns N' Roses, Police and Van Halen regularly sold quantities of albums unheard of in previous decades. Prince's *Purple Rain* shipped a million copies in its first week and was one of the many sound-track albums in the 1980s to pass the magic million mark in America. British record buyers bought many compilation albums and especially successful were the *Now That's What I Call Music!* and *Hits* series. They also bought vast quantities of Dire Straits' sixth album *Brothers In Arms*. It became the decade's best seller in Britain; its success was partly due to MTV and partly to the compact disk – yet another tech-nological leap forward. The new 'unscratchable' format first found favor among older, more affluent record-buyers who not only flocked to the shops to stock up on the latest releases from U2, Bon Jovi and Phil Collins but also to renew their worn-out collections of vinyl.

Nevertheless, it wasn't all AOR (Adult Oriented Rock) – dance music and pure pop also sold millions of albums on both sides of the Atlantic. Madonna, Whitney Houston, Gloria Estefan and Janet Jackson achieved phe-nomenal transatlantic sales and, in Britain, Kylie Minogue shifted over two million copies of her eponymous 1988 debut album. These artists' achievements were not only a victory for pop, but also a victory for women; who more than proved that they could hold their own in an industry that had previously excluded and patronized them.

However, the 1980s will probably be remembered in history as the decade when rock came of age. Top stars could not only sell out stadiums right around the globe, they also found they could actually make a difference to the world by making people aware of ecological problems and by raising money for those who needed it.

TOP US ALBUM ACTS OF THE 1980s

1. Michael Jackson
2. Bruce Springsteen
3. Def Leppard
4. Lionel Richie
5. Prince
6. Billy Joel
7. The Police
8. Whitney Houston
9. Bon Jovi
10. Van Halen
11. Journey
12. John Cougar Mellencamp
13. Madonna
14. Guns N' Roses
15. Janet Jackson
16. The Rolling Stones
17. Phil Collins
18. Huey Lewis & The News
19. Paula Abdul
20. George Michael

TOP UK ALBUM ACTS OF THE 1980s

1. Michael Jackson
2. Dire Straits
3. Phil Collins
4. Queen
5. Madonna
6. Eurythmics
7. Kylie Minogue
8. U2
9. Lionel Richie
10. Roxy Music
11. Simply Red
12. Adam & The Ants
13. Barbra Streisand
14. Bruce Springsteen
15. The Police
16. Fleetwood Mac
17. Paul Young
18. Wham!
19. Tears For Fears
20. Genesis

Queen

Dire Straits

TOP BRITISH ALBUMS OF THE 1980s

1	**Thriller**	Michael Jackson
2	**Brothers In Arms**	Dire Straits
3	**. . . But Seriously**	Phil Collins
4	**Can't Slow Down**	Lionel Ritchie
5	**Kings Of The Wild Frontier**	Adam & the Ants
6	**Born in the USA**	Bruce Springsteen
7	**Graceland**	Paul Simon
8	**True Blue**	Madonna
9	**No Jacket Required**	Phil Collins
10	**Kylie Minogue**	Kylie Minogue
11	**Tango In The Night**	Fleetwood Mac
12	**Bad**	Michael Jackson
13	**No Parlez**	Paul Young
14	**Kids From Fame**	Kids From Fame
15	**A New Flame**	Simply Red
16	**Ten Good Reasons**	Jason Donovan
17	**The Joshua Tree**	U2
18	**Songs From The Big Chair**	Tears For Fears
19	**An Innocent Man**	Billy Joel
20	**Diamond Life**	Sade

The Commodores

TOP AMERICAN ALBUMS OF THE 1980s

1	**Thriller**	Michael Jackson
2	**Born In The USA**	Bruce Springsteen
3	**Hysteria**	Def Leppard
4	**Dirty Dancing**	Soundtrack
5	**Forever Your Girl**	Paula Abdul
6	**Can't Slow Down**	Lionel Ritchie
7	**Faith**	George Michael
8	**Slippery When Wet**	Bon Jovi
9	**Appetite For Destruction**	Guns N' Roses
10	**Whitney Houston**	Whitney Houston
11	**Synchronicity**	The Police
12	**Don't Be Cruel**	Bobby Brown
13	**Girl You Know It's True**	Milli Vanilli
14	**Bad**	Michael Jackson
15	**Purple Rain**	Prince
16	**Whitesnake**	Whitesnake
17	**4**	Foreigner
18	**Sports**	Huey Lewis & The News
19	**Escape**	Journey
20	**Janet Jackson's Rhythm Nation 1814**	Janet Jackson

Genesis

Boy George

UK 1980 JAN-MAR

• Madness, The Specials and The Selecter put 2-Tone music into the Top 10 in Britain and the former two even cracked the US Top 200. The Specials also made their American live debut at New York's new wave club Hurrah.

• Interesting acts debuting in first charts of the new decade included Genesis member Mike Rutherford with **Smallcreep's Day**, Shakin' Stevens with **Take One** and youthful heavy metal act Def Leppard with **On Through The Night**. Other newcomers included The Psychedelic Furs' eponymous album, and Trevor Horn's group, Buggles, with **The Age Of Plastic**.

• Britain's first independent – Indie – Album Chart was headed by **Dirk Wears White Sox** by Adam & The Ants. **Unknown Pleasures** by Joy Division and **Stations Of The Crass** by Crass were among the quarter's other chart toppers.

January 1980

This Mnth	Last Mnth	Title	Artist	Label	Wks in 10	US Pos	
1	2	Greatest Hits Vol. 2	Abba	Epic	13	46	
2	1	Greatest Hits	Rod Stewart	Riva	12	22	
3	3	Reggatta De Blanc	Police	A&M	26	25	
4	4	The Wall	Pink Floyd	Columbia	9	1	
5	-	Pretenders	Pretenders	Real	9	9	F
6	8	20 Hottest Hits	Hot Chocolate	RAK	6		
7	-	Bee Gees Greatest	Bee Gees	RSO	6	1	
8	-	One Step Beyond	Madness	Stiff	9	128	F
9	-	Video Stars	Various	K-Tel	3		
10	5	Love Songs	Elvis Presley	K-Tel	6		

February 1980

This Mnth	Last Mnth	Title	Artist	Label	Wks in 10	US Pos	
1	5	Pretenders	Pretenders	Real	9	9	F
2	-	The Last Dance	Various	Motown	7		
3	8	One Step Beyond	Madness	Stiff	9	128	F
4	-	Short Stories	Jon & Vangelis	Polydor	5	125	F
5	-	Permanent Waves	Rush	Mercury	3	4	F
6	3	Reggatta De Blanc	Police	A&M	26	25	
7	-	Golden Collection	Charley Pride	K-Tel	3		FL
8	-	Get Happy	Elvis Costello	F-Beat	5	11	
9	-	String Of Hits	Shadows	EMI	12		
10	-	Specials	Specials	2-Tone	6	84	F

March 1980

This Mnth	Last Mnth	Title	Artist	Label	Wks in 10	US Pos	
1	9	String Of Hits	Shadows	EMI	12		
2	-	Tell Me On A Sunday	Marti Webb	Polydor	8		FL
3	-	Greatest Hits	Rose Royce	Whitfield	13		L
4	8	Get Happy	Elvis Costello	F-Beat	5	11	
5	-	Tears And Laughter	Johnny Mathis	CBS	6		
6	2	The Last Dance	Various	Motown	7		
7	6	Reggatta De Blanc	Police	A&M	26	25	
8	1	Pretenders	Pretenders	Real	9	9	F
9	-	Heartbreakers	Matt Monro	EMI	4		FL
10	-	Off The Wall	Michael Jackson	Epic	21	3	F

US 1980 JAN-MAR

January 1980

This Mnth	Last Mnth	Title	Artist	Label	Wks in 10	UK Pos	
1	2	**On The Radio-Greatest Hits - Volumes I & II**	Donna Summer	Casablanca	18	24	**2P**
2	-	**The Wall**	Pink Floyd	Columbia	27	3	**8P**
3	6	**Bee Gees Greatest**	Bee Gees	RSO	13	6	**P**
4	1	**The Long Run**	Eagles	Asylum	21	4	**4P**
5	10	**Damn The Torpedoes**	Tom Petty & The Heartbreakers	Backstreet	20	57	**F2P**
6	4	**Journey Through The Secret Life Of Plants**	Stevie Wonder	Tamla	9	8	
7	3	**Cornerstone**	Styx	A&M	18	36	**2P**
8	-	**Kenny**	Kenny Rogers	UA	10	7	**FP**
9	-	**Off The Wall**	Michael Jackson	Epic	29	5	**6P**
10	5	**In Through The Out Door**	Led Zeppelin	Swan Song	18	1	**5P**

February 1980

This Mnth	Last Mnth	Title	Artist	Label	Wks in 10	UK Pos	
1	2	**The Wall**	Pink Floyd	Columbia	27	3	**8P**
2	5	**Damn The Torpedoes**	Tom Petty & The Heartbreakers	Backstreet	20	57	**F2P**
3	4	**The Long Run**	Eagles	Asylum	21	4	**4P**
4	9	**Off The Wall**	Michael Jackson	Epic	29	5	**6P**
5	-	**Phoenix**	Dan Fogelberg	Full Moon	10	42	**P**
6	8	**Kenny**	Kenny Rogers	UA	10	7	**FP**
7	1	**On The Radio-Greatest Hits - Volumes I & II**	Donna Summer	Casablanca	18	24	**2P**
8	-	**Tusk**	Fleetwood Mac	Warner	16	1	**2P**
9	7	**Cornerstone**	Styx	A&M	18	36	**2P**
10	3	**Bee Gees Greatest**	Bee Gees	RSO	13	6	**P**

March 1980

This Mnth	Last Mnth	Title	Artist	Label	Wks in 10	UK Pos	
1	1	**The Wall**	Pink Floyd	Columbia	27	3	**8P**
2	2	**Damn The Torpedoes**	Tom Petty & The Heartbreakers	Backstreet	20	57	**F2P**
3	5	**Phoenix**	Dan Fogelberg	Full Moon	10	42	**P**
4	-	**Permanent Waves**	Rush	Mercury	5	3	**F**
5	-	**Mad Love**	Linda Ronstadt	Asylum	12	65	**P**
6	4	**Off The Wall**	Michael Jackson	Epic	29	5	**6P**
7	-	**Bebe Le Strange**	Heart	Epic	4		
8	-	**The Whispers**	Whispers	Solar	9		**FPL**
9	-	**Against The Wind**	Bob Seger & The Silver Bullet Band	Capitol	22	26	**4P**
10	7	**On The Radio-Greatest Hits - Volumes I & II**	Donna Summer	Casablanca	18	24	**2P**

• As the new decade dawned, Pink Floyd headed to the top with **The Wall**. It fought off all competition for 15 weeks and went on to become the year's most successful album. The first single from the album, 'Another Brick In The Wall' was a transatlantic Number 1, although, surprisingly, the parent album only reached Number 3 in the group's homeland. Pink Floyd also beat the longevity record for rock records set by Carole King's **Tapestry**, when **Dark Side Of The Moon** spent its 303rd week on the Top 200. Incidentally, **The Wall** was Pink Floyd's last US chart topper for 15 years.

• Established soul group The Whispers and ex-Moments, Ray, Goodman & Brown enjoyed their biggest pop hits with self-titled LPs. Other R&B albums in the Top 20 included **Light Up The Night** by The Brothers Johnson and **Where There's Smoke** by ex-Miracle man, Smokey Robinson.

• Movies in the news included Bette Midler's *The Rose*, country singer Loretta Lynn's bio-pic, *Coal Miner's Daughter*, and *American Gigolo*. All their soundtrack albums reached the Top 40 and Blondie's 'Call Me' from the latter film, topped the singles chart.

UK 1980 APR-JUNE

• Genesis, with the now noticeable influence of Phil Collins, had their biggest transatlantic hit with **Duke**, which topped the UK chart and narrowly missed the US Top 10. Shortly afterwards their ex-lead vocalist, Peter Gabriel, had a UK Number 1 with his third eponymous album.

• Heavy metal was riding on the crest of a wave. Crashing into the Top 10 were **British Steel** from Judas Priest, **Wheels Of Steel** by Saxon, **Heaven & Hell** by Black Sabbath, **Ready And Willing** from Whitesnake and a self-titled set from Iron Maiden. Movements within the heavy metal camp included Brian Johnson, previously of Geordie who took over lead vocals in AC/DC, Peter Criss left Kiss and Ronnie James Dio, ex-Rainbow, played his first gigs as Ozzy Osbourne's replacement in Black Sabbath. Led Zeppelin started their first European tour since 1973 – which they abandoned when drummer Jon Bonham died.

April 1980

This Mnth	Last Mnth	Title	Artist	Label	Wks in 10	US Pos	
1	3	**Greatest Hits**	Rose Royce	Whitfield	13		L
2	-	**Duke**	Genesis	Charisma	8	11	
3	-	**12 Gold Bars**	Status Quo	Vertigo	9		
4	5	**Tears And Laughter**	Johnny Mathis	CBS	6		
5	9	**Heartbreakers**	Matt Monro	EMI	4		FL
6	-	**British Steel**	Judas Priest	CBS	2	34	L
7	2	**Tell Me On A Sunday**	Marti Webb	Polydor	8		FL
8	-	**Star Tracks**	Various	K-Tel	2		
9	-	**Iron Maiden**	Iron Maiden	EMI	2		F
10	-	**Wheels Of Steel**	Saxon	Carrere	2		F

May 1980

This Mnth	Last Mnth	Title	Artist	Label	Wks in 10	US Pos	
1	-	**The Magic Of Boney M**	Boney M	Atlantic/Hansa	9		L
2	-	**Sky 2**	Sky	Ariola	16		
3	1	**Greatest Hits**	Rose Royce	Whitfield	13		L
4	2	**Duke**	Genesis	Charisma	8	11	
5	-	**Just One Night**	Eric Clapton	RSO	3	2	
6	-	**Suzi Quatro's Greatest Hits**	Suzi Quatro	RAK	4		FL
7	3	**12 Gold Bars**	Status Quo	Vertigo	9		
8	-	**McCartney II**	Paul McCartney	Parlophone	8	3	
9	-	**Off The Wall**	Michael Jackson	Epic	21	3	F
10	-	**Just Can't Stop It**	Beat	Go-Feet	7		F

June 1980

This Mnth	Last Mnth	Title	Artist	Label	Wks in 10	US Pos	
1	-	**Flesh And Blood**	Roxy Music	Polydor	17	35	
2	-	**Peter Gabriel**	Peter Gabriel	Charisma	6		
3	8	**McCartney II**	Paul McCartney	Parlophone	8	3	
4	10	**Just Can't Stop It**	Beat	Go-Feet	7		F
5	-	**Me Myself I**	Joan Armatrading	A&M	10	28	
6	-	**Hot Wax**	Various	K-Tel	3		
7	2	**Sky 2**	Sky	Ariola	16		
8	-	**Ready And Willing**	Whitesnake	UA	4		F
9	-	**The Photos**	Photos	CBS	2		FL
10	-	**Saved**	Bob Dylan	CBS	3	24	

US 1980 APR-JUNE

April 1980

This Mnth	Last Mnth	Title	Artist	Label	Wks in 10	UK Pos	
1	1	**The Wall**	Pink Floyd	Columbia	27	3	**8P**
2	9	**Against The Wind**	Bob Seger & The Silver Bullet Band	Capitol	22	26	**4P**
3	-	**Glass Houses**	Billy Joel	Columbia	25	9	**7P**
4	5	**Mad Love**	Linda Ronstadt	Asylum	12	65	**P**
5	6	**Off The Wall**	Michael Jackson	Epic	29	5	**6P**
6	8	**The Whispers**	Whispers	Solar	9		**FPL**
7	-	**Light Up The Night**	Brothers Johnson	A&M	7	22	**PL**
8	2	**Damn The Torpedoes**	Tom Petty & The Heartbreakers	Backstreet	20	57	**F2P**
9	-	**American Gigolo**	Soundtrack	Polydor	5		
10	-	**Departure**	Journey	Columbia	5		**F3P**

May 1980

This Mnth	Last Mnth	Title	Artist	Label	Wks in 10	UK Pos	
1	2	**Against The Wind**	Bob Seger & The Silver Bullet Band	Capitol	22	26	**4P**
2	1	**The Wall**	Pink Floyd	Columbia	27	3	**8P**
3	3	**Glass Houses**	Billy Joel	Columbia	25	9	**7P**
4	4	**Mad Love**	Linda Ronstadt	Asylum	12	65	**P**
5	-	**Women And Children First**	Van Halen	Warner	9	15	**3P**
6	-	**Just One Night**	Eric Clapton	RSO	11	3	
7	-	**Christopher Cross**	Christopher Cross	Warner	15	14	**F5PL**
8	5	**Off The Wall**	Michael Jackson	Epic	29	5	**6P**
9	7	**Light Up The Night**	Brothers Johnson	A&M	7	22	**PL**
10	-	**Go All The Way**	Isley Brothers	T-Neck	4		**PL**

June 1980

This Mnth	Last Mnth	Title	Artist	Label	Wks in 10	UK Pos	
1	3	**Glass Houses**	Billy Joel	Columbia	25	9	**7P**
2	1	**Against The Wind**	Bob Seger & The Silver Bullet Band	Capitol	22	26	**4P**
3	6	**Just One Night**	Eric Clapton	RSO	11	3	
4	2	**The Wall**	Pink Floyd	Columbia	27	3	**8P**
5	-	**Mouth To Mouth**	Lipps Inc.	Casablanca	7		**FL**
6	-	**McCartney II**	Paul McCartney	Columbia	8	1	
7	5	**Women And Children First**	Van Halen	Warner	9	15	**3P**
8	-	**Empire Strikes Back**	Soundtrack	RSO	9		
9	7	**Christopher Cross**	Christopher Cross	Warner	15	14	**F5PL**
10	-	**Middle Man**	Boz Scaggs	Columbia	4	52	**PL**

• New York's world famous Studio 54 club closed its doors putting another nail into the coffin of disco music. Simultaneously, the movie *Urban Cowboy* opened, and before long clubs all over the US were installing bucking bronco machines and playing country music in the hope of attracting more customers. John Travolta, who had helped popularize disco via his film *Saturday Night Fever*, also starred in *Urban Cowboy*. Simultaneously, the stage musical *Grease* – the film version of which had also starred Travolta – closed on Broadway after 3,883 performances. During its record run, it grossed over $8 million.

• The films *The Blues Brothers* and *Roadie* opened. The former, which featured Aretha Franklin, James Brown and Ray Charles, was a box office smash, while the latter, which included Meat Loaf, Blondie, Alice Cooper and Roy Orbison failed to draw the expected crowds.

• The Budokan Theater in Japan was becoming the fashionable venue to record live albums. Recently both Cheap Trick and Bob Dylan had recorded hit albums there and now it was the turn of Eric Clapton. His live double album, **Just One Night**, was his biggest hit for six years, and only Billy Joel's seven million seller **Glass Houses** stopped it hitting the top.

UK 1980 JULY-SEPT

• Queen scored the only transatlantic Number 1 of their career with **The Game** as The Rolling Stones clocked up their fourth with **Emotional Rescue**. The former album included their only US Number 1 singles 'Crazy Little Thing Called Love' and 'Another One Bites The Dust', while the Stones set included the American chart topper 'Miss You'.

• Groups building their fan following via live gigs included Simple Minds, who supported The Skids, Ultravox, Duran Duran, UB40, who supported The Police, and New Order. Adam & The Ants signed to CBS and American rockabilly trio The Stray Cats joined Arista, after an all-out label war for their signature. Meanwhile in the USA, Polydor signed New York group Blue Angel, who featured future solo star Cyndi Lauper.

• The Monsters Of Rock Festival at Donington starred British bands Judas Priest, Rainbow and Saxon. Also headlining were Germany's Scorpions and Canada's April Wine.

July 1980

This Mnth	Last Mnth	Title	Artist	Label	Wks in 10	US Pos	
1	-	**Emotional Rescue**	Rolling Stones	Rolling Stones	6	1	
2	1	**Flesh And Blood**	Roxy Music	Polydor	17	35	
3	-	**The Game**	Queen	EMI	4	1	
4	-	**Deepest Purple**	Deep Purple	Harvest	7	148	
5	-	**Uprising**	Bob Marley & The Wailers	Island	5	45	
6	2	**Peter Gabriel**	Peter Gabriel	Charisma	6		
7	-	**Xanadu**	Olivia Newton-John	Jet	8	4	F
8	10	**Saved**	Bob Dylan	CBS	3	24	
9	5	**Me Myself I**	Joan Armatrading	A&M	10	28	
10	-	**Black Sabbath Live At Last**	Black Sabbath	Nems	2		

August 1980

This Mnth	Last Mnth	Title	Artist	Label	Wks in 10	US Pos	
1	2	**Flesh And Blood**	Roxy Music	Polydor	17	35	
2	-	**Back In Black**	AC/DC	Atlantic	6	4	
3	4	**Deepest Purple**	Deep Purple	Harvest	7	148	
4	7	**Xanadu**	Olivia Newton-John	Jet	8	4	F
5	-	**Give Me The Night**	George Benson	Warner	9	3	F
6	-	**Glory Road**	Gillan	Virgin	4	183	F
7	1	**Emotional Rescue**	Rolling Stones	Rolling Stones	6	1	
8	-	**Searching For The Young Soul Rebels**	Dexy's Midnight Runners	Parlophone	5		F
9	-	**Kaleidoscope**	Siouxsie & The Banshees	Polydor	3		F
10	-	**Off The Wall**	Michael Jackson	Epic	21	3	F

September 1980

This Mnth	Last Mnth	Title	Artist	Label	Wks in 10	US Pos	
1	-	**Signing Off**	UB40	Graduate	5		F
2	-	**Telekon**	Gary Numan	Beggars Banquet	3	64	
3	1	**Flesh And Blood**	Roxy Music	Polydor	17	35	
4	-	**Never For Ever**	Kate Bush	EMI	8		
5	-	**Manilow Magic**	Barry Manilow	Arista	32		F
6	5	**Give Me The Night**	George Benson	Warner	9	3	F
7	-	**I'm No Hero**	Cliff Richard	EMI	3	80	
8	-	**Drama**	Yes	Atlantic	3	18	
9	-	**Scary Monsters And Super Creeps**	David Bowie	RCA	5	12	
10	2	**Back In Black**	AC/DC	Atlantic	6	4	

UK 1980 JULY-SEPT

July 1980

This Mnth	Last Mnth	Title	Artist	Label	Wks in 10	UK Pos	
1	1	**Glass Houses**	Billy Joel	Columbia	25	9	**7P**
2	3	**Just One Night**	Eric Clapton	RSO	11	3	
3	8	**Empire Strikes Back**	Soundtrack	RSO	9		
4	6	**McCartney II**	Paul McCartney	Columbia	8	1	
5	-	**Empty Glass**	Pete Townshend	Atco	9	11	**FL**
6	-	**Let's Get Serious**	Jermaine Jackson	Motown	5	22	**FL**
7	-	**Heroes**	Commodores	Motown	5	50	**PL**
8	-	**Emotional Rescue**	Rolling Stones	Rolling Stones	14	1	**P**
9	2	**Against The Wind**	Bob Seger & The Silver Bullet Band	Capitol	22	26	**4P**
10	-	**Urban Cowboy**	Soundtrack	Asylum	14		**P**

August 1980

This Mnth	Last Mnth	Title	Artist	Label	Wks in 10	UK Pos	
1	8	**Emotional Rescue**	Rolling Stones	Rolling Stones	14	1	**P**
2	-	**Hold Out**	Jackson Browne	Asylum	13	44	**P**
3	1	**Glass Houses**	Billy Joel	Columbia	25	9	**7P**
4	10	**Urban Cowboy**	Soundtrack	Asylum	14		**P**
5	-	**The Game**	Queen	Elektra	21	1	**P**
6	-	**Diana**	Diana Ross	Motown	18	12	**PL**
7	-	**Christopher Cross**	Christopher Cross	Warner	15	14	**F5PL**
8	5	**Empty Glass**	Pete Townshend	Atco	9	11	**FL**
9	3	**Empire Strikes Back**	Soundtrack	RSO	9		
10	-	**Fame**	Soundtrack	RSO	5	1	**P**

September 1980

This Mnth	Last Mnth	Title	Artist	Label	Wks in 10	UK Pos	
1	2	**Hold Out**	Jackson Browne	Asylum	13	44	**P**
2	5	**The Game**	Queen	Elektra	21	1	**P**
3	1	**Emotional Rescue**	Rolling Stones	Rolling Stones	14	1	**P**
4	6	**Diana**	Diana Ross	Motown	18	12	**PL**
5	4	**Urban Cowboy**	Soundtrack	Asylum	14		**P**
6	7	**Christopher Cross**	Christopher Cross	Warner	15	14	**F5PL**
7	-	**Give Me The Night**	George Benson	Warner	10	3	**PL**
8	-	**Panorama**	Cars	Elektra	6		**P**
9	-	**Xanadu (Soundtrack)**	Olivia Newton-John	MCA	8	2	**2P**
10	10	**Fame**	Soundtrack	RSO	5	1	**P**

• Christopher Cross' eponymous debut took the Grammy for Album of the Year. Billy Joel's **Glass Houses** earned him the trophy for Best Male Rock Vocal Performance and Bob Seger & The Silver Bullet Band's **Against The Wind** won the award for Best Rock Vocal Group Performance.

• The Beach Boys attracted 500,000 to a July 4 day concert in Washington, D.C., and country outlaw Willie Nelson hosted a very well attended all-star picnic on the same day. Both were to become regular Independence Day events.

• David Bowie and Linda Ronstadt starred in New York stage productions. Bowie was seen on Broadway in *The Elephant Man* and Ronstadt appeared in a production of *The Pirates Of Penzance*. Other noteworthy New York events included Elton John's free show in Central Park which attracted 400,000 fans, and the recording of John Lennon's first album for five years, **Double Fantasy**.

• The soundtrack albums to **Urban Cowboy, The Empire Strikes Back** and Willie Nelson's **Honeysuckle Rose** added to the number of double albums in the Top 20. Frank Sinatra clicked with the triple album **Trilogy: Past, Present And Future** and the eight album set **Elvis Aaron Presley** only narrowly missed the Top 20.

UK 1980 OCT-DEC

October 1980

This Mnth	Last Mnth	Title	Artist	Label	Wks in 10	US Pos	
1	-	**Zenyatta Mondatta**	Police	A&M	15	5	
2	-	**Absolutely**	Madness	Stiff	5	146	
3	9	**Scary Monsters And Super Creeps**	David Bowie	RCA	5	12	
4	-	**Mounting Excitement**	Various	K-Tel	4		
5	4	**Never For Ever**	Kate Bush	EMI	8		
6	-	**Guilty**	Barbra Streisand	CBS	17	1	
7	-	**The Very Best Of Don Mclean**	Don McLean	UA	4		L
8	-	**More Specials**	Specials	2-Tone	3	98	
9	-	**The River**	Bruce Springsteen	CBS	3	1	F
10	-	**Just Supposin'**	Status Quo	Vertigo	3		

November 1980

This Mnth	Last Mnth	Title	Artist	Label	Wks in 10	US Pos	
1	6	**Guilty**	Barbra Streisand	CBS	17	1	
2	1	**Zenyatta Mondatta**	Police	A&M	15	5	
3	-	**Hotter Than July**	Stevie Wonder	Motown	16	3	
4	-	**Super Trouper**	Abba	Epic	11	17	P
5	-	**Kings Of The Wild Frontier**	Adam & The Ants	CBS	33	44	FL
6	-	**Ace Of Spades**	Motorhead	Bronze	3		F
7	-	**Not The 9 O'Clock News**	Not The 9 O'Clock News Cast	BBC	10		F
8	-	**Organisation**	Orchestral Manoeuvres In The Dark	Dindisc	3		F
9	9	**The River**	Bruce Springsteen	CBS	3	1	F
10	10	**Just Supposin'**	Status Quo	Vertigo	3		

December 1980

This Mnth	Last Mnth	Title	Artist	Label	Wks in 10	US Pos	
1	4	**Super Trouper**	Abba	Epic	11	17	P
2	-	**Dr. Hook's Greatest Hits**	Dr. Hook	Capitol	10	142	
3	1	**Guilty**	Barbra Streisand	CBS	17	1	
4	-	**Manilow Magic**	Barry Manilow	Arista	32		F
5	-	**Double Fantasy**	John Lennon	Geffen	16	1	
6	-	**Sound Affects**	Jam	Polydor	2	72	
7	7	**Not The 9 O'Clock News**	Not The 9 O'Clock News Cast	BBC	10		F
8	2	**Zenyatta Mondatta**	Police	A&M	15	5	
9	-	**Autoamerican**	Blondie	Chrysalis	3	7	
10	-	**Inspiration**	Elvis Presley	K-Tel	4		

• Abba's **Super Trouper** amassed record advance orders in the UK of over one million and gave the Swedish quartet their sixth successive British Number 1.

• Status Quo also continued their staggering run of hits when **Just Supposin'** became their 11th successive Top 5 entry.

• Two of the world's most successful groups hit the headlines. The Bee Gees sued their label and ex-manager for $200 million for alleged fraud and Led Zeppelin announced that they would not continue after the death of drummer John Bonham.

• Seventies superstar Gary Glitter was declared bankrupt as he launched a comeback tour.

• Paul Simon made his first British concert appearance for five years, and his fellow folk/rock superstar Bob Dylan hit the road in the USA with a born-again slanted tour.

• Bob Marley, who had recently headlined at Madison Square Garden with The Commodores, assured worried fans that he was not dead. He also denied rumours that he had got cancer and said he was merely resting after collapsing on stage in Pittsburgh.

US 1980

OCT-DEC

October 1980

This Mnth	Last Mnth	Title	Artist	Label	Wks in 10	UK Pos	
1	2	**The Game**	Queen	Elektra	21	1	P
2	4	**Diana**	Diana Ross	Motown	18	12	PL
3	9	**Xanadu (Soundtrack)**	Olivia Newton-John	MCA	8	2	2P
4	7	**Give Me The Night**	George Benson	Warner	10	3	PL
5	-	**Guilty**	Barbra Streisand	Columbia	18	1	5P
6	-	**Crimes Of Passion**	Pat Benatar	Chrysalis	29		F4P
7	8	**Panorama**	Cars	Elektra	6		P
8	-	**One Step Closer**	Doobie Brothers	Warner	7	53	PL
9	3	**Emotional Rescue**	Rolling Stones	Rolling Stones	14	1	P
10	5	**Urban Cowboy**	Soundtrack	Asylum	14		P

November 1980

This Mnth	Last Mnth	Title	Artist	Label	Wks in 10	UK Pos	
1	-	**The River**	Bruce Springsteen	Columbia	8	8	3P
2	5	**Guilty**	Barbra Streisand	Columbia	18	1	5P
3	-	**Kenny Rogers' Greatest Hits**	Kenny Rogers	Liberty	20		P
4	1	**The Game**	Queen	Elektra	21	1	P
5	6	**Crimes Of Passion**	Pat Benatar	Chrysalis	29		F4P
6	8	**One Step Closer**	Doobie Brothers	Warner	7	53	PL
7	-	**Hotter Than July**	Stevie Wonder	Tamla	16	2	P
8	2	**Diana**	Diana Ross	Motown	18	12	PL
9	-	**Back In Black**	AC/DC	Atlantic	23	1	F10P
10	-	**Paris**	Supertramp	A&M	3	7	

December 1980

This Mnth	Last Mnth	Title	Artist	Label	Wks in 10	UK Pos	
1	2	**Guilty**	Barbra Streisand	Columbia	18	1	5P
2	3	**Kenny Rogers' Greatest Hits**	Kenny Rogers	Liberty	20		P
3	7	**Hotter Than July**	Stevie Wonder	Tamla	16	2	P
4	9	**Back In Black**	AC/DC	Atlantic	23	1	F10P
5	5	**Crimes Of Passion**	Pat Benatar	Chrysalis	29		F4P
6	1	**The River**	Bruce Springsteen	Columbia	8	8	3P
7	-	**Eagles Live**	Eagles	Asylum	7	24	2P
8	-	**Zenyatta Mondatta**	Police	A&M	21	1	FP
9	-	**Double Fantasy**	John Lennon	Geffen	22	1	3PL
10	4	**The Game**	Queen	Elektra	21	1	P

• John Lennon's murder shocked the world just as much as Elvis Presley's death had three years earlier. Lennon's comeback album, **Double Fantasy**, and single, '(Just Like) Starting Over', shot to the top on both sides of the Atlantic. The album topped the US chart for two months and was voted Album of the Year at the Grammys. In Britain, three of his singles reached Number 1 in the first two months after his death.

• Sales of records and tapes continued to decrease in 1980, when 34 million fewer units were sold than in the previous year. Pre-recorded audio tapes now accounted for 39% of all album sales.

• As the Seventies stalwarts Diana Ross, The Doobie Brothers and Steely Dan visited the Top 10 for the last time, debuts were made by Eighties regulars AC/DC, Pat Benatar and The Police.

• Paul McCartney received a rhodium record from the *Guinness Book Of Records* to celebrate his being the most successful songwriter of all time.

UK 1981 JAN-MAR

• Overnight everyone was talking about New Romantic music in Britain. The first hit albums to come from the genre were **Journey To Glory** from Spandau Ballet, **Vienna** by Ultravox, the quaintly titled **From The Tearooms Of Mars To The Hellholes Of Uranus** by Landscape, and a self-titled set from Visage. On the singles chart, Birmingham band Duran Duran were clocking up their first hit with 'Planet Earth'.

• The film *Dance Craze* opened. Its stars included Ska/2-Tone artists Bad Manners, The Beat, The Selecter and The Specials. The soundtrack album reached the Top 10. Meanwhile, 2-Tone superstars Madness starting filming *Take It Or Leave It*.

• As Billy Idol left Generation X, Pete Shelley quit The Buzzcocks and Dave Stewart and Annie Lennox disbanded The Tourists, rumours were rife that The Police and Blondie would be the next acts to call it a day.

• Phil Collins' first solo album **Face Value** entered the UK chart at Number 1 and was still on the chart five years later.

• **Remixture**, the first compilation album containing re-mixes of current club hits, was released. It topped the dance album chart and entered the pop lists. It was a forerunner of a very successful series of albums on the Street Sounds label.

January 1981

This Mnth	Last Mnth	Title	Artist	Label	Wks in 10	US Pos	
1	5	**Double Fantasy**	John Lennon	Geffen	16	1	
2	1	**Super Trouper**	Abba	Epic	11	17	P
3	2	**Dr. Hook's Greatest Hits**	Dr. Hook	Capitol	10	142	
4	-	**Kings Of The Wild Frontier**	Adam & The Ants	CBS	33	44	FL
5	3	**Guilty**	Barbra Streisand	CBS	17	1	
6	4	**Manilow Magic**	Barry Manilow	Arista	32		F
7	-	**Very Best Of David Bowie**	David Bowie	K-Tel	5		
8	8	**Zenyatta Mondatta**	Police	A&M	15	5	
9	7	**Not The 9 O'Clock News**	Not The 9 O'Clock News Cast	BBC	10		F
10	-	**Barry**	Barry Manilow	Arista	6	15	

February 1981

This Mnth	Last Mnth	Title	Artist	Label	Wks in 10	US Pos	
1	1	**Double Fantasy**	John Lennon	Geffen	16	1	
2	4	**Kings Of The Wild Frontier**	Adam & The Ants	CBS	33	44	FL
3	-	**Face Value**	Phil Collins	Virgin	15	7	FP
4	-	**Vienna**	Ultravox	Chrysalis	8	164	F
5	7	**Very Best Of David Bowie**	David Bowie	K-Tel	5		
6	-	**Difficult To Cure**	Rainbow	Polydor	5	50	
7	-	**Moving Pictures**	Rush	Mercury	3	3	
8	6	**Manilow Magic**	Barry Manilow	Arista	32		F
9	-	**Makin' Movies**	Dire Straits	Vertigo	10	19	
10	-	**Dance Craze**	Soundtrack	2-Tone	6		

March 1981

This Mnth	Last Mnth	Title	Artist	Label	Wks in 10	US Pos	
1	2	**Kings Of The Wild Frontier**	Adam & The Ants	CBS	33	44	FL
2	3	**Face Value**	Phil Collins	Virgin	15	7	FP
3	-	**The Jazz Singer (Soundtrack)**	Neil Diamond	Capitol	13	3	
4	4	**Vienna**	Ultravox	Chrysalis	8	164	F
5	1	**Double Fantasy**	John Lennon	Geffen	16	1	
6	10	**Dance Craze**	Soundtrack	2-Tone	6		
7	-	**Journey To Glory**	Spandau Ballet	Reformation	3		F
8	-	**Never Too Late**	Status Quo	Vertigo	3		
9	-	**Stray Cats**	Stray Cats	Arista	4		FL
10	-	**Very Best Of**	Rita Coolidge	A&M	2		L

US 1981 JAN-MAR

January 1981

This Mnth	Last Mnth	Title	Artist	Label	Wks in 10	UK Pos	
1	9	**Double Fantasy**	John Lennon	Geffen	22	1	**3PL**
2	5	**Crimes Of Passion**	Pat Benatar	Chrysalis	29		**F4P**
3	3	**Hotter Than July**	Stevie Wonder	Tamla	16	2	**P**
4	2	**Kenny Rogers' Greatest Hits**	Kenny Rogers	Liberty	20		**P**
5	1	**Guilty**	Barbra Streisand	Columbia	18	1	**5P**
6	4	**Back In Black**	AC/DC	Atlantic	23	1	**F10P**
7	-	**The Jazz Singer (Soundtrack)**	Neil Diamond	Capitol	19	3	**5P**
8	8	**Zenyatta Mondatta**	Police	A&M	21	1	**FP**
9	7	**Eagles Live**	Eagles	Asylum	7	24	**2P**
10	-	**Gaucho**	Steely Dan	MCA	6	27	**PL**

February 1981

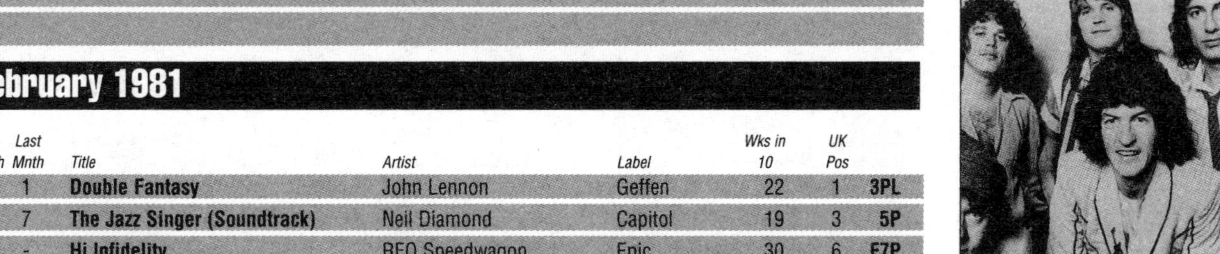

This Mnth	Last Mnth	Title	Artist	Label	Wks in 10	UK Pos	
1	1	**Double Fantasy**	John Lennon	Geffen	22	1	**3PL**
2	7	**The Jazz Singer (Soundtrack)**	Neil Diamond	Capitol	19	3	**5P**
3	-	**Hi Infidelity**	REO Speedwagon	Epic	30	6	**F7P**
4	2	**Crimes Of Passion**	Pat Benatar	Chrysalis	29		**F4P**
5	8	**Zenyatta Mondatta**	Police	A&M	21	1	**FP**
6	-	**Paradise Theater**	Styx	A&M	27	8	**3P**
7	4	**Kenny Rogers' Greatest Hits**	Kenny Rogers	Liberty	20		**P**
8	-	**Autoamerican**	Blondie	Chrysalis	9	3	**PL**
9	6	**Back In Black**	AC/DC	Atlantic	23	1	**F10P**
10	3	**Hotter Than July**	Stevie Wonder	Tamla	16	2	**P**

March 1981

This Mnth	Last Mnth	Title	Artist	Label	Wks in 10	UK Pos	
1	3	**Hi Infidelity**	REO Speedwagon	Epic	30	6	**F7P**
2	6	**Paradise Theater**	Styx	A&M	27	8	**3P**
3	1	**Double Fantasy**	John Lennon	Geffen	22	1	**3PL**
4	2	**The Jazz Singer (Soundtrack)**	Neil Diamond	Capitol	19	3	**5P**
5	5	**Zenyatta Mondatta**	Police	A&M	21	1	**FP**
6	4	**Crimes Of Passion**	Pat Benatar	Chrysalis	29		**F4P**
7	8	**Autoamerican**	Blondie	Chrysalis	9	3	**PL**
8	-	**Moving Pictures**	Rush	Mercury	14	3	**4P**
9	7	**Kenny Rogers' Greatest Hits**	Kenny Rogers	Liberty	20		**P**
10	-	**Captured**	Journey	Columbia	4		**2P**

• A new breed of North American rock group was taking over. Currently leading the field were REO Speedwagon, whose **Hi-Infidelity** spent 15 weeks at the top and sold over seven million copies. Also hitting the Top 10 were Journey, Styx and Canadian band, Rush.

• British acts U2, Sheena Easton and Adam & the Ants debuted on the album chart with **Boy**, which finally turned gold in 1994, **Sheena Easton** and **Kings Of The Wild Frontie**r respectively. In February, Adam & The Ants had five singles and two albums in the British charts. Their album was top for three months and became the biggest UK hit of the year. Easton, who rose to fame after appearing on the UK TV show *The Big Time*, scooped the Grammy for Best New Artist of 1981.

• Bill Haley died. He was the man most responsible for the initial spread of rock 'n' roll. His album **Rock Around The Clock** had been the first rock album to chart back in January 1956.

UK 1981 APR-JUNE

April 1981

This Mnth	Last Mnth	Title	Artist	Label	Wks in 10	US Pos	
1	1	**Kings Of The Wild Frontier**	Adam & The Ants	CBS	33	44	FL
2	-	**Hotter Than July**	Stevie Wonder	Motown	16	3	
3	3	**The Jazz Singer (Soundtrack)**	Neil Diamond	Capitol	13	3	
4	-	**Sky 3**	Sky	Ariola	4	181	
5	-	**Face Dances**	Who	Polydor	3	4	
6	-	**Come And Get It**	Whitesnake	Liberty	4		
7	-	**This Ole House**	Shakin' Stevens	Epic	11		F
8	2	**Face Value**	Phil Collins	Virgin	15	7	FP
9	8	**Never Too Late**	Status Quo	Vertigo	3		
10	-	**Makin' Movies**	Dire Straits	Vertigo	10	19	

• The first album from the Netherlands to head the British charts was **Stars On 45** by a Dutch session band tagged Starsound in the UK and Stars On in America. The album's title track launched a craze for medley singles.

May 1981

This Mnth	Last Mnth	Title	Artist	Label	Wks in 10	US Pos	
1	1	**Kings Of The Wild Frontier**	Adam & The Ants	CBS	33	44	FL
2	7	**This Ole House**	Shakin' Stevens	Epic	11		F
3	2	**Hotter Than July**	Stevie Wonder	Motown	16	3	
4	-	**Stars On 45**	Starsound	CBS	13	9	FL
5	-	**Future Shock**	Gillan	Virgin	4		L
6	-	**Wha'ppen**	Beat	Go-Feet	4		
7	-	**Chartbusters 81**	Various	K-Tel	3		
8	-	**Living Ornaments 1979-1980**	Gary Numan	Beggars Banquet	2		
9	-	**Roll On**	Various	Polydor	3		
10	6	**Come And Get It**	Whitesnake	Liberty	4		

• Another handful of top acts announced that they were disbanding: Wings, Steely Dan and Yes (above; Steve Howe and Geoff Downes then formed Asia). It was also rumoured that Abba were going their separate ways.

June 1981

This Mnth	Last Mnth	Title	Artist	Label	Wks in 10	US Pos	
1	4	**Stars On 45**	Starsound	CBS	13	9	FL
2	-	**Disco Daze And Disco Nites**	Various	Ronco	9		
3	-	**Anthem**	Toyah	Safari	9		F
4	-	**Present Arms**	UB40	DEP International	10		
5	1	**Kings Of The Wild Frontier**	Adam & The Ants	CBS	33	44	FL
6	-	**Themes**	Various	K-Tel	4		
7	2	**This Ole House**	Shakin' Stevens	Epic	11		F
8	-	**Chariots Of Fire (Soundtrack)**	Vangelis	Polydor	8	1	FL
9	-	**No Sleep Til Hammersmith**	Motorhead	Bronze	7		
10	-	**Magnetic Fields**	Jean-Michel Jarre	Polydor	2	98	

• A new crop of British acts made their presence felt on the album chart. Debuting in the Top 10 were actress/singer Toyah with **Anthem**, female rockers Girlschool with **Hit 'n'Run**, Echo & The Bunnymen with **Heaven Up Here** and soul duo Linx with **Intuition**. New faces hot on their heels included Teardrop Explodes with **Kilimanjaro**, Tygers Of Pan Tang with **Spellbound**, A Certain Ratio **To Each** and Brit Funk pioneers Incognito with **Jazz Funk**.

US 1981 APR-JUNE

April 1981

This Mnth	Last Mnth	Title	Artist	Label	Wks in 10	UK Pos	
1	1	**Hi Infidelity**	REO Speedwagon	Epic	30	6	**F7P**
2	2	**Paradise Theater**	Styx	A&M	27	8	**3P**
3	-	**Arc Of A Diver**	Steve Winwood	Island	13	13	**FP**
4	8	**Moving Pictures**	Rush	Mercury	14	3	**4P**
5	-	**Winelight**	Grover Washington Jr.	Elektra	8	34	**PL**
6	-	**Face Dances**	Who	MCA	8	2	**P**
7	3	**Double Fantasy**	John Lennon	Geffen	22	1	**3PL**
8	5	**Zenyatta Mondatta**	Police	A&M	21	1	**FP**
9	-	**Another Ticket**	Eric Clapton	RSO	8	18	
10	4	**The Jazz Singer (Soundtrack)**	Neil Diamond	Capitol	19	3	**5P**

May 1981

This Mnth	Last Mnth	Title	Artist	Label	Wks in 10	UK Pos	
1	1	**Hi Infidelity**	REO Speedwagon	Epic	30	6	**F7P**
2	2	**Paradise Theater**	Styx	A&M	27	8	**3P**
3	3	**Arc Of A Diver**	Steve Winwood	Island	13	13	**FP**
4	5	**Winelight**	Grover Washington Jr.	Elektra	8	34	**PL**
5	-	**Dirty Deeds Done Dirt Cheap**	AC/DC	Atlantic	13		
6	6	**Face Dances**	Who	MCA	8	2	**P**
7	4	**Moving Pictures**	Rush	Mercury	14	3	**4P**
8	9	**Another Ticket**	Eric Clapton	RSO	8	18	
9	7	**Double Fantasy**	John Lennon	Geffen	22	1	**3PL**
10	-	**Mistaken Identity**	Kim Carnes	EMI America	12	26	**FL**

June 1981

This Mnth	Last Mnth	Title	Artist	Label	Wks in 10	UK Pos	
1	1	**Hi Infidelity**	REO Speedwagon	Epic	30	6	**F7P**
2	10	**Mistaken Identity**	Kim Carnes	EMI America	12	26	**FL**
3	5	**Dirty Deeds Done Dirt Cheap**	AC/DC	Atlantic	13		
4	2	**Paradise Theater**	Styx	A&M	27	8	**3P**
5	-	**Fair Warning**	Van Halen	Warner	5	49	**2P**
6	-	**Hard Promises**	Tom Petty & The Heartbreakers	Backstreet	11	32	**P**
7	3	**Arc Of A Diver**	Steve Winwood	Island	13	13	**FP**
8	-	**Face Value**	Phil Collins	Atlantic	10	1	**F**
9	-	**Zebop!**	Santana	Columbia	7	33	**L**
10	7	**Moving Pictures**	Rush	Mercury	14	3	**4P**

• Bob Marley, the person most responsible for making reggae popular around the world, died of cancer. He received a statesman's funeral in Jamaica.

• One hundred years after the birth of Emile Berliner, the inventor of the flat record, which had replaced cylinder shaped ones, the first demonstration of the compact disk took place in Europe. This revolutionary digital playback system, which utilized laser beam technology, eventually replaced vinyl as the most popular format for carrying recorded sound.

• British-based American singer and noted choreographer Toni Basil's **Word Of Mouth** was released simultaneously on record and video – the first LP to do so. The album included the worldwide hit 'Mickey'.

• 1981 was another great year for R&B – currently being called 'Black Music'. Grover Washington, Kool & The Gang and Smokey Robinson cracked the Top 10 with **Winelight**, **Celebrate** and **Being With You** respectively. Hitting the Top 20 were such albums as **The Two Of Us** by Yarbrough And Peoples**, Gap Band III** and **The Dude** from Quincy Jones. Also scoring were Ray Parker Jr.'s **A Woman Needs Love**, Chaka Khan's **What Cha' Gonna Do For Me** and punk funk superstar Rick James' **Street Songs**.

UK 1981 JULY-SEPT

July 1981

This Mnth	Last Mnth	Title	Artist	Label	Wks in 10	US Pos	
1	-	**Love Songs**	Cliff Richard	EMI	13		
2	1	**Stars On 45**	Starsound	CBS	13	9	FL
3	9	**No Sleep Til Hammersmith**	Motorhead	Bronze	7		
4	-	**Secret Combination**	Randy Crawford	Warner	12	71	
5	2	**Disco Daze And Disco Nites**	Various	Ronco	9		
6	3	**Anthem**	Toyah	Safari	9		F
7	-	**Kim Wilde**	Kim Wilde	RAK	6	86	F
8	5	**Kings Of The Wild Frontier**	Adam & The Ants	CBS	33	44	FL
9	4	**Present Arms**	UB40	DEP International	10		
10	-	**Duran Duran**	Duran Duran	EMI	10	10	F

August 1981

This Mnth	Last Mnth	Title	Artist	Label	Wks in 10	US Pos	
1	1	**Love Songs**	Cliff Richard	EMI	13		
2	-	**Time**	Electric Light Orchestra	Jet	7	16	
3	4	**Secret Combination**	Randy Crawford	Warner	12	71	
4	-	**The Official BBC Album Of The Royal Wedding**	Various	BBC	4		
5	10	**Duran Duran**	Duran Duran	EMI	10	10	F
6	-	**Hi Infidelity**	REO Speedwagon	Epic	8	1	FL
7	2	**Stars On 45**	Starsound	CBS	13	9	FL
8	7	**Kim Wilde**	Kim Wilde	RAK	6	86	F
9	-	**Hotter Than July**	Stevie Wonder	Motown	16	3	
10	-	**Pretenders Ii**	Pretenders	Real	4	10	

September 1981

This Mnth	Last Mnth	Title	Artist	Label	Wks in 10	US Pos	
1	-	**Dead Ringer**	Meat Loaf	Epic	10	45	
2	-	**Tattoo You**	Rolling Stones	Rolling Stones	6	1	
3	2	**Time**	Electric Light Orchestra	Jet	7	16	
4	1	**Love Songs**	Cliff Richard	EMI	13		
5	-	**Dance**	Gary Numan	Beggars Banquet	2	167	
6	3	**Secret Combination**	Randy Crawford	Warner	12	71	
7	-	**Rage In Eden**	Ultravox	Chrysalis	3	144	
8	5	**Duran Duran**	Duran Duran	EMI	10	10	F
9	-	**Abacab**	Genesis	Charisma	5	7	
10	-	**Present Arms**	UB40	DEP International	10		

• Two days after the Royal Wedding, BBC Records had a recording of Prince Charles and Princess Diana's nuptials on sale. Before the couple returned from their honeymoon it had topped the chart and was on the way down.

• In its 176th chart week, Meat Loaf's **Bat Out Of Hell** reached its peak in the UK chart at Number 9. His long-awaited follow-up, **Dead Ringer**, was also a record breaker; it entered the chart at Number 1 – the first American album to accomplish this feat.

• Kim Wilde, daughter of Fifties pop idol Marty Wilde, debuted with a self-titled album co-written and produced by her father. Other females in the news included Olivia Newton-John, who was given a star on the Hollywood Walk Of Fame and American Chrissie Hynde, whose group The Pretenders' second album was in the transatlantic Top 10.

• Two Irish acts debuted on the British chart, U2 and Chris DeBurgh. The rock group entered with **Boy** and the singer/songwriter charted with **Best Moves**.

• Cliff Richard, who had recently been awarded an MBE by the Queen, hit the top with **Love Songs**. The album, which contained ballads from various stages of his career, was his first Number 1 hit since 1977.

US 1981

JULY-SEPT

July 1981

This Mnth	Last Mnth	Title	Artist	Label	Wks in 10	UK Pos	
1	2	**Mistaken Identity**	Kim Carnes	EMI America	12	26	FL
2	1	**Hi Infidelity**	REO Speedwagon	Epic	30	6	F7P
3	-	**Long Distance Voyager**	Moody Blues	Threshold	12	7	P
4	4	**Paradise Theater**	Styx	A&M	27	8	3P
5	6	**Hard Promises**	Tom Petty & The Heartbreakers	Backstreet	11	32	P
6	3	**Dirty Deeds Done Dirt Cheap**	AC/DC	Atlantic	13		
7	-	**Street Songs**	Rick James	Gordy	12		FPL
8	8	**Face Value**	Phil Collins	Atlantic	10	1	F
9	-	**Stars On Long Play**	Stars On	Radio	5	1	FL
10	9	**Zebop!**	Santana	Columbia	7	33	L

August 1981

This Mnth	Last Mnth	Title	Artist	Label	Wks in 10	UK Pos	
1	-	**Precious Time**	Pat Benatar	Chrysalis	14	30	2P
2	3	**Long Distance Voyager**	Moody Blues	Threshold	12	7	P
3	-	**4**	Foreigner	Atlantic	33	5	6P
4	7	**Street Songs**	Rick James	Gordy	12		FPL
5	-	**Escape**	Journey	Columbia	39	32	9P
6	-	**Share Your Love**	Kenny Rogers	Liberty	5		P
7	-	**Bella Donna**	Stevie Nicks	Modern	26	11	F4P
8	1	**Mistaken Identity**	Kim Carnes	EMI America	12	26	FL
9	2	**Hi Infidelity**	REO Speedwagon	Epic	30	6	F7P
10	5	**Hard Promises**	Tom Petty & The Heartbreakers	Backstreet	11	32	P

September 1981

This Mnth	Last Mnth	Title	Artist	Label	Wks in 10	UK Pos	
1	7	**Bella Donna**	Stevie Nicks	Modern	26	11	F4P
2	5	**Escape**	Journey	Columbia	39	32	9P
3	3	**4**	Foreigner	Atlantic	33	5	6P
4	-	**Tattoo You**	Rolling Stones	Rolling Stones	22	2	3P
5	1	**Precious Time**	Pat Benatar	Chrysalis	14	30	2P
6	-	**Don't Say No**	Billy Squier	Capitol	7		F3P
7	-	**Pirates**	Rickie Lee Jones	Warner	8	37	L
8	-	**Working Class Dog**	Rick Springfield	RCA	5		FP
9	4	**Street Songs**	Rick James	Gordy	12		FPL
10	-	**Pretenders II**	Pretenders	Sire	3	7	

• It was ladies first on the US album charts with Pat Benatar, Kim Carnes and Stevie Nicks reaching the top spot with **Precious Time, Mistaken Identity** and **Bella Donna** respectively. Benatar and Nicks also entered the UK charts where they joined two other American women, Randy Crawford and Debbie Harry.

• Among the most talented new black acts on the album chart were smooth soul vocalist Luther Vandross with **Never Too Much** and The Time, who included later superstar producers/composers Jimmy Jam and Terry Lewis, with a self-titled set. Simultaneously, another superior song stylist, Al Jarreau, clocked up his first Top 20 entry with **Breakin' Away**.

• AC/DC were not the only Australian act riding high in the USA. AOR duo Air Supply, whose first seven hit singles all reached the US Top 5, scored their first Top 10 album with **The One That You Love**, and actor/rock singer Rick Springfield clicked with **Working Class Dog**.

• The first country group to ever crack the Top 20 pop chart were The Oak Ridge Boys with **Fancy Free**. Three weeks later they were joined by a second, Alabama, with **Feels So Right**. The latter group went on to score nine consecutive platinum albums – a feat only bettered by Chicago.

UK 1981 OCT-DEC

• Queen's **Greatest Hits** album entered at Number 1. It spent over 300 weeks on the chart and sold over three million copies in Britain alone. The Police made it three Number 1 albums in a row with **Ghost In The Machine**, and rock'n'roller Shakin' Stevens – one of the most consistent singles acts of the decade had his only Number 1 album, **Shaky**.

• The late Ian Curtis' group, Joy Division, reached the Top 10 and led the Indie charts with **Still**. Those chart feats were then repeated by their off-shoot group, New Order, with their debut album, **Movement**.

• British synth-rockers Depeche Mode reached the Top 10 for the first time with **Speak And Spell**. They went on to amass seven further entries before the end of the decade. The group, who lost keyboard playing songwriter Vince Clarke, also had a minor US success with the album.

• Still more noteworthy new British groups debuted on the chart: Altered Images, fronted by actress/singer Clare Grogan with **Happy Birthday**, Bow Wow Wow with the oddly titled **See Jungle! See Jungle! Go Join Your Gang Yeah City All Over! Go Ape Crazy** and Soft Cell with **Non-Stop Erotic Cabaret**.

October 1981

This Mnth	Last Mnth	Title	Artist	Label	Wks in 10	US Pos	
1	-	**Ghost In The Machine**	Police	A&M	13	2	
2	-	**Shaky**	Shakin' Stevens	Epic	13		
3	-	**Super Hits 1 & 2**	Various	Ronco	6		
4	-	**Hooked On Classics**	Royal Philharmonic Orchestra	K-Tel	7	4	**FL**
5	9	**Abacab**	Genesis	Charisma	5	7	
6	-	**Dare**	Human League	Virgin	22	3	**F**
7	-	**If I Should Love Again**	Barry Manilow	Arista	4	14	
8	1	**Dead Ringer**	Meat Loaf	Epic	10	45	
9	-	**Wired For Sound**	Cliff Richard	EMI	7	132	
10	-	**Madness 7**	Madness	Stiff	3		

November 1981

This Mnth	Last Mnth	Title	Artist	Label	Wks in 10	US Pos	
1	-	**Greatest Hits**	Queen	EMI	23	11	**3P**
2	2	**Shaky**	Shakin' Stevens	Epic	13		
3	-	**Prince Charming**	Adam Ant	CBS	10	94	**F**
4	6	**Dare**	Human League	Virgin	22	3	**F**
5	-	**Architecture And Morality**	Orchestral Manoeuvres In The Dark	Dindisc	14	144	
6	-	**Best Of Blondie**	Blondie	Chrysalis	10	30	
7	1	**Ghost In The Machine**	Police	A&M	13	2	
8	-	**Chart Hits 81**	Various	K-Tel	8		
9	-	**Exit Stage Left**	Rush	Mercury	2	10	
10	-	**Tonight I'm Yours**	Rod Stewart	Riva	2	11	

December 1981

This Mnth	Last Mnth	Title	Artist	Label	Wks in 10	US Pos	
1	1	**Greatest Hits**	Queen	EMI	23	11	**3P**
2	8	**Chart Hits 81**	Various	K-Tel	8		
3	3	**Prince Charming**	Adam Ant	CBS	10	94	**F**
4	4	**Dare**	Human League	Virgin	22	3	**F**
5	-	**Pearls**	Elkie Brooks	A&M	18		**F**
6	-	**The Visitors**	Abba	Epic	7	29	
7	-	**The Simon And Garfunkel Collection**	Simon & Garfunkel	CBS	5		
8	6	**Best Of Blondie**	Blondie	Chrysalis	10	30	
9	-	**For Those About To Rock**	AC/DC	Atlantic	2	1	
10	-	**Begin The Beguine**	Julio Iglesias	CBS	8		**F**

US 1981 OCT-DEC

October 1981

This Mnth	Last Mnth	Title	Artist	Label	Wks in 10	UK Pos	
1	4	**Tattoo You**	Rolling Stones	Rolling Stones	22	2	3P
2	2	**Escape**	Journey	Columbia	39	32	9P
3	3	**4**	Foreigner	Atlantic	33	5	6P
4	-	**Nine Tonight**	Bob Seger & The Silver Bullet Band	Capitol	10	24	3P
5	1	**Bella Donna**	Stevie Nicks	Modern	26	11	F4P
6	-	**The Innocent Age**	Dan Fogelberg	Full Moon	8		PL
7	5	**Precious Time**	Pat Benatar	Chrysalis	14	30	2P
8	7	**Pirates**	Rickie Lee Jones	Warner	8	37	L
9	-	**Songs In The Attic**	Billy Joel	Columbia	5	57	2PP
10	-	**Breakin' Away**	Al Jarreau	Warner	4	60	FPL

November 1981

This Mnth	Last Mnth	Title	Artist	Label	Wks in 10	UK Pos	
1	1	**Tattoo You**	Rolling Stones	Rolling Stones	22	2	3P
2	3	**4**	Foreigner	Atlantic	33	5	6P
3	2	**Escape**	Journey	Columbia	39	32	9P
4	-	**Ghost In The Machine**	Police	A&M	24	1	2P
5	4	**Nine Tonight**	Bob Seger & The Silver Bullet Band	Capitol	10	24	3P
6	5	**Bella Donna**	Stevie Nicks	Modern	26	11	F4P
7	-	**Raise!**	Earth, Wind & Fire	Arc	10	14	PL
8	6	**The Innocent Age**	Dan Fogelberg	Full Moon	8		PL
9	-	**Abacab**	Genesis	Atlantic	6	1	F2P
10	-	**Private Eyes**	Daryl Hall & John Oates	RCA	13	8	FP

December 1981

This Mnth	Last Mnth	Title	Artist	Label	Wks in 10	UK Pos	
1	2	**4**	Foreigner	Atlantic	33	5	6P
2	4	**Ghost In The Machine**	Police	A&M	24	1	2P
3	3	**Escape**	Journey	Columbia	39	32	9P
4	7	**Raise!**	Earth, Wind & Fire	Arc	10	14	PL
5	1	**Tattoo You**	Rolling Stones	Rolling Stones	22	2	3P
6	-	**For Those About To Rock We Salute You**	AC/DC	Atlantic	12	3	2P
7	-	**Physical**	Olivia Newton-John	MCA	14	11	2PL
8	6	**Bella Donna**	Stevie Nicks	Modern	26	11	F4P
9	5	**Nine Tonight**	Bob Seger & The Silver Bullet Band	Capitol	10	24	3P
10	9	**Abacab**	Genesis	Atlantic	6	1	F2P

• In 1981, over one and half million Sony Walkmans were sold and compact disks were first demonstrated in America. It was also the year that MTV first appeared on the small screen and home video games started to take off.

• The Rolling Stones packed them in on a US stadium tour that was seen by over two million fans and grossed $50 million. It replaced the Jacksons' Triumph tour as the year's most successful series of concerts. Live shows hitting the headlines in Britain included ZZ Top's appearance at Hammersmith Odeon and Adam Ant's Prince Charming Revue and his appearance in a Royal Variety Show.

• As Dan Fogelberg and Olivia Newton-John bowed out of the Top 10 for the last time, two of the decade's top acts made their debut, Daryl Hall & John Oates and Genesis.

UK 1982 JAN-MAR

• Several acts from continental Europe were enjoying chart success. Greek keyboard player Vangelis was heading to the top in the USA with **Chariots Of Fire** and clicking in Britain with **The Friends Of Mr. Cairo**, an album recorded with ex-Yes man Jon Anderson. Spanish operatic star Placido Domingo had a transatlantic Top 20 entry with **Perhaps Love** and Abba scored their seventh successive UK Number 1 with **The Visitors**. It was to be the last newly recorded album by the Swedish quartet, who performed their final show on New Year's Day.

• Pop/reggae group UB40 signed a record deal with DEP International that was described by the music media as "The best since Paul McCartney signed with Columbia".

• The Jam, who made a habit of entering the singles chart at Number 1, repeated that feat on the album chart with **The Gift**.

• Winners at the first BRIT awards included Cliff Richard (Best Male Artist), The Police (Best Group), **Kings Of The Wild Frontier** by Adam & The Ants (Album of the Year) and Human League (Best Newcomer). American songstress Randy Crawford was voted Best Female Artist and John Lennon posthumously received an award for his Outstanding Contribution to British Music.

January 1982

This Mnth	Last Mnth	Title	Artist	Label	Wks in 10	US Pos	
1	4	**Dare**	Human League	Virgin	22	3	F
2	1	**Greatest Hits**	Queen	EMI	23	11	3P
3	6	**The Visitors**	Abba	Epic	7	29	
4	-	**Hits Hits Hits**	Various	Ronco	4		
5	5	**Pearls**	Elkie Brooks	A&M	18		F
6	2	**Chart Hits 81**	Various	K-Tel	8		
7	3	**Prince Charming**	Adam Ant	CBS	10	94	F
8	-	**Love Songs**	Barbra Streisand	CBS	16		
9	-	**Ghost In The Machine**	Police	A&M	13	2	
10	-	**Modern Dance**	Various	K-Tel	3		

February 1982

This Mnth	Last Mnth	Title	Artist	Label	Wks in 10	US Pos	
1	8	**Love Songs**	Barbra Streisand	CBS	16		
2	5	**Pearls**	Elkie Brooks	A&M	18		F
3	-	**Architecture And Morality**	Orchestral Manoeuvres In The Dark	Dindisc	14	144	
4	1	**Dare**	Human League	Virgin	22	3	F
5	-	**Dead Ringer**	Meat Loaf	Epic	10	45	
6	-	**Non-Stop Erotic Cabaret**	Soft Cell	Some Bizzare	6	22	F
7	-	**The Friends Of Mr. Cairo**	Jon & Vangelis	Polydor	4	64	L
8	-	**4**	Foreigner	Atlantic	5	1	F
9	-	**Dreaming**	Various	K-Tel	4		
10	-	**English Settlement**	XTC	Virgin	2	48	FL

March 1982

This Mnth	Last Mnth	Title	Artist	Label	Wks in 10	US Pos	
1	1	**Love Songs**	Barbra Streisand	CBS	16		
2	-	**Action Trax**	Various	K-Tel	5		
3	-	**Pelican West**	Haircut 100	Arista	11	31	FL
4	-	**All For A Song**	Barbara Dickson	Epic	9		
5	-	**The Gift**	Jam	Polydor	5	82	
6	2	**Pearls**	Elkie Brooks	A&M	18		F
7	9	**Dreaming**	Various	K-Tel	4		
8	-	**One Night At Budokan**	Michael Schenker Group	Chrysalis	2		L
9	6	**Non-Stop Erotic Cabaret**	Soft Cell	Some Bizzare	6	22	F
10	-	**Fun Boy Three**	Fun Boy Three	Chrysalis	3		FL

US 1982 JAN-MAR

January 1982

This Mnth	Last Mnth	Title	Artist	Label	Wks in 10	UK Pos	
1	1	**4**	Foreigner	Atlantic	33	5	**6P**
2	3	**Escape**	Journey	Columbia	39	32	**9P**
3	6	**For Those About To Rock We Salute You**	AC/DC	Atlantic	12	3	**2P**
4	2	**Ghost In The Machine**	Police	A&M	24	1	**2P**
5	5	**Tattoo You**	Rolling Stones	Rolling Stones	22	2	**3P**
6	8	**Bella Donna**	Stevie Nicks	Modern	26	11	**F4P**
7	-	**Hooked On Classics**	Royal Philharmonic Orchestra	RCA	9	4	**FPL**
8	4	**Raise!**	Earth, Wind & Fire	Arc	10	14	**PL**
9	-	**Freeze Frame**	J. Geils Band	EMI America	19	12	**PL**
10	7	**Physical**	Olivia Newton-John	MCA	14	11	**2PL**

February 1982

This Mnth	Last Mnth	Title	Artist	Label	Wks in 10	UK Pos	
1	9	**Freeze Frame**	J. Geils Band	EMI America	19	12	**PL**
2	2	**Escape**	Journey	Columbia	39	32	**9P**
3	1	**4**	Foreigner	Atlantic	33	5	**6P**
4	7	**Hooked On Classics**	Royal Philharmonic Orchestra	RCA	9	4	**FPL**
5	-	**Private Eyes**	Daryl Hall & John Oates	RCA	13	8	**FP**
6	-	**Beauty And The Beat**	Go-Go's	IRS	15		**F2P**
7	4	**Ghost In The Machine**	Police	A&M	24	1	**2P**
8	3	**For Those About To Rock We Salute You**	AC/DC	Atlantic	12	3	**2P**
9	6	**Bella Donna**	Stevie Nicks	Modern	26	11	**F4P**
10	5	**Tattoo You**	Rolling Stones	Rolling Stones	22	2	**3P**

March 1982

This Mnth	Last Mnth	Title	Artist	Label	Wks in 10	UK Pos	
1	6	**Beauty And The Beat**	Go-Go's	IRS	15		**F2P**
2	1	**Freeze Frame**	J. Geils Band	EMI America	19	12	**PL**
3	-	**I Love Rock-N-Roll**	Joan Jett & The Blackhearts	Boardwalk	12	25	**FPL**
4	2	**Escape**	Journey	Columbia	39	32	**9P**
5	3	**4**	Foreigner	Atlantic	33	5	**6P**
6	7	**Ghost In The Machine**	Police	A&M	24	1	**2P**
7	-	**Chariots Of Fire (Soundtrack)**	Vangelis	Polydor	15	5	**FPL**
8	-	**Physical**	Olivia Newton-John	MCA	14	11	**2PL**
9	4	**Hooked On Classics**	Royal Philharmonic Orchestra	RCA	9	4	**FPL**
10	-	**Quarterflash**	Quarterflash	Geffen	4		**FPL**

• Anglo-American rock group Foreigner's only chart topper, **4**, led the field for 10 weeks taking turns at Number 1 with AC/DC, the first Australian act to head the US lists. On the subject of Number 1 firsts, The Go-Go's became the first female rock band to reach the summit when **Beauty & The Beat** hit the top in its 32nd chart week.

• Al Jarreau's album, **Breakin' Away**, earned him the trophy for Male Vocal Performance at the Grammy Awards. The late John Lennon's **Double Fantasy** was named Album of the Year. Ex-Monkees member Mike Nesmith grabbed an award for video production.

• Canadian acts were also faring well in the USA: Loverboy with **Get Lucky** and newcomer Bryan Adams with **You Want It, You Got It**. There was also a self-titled album from Aldo Nova and comedy duo Bob & Doug McKenzie's **Great White North**. By the way, top movie star Rick Moranis was a member of the latter duo.

UK 1982 APR-JUNE

• The Rolling Stones attracted 140,000 fans to Wembley Stadium for their first UK gigs in six years. Also appearing at Wembley was Diana Ross who charged a then record £25 ($37) for tickets.

• Adam & The Ants, the top British act of the early years of the decade split up, as the next major British superstars Culture Club, featuring Boy George, signed to Virgin.

• Even though their US success was confined to the club scene, New York's latin-oriented dance act, Kid Creole & The Coconuts, were one of the most successful US acts in Britain. In 1982, the distinctive group clocked up three Top 10 singles and had a Top 3 album, **Tropical Gangsters**. The 13-piece ensemble even bagged the award for Top International Act at 1983's BRIT Awards ceremony.

• It was Eurovision Song Contest time again. In the UK, Q-Feel, which included future hit composer and singer Martin Page, failed in their bid to represent Britain and a similar fate befell The Force, later known internationally as Europe, in Sweden. Interestingly, last year's contest winners Bucks Fizz were enjoying their only Top 10 LP, **Are You Ready?**

April 1982

This Mnth	Last Mnth	Title	Artist	Label	Wks in 10	US Pos	
1	1	**Love Songs**	Barbra Streisand	CBS	16		
2	3	**Pelican West**	Haircut 100	Arista	11	31	FL
3	-	**The Number Of The Beast**	Iron Maiden	EMI	9	33	
4	4	**All For A Song**	Barbara Dickson	Epic	9		
5	-	**James Bond's Greatest Hits**	Various	Liberty	3		
6	5	**The Gift**	Jam	Polydor	5	82	
7	-	**1982**	Status Quo	Vertigo	3		
8	-	**Begin The Beguine**	Julio Iglesias	CBS	8		F
9	-	**Sky 4-Forthcoming**	Sky	Ariola	4		L
10	-	**The Anvil**	Visage	Polydor	2		FL

May 1982

This Mnth	Last Mnth	Title	Artist	Label	Wks in 10	US Pos	
1	-	**Complete Madness**	Madness	Stiff	19		
2	-	**Barry Live In Britain**	Barry Manilow	Arista	7		
3	-	**Tug Of War**	Paul McCartney	Parlophone	5	1	
4	2	**Pelican West**	Haircut 100	Arista	11	31	FL
5	-	**Rio**	Duran Duran	EMI	24	6	
6	7	**1982**	Status Quo	Vertigo	3		
7	-	**Night Birds**	Shakatak	Polydor	7		FL
8	-	**Combat Rock**	Clash	CBS	2	7	
9	-	**Chartbusters**	Various	Ronco	3		
10	-	**Hot Space**	Queen	EMI	3	22	

June 1982

This Mnth	Last Mnth	Title	Artist	Label	Wks in 10	US Pos	
1	-	**Avalon**	Roxy Music	EG	11	53	
2	1	**Complete Madness**	Madness	Stiff	19		
3	-	**3 Sides Live**	Genesis	Charisma	4	10	
4	5	**Rio**	Duran Duran	EMI	24	6	
5	-	**Still Life (American Concerts 1981)**	Rolling Stones	Rolling Stones	8	5	
6	7	**Night Birds**	Shakatak	Polydor	7		FL
7	-	**The Number Of The Beast**	Iron Maiden	EMI	9	33	
8	-	**Tropical Gangsters**	Kid Creole & The Coconuts	Ze	11		FL
9	-	**The Changeling**	Toyah	Safari	3		L
10	3	**Tug Of War**	Paul McCartney	Parlophone	5	1	

US 1982 APR-JUNE

April 1982

This Mnth	Last Mnth	Title	Artist	Label	Wks in 10	UK Pos	
1	1	**Beauty And The Beat**	Go-Go's	IRS	15		**F2P**
2	7	**Chariots Of Fire (Soundtrack)**	Vangelis	Polydor	15	5	**FPL**
3	3	**I Love Rock-N-Roll**	Joan Jett & The Blackhearts	Boardwalk	12	25	**FPL**
4	2	**Freeze Frame**	J. Geils Band	EMI America	19	12	**PL**
5	-	**Success Hasn't Spoiled Me Yet**	Rick Springfield	RCA	12		**PL**
6	-	**The Concert In Central Park**	Simon & Garfunkel	Warner	5	6	**PL**
7	8	**Physical**	Olivia Newton-John	MCA	14	11	**2PL**
8	-	**Asia**	Asia	Geffen	27	11	**F3P**
9	-	**Get Lucky**	Loverboy	Columbia	14		**F4P**
10	4	**Escape**	Journey	Columbia	39	32	**9P**

May 1982

This Mnth	Last Mnth	Title	Artist	Label	Wks in 10	UK Pos	
1	8	**Asia**	Asia	Geffen	27	11	**F3P**
2	2	**Chariots Of Fire (Soundtrack)**	Vangelis	Polydor	15	5	**FPL**
3	5	**Success Hasn't Spoiled Me Yet**	Rick Springfield	RCA	12		**PL**
4	1	**Beauty And The Beat**	Go-Go's	IRS	15		**F2P**
5	3	**I Love Rock-N-Roll**	Joan Jett & The Blackhearts	Boardwalk	12	25	**FPL**
6	4	**Freeze Frame**	J. Geils Band	EMI America	19	12	**PL**
7	-	**Tug Of War**	Paul McCartney	Columbia	9	1	**PL**
8	-	**Diver Down**	Van Halen	Warner	9	36	**3P**
9	9	**Get Lucky**	Loverboy	Columbia	14		**F4P**
10	-	**Aldo Nova**	Aldo Nova	Portrait	8		**FPL**

June 1982

This Mnth	Last Mnth	Title	Artist	Label	Wks in 10	UK Pos	
1	7	**Tug Of War**	Paul McCartney	Columbia	9	1	**PL**
2	1	**Asia**	Asia	Geffen	27	11	**F3P**
3	8	**Diver Down**	Van Halen	Warner	9	36	**3P**
4	-	**Stevie Wonder's Original Musiquarium I**	Stevie Wonder	Tamla	6	8	
5	-	**Dare**	Human League	A&M	9	1	**FL**
6	3	**Success Hasn't Spoiled Me Yet**	Rick Springfield	RCA	12		**PL**
7	-	**Always On My Mind**	Willie Nelson	Columbia	15		**F4PL**
8	10	**Aldo Nova**	Aldo Nova	Portrait	8		**FPL**
9	-	**Toto IV**	Toto	Columbia	22	4	**3PL**
10	2	**Chariots Of Fire (Soundtrack)**	Vangelis	Polydor	15	5	**FPL**

• The latest British supergroup, Asia, took their eponymous debut album to the top for nine weeks. The album, which missed the Top 10 in their homeland, was the most successful debut since The Monkees.

• Joan Jett, who had been a member of the pioneering girl rock group The Runaways, narrowly missed the top of the chart with her first album backed by The Blackhearts, **I Love Rock-n-Roll**, named after her chart topping single. Coincidentally, the record that halted their path was by The Go-Go's, a girl group in The Runaways tradition.

• As ex-Beatle Paul McCartney scored his last American Top 10 album entry with the transatlantic Number 1 **Tug Of War**, The Human League led the second major British Invasion of the US singles charts. The synth-led Sheffield band were the first of the new wave of British groups to break through Stateside. However, unlike The Beatles, who led the first invasion, they only managed one US Top 10 album, **Dare**.

UK 1982 JULY-SEPT

• Two years after it had been successful Stateside, the soundtrack album from **Fame** topped the British chart. Its delayed chart action was due to the UK success of the TV series of the same name. Amazingly, it was replaced at the summit by **Kids From Fame** from the TV series itself. In all, the series spawned five UK hit albums and four hit singles – none of which charted in America.

• The first Prince's Trust Rock Gala, co-organized by Phil Collins, was held in London, with Prince Charles and Princess Diana in attendance. One of the highlights of the show was the performance of a super group which included Phil Collins, Pete Townshend, Robert Plant, Midge Ure and Kate Bush. Collins' ex-group mate, Peter Gabriel, organized the first World Of Music Arts And Dance (Womad) Festival in Somerset, England. It featured a variety of music from around the world and pre-dated the craze for World Music.

• Twelve years after they split-up, all the members of The Beatles had roads named after them in their hometown, Liverpool: John Lennon Drive, Paul McCartney Way, George Harrison Close and Ringo Starr Drive.

July 1982

This Mnth	Last Mnth	Title	Artist	Label	Wks in 10	US Pos	
1	-	**The Lexicon Of Love**	ABC	Neutron	16	24	F
2	1	**Avalon**	Roxy Music	EG	11	53	
3	-	**Pictures At Eleven**	Robert Plant	Swan Song	4	5	F
4	-	**Fame**	Soundtrack	RSO	7	7	
5	-	**Love And Dancing**	League Unlimited Orchestra	Virgin	9		
6	2	**Complete Madness**	Madness	Stiff	19		
7	5	**Still Life (American Concerts 1981)**	Rolling Stones	Rolling Stones	8	5	
8	-	**Mirage**	Fleetwood Mac	Warner	5	1	
9	8	**Tropical Gangsters**	Kid Creole & The Coconuts	Ze	11		FL
10	-	**Kids From Fame**	Kids From Fame	BBC	24	146	FP

August 1982

This Mnth	Last Mnth	Title	Artist	Label	Wks in 10	US Pos	
1	10	**Kids From Fame**	Kids From Fame	BBC	24	146	FP
2	-	**Too-Rye-Ay**	Dexy's Midnight Runners	Mercury	8	14	L
3	5	**Love And Dancing**	League Unlimited Orchestra	Virgin	9		
4	4	**Fame**	Soundtrack	RSO	7	7	
5	9	**Tropical Gangsters**	Kid Creole & The Coconuts	Ze	11		FL
6	1	**The Lexicon Of Love**	ABC	Neutron	16	24	F
7	6	**Complete Madness**	Madness	Stiff	19		
8	-	**Love Songs**	Commodores	K-Tel	4		L
9	-	**Talking Back To The Night**	Steve Winwood	Island	3	28	F
10	2	**Avalon**	Roxy Music	EG	11	53	

Setember 1982

This Mnth	Last Mnth	Title	Artist	Label	Wks in 10	US Pos	
1	1	**Kids From Fame**	Kids From Fame	BBC	24	146	FP
2	-	**Upstairs At Eric's**	Yazoo	Mute	8	92	F
3	6	**The Lexicon Of Love**	ABC	Neutron	16	24	F
4	-	**Rio**	Duran Duran	EMI	24	6	
5	2	**Too-Rye-Ay**	Dexy's Midnight Runners	Mercury	8	14	L
6	-	**Chartbeat/Chartheat**	Various	K-Tel	4		
7	-	**Breakout**	Various	Ronco	3		
8	-	**Now You See Me, Now You Don't**	Cliff Richard	EMI	2		
9	-	**Signals**	Rush	Mercury	2	10	
10	-	**In The Heat Of The Night**	Imagination	R&B	4		F

US 1982

JULY-SEPT

July 1982

This Mnth	Last Mnth	Title	Artist	Label	Wks in 10	UK Pos	
1	2	**Asia**	Asia	Geffen	27	11	F3P
2	7	**Always On My Mind**	Willie Nelson	Columbia	15		F4PL
3	9	**Toto IV**	Toto	Columbia	22	4	3PL
4	5	**Dare**	Human League	A&M	9	1	FL
5	-	**Still Life (American Concert 1981)**	Rolling Stones	Rolling Stones	5	4	
6	-	**American Fool**	John Cougar Mellencamp	Riva	22	37	F4P
7	1	**Tug Of War**	Paul McCartney	Columbia	9	1	PL
8	-	**Eye Of The Tiger**	Survivor	Scotti Bros	12	12	FPL
9	-	**Mirage**	Fleetwood Mac	Warner	18	5	2P
10	-	**Get Lucky**	Loverboy	Columbia	14		F4P

August 1982

This Mnth	Last Mnth	Title	Artist	Label	Wks in 10	UK Pos	
1	9	**Mirage**	Fleetwood Mac	Warner	18	5	2P
2	8	**Eye Of The Tiger**	Survivor	Scotti Bros	12	12	FPL
3	1	**Asia**	Asia	Geffen	27	11	F3P
4	6	**American Fool**	John Cougar Mellencamp	Riva	22	37	F4P
5	-	**Pictures At Eleven**	Robert Plant	Swan Song	9	2	FP
6	-	**Abracadabra**	Steve Miller Band	Capitol	12	10	PL
7	-	**Good Trouble**	REO Speedwagon	Epic	10	29	P
8	-	**Daylight Again**	Crosby, Stills & Nash	Atlantic	6		PL
9	3	**Toto IV**	Toto	Columbia	22	4	3PL
10	-	**Vacation**	Go-Go's	IRS	9	75	L

September 1982

This Mnth	Last Mnth	Title	Artist	Label	Wks in 10	UK Pos	
1	4	**American Fool**	John Cougar Mellencamp	Riva	22	37	F4P
2	1	**Mirage**	Fleetwood Mac	Warner	18	5	2P
3	6	**Abracadabra**	Steve Miller Band	Capitol	12	10	PL
4	3	**Asia**	Asia	Geffen	27	11	F3P
5	5	**Pictures At Eleven**	Robert Plant	Swan Song	9	2	FP
6	2	**Eye Of The Tiger**	Survivor	Scotti Bros	12	12	FPL
7	7	**Good Trouble**	REO Speedwagon	Epic	10	29	P
8	-	**Emotions In Motion**	Billy Squier	Capitol	9		2PL
9	10	**Vacation**	Go-Go's	IRS	9	75	L
10	8	**Daylight Again**	Crosby, Stills & Nash	Atlantic	6		PL

• Interesting Top 20 albums included **Vinyl Confessions**, the last major hit for Kansas, and **All Four One** and **Quiet Lies**, the biggest hits for Los Angeles quintet The Motels and country rocker Juice Newton. Other noteworthy entrants included Britain's A Flock Of Seagulls with their eponymous debut album and the original cast album **Dream Girls** – based on The Supremes story.

• John Cougar, who had initially been launched as would-be teen idol Johnny Cougar on Rod Stewart's Riva label, had his first Top 20 entry, **American Fool**. It led the field for nine weeks and was his last album released under that surname. Henceforth he would be known as John Cougar Mellencamp.

• Wedding bells chimed as Ozzy Osbourne wed manager Don Arden's daughter, Sharon. The band at Southside Johnny's wedding reception was led by his boss Bruce Springsteen. In California, both Duran Duran's Andy Taylor and Jefferson Starship vocalist Mickey Thomas were married.

UK 1982 OCT-DEC

• After two months at the top, the **Kids From Fame** album shifted to allow Dire Straits' to score their first Number 1, **Love Over Gold**. The Kids album then returned to the top and stopped their second album, **Kids From Fame Again** from reaching the summit. It also halted the progress of Phil Collins' **Hello I Must Be Going**, which he promoted during his first solo tour. For the record books, **Kids From Fame** was the only million selling album in Britain in 1982.

• Abba, who had disbanded earlier in the year, scored their eighth successive Number 1, **The Singles – The First Ten Years**. It was one of several greatest hits albums that charted over the Christmas period. Among the others were sets by such varied acts as Nat 'King' Cole, Diana Ross, Squeeze and Olivia Newton-John. Other Top 10 hit compilations included **The John Lennon Collection** and **20 Greatest Hits** from The Beatles. The Beatles set commemorated the 20th anniversary of the release of their first single, 'Love Me Do', which now entered the UK Top 10 for the first time. At the same time, in Japan, The Beatles complete output, including all solo projects, was released in an 83 album set selling for £800 ($1200)!

October 1982

This Mnth	Last Mnth	Title	Artist	Label	Wks in 10	US Pos	
1	-	**Love Over Gold**	Dire Straits	Vertigo	7	19	
2	1	**Kids From Fame**	Kids From Fame	BBC	24	146	FP
3	-	**Kids From Fame Again**	Kids From Fame	RCA	5		
4	2	**Upstairs At Eric's**	Yazoo	Mute	8	92	F
5	-	**Nebraska**	Bruce Springsteen	CBS	3	3	
6	-	**Reflections**	Various	CBS	7		
7	-	**UB44**	UB40	DEP International	2		
8	3	**The Lexicon Of Love**	ABC	Neutron	16	24	F
9	-	**Give Me Your Heart Tonight**	Shakin' Stevens	Epic	3		
10	-	**New Gold Dream (81,82,83,84)**	Simple Minds	Virgin	3	69	F

November 1982

This Mnth	Last Mnth	Title	Artist	Label	Wks in 10	US Pos	
1	2	**Kids From Fame**	Kids From Fame	BBC	24	146	FP
2	-	**Hello I Must Be Going**	Phil Collins	Virgin	10	8	
3	-	**Heartbreaker**	Dionne Warwick	Arista	15	25	
4	3	**Kids From Fame Again**	Kids From Fame	RCA	5		
5	-	**Singles-45s And Under**	Squeeze	A&M	3	47	F
6	6	**Reflections**	Various	CBS	7		
7	-	**The Singles - The First Ten Years**	Abba	Epic	9	62	
8	-	**From The Makers Of...**	Status Quo	Vertigo	8		
9	1	**Love Over Gold**	Dire Straits	Vertigo	7	19	
10	-	**Famous Last Words**	Supertramp	A&M	3	5	

December 1982

This Mnth	Last Mnth	Title	Artist	Label	Wks in 10	US Pos	
1	-	**The John Lennon Collection**	John Lennon	Parlophone	14	33	
2	7	**The Singles - The First Ten Years**	Abba	Epic	9	62	
3	-	**Rio**	Duran Duran	EMI	24	6	
4	1	**Kids From Fame**	Kids From Fame	BBC	24	146	F
5	-	**Pearls II**	Elkie Brooks	A&M	6		
6	-	**Dig The New Breed**	Jam	Polydor	3	131	
7	3	**Heartbreaker**	Dionne Warwick	Arista	15	25	
8	-	**Greatest Love Songs**	Nat 'King' Cole	Capitol	5		L
9	-	**Coda**	Led Zeppelin	Atlantic	2	6	
10	-	**Love Songs**	Diana Ross	K-Tel	5		

US 1982 OCT-DEC

October 1982

This Mnth	Last Mnth	Title	Artist	Label	Wks in 10	UK Pos	
1	1	**American Fool**	John Cougar Mellencamp	Riva	22	37	**F4P**
2	2	**Mirage**	Fleetwood Mac	Warner	18	5	**2P**
3	3	**Abracadabra**	Steve Miller Band	Capitol	12	10	**PL**
4	8	**Emotions In Motion**	Billy Squier	Capitol	9		**2PL**
5	-	**If That's What It Takes**	Michael McDonald	Warner	6		**FL**
6	-	**Nebraska**	Bruce Springsteen	Columbia	7	3	**P**
7	-	**Eye In The Sky**	Alan Parsons Project	Arista	7	28	**PL**
8	4	**Asia**	Asia	Geffen	27	11	**F3P**
9	-	**Business As Usual**	Men At Work	Columbia	31	1	**F6P**
10	9	**Vacation**	Go-Go's	IRS	9	75	**L**

November 1982

This Mnth	Last Mnth	Title	Artist	Label	Wks in 10	UK Pos	
1	9	**Business As Usual**	Men At Work	Columbia	31	1	**F6P**
2	2	**Mirage**	Fleetwood Mac	Warner	18	5	**2P**
3	6	**Nebraska**	Bruce Springsteen	Columbia	7	3	**P**
4	-	**Lionel Richie**	Lionel Richie	Motown	21	9	**F4P**
5	-	**Built For Speed**	Stray Cats	EMI America	20		**FPL**
6	1	**American Fool**	John Cougar Mellencamp	Riva	22	37	**F4P**
7	-	**Night And Day**	Joe Jackson	A&M	7	3	**FL**
8	-	**The Nylon Curtain**	Billy Joel	Columbia	7	27	**2P**
9	-	**It's Hard**	Who	MCA	7	11	**L**
10	7	**Eye In The Sky**	Alan Parsons Project	Arista	7	28	**PL**

December 1982

This Mnth	Last Mnth	Title	Artist	Label	Wks in 10	UK Pos	
1	1	**Business As Usual**	Men At Work	Columbia	31	1	**F6P**
2	5	**Built For Speed**	Stray Cats	EMI America	20		**FPL**
3	4	**Lionel Richie**	Lionel Richie	Motown	21	9	**F4P**
4	7	**Night And Day**	Joe Jackson	A&M	7	3	**FL**
5	-	**...Famous Last Words...**	Supertramp	A&M	7	6	**L**
6	-	**H2O**	Daryl Hall & John Oates	RCA	33	24	
7	-	**Midnight Love**	Marvin Gaye	Columbia	7	10	**2PL**
8	8	**The Nylon Curtain**	Billy Joel	Columbia	7	27	**2P**
9	-	**Get Nervous**	Pat Benatar	Chrysalis	12	73	**PL**
10	-	**Coda**	Led Zeppelin	Swan Song	7	4	**PL**

• For the fourth consecutive year record and tape sales slipped; this time they were down 3% to $3.59 billion. It was also the year videos came of age and proved themselves to be a vital promotional tool. An example was the success of Australian group Men At Work's heavily MTV promoted album **Business As Usual**. It topped the chart for 15 weeks, breaking the record for debut albums set 16 years earlier by The Monkees.

• **Coda**, a collection of previously unreleased tracks by Led Zeppelin, became their tenth successive gold album.

• The Carpenters' (above) appearance at a school in Sherman Oaks, California, attended by Karen Carpenter's godchildren, was the last made by the top selling duo before her death six weeks later. The Who announced that their gig at Toronto's Maple Leaf Garden would be their last. In Britain, chart topping act The Jam played their final dates, as did Japan, in Japan, naturally.

UK 1983 JAN-MAR

• The new British Invasion of the US charts had started, and by March one third of the singles on the Hot 100 were by British born acts. On the album chart, Top 10 debuts were made by British groups The Clash with **Combat Rock**, Duran Duran with **Rio** and Def Leppard with **Pyromania**. The Top 20 welcomed Culture Club with **Kissing To Be Clever**, Adam Ant with **Friend Or Foe**, Thomas Dolby with **Blinded By Science** and Dexy's Midnight Runners with **Too-Rye-Ay**. The photogenic pop act Duran Duran proved especially popular. They were mobbed by thousands of fans when they made a personal appearance in New York, reminding many of the early days of Beatlemania.

• Winners at the BRIT awards included Paul McCartney (Top Male), Kim Wilde (Top Female), Dire Straits (Top Group), Yazoo (Top Newcomers) and The Beatles picked up an award for their Outstanding Contribution to British Music.

• The recently disbanded Jam broke a record set by Elvis Presley when 15 of their singles simultaneously entered the UK Top 100. Their ex-lead vocalist Paul Weller signed a very lucrative deal with Polydor Records. However, the advance he received paled into insignificance when compared to the $10 million paid to David Bowie for putting his signature on an EMI contract.

January 1983

This Mnth	Last Mnth	Title	Artist	Label	Wks in 10	US Pos	
1	1	**The John Lennon Collection**	John Lennon	Parlophone	14	33	
2	-	**Raiders Of The Pop Charts**	Various	Ronco	6		
3	7	**Heartbreaker**	Dionne Warwick	Arista	15	25	
4	-	**Hello I Must Be Going**	Phil Collins	Virgin	10	8	
5	3	**Rio**	Duran Duran	EMI	24	6	
6	2	**The Singles - The First Ten Years**	Abba	Epic	9	62	
7	-	**Business As Usual**	Men At Work	Epic	7	1	F
8	-	**Feline**	Stranglers	Epic	3		
9	-	**Richard Clayderman**	Richard Clayderman	Decca	8		FL
10	5	**Pearls II**	Elkie Brooks	A&M	6		

February 1983

This Mnth	Last Mnth	Title	Artist	Label	Wks in 10	US Pos	
1	7	**Business As Usual**	Men At Work	Epic	7	1	F
2	1	**The John Lennon Collection**	John Lennon	Parlophone	14	33	
3	-	**Porcupine**	Echo & The Bunnymen	Korova	3	137	
4	9	**Richard Clayderman**	Richard Clayderman	Decca	8		FL
5	-	**Night And Day**	Joe Jackson	A&M	4	4	F
6	-	**Thriller**	Michael Jackson	Epic	76	1	2P
7	4	**Hello I Must Be Going**	Phil Collins	Virgin	10	8	
8	-	**Another Page**	Christopher Cross	Warner	3	11	FL
9	-	**Visions**	Various	K-Tel	5		
10	2	**Raiders Of The Pop Charts**	Various	Ronco	6		

March 1983

This Mnth	Last Mnth	Title	Artist	Label	Wks in 10	US Pos	
1	6	**Thriller**	Michael Jackson	Epic	76	1	2P
2	-	**War**	U2	Island	7	12	F
3	-	**Hotline**	Various	K-Tel	4		
4	-	**The Hurting**	Tears For Fears	Mercury	12	73	F
5	-	**Sweet Dreams (Are Made Of This)**	Eurythmics	RCA	10	15	F
6	-	**Quick Step And Side Kick**	Thompson Twins	Arista	2		F
7	-	**Toto IV**	Toto	Columbia	4	4	FL
8	-	**Dazzle Ships**	Orchestral Manoeuvres In The Dark	Dindisc	2	162	
9	-	**Thunder And Lightning**	Thin Lizzy	Vertigo	2	159	
10	1	**Business As Usual**	Men At Work	Epic	7	1	F

US 1983

JAN-MAR

January 1983

This Mnth	Last Mnth	Title	Artist	Label	Wks in 10	UK Pos	
1	1	**Business As Usual**	Men At Work	Columbia	31	1	**F6P**
2	2	**Built For Speed**	Stray Cats	EMI America	20		**FPL**
3	6	**H20**	Daryl Hall & John Oates	RCA	33	24	
4	9	**Get Nervous**	Pat Benatar	Chrysalis	12	73	**PL**
5	3	**Lionel Richie**	Lionel Richie	Motown	21	9	**F4P**
6	10	**Coda**	Led Zeppelin	Swan Song	7	4	**PL**
7	-	**Thriller**	Michael Jackson	Epic	78	1	**24P**
8	5	**...Famous Last Words...**	Supertramp	A&M	7	6	**L**
9	-	**Combat Rock**	Clash	Epic	10	2	**FL**
10	7	**Midnight Love**	Marvin Gaye	Columbia	7	10	**2PL**

February 1983

This Mnth	Last Mnth	Title	Artist	Label	Wks in 10	UK Pos	
1	1	**Business As Usual**	Men At Work	Columbia	31	1	**F6P**
2	2	**Built For Speed**	Stray Cats	EMI America	20		**FPL**
3	3	**H20**	Daryl Hall & John Oates	RCA	33	24	
4	7	**Thriller**	Michael Jackson	Epic	78	1	**24P**
5	-	**The Distance**	Bob Seger & The Silver Bullet Band	Capitol	14	45	**P**
6	4	**Get Nervous**	Pat Benatar	Chrysalis	12	73	**PL**
7	9	**Combat Rock**	Clash	Epic	10	2	**FL**
8	-	**Hello, I Must Be Going!**	Phil Collins	Atlantic	7	2	**2P**
9	-	**Toto IV**	Toto	Columbia	22	4	**3PL**
10	-	**Frontiers**	Journey	Columbia	22	6	**5P**

March 1983

This Mnth	Last Mnth	Title	Artist	Label	Wks in 10	UK Pos	
1	4	**Thriller**	Michael Jackson	Epic	78	1	**24P**
2	10	**Frontiers**	Journey	Columbia	22	6	**5P**
3	3	**H20**	Daryl Hall & John Oates	RCA	33	24	
4	1	**Business As Usual**	Men At Work	Columbia	31	1	**F6P**
5	5	**The Distance**	Bob Seger & The Silver Bullet Band	Capitol	14	45	**P**
6	-	**Rio**	Duran Duran	Harvest	11	2	**F2P**
7	-	**Lionel Richie**	Lionel Richie	Motown	21	9	**F4P**
8	2	**Built For Speed**	Stray Cats	EMI America	20		**FPL**
9	9	**Toto IV**	Toto	Columbia	22	4	**3PL**
10	-	**Pyromania**	Def Leppard	Mercury	38	18	**F9P**

• When Michael Jackson's **Thriller** entered the chart, few people could have prophesied it would become the world's biggest selling record, singles included. **Thriller** topped the chart for a staggering 37 weeks and went on to sell over 45 million copies globally. This figure included 24 million in America and almost 3 million in the UK.

• Toto picked up a record five Grammy awards including Album of the Year for **Toto IV**.

• Actress Jane Fonda became the only person to ever reach the Top 20 with an aerobics record. **Jane Fonda's Workout Record** was an even bigger chart hit across the Atlantic.

• Hardware giants Sony and Philips jointly launched the first compact disk players on the international market. Another technological advance was made when The Human League released the supposed first video single. It contained three of their British hits, 'Love Action', 'Don't You Want Me' and 'Mirror Man' and sold for £12 ($18).

UK 1983 APR-JUNE

• Spandau Ballet's 'True' topped the singles chart used on the 1000th edition of TV's *Top Of The Pops*. Later in the year, that single, and the album of the same name, gave the leading New Romantic act their only American Top 20 entries.

• As Meat Loaf's **Midnight At The Lost And Found** cracked the Top 10 it was reported that he had filed for bankruptcy with debts of over $1 million. Another story circulating was that the big US rocker had lost 70lbs dieting.

• Lower down the chart, two folk-based Irish acts debuted: Clannad with **Magical Ring** and Foster And Allen with **Maggie**. Both acts would become UK chart regulars.

• The much hyped Kajagoogoo had their only Top 10 entry, as did Welsh singer Bonnie Tyler, and music media favourites Heaven 17 and Japan. Other new acts in the headlines included Paul Weller's group The Style Council, who played their first gigs, and distinctive Manchester band The Smiths, who released their first single, 'Hand In Glove'.

• Groups who reunited, albeit briefly, included The Everly Brothers, The Hollies, The Animals and Yes.

April 1983

This Mnth	Last Mnth	Title	Artist	Label	Wks in 10	US Pos	
1	1	**Thriller**	Michael Jackson	Epic	76	1	2P
2	-	**The Final Cut**	Pink Floyd	Harvest	5	6	
3	4	**The Hurting**	Tears For Fears	Mercury	12	73	F
4	5	**Sweet Dreams (Are Made Of This)**	Eurythmics	RCA	10	15	F
5	-	**Faster Than The Speed Of Night**	Bonnie Tyler	CBS	6	4	FL
6	-	**Let's Dance**	David Bowie	EMI America	18	4	
7	-	**Chart Runners**	Various	Ronco	5		
8	2	**War**	U2	Island	7	12	F
9	-	**True**	Spandau Ballet	Reformation	22	19	
10	-	**Deep Sea Skiving**	Bananarama	London	3	63	F

May 1983

This Mnth	Last Mnth	Title	Artist	Label	Wks in 10	US Pos	
1	1	**Thriller**	Michael Jackson	Epic	76	1	2P
2	9	**True**	Spandau Ballet	Reformation	22	19	
3	6	**Let's Dance**	David Bowie	EMI America	18	4	
4	-	**The Luxury Gap**	Heaven 17	Virgin	11	72	FL
5	3	**The Hurting**	Tears For Fears	Mercury	12	73	F
6	-	**Power Corruption And Lies**	New Order	Factory	2		F
7	5	**Faster Than The Speed Of Night**	Bonnie Tyler	CBS	6	4	FL
8	4	**Sweet Dreams (Are Made Of This)**	Eurythmics	RCA	10	15	F
9	-	**Piece Of Mind**	Iron Maiden	EMI	3	14	
10	-	**Twice As Kool**	Kool & The Gang	De-Lite	6		

June 1983

This Mnth	Last Mnth	Title	Artist	Label	Wks in 10	US Pos	
1	1	**Thriller**	Michael Jackson	Epic	76	1	2P
2	3	**Let's Dance**	David Bowie	EMI America	18	4	
3	10	**Twice As Kool**	Kool & The Gang	De-Lite	6		
4	2	**True**	Spandau Ballet	Reformation	22	19	
5	-	**In Your Eyes**	George Benson	Warner	5	27	
6	-	**Confrontation**	Bob Marley & The Wailers	Island	3	55	
7	-	**Synchronicity**	Police	A&M	8	1	
8	-	**Oil On Canvas**	Japan	Virgin	2		FL
9	-	**Chart Encounters Of The Hit Kind**	Various	Ronco	3		
10	4	**The Luxury Gap**	Heaven 17	Virgin	11	72	FL

US 1983 APR-JUNE

April 1983

This Mnth	Last Mnth	Title	Artist	Label	Wks in 10	UK Pos	
1	1	**Thriller**	Michael Jackson	Epic	78	1	24P
2	2	**Frontiers**	Journey	Columbia	22	6	5P
3	3	**H2O**	Daryl Hall & John Oates	RCA	33	24	
4	4	**Business As Usual**	Men At Work	Columbia	31	1	F6P
5	-	**Kilroy Was Here**	Styx	A&M	16	67	PL
6	6	**Rio**	Duran Duran	Harvest	11	2	F2P
7	7	**Lionel Richie**	Lionel Richie	Motown	21	9	F4P
8	10	**Pyromania**	Def Leppard	Mercury	38	18	F9P
9	9	**Toto IV**	Toto	Columbia	22	4	3PL
10	-	**The Final Cut**	Pink Floyd	Columbia	5	1	P

May 1983

This Mnth	Last Mnth	Title	Artist	Label	Wks in 10	UK Pos	
1	1	**Thriller**	Michael Jackson	Epic	78	1	24P
2	8	**Pyromania**	Def Leppard	Mercury	38	18	F9P
3	2	**Frontiers**	Journey	Columbia	22	6	5P
4	-	**Cargo**	Men At Work	Columbia	14	8	3PL
5	5	**Kilroy Was Here**	Styx	A&M	16	67	PL
6	-	**Flashdance**	Soundtrack	Casablanca	25	9	5P
7	-	**Let's Dance**	David Bowie	EMI America	16	1	PL
8	4	**Business As Usual**	Men At Work	Columbia	31	1	F6P
9	3	**H2O**	Daryl Hall & John Oates	RCA	33	24	
10	10	**The Final Cut**	Pink Floyd	Columbia	5	1	P

June 1983

This Mnth	Last Mnth	Title	Artist	Label	Wks in 10	UK Pos	
1	1	**Thriller**	Michael Jackson	Epic	78	1	24P
2	6	**Flashdance**	Soundtrack	Casablanca	25	9	5P
3	4	**Cargo**	Men At Work	Columbia	14	8	3PL
4	2	**Pyromania**	Def Leppard	Mercury	38	18	F9P
5	7	**Let's Dance**	David Bowie	EMI America	16	1	PL
6	3	**Frontiers**	Journey	Columbia	22	6	5P
7	9	**H2O**	Daryl Hall & John Oates	RCA	33	24	
8	5	**Kilroy Was Here**	Styx	A&M	16	67	PL
9	-	**Cuts Like A Knife**	Bryan Adams	A&M	6	30	FP
10	-	**Prince **1999****	Prince	Warner	11	30	F3P

• Over 60% of the Hot 100 singles were by non-American artists, the vast majority being British, a figure not bettered even when The Beatles were at the height of their career.

• Van Halen and David Bowie were paid over $1 million to appear at the US '83 Festival. Perhaps not surprisingly, the festival lost money even though 300,000 fans attended.

• New faces on the Top 200 album chart included R.E.M. with **Murmur**, Tears For Fears with **The Hurting**, Eurythmics with **Sweet Dreams** and Michael Bolton with a self-titled album.

• The Police ended their recording career while at the top. Not only was **Synchonicity** a transatlantic Number 1 (it headed the US field for 17 weeks) but their single 'Every Breath You Take' also repeated that feat. Moreover, the Grammy winning **Synchronicity** was their fourth successive LP to enter at Number 1 in Britain.

UK 1983

JULY-SEPT

• Barry Manilow attracted 40,000 fans to a show at Blenheim Palace and Duran Duran and Dire Straits were among the acts who participated in this year's Prince's Trust Gala.

• At times, British artists hogged half of the Top 30 slots on the US singles chart. David Bowie, whose Serious Moonlight tour was filling stadiums around the world, had ten albums simultaneously in the British Top 100 – a feat that only Elvis Presley had bettered.

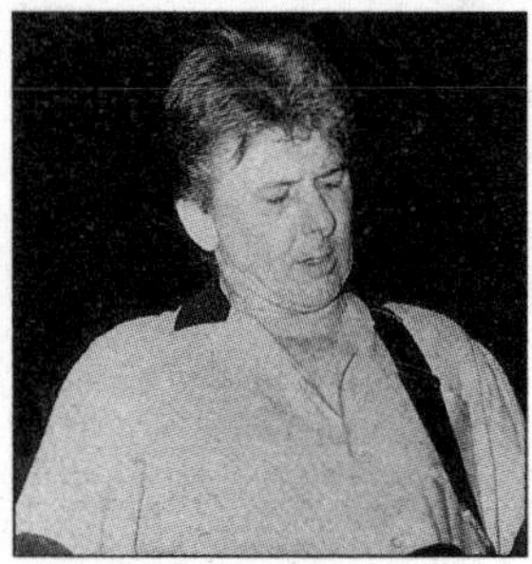

• Among the hit making British groups who disbanded were Bad Company (above), Haircut 100, Fun Boy Three, The Beat and Yazoo,

• Two American groups topped the UK charts with collections of old hits: The Beach Boys, with a 36-tracker, and The Jacksons, with an album half the size. Among the other chart toppers this quarter were newcomer Paul Young's **No Parlez**, which sold over 1.2 million in the UK, and UB40's **Labour Of Love**, the first reggae album to reach the summit.

July 1983

This Mnth	Last Mnth	Title	Artist	Label	Wks in 10	US Pos	
1	7	**Synchronicity**	Police	A&M	8	1	
2	1	**Thriller**	Michael Jackson	Epic	76	1	**2P**
3	-	**Fantastic**	Wham!	Inner Vision	20		**F**
4	-	**You And Me Both**	Yazoo	Mute	6	69	**L**
5	2	**Let's Dance**	David Bowie	EMI America	18	4	
6	-	**Julio**	Julio Iglesias	CBS	4	32	
7	-	**Crisis**	Mike Oldfield	Virgin	7		
8	-	**Body Wishes**	Rod Stewart	Warner	4	30	
9	-	**Secret Messages**	Electric Light Orchestra	Jet	3	36	
10	10	**The Luxury Gap**	Heaven 17	Virgin	11	72	**FL**

August 1983

This Mnth	Last Mnth	Title	Artist	Label	Wks in 10	US Pos	
1	-	**18 Greatest Hits**	Michael Jackson & The Jackson Five	Telstar	9		
2	-	**The Very Best Of The Beach Boys**	Beach Boys	Capitol	9		
3	3	**Fantastic**	Wham!	Inner Vision	20		**F**
4	2	**Thriller**	Michael Jackson	Epic	76	1	**2P**
5	-	**No Parlez**	Paul Young	CBS	31	79	**FP**
6	-	**Punch The Clock**	Elvis Costello	F-Beat	3	24	
7	-	**The Crossing**	Big Country	Mercury	14	18	**F**
8	-	**Alpha**	Asia	Geffen	2	6	**FL**
9	4	**You And Me Both**	Yazoo	Mute	6	69	**L**
10	-	**True**	Spandau Ballet	Reformation	22	19	

September 1983

This Mnth	Last Mnth	Title	Artist	Label	Wks in 10	US Pos	
1	2	**The Very Best Of The Beach Boys**	Beach Boys	Capitol	9		
2	1	**18 Greatest Hits**	Michael Jackson & The Jackson Five	Telstar	9		
3	3	**Fantastic**	Wham!	Inner Vision	20		**F**
4	5	**No Parlez**	Paul Young	CBS	31	79	**FP**
5	10	**True**	Spandau Ballet	Reformation	22	19	
6	4	**Thriller**	Michael Jackson	Epic	76	1	**2P**
7	7	**The Crossing**	Big Country	Mercury	14	18	**F**
8	-	**Labour Of Love**	UB40	DEP International	9	14	
9	-	**Construction Time Again**	Depeche Mode	Mute	3		
10	-	**Flick Of The Switch**	AC/DC	Atlantic	2	15	

US 1983

JULY-SEPT

July 1983

This Mnth	Last Mnth	Title	Artist	Label	Wks in 10	UK Pos	
1	1	**Thriller**	Michael Jackson	Epic	78	1	**24P**
2	2	**Flashdance**	Soundtrack	Casablanca	25	9	**5P**
3	4	**Pyromania**	Def Leppard	Mercury	38	18	**F9P**
4	-	**Synchronicity**	Police	A&M	40	1	**4P**
5	5	**Let's Dance**	David Bowie	EMI America	16	1	**PL**
6	3	**Cargo**	Men At Work	Columbia	14	8	**3PL**
7	-	**The Wild Heart**	Stevie Nicks	Modern	11	28	**2P**
8	-	**Keep It Up**	Loverboy	Columbia	7		**2PL**
9	6	**Frontiers**	Journey	Columbia	22	6	**5P**
10	10	**Prince **1999****	Prince	Warner	11	30	**F3P**

August 1983

This Mnth	Last Mnth	Title	Artist	Label	Wks in 10	UK Pos	
1	4	**Synchronicity**	Police	A&M	40	1	**4P**
2	1	**Thriller**	Michael Jackson	Epic	78	1	**24P**
3	2	**Flashdance**	Soundtrack	Casablanca	25	9	**5P**
4	3	**Pyromania**	Def Leppard	Mercury	38	18	**F9P**
5	7	**The Wild Heart**	Stevie Nicks	Modern	11	28	**2P**
6	5	**Let's Dance**	David Bowie	EMI America	16	1	**PL**
7	8	**Keep It Up**	Loverboy	Columbia	7		**2PL**
8	-	**Staying Alive**	Soundtrack	RSO	6		
9	6	**Cargo**	Men At Work	Columbia	14	8	**3PL**
10	9	**Frontiers**	Journey	Columbia	22	6	**5P**

September 1983

This Mnth	Last Mnth	Title	Artist	Label	Wks in 10	UK Pos	
1	1	**Synchronicity**	Police	A&M	40	1	**4P**
2	2	**Thriller**	Michael Jackson	Epic	78	1	**24P**
3	3	**Flashdance**	Soundtrack	Casablanca	25	9	**5P**
4	4	**Pyromania**	Def Leppard	Mercury	38	18	**F9P**
5	-	**An Innocent Man**	Billy Joel	Columbia	30	2	**7P**
6	-	**Alpha**	Asia	Geffen	5	5	**PL**
7	5	**The Wild Heart**	Stevie Nicks	Modern	11	28	**2P**
8	8	**Staying Alive**	Soundtrack	RSO	6		
9	-	**Lawyers In Love**	Jackson Browne	Asylum	4	37	**L**
10	-	**Reach The Beach**	Fixx	MCA	10	91	**FPL**

• As usual there were many noteworthy gigs during the summer. In New York, more than 70,000 paid to see The Police perform at the Shea Stadium and approximately twice as many attended a rained-out free concert given by Diana Ross in Central Park. Run-D.M.C. and LL Cool J. were the stars of a controversial rap tour and Simon & Garfunkel launched a very successful reunion tour. Simon wed actress Carrie Fisher, whose mother, Debbie Reynolds, father, Eddie Fisher, and step-mother, Connie Stevens, had all had hit records in their own right.

• The Rolling Stones signed to CBS for a record $25 million and Bon Jovi joined Mercury Records for a far smaller advance.

• American news stories included the arrest of Harold Melvin and three of his group, The Blue Notes, on drug charges – their last hit was, ironically, titled 'Bad Luck' – and the sentencing of David Crosby of Crosby, Stills & Nash, to five years imprisonment for drug possession and for carrying a gun.

• After a three-year break Willie Nelson held another Independence Day picnic, James Taylor embarked on a US tour and Bob Dylan and Santana started a European jaunt together.

UK 1983 OCT-DEC

October 1983

This Mnth	Last Mnth	Title	Artist	Label	Wks in 10	US Pos	
1	8	**Labour Of Love**	UB40	DEP International	9	14	
2	4	**No Parlez**	Paul Young	CBS	31	79	**FP**
3	-	**Genesis**	Genesis	Charisma	9	9	
4	7	**The Crossing**	Big Country	Mercury	14	18	**F**
5	-	**Colour By Numbers**	Culture Club	Virgin	17	2	
6	-	**Let's Dance**	David Bowie	EMI America	18	4	
7	3	**Fantastic**	Wham!	Inner Vision	20		**F**
8	-	**Snap**	Jam	Polydor	4		
9	-	**The Hit Squad - Chart Tracking**	Various	Ronco	2		
10	-	**Voice Of The Heart**	Carpenters	A&M	4	46	

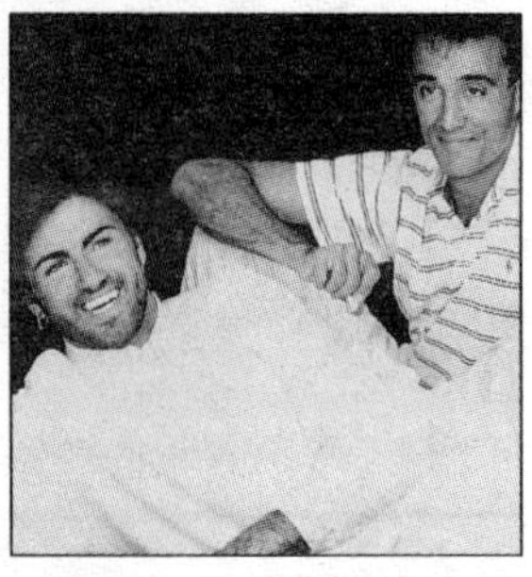

• Wham!, arguably the hottest act in Britain, were mobbed on their first nationwide tour. The duo, fronted by multi-talented George Michael were also in the midst of their first major legal battle with a record label – which resulted in their recording career being put on ice for several months.

• Pink Floyd's **Dark Side of The Moon**, which already held the record for most weeks on the US chart by a rock album, spent its 491st week on the Top 200. This beat the all time longevity record set by **Johnny Mathis' Greatest Hits**.

• The Who, whose US tour was the year's biggest earner, officially split, as did trendsetting soul trio Shalamar, and lead singer Peter Wolf left the J. Geils Band after 15 years.

• American rock superstars Kiss gave up their outrageous stage make-up, and ironically finally scored a Top 10 UK hit with **Lick It Up**.

November 1983

This Mnth	Last Mnth	Title	Artist	Label	Wks in 10	US Pos	
1	5	**Colour By Numbers**	Culture Club	Virgin	17	2	
2	-	**Can't Slow Down**	Lionel Richie	Motown	49	1	**P**
3	-	**Thriller**	Michael Jackson	Epic	76	1	**2P**
4	1	**Labour Of Love**	UB40	DEP International	9	14	
5	-	**The Two Of Us**	Various	K-Tel	4	3	
6	-	**Undercover**	Rolling Stones	Rolling Stones	2	4	
7	8	**Snap**	Jam	Polydor	4		
8	3	**Genesis**	Genesis	Charisma	9	9	
9	2	**No Parlez**	Paul Young	CBS	31	79	**FP**
10	-	**An Innocent Man**	Billy Joel	CBS	33	4	

December 1983

This Mnth	Last Mnth	Title	Artist	Label	Wks in 10	US Pos	
1	9	**No Parlez**	Paul Young	CBS	31	79	**FP**
2	1	**Colour By Numbers**	Culture Club	Virgin	17	2	
3	-	**Stages**	Elaine Paige	K-Tel	7		**F**
4	-	**Now That's What I Call Music**	Various	EMI/Virgin	11		
5	3	**Thriller**	Michael Jackson	Epic	76	1	**2P**
6	-	**Seven And The Ragged Tiger**	Duran Duran	EMI	5	8	
7	-	**U2 Live: Under A Blood Red Sky**	U2	Island	8	12	
8	-	**Formula 30**	Various	Decca/Mercury	2		
9	-	**Chas & Dave's Knees Up - Jamboree Bag No. 2**	Chas & Dave	Rockney	4		**FL**
10	2	**Can't Slow Down**	Lionel Richie	Motown	49	1	**P**

US 1983 OCT-DEC

October 1983

This Mnth	Last Mnth	Title	Artist	Label	Wks in 10	UK Pos	
1	1	**Synchronicity**	Police	A&M	40	1	**4P**
2	2	**Thriller**	Michael Jackson	Epic	78	1	**24P**
3	3	**Flashdance**	Soundtrack	Casablanca	25	9	**5P**
4	5	**An Innocent Man**	Billy Joel	Columbia	30	2	**7P**
5	-	**Metal Health**	Quiet Riot	Pasha	17	F	**4PL**
6	4	**Pyromania**	Def Leppard	Mercury	38	18	**F9P**
7	-	**Faster Than The Speed Of Night**	Bonnie Tyler	RCA	7	1	**FPL**
8	10	**Reach The Beach**	Fixx	MCA	10	91	**FPL**
9	-	**Greatest Hits**	Air Supply	Arista	8		**5PL**
10	-	**The Principle Of Moments**	Robert Plant	Es Paranza	5	7	**P**

November 1983

This Mnth	Last Mnth	Title	Artist	Label	Wks in 10	UK Pos	
1	1	**Synchronicity**	Police	A&M	40	1	**4P**
2	5	**Metal Health**	Quiet Riot	Pasha	17		**F4PL**
3	2	**Thriller**	Michael Jackson	Epic	78	1	**24P**
4	4	**An Innocent Man**	Billy Joel	Columbia	30	2	**7P**
5	-	**Eyes That See In The Dark**	Kenny Rogers	RCA	8	53	**PL**
6	-	**Can't Slow Down**	Lionel Richie	Motown	59	1	**10P**
7	7	**Faster Than The Speed Of Night**	Bonnie Tyler	RCA	7	1	**FPL**
8	9	**Greatest Hits**	Air Supply	Arista	8		**5PL**
9	6	**Pyromania**	Def Leppard	Mercury	38	18	**F9P**
10	-	**What's New**	Linda Ronstadt	Asylum	15	31	**3P**

December 1983

This Mnth	Last Mnth	Title	Artist	Label	Wks in 10	UK Pos	
1	6	**Can't Slow Down**	Lionel Richie	Motown	59	1	**10P**
2	3	**Thriller**	Michael Jackson	Epic	78	1	**24P**
3	1	**Synchronicity**	Police	A&M	40	1	**4P**
4	10	**What's New**	Linda Ronstadt	Asylum	15	31	**3P**
5	2	**Metal Health**	Quiet Riot	Pasha	17		**F4PL**
6	-	**Undercover**	Rolling Stones	Rolling Stones	4	3	**P**
7	4	**An Innocent Man**	Billy Joel	Columbia	30	2	**7P**
8	5	**Eyes That See In The Dark**	Kenny Rogers	RCA	8	53	**PL**
9	-	**Colour By Numbers**	Culture Club	Epic	30	1	**F4PL**
10	-	**90125**	Yes	Atco	12	16	**PL**

• In 1983, tapes outsold records for the first time with total sales increasing 3% to $3.7 billion. It was also the year that videos showed they could make or break an act. They were a great boost to many heavy metal outfits and visual acts like Prince and Michael Jackson. Videos also benefited a lot of British groups, whose image seemed almost as important as their sound. On the subject of videos, Michael Jackson, ZZ Top, Duran Duran and Eurythmics were among the winners in the first *Billboard* Video Awards.

• CBS announced that Michael Jackson's **Thriller** was the biggest selling album of all time, and that Jackson's seven US Top 10 singles in 1983 was the best performance by any artist since The Beatles record-shattering 11 entries in 1964! Jackson's latest video, a 14 minute epic promoting his single 'Thriller' cost a record-breaking $1.1 million.

• The formation of a Rock And Roll Hall of Fame was announced. The first artists were inducted in1986. The actual Hall of Fame building was due to be opened in Cleveland in the mid-Nineties.

• New US rock bands who debuted in the Top 200 included Motley Crue with **Shoot At The Devil** and Dokken with **Breaking The Chains**.

UK 1984 JAN-MAR

• **Now That's What I Call Music** was the first in the most successful album series ever in Britain. The albums, which included hit singles of the previous quarter, almost always reached Number 1, and were showing no signs of losing popularity at the end of the period covered by this book, when volume 29 sold nearly 1.5 million copies.

• First of the Class of '84 to enter the UK Top 10 included top selling acts of the decade The Style Council, Howard Jones and The Smiths. The latter act, who were voted Best New Group in the *NME*, saw their first trio of singles take the top three places on the Indie singles chart.

• BRIT winners included David Bowie (Top Male), Annie Lennox (Top Female), Culture Club (Top Group), Paul Young (Top Newcomer) and Michael Jackson's **Thriller** (Top Album).

• As John Lennon's **Milk And Honey** became his last transatlantic Top 20 entry, his wife Yoko Ono, who sang on half the tracks, pledged £250,000 to Strawberry Fields, the Liverpool old people's home that John had made world famous. Also, twenty years after they had put their hometown on the musical map, The Beatles were made Freemen of the City Of Liverpool, and it was announced that The Beatle City Exhibition Center would soon open.

January 1984

This Mnth	Last Mnth	Title	Artist	Label	Wks in 10	US Pos	
1	4	**Now That's What I Call Music**	Various	EMI/Virgin	11		
2	1	**No Parlez**	Paul Young	CBS	31	79	**FP**
3	5	**Thriller**	Michael Jackson	Epic	76	1	**2P**
4	-	**An Innocent Man**	Billy Joel	CBS	33	4	
5	2	**Colour By Numbers**	Culture Club	Virgin	17	2	
6	-	**Pipes Of Peace**	Paul McCartney	Parlophone	7	15	
7	10	**Can't Slow Down**	Lionel Richie	Motown	49	1	**P**
8	-	**Touch**	Eurythmics	RCA	11	7	
9	7	**U2 Live: Under A Blood Red Sky**	U2	Island	8	12	
10	-	**Portrait**	Diana Ross	Telstar	3		

February 1984

This Mnth	Last Mnth	Title	Artist	Label	Wks in 10	US Pos	
1	8	**Touch**	Eurythmics	RCA	11	7	
2	3	**Thriller**	Michael Jackson	Epic	76	1	**2P**
3	4	**An Innocent Man**	Billy Joel	CBS	33	4	
4	2	**No Parlez**	Paul Young	CBS	31	79	**FP**
5	-	**Sparkle In The Rain**	Simple Minds	Virgin	5	64	
6	7	**Can't Slow Down**	Lionel Richie	Motown	49	1	**P**
7	-	**Milk And Honey**	John Lennon	Polydor	2	11	**L**
8	1	**Now That's What I Call Music**	Various	EMI/Virgin	11		
9	-	**Into The Gap**	Thompson Twins	Arista	15	10	
10	-	**The Crossing**	Big Country	Mercury	14	18	**F**

March 1984

This Mnth	Last Mnth	Title	Artist	Label	Wks in 10	US Pos	
1	9	**Into The Gap**	Thompson Twins	Arista	15	10	
2	3	**An Innocent Man**	Billy Joel	CBS	33	4	
3	2	**Thriller**	Michael Jackson	Epic	76	1	**2P**
4	-	**Human's Lib**	Howard Jones	WEA	12	59	**F**
5	6	**Can't Slow Down**	Lionel Richie	Motown	49	1	**P**
6	-	**The Smiths**	Smiths	Rough Trade	4		**F**
7	-	**The Works**	Queen	EMI	25	23	
8	-	**Alchemy-Dire Straits Live**	Dire Straits	Vertigo	7	46	
9	1	**Touch**	Eurythmics	RCA	11	7	
10	-	**Cafe Bleu**	Style Council	Polydor	4		**F**

US 1984 JAN-MAR

January 1984

This Mnth	Last Mnth	Title	Artist	Label	Wks in 10	UK Pos	
1	2	**Thriller**	Michael Jackson	Epic	78	1	**24P**
2	1	**Can't Slow Down**	Lionel Richie	Motown	59	1	**10P**
3	4	**What's New**	Linda Ronstadt	Asylum	15	31	**3P**
4	3	**Synchronicity**	Police	A&M	40	1	**4P**
5	9	**Colour By Numbers**	Culture Club	Epic	30	1	**F4PL**
6	10	**90125**	Yes	Atco	12	16	**PL**
7	5	**Metal Health**	Quiet Riot	Pasha	17		**F4PL**
8	7	**An Innocent Man**	Billy Joel	Columbia	30	2	**7P**
9	-	**Rock 'n Soul Part 1**	Daryl Hall & John Oates	RCA	11	16	**2P**
10	-	**Yentl (Soundtrack)**	Barbra Streisand	Columbia	2	21	**P**

February 1984

This Mnth	Last Mnth	Title	Artist	Label	Wks in 10	UK Pos	
1	1	**Thriller**	Michael Jackson	Epic	78	1	**24P**
2	5	**Colour By Numbers**	Culture Club	Epic	30	1	**F4PL**
3	2	**Can't Slow Down**	Lionel Richie	Motown	59	1	**10P**
4	-	**1984 (MCMLXXXIV)**	Van Halen	Warner	27	15	**7P**
5	4	**Synchronicity**	Police	A&M	40	1	**4P**
6	8	**An Innocent Man**	Billy Joel	Columbia	30	2	**7P**
7	6	**90125**	Yes	Atco	12	16	**PL**
8	-	**Learning To Crawl**	Pretenders	Sire	10	11	**PL**
9	-	**Seven And The Ragged Tiger**	Duran Duran	Capitol	14	1	**2P**
10	9	**Rock 'n Soul Part 1**	Daryl Hall & John Oates	RCA	11	16	**2P**

March 1984

This Mnth	Last Mnth	Title	Artist	Label	Wks in 10	UK Pos	
1	1	**Thriller**	Michael Jackson	Epic	78	1	**24P**
2	4	**1984 (MCMLXXXIV)**	Van Halen	Warner	27	15	**7P**
3	2	**Colour By Numbers**	Culture Club	Epic	30	1	**F4PL**
4	3	**Can't Slow Down**	Lionel Richie	Motown	59	1	**10P**
5	8	**Learning To Crawl**	Pretenders	Sire	10	11	**PL**
6	-	**Sports**	Huey Lewis & The News	Chrysalis	42	23	**F7P**
7	5	**Synchronicity**	Police	A&M	40	1	**4P**
8	-	**Footloose**	Soundtrack	Columbia	20	7	**8P**
9	6	**An Innocent Man**	Billy Joel	Columbia	30	2	**7P**
10	-	**Touch**	Eurythmics	RCA	6	1	**FP**

• Michael Jackson walked away with a record eight Grammy Awards and seven American Music Awards. His video *The Making Of Thriller* had record advance orders. **Thriller** again hogged the top spot for the quarter stopping both Van Halen's **1984 (MCMLXXXIV)**

and Culture Club's **Colour By Numbers** from reaching the summit. Culture Club, who featured 'gender bender' vocalist Boy George (above), were mobbed when they arrived for a US tour, and not surprisingly won the Grammy for Best New Artist. Apart from Michael Jackson the only other act who had an outstanding Grammy night were The Police, who collected three awards.

• The only album that managed to unseat **Thriller**, albeit for a short period, was Lionel Richie's transatlantic topper **Can't Slow Down**. It went on to sell over 10 million copies in the USA and bagged the Album of the Year Grammy twelve months later. In Britain, it sold 1.7 million and was the top album of 1984.

UK 1984 APR-JUNE

• Over 75,000 fans attended Elton John's concert at Wembley Stadium, on which he was supported by Kool & The Gang, Paul Young and Nik Kershaw. Elton's latest album, **Breaking Hearts**, became his biggest hit for nine years in his homeland.

• The most successful reggae album of all time, **Legend** by Bob Marley & The Wailers, topped the chart. It went on to sell over a million copies in the UK and in excess of five million copies in America.

• New York happenings included the marriage of Jim Kerr, the leader of British band Simple Minds, with Chrissie Hynde, the lead singer of The Pretenders. The Rolling Stones became the first rock act inaugurated into the Madison Square Garden Hall Of Fame and fellow Britons Judas Priest caused riots when they appeared at that venue. Anglo-American spoof heavy rockers Spinal Tap had their debut gig at CBGBs.

• There were many legal battles in progress. Producer Jack Douglas sued Yoko Ono over royalties due on John Lennon's **Double Fantasy**. The Rolling Stones sued manager Allen Klein in an attempt to regain control of some early copyrights. Neil Diamond sued CBS to get them to release his album **Primitive**. The Jacksons sued promoters who supposedly reneged on an agreement, but The Animals withdrew their suit against EMI over past royalty payments.

April 1984

This Mnth	Last Mnth	Title	Artist	Label	Wks in 10	US Pos	
1	-	**Now That's What I Call Music 2**	Various	EMI/Virgin	12		
2	5	**Can't Slow Down**	Lionel Richie	Motown	49	1	P
3	1	**Into The Gap**	Thompson Twins	Arista	15	10	
4	3	**Thriller**	Michael Jackson	Epic	76	1	2P
5	4	**Human's Lib**	Howard Jones	WEA	12	59	F
6	2	**An Innocent Man**	Billy Joel	Columbia	33	4	
7	8	**Alchemy-Dire Straits Live**	Dire Straits	Vertigo	7	46	
8	7	**The Works**	Queen	EMI	25	23	
9	-	**Grace Under Pressure**	Rush	Vertigo	2	10	
10	10	**Cafe Bleu**	Style Council	Polydor	4		F

May 1984

This Mnth	Last Mnth	Title	Artist	Label	Wks in 10	US Pos	
1	1	**Now That's What I Call Music 2**	Various	EMI/Virgin	12		
2	2	**Can't Slow Down**	Lionel Richie	Motown	49	1	P
3	8	**The Works**	Queen	EMI	25	23	
4	4	**Thriller**	Michael Jackson	Epic	76	1	2P
5	-	**Legend**	Bob Marley & The Wailers	Island	20	54	P
6	-	**Footloose**	Soundtrack	CBS	6	1	
7	-	**Hysteria**	Human League	Virgin	2	62	
8	3	**Into The Gap**	Thompson Twins	Arista	15	10	
9	-	**Ocean Rain**	Echo & The Bunnymen	Korova	2	87	
10	-	**And I Love You So**	Howard Keel	Warwick	3		FL

June 1984

This Mnth	Last Mnth	Title	Artist	Label	Wks in 10	US Pos	
1	5	**Legend**	Bob Marley & The Wailers	Island	20	54	P
2	3	**The Works**	Queen	EMI	25	23	
3	-	**An Innocent Man**	Billy Joel	Columbia	33	4	
4	2	**Can't Slow Down**	Lionel Richie	Motown	49	1	P
5	1	**Now That's What I Call Music 2**	Various	EMI/Virgin	12		
6	-	**Born In The USA**	Bruce Springsteen	CBS	35	1	
7	-	**Then Came Rock 'n' Roll**	Various	EMI	4		
8	4	**Thriller**	Michael Jackson	Epic	76	1	2P
9	-	**Hungry For Hits**	Various	K-Tel	3		
10	-	**American Heartbeat**	Various	Epic	4		

US 1984 APR-JUNE

April 1984

This Mnth	Last Mnth	Title	Artist	Label	Wks in 10	UK Pos	
1	8	**Footloose**	Soundtrack	Columbia	20	7	**8P**
2	1	**Thriller**	Michael Jackson	Epic	78	1	**24P**
3	2	**1984 (MCMLXXXIV)**	Van Halen	Warner	27	15	**7P**
4	4	**Can't Slow Down**	Lionel Richie	Motown	59	1	**10P**
5	3	**Colour By Numbers**	Culture Club	Epic	30	1	**F4PL**
6	6	**Sports**	Huey Lewis & The News	Chrysalis	42	23	**F7P**
7	10	**Touch**	Eurythmics	RCA	6	1	**FP**
8	-	**Love At First Sting**	Scorpions	Mercury	13	17	**2P**
9	-	**Heartbeat City**	Cars	Elektra	31	25	**3PL**
10	5	**Learning To Crawl**	Pretenders	Sire	10	11	**PL**

May 1984

This Mnth	Last Mnth	Title	Artist	Label	Wks in 10	UK Pos	
1	1	**Footloose**	Soundtrack	Columbia	20	7	**8P**
2	4	**Can't Slow Down**	Lionel Richie	Motown	59	1	**10P**
3	2	**Thriller**	Michael Jackson	Epic	78	1	**24P**
4	3	**1984 (MCMLXXXIV)**	Van Halen	Warner	27	15	**7P**
5	6	**Sports**	Huey Lewis & The News	Chrysalis	42	23	**F7P**
6	5	**Colour By Numbers**	Culture Club	Epic	30	1	**F4PL**
7	9	**Heartbeat City**	Cars	Elektra	31	25	**3PL**
8	8	**Love At First Sting**	Scorpions	Mercury	13	17	**2P**
9	-	**She's So Unusual**	Cyndi Lauper	Portrait	21	16	**F5P**
10	-	**Into The Gap**	Thompson Twins	Arista	2	1	**FPL**

June 1984

This Mnth	Last Mnth	Title	Artist	Label	Wks in 10	UK Pos	
1	1	**Footloose**	Soundtrack	Columbia	20	7	**8P**
2	5	**Sports**	Huey Lewis & The News	Chrysalis	42	23	**F7P**
3	2	**Can't Slow Down**	Lionel Richie	Motown	59	1	**10P**
4	9	**She's So Unusual**	Cyndi Lauper	Portrait	21	16	**F5P**
5	7	**Heartbeat City**	Cars	Elektra	31	25	**3PL**
6	8	**Love At First Sting**	Scorpions	Mercury	13	17	**2P**
7	3	**Thriller**	Michael Jackson	Epic	78	1	**24P**
8	4	**1984 (MCMLXXXIV)**	Van Halen	Warner	27	15	**7P**
9	6	**Colour By Numbers**	Culture Club	Epic	30	1	**F4PL**
10	-	**Born In The USA**	Bruce Springsteen	Columbia	84	1	**14P**

• Two New York-based female singers were battling it out in the Top 20; Cyndi Lauper and Madonna. Lauper, who was leading the way with **She's So Unusual**, went on to win the Grammy for Best New Artist of the year. Madonna's self-titled debut album finally reached the Top 20 after spending almost a year on the chart.

• One of the year's most successful US tours was jointly headed by Tina Turner and Lionel Richie. Tina, who had made her chart debut in 1960, was more popular than ever; her latest album, **Private Dancer**, went on to sell over 15 million copies around the world.

• The soundtrack album from the film **Footloose**, finally dethroned **Thriller**. Other soundtrack albums that crashed into the Top 20 included **Against All Odds**, which included Phil Collins' Number 1 of that title, and **Hard To Hold**, which featured Rick Springfield. There were also the albums from the dance movies **Breakin'** and **Beat Street**.

UK 1984 JULY-SEPT

July 1984

This Mnth	Last Mnth	Title	Artist	Label	Wks in 10	US Pos	
1	1	**Legend**	Bob Marley & The Wailers	Island	20	54	P
2	-	**Parade**	Spandau Ballet	Reformation	10	50	
3	4	**Can't Slow Down**	Lionel Richie	Motown	49	1	P
4	-	**Breaking Hearts**	Elton John	Rocket	5	20	
5	3	**An Innocent Man**	Billy Joel	CBS	33	4	
6	-	**Human Racing**	Nik Kershaw	MCA	7	70	F
7	-	**Victory**	Jacksons	Epic	2	4	
8	10	**American Heartbeat**	Various	Epic	4		
9	-	**Diamond Life**	Sade	Epic	30	5	F
10	-	**The Last In Line**	Dio	Vertigo	2	23	F

• Phil Collins tied the knot as did the Godfather of Funk, James Brown. The youngest member of the world famous Jackson family, Janet, married James DeBarge, from another well-known R&B singing family, Debarge. Janet also teamed up, this time only on record, with Britain's most successful solo artist, Cliff Richard. Their single 'Two To The Power' failed to click on either side of the Atlantic.

• Interesting live shows included Status Quo at Milton Keynes Bowl and Van Halen, AC/DC and Motley Crue at Castle Donington. Madonna started a US tour supported by The Beastie Boys and Iron Maiden opened their world tour in Poland.

• Spandau Ballet's **Parade** album amassed British advance orders of 300,000. Pin-up model Samantha Fox, who later had a successful transatlantic recording career of her own, was seen in a revealing pose on the album's cover.

• Billy Joel joined the elite few who could boast six or more albums simultaneously on the UK chart. The reason for the upsurge in sales was his sell-out British tour, including a Wembley show which was seen on nationwide TV.

August 1984

This Mnth	Last Mnth	Title	Artist	Label	Wks in 10	US Pos	
1	1	**Legend**	Bob Marley & The Wailers	Island	20	54	P
2	9	**Diamond Life**	Sade	Epic	30	5	F
3	-	**Now That's What I Call Music 3**	Various	EMI/Virgin	13		
4	-	**Private Dancer**	Tina Turner	Capitol	17	3	F
5	3	**Can't Slow Down**	Lionel Richie	Motown	49	1	P
6	-	**The Works**	Queen	EMI	25	23	
7	-	**Thriller**	Michael Jackson	Epic	76	1	2P
8	5	**An Innocent Man**	Billy Joel	CBS	33	4	
9	2	**Parade**	Spandau Ballet	Reformation	10	50	
10	-	**Break Out**	Pointer Sisters	Planet	5	8	FL

September 1984

This Mnth	Last Mnth	Title	Artist	Label	Wks in 10	US Pos	
1	3	**Now That's What I Call Music 3**	Various	EMI/Virgin	13		
2	2	**Diamond Life**	Sade	Epic	30	5	F
3	4	**Private Dancer**	Tina Turner	Capitol	17	3	F
4	5	**Can't Slow Down**	Lionel Richie	Motown	49	1	P
5	-	**Powerslave**	Iron Maiden	EMI	3	21	
6	6	**The Works**	Queen	EMI	25	23	
7	-	**Woman In Red (Soundtrack)**	Stevie Wonder	Motown	6	4	
8	9	**Parade**	Spandau Ballet	Reformation	10	50	
9	1	**Legend**	Bob Marley & The Wailers	Island	20	54	P
10	-	**Eliminator**	ZZ Top	Warner	22	9	F

US 1984

JULY-SEPT

July 1984

This Mnth	Last Mnth	Title	Artist	Label	Wks in 10	UK Pos	
1	10	**Born In The USA**	Bruce Springsteen	Columbia	84	1	**14P**
2	2	**Sports**	Huey Lewis & The News	Chrysalis	42	23	**F7P**
3	5	**Heartbeat City**	Cars	Elektra	31	25	**3PL**
4	3	**Can't Slow Down**	Lionel Richie	Motown	59	1	**10P**
5	1	**Footloose**	Soundtrack	Columbia	20	7	**8P**
6	-	**Purple Rain (Soundtrack)**	Prince & The Revolution	Warner	32	7	**11P**
7	-	**Rebel Yell**	Billy Idol	Chrysalis	5	36	**F2P**
8	8	**1984 (MCMLXXXIV)**	Van Halen	Warner	27	15	**7P**
9	-	**Breakin'**	Soundtrack	Polydor	4		**P**
10	4	**She's So Unusual**	Cyndi Lauper	Portrait	21	16	**F5P**

August 1984

This Mnth	Last Mnth	Title	Artist	Label	Wks in 10	UK Pos	
1	6	**Purple Rain (Soundtrack)**	Prince & The Revolution	Warner	32	7	**11P**
2	1	**Born In The USA**	Bruce Springsteen	Columbia	84	1	**14P**
3	2	**Sports**	Huey Lewis & The News	Chrysalis	42	23	**F7P**
4	-	**Victory**	Jacksons	Epic	8	3	**2PL**
5	3	**Heartbeat City**	Cars	Elektra	31	25	**3PL**
6	4	**Can't Slow Down**	Lionel Richie	Motown	59	1	**10P**
7	-	**Ghostbusters**	Soundtrack	Arista	9	24	**P**
8	-	**Private Dancer**	Tina Turner	Capitol	39	2	**F5P**
9	-	**Out Of The Cellar**	Ratt	Atlantic	9		**F3P**
10	9	**Breakin'**	Soundtrack	Polydor	4		**P**

September 1984

This Mnth	Last Mnth	Title	Artist	Label	Wks in 10	UK Pos	
1	1	**Purple Rain (Soundtrack)**	Prince & The Revolution	Warner	32	7	**11P**
2	2	**Born In The USA**	Bruce Springsteen	Columbia	84	1	**14P**
3	3	**Sports**	Huey Lewis & The News	Chrysalis	42	23	**F7P**
4	8	**Private Dancer**	Tina Turner	Capitol	39	2	**F5P**
5	5	**Heartbeat City**	Cars	Elektra	31	25	**3PL**
6	6	**Can't Slow Down**	Lionel Richie	Motown	59	1	**10P**
7	9	**Out Of The Cellar**	Ratt	Atlantic	9		**F3P**
8	-	**1100 Bel Air Place**	Julio Iglesias	Columbia	11	14	**F4PL**
9	7	**Ghostbusters**	Soundtrack	Arista	9	24	**P**
10	4	**Victory**	Jacksons	Epic	8	3	**2PL**

• Fourteen years after their chart debut, The Jacksons had their last Top 10 album, **Victory**. Michael Jackson joined them on their Victory tour, which included many of the year's top grossing dates. It was reported that Michael gave his $5 million share of earnings from that tour to charity.

• Bruce Springsteen's **Born In The USA** hit the top spot in the USA – a feat it finally repeated in Britain over six months later. The album proved to be one of the biggest sellers of all time, with US sales alone accounting for over 14 million. Also Springsteen's Born In The USA tour hit the road; it would play 158 dates in 11 countries and be seen by five million people.

• Prince's **Purple Rain** album equaled the record set by **Saturday Night Fever** for rock soundtracks, when it too topped the US chart for 24 weeks. The album reportedly sold over a million in its first week. It was America's top selling LP of 1984 and earned two Grammy awards.

UK 1984

OCT-DEC

• Ex-Boomtown Rats vocalist Bob Geldof and Ultravox front man Midge Ure organized Band Aid, an all-star group whose 'Do They Know It's Christmas' single raised much money to help the starving in Ethiopia, and with sales of 3.5 million became Britain's biggest selling single ever. Many other acts donated proceeds of live shows to this good cause and Geldof started planning a massive charity fund-raising show for the following summer.

• Frankie Goes To Hollywood, Britain's top selling singles act of 1984, amassed record advance orders of over a million, 400,000 being for the cassette for their debut album, **Welcome To The Pleasure Dome**. The act also made their live debut – it was in Hollywood naturally.

• The ultra successful multi-label hit compilation series **Now That's What I Call Music** had its first real competition when CBS and WEA joined together and launched the similar **Hits** series. In their first chart battle the newcomer outsold **Now! 4**.

• John Lennon's son Julian cracked the transatlantic Top 20 with his debut **Valotte**. In America, it fared better than Paul McCartney's **Give My Regards To Broad Street**. In the UK, however, the latter, which included 13 Lennon and McCartney tunes, hit the top.

October 1984

This Mnth	Last Mnth	Title	Artist	Label	Wks in 10	US Pos	
1	2	**Diamond Life**	Sade	Epic	30	5	F
2	-	**The Unforgettable Fire**	U2	Island	8	12	
3	-	**Tonight**	David Bowie	EMI America	3	11	
4	7	**Woman In Red (Soundtrack)**	Stevie Wonder	Motown	6	4	
5	1	**Now That's What I Call Music 3**	Various	EMI/Virgin	13		
6	-	**Geffrey Morgan**	UB40	DEP International	2	60	
7	-	**The Age Of Consent**	Bronski Beat	Forbidden Fruit	9	36	FL
8	10	**Eliminator**	ZZ Top	Warner	22	9	F
9	-	**Steeltown**	Big Country	Mercury	3	70	
10	-	**Hits Hits Hits - 18 Smash Originals**	Various	Telstar	2		

November 1984

This Mnth	Last Mnth	Title	Artist	Label	Wks in 10	US Pos	
1	-	**Welcome To The Pleasure Dome**	Frankie Goes To Hollywood	ZTT	14	33	FP
2	-	**The Collection**	Ultravox	Chrysalis	13		
3	1	**Diamond Life**	Sade	Epic	30	5	F
4	-	**Give My Regards To Broad Street**	Paul McCartney	Parlophone	5	21	
5	8	**Eliminator**	ZZ Top	Warner	22	9	F
6	-	**Make It Big**	Wham!	Epic	16	1	
7	-	**Alf**	Alison Moyet	CBS	25	45	F
8	-	**Waking Up With The House On Fire**	Culture Club	Virgin	2	26	
9	-	**Perfect Strangers**	Deep Purple	Polydor	2	17	
10	9	**Steeltown**	Big Country	Mercury	3	70	

December 1984

This Mnth	Last Mnth	Title	Artist	Label	Wks in 10	US Pos	
1	-	**The Hits Album**	Various	CBS/WEA	9		
2	6	**Make It Big**	Wham!	Epic	16	1	
3	-	**Now That's What I Call Music 4**	Various	EMI/Virgin	8		
4	2	**The Collection**	Ultravox	Chrysalis	13		
5	1	**Welcome To The Pleasure Dome**	Frankie Goes To Hollywood	ZTT	14	33	FP
6	7	**Alf**	Alison Moyet	CBS	25	45	F
7	-	**Party Party - 16 Great Party Icebreakers**	Black Lace	Telstar	5		FL
8	3	**Diamond Life**	Sade	Portrait	30	5	F
9	-	**Greatest Hits**	Shakin' Stevens	Epic	7		L
10	-	**Arena**	Duran Duran	EMI	6	4	

US 1984 OCT-DEC

October 1984

This Mnth	Last Mnth	Title	Artist	Label	Wks in 10	UK Pos	
1	1	**Purple Rain (Soundtrack)**	Prince & The Revolution	Warner	32	7	**11P**
2	2	**Born In The USA**	Bruce Springsteen	Columbia	84	1	**14P**
3	4	**Private Dancer**	Tina Turner	Capitol	39	2	**F5P**
4	3	**Sports**	Huey Lewis & The News	Chrysalis	42	23	**F7P**
5	5	**Heartbeat City**	Cars	Elektra	31	25	**3PL**
6	8	**1100 Bel Air Place**	Julio Iglesias	Columbia	11	14	**F4PL**
7	6	**Can't Slow Down**	Lionel Richie	Motown	59	1	**10P**
8	-	**The Woman In Red (Soundtrack)**	Stevie Wonder	Motown	11	2	**P**
9	-	**Madonna**	Madonna	Sire	5	6	**F4P**
10	-	**Eddie And The Cruisers**	John Cafferty & The Beaver Brown Band	Scotti Bros	6		**F2PL**

November 1984

This Mnth	Last Mnth	Title	Artist	Label	Wks in 10	UK Pos	
1	1	**Purple Rain (Soundtrack)**	Prince & The Revolution	Warner	32	7	**11P**
2	2	**Born In The USA**	Bruce Springsteen	Columbia	84	1	**14P**
3	3	**Private Dancer**	Tina Turner	Capitol	39	2	**F5P**
4	8	**The Woman In Red (Soundtrack)**	Stevie Wonder	Motown	11	2	**P**
5	4	**Sports**	Huey Lewis & The News	Chrysalis	42	23	**F7P**
6	6	**1100 Bel Air Place**	Julio Iglesias	Columbia	11	14	**F4PL**
7	7	**Can't Slow Down**	Lionel Richie	Motown	59	1	**10P**
8	5	**Heartbeat City**	Cars	Elektra	31	25	**3PL**
9	-	**Volume One**	Honeydrippers	Es Paranza	10	56	**FPL**
10	-	**Big Bam Boom**	Daryl Hall & John Oates	RCA	12	28	**2PL**

December 1984

This Mnth	Last Mnth	Title	Artist	Label	Wks in 10	UK Pos	
1	1	**Purple Rain (Soundtrack)**	Prince & The Revolution	Warner	32	7	**11P**
2	2	**Born In The USA**	Bruce Springsteen	Columbia	84	1	**14P**
3	3	**Private Dancer**	Tina Turner	Capitol	39	2	**F5P**
4	9	**Volume One**	Honeydrippers	Es Paranza	10	56	**FPL**
5	10	**Big Bam Boom**	Daryl Hall & John Oates	RCA	12	28	**2PL**
6	-	**Like A Virgin**	Madonna	Sire	33	1	**7P**
7	4	**The Woman In Red (Soundtrack)**	Stevie Wonder	Motown	11	2	**P**
8	-	**Arena**	Duran Duran	Capitol	8	6	**2P**
9	7	**Can't Slow Down**	Lionel Richie	Motown	59	1	**10P**
10	5	**Sports**	Huey Lewis & The News	Chrysalis	42	23	**F7P**

• 1984 was the best year yet for American album and tape sales which hit $4.46 billion, an increase of 17% on the previous twelve months. Sales of pre-recorded cassettes doubled and compact disks accounted for $4.2 million.

• Madonna's self-titled debut album reached the Top 10 in its 58th chart week. Soon afterwards her sophomore set, **Like A Virgin**, crashed into the Top 10 in only its second chart week: in the UK it finally hit Number 1 after spending 44 weeks on the chart. Madonna's album was produced by ex-Chic member Nile Rodgers, who also produced the transatlantic Top 10 LP **We Are Family** by Sister Sledge and David Bowie's chart-topping **Let's Dance**. Added to that success, Rodgers was a member of The Honeydrippers, which also included Jimmy Page and Robert Plant from Led Zeppelin and Jeff Beck, who reached the US album Top 10 with their sole recording, the 20 minute short **Volume One**.

UK 1985

JAN-MAR

• Two BRIT winners scored Number 1 albums: Wham! had their second topper with **Make It Big!** and ex-Yazoo vocalist Alison Moyet reached the summit with her debut album, **Alf**. Also newcomer Sade whose **Diamond Life** was voted Best Album, reached runner-up spot behind U2's **The Unforgettable Fire** – the 100th album to enter the UK chart in pole position.

• At the BRIT awards ceremony, Prince made a memorable appearance collecting his award for Best International Solo Artist in the company of two quite unnecessary bodyguards. Across the Atlantic, veteran vocalist Tina Turner grabbed four Grammy Awards while Prince received a record 10 American Music Award nominations.

• Producers Stock, Aitken & Waterman scored their first Top 20 hit single, 'You Spin Me Round' by Dead Or Alive. They went on to become the most successful singles producers ever in Britain, with 46 Top 10 entries in the Eighties alone!

January 1985

This Mnth	Last Mnth	Title	Artist	Label	Wks in 10	US Pos	
1	6	**Alf**	Alison Moyet	CBS	25	45	F
2	1	**The Hits Album**	Various	CBS/WEA	9		
3	4	**The Collection**	Ultravox	Chrysalis	13		
4	2	**Make It Big**	Wham!	Columbia	16	1	
5	3	**Now That's What I Call Music 4**	Various	EMI/Virgin	8		
6	-	**Agent Provocateur**	Foreigner	Atlantic	6	4	L
7	5	**Welcome To The Pleasure Dome**	Frankie Goes To Hollywood	ZTT	14	33	FP
8	-	**Eliminator**	ZZ Top	Warner	22	9	F
9	8	**Diamond Life**	Sade	Epic	30	5	F
10	7	**Party Party - 16 Great Party Icebreakers**	Black Lace	Telstar	5		FL

February 1985

This Mnth	Last Mnth	Title	Artist	Label	Wks in 10	US Pos	
1	-	**Born In The USA**	Bruce Springsteen	CBS	35	1	
2	6	**Agent Provocateur**	Foreigner	Atlantic	6	4	L
3	1	**Alf**	Alison Moyet	CBS	25	45	F
4	-	**Hits Out Of Hell**	Meat Loaf	Epic	9		
5	-	**The Barbara Dickson Songbook**	Barbara Dickson	K-Tel	4		L
6	-	**The Age Of Consent**	Bronski Beat	Forbidden Fruit	9	36	FL
7	8	**Eliminator**	ZZ Top	Warner	22	9	F
8	-	**Meat Is Murder**	Smiths	Rough Trade	3	110	
9	-	**The Very Best Of Chris De Burgh**	Chris De Burgh	Telstar	3		F
10	-	**Steps In Time**	King	CBS	2		FL

March 1985

This Mnth	Last Mnth	Title	Artist	Label	Wks in 10	US Pos	
1	-	**No Jacket Required**	Phil Collins	Virgin	36	1	P
2	1	**Born In The USA**	Bruce Springsteen	CBS	35	1	
3	3	**Alf**	Alison Moyet	CBS	25	45	F
4	-	**Songs From The Big Chair**	Tears For Fears	Mercury	30	1	
5	4	**Hits Out Of Hell**	Meat Loaf	Epic	9		
6	-	**Dream Into Action**	Howard Jones	WEA	7	10	
7	8	**Meat Is Murder**	Smiths	Rough Trade	3	110	
8	7	**Eliminator**	ZZ Top	Warner	22	9	F
9	-	**Private Dancer**	Tina Turner	Capitol	17	3	F
10	-	**Reckless**	Bryan Adams	A&M	3	1	F

US 1985 JAN-MAR

January 1985

This Mnth	Last Mnth	Title	Artist	Label	Wks in 10	UK Pos	
1	2	**Born In The USA**	Bruce Springsteen	Columbia	84	1	**14P**
2	1	**Purple Rain (Soundtrack)**	Prince & The Revolution	Warner	32	7	**11P**
3	6	**Like A Virgin**	Madonna	Sire	33	1	**7P**
4	8	**Arena**	Duran Duran	Capitol	8	6	**2P**
5	-	**Chicago 17**	Chicago	Full Moon	12	24	**5PL**
6	3	**Private Dancer**	Tina Turner	Capitol	39	2	**F5P**
7	5	**Big Bam Boom**	Daryl Hall & John Oates	RCA	12	28	**2PL**
8	4	**Volume One**	Honeydrippers	Es Paranza	10	56	**FPL**
9	-	**Reckless**	Bryan Adams	A&M	40	7	**5P**
10	-	**She's So Unusual**	Cyndi Lauper	Portrait	21	16	**F5P**

February 1985

This Mnth	Last Mnth	Title	Artist	Label	Wks in 10	UK Pos	
1	3	**Like A Virgin**	Madonna	Sire	33	1	**7P**
2	1	**Born In The USA**	Bruce Springsteen	Columbia	84	1	**14P**
3	-	**Make It Big**	Wham!	Columbia	25	1	**F6P**
4	-	**Agent Provocateur**	Foreigner	Atlantic	12	1	**2PL**
5	2	**Purple Rain (Soundtrack)**	Prince & The Revolution	Warner	32	7	**11P**
6	5	**Chicago 17**	Chicago	Full Moon	12	24	**5PL**
7	-	**Centerfield**	John Fogerty	Warner	15	48	**F2PL**
8	9	**Reckless**	Bryan Adams	A&M	40	7	**5P**
9	-	**New Edition**	New Edition	MCA	6		**FPL**
10	6	**Private Dancer**	Tina Turner	Capitol	39	2	**F5P**

March 1985

This Mnth	Last Mnth	Title	Artist	Label	Wks in 10	UK Pos	
1	7	**Centerfield**	John Fogerty	Warner	15	48	**F2PL**
2	3	**Make It Big**	Wham!	Columbia	25	1	**F6P**
3	2	**Born In The USA**	Bruce Springsteen	Columbia	84	1	**14P**
4	1	**Like A Virgin**	Madonna	Sire	33	1	**7P**
5	-	**Beverly Hills Cop**	Soundtrack	MCA	22	24	**2P**
6	-	**No Jacket Required**	Phil Collins	Atlantic	31	1	**7P**
7	4	**Agent Provocateur**	Foreigner	Atlantic	12	1	**2PL**
8	10	**Private Dancer**	Tina Turner	Capitol	39	2	**F5P**
9	-	**Wheels Are Turnin'**	REO Speedwagon	Epic	7		**2PL**
10	9	**New Edition**	New Edition	MCA	6		**FPL**

• American acts were not slow to follow the lead of Band Aid, and an all-star group was quickly assembled to raise money for Ethiopia and other charities. The act's single 'We Are The World' sold in excess of four million in the USA, and the album of the same name topped the chart in just two weeks and sold more than three million copies. The only black mark over this charitable project was the fact that some chain stores refused to stock the records, as there was no profit in it for them. A similar fate befell Bob Geldof's planned Live Aid show, which Wembley Stadium initially refused to stage for free.

• Rock giants enjoying their last Top 10 albums were Hall & Oates, Chicago, REO Speedwagon and Foreigner. The latter group's last major hit **Agent Provocateur** gave the Anglo-American act their only British chart topper.

• Many Top 20 album artists had previously been a part of hit bands. Numbered among these were John Fogerty, ex-Creedence Clearwater Revival, Don Henley, ex-Eagles and Lionel Richie, ex-Commodores. While taking sabbaticals from their regular groups to get solo successes were David Lee Roth of Van Halen, Phil Collins of Genesis and Mick Jagger of The Rolling Stones.

UK 1985 APR-JUNE

• Phil Collins added a second solo Number 1 to his tally of three with Genesis. **No Jacket Required** was to be his last solo album for nearly five years.

• The Firm and Power Station were the latest in a long line of supergroups. The former included Jimmy Page, ex-Led Zeppelin and Honeydrippers, and vocalist Paul Rodgers, ex-Free and Bad Company. The line-up of Power Station included Duran Duran members John and Andy Taylor and lead singer Robert Palmer.

• **Brothers In Arms** by Dire Straits gave the British group their only transatlantic Number 1 – in fact, it topped the charts in 22 countries. The album sold over 3.6 million in the UK alone – a figure only bettered by The Beatles' **Sergeant Pepper**.

• Bruce Springsteen's UK tour was an amazing success. The Boss packed out shows nationwide and all his seven albums simultaneously reached the British Top 100.

April 1985

This Mnth	Last Mnth	Title	Artist	Label	Wks in 10	US Pos	
1	-	**The Secret Of Association**	Paul Young	CBS	10	19	
2	1	**No Jacket Required**	Phil Collins	Virgin	36	1	P
3	4	**Songs From The Big Chair**	Tears For Fears	Mercury	30	1	
4	-	**Hits 2**	Various	CBS/WEA	10		
5	-	**Requiem**	Andrew Lloyd Webber	HMV	5		L
6	2	**Born In The USA**	Bruce Springsteen	CBS	35	1	
7	3	**Alf**	Alison Moyet	CBS	25	45	F
8	6	**Dream Into Action**	Howard Jones	WEA	7	10	
9	-	**Welcome To The Pleasure Dome**	Frankie Goes To Hollywood	ZTT	14	33	FP
10	-	**Go West/ Bangs And Crashes**	Go West	Chrysalis	10	60	F

May 1985

This Mnth	Last Mnth	Title	Artist	Label	Wks in 10	US Pos	
1	4	**Hits 2**	Various	CBS/WEA	10		
2	2	**No Jacket Required**	Phil Collins	Virgin	36	1	P
3	3	**Songs From The Big Chair**	Tears For Fears	Mercury	30	1	
4	-	**Be Yourself Tonight**	Eurythmics	RCA	21	9	
5	1	**The Secret Of Association**	Paul Young	CBS	10	19	
6	6	**Born In The USA**	Bruce Springsteen	CBS	35	1	
7	-	**Brothers In Arms**	Dire Straits	Vertigo	65	1	3P
8	-	**Mr. Bad Guy**	Freddie Mercury	CBS	2	159	F
9	-	**Out Now!**	Various	Chrysalis/MCA	8		
10	-	**Around The World In A Day**	Prince & The Revolution	Warner	2	1	

June 1985

This Mnth	Last Mnth	Title	Artist	Label	Wks in 10	US Pos	
1	7	**Brothers In Arms**	Dire Straits	Vertigo	65	1	3P
2	9	**Out Now!**	Various	Chrysalis/MCA	8		
3	-	**Now Dance**	Various	EMI/Virgin	4		
4	-	**Boys And Girls**	Bryan Ferry	EG	8	63	
5	6	**Born In The USA**	Bruce Springsteen	CBS	35	1	
6	-	**Best Of The 20th Century Boy**	T. Rex	K-Tel	6		L
7	3	**Songs From The Big Chair**	Tears For Fears	Mercury	30	1	
8	-	**Our Favourite Shop**	Style Council	Polydor	3		
9	-	**Cupid And Psyche '85**	Scritti Politti	Virgin	4	50	F
10	2	**No Jacket Required**	Phil Collins	Virgin	36	1	P

US 1985

APR-JUNE

April 1985

This Mnth	Last Mnth	Title	Artist	Label	Wks in 10	UK Pos	
1	6	**No Jacket Required**	Phil Collins	Atlantic	31	1	**7P**
2	3	**Born In The USA**	Bruce Springsteen	Columbia	84	1	**14P**
3	1	**Centerfield**	John Fogerty	Warner	15	48	**F2PL**
4	5	**Beverly Hills Cop**	Soundtrack	MCA	22	24	**2P**
5	8	**Private Dancer**	Tina Turner	Capitol	39	2	**F5P**
6	4	**Like A Virgin**	Madonna	Sire	33	1	**7P**
7	2	**Make It Big**	Wham!	Columbia	25	1	**F6P**
8	-	**We Are The World**	USA For Africa	Columbia	7	31	**F3PL**
9	9	**Wheels Are Turnin'**	REO Speedwagon	Epic	7		**2PL**
10	-	**Diamond Life**	Sade	Portrait	10	2	**F3P**

May 1985

This Mnth	Last Mnth	Title	Artist	Label	Wks in 10	UK Pos	
1	1	**No Jacket Required**	Phil Collins	Atlantic	31	1	**7P**
2	8	**We Are The World**	USA For Africa	Columbia	7	31	**F3PL**
3	2	**Born In The USA**	Bruce Springsteen	Columbia	84	1	**14P**
4	4	**Beverly Hills Cop**	Soundtrack	MCA	22	24	**2P**
5	10	**Diamond Life**	Sade	Portrait	10	2	**F3P**
6	6	**Like A Virgin**	Madonna	Sire	33	1	**7P**
7	-	**Around The World In A Day**	Prince	Paisley Park	14	5	**2P**
8	-	**Southern Accents**	Tom Petty & The Heartbreakers	MCA	6	23	**P**
9	3	**Centerfield**	John Fogerty	Warner	15	48	**F2PL**
10	7	**Make It Big**	Wham!	Columbia	25	1	**F6P**

June 1985

This Mnth	Last Mnth	Title	Artist	Label	Wks in 10	UK Pos	
1	7	**Around The World In A Day**	Prince	Paisley Park	14	5	**2P**
2	1	**No Jacket Required**	Phil Collins	Atlantic	31	1	**7P**
3	4	**Beverly Hills Cop**	Soundtrack	MCA	22	24	**2P**
4	3	**Born In The USA**	Bruce Springsteen	Columbia	84	1	**14P**
5	-	**Songs From The Big Chair**	Tears For Fears	Mercury	32	2	**F4P**
6	10	**Make It Big**	Wham!	Columbia	25	1	**F6P**
7	-	**Reckless**	Bryan Adams	A&M	40	7	**5P**
8	5	**Diamond Life**	Sade	Portrait	10	2	**F3P**
9	6	**Like A Virgin**	Madonna	Sire	33	1	**7P**
10	-	**The Power Station**	Power Station	Capitol	11	12	**FPL**

• Multi-artist film soundtracks were becoming regular chart visitors. **Beverly Hills Cop**, which included Patti LaBelle, The Pointer Sisters and Glenn Frey, reached the summit, while **Vision Quest**, featuring Madonna, Foreigner and Journey, and **The Breakfast Club**, which included British groups Simple Minds and Wang Chung, both graced the Top 20.

• R&B acts cracking the pop Top 20 included Kool & The Gang with **Emergency**, Luther Vandross with **The Night I Fell In Love**, Rick James' protégées the Mary Jane Girls with **Only Four You**, Debarge with **Rhythm Of The Night** and British-based Billy Ocean with **Suddenly**.

• British acts were again very successful in the US, and at times accounted for 75% of the singles Top 10. On the album front, UK newcomers Sade, Tears For Fears and Howard Jones debuted in the Top 10. Londoner Phil Collins had a transatlantic Number 1 with **No Jacket Required**, which sold nearly two million in his homeland and won the Grammy for Best Album of 1985.

• The teaming of The Temptations and Hall & Oates at the re-opening of the famed Apollo Theater in New York attracted a lot of press interest, as did the fact that the 20,000 tickets for U2's Madison Square Garden show were sold in a record breaking one hour.

UK 1985 JULY-SEPT

July 1985

This Mnth	Last Mnth	Title	Artist	Label	Wks in 10	US Pos	
1	5	**Born In The USA**	Bruce Springsteen	CBS	35	1	
2	1	**Brothers In Arms**	Dire Straits	Vertigo	65	1	**3P**
3	-	**All Through The Night**	Aled Jones	BBC	7		**L**
4	7	**Songs From The Big Chair**	Tears For Fears	Mercury	30	1	
5	-	**Misplaced Childhood**	Marillion	EMI	9	47	
6	-	**The Dream Of The Blue Turtles**	Sting	A&M	9	2	**F**
7	-	**Be Yourself Tonight**	Eurythmics	RCA	21	9	
8	9	**Cupid And Psyche '85**	Scritti Politti	Virgin	4	50	**F**
9	-	**Greatest Hits Volume I & Volume II**	Billy Joel	CBS	4	6	
10	-	**The Secret Of Association**	Paul Young	CBS	10	19	

August 1985

This Mnth	Last Mnth	Title	Artist	Label	Wks in 10	US Pos	
1	2	**Brothers In Arms**	Dire Straits	Vertigo	65	1	**3P**
2	1	**Born In The USA**	Bruce Springsteen	CBS	35	1	
3	-	**Now That's What I Call Music 5**	Various	EMI/Virgin	10		
4	-	**Like A Virgin**	Madonna	Sire	30	1	**P**
5	7	**Be Yourself Tonight**	Eurythmics	RCA	21	9	
6	4	**Songs From The Big Chair**	Tears For Fears	Mercury	30	1	
7	-	**No Jacket Required**	Phil Collins	Virgin	36	1	**P**
8	-	**The Kenny Rogers Story**	Kenny Rogers	Liberty	11		**L**
9	-	**Madonna/The First Album**	Madonna	Sire	10	8	**F**
10	10	**The Secret Of Association**	Paul Young	CBS	10	19	

September 1985

This Mnth	Last Mnth	Title	Artist	Label	Wks in 10	US Pos	
1	4	**Like A Virgin**	Madonna	Sire	30	1	**P**
2	3	**Now That's What I Call Music 5**	Various	EMI/Virgin	10		
3	1	**Brothers In Arms**	Dire Straits	Vertigo	65	1	**3P**
4	8	**The Kenny Rogers Story**	Kenny Rogers	Liberty	11		**L**
5	6	**Songs From The Big Chair**	Tears For Fears	Mercury	30	1	
6	7	**No Jacket Required**	Phil Collins	Virgin	36	1	**P**
7	-	**Hounds Of Love**	Kate Bush	EMI	11	30	
8	9	**Madonna/The First Album**	Madonna	Sire	10	8	**F**
9	-	**Misplaced Childhood**	Marillion	EMI	9	47	
10	-	**The Head On The Door**	Cure	Fiction	4	59	

• Madonna, now the most talked about female artist on either side of the Atlantic, married actor Sean Penn as her own film, *Desperately Seeking Susan*, was released. In Britain, she became the first female to hold the Top 2 singles chart placings. However, she was not the only female singer/songwriter in the news: Kate Bush hit the headlines when she scored her second Number 1 album, **Hounds Of Love**.

• The fact that there was a record number of reissued singles in the UK Top 40 did not mean that there was a shortage of new acts on the way up. In London, many people raved about Sigue Sigue Sputnik, a band formed by ex-Generation X member, Tony James. Meanwhile in Manchester, two popular local bands released their first singles, Stone Roses and Happy Mondays. Sigue Sigue Sputnik became a well-hyped one hit wonder and the latter acts led the Manchester invasion of the UK charts later in the decade.

• Apart from Live Aid there were several other noteworthy UK live shows. James Brown played to sell-out crowds in London supported by newcomers Simply Red. Dire Straits, another Live Aid act, played 10 straight nights at Wembley Arena, and US superstars ZZ Top, Bon Jovi and Metallica made successful appearances at Donington '85.

US 1985

JULY-SEPT

July 1985

This Mnth	Last Mnth	Title	Artist	Label	Wks in 10	UK Pos	
1	5	**Songs From The Big Chair**	Tears For Fears	Mercury	32	2	**F4P**
2	2	**No Jacket Required**	Phil Collins	Atlantic	31	1	**7P**
3	7	**Reckless**	Bryan Adams	A&M	40	7	**5P**
4	1	**Around The World In A Day**	Prince	Paisley Park	14	5	**2P**
5	4	**Born In The USA**	Bruce Springsteen	Columbia	84	1	**14P**
6	3	**Beverly Hills Cop**	Soundtrack	MCA	22	24	**2P**
7	10	**The Power Station**	Power Station	Capitol	11	12	**FPL**
8	6	**Make It Big**	Wham!	Columbia	25	1	**F6P**
9	9	**Like A Virgin**	Madonna	Sire	33	1	**7P**
10	-	**Invasion Of Your Privacy**	Ratt	Atlantic	6	50	**PL**

August 1985

This Mnth	Last Mnth	Title	Artist	Label	Wks in 10	UK Pos	
1	1	**Songs From The Big Chair**	Tears For Fears	Mercury	32	2	**F4P**
2	3	**Reckless**	Bryan Adams	A&M	40	7	**5P**
3	2	**No Jacket Required**	Phil Collins	Atlantic	31	1	**7P**
4	-	**The Dream Of The Blue Turtles**	Sting	A&M	19	3	**F3P**
5	5	**Born In The USA**	Bruce Springsteen	Columbia	84	1	**14P**
6	-	**Brothers In Arms**	Dire Straits	Warner	37	1	**7PL**
7	-	**Theatre Of Pain**	Motley Crue	Elektra	9	36	**F2P**
8	7	**The Power Station**	Power Station	Capitol	11	12	**FPL**
9	4	**Around The World In A Day**	Prince	Paisley Park	14	5	**2P**
10	10	**Invasion Of Your Privacy**	Ratt	Atlantic	6	50	**PL**

September 1985

This Mnth	Last Mnth	Title	Artist	Label	Wks in 10	UK Pos	
1	6	**Brothers In Arms**	Dire Straits	Warner	37	1	**7PL**
2	4	**The Dream Of The Blue Turtles**	Sting	A&M	19	3	**F3P**
3	1	**Songs From The Big Chair**	Tears For Fears	Mercury	32	2	**F4P**
4	5	**Born In The USA**	Bruce Springsteen	Columbia	84	1	**14P**
5	2	**Reckless**	Bryan Adams	A&M	40	7	**5P**
6	3	**No Jacket Required**	Phil Collins	Atlantic	31	1	**7P**
7	-	**Greatest Hits Volume 1 & Volume 2**	Billy Joel	Columbia	9	7	**6P**
8	-	**Whitney Houston**	Whitney Houston	Arista	46	2	**F11P**
9	7	**Theatre Of Pain**	Motley Crue	Elektra	9	36	**F2P**
10	-	**Heart**	Heart	Capitol	37	19	**5P**

• Few could argue that Live Aid was not the most important live event of the rock era. The show which was staged in both London and Philadelphia included over two dozen of the world's top rock acts. Among the superstars on show were Bryan Adams, Beach Boys, Black Sabbath, David Bowie, Phil Collins, Crosby, Stills & Nash and Bob Dylan. Also among the star-studded throng were INXS (above), Mick Jagger, a reformed Led Zeppelin, Madonna, Paul McCartney, Queen, Tina Turner, U2 and The Who, reunited for the event. Live Aid was seen in 170 countries by a TV audience of approximately 1.6 billion. It raised the remarkable sum of $80 million (£50 million) for famine relief in Africa.

• As British acts continued to have a great run Stateside, several noteworthy American groups made their UK chart debuts. Among them were R.E.M. with **Fables Of The Reconstruction**, Huey Lewis & The News with **Sports** and heavy metal acts Motley Crue and Ratt with **Theatre of Pain** and **Invasion Of Your Privacy** respectively.

UK 1985 OCT-DEC

• In Britain, for the first time, the sales of cassettes passed those of vinyl albums, and all but a rare few hit singles were available in both 7" and 12" formats. The sales of records and tapes in the USA remained roughly static, however the sales of compact disks increased by a remarkable 250% and now accounted for 21 million of the 643 million units sold.

• Despite taking legal steps, Spandau Ballet failed to stop Chrysalis from releasing their **Greatest Hits**. It became one of five such collections in December's Top 10. Another case that hit the headlines was that of Badfinger, who won an 11 year battle over royalties. Tragically, by then, the group's two main writers, Pete Ham and Tom Evans, had already committed suicide.

• British groups going through personnel changes included The Clash, The Alarm, Sixties stars The Searchers and Bronski Beat, the latter replacing their distinctive lead singer Jimmy Somerville with John Foster.

• Rod Stewart's Manager, Billy Gaff, purchased London's internationally renowned Marquee Club and there was also a lot of interest in the new Mother label launched by U2 to help new acts break into the record business.

October 1985

This Mnth	Last Mnth	Title	Artist	Label	Wks in 10	US Pos	
1	7	**Hounds Of Love**	Kate Bush	EMI	11	30	
2	1	**Like A Virgin**	Madonna	Sire	30	1	**P**
3	3	**Brothers In Arms**	Dire Straits	Vertigo	65	1	**3P**
4	2	**Now That's What I Call Music 5**	Various	EMI/Virgin	10		
5	-	**The Love Songs**	George Benson	K-Tel	12		**L**
6	9	**Misplaced Childhood**	Marillion	EMI	9	47	
7	-	**The Gift**	Midge Ure	Chrysalis	2	F	
8	-	**In Square Circle**	Stevie Wonder	Motown	3	5	**L**
9	-	**Live After Death**	Iron Maiden	EMI	2	19	
10	8	**Madonna/The First Album**	Madonna	Sire	10	8	**F**

November 1985

This Mnth	Last Mnth	Title	Artist	Label	Wks in 10	US Pos	
1	5	**The Love Songs**	George Benson	K-Tel	12		**L**
2	3	**Brothers In Arms**	Dire Straits	Vertigo	65	1	**3P**
3	-	**Once Upon A Time**	Simple Minds	Virgin	10	10	
4	-	**Promise**	Sade	Epic	10	1	
5	-	**The Greatest Hits Of 1985**	Various	Telstar	8		
6	-	**Afterburner**	ZZ Top	Warner	2	4	
7	-	**Out Now! 2**	Various	Chrysalis/MCA	4		
8	-	**Ice On Fire**	Elton John	Rocket	2	48	
9	1	**Hounds Of Love**	Kate Bush	EMI	11	30	
10	2	**Like A Virgin**	Madonna	Sire	30	1	**P**

December 1985

This Mnth	Last Mnth	Title	Artist	Label	Wks in 10	US Pos	
1	-	**Now That's What I Call Music 6**	Various	EMI/Virgin	8		
2	-	**Now - The Christmas Album**	Various	EMI/Virgin	8		
3	-	**Hits 3**	Various	CBS/WEA	6		
4	-	**The Singles Collection**	Spandau Ballet	Chrysalis	9		
5	2	**Brothers In Arms**	Dire Straits	Vertigo	65	1	**3P**
6	1	**The Love Songs**	George Benson	K-Tel	12		**L**
7	4	**Promise**	Sade	Epic	10	1	
8	5	**The Greatest Hits Of 1985**	Various	Telstar	8		
9	10	**Like A Virgin**	Madonna	Sire	30	1	**P**
10	-	**The Love Album**	Various	Telstar	4		

US 1985 OCT-DEC

October 1985

This Mnth	Last Mnth	Title	Artist	Label	Wks in 10	UK Pos	
1	1	**Brothers In Arms**	Dire Straits	Warner	37	1	**7PL**
2	8	**Whitney Houston**	Whitney Houston	Arista	46	2	**F11P**
3	2	**The Dream Of The Blue Turtles**	Sting	A&M	19	3	**F3P**
4	3	**Songs From The Big Chair**	Tears For Fears	Mercury	32	2	**F4P**
5	4	**Born In The USA**	Bruce Springsteen	Columbia	84	1	**14P**
6	-	**Scarecrow**	John Cougar Mellencamp	Riva	29		**3P**
7	-	**Miami Vice**	Soundtrack - TV	MCA	18	11	**4P**
8	5	**Reckless**	Bryan Adams	A&M	40	7	**5P**
9	10	**Heart**	Heart	Capitol	37	19	**5P**
10	7	**Greatest Hits Volume 1 & Volume 2**	Billy Joel	Columbia	9	7	**6P**

November 1985

This Mnth	Last Mnth	Title	Artist	Label	Wks in 10	UK Pos	
1	7	**Miami Vice**	Soundtrack - TV	MCA	18	11	**4P**
2	6	**Scarecrow**	John Cougar Mellencamp	Riva	29		**3P**
3	1	**Brothers In Arms**	Dire Straits	Warner	37	1	**7PL**
4	2	**Whitney Houston**	Whitney Houston	Arista	46	2	**F11P**
5	9	**Heart**	Heart	Capitol	37	19	**5P**
6	-	**In Square Circle**	Stevie Wonder	Tamla	14	5	**2PL**
7	4	**Songs From The Big Chair**	Tears For Fears	Mercury	32	2	**F4P**
8	3	**The Dream Of The Blue Turtles**	Sting	A&M	19	3	**F3P**
9	5	**Born In The USA**	Bruce Springsteen	Columbia	84	1	**14P**
10	-	**Afterburner**	ZZ Top	Warner	15	2	**4P**

December 1985

This Mnth	Last Mnth	Title	Artist	Label	Wks in 10	UK Pos	
1	1	**Miami Vice**	Soundtrack - TV	MCA	18	11	**4P**
2	5	**Heart**	Heart	Capitol	37	19	**5P**
3	2	**Scarecrow**	John Cougar Mellencamp	Riva	29		**3P**
4	10	**Afterburner**	ZZ Top	Warner	15	2	**4P**
5	3	**Brothers In Arms**	Dire Straits	Warner	37	1	**7PL**
6	6	**In Square Circle**	Stevie Wonder	Tamla	14	5	**2PL**
7	-	**The Broadway Album**	Barbra Streisand	Columbia	18	3	**4P**
8	9	**Born In The USA**	Bruce Springsteen	Columbia	84	1	**14P**
9	4	**Whitney Houston**	Whitney Houston	Arista	46	2	**F11P**
10	7	**Songs From The Big Chair**	Tears For Fears	Mercury	32	2	**F4P**

• 1985 was not only the year of Live Aid, it was the time when rock stars realized that they could actually make a difference in many areas. Various acts helped numerous good causes around the world, and also made people aware of other serious issues such as AIDS and the environment.

• In the last months of 1985, the grandfather of rock'n'roll, Joe Turner, and Ian Stewart, an original Rolling Stone died. Early rock superstar Ricky Nelson was killed in a plane crash and Ricky Wilson of The B-52's died of complications from AIDS.

• The self-titled debut album by Whitney Houston (above) went on to become the biggest selling album ever by a female artist, and also the top selling debut LP of all time, with US sales alone passing the 11 million mark. In Britain, it narrowly missed the top spot and sold over a million. Simultaneously, another American, Jennifer Rush became the first female to sell a million copies of a single in the UK with 'The Power Of Love'.

UK 1986

JAN-MAR

• Phil Collins grabbed both the BRIT and Grammy award for Top Album with **No Jacket Required**, as well as being voted Top Male Artist at the BRITs. Other BRIT winners included Dire Straits (above) (Top Group), Annie Lennox (Top Female), Go West (Best Newcomers) and Bruce Springsteen (Top International Solo Artist). Meanwhile, over at the Grammy Awards in Los Angeles, British-based Sade picked up the trophy for Best New Artist.

• The latest act to put a handful of their albums simultaneously into the UK chart was Dire Straits, whose complete output of six LPs hit after one of their concerts was shown on TV.

• **Once Upon A Time** gave Scotland's Simple Minds their only US Top 20 album and the single taken from it, 'Alive & Kicking', reached the Top 3. Another act who visited the US Top 20 for the only time was Austrian Falco with **Falco 3**, which included the transatlantic Number 1 single 'Rock Me Amadeus'.

January 1986

This Mnth	Last Mnth	Title	Artist	Label	Wks in 10	US Pos	
1	5	**Brothers In Arms**	Dire Straits	Vertigo	65	1	**3P**
2	1	**Now That's What I Call Music 6**	Various	EMI/Virgin	8		
3	9	**Like A Virgin**	Madonna	Sire	30	1	**P**
4	-	**Hunting High And Low**	A-Ha	Warner	18	15	**F**
5	3	**Hits 3**	Various	CBS/WEA	6		
6	-	**World Machine**	Level 42	Polydor	14	18	
7	-	**The Broadway Album**	Barbra Streisand	CBS	8	1	
8	7	**Promise**	Sade	Epic	10	1	
9	-	**Island Life**	Grace Jones	Island	7	161	**FL**
10	-	**The Dream Of The Blue Turtles**	Sting	A&M	9	2	**F**

February 1986

This Mnth	Last Mnth	Title	Artist	Label	Wks in 10	US Pos	
1	1	**Brothers In Arms**	Dire Straits	Vertigo	65	1	**3P**
2	4	**Hunting High And Low**	A-Ha	Warner	18	15	**F**
3	7	**The Broadway Album**	Barbra Streisand	CBS	8	1	
4	6	**World Machine**	Level 42	Polydor	14	18	
5	-	**Be Yourself Tonight**	Eurythmics	RCA	21	9	
6	9	**Island Life**	Grace Jones	Island	7	161	**FL**
7	-	**Whitney Houston**	Whitney Houston	Arista	22	1	**FP**
8	10	**The Dream Of The Blue Turtles**	Sting	A&M	9	2	**F**
9	-	**No Jacket Required**	Phil Collins	Atlantic	36	1	**P**
10	-	**Rocky IV**	Soundtrack	Scotti Bros	8	10	

March 1986

This Mnth	Last Mnth	Title	Artist	Label	Wks in 10	US Pos	
1	1	**Brothers In Arms**	Dire Straits	Vertigo	65	1	**3P**
2	7	**Whitney Houston**	Whitney Houston	Arista	22	1	**FP**
3	9	**No Jacket Required**	Phil Collins	Virgin	36	1	**P**
4	10	**Rocky IV**	Soundtrack	Scotti Bros	8	10	
5	-	**Hits For Lovers**	Various	Epic	6		
6	5	**Be Yourself Tonight**	Eurythmics	RCA	21	9	
7	-	**Hounds Of Love**	Kate Bush	EMI	11	30	
8	-	**Jonathan King's Entertainment USA**	Various	Stylus	3		
9	-	**Hits 4**	Various	CBS/WEA	9		
10	-	**Black Celebration**	Depeche Mode	Mute	1	90	

US 1986 JAN-MAR

January 1986

This Mnth	Last Mnth	Title	Artist	Label	Wks in 10	UK Pos	
1	1	**Miami Vice**	Soundtrack - TV	MCA	18	11	**4P**
2	7	**The Broadway Album**	Barbra Streisand	Columbia	18	3	**4P**
3	2	**Heart**	Heart	Capitol	37	19	**5P**
4	3	**Scarecrow**	John Cougar Mellencamp	Riva	29		**3P**
5	4	**Afterburner**	ZZ Top	Warner	15	2	**4P**
6	5	**Brothers In Arms**	Dire Straits	Warner	37	1	**7PL**
7	-	**Promise**	Sade	Portrait	16	1	**3P**
8	8	**Born In The USA**	Bruce Springsteen	Columbia	84	1	**14P**
9	6	**In Square Circle**	Stevie Wonder	Tamla	14	5	**2PL**
10	-	**Knee Deep In The Hoopla**	Starship	Grunt	15		**PL**

February 1986

This Mnth	Last Mnth	Title	Artist	Label	Wks in 10	UK Pos	
1	7	**Promise**	Sade	Portrait	16	1	**3P**
2	2	**The Broadway Album**	Barbra Streisand	Columbia	18	3	**4P**
3	3	**Heart**	Heart	Capitol	37	19	**5P**
4	-	**Welcome To The Real World**	Mr. Mister	RCA	12	6	**FPL**
5	4	**Scarecrow**	John Cougar Mellencamp	Riva	29		**3P**
6	-	**Whitney Houston**	Whitney Houston	Arista	46	2	**F11P**
7	6	**Brothers In Arms**	Dire Straits	Warner	37	1	**7PL**
8	1	**Miami Vice**	Soundtrack - TV	MCA	18	11	**4P**
9	5	**Afterburner**	ZZ Top	Warner	15	2	**4P**
10	10	**Knee Deep In The Hoopla**	Starship	Grunt	15		**PL**

March 1986

This Mnth	Last Mnth	Title	Artist	Label	Wks in 10	UK Pos	
1	6	**Whitney Houston**	Whitney Houston	Arista	46	2	**F11P**
2	1	**Promise**	Sade	Portrait	16	1	**3P**
3	4	**Welcome To The Real World**	Mr. Mister	RCA	12	6	**FPL**
4	3	**Heart**	Heart	Capitol	37	19	**5P**
5	2	**The Broadway Album**	Barbra Streisand	Columbia	18	3	**4P**
6	5	**Scarecrow**	John Cougar Mellencamp	Riva	29		**3P**
7	7	**Brothers In Arms**	Dire Straits	Warner	37	1	**7PL**
8	10	**Knee Deep In The Hoopla**	Starship	Grunt	15		**PL**
9	-	**The Ultimate Sin**	Ozzy Osbourne	CBS Associated	8	8	**F2PP**
10	-	**Once Upon A Time**	Simple Minds	A&M	5	1	**FL**

• Female singers achieved far more success than ever before, and in March a record four of the Top 5, and 13 of the Top 40 albums featured female vocalists. The Wilson sisters' group, Heart, were followed at Number 1 by Barbra Streisand, who was replaced by Sade. The all male Mr. Mister managed a week at the top before Whitney Houston dethroned them. Other ladies in the Top 20 were: Whitney's cousin Dionne Warwick with **Friends**, R&B girl group Klymaxx with **Meeting In The Ladies Room**, Stevie Nicks with **Rock A Little** and The Bangles, whose **Different Light** finally reached the Top 5 after 51 weeks on the chart. There were two mixed groups in The Top 20; Atlantic Starr with **As The Band Turns** and Britain's Dream Academy with a self-titled set.

• The latest collection of mixed artist soundtrack albums to click were **White Nights**, featuring Phil Collins, Robert Plant and Chaka Khan, **Rocky IV** featuring James Brown, Survivor and John Cafferty and **Pretty in Pink** featuring The Psychedelic Furs, Orchestral Manoeuvres In The Dark and The Smiths. The most successful of the current batch was the soundtrack to the TV series **Miami Vice** which included Top 10 singles hits from Tina Turner, Phil Collins, Jan Hammer and Glenn Frey.

UK 1986 APR-JUNE

April 1986

This Mnth	Last Mnth	Title	Artist	Label	Wks in 10	US Pos	
1	9	**Hits 4**	Various	CBS/WEA	9		
2	1	**Brothers In Arms**	Dire Straits	Vertigo	65	1	**3P**
3	-	**Please**	Pet Shop Boys	Parlophone	5	7	**F**
4	2	**Whitney Houston**	Whitney Houston	Arista	22	1	**FP**
5	-	**Hunting High And Low**	A-Ha	Warner	18	15	**F**
6	-	**Parade - Music From 'Under The Cherry Moon' (Soundtrack)**	Prince & The Revolution	Warner	2	3	
7	-	**Street Life-20 Great Hits**	Bryan Ferry/Roxy Music	EG	11	100	
8	-	**Dirty Work**	Rolling Stones	Rolling Stones	2	4	
9	-	**Welcome To The Real World**	Mr. Mister	RCA	4	1	**FL**
10	3	**No Jacket Required**	Phil Collins	Virgin	36	1	**P**

May 1986

This Mnth	Last Mnth	Title	Artist	Label	Wks in 10	US Pos	
1	7	**Street Life-20 Great Hits**	Bryan Ferry/Roxy Music	EG	11	100	
2	2	**Brothers In Arms**	Dire Straits	Vertigo	65	1	**3P**
3	4	**Whitney Houston**	Whitney Houston	Arista	22	1	**FP**
4	-	**Love Zone**	Billy Ocean	Jive	5	6	**L**
5	1	**Hits 4**	Various	CBS/WEA	9		
6	-	**The Collection**	Earth, Wind & Fire	K-Tel	4		**L**
7	-	**The Greatest Hits**	Shalamar	Stylus	4		
8	5	**Hunting High And Low**	A-Ha	Warner	18	15	**F**
9	-	**Once Upon A Time**	Simple Minds	A&M	10	10	
10	-	**So**	Peter Gabriel	Virgin	10	2	

June 1986

This Mnth	Last Mnth	Title	Artist	Label	Wks in 10	US Pos	
1	10	**So**	Peter Gabriel	Virgin	10	2	
2	-	**Picture Book**	Simply Red	Elektra	19	16	**F**
3	-	**A Kind Of Magic**	Queen	EMI	16	46	
4	2	**Brothers In Arms**	Dire Straits	Vertigo	65	1	**3P**
5	-	**Invisible Touch**	Genesis	Charisma	18	3	**P**
6	1	**Street Life-20 Great Hits**	Bryan Ferry/Roxy Music	EG	11	100	
7	4	**Love Zone**	Billy Ocean	Jive	5	6	**L**
8	-	**The Queen Is Dead**	Smiths	Rough Trade	2	70	
9	-	**Standing On A Beach - The Singles**	Cure	Fiction	3	48	
10	8	**Hunting High And Low**	A-Ha	Warner	18	15	**F**

• New albums from Genesis, **Invisible Touch**, and their ex-lead vocalist Peter Gabriel, **So**, entered the UK chart at Number 1 and they both reached the US Top 5.

• Wham! split up. The duo who sold nearly 40 million records in their short career gave their final concert in front of 72,000 fans at Wembley Stadium.

• Bob Geldof, the mainman behind Band Aid and Live Aid, had his first book published, *Is That It?* and it was announced that he would receive an honorary knighthood from the Queen. Many more charitable musical events also took place; among these were the 'Race Against Time' in which 36 million people around the world ran to raise money for Ethiopia. There were also numerous live shows for good causes such as Artists Against Apartheid, Amnesty International, Greenpeace, and The Prince's Trust. Many top acts became involved including Boy George, Phil Collins, Elton John, Paul McCartney, Van Morrison, Sting, Tina Turner and U2.

US 1986 APR-JUNE

April 1986

This Mnth	Last Mnth	Title	Artist	Label	Wks in 10	UK Pos	
1	1	**Whitney Houston**	Whitney Houston	Arista	46	2	**F11P**
2	4	**Heart**	Heart	Capitol	37	19	**5P**
3	2	**Promise**	Sade	Portrait	16	1	**3P**
4	-	**Falco 3**	Falco	A&M	6	32	**FL**
5	-	**5150**	Van Halen	Warner	14	16	**5P**
6	6	**Scarecrow**	John Cougar Mellencamp	Riva	29		**3P**
7	9	**The Ultimate Sin**	Ozzy Osbourne	CBS Associated	8	8	**F2PP**
8	-	**Pretty In Pink**	Soundtrack	A&M	9		
9	7	**Brothers In Arms**	Dire Straits	Warner	37	1	**7PL**
10	3	**Welcome To The Real World**	Mr. Mister	RCA	12	6	**FPL**

May 1986

This Mnth	Last Mnth	Title	Artist	Label	Wks in 10	UK Pos	
1	1	**Whitney Houston**	Whitney Houston	Arista	46	2	**F11P**
2	5	**5150**	Van Halen	Warner	14	16	**5P**
3	-	**Parade (Soundtrack)**	Prince	Paisley Park	9	4	**P**
4	-	**Like A Rock**	Bob Seger &				
			The Silver Bullet Band	Capitol	15	35	**P**
5	8	**Pretty In Pink**	Soundtrack	A&M	9		
6	-	**Dirty Work**	Rolling Stones	Rolling Stones	7	4	**P**
7	-	**Raised On Radio**	Journey	Columbia	7		
8	-	**Control**	Janet Jackson	A&M	37	8	**F5P**
9	-	**Riptide**	Robert Palmer	Island	4	5	**FPL**
10	2	**Heart**	Heart	Capitol	37	19	**5P**

June 1986

This Mnth	Last Mnth	Title	Artist	Label	Wks in 10	UK Pos	
1	1	**Whitney Houston**	Whitney Houston	Arista	46	2	**F11P**
2	-	**Winner In You**	Patti Labelle	MCA	12	30	**FPL**
3	2	**5150**	Van Halen	Warner	14	16	**5P**
4	4	**Like A Rock**	Bob Seger &				
			The Silver Bullet Band	Capitol	15	35	**P**
5	8	**Control**	Janet Jackson	A&M	37	8	**F5P**
6	-	**Please**	Pet Shop Boys	EMI America	6	3	**FPL**
7	-	**Raised On Radio**	Journey	Columbia	7		
8	3	**Parade (Soundtrack)**	Prince	Paisley Park	9	4	**P**
9	-	**Love Zone**	Billy Ocean	Jive	12	2	**2PL**
10	-	**Play Deep**	Outfield	Columbia	6		**F2PL**

• In June, for the first time, female singers took the top three slots. Incidentally, it was also the first time Afro-Americans had achieved this feat. On the singles chart, Houston became the first female to score three successive Number 1 singles. Her latest, 'The Greatest Love Of All', was penned by Linda Creed, who died of cancer as the record headed up the chart.

• Kentucky-born Dwight Yoakam became the first of the so-called 'New Country' acts to reach the pop chart with his **Guitars Cadillacs Etc, Etc**. However, by the year's end, it was Randy Travis who had replaced him as the top selling New Country act.

• For the only time, half of the US Top 40 singles were by British acts. UK artists were also increasing their share of the LP market. Among those enjoying their first taste of the Top 20 were Robert Palmer with **Riptide**, The Pet Shop Boys with **Please**, the locally unsuccessful band Outfield with **Play Deep**, Level 42 with **World Machine** and Simply Red with **Picture Book**. The latter group's leader Mick Hucknall was now writing with top American composer Lamont Dozier, who had written numerous Motown hits.

UK 1986

JULY-SEPT

• Madonna became the first American female singer to have an album enter the UK charts at Number 1: **True Blue**, which went on to sell over 1.5 million copies in Britain, was her second successive transatlantic chart topper.

• RCA said goodbye to John Denver, their biggest selling artist of the Seventies. Soon after, the world famous American label, whose top international stars included Glenn Miller, Perry Como, Elvis Presley, Jim Reeves and Jefferson Airplane, was sold to German company BMG.

• Family group Five Star became the youngest group and the first black British group to top the charts. Their debut album **Silk And Steel** sold over a million in the UK alone.

• Among the acts who packed the crowds in at Wembley were Rod Stewart, Queen, Status Quo and Prince, who played his first London gig for five years.

July 1986

This Mnth	Last Mnth	Title	Artist	Label	Wks in 10	US Pos	
1	-	**True Blue**	Madonna	Sire	36	1	P
2	3	**A Kind Of Magic**	Queen	EMI	16	46	
3	5	**Invisible Touch**	Genesis	Charisma	18	3	P
4	-	**Revenge**	Eurythmics	RCA	21	12	
5	-	**Every Beat Of My Heart**	Rod Stewart	Warner	5		
6	-	**The Final**	Wham!	Epic	7		L
7	-	**London 0 Hull 4**	Housemartins	Go! Discs	3	124	F
8	-	**The Seer**	Big Country	Mercury	2	59	
9	2	**Picture Book**	Simply Red	Elektra	19	16	F
10	-	**Now - The Summer Album**	Various	EMI/Virgin	2		

August 1986

This Mnth	Last Mnth	Title	Artist	Label	Wks in 10	US Pos	
1	1	**True Blue**	Madonna	Sire	36	1	P
2	-	**Into The Light**	Chris De Burgh	A&M	10	25	
3	2	**A Kind Of Magic**	Queen	EMI	16	46	
4	6	**The Final**	Wham!	Epic	7		L
5	-	**Now That's What I Call Music 7**	Various	EMI/Virgin	9		
6	4	**Revenge**	Eurythmics	RCA	21	12	
7	-	**Riptide**	Robert Palmer	Island	4	8	F
8	-	**Dancing On The Ceiling**	Lionel Richie	Motown	5	1	
9	-	**Brothers In Arms**	Dire Straits	Vertigo	65	1	3P
10	9	**Picture Book**	Simply Red	Elektra	19	16	F

September 1986

This Mnth	Last Mnth	Title	Artist	Label	Wks in 10	US Pos	
1	5	**Now That's What I Call Music 7**	Various	EMI/Virgin	9		
2	-	**Silk And Steel**	Five Star	Tent	28	80	FP
3	1	**True Blue**	Madonna	Sire	36	1	P
4	-	**Graceland**	Paul Simon	Warner	33	3	P
5	6	**Revenge**	Eurythmics	RCA	21	12	
6	8	**Dancing On The Ceiling**	Lionel Richie	Motown	5	1	
7	-	**Break Every Rule**	Tina Turner	Capitol	4	4	
8	3	**A Kind Of Magic**	Queen	EMI	16	46	
9	2	**Into The Light**	Chris De Burgh	A&M	10	25	
10	-	**In The Army Now**	Status Quo	Vertigo	1		

US 1986

JULY-SEPT

July 1986

This Mnth	Last Mnth	Title	Artist	Label	Wks in 10	UK Pos	
1	5	**Control**	Janet Jackson	A&M	37	8	**F5P**
2	2	**Winner In You**	Patti Labelle	MCA	12	30	**FPL**
3	-	**So**	Peter Gabriel	Atco	12	1	**F4P**
4	1	**Whitney Houston**	Whitney Houston	Arista	46	2	**F11P**
5	-	**Top Gun**	Soundtrack	Columbia	20	4	**7P**
6	-	**Invisible Touch**	Genesis	Atlantic	26	1	**5P**
7	9	**Love Zone**	Billy Ocean	Jive	12	2	**2PL**
8	4	**Like A Rock**	Bob Seger & The Silver Bullet Band	Capitol	15	35	**P**
9	-	**The Other Side Of Life**	Moody Blues	Threshold	6		**PL**
10	3	**5150**	Van Halen	Warner	14	16	**5P**

August 1986

This Mnth	Last Mnth	Title	Artist	Label	Wks in 10	UK Pos	
1	5	**Top Gun**	Soundtrack	Columbia	20	4	**7P**
2	-	**True Blue**	Madonna	Sire	25	1	**5P**
3	3	**So**	Peter Gabriel	Atco	12	1	**F4P**
4	6	**Invisible Touch**	Genesis	Atlantic	26	1	**5P**
5	1	**Control**	Janet Jackson	A&M	37	8	**F5P**
6	-	**Eat 'Em And Smile**	David Lee Roth	Warner	8	28	**FP**
7	7	**Love Zone**	Billy Ocean	Jive	12	2	**2PL**
8	-	**Raising Hell**	Run-D.M.C.	Profile	14	41	**F2P**
9	2	**Winner In You**	Patti Labelle	MCA	12	30	**FPL**
10	-	**Back In The High Life**	Steve Winwood	Island	14	8	**3P**

September 1986

This Mnth	Last Mnth	Title	Artist	Label	Wks in 10	UK Pos	
1	1	**Top Gun**	Soundtrack	Columbia	20	4	**7P**
2	2	**True Blue**	Madonna	Sire	25	1	**5P**
3	10	**Back In The High Life**	Steve Winwood	Island	14	8	**3P**
4	8	**Raising Hell**	Run-D.M.C.	Profile	14	41	**F2P**
5	6	**Eat 'Em And Smile**	David Lee Roth	Warner	8	28	**FP**
6	-	**Dancing On The Ceiling**	Lionel Richie	Motown	20	2	**4PL**
7	4	**Invisible Touch**	Genesis	Atlantic	26	1	**5P**
8	-	**The Bridge**	Billy Joel	Columbia	11	38	**2P**
9	5	**Control**	Janet Jackson	A&M	37	8	**F5P**
10	-	**Fore!**	Huey Lewis & The News	Chrysalis	26	8	**3PL**

• The first rap act to reach the Top 20 were New Yorkers Run-D.M.C. with **Raising Hell**, which was also the first platinum selling rap album. Riots were reported during their tour on which support acts were fellow rappers LL Cool J, Whodini and The Beastie Boys.

• Twenty-year-old Janet Jackson became the youngest singer to reach Number 1 in the USA since Little Stevie Wonder in 1963. Other American women in the news included Tina Turner who was given a star on the Hollywood Walk Of Fame, just outside her record company, Capitol, and Dolly Parton who opened her own 400-acre theme park, Dollywood.

• The top selling film soundtrack for the quarter was **Top Gun**: it included hits from Kenny Loggins, Loverboy and Berlin. Prince's latest movie *Under The Cherry Moon* premiered as did Talking Head's *True Stories* and *Sid And Nancy*; based on The Sex Pistols Sid Vicious' story.

• Ex-Van Halen vocalist David Lee Roth, whose second solo album **Eat 'Em And Smile** reached the Top 10, was voted the second 'Hunkiest Pop Star' in America – overall winner was Australian Michael Hutchence, front man of INXS. Roth, set off on a 10-month US tour.

UK 1986 OCT-DEC

• For the first time, female vocalists sang on the Top 5 British singles in November. On the album chart, Kate Bush became the first British female to amass three Number 1 albums. Her latest, **The Whole Story**, included a new recording of her chart topping debut single 'Wuthering Heights'.

• Fourteen years after he had last topped the UK chart, Paul Simon's critically acclaimed album **Graceland** reached Number 1. Soon after, Simon was voted Top International Solo Artist at the BRIT awards and **Graceland** won the Grammy award for Album Of The Year.

• Norwegian teen idols A-Ha scored the second of their three Number 2s with **Scoundrel Days**. Thousands of their fans brought London's traffic to a halt when the trio appeared at a West End store.

• Ex-Pink Floyd singer Roger Waters tried unsuccessfully to stop the other members from using the group's name. Other British bands in the headlines included chart acts Bronski Beat, The Pogues, King and The Smiths, who all had personnel changes. Furthermore, the latter act, who were the country's best known indie band, signed with EMI, the biggest UK major label.

October 1986

This Mnth	Last Mnth	Title	Artist	Label	Wks in 10	US Pos	
1	4	**Graceland**	Paul Simon	Warner	33	3	**P**
2	2	**Silk And Steel**	Five Star	Tent	28	80	**FP**
3	3	**True Blue**	Madonna	Sire	36	1	**P**
4	5	**Revenge**	Eurythmics	RCA	21	12	
5	-	**Scoundrel Days**	A-Ha	Warner	4	74	
6	-	**South Pacific**	Studio Cast	CBS	3		
7	1	**Now That's What I Call Music 7**	Various	EMI/Virgin	9		
8	-	**Somewhere In Time**	Iron Maiden	EMI	2	11	
9	-	**Communards**	Communards	London	4	90	**F**
10	-	**Word Up**	Cameo	Club	2	8	**FL**

November 1986

This Mnth	Last Mnth	Title	Artist	Label	Wks in 10	US Pos	
1	-	**Every Breath You Take - The Singles**	Police	A&M	11	7	
2	1	**Graceland**	Paul Simon	Warner	33	3	**P**
3	3	**True Blue**	Madonna	Sire	36	1	**P**
4	-	**Now Dance '86**	Various	EMI/Virgin	4		
5	-	**Top Gun**	Soundtrack	CBS	7	1	
6	2	**Silk And Steel**	Five Star	Tent	28	80	**FP**
7	-	**Hits 5**	Various	CBS/WEA	8		
8	-	**The Whole Story**	Kate Bush	EMI	14	76	**P**
9	-	**Slippery When Wet**	Bon Jovi	Vertigo	10	1	**FP**
10	5	**Scoundrel Days**	A-Ha	Warner	4	74	

December 1986

This Mnth	Last Mnth	Title	Artist	Label	Wks in 10	US Pos	
1	-	**Now That's What I Call Music 8**	Various	EMI/Virgin/ PolyGram	9		
2	7	**Hits 5**	Various	CBS/WEA	8		
3	8	**The Whole Story**	Kate Bush	EMI	14	76	**P**
4	1	**Every Breath You Take - The Singles**	Police	A&M	11	7	
5	2	**Graceland**	Paul Simon	Warner	33	3	**P**
6	3	**True Blue**	Madonna	Sire	36	1	**P**
7	-	**Live Magic**	Queen	EMI	16		
8	6	**Silk And Steel**	Five Star	Tent	28	80	**FP**
9	5	**Top Gun**	Soundtrack	CBS	7	1	
10	9	**Slippery When Wet**	Bon Jovi	Vertigo	10	1	**FP**

US 1986 OCT-DEC

October 1986

This Mnth	Last Mnth	Title	Artist	Label	Wks in 10	UK Pos	
1	10	**Fore!**	Huey Lewis & The News	Chrysalis	26	8	**3PL**
2	1	**Top Gun**	Soundtrack	Columbia	20	4	**7P**
3	6	**Dancing On The Ceiling**	Lionel Richie	Motown	20	2	**4PL**
4	-	**Slippery When Wet**	Bon Jovi	Mercury	46	6	**F11P**
5	4	**Raising Hell**	Run-D.M.C.	Profile	14	41	**F2P**
6	2	**True Blue**	Madonna	Sire	25	1	**5P**
7	3	**Back In The High Life**	Steve Winwood	Island	14	8	**3P**
8	8	**The Bridge**	Billy Joel	Columbia	11	38	**2P**
9	-	**Third Stage**	Boston	MCA	20	37	**4P**
10	7	**Invisible Touch**	Genesis	Atlantic	26	1	**5P**

November 1986

This Mnth	Last Mnth	Title	Artist	Label	Wks in 10	UK Pos	
1	9	**Third Stage**	Boston	MCA	20	37	**4P**
2	4	**Slippery When Wet**	Bon Jovi	Mercury	46	6	**F11P**
3	1	**Fore!**	Huey Lewis & The News	Chrysalis	26	8	**3PL**
4	-	**True Colors**	Cyndi Lauper	Portrait	6	25	**2PL**
5	-	**Break Every Rule**	Tina Turner	Capitol	6	2	**PL**
6	3	**Dancing On The Ceiling**	Lionel Richie	Motown	20	2	**4PL**
7	2	**Top Gun**	Soundtrack	Columbia	20	4	**7P**
8	7	**Back In The High Life**	Steve Winwood	Island	14	8	**3P**
9	-	**Bruce Springsteen & The E Street Band Live/1975-1985**	Bruce Springsteen	Columbia	11	4	**12P**
10	-	**Graceland**	Paul Simon	Columbia	24	1	**5P**

December 1986

This Mnth	Last Mnth	Title	Artist	Label	Wks in 10	UK Pos	
1	9	**Bruce Springsteen & The E Street Band Live/1975-1985**	Bruce Springsteen	Columbia	11	4	**12P**
2	2	**Slippery When Wet**	Bon Jovi	Mercury	46	6	**F11P**
3	1	**Third Stage**	Boston	MCA	20	37	**4P**
4	3	**Fore!**	Huey Lewis & The News	Chrysalis	26	8	**3PL**
5	-	**The Way It Is**	Bruce Hornsby & The Range	RCA	23	16	**F3P**
6	10	**Graceland**	Paul Simon	Columbia	24	1	**5P**
7	6	**Dancing On The Ceiling**	Lionel Richie	Motown	20	2	**4PL**
8	-	**Whiplash Smile**	Billy Idol	Chrysalis	5	8	**P**
9	-	**Every Breath You Take - The Singles**	Police	A&M	4	1	**3PL**
10	-	**Word Up!**	Cameo	Atlanta Artists	3	7	**FPL**

• Album sales continued to rise as single sales decreased by 22% in 1986. Compact disk sales increased 139% and almost reached $1 billion. In total, records and tape sales in America were $4.65 billion – a rise of 6% on the previous year.

• Even though UK acts had a wonderful year Stateside, no British born artists topped the album charts in 1986. The year ended with American acts Huey Lewis & The News (above), Bon Jovi, Boston and Bruce Springsteen & The E Street Band following each other at the peak. Boston's **Third Stage** was their first album for eight years and contained their only Number 1 single, 'Amanda'. Springsteen's five album live set was only the fourth album to enter the US chart at Number 1 – the others being two single albums by Elton John and a double by Stevie Wonder.

• The first acts inducted into the Rock And Roll Hall Of Fame were: Chuck Berry, James Brown, Sam Cooke, Fats Domino, the Everly Brothers, DJ Alan Freed, Buddy Holly, Jerry Lee Lewis, Little Richard and Elvis Presley.

UK 1987 JAN-MAR

• Picking up trophies at the BRIT awards were: Peter Gabriel (Best Male), Kate Bush (Best Female), Five Star (Best Group), **Brothers In Arms** by Dire Straits (Best Album), The Housemartins (Best Newcomer), The Bangles (Top International Group) and Eric Clapton (Outstanding Contribution to British Music).

• The first original cast album to top the UK charts was **Phantom Of The Opera**. The double album, which featured the London stage cast including noted actor Michael Crawford, has been a frequent visitor to the charts on both sides of the Atlantic ever since.

• Both Level 42 and Simply Red scored their second successive Number 2 hits with **Running In The Family** and **Men And Women** respectively, and in Simply Red's case both their albums were simultaneously in the Top 10. They were not the only current hit act to find themselves in runner-up spot more often than they would have liked. Manchester group The Smiths' **The World Won't Listen** was one of five Number 2 hits they racked up in less than five years.

• The long awaited release of The Beatles' first four British albums on compact disc: **Please Please Me**, **With The Beatles**, **A Hard Day's Night** and **Beatles For Sale** briefly gave the group the Top 4 places on the compact disk chart.

January 1987

This Mnth	Last Mnth	Title	Artist	Label	Wks in 10	US Pos	
1	3	**The Whole Story**	Kate Bush	EMI	14	76	P
2	5	**Graceland**	Paul Simon	Warner	33	3	P
3	6	**True Blue**	Madonna	Sire	36	1	P
4	1	**Now That's What I Call Music 8**	Various	EMI/Virgin/ PolyGram	9		
5	7	**Live Magic**	Queen	EMI	16		
6	-	**Different Light**	Bangles	CBS	7	2	F
7	10	**Slippery When Wet**	Bon Jovi	Vertigo	10	1	FP
8	8	**Silk And Steel**	Five Star	Tent	28	80	FP
9	4	**Every Breath You Take - The Singles**	Police	A&M	11	7	
10	2	**Hits 5**	Various	CBS/WEA	8		

February 1987

This Mnth	Last Mnth	Title	Artist	Label	Wks in 10	US Pos	
1	2	**Graceland**	Paul Simon	Warner	33	3	P
2	-	**August**	Eric Clapton	Duck	7	37	
3	6	**Different Light**	Bangles	CBS	7	2	F
4	-	**Phantom Of The Opera**	Original London Cast	Polydor	7	33	P
5	1	**The Whole Story**	Kate Bush	EMI	14	76	P
6	-	**The Very Best Of Hot Chocolate**	Hot Chocolate	RAK	7		
7	8	**Silk And Steel**	Five Star	Tent	28	80	FP
8	5	**Live Magic**	Queen	EMI	16		
9	-	**No More The Fool**	Elkie Brooks	Legend	3		
10	-	**Picture Book**	Simply Red	Elektra	19	16	F

March 1987

This Mnth	Last Mnth	Title	Artist	Label	Wks in 10	US Pos	
1	6	**The Very Best Of Hot Chocolate**	Hot Chocolate	RAK	7		
2	4	**Phantom Of The Opera**	Original London Cast	Polydor	7	33	P
3	1	**Graceland**	Paul Simon	Warner	33	3	P
4	-	**The World Won't Listen**	Smiths	Rough Trade	3		
5	-	**The Joshua Tree**	U2	Island	28	1	P
6	-	**Men And Women**	Simply Red	WEA	7	31	
7	10	**Picture Book**	Simply Red	Elektra	19	16	F
8	7	**Silk And Steel**	Five Star	Tent	28	80	FP
9	-	**Move Closer**	Various	CBS	6		
10	-	**Running In The Family**	Level 42	Polydor	12		

US 1987 JAN-MAR

January 1987

This Mnth	Last Mnth	Title	Artist	Label	Wks in 10	UK Pos	
1	2	**Slippery When Wet**	Bon Jovi	Mercury	46	6	**F11P**
2	1	**Bruce Springsteen & The E Street Band Live/1975-1985**	Bruce Springsteen	Columbia	11	4	**12P**
3	3	**Third Stage**	Boston	MCA	20	37	**4P**
4	5	**The Way It Is**	Bruce Hornsby & The Range	RCA	23	16	**F3P**
5	-	**Different Light**	Bangles	Columbia	9	3	**F3PL**
6	4	**Fore!**	Huey Lewis & The News	Chrysalis	26	8	**3PL**
7	-	**Night Songs**	Cinderella	Mercury	15		**F3P**
8	-	**True Blue**	Madonna	Sire	25	1	**5P**
9	7	**Dancing On The Ceiling**	Lionel Richie	Motown	20	2	**4PL**
10	6	**Graceland**	Paul Simon	Columbia	24	1	**5P**

February 1987

This Mnth	Last Mnth	Title	Artist	Label	Wks in 10	UK Pos	
1	1	**Slippery When Wet**	Bon Jovi	Mercury	46	6	**F11P**
2	-	**Licensed To Ill**	Beastie Boys	Def Jam	19	7	**F5P**
3	7	**Night Songs**	Cinderella	Mercury	15		**F3P**
4	5	**Different Light**	Bangles	Columbia	9	3	**F3PL**
5	4	**The Way It Is**	Bruce Hornsby & The Range	RCA	23	16	**F3P**
6	-	**Control**	Janet Jackson	A&M	37	8	**F5P**
7	3	**Third Stage**	Boston	MCA	20	37	**4P**
8	-	**Invisible Touch**	Genesis	Atlantic	26	1	**5P**
9	-	**Georgia Satellites**	Georgia Satellites	Elektra	5	52	**FPL**
10	6	**Fore!**	Huey Lewis & The News	Chrysalis	26	8	**3PL**

March 1987

This Mnth	Last Mnth	Title	Artist	Label	Wks in 10	UK Pos	
1	2	**Licensed To Ill**	Beastie Boys	Def Jam	19	7	**F5P**
2	1	**Slippery When Wet**	Bon Jovi	Mercury	46	6	**F11P**
3	5	**The Way It Is**	Bruce Hornsby & The Range	RCA	23	16	**F3P**
4	8	**Invisible Touch**	Genesis	Atlantic	26	1	**5P**
5	6	**Control**	Janet Jackson	A&M	37	8	**F5P**
6	-	**Graceland**	Paul Simon	Columbia	24	1	**5P**
7	3	**Night Songs**	Cinderella	Mercury	15		**F3P**
8	9	**Georgia Satellites**	Georgia Satellites	Elektra	5	52	**FPL**
9	-	**Life, Love And Pain**	Club Nouveau	Warner	7		**FPL**
10	-	**The Final Countdown**	Europe	Epic	10	9	**F3PL**

• There was a lot of media interest in the forthcoming launch of both DAT (digital audio tapes) and CDV (compact disk videos) machines. However, neither format took off with the public on either side of the Atlantic.

• **Licensed To Ill** by white rap trio The Beastie Boys was the first Number 1 rap album.

• **The Broadway Album** won Barbra Streisand the Grammy for Best Female Vocal Performance and **Break Every Rule** by Tina Turner took the trophy for Best Rock Female Performance. Bruce Hornsby & The Range, who were in the Top 3 with their debut Album **The Way It Is**, were voted Best Newcomers.

• Eight of the acts on the March chart were making their first entries in the Top 10; The Beastie Boys, Bon Jovi, Bruce Hornsby & The Range, Janet Jackson, Pennsylvania rockers Cinderella, Georgia Satellites, Club Nouveau and Swedish band Europe.

UK 1987 APR-MAR

• Curiosity Killed The Cat, who were being mobbed on their first major British tour, topped the album chart with their debut, **Keep Your Distance**. They were followed into the top slot by another much talked about new band: Swing Out Sister with **It's Better To Travel**. Simple Minds then scored their third successive Number 1 with the live double album **Live In The City Of Light**. All three albums entered first week at Number 1 – a feat that was no longer a rarity in Britain.

• After five years on the small screen, *The Tube* was seen for the final time. Guests on the last show included The Cure, Tina Turner and U2. At the same time, *The Roxy* was launched as a rival to *Top Of The Pops* – its challenge lasted only a matter of months.

• EMI announced that The Beatles' **Sergeant Pepper** was the biggest selling album ever in Britain, and to celebrate its 20th birthday this classic album was reissued and again reached the Top 10.

• Among the celebrities who died this quarter were world renowned jazz drummer Buddy Rich, noted folk composer Elizabeth Cotton, internationally famous guitarist Andres Segovia and pioneer white blues performer Paul Butterfield.

April 1987

This Mnth	Last Mnth	Title	Artist	Label	Wks in 10	US Pos	
1	-	**Now That's What I Call Music 9**	Various	EMI/Virgin/			
				PolyGram	8		
2	5	**The Joshua Tree**	U2	Island	28	1	**P**
3	10	**Running In The Family**	Level 42	Polydor	12		
4	9	**Move Closer**	Various	CBS	6		
5	-	**Raindancing**	Alison Moyet	CBS	13	94	**L**
6	6	**Men And Women**	Simply Red	WEA	7	31	
7	3	**Graceland**	Paul Simon	Warner	33	3	**P**
8	-	**Sign 'O' The Times**	Prince	Paisley Park	2	6	
9	-	**F.L.M.**	Mel & Kim	Supreme	11		**FL**
10	-	**Electric**	Cult	Beggars Banquet	1		

May 1987

This Mnth	Last Mnth	Title	Artist	Label	Wks in 10	US Pos	
1	-	**Keep Your Distance**	Curiosity Killed The Cat	Mercury	13	55	**FL**
2	-	**Solitude Standing**	Suzanne Vega	A&M	9	11	**F**
3	3	**Running In The Family**	Level 42	Polydor	12		
4	2	**The Joshua Tree**	U2	Island	28	1	**P**
5	-	**Tango In The Night**	Fleetwood Mac	Warner	38	7	**P**
6	5	**Raindancing**	Alison Moyet	CBS	13	94	**L**
7	1	**Now That's What I Call Music 9**	Various	EMI/Virgin/			
				PolyGram	8		
8	-	**It's Better To Travel**	Swing Out Sister	Mercury	7	40	**F**
9	-	**Invisible Touch**	Genesis	Atlantic	18	3	**P**
10	9	**F.L.M.**	Mel & Kim	Supreme	11		**FL**

June 1987

This Mnth	Last Mnth	Title	Artist	Label	Wks in 10	US Pos	
1	-	**Live In The City Of Light**	Simple Minds	Virgin	7	96	
2	4	**The Joshua Tree**	U2	Island	28	1	**P**
3	-	**Whitney**	Whitney Houston	Arista	23	1	**2P**
4	2	**Solitude Standing**	Suzanne Vega	A&M	9	11	**F**
5	1	**Keep Your Distance**	Curiosity Killed The Cat	Mercury	13	55	**FL**
6	8	**It's Better To Travel**	Swing Out Sister	Mercury	7	40	**F**
7	-	**Sergeant Pepper's Lonely Hearts**					
		Club Band	Beatles	Capitol	51	1	**4P**
8	-	**Licence To Ill**	Beastie Boys	Def Jam	2	1	**F**
9	6	**Raindancing**	Alison Moyet	CBS	13	94	**L**
10	5	**Tango In The Night**	Fleetwood Mac	Warner	38	7	**P**

US 1987

APR-MAR

April 1987

This Mnth	Last Mnth	Title	Artist	Label	Wks in 10	UK Pos	
1	1	**Licensed To Ill**	Beastie Boys	Def Jam	19	7	**F5P**
2	2	**Slippery When Wet**	Bon Jovi	Mercury	46	6	**F11P**
3	-	**The Joshua Tree**	U2	Island	35	1	**F5P**
4	6	**Graceland**	Paul Simon	Columbia	24	1	**5P**
5	3	**The Way It Is**	Bruce Hornsby & The Range	RCA	23	16	**F3P**
6	-	**Look What The Cat Dragged In**	Poison	Enigma	17		**F2P**
7	4	**Invisible Touch**	Genesis	Atlantic	26	1	**5P**
8	9	**Life, Love And Pain**	Club Nouveau	Warner	7		**FPL**
9	5	**Control**	Janet Jackson	A&M	37	8	**F5P**
10	10	**The Final Countdown**	Europe	Epic	10	9	**F3PL**

May 1987

This Mnth	Last Mnth	Title	Artist	Label	Wks in 10	UK Pos	
1	3	**The Joshua Tree**	U2	Island	35	1	**F5P**
2	2	**Slippery When Wet**	Bon Jovi	Mercury	46	6	**F11P**
3	1	**Licensed To Ill**	Beastie Boys	Def Jam	19	7	**F5P**
4	6	**Look What The Cat Dragged In**	Poison	Enigma	17		**F2P**
5	4	**Graceland**	Paul Simon	Columbia	24	1	**5P**
6	-	**Whitesnake**	Whitesnake	Geffen	41	8	**F6P**
7	-	**Sign 'O' The Times**	Prince	Paisley Park	4	4	**P**
8	-	**Into The Fire**	Bryan Adams	A&M	5	10	**P**
9	-	**Tango In The Night**	Fleetwood Mac	Warner	6	1	**2PL**
10	-	**Trio**	Dolly Parton, Emmylou Harris & Linda Ronstadt	Warner	3	60	**FL**

June 1987

This Mnth	Last Mnth	Title	Artist	Label	Wks in 10	UK Pos	
1	1	**The Joshua Tree**	U2	Island	35	1	**F5P**
2	6	**Whitesnake**	Whitesnake	Geffen	41	8	**F6P**
3	2	**Slippery When Wet**	Bon Jovi	Mercury	46	6	**F11P**
4	-	**Girls Girls Girls**	Motley Crue	Elektra	12	14	**2P**
5	4	**Look What The Cat Dragged In**	Poison	Enigma	17		**F2P**
6	-	**Tribute**	Ozzy Osbourne	CBS Associated	6	13	**P**
7	5	**Graceland**	Paul Simon	Columbia	24	1	**5P**
8	-	**Whitney**	Whitney Houston	Arista	31	1	**8P**
9	-	**Spanish Fly**	Lisa Lisa & Cult Jam	Columbia	7		**FPL**
10	9	**Tango In The Night**	Fleetwood Mac	Warner	6	1	**2PL**

• It seemed that New York rap trio The Beastie Boys stirred up controversy wherever they went on European territory. Whilst on tour in Britain, group member King Ad-Rock was charged with injuring a fan with a can of drink at a show in Liverpool. Also the group were blamed when hundreds of Volkswagen car logos were stolen and worn as medallions by UK fans copying their idols' stage wear. To top this off, the British tabloids reported that the group insulted terminally ill children at the Montreux Rock Festival but they vehemently denied this.

• Other stars who appeared at Montreux for the internationally renowned Swiss Festival included Whitney Houston, Cameo, Run-D.M.C., Duran Duran, Spandau Ballet and UB40 (above).

• Chappell's, once the world's biggest music publisher, was sold to Warner Brothers for $180 million (£120 million).

UK 1987 JULY-SEPT

• U2 became the first Irish act to score a transatlantic chart topper with **The Joshua Tree**. The album shipped over two million in America in just six weeks and held the top spot for two months. In Britain, 250,000 were sold in the first week and total sales were in the region of 1.5 million. The album went on to win the Grammy for Best Album of 1987 and helped earn U2 the BRIT award for Best International Group.

• Michael Jackson's **Bad** broke sales records on both sides of the Atlantic. In his homeland, the initial shipment was more than 2.25 million copies, while in Britain over 380,000 were sold in the first week.

• Terence Trent D'Arby became the first American artist to enter the UK chart at Number 1 with a debut album. The performer sold over 1.4 million copies of **Introducing The Hardline According To Terence Trent D'Arby** in Britain. His UK success was later echoed in his homeland where it eventually reached the Top 5 and sold over two million.

July 1987

This Mnth	Last Mnth	Title	Artist	Label	Wks in 10	US Pos	
1	3	**Whitney**	Whitney Houston	Arista	23	1	2P
2	2	**The Joshua Tree**	U2	Island	28	1	P
3	-	**Invisible Touch**	Genesis	Charisma	18	3	P
4	-	**The Return Of Bruno**	Bruce Willis	Motown	6	14	FL
5	5	**Keep Your Distance**	Curiosity Killed The Cat	Mercury	13	55	FL
6	1	**Live In The City Of Light**	Simple Minds	Virgin	7	96	
7	-	**Clutching At Straws**	Marillion	EMI	2	103	
8	-	**Introducing The Hardline According To Terence Trent D'arby**	Terence Trent D'arby	CBS	23	4	FP
9	-	**Hits 6**	Various	CBS/WEA	9		
10	-	**Echo & The Bunnymen**	Echo & The Bunnymen	WEA	1	51	L

August 1987

This Mnth	Last Mnth	Title	Artist	Label	Wks in 10	US Pos	
1	9	**Hits 6**	Various	CBS/WEA	9		
2	8	**Introducing The Hardline According To Terence Trent D'arby**	Terence Trent D'arby	CBS	23	4	FP
3	1	**Whitney**	Whitney Houston	Arista	23	1	2P
4	-	**Sixties Mix**	Various	Stylus	6		
5	-	**Who's That Girl (Soundtrack)**	Madonna	Sire	6	7	
6	2	**The Joshua Tree**	U2	Island	28	1	P
7	-	**Bad Animals**	Heart	Capitol	5	2	F
8	3	**Invisible Touch**	Genesis	Charisma	18	3	P
9	-	**Hysteria**	Def Leppard	Bludgeon Riffola	7	1	FP
10	-	**Substance**	New Order	Factory	4	36	

September 1987

This Mnth	Last Mnth	Title	Artist	Label	Wks in 10	US Pos	
1	-	**Bad**	Michael Jackson	Epic	38	1	3P
2	1	**Hits 6**	Various	CBS/WEA	9		P
3	9	**Hysteria**	Def Leppard	Mercury	7	1	FP
4	10	**Substance**	New Order	Factory	4	36	
5	-	**Pet Shop Boys, Actually**	Pet Shop Boys	Parlophone	15	25	P
6	3	**Whitney**	Whitney Houston	Arista	23	1	2P
7	-	**Changing Faces - The Very Best Of 10 CC**	10 C.C. & Godley & Creme	Pro TV	5		L
8	6	**The Joshua Tree**	U2	Island	28	1	P
9	-	**A Momentary Lapse Of Reason**	Pink Floyd	EMI	2	3	
10	-	**Presley - The All Time Greatest Hits**	Elvis Presley	RCA	4		L

US 1987

JULY-SEPT

July 1987

This Mnth	Last Mnth	Title	Artist	Label	Wks in 10	UK Pos	
1	8	**Whitney**	Whitney Houston	Arista	31	1	**8P**
2	1	**The Joshua Tree**	U2	Island	35	1	**F5P**
3	4	**Girls Girls Girls**	Motley Crue	Elektra	12	14	**2P**
4	2	**Whitesnake**	Whitesnake	Geffen	41	8	**F6P**
5	-	**Bad Animals**	Heart	Capitol	18	7	**3P**
6	-	**Duotones**	Kenny G	Arista	10	28	**F4P**
7	3	**Slippery When Wet**	Bon Jovi	Mercury	46	6	**F11P**
8	-	**Bigger And Deffer**	LL Cool J	Def Jam	13	54	**F2P**
9	9	**Spanish Fly**	Lisa Lisa & Cult Jam	Columbia	7		**FPL**
10	5	**Look What The Cat Dragged In**	Poison	Enigma	17		**F2P**

August 1987

This Mnth	Last Mnth	Title	Artist	Label	Wks in 10	UK Pos	
1	1	**Whitney**	Whitney Houston	Arista	31	1	**8P**
2	4	**Whitesnake**	Whitesnake	Geffen	41	8	**F6P**
3	5	**Bad Animals**	Heart	Capitol	18	7	**3P**
4	8	**Bigger And Deffer**	LL Cool J	Def Jam	13	54	**F2P**
5	2	**The Joshua Tree**	U2	Island	35	1	**F5P**
6	3	**Girls Girls Girls**	Motley Crue	Elektra	12	14	**2P**
7	-	**In The Dark**	Grateful Dead	Arista	7	57	**FPL**
8	6	**Duotones**	Kenny G	Arista	10	28	**F4P**
9	-	**La Bamba**	Soundtrack	Warner	11	24	**2P**
10	-	**Beverly Hills Cop II**	Soundtrack	MCA	6	71	**P**

September 1987

This Mnth	Last Mnth	Title	Artist	Label	Wks in 10	UK Pos	
1	9	**La Bamba**	Soundtrack	Warner	11	24	**2P**
2	1	**Whitney**	Whitney Houston	Arista	31	1	**8P**
3	2	**Whitesnake**	Whitesnake	Geffen	41	8	**F6P**
4	-	**Hysteria**	Def Leppard	Mercury	78	1	**11P**
5	3	**Bad Animals**	Heart	Capitol	18	7	**3P**
6	4	**Bigger And Deffer**	LL Cool J	Def Jam	13	54	**F2P**
7	-	**Who's That Girl (Soundtrack)**	Madonna	Sire	3	4	**P**
8	-	**Bad**	Michael Jackson	Epic	39	1	**8P**
9	7	**In The Dark**	Grateful Dead	Arista	7	57	**FPL**
10	-	**Crushin'**	Fat Boys	Tin Pan Apple	4	49	**FPL**

• Whitney Houston's sophomore album, **Whitney**, was the first album ever to enter both the American and UK charts at the top spot. It was also the first album by a female to reach Number 1 in the USA in its first week. In total, **Whitney** clocked up sales of over eight million in the USA and passed the two million mark in Britain.

• For the first time since 1955, six different female singers had records on the US Top 10 singles chart. The ladies were not so successful on the LP chart, but there was room in the Top 10 for Jody Watley's eponymous debut. Watley, the god-daughter of Jackie Wilson, had previously been a member of the hit trio Shalamar. Her first solo set contained three Top 10 singles and helped win her the Grammy for Best New Artist of 1987.

• Numbered among the American acts hitting the road were Motley Crue, supported by Guns N' Roses, and Roy Orbison who both started US tours and Madonna, who played to a sell-out crowd at London's Wembley Stadium, despite the protests of local residents. Among the other acts who appeared at Wembley this summer were Stevie Wonder, David Bowie and Genesis.

UK 1987 OCT-DEC

• Among the noteworthy British acts debuting on the UK Top 10 were Scottish group Wet Wet Wet with **Popped In Souled Out** and T'Pau with their chart topping debut **Bridge Of Spies**. Also clocking up his first hit album was blue-eyed soul singer Rick Astley with **Whenever You Need Somebody**.

• Ground-breaking British group The Smiths played their last gigs as **Strangeways Here We Come** narrowly missed the top spot. Although their US success was relatively minor, this album was one of three which turned gold there.

• Ex-Wham! Star George Michael's first solo set, **Faith**, took him to the top of the charts on both sides of the Atlantic and sold 15 million worldwide. Michael sang, wrote, produced, arranged and played every instrument on the album. It was not only the first album by a male artist to sell a million compact discs but he was also the first white male soloist to top the US R&B album chart.

• Bruce Springsteen's second transatlantic Number 1, **Tunnel Of Love**, went on to earn him the Grammy for Best Male Rock Performance, while another UK and US hit, Sting's **Nothing Like The Sun**, was voted Album of The Year at the 1988 BRIT awards.

October 1987

This Mnth	Last Mnth	Title	Artist	Label	Wks in 10	US Pos	
1	1	**Bad**	Michael Jackson	Epic	38	1	3P
2	-	**The Cream Of Eric Clapton**	Eric Clapton	Polydor	6		P
3	-	**Tunnel Of Love**	Bruce Springsteen	CBS	4	1	
4	-	**Popped In Souled Out**	Wet Wet Wet	Precious	31	123	FP
5	5	**Pet Shop Boys, Actually**	Pet Shop Boys	Parlophone	15	25	P
6	-	**Nothing Like The Sun**	Sting	A&M	3	9	
7	-	**Tango In The Night**	Fleetwood Mac	Warner	38	7	P
8	-	**Strangeways Here We Come**	Smiths	Rough Trade	3	55	
9	-	**Wonderful Life**	Black	A&M	4		FL
10	-	**Dancing With Strangers**	Chris Rea	Magnet	5		F

November 1987

This Mnth	Last Mnth	Title	Artist	Label	Wks in 10	US Pos	
1	-	**Bridge Of Spies**	T'Pau	Siren	18	31	FP
2	7	**Tango In The Night**	Fleetwood Mac	Warner	38	7	P
3	-	**The Best Of UB40 Vol. I**	UB40	Virgin	7		P
4	-	**All The Best !**	Paul McCartney	Parlophone	9	62	
5	-	**Faith**	George Michael	Epic	8	1	FP
6	-	**The Singles**	Pretenders	WEA	9	69	
7	-	**Best Shots**	Pat Benatar	Chrysalis	4	67	FL
8	-	**Whenever You Need Somebody**	Rick Astley	RCA	15	10	FP
9	-	**Crazy Nights**	Kiss	Vertigo	1	18	
10	6	**Nothing Like The Sun**	Sting	A&M	3	9	

December 1987

This Mnth	Last Mnth	Title	Artist	Label	Wks in 10	US Pos	
1	-	**Now That's What I Call Music 10**	Various	EMI/Virgin/ PolyGram	7		P
2	8	**Whenever You Need Somebody**	Rick Astley	RCA	15	10	FP
3	-	**Hits 7**	Various	CBS/WEA	6		
4	1	**Bridge Of Spies**	T'Pau	Siren	18	31	FP
5	4	**All The Best !**	Paul McCartney	Parlophone	9	62	
6	-	**Bad**	Michael Jackson	Epic	38	1	3P
7	6	**The Singles**	Pretenders	WEA	9	69	
8	2	**Tango In The Night**	Fleetwood Mac	Warner	38	7	P
9	3	**The Best Of UB40 Vol. I**	UB40	Virgin	7		P
10	-	**Raindancing**	Alison Moyet	CBS	13	94	L

US 1987

OCT-DEC

October 1987

This Mnth	Last Mnth	Title	Artist	Label	Wks in 10	UK Pos	
1	8	**Bad**	Michael Jackson	Epic	39	1	**8P**
2	3	**Whitesnake**	Whitesnake	Geffen	41	8	**F6P**
3	2	**Whitney**	Whitney Houston	Arista	31	1	**8P**
4	4	**Hysteria**	Def Leppard	Mercury	78	1	**11P**
5	-	**A Momentary Lapse Of Reason**	Pink Floyd	Columbia	15	3	**3P**
6	-	**Dirty Dancing**	Soundtrack	RCA	48	4	**11P**
7	1	**La Bamba**	Soundtrack	Warner	11	24	**2P**
8	-	**The Lonesome Jubilee**	John Cougar Mellencamp	Mercury	27	31	**4P**
9	-	**The Joshua Tree**	U2	Island	35	1	**F5P**
10	-	**Tunnel Of Love**	Bruce Springsteen	Columbia	10	1	**3P**

November 1987

This Mnth	Last Mnth	Title	Artist	Label	Wks in 10	UK Pos	
1	6	**Dirty Dancing**	Soundtrack	RCA	48	4	**11P**
2	10	**Tunnel Of Love**	Bruce Springsteen	Columbia	10	1	**3P**
3	1	**Bad**	Michael Jackson	Epic	39	1	**8P**
4	2	**Whitesnake**	Whitesnake	Geffen	41	8	**F6P**
5	5	**A Momentary Lapse Of Reason**	Pink Floyd	Columbia	15	3	**3P**
6	4	**Hysteria**	Def Leppard	Mercury	78	1	**11P**
7	8	**The Lonesome Jubilee**	John Cougar Mellencamp	Mercury	27	31	**4P**
8	3	**Whitney**	Whitney Houston	Arista	31	1	**8P**
9	9	**The Joshua Tree**	U2	Island	35	1	**F5P**
10	-	**Nothing Like The Sun**	Sting	A&M	4	1	**2P**

December 1987

This Mnth	Last Mnth	Title	Artist	Label	Wks in 10	UK Pos	
1	1	**Dirty Dancing**	Soundtrack	RCA	48	4	**11P**
2	3	**Bad**	Michael Jackson	Epic	39	1	**8P**
3	4	**Whitesnake**	Whitesnake	Geffen	41	8	**F6P**
4	-	**Faith**	George Michael	Columbia	51	1	**F9P**
5	5	**A Momentary Lapse Of Reason**	Pink Floyd	Columbia	15	3	**3P**
6	7	**The Lonesome Jubilee**	John Cougar Mellencamp	Mercury	27	31	**4P**
7	2	**Tunnel Of Love**	Bruce Springsteen	Columbia	10	1	**3P**
8	6	**Hysteria**	Def Leppard	Mercury	78	1	**11P**
9	-	**Tiffany**	Tiffany	MCA	22	5	**F4PL**
10	10	**Nothing Like The Sun**	Sting	A&M	4	1	**2P**

• Compact disk sales rocketed up 93% to 100 million in the US, which helped push the total record and tape business up by 19.7% to $5.56 billion.

• It had been a bumper year for soundtracks with **Dirty Dancing** hitting the top shortly after **La Bamba** had vacated that position. The former album passed the 11 million mark in the USA and moved over a million in the UK. The success of the Ritchie Valens bio-pic, also helped push **The Best Of Ritchie Valens** into the chart. Other soundtracks selling huge quantities included Madonna's **Who's That Girl**, **The Lost Boys** and **Beverly Hills Cop II**.

• There was an upsurge of interest in heavy metal and hard rock with Britain's Def Leppard (above) and Whitesnake leading the way. Also reaching the Top 20 were such acts as Aerosmith, Dokken, Europe, Sammy Hagar, INXS Kiss and Rush. For the record, Def Leppard's **Hysteria** went on to sell over 12 million copies in America alone.

UK 1988 JAN-MAR

• BRIT winners included George Michael (Best Male), Alison Moyet (Best Female), Pet Shop Boys (Best Group), Wet Wet Wet (Best Newcomer). International awards went to Michael Jackson (Best Solo Artist), U2 (Best Group) and Terence Trent D'Arby (Best Newcomer). An award for outstanding contribution to British music was awarded to The Who, who reunited to perform at the ceremony.

• As George Michael's global tour started in Japan, the album **Faith** spent the first of 12 weeks at the top of the US chart – a record for a solo British artist.

• It was unusual for dance music acts to crack the album Top 10 but America's Joyce Sims with **Come Into My Life** and British session group Mirage with **The Best Of Mirage – Jack Mix '88** were exceptions. Dance music was rapidly growing in importance in the singles market and the sampling of records was becomming commonplace in that field of music.

January 1988

This Mnth	Last Mnth	Title	Artist	Label	Wks in 10	US Pos	
1	6	**Bad**	Michael Jackson	Epic	38	1	**3P**
2	-	**Popped In Souled Out**	Wet Wet Wet	Precious	31	123	**FP**
3	2	**Whenever You Need Somebody**	Rick Astley	RCA	15	10	**FP**
4	-	**Introducing The Hardline According To Terence Trent D'arby**	Terence Trent D'arby	CBS	23	4	**FP**
5	1	**Now That's What I Call Music 10**	Various	EMI/Virgin/ PolyGram	7		**P**
6	-	**Turn Back The Clock**	Johnny Hates Jazz	Virgin	12	56	**FL**
7	-	**The Christians**	Christians	Island	13	158	**F**
8	4	**Bridge Of Spies**	T'Pau	Siren	18	31	**FP**
9	3	**Hits 7**	Various	CBS/WEA	6		
10	-	**Pet Shop Boys, Actually**	Pet Shop Boys	Parlophone	15	25	**P**

February 1988

This Mnth	Last Mnth	Title	Artist	Label	Wks in 10	US Pos	
1	4	**Introducing The Hardline According To Terence Trent D'arby**	Terence Trent D'arby	Columbia	23	4	**FP**
2	7	**The Christians**	Christians	Island	13	158	**F**
3	8	**Bridge Of Spies**	T'Pau	Siren	18	31	**FP**
4	2	**Popped In Souled Out**	Wet Wet Wet	Precious	31	123	**FP**
5	6	**Turn Back The Clock**	Johnny Hates Jazz	Virgin	12	56	**FL**
6	-	**Blow Up Your Video**	AC/DC	Atlantic	2	12	
7	-	**Come Into My Life**	Joyce Sims	London	5		**FL**
8	3	**Whenever You Need Somebody**	Rick Astley	RCA	15	10	**FP**
9	-	**The Best Of Mirage-Jack Mix '88**	Mirage	Stylus	4		**F**
10	-	**If I Should Fall From Grace With God**	Pogues	Stiff	2	88	**F**

March 1988

This Mnth	Last Mnth	Title	Artist	Label	Wks in 10	US Pos	
1	1	**Introducing The Hardline According To Terence Trent D'arby**	Terence Trent D'arby	CBS	23	4	**FP**
2	-	**The Best Of OMD**	OMD	Virgin	9		**L**
3	8	**Whenever You Need Somebody**	Rick Astley	RCA	15	10	**FP**
4	-	**Give Me The Reason**	Luther Vandross	Epic	7	14	**F**
5	4	**Popped In Souled Out**	Wet Wet Wet	Precious	31	123	**FP**
6	3	**Bridge Of Spies**	T'Pau	Siren	18	31	**FP**
7	-	**Hearsay/All Mixed Up**	Alexander O'Neal	Tabu	5	29	**FP**
8	-	**Unforgettable**	Various	EMI	3		
9	-	**Tear Down These Walls**	Billy Ocean	Jive	2	18	
10	5	**Turn Back The Clock**	Johnny Hates Jazz	Virgin	12	56	**FL**

US 1988 JAN-MAR

January 1988

This Mnth	Last Mnth	Title	Artist	Label	Wks in 10	UK Pos	
1	1	**Dirty Dancing**	Soundtrack	RCA	48	4	**11P**
2	4	**Faith**	George Michael	Columbia	51	1	**F9P**
3	9	**Tiffany**	Tiffany	MCA	22	5	**F4PL**
4	2	**Bad**	Michael Jackson	Epic	39	1	**8P**
5	3	**Whitesnake**	Whitesnake	Geffen	41	8	**F6P**
6	6	**The Lonesome Jubilee**	John Cougar Mellencamp	Mercury	27	31	**4P**
7	-	**Kick**	INXS	Atlantic	22	9	**F4P**
8	-	**Whitney**	Whitney Houston	Arista	31	1	**8P**
9	8	**Hysteria**	Def Leppard	Mercury	78	1	**11P**
10	5	**A Momentary Lapse Of Reason**	Pink Floyd	Columbia	15	3	**3P**

February 1988

This Mnth	Last Mnth	Title	Artist	Label	Wks in 10	UK Pos	
1	2	**Faith**	George Michael	Columbia	51	1	**F9P**
2	1	**Dirty Dancing**	Soundtrack	RCA	48	4	**11P**
3	3	**Tiffany**	Tiffany	MCA	22	5	**F4PL**
4	7	**Kick**	INXS	Atlantic	22	9	**F4P**
5	4	**Bad**	Michael Jackson	Epic	39	1	**8P**
6	6	**The Lonesome Jubilee**	John Cougar Mellencamp	Mercury	27	31	**4P**
7	9	**Hysteria**	Def Leppard	Mercury	78	1	**11P**
8	-	**Out Of The Blue**	Debbie Gibson	Atlantic	13	26	**F3P**
9	-	**Skyscraper**	David Lee Roth	Warner	8	11	**PL**
10	5	**Whitesnake**	Whitesnake	Geffen	41	8	**F6P**

March 1988

This Mnth	Last Mnth	Title	Artist	Label	Wks in 10	UK Pos	
1	2	**Dirty Dancing**	Soundtrack	RCA	48	4	**11P**
2	1	**Faith**	George Michael	Columbia	51	1	**F9P**
3	4	**Kick**	INXS	Atlantic	22	9	**F4P**
4	5	**Bad**	Michael Jackson	Epic	39	1	**8P**
5	3	**Tiffany**	Tiffany	MCA	22	5	**F4PL**
6	9	**Skyscraper**	David Lee Roth	Warner	8	11	**PL**
7	7	**Hysteria**	Def Leppard	Mercury	78	1	**11P**
8	8	**Out Of The Blue**	Debbie Gibson	Atlantic	13	26	**F3P**
9	6	**The Lonesome Jubilee**	John Cougar Mellencamp	Mercury	27	31	**4P**
10	-	**Whenever You Need Somebody**	Rick Astley	RCA	2	1	**F2PL**

• Whitney Houston was the first female artist to sell over five million copies of her first two albums, **Whitney Houston** and **Whitney**. At the same time, on the singles chart, her 'Where Do Broken Hearts Go' was heading towards the top – her seventh single in a row to accomplish that feat.

• Outspoken and controversial rap group Public Enemy debuted on the chart with **Yo! Bum Rush The Show**. Other rappers enjoying crossover success included teenager LL Cool J with the hard hitting **Bigger & Deffer**, West coast rapper Ice-T with **Rhyme Pays** and New York heavyweights, The Fat Boys with **Crushin'**.

• Teenage female singers were suddenly in vogue with Tiffany and Debbie Gibson being the most successful. 16-year-old Tiffany (Darwisch) topped the chart with her self-titled debut album, which included the Number 1 singles 'I Think We're Alone Now' and 'Could've Been'. She was the first female teenager to top the album chart and the first teenager since (Little) Stevie Wonder in 1963. The success of 17-year-old Debbie Gibson was even more impressive as she also co-wrote and co-produced **Out Of The Blue**, which despite its lowly UK chart placing sold over 200,000 copies.

UK 1988 APR-JUNE

• Female artists were also having a very successful period in Britain, and at times there were a record 13 in the singles Top 40. Among the ladies adding to their Top 10 album totals were Sade with **Stronger Than Pride** and Tina Turner with **Live In Europe**, which earned her a Grammy the following year. Americans Belinda Carlisle and Nanci Griffith debuted on the charts with **Heaven On Earth** and **Little Love Affairs** respectively. Female-fronted groups, Fairground Attraction with **The First Of A Million Kisses**, The Primitives with **Lovely** and The Sugarcubes with **Life's Too Good** also opened their chart accounts. For the record, the latter act's vocalist, Bjork, became one of the most critically acclaimed artists of the mid-Nineties.

• As **Hip Hop And Rapping In The House** became the first specialist dance compilation album to crack the UK Top 10, Londoner Derek B's debut set, **Bullet From A Gun**, became the first local rap record to reach the Top 20.

April 1988

This Mnth	Last Mnth	Title	Artist	Label	Wks in 10	US Pos	
1	-	**Now That's What I Call Music 11**	Various	EMI/Virgin/ PolyGram	7		
2	2	**The Best Of OMD**	OMD	Virgin	9		L
3	-	**Push**	Bros	CBS	16	171	FP
4	5	**Popped In Souled Out**	Wet Wet Wet	Precious	31	123	FP
5	-	**Tango In The Night**	Fleetwood Mac	Warner	38	7	P
6	-	**Seventh Son Of A Seventh Son**	Iron Maiden	EMI	2	12	
7	-	**Dirty Dancing**	Soundtrack	RCA	19	1	P
8	1	**Introducing The Hardline According To Terence Trent D'arby**	Terence Trent D'arby	CBS	23	4	FP
9	-	**The Innocents**	Erasure	Mute	11	49	P
10	-	**Hip Hop And Rapping In The House**	Various	Stylus	4		

May 1988

This Mnth	Last Mnth	Title	Artist	Label	Wks in 10	US Pos	
1	5	**Tango In The Night**	Fleetwood Mac	Warner	38	7	P
2	7	**Dirty Dancing**	Soundtrack	RCA	19	1	P
3	-	**Lovesexy**	Prince	Paisley Park	2	11	
4	-	**Stronger Than Pride**	Sade	Epic	7	7	
5	-	**The Christians**	Christians	Island	13	158	F
6	-	**More Dirty Dancing**	Various	RCA	6	3	
7	4	**Popped In Souled Out**	Wet Wet Wet	Precious	31	123	FP
8	9	**The Innocents**	Erasure	Mute	11	49	P
9	1	**Now That's What I Call Music 11**	Various	EMI/Virgin/ PolyGram	7		
10	-	**Stay On These Roads**	A-Ha	Warner	2	148	L

June 1988

This Mnth	Last Mnth	Title	Artist	Label	Wks in 10	US Pos	
1	-	**Nite Flite**	Various	CBS	7		
2	1	**Tango In The Night**	Fleetwood Mac	Warner	38	7	P
3	-	**Motown Dance Party**	Various	Motown	4		
4	-	**Heaven On Earth**	Belinda Carlisle	Virgin	9	13	F
5	7	**Popped In Souled Out**	Wet Wet Wet	Precious	31	123	FP
6	2	**Dirty Dancing**	Soundtrack	RCA	19	1	P
7	4	**Stronger Than Pride**	Sade	Epic	7	7	
8	-	**Whitney**	Whitney Houston	Arista	23	1	2P
9	6	**More Dirty Dancing**	Various	RCA	6	3	
10	-	**Tracy Chapman**	Tracy Chapman	Elektra	16	1	FP

US 1988 APR-JUNE

April 1988

This Mnth	Last Mnth	Title	Artist	Label	Wks in 10	UK Pos	
1	1	**Dirty Dancing**	Soundtrack	RCA	48	4	**11P**
2	2	**Faith**	George Michael	Columbia	51	1	**F9P**
3	4	**Bad**	Michael Jackson	Epic	39	1	**8P**
4	3	**Kick**	INXS	Atlantic	22	9	**F4P**
5	-	**More Dirty Dancing**	Various	RCA	13	3	**4P**
6	5	**Tiffany**	Tiffany	MCA	22	5	**F4PL**
7	-	**Now And Zen**	Robert Plant	Es Paranza	10	10	**PL**
8	-	**Introducing The Hardline According To Terence Trent D'arby**	Terence Trent D'arby	Columbia	8	1	**F2PL**
9	6	**Skyscraper**	David Lee Roth	Warner	8	11	**PL**
10	7	**Hysteria**	Def Leppard	Mercury	78	1	**11P**

May 1988

This Mnth	Last Mnth	Title	Artist	Label	Wks in 10	UK Pos	
1	2	**Faith**	George Michael	Columbia	51	1	**F9P**
2	1	**Dirty Dancing**	Soundtrack	RCA	48	4	**11P**
3	5	**More Dirty Dancing**	Various	RCA	13	3	**4P**
4	3	**Bad**	Michael Jackson	Epic	39	1	**8P**
5	8	**Introducing The Hardline According To Terence Trent D'arby**	Terence Trent D'arby	Columbia	8	1	**F2PL**
6	4	**Kick**	INXS	Atlantic	22	9	**F4P**
7	7	**Now And Zen**	Robert Plant	Es Paranza	10	10	**PL**
8	-	**Appetite For Destruction**	Guns N' Roses	Geffen	52	5	**F10P**
9	-	**Let It Loose**	Gloria Estefan & The Miami Sound Machine	Epic	9	1	**F3P**
10	6	**Tiffany**	Tiffany	MCA	22	5	**F4PL**

June 1988

This Mnth	Last Mnth	Title	Artist	Label	Wks in 10	UK Pos	
1	1	**Faith**	George Michael	Columbia	51	1	**F9P**
2	-	**Open Up And Say Ahh**	Poison	Enigma	27	18	**5P**
3	2	**Dirty Dancing**	Soundtrack	RCA	48	4	**11P**
4	-	**Hysteria**	Def Leppard	Mercury	78	1	**11P**
5	-	**Savage Amusement**	Scorpions	Mercury	7	18	**PL**
6	-	**OU812**	Van Halen	Warner	16	16	**3P**
7	4	**Bad**	Michael Jackson	Epic	39	1	**8P**
8	-	**Scenes From The Southside**	Bruce Hornsby & The Range	RCA	7	18	**PL**
9	9	**Let It Loose**	Gloria Estefan & The Miami Sound Machine	Epic	9	1	**F3P**
10	8	**Appetite For Destruction**	Guns N' Roses	Geffen	52	5	**F10P**

• For the only time, two albums linked to the same film were simultaneously in the Top 3. The movie was *Dirty Dancing* and the albums, **Dirty Dancing** and **More Dirty Dancing**, mostly contained hits from the Sixties. Featured artists included The Ronettes, Maurice Williams & The Zodiacs, The Four Seasons, The Contours and The Shirelles. The ten million selling first album also included two mid-Fifties classics 'In The Still Of The Night' by the Five Satins and Bo Diddley's song 'Love Is Strange' from Mickey & Sylvia.

• Pink Floyd's **Dark Side Of The Moon** dropped off the Top 200 chart with 725 chart weeks (14 years) under its belt! When *Billboard* introduced the catalogue chart for albums that had been off the Top 200 for three months, **Dark Side Of The Moon** became an immovable fixture on it.

• The biggest event of the year was Nelson Mandela's 70th Birthday Tribute at Wembley. The all-star extravaganza was seen all around the world on TV and showcased such acts as Bryan Adams, The Bee Gees, Natalie Cole, Phil Collins, Dire Straits, Eurythmics, Al Green, Whitney Houston, George Michael, Salt-N-Pepa, Sting and Stevie Wonder.

UK 1988 JULY-SEPT

July 1988

This Mnth	Last Mnth	Title	Artist	Label	Wks in 10	US Pos	
1	10	**Tracy Chapman**	Tracy Chapman	Elektra	16	1	**FP**
2	-	**Idol Songs: 11 Of The Best**	Billy Idol	Chrysalis	10		**L**
3	-	**Push**	Bros	CBS	16	171	**FP**
4	-	**Kylie**	Kylie Minogue	PWL	29	53	**F2P**
5	-	**Now That's What I Call Music 12**	Various	EMI/Virgin/			
				PolyGram	9		
6	2	**Tango In The Night**	Fleetwood Mac	Warner	38	7	**P**
7	-	**Roll With It**	Steve Winwood	Virgin	3	1	**L**
8	-	**Bad**	Michael Jackson	Epic	38	1	**3P**
9	6	**Dirty Dancing**	Soundtrack	RCA	19	1	**P**
10	-	**The Collection**	Barry White	Mercury	3		**L**

August 1988

This Mnth	Last Mnth	Title	Artist	Label	Wks in 10	US Pos	
1	5	**Now That's What I Call Music 12**	Various	EMI/Virgin/			
				PolyGram	9		
2	4	**Kylie**	Kylie Minogue	PWL	29	53	**F2P**
3	1	**Tracy Chapman**	Tracy Chapman	Elektra	16	1	**FP**
4	-	**Hits 8**	Various	CBS/WEA	5		
5	8	**Bad**	Michael Jackson	Epic	38	1	**3P**
6	-	**The First Of A Million Kisses**	Fairground Attraction	RCA	9	137	**FL**
7	2	**Idol Songs: 11 Of The Best**	Billy Idol	Chrysalis	10		**L**
8	3	**Push**	Bros	CBS	16	171	**FP**
9	-	**The Greatest Ever Rock 'n' Roll Mix**	Various	Stylus	5		
10	9	**Dirty Dancing**	Soundtrack	RCA	19	1	**P**

September 1988

This Mnth	Last Mnth	Title	Artist	Label	Wks in 10	US Pos	
1	2	**Kylie**	Kylie Minogue	PWL	29	53	**F2P**
2	-	**Hot City Nights**	Various	Vertigo	6		
3	3	**Tracy Chapman**	Tracy Chapman	Elektra	16	1	**FP**
4	6	**The First Of A Million Kisses**	Fairground Attraction	RCA	9	137	**FL**
5	-	**Rap Trax**	Various	Stylus	5		
6	5	**Bad**	Michael Jackson	Epic	38	1	**3P**
7	1	**Now That's What I Call Music 12**	Various	EMI/Virgin/			
				PolyGram	9		
8	-	**Rank**	Smiths	Rough Trade	1	77	
9	-	**...And Justice For All**	Metallica	Vertigo	1	6	**F**
10	-	**So Good**	Mica Paris	4th & Broadway	2	86	**FL**

• The sales of singles in the UK continued to drop but one act who still sold singles by the ton was Australian actress/singer Kylie Minogue. Her debut album, **Kylie**, was the first album by an Australian solo act to top the charts. It went on to sell over two million copies in the UK alone – the biggest selling female debut in Britain.

• Michael Jackson packed in over 500,000 for his seven nights at Wembley stadium. As often happens when a major celebrity tours the UK, Jackson's visit helped push six of his albums into the chart.

• The biggest all-star line-up at Wembley was the 'Human Rights Now' tour in aid of an Amnesty International and starred Bruce Springsteen, Sting, Tracy Chapman and Peter Gabriel.

• Rock-related films on release included *Buster* starring Phil Collins, *Tougher Than Leather* starring Run-D.M.C., *Sign O'The Times* starring Prince and *The Krays* starring Gary & Martin Kemp of Spandau Ballet.

• British metal merchants Def Leppard headed the chart with **Hysteria**, which went on to sell over 11 million copies in the USA – a record unsurpassed by any British group, including The Beatles and The Rolling Stones

US 1988

JULY-SEPT

July 1988

This Mnth	Last Mnth	Title	Artist	Label	Wks in 10	UK Pos	
1	6	**OU812**	Van Halen	Warner	16	16	**3P**
2	4	**Hysteria**	Def Leppard	Mercury	78	1	**11P**
3	3	**Dirty Dancing**	Soundtrack	RCA	48	4	**11P**
4	1	**Faith**	George Michael	Columbia	51	1	**F9P**
5	10	**Appetite For Destruction**	Guns N' Roses	Geffen	52	5	**F10P**
6	2	**Open Up And Say Ahh**	Poison	Enigma	27	18	**5P**
7	-	**Stronger Than Pride**	Sade	Epic	6	3	**3P**
8	8	**Scenes From The Southside**	Bruce Hornsby & The Range	RCA	7	18	**PL**
9	-	**Tracy Chapman**	Tracy Chapman	Elektra	18	1	**F3P**
10	-	**Roll With It**	Steve Winwood	Virgin	14	4	**2PL**

August 1988

This Mnth	Last Mnth	Title	Artist	Label	Wks in 10	UK Pos	
1	2	**Hysteria**	Def Leppard	Mercury	78	1	**11P**
2	10	**Roll With It**	Steve Winwood	Virgin	14	4	**2PL**
3	5	**Appetite For Destruction**	Guns N' Roses	Geffen	52	5	**F10P**
4	9	**Tracy Chapman**	Tracy Chapman	Elektra	18	1	**F3P**
5	3	**Dirty Dancing**	Soundtrack	RCA	48	4	**11P**
6	-	**He's The DJ I'm The Rapper**	DJ Jazzy Jeff & The Fresh Prince	Jive	10	68	**F2PL**
7	4	**Faith**	George Michael	Columbia	51	1	**F9P**
8	1	**OU812**	Van Halen	Warner	16	16	**3P**
9	6	**Open Up And Say Ahh**	Poison	Enigma	27	18	**5P**
10	-	**Let It Loose**	Gloria Estefan & The Miami Sound Machine	Epic	9	1	**F3P**

September 1988

This Mnth	Last Mnth	Title	Artist	Label	Wks in 10	UK Pos	
1	1	**Hysteria**	Def Leppard	Mercury	78	1	**11P**
2	3	**Appetite For Destruction**	Guns N' Roses	Geffen	52	5	**F10P**
3	4	**Tracy Chapman**	Tracy Chapman	Elektra	18	1	**F3P**
4	2	**Roll With It**	Steve Winwood	Virgin	14	4	**2PL**
5	6	**He's The DJ I'm The Rapper**	DJ Jazzy Jeff & The Fresh Prince	Jive	10	68	**F2PL**
6	7	**Faith**	George Michael	Columbia	51	1	**F9P**
7	8	**OU812**	Van Halen	Warner	16	16	**3P**
8	-	**Richard Marx**	Richard Marx	EMI Manhattan	4	68	**F3P**
9	9	**Open Up And Say Ahh**	Poison	Enigma	27	18	**5P**
10	-	**Cocktail**	Soundtrack	Elektra	19	2	**4P**

• Arguably the most talked about new performer was black folk singer/songwriter Tracy Chapman, who become a world-wide sensation overnight after appearing on the Nelson Mandela 70th Birthday Tribute. Her self-titled debut LP was the first folk album to top the US charts for 16 years, and was the first debut by a female to top the UK charts. In total, the record sold over 10 million copies worldwide and helped her to win the Grammy for Best New Artist and two BRIT awards.

• R&B music was again well represented in the Top 20 with hits coming from newcomers Al B. Sure! with **In Effect Mode**, Keith Sweat with **Make It Last Forever** and Pebbles with **Pebbles**. Also hitting the heights were rap groups Run-D.M.C. with **Tougher Than Leather** and DJ Jazzy Jeff & The Fresh Prince with **He's The DJ, I'm The Rapper**. The Fresh Prince (aka Will Smith) went on to become, arguably, the world's best known rap artist, thanks to his hit TV series *The Fresh Prince of Bel Air*.

UK 1988 OCT-DEC

• As Cliff Richard celebrated his 30th anniversary in show business, his double album **Private Collection** moved to the top. It was his first Number 1 LP since mid-1981 and his first album to sell over a million in the UK alone.

• Bros-mania was reaching its peak. The act, who were about to take the BRIT trophy for Best Newcomers, sold a record 90,000 copies of their live video in one day. The photogenic British group were also mobbed by 6,000 fans when touring Australia.

• The most talked about musical event in Britain was Frenchman Jean-Michel Jarre's spectacular laser show, 'Destination Docklands' on the River Thames. The media attention helped push **Revolutions** into the runner-up spot. Incidentally, the album and live extravaganza featured Hank Marvin of The Shadows.

• More than half of the top selling albums over Christmas were greatest hits compilations. Among the acts involved were: Cliff Richard, Dire Straits, Human League, Fleetwood Mac, Bananarama, Bryan Ferry & Roxy Music and Roy Orbison.

• As Mecca, owner of a large chain of clubs, and *Top Of The Pops* banned the playing of Acid House records, various clothes shops refused to stock Smiley Face T-shirts, which were associated with this musical movement. Despite this, Acid House ruled in British clubs.

October 1988

This Mnth	Last Mnth	Title	Artist	Label	Wks in 10	US Pos	
1	-	**New Jersey**	Bon Jovi	Vertigo	3	1	
2	-	**Revolutions**	Jean-Michel Jarre	Polydor	3		L
3	1	**Kylie**	Kylie Minogue	PWL	29	53	F2P
4	-	**Staring At The Sun**	Level 42	Polydor	3	128	
5	-	**Rattle And Hum**	U2	Island	4	1	P
6	-	**Conscience**	Womack And Womack	4th & Broadway	5		F
7	-	**Introspective**	Pet Shop Boys	Parlophone	5	34	
8	-	**Flying Colours**	Chris De Burgh	A&M	2		
9	-	**Moonlighting (TV Soundtrack)**	Various	WEA	3	50	
10	-	**To Whom It May Concern**	Pasadenas	CBS	2	89	F

November 1988

This Mnth	Last Mnth	Title	Artist	Label	Wks in 10	US Pos	
1	3	**Kylie**	Kylie Minogue	PWL	29	53	F2P
2	-	**Money For Nothing**	Dire Straits	Vertigo	13	62	P
3	-	**Greatest Hits**	Human League	Virgin	3		L
4	5	**Rattle And Hum**	U2	Island	4	1	P
5	-	**Private Collection**	Cliff Richard	EMI	9		P
6	-	**Watermark**	Enya	WEA	11	25	FP
7	-	**New Light Through Old Windows**	Chris Rea	WEA	4	92	
8	-	**The Memphis Sessions**	Wet Wet Wet	Precious	2		
9	-	**Smash Hits Party '88**	Various	Dover	4		
10	-	**Rage**	T'Pau	Siren	2		

December 1988

This Mnth	Last Mnth	Title	Artist	Label	Wks in 10	US Pos	
1	-	**Now That's What I Call Music 13**	Various	EMI/Virgin/ PolyGram	6		
2	5	**Private Collection**	Cliff Richard	EMI	9		P
3	1	**Kylie**	Kylie Minogue	PWL	29	53	F2P
4	-	**The Premiere Collection**	Various	Polydor	6		P
5	-	**Greatest Hits**	Fleetwood Mac	Warner	11	14	
6	2	**Money For Nothing**	Dire Straits	Vertigo	13	62	P
7	-	**The Hits Album**	Various	CBS/WEA	4		
8	-	**The Greatest Hits Collection**	Bananarama	London	12	151	L
9	-	**The Ultimate Collection**	Bryan Ferry/Roxy Music	EG	7		
10	-	**Wanted**	Yazz	Big Life	7		FL

US 1988 OCT-DEC

October 1988

This Mnth	Last Mnth	Title	Artist	Label	Wks in 10	UK Pos	
1	2	**Appetite For Destruction**	Guns N' Roses	Geffen	52	5	**F10P**
2	1	**Hysteria**	Def Leppard	Mercury	78	1	**11P**
3	10	**Cocktail**	Soundtrack	Elektra	19	2	**4P**
4	-	**New Jersey**	Bon Jovi	Mercury	22	1	**6P**
5	3	**Tracy Chapman**	Tracy Chapman	Elektra	18	1	**F3P**
6	-	**Simple Pleasures**	Bobby McFerrin	EMI Manhattan	7	92	**FPL**
7	-	**...And Justice For All**	Metallica	Elektra	11	4	**F3P**
8	4	**Roll With It**	Steve Winwood	Virgin	14	4	**2PL**
9	6	**Faith**	George Michael	Columbia	51	1	**F9P**
10	-	**Don't Be Cruel**	Bobby Brown	MCA	45	3	**F6P**

November 1988

This Mnth	Last Mnth	Title	Artist	Label	Wks in 10	UK Pos	
1	-	**Rattle And Hum**	U2	Island	14	1	**3P**
2	1	**Appetite For Destruction**	Guns N' Roses	Geffen	52	5	**F10P**
3	4	**New Jersey**	Bon Jovi	Mercury	22	1	**6P**
4	3	**Cocktail**	Soundtrack	Elektra	19	2	**4P**
5	2	**Hysteria**	Def Leppard	Mercury	78	1	**11P**
6	-	**Giving You The Best That I Got**	Anita Baker	Elektra	18	9	**F3P**
7	10	**Don't Be Cruel**	Bobby Brown	MCA	45	3	**F6P**
8	9	**Faith**	George Michael	Columbia	51	1	**9P**
9	6	**Simple Pleasures**	Bobby McFerrin	EMI Manhattan	7	92	**FPL**
10	-	**Silhouette**	Kenny G	Arista	9		**3P**

December 1988

This Mnth	Last Mnth	Title	Artist	Label	Wks in 10	UK Pos	
1	1	**Rattle And Hum**	U2	Island	14	1	**3P**
2	6	**Giving You The Best That I Got**	Anita Baker	Elektra	18	9	**F3P**
3	4	**Cocktail**	Soundtrack	Elektra	19	2	**4P**
4	2	**Appetite For Destruction**	Guns N' Roses	Geffen	52	5	**F10P**
5	3	**New Jersey**	Bon Jovi	Mercury	22	1	**6P**
6	7	**Don't Be Cruel**	Bobby Brown	MCA	45	3	**F6P**
7	5	**Hysteria**	Def Leppard	Mercury	78	1	**11P**
8	-	**Traveling Wilburys Volume 1**	Traveling Wilburys	Wilbury	22	16	**F3PL**
9	10	**Silhouette**	Kenny G	Arista	9		**3P**
10	-	**Open Up And Say Ahh**	Poison	Enigma	27	18	**5P**

• Compact disk sales were up 47%, as the total American record and tape shipments reached a record $6.25 billion. Business in Britain was also booming. Compact disk business was up 60% and total sales passed the $1 billion mark.

• As New Edition had their last major hit album with, **Heart Break**, their former vocalist Bobby Brown's second LP, **Don't Be Cruel**, made him the first teenage male to top the chart for 15 years.

• U2 scored their second successive transatlantic Number 1 with music from their film **Rattle And Hum**. In its first week, the album sold a record million copies in America and 300,000 in Britain.

• Roy Orbison died days after his latest recording project, **The Traveling Wilburys**, took him into the album Top 10 for the first time in his long career. His last live show was in Cleveland, the home of the Rock And Roll Hall Of Fame, to which he had recently been elected.

UK 1989 JAN-MAR

• George Michael's **Faith** was selected as Album Of The Year at The Grammy Awards, and to many people's surprise he was voted Top R&B Male Artist and **Faith** Top R&B Album at the American Music Awards. Multi-Grammy winners this year were Bobby McFerrin, Tracy Chapman, U2 and Anita Baker.

• Compilation and various artists albums were given their own chart in Britain. This meant that albums like the top selling series, **Now That's What I Call Music** and **Hits** and any various artist soundtracks would no longer appear in the regular Top 10 chart.

• U2's **The Joshua Tree**, Def Leppard's **Hysteria**, George Michael's **Faith** and the soundtrack album to **Dirty Dancing** were the first compact disks to sell over a million copies. Equally impressive were the sales of videos by U2 (*Rattle & Hum*), Bruce Springsteen (*Anthology 1978-1988)*, and Michael Jackson (*Moon Walker*). The former two sold over 350,000 copies and the latter doubled that figure to become one of the biggest selling music videos to date.

• Among the latest headliners at Wembley were Level 42, Simply Red, Bryan Ferry and Luther Vandross whose 10 shows in front of 115,000 fans at the Arena grossed a record $3.65 million.

January 1989

This Mnth	Last Mnth	Title	Artist	Label	Wks in 10	US Pos	
1	5	**Greatest Hits**	Fleetwood Mac	Warner	11	14	
2	-	**The Innocents**	Erasure	Mute	11	49	**P**
3	-	**The Legendary Roy Orbison**	Roy Orbison	Telstar	9		
4	3	**Kylie**	Kylie Minogue	PWL	29	53	**F2P**
5	8	**The Greatest Hits Collection**	Bananarama	London	12	151	**L**
6	-	**Bad**	Michael Jackson	Epic	38	1	**3P**
7	-	**Anything For You**	Gloria Estefan & The Miami Sound Machine	Epic	17	6	**FP**
8	1	**Now That's What I Call Music 13**	Various	EMI/Virgin/ PolyGram	6		
9	-	**Watermark**	Enya	WEA	11	25	**FP**
10	2	**Private Collection**	Cliff Richard	EMI	9		**P**

February 1989

This Mnth	Last Mnth	Title	Artist	Label	Wks in 10	US Pos	
1	3	**The Legendary Roy Orbison**	Roy Orbison	Telstar	9		
2	7	**Anything For You**	Gloria Estefan & The Miami Sound Machine	Epic	17	6	**FP**
3	-	**Mystery Girl**	Roy Orbison	Virgin	5	5	**L**
4	-	**Ancient Heart**	Tanita Tikaram	WEA	9	59	**F**
5	-	**The Living Years**	Mike + The Mechanics	WEA	5	13	**FL**
6	-	**The Raw And The Cooked**	Fine Young Cannibals	London	17	1	**FPL**
7	-	**Technique**	New Order	Factory	2	32	
8	2	**The Innocents**	Erasure	Mute	11	49	**P**
9	-	**A New Flame**	Simply Red	Elektra	26	22	**P**
10	9	**Watermark**	Enya	WEA	11	25	**FP**

March 1989

This Mnth	Last Mnth	Title	Artist	Label	Wks in 10	US Pos	
1	9	**A New Flame**	Simply Red	Elektra	26	22	**P**
2	2	**Anything For You**	Gloria Estefan & The Miami Sound Machine	Epic	17	6	**FP**
3	4	**Ancient Heart**	Tanita Tikaram	WEA	9	59	**F**
4	-	**Stop**	Sam Brown	A&M	5		**FL**
5	-	**Singular Adventures Of The Style Council**	Style Council	Polydor	5		**L**
6	-	**Don't Be Cruel**	Bobby Brown	MCA	21	1	**FL**
7	6	**The Raw And The Cooked**	Fine Young Cannibals	London	17	1	**FPL**
8	-	**Southside**	Texas	Mercury	3	88	**FL**
9	3	**Mystery Girl**	Roy Orbison	Virgin	5	5	**L**
10	-	**The Big Area**	Then Jerico	London	1		**FL**

US 1989 JAN-MAR

January 1989

This Mnth	Last Mnth	Title	Artist	Label	Wks in 10	UK Pos	
1	6	**Don't Be Cruel**	Bobby Brown	MCA	45	3	**F6P**
2	2	**Giving You The Best That I Got**	Anita Baker	Elektra	18	9	**F3P**
3	4	**Appetite For Destruction**	Guns N' Roses	Geffen	52	5	**F10P**
4	5	**New Jersey**	Bon Jovi	Mercury	22	1	**6P**
5	7	**Hysteria**	Def Leppard	Mercury	78	1	**11P**
6	1	**Rattle And Hum**	U2	Island	14	1	**3P**
7	3	**Cocktail**	Soundtrack	Elektra	19	2	**4P**
8	8	**Traveling Wilburys**	Traveling Wilburys	Wilbury	22	16	**F3PL**
9	10	**Open Up And Say Ahh**	Poison	Enigma	27	18	**5P**
10	-	**G N' R Lies**	Guns N' Roses	Geffen	18	32	**4P**

February 1989

This Mnth	Last Mnth	Title	Artist	Label	Wks in 10	UK Pos	
1	1	**Don't Be Cruel**	Bobby Brown	MCA	45	3	**F6P**
2	3	**Appetite For Destruction**	Guns N' Roses	Geffen	52	5	**F10P**
3	8	**Traveling Wilburys Volume 1**	Traveling Wilburys	Wilbury	22	16	**F3PL**
4	10	**G N' R Lies**	Guns N' Roses	Geffen	18	32	**4P**
5	-	**Shooting Rubberbands At The Stars**	Edie Brickell & The New Bohemians	Geffen	8	25	**FPL**
6	5	**Hysteria**	Def Leppard	Mercury	78	1	**11P**
7	9	**Open Up And Say Ahh**	Poison	Enigma	27	18	**5P**
8	4	**New Jersey**	Bon Jovi	Mercury	22	1	**6P**
9	2	**Giving You The Best That I Got**	Anita Baker	Elektra	18	9	**F3P**
10	-	**Electric Youth**	Debbie Gibson	Atlantic	13	8	**2PL**

March 1989

This Mnth	Last Mnth	Title	Artist	Label	Wks in 10	UK Pos	
1	10	**Electric Youth**	Debbie Gibson	Atlantic	13	8	**2PL**
2	1	**Don't Be Cruel**	Bobby Brown	MCA	45	3	**F6P**
3	2	**Appetite For Destruction**	Guns N' Roses	Geffen	52	5	**F10P**
4	3	**Traveling Wilburys Volume 1**	Traveling Wilburys	Wilbury	22	16	**F3PL**
5	-	**Forever Your Girl**	Paula Abdul	Virgin	64	5	**F7P**
6	5	**Shooting Rubberbands At The Stars**	Edie Brickell & The New Bohemians	Geffen	8	25	**FPL**
7	-	**Mystery Girl**	Roy Orbison	Virgin	8	2	**FPL**
8	4	**G N' R Lies**	Guns N' Roses	Geffen	18	32	**4P**
9	-	**Loc-Ed After Dark**	Tone Loc	Delicious	12	68	**F2PL**
10	6	**Hysteria**	Def Leppard	Mercury	78	1	**11P**

• Paula Abdul, who had previously been best known for her award winning choreography on Janet Jackson's videos, was now a top album act in her own right. Her album **Forever Your Girl**, which sold over seven million copies, was the first debut album to include four Number 1 singles; 'Straight Up', 'Forever Your Girl', 'Cold Hearted' and 'Opposites Attract'.

• Debbie Gibson became the third teenager in less than a year to top the chart. She also became the first teenage girl to simultaneously top the singles and album chart. The act Debbie dethroned, fellow teenager Bobby Brown, was arrested for alleged lewdness on stage.

• Buddy Holly, Jimi Hendrix, Marvin Gaye and Roy Orbison's names were added to the Hollywood Rock Walk. A collection of previous Holly hits, **True Love Ways**, was in the UK Top 10, and Roy Orbison, was featured on America's Top 2 compact disks and had two entries in the Top 3 in the UK, Canada and Australia.

UK 1989 APR-JUNE

• Albums entering the UK chart at Number 1 were now a regular event. The latest ones to achieve this feat included ex-Frankie Goes To Hollywood front man Holly Johnson's debut, **Blast**, Queen's sixth chart topper **The Miracle** and Simply Red's (below) **A New Flame**. Other records instantly hitting the summit were Simple Minds' fourth successive Number 1 entry, **Street Fighting Years**, Deacon Blue's first chart topper, **When The World Knows Your Name** and Madonna's **Like A Prayer**. Incidentally, the title song for the latter album was Madonna's 18th Top 5 single in Britain – a record for a female vocalist.

•Producers Stock, Aitken & Waterman scored three successive Number 1 singles (Kylie Minogue, Jason Donovan and Ferry Aid). The trio had notched up over 80 UK chart records in less than five years, most of which they had also composed. They were also the first producers to have Number 1 hits by ten different artists!

April 1989

This Mnth	Last Mnth	Title	Artist	Label	Wks in 10	US Pos	
1	1	**A New Flame**	Simply Red	Elektra	26	22	**P**
2	2	**Anything For You**	Gloria Estefan & The Miami Sound Machine	Epic	17	6	**FP**
3	-	**Like A Prayer**	Madonna	Sire	12	1	**P**
4	-	**When The World Knows Your Name**	Deacon Blue	CBS	10		**F**
5	6	**Don't Be Cruel**	Bobby Brown	MCA	21	1	**FL**
6	7	**The Raw And The Cooked**	Fine Young Cannibals	London	17	1	**FPL**
7	-	**Appetite For Destruction**	Guns N' Roses	Geffen	15	1	**P**
8	-	**Club Classics Vol. One**	Soul II Soul	Virgin/10	17	14	**FP**
9	5	**Singular Adventures Of The Style Council**	Style Council	Polydor	5		**L**
10	-	**Original Soundtrack**	S'Express	Rhythm King	2		**FL**

May 1989

This Mnth	Last Mnth	Title	Artist	Label	Wks in 10	US Pos	
1	-	**Ten Good Reasons**	Jason Donovan	PWL	29		**FP**
2	-	**Street Fighting Years**	Simple Minds	Virgin	8	70	
3	6	**The Raw And The Cooked**	Fine Young Cannibals	London	17	1	**FPL**
4	-	**Blast**	Holly Johnson	MCA	4		**FL**
5	1	**A New Flame**	Simply Red	Elektra	26	22	
6	-	**Paradise**	Inner City	10	3		**FL**
7	4	**When The World Knows Your Name**	Deacon Blue	CBS	10		**F**
8	2	**Anything For You**	Gloria Estefan & The Miami Sound Machine	Epic	17	6	**FP**
9	-	**Everything**	Bangles	CBS	3	15	
10	-	**Pastpresent**	Clannad	RCA	9		**F**

June 1989

This Mnth	Last Mnth	Title	Artist	Label	Wks in 10	US Pos	
1	1	**Ten Good Reasons**	Jason Donovan	PWL	29		**FP**
2	-	**The Miracle**	Queen	Parlophone	9	24	
3	-	**Flowers In The Dirt**	Paul McCartney	Parlophone	3	21	
4	-	**Raw Like Sushi**	Neneh Cherry	Circa	9	40	**FL**
5	-	**Club Classics Vol. One**	Soul II Soul	Virgin/10	17	14	**FP**
6	-	**Don't Be Cruel**	Bobby Brown	MCA	21	1	**FL**
7	-	**The Other Side Of The Mirror**	Stevie Nicks	EMI	3	10	**FL**
8	7	**When The World Knows Your Name**	Deacon Blue	CBS	10		**F**
9	10	**Pastpresent**	Clannad	RCA	9		**F**
10	-	**Tin Machine**	Tin Machine	EMU USA	2	28	**FL**

US 1989 APR-JUNE

April 1989

This Mnth	Last Mnth	Title	Artist	Label	Wks in 10	UK Pos	
1	1	**Electric Youth**	Debbie Gibson	Atlantic	13	8	**2PL**
2	9	**Loc-Ed After Dark**	Tone Loc	Delicious	12	68	**F2PL**
3	2	**Don't Be Cruel**	Bobby Brown	MCA	45	3	**F6P**
4	-	**Like A Prayer**	Madonna	Sire	16	1	**3P**
5	7	**Mystery Girl**	Roy Orbison	Virgin	8	2	**FPL**
6	4	**Traveling Wilburys Volume 1**	Traveling Wilburys	Wilbury	22	16	**F3PL**
7	-	**The Raw & The Cooked**	Fine Young Cannibals	IRS/MCA	27	1	**F2PL**
8	5	**Forever Your Girl**	Paula Abdul	Virgin	64	5	**F7P**
9	3	**Appetite For Destruction**	Guns N' Roses	Geffen	52	5	**F10P**
10	-	**Hangin' Tough**	New Kids On The Block	Columbia	45	2	**F8P**

May 1989

This Mnth	Last Mnth	Title	Artist	Label	Wks in 10	UK Pos	
1	4	**Like A Prayer**	Madonna	Sire	16	1	**3P**
2	2	**Loc-Ed After Dark**	Tone Loc	Delicious	12	68	**F2PL**
3	-	**G N' R Lies**	Guns N' Roses	Geffen	18	32	**4P**
4	7	**The Raw & The Cooked**	Fine Young Cannibals	IRS/MCA	27	1	**F2PL**
5	3	**Don't Be Cruel**	Bobby Brown	MCA	45	3	**F6P**
6	-	**Beaches (Soundtrack)**	Bette Midler	Atlantic	11		**3P**
7	10	**Hangin' Tough**	New Kids On The Block	Columbia	45	2	**F8P**
8	-	**Vivid**	Living Colour	Epic	8		**F2PL**
9	8	**Forever Your Girl**	Paula Abdul	Virgin	64	5	**F7P**
10	1	**Electric Youth**	Debbie Gibson	Atlantic	13	8	**2PL**

June 1989

This Mnth	Last Mnth	Title	Artist	Label	Wks in 10	UK Pos	
1	4	**The Raw & The Cooked**	Fine Young Cannibals	IRS/MCA	27	1	**F2PL**
2	6	**Beaches (Soundtrack)**	Bette Midler	Atlantic	11		**3P**
3	1	**Like A Prayer**	Madonna	Sire	16	1	**3P**
4	5	**Don't Be Cruel**	Bobby Brown	MCA	45	3	**F6P**
5	9	**Forever Your Girl**	Paula Abdul	Virgin	64	5	**F7P**
6	-	**Full Moon Fever**	Tom Petty	MCA	35	8	**2P**
7	3	**G N' R Lies**	Guns N' Roses	Geffen	18	32	**4P**
8	7	**Hangin' Tough**	New Kids On The Block	Columbia	45	2	**F8P**
9	-	**Big Daddy**	John Cougar Mellencamp	Mercury	4	25	**P**
10	-	**Sonic Temple**	Cult	Sire/Reprise	4	3	**FPL**

• In the tenth year since it first charted, rap was becoming a major force on the album chart. Tone Loc's **Loc-ed After Dark** became the first album by a black rap act to top the pop charts, and N.W.A., MC Hammer and Kool Moe Dee debuted in the Top 40 with **Straight Outta Compton**, **Let's Get It Started** and **Knowledge Is King** respectively. For the first time, over half the Top 10 R&B albums were by rap artists and *Billboard* introduced its first all-rap chart. However, rap was still picking up a lot of bad press: N.W.A. and Too Short were charged with disorderly conduct and using bad language on stage, N.W.A. were banned by MTV for being too "pro-gang" and Public Enemy's Professor Griff was accused of making anti-Semitic remarks. In Britain, UK rapper Merlin (of 'Who's In The House' fame) was found guilty of housebreaking and American rapper Cash Money was deported.

• Vinyl was vanishing; for the first time singles that were not available on vinyl were making the US chart, and it was reported that only 30% of albums sold in the UK were on vinyl.

UK 1989 JULY-SEPT

• The Beatles and The Rolling Stones were the first British acts inducted into the Rock And Roll Hall Of Fame. Other recent entrants were The Beach Boys, Dion, Bob Dylan, The Drifters, Otis Redding, The Supremes, The Temptations and Stevie Wonder.

• The Who appeared in a benefit performance of *Tommy* in Los Angeles which also starred Phil Collins, Steve Winwood, Patti LaBelle and Billy Idol. Other noteworthy live shows included the Moscow Peace Festival headlined by Bon Jovi, Ozzy Osbourne, Motley Crue, The Scorpions and Skid Row, and the Reading Festival with bill toppers New Order, The Pogues, The Mission, Billy Bragg and New Model Army.

• U2, as shareholders of Island Records, made an estimated $48 (£30) million when Phonogram bought the British label for $480 (£300) million. Herb Alpert was also a little richer when his label A&M was sold to Phonogram for $460 million.

• In 1989, British acts had their least successful year on the US charts since 1980. There were also more European records than ever selling in the UK, with Italian records at times holding the Top 3 places on the British dance music chart. The brightest hope among the new UK bands appeared to be Manchester's Stone Roses who were packing the crowds in on tour.

July 1989

This Mnth	Last Mnth	Title	Artist	Label	Wks in 10	US Pos	
1	5	**Club Classics Vol. One**	Soul II Soul	Virgin/10	17	14	**FP**
2	6	**Don't Be Cruel**	Bobby Brown	MCA	21	1	**FL**
3	-	**Batman (Soundtrack)**	Prince	Warner	11	1	
4	1	**Ten Good Reasons**	Jason Donovan	PWL	29		**FP**
5	-	**Velveteen**	Transvision Vamp	MCA	8		**L**
6	-	**A New Flame**	Simply Red	Elektra	26	22	**P**
7	-	**Appetite For Destruction**	Guns N' Roses	Geffen	15	1	**P**
8	9	**Pastpresent**	Clannad	RCA	9		**F**
9	4	**Raw Like Sushi**	Neneh Cherry	Circa	9	40	**FL**
10	-	**The Twelve Commandments Of Dance**	London Boys	WEA	7		**FL**

August 1989

This Mnth	Last Mnth	Title	Artist	Label	Wks in 10	US Pos	
1	-	**Cuts Both Ways**	Gloria Estefan	Epic	13	8	**P**
2	6	**A New Flame**	Simply Red	Elektra	26	22	**P**
3	4	**Ten Good Reasons**	Jason Donovan	PWL	29		**FP**
4	10	**The Twelve Commandments Of Dance**	London Boys	WEA	7		**FL**
5	2	**Don't Be Cruel**	Bobby Brown	MCA	21	1	**FL**
6	5	**Velveteen**	Transvision Vamp	MCA	8		**L**
7	1	**Club Classics Vol. One**	Soul II Soul	Virgin/10	17	14	**FP**
8	-	**Trash**	Alice Cooper	Epic	4	20	
9	3	**Batman (Soundtrack)**	Prince	Warner	11	1	
10	-	**Big Bang**	Fuzzbox	WEA	1		**FL**

September 1989

This Mnth	Last Mnth	Title	Artist	Label	Wks in 10	US Pos	
1	1	**Cuts Both Ways**	Gloria Estefan	Epic	13	8	**P**
2	3	**Ten Good Reasons**	Jason Donovan	PWL	29		**FP**
3	2	**A New Flame**	Simply Red	Elektra	26	22	**P**
4	-	**We Two Are One**	Eurythmics	RCA	5	34	
5	-	**Imagination**	Imagination	Stylus	4		**L**
6	8	**Trash**	Alice Cooper	Epic	4	20	
7	-	**Aspects Of Love**	Original Cast	Polydor	2		
8	-	**Steel Wheels**	Rolling Stones	CBS	2	3	
9	-	**Pump**	Aerosmith	Geffen	3	5	**F**
10	-	**Foreign Affair**	Tina Turner	Capitol	18	31	**P**

US 1989 JULY-SEPT

July 1989

This Mnth	Last Mnth	Title	Artist	Label	Wks in 10	UK Pos	
1	1	**The Raw & The Cooked**	Fine Young Cannibals	IRS/MCA	27	1	**F2PL**
2	4	**Don't Be Cruel**	Bobby Brown	MCA	45	3	**F6P**
3	6	**Full Moon Fever**	Tom Petty	MCA	35	8	**2P**
4	8	**Hangin' Tough**	New Kids On The Block	Columbia	45	2	**F8P**
5	-	**Batman (Soundtrack)**	Prince	Paisley Park	10	1	**2P**
6	-	**Girl You Know It's True**	Milli Vanilli	Arista	41		**F6PL**
7	3	**Like A Prayer**	Madonna	Sire	16	1	**3P**
8	2	**Beaches (Soundtrack)**	Bette Midler	Atlantic	11		**3P**
9	5	**Forever Your Girl**	Paula Abdul	Virgin	64	5	**F7P**
10	-	**Walking With A Panther**	LL Cool J	Def Jam	5	43	**P**

August 1989

This Mnth	Last Mnth	Title	Artist	Label	Wks in 10	UK Pos	
1	5	**Batman (Soundtrack)**	Prince	Paisley Park	10	1	**2P**
2	4	**Hangin' Tough**	New Kids On The Block	Columbia	45	2	**F8P**
3	-	**Repeat Offender**	Richard Marx	EMI	12	8	**3PL**
4	1	**The Raw & The Cooked**	Fine Young Cannibals	IRS/MCA	27	1	**F2PL**
5	3	**Full Moon Fever**	Tom Petty	MCA	35	8	**2P**
6	9	**Forever Your Girl**	Paula Abdul	Virgin	64	5	**F7P**
7	6	**Girl You Know It's True**	Milli Vanilli	Arista	41		**F6PL**
8	2	**Don't Be Cruel**	Bobby Brown	MCA	45	3	**F6P**
9	-	**Skid Row**	Skid Row	Atlantic	11	61	**F3P**
10	10	**Walking With A Panther**	L.L. Cool J	Def Jam	5	43	**P**

September 1989

This Mnth	Last Mnth	Title	Artist	Label	Wks in 10	UK Pos	
1	2	**Hangin' Tough**	New Kids On The Block	Columbia	45	2	**F8P**
2	7	**Girl You Know It's True**	Milli Vanilli	Arista	41		**F6PL**
3	3	**Repeat Offender**	Richard Marx	EMI	12	8	**3PL**
4	6	**Forever Your Girl**	Paula Abdul	Virgin	64	5	**F7P**
5	5	**Full Moon Fever**	Tom Petty	MCA	35	8	**2P**
6	9	**Skid Row**	Skid Row	Atlantic	11	61	**F3P**
7	1	**Batman (Soundtrack)**	Prince	Paisley Park	10	1	**2P**
8	4	**The Raw & The Cooked**	Fine Young Cannibals	IRS/MCA	27	1	**F2PL**
9	-	**Cuts Both Ways**	Gloria Estefan	Epic	4	1	**3P**
10	-	**The End Of The Innocence**	Don Henley	Geffen	5	17	**F3PL**

• Many long established rock acts were attracting large audiences on US tours. Among them were The Beach Boys, Chicago, the reformed Allman Brothers, Bob Dylan, Ringo Starr, on his first tour since the break up of The Beatles and The Who, the latter act earning $30 million from their tour.

• After over a year on the US album chart, New Kids On The Block, America's hottest new singles act, reached Number 1 with **Hangin' Tough**. It was the first album by a teen group to sell over two million copies.

• Among the noteworthy acts debuting in the US Top 20 were American rock bands Warrant with **Dirty Rotten Filthy Stinking Rich**, Great White with **Twice Shy** and Skid Row with **Skid Row**, and rap acts Heavy D & The Boys with **Big Tyme** and The D.O.C. with **No One Can Do It Better**. Also getting their first major hits were British bands, The Cult with **Sonic Temple**, The Cure with **Disintegration** and Fine Young Cannibals (above) with a self-titled set.

UK 1989 OCT-DEC

• It was a record breaking year for albums entering the UK chart in pole position. An amazing 27 of them first appeared at Number 1, with a staggering seven doing it in consecutive weeks between September and October.

• Producers Stock, Aitken & Waterman were responsible for 11 of the years Top 40 singles in the UK.

• Another array of top line talent played at Wembley in the run-up to Christmas. Included among them were US acts Aerosmith, Motley Crue, Alexander O'Neal, Stevie Nicks and Skid Row. There was also The Cult, top world music group The Gypsy Kings, Status Quo, Wet Wet Wet and The Who.

• The most successful transatlantic singles chart artist of the Eighties was Madonna. The most prolific hit maker of the era was also now arguably the most controversial. Her 1989 video for 'Like A Prayer' upset both Catholics and Muslims and lost her a multi-million dollar sponsorship deal with Pepsi.

• America's top 20 grossing shows of the year included 15 by the Rolling Stones and three by The Who. The latest veteran British performer to successfully launch an American tour was Paul McCartney. His first visit for 13 years also proved to be a stadium sell-out.

October 1989

This Mnth	Last Mnth	Title	Artist	Label	Wks in 10	US Pos	
1	10	**Foreign Affair**	Tina Turner	Capitol	18	31	P
2	1	**Cuts Both Ways**	Gloria Estefan	Epic	13	8	P
3	-	**The Seeds Of Love**	Tears For Fears	Fontana	4	8	
4	-	**Crossroads**	Tracy Chapman	Elektra	4	9	L
5	-	**Enjoy Yourself**	Kylie Minogue	PWL	16		P
6	4	**We Two Are One**	Eurythmics	RCA	5	34	
7	-	**Like A Prayer**	Madonna	Sire	12	1	P
8	-	**Wild!**	Erasure	Mute	3	57	
9	-	**The Sensual World**	Kate Bush	EMI	2	43	
10	-	**The Time**	Bros	CBS	1		L

November 1989

This Mnth	Last Mnth	Title	Artist	Label	Wks in 10	US Pos	
1	5	**Enjoy Yourself**	Kylie Minogue	PWL	16		P
2	-	**The Road To Hell**	Chris Rea	WEA	20	107	P
3	-	**Runaway Horses**	Belinda Carlisle	Virgin	6	37	
4	-	**Greatest Hits**	Billy Ocean	Jive	4	77	
5	8	**Wild!**	Erasure	Mute	3	57	
6	-	**Journeyman**	Eric Clapton	Duck	9	16	
7	-	**All Or Nothing/2 X 2**	Milli Vanilli	Cooltempo	4		FL
8	-	**Welcome To The Beautiful South**	Beautiful South	Go! Discs	2		F
9	-	**From A Spark To A Flame - The Very Best Of Chris De Burgh**	Chris De Burgh	A&M	8		
10	-	**Holding Back The River**	Wet Wet Wet	Precious	7		

December 1989

This Mnth	Last Mnth	Title	Artist	Label	Wks in 10	US Pos	
1	-	**...But Seriously**	Phil Collins	Atlantic	42	1	2P
2	-	**Jive Bunny - The Album**	Jive Bunny & The Mastermixers	Telstar	7	26	FL
3	1	**Enjoy Yourself**	Kylie Minogue	PWL	16		P
4	2	**The Road To Hell**	Chris Rea	WEA	20	107	P
5	-	**Affection**	Lisa Stansfield	Arista	16	9	F
6	-	**Foreign Affair**	Tina Turner	Capitol	18	31	P
7	-	**The Best Of Rod Stewart**	Rod Stewart	Warner	11		P
8	-	**Ten Good Reasons**	Jason Donovan	PWL	29		FP
9	9	**From A Spark To A Flame - The Very Best Of Chris De Burgh**	Chris De Burgh	A&M	8		
10	10	**Holding Back The River**	Wet Wet Wet	Precious	7		

US 1989 OCT-DEC

October 1989

This Mnth	Last Mnth	Title	Artist	Label	Wks in 10	UK Pos	
1	-	**Dr. Feelgood**	Motley Crue	Elektra	11	4	**4P**
2	2	**Girl You Know It's True**	Milli Vanilli	Arista	41		**F6PL**
3	4	**Forever Your Girl**	Paula Abdul	Virgin	64	5	**F7P**
4	-	**Steel Wheels**	Rolling Stones	Columbia	13	2	**2P**
5	-	**Rhythm Nation 1814**	Janet Jackson	A&M	35	4	**6P**
6	1	**Hangin' Tough**	New Kids On The Block	Columbia	45	2	**F8P**
7	-	**Pump**	Aerosmith	Geffen	30	3	**5P**
8	5	**Full Moon Fever**	Tom Petty	MCA	35	8	**2P**
9	6	**Skid Row**	Skid Row	Atlantic	11	61	**F3P**
10	3	**Repeat Offender**	Richard Marx	EMI	12	8	**3PL**

November 1989

This Mnth	Last Mnth	Title	Artist	Label	Wks in 10	UK Pos	
1	5	**Rhythm Nation 1814**	Janet Jackson	A&M	35	4	**6P**
2	2	**Girl You Know It's True**	Milli Vanilli	Arista	41		**F6PL**
3	4	**Steel Wheels**	Rolling Stones	Columbia	13	2	**2P**
4	3	**Forever Your Girl**	Paula Abdul	Virgin	64	5	**F7P**
5	7	**Pump**	Aerosmith	Geffen	30	3	**5P**
6	-	**Dr. Feelgood**	Motley Crue	Elektra	11	4	**4P**
7	6	**Hangin' Tough**	New Kids On The Block	Columbia	45	2	**F8P**
8	-	**Storm Front**	Billy Joel	Columbia	19	5	**4P**
9	-	**The Seeds Of Love**	Tears For Fears	Fontana	3	1	**PL**
10	-	**Crossroads**	Tracy Chapman	Elektra	4	1	**PL**

December 1989

This Mnth	Last Mnth	Title	Artist	Label	Wks in 10	UK Pos	
1	2	**Girl You Know It's True**	Milli Vanilli	Arista	41		**F6PL**
2	8	**Storm Front**	Billy Joel	Columbia	19	5	**4P**
3	1	**Rhythm Nation 1814**	Janet Jackson	A&M	35	4	**6P**
4	4	**Forever Your Girl**	Paula Abdul	Virgin	64	5	**F7P**
5	7	**Hangin' Tough**	New Kids On The Block	Columbia	45	2	**F8P**
6	-	**...But Seriously**	Phil Collins	Atlantic	20	1	**4PL**
7	-	**Cosmic Thing**	B-52's	Warner	22	8	**F2PL**
8	5	**Pump**	Aerosmith	Geffen	30	3	**5P**
9	3	**Steel Wheels**	Rolling Stones	Columbia	13	2	**2P**
10	-	**Merry Merry Christmas**	New Kids On The Block	Columbia	3		**2P**

• As the first non-vinyl albums cracked the chart, it was announced that in 1989 compact disk sales rose by 24% and vinyl figures were down 59%. Even though singles business decreased 35%, cassette single sales were up an amazing 240%, which pushed the total record and tape figure to $6.46 billion. In Britain, compact disks now outsold vinyl albums and cassette single sales were up an estimated 700%!

• The most successful decade yet for female artists ended with the women still on top. Between them, Janet Jackson and her ex-choreographer Paula Abdul, topped the album chart for most of the last quarter with **Rhythm Nation 1814**, which was crammed full of future Top 5 hits, and **Forever Your Girl** respectively. In Britain, seven of the Top 10 LPs in October featured female vocalists and of these Gloria Estefan, Eurythmics, Tina Turner, Tracy Chapman and Kylie Minogue hit the top spot. In fact, at times female vocalists held the Top 4 rungs on the British chart – an unprecedented event.

Kurt Cobain, Nirvana

the 1990s

Ace of Base

Roxette

Bryan Adams

TOP UK ACTS ON THE US CHARTS IN THE 1990s	
1	Eric Clapton
2	U2
3	Sinead O'Connor
4	Sting
5	Def Leppard
6	Rod Stewart
7	Pink Floyd
8	Depeche Mode
9	George Michael
10	Queen

In the early 1990's, the media noticed that many young people spent their money on computer games rather than compact disks, and they seemed convinced that this was the end of the road for rock. However, it was just a blip on the screen, and the sales of rock, pop, R&B and country continued to grow throughout the decade. British acts lost a lot of ground to their US counterparts in the 1990's; in fact, the mid-1990's was the worst period for UK acts on the American chart since the pre-Beatles era. However, there was no shortage of new American rock with acts like Nirvana,

TOP US ACTS ON THE UK CHARTS IN THE 1990s	
1	REM
2	Madonna
3	Michael Bolton
4	Mariah Carey
5	Cher
6	Meat Loaf
7	Tina Turner
8	Lionel Richie
9	Prince
10	Michael Jackson

the 1990s

Pearl Jam, Soundgarden, Alice In Chains and the Stone Temple Pilots each topping the US lists. New Country was another American success story.

On many occasions, several country albums were simultaneously in the pop Top 10, and the genre's top artist, Garth Brooks, sold over 50 million albums in the early years of the decade. Rap, which had initially been considered a passing fad, sold in unimagined quantities thanks to performers like Hammer, NWA, Ice Cube, Dr. Dre, Snoop Doggy Dogg and Arrested Development. In Britain, dance music, including its offshoots, rave, techno and ragga, which ruled the singles chart, sold in vast quantities on compilation albums. In America, where a Various Artists album usually meant a soundtrack album: *Forrest Gump*, *Sleepless in Seattle* and, the best selling album of the 1990's so far, *The Bodyguard*, all reached Number 1. There was also room on the transatlantic charts for such varied styles as New Age, World Music and Opera with Enya, Enigma, Yanni and The Three Tenors (Pavarotti, Domingo and Carreras) earning gold and platinum discs.

Many stars of the previous decade, survived and flourished. R.E.M., Madonna, Simply Red, Genesis, Janet and Michael Jackson, Metallica Guns N' Roses were among the many relative veterans who added to their impressive hit tallies. As ever, new teen idols were still in great demand: America's New Kids On The Block smashed records on both sides of the Atlantic and Britain's Take That accomplished some outstanding sales feats in their homeland. The early 1990's will also be remembered for such successful acts as Mariah Carey, Michael Bolton, Boyz II Men and Sweden's Ace Of Base.

On the format front, the compact disk finally wiped the floor with vinyl and resisted the challenge from Digital Compact Cassette and MiniDisk. However, technology is moving at such a pace that it is almost impossible to prophesy what the rest of the decade will bring. Already, interactive CD-ROMs, digital radio and CDVs are making their presence felt and soon recordable compact disks and quality music of your choice via telephone or cable will be available to everyone. Whatever happens, it will be an exciting time and one where albums still play an essential role.

TOP UK ALBUM ACTS OF THE 1990s

1. REM
2. Simply Red
3. Luciano Pavarotti
4. Madonna
5. Michael Bolton
6. Mariah Carey
7. Cher
8. Elton John
9. Genesis
10. Wet Wet Wet
11. Queen
12. Meatloaf
13. Eurythmics
14. Deacon Blue
15. Placido Domingo
16. Jose Carreras
17. Tina Turner
18. Phil Collins
19. Seal
20. Take That

TOP US ALBUM ACTS OF THE 1990s

1. Garth Brooks
2. Mariah Carey
3. Hammer
4. Michael Bolton
5. Billy Ray Cyrus
6. Eric Clapton
7. Pearl Jam
8. Wilson Philips
9. Kenny G
10. Nirvana
11. Boyz II Men
12. Ace Of Base
13. Vanilla Ice
14. Janet Jackson
15. REM
16. Bonnie Raitt
17. Stone Temple Pilots
18. Madonna
19. Kriss Kross
20. C&C Music Factory

Seal

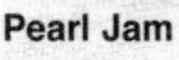

Pearl Jam

TOP BRITISH ALBUMS OF THE 1990s

1	**Stars**	Simply Red
2	**Automatic For The People**	REM
3	**Music Box**	Mariah Carey
4	**Bat Out Of Hell 2**	Meatloaf
5	**Out Of Time**	REM
6	**The Immaculate Collection**	Madonna
7	**Greatest Hits**	Eurythmics
8	**In Concert**	Luciano Pavarotti & Placido Domingo
9	**Back To Front**	Lionel Richie
10	**The Very Best Of Elton John**	Elton John
11	**So Close**	Dina Carroll
12	**End Of Part One (Their Greatest Hits)**	Wet Wet Wet
13	**Diva**	Annie Lennox
14	**Queen's Greatest Hits**	Queen
15	**Dangerous**	Michael Jackson
16	**One Woman - The Ultimate Collection**	Diana Ross
17	**Simply The Best**	Tina Turner
18	**We Can't Dance**	Genesis
19	**Seal**	Seal
20	**Love Hurts**	Cher

TOP AMERICAN ALBUMS OF THE 1990s

1	**Please Hammer, Don't Hurt 'em**	Hammer
2	**Mariah Carey**	Mariah Carey
3	**Ropin' The Wind**	Garth Brooks
4	**Some Gave All**	Billy Ray Cyrus
5	**The Bodyguard**	Soundtrack
6	**Wilson Philips**	Wilson Philips
7	**Unplugged**	Eric Clapton
8	**Music Box**	Mariah Carey
9	**The Sign**	Ace Of Base
10	**Breathless**	Kenny G
11	**To The Extreme**	Vanilla Ice
12	**Janet**	Janet Jackson
13	**Totally Krossed Out**	Kriss Kross
14	**Gonna Make You Sweat**	C&C Music Factory
15	**Never Mind**	Nirvana
16	**Ten**	Pearl Jam
17	**The Lion King**	Soundtrack
18	**Time, Love & Tenderness**	Michael Bolton
19	**Unforgettable**	Natalie Cole
20	**No Fences**	Garth Brooks

Wilson Philips

Take That

Vanilla Ice

UK 1990 JAN-MAR

• Phil Collins, who at times was the only male on the UK Top 10 singles chart, headed the album list with **...But Seriously**. It sold over a million in the UK in a record five weeks, and held off competition at Number 1 for 15 weeks – the longest stay at the summit by a solo act for 30 years. It was the world's top seller in 1990 and sold over 13 million copies. **...But Seriously** stopped Eric Clapton, Lisa Stansfield, The Quireboys, Technotronic and New Kids On The Block from getting their first chart toppers.

• BRIT winners included Phil Collins (Best Male) Annie Lennox (Best Female), Lisa Stansfield (Best Newcomer), Neneh Cherry (Best International Solo Artist and Newcomer) and U2 (Best International Group). Fine Young Cannibals, the winners of Best British Group and Best Album award, returned their trophies in protest over Prime Minister Margaret Thatcher's appearance on the awards show.

• The hottest teen attraction on both sides of the Atlantic were New Kids On The Block. Their **Hangin' Tough** became the first music video to sell over a million copies and its title song was a transatlantic Number 1. They scored more Top 10 hits in the UK and US in 1990 than any previous American group.

January 1990

This Mnth	Last Mnth	Title	Artist	Label	Wks in 10	US Pos	
1	1	**...But Seriously**	Phil Collins	Virgin	42	1	**2P**
2	3	**Enjoy Yourself**	Kylie Minogue	PWL	16		**P**
3	6	**Foreign Affair**	Tina Turner	Capitol	18	31	**P**
4	-	**Hangin' Tough**	New Kids On The Block	CBS	9	1	**F**
5	2	**Jive Bunny - The Album**	Jive Bunny & The Mastermixers	Telstar	7	26	**FL**
6	5	**Affection**	Lisa Stansfield	Arista	16	9	**F**
7	8	**Ten Good Reasons**	Jason Donovan	PWL	29		**FP**
8	4	**The Road To Hell**	Chris Rea	WEA	20	107	**P**
9	-	**Colour**	Christians	Island	3		**L**
10	-	**Reading Writing & Arithmetic**	Sundays	Rough Trade	1	39	**FL**

February 1990

This Mnth	Last Mnth	Title	Artist	Label	Wks in 10	US Pos	
1	1	**...But Seriously**	Phil Collins	Virgin	42	1	**2P**
2	-	**Journeyman**	Eric Clapton	Duck	9	16	
3	6	**Affection**	Lisa Stansfield	Arista	16	9	**F**
4	-	**The Very Best Of Cat Stevens**	Cat Stevens	A&M	4		**L**
5	-	**Pump Up The Jam**	Technotronic	Swanyard	6	10	**F**
6	9	**Colour**	Christians	Island	3		**L**
7	-	**The Sweetkeeper**	Tanita Tikaram	East West	2	124	**L**
8	4	**Hangin' Tough**	New Kids On The Block	CBS	9	1	**F**
9	8	**The Road To Hell**	Chris Rea	WEA	20	107	**P**
10	-	**A Bit Of What You Fancy**	Quireboys	Parlophone	1		**FL**

March 1990

This Mnth	Last Mnth	Title	Artist	Label	Wks in 10	US Pos	
1	1	**...But Seriously**	Phil Collins	Virgin	42	1	**2P**
2	9	**The Road To Hell**	Chris Rea	WEA	20	107	**P**
3	-	**Vivaldi Four Seasons**	Nigel Kennedy with the English Chamber Orchestra	EMI	10		**FL**
4	-	**Changesbowie**	David Bowie	EMI	6	39	
5	5	**Pump Up The Jam**	Technotronic	Swanyard	6	10	**F**
6	-	**I Do Not Want What I Haven't Got**	Sinead O'Connor	Ensign	4	1	**F**
7	3	**Affection**	Lisa Stansfield	Arista	16	9	**F**
8	-	**Missing...Presumed Having A Good Time**	Notting Hillbillies	Vertigo	2	52	**FL**
9	-	**Foreign Affair**	Tina Turner	Capitol	18	31	**P**
10	-	**The Best Of Rod Stewart**	Rod Stewart	Warner	11		**P**

US 1990

JAN-MAR

January 1990

This Mnth	Last Mnth	Title	Artist	Label	Wks in 10	UK Pos	
1	6	...But Seriously	Phil Collins	Atlantic	20	1	4PL
2	1	Girl You Know It's True	Milli Vanilli	Arista	41		F6PL
3	2	Storm Front	Billy Joel	Columbia	19	5	4P
4	4	Forever Your Girl	Paula Abdul	Virgin	64	5	F7P
5	3	Rhythm Nation 1814	Janet Jackson	A&M	35	4	6P
6	8	Pump	Aerosmith	Geffen	30	3	5P
7	5	Hangin' Tough	New Kids On The Block	Columbia	45	2	F8P
8	7	Cosmic Thing	B-52's	Warner	22	8	F2PL
9	-	Full Moon Fever	Tom Petty	MCA	35	8	2P
10	-	Cry Like A Rainstorm, Howl Like The Wind	Linda Ronstadt	Elektra	6	43	2PL

February 1990

This Mnth	Last Mnth	Title	Artist	Label	Wks in 10	UK Pos	
1	4	Forever Your Girl	Paula Abdul	Virgin	64	5	F7P
2	2	Girl You Know It's True	Milli Vanilli	Arista	41		F6PL
3	5	Rhythm Nation 1814	Janet Jackson	A&M	35	4	6P
4	1	...But Seriously	Phil Collins	Atlantic	20	1	4PL
5	8	Cosmic Thing	B-52's	Warner	22	8	F2PL
6	3	Storm Front	Billy Joel	Columbia	19	5	4P
7	6	Pump	Aerosmith	Geffen	30	3	5P
8	9	Full Moon Fever	Tom Petty	MCA	35	8	2P
9	-	Dance!...Ya Know It	Bobby Brown	MCA	5	26	P
10	-	Back On The Block	Quincy Jones	Qwest	3	26	PL

March 1990

This Mnth	Last Mnth	Title	Artist	Label	Wks in 10	UK Pos	
1	1	Forever Your Girl	Paula Abdul	Virgin	64	5	F7P
2	3	Rhythm Nation 1814	Janet Jackson	A&M	35	4	6P
3	4	...But Seriously	Phil Collins	Atlantic	20	1	4PL
4	5	Cosmic Thing	B-52's	Warner	22	8	F2PL
5	2	Girl You Know It's True	Milli Vanilli	Arista	41		F6PL
6	-	Soul Provider	Michael Bolton	Columbia	21	4	F6P
7	6	Storm Front	Billy Joel	Columbia	19	5	4P
8	-	Nick Of Time	Bonnie Raitt	Capitol	11	51	F4P
9	-	Alannah Myles	Alannah Myles	Atlantic	8	3	FPL
10	-	Cry Like A Rainstorm, Howl Like The Wind	Linda Ronstadt	Elektra	6	43	2PL

• Among the interesting Grammy winners were Bonnie Raitt, Soul II Soul and Milli Vanilli (above). Raitt's **Nick Of Time**, which had dropped out of the Top 100, grabbed a handful of awards and shot to the top exactly one year after it had first entered. Soul II Soul were the first black British act to grab any Grammy award. The London band also picked up trophies from the American Music Awards and from *Rolling Stone* and TV's *Soul Train*. German-based Milli Vanilli were named Best Newcomers; an award the duo had to return later in the year when it came to light that they had neither sung on their six million selling album nor on their five US Top 5 singles.

• The first album by a female artist to spend 50 weeks in the US Top 10 was Paula Abdul's **Forever Your Girl**. The album, which also spent longer in the Top 10 than any other debut album, returned to Number 1 in its 81st chart week – another record for Abdul.

UK 1990 APR-JUNE

• A show celebrating Nelson Mandela's release from prison was held at Wembley stadium. The headliners included Tracy Chapman, Peter Gabriel, Patti LaBelle, Simple Minds and Neil Young. There was also a star-studded tribute show to John Lennon held in Liverpool. Among the acts performing were Natalie Cole, Terence Trent D'Arby, Roberta Flack, Hall & Oates, Cyndi Lauper, Kylie Minogue, Wet Wet Wet and Lennon's wife Yoko Ono.

• As a record number of European acts reached the UK singles chart, Luciano Pavarotti became the first Italian to top the LP charts. Pavarotti was joined in the top 10 by another classical artist, violinist Nigel Kennedy, with Vivaldi's **Four Seasons**.

• Paul McCartney broke the record for the largest paying audience when 184,000 Brazilians saw him at the Maracana Stadium. Another record breaking act were Iron Maiden who had ten double 12" singles reach the UK album Top 20 in consecutive weeks.

April 1990

This Mnth	Last Mnth	Title	Artist	Label	Wks in 10	US Pos	
1	-	**Only Yesterday**	Carpenters	A&M	13		PL
2	4	**Changesbowie**	David Bowie	EMI	6	39	
3	1	**...But Seriously**	Phil Collins	Virgin	42	1	2P
4	-	**Behind The Mask**	Fleetwood Mac	Warner	6	18	L
5	-	**Brigade**	Heart	Capitol	4	3	L
6	-	**The Best Of Van Morrison**	Van Morrison	Polydor	3	41	F
7	6	**I Do Not Want What I Haven't Got**	Sinead O'Connor	Ensign	4	1	F
8	3	**Vivaldi Four Seasons**	Nigel Kennedy with the English Chamber Orchestra	EMI	10		FL
9	-	**Labour Of Love II**	UB40	DEP International	12	30	
10	-	**Alannah Myles**	Alannah Myles	Atlantic	5	5	FL

May 1990

This Mnth	Last Mnth	Title	Artist	Label	Wks in 10	US Pos	
1	1	**Only Yesterday**	Carpenters	A&M	13		PL
2	3	**...But Seriously**	Phil Collins	Virgin	42	1	2P
3	9	**Labour Of Love II**	UB40	DEP International	12	30	
4	10	**Alannah Myles**	Alannah Myles	Atlantic	5	5	FL
5	-	**Forever Your Girl**	Paula Abdul	Siren	6	1	F
6	8	**Vivaldi Four Seasons**	Nigel Kennedy with the English Chamber Orchestra	EMI	10		FL
7	4	**Behind The Mask**	Fleetwood Mac	Warner	6	18	L
8	-	**Life**	Inspiral Carpets	Cow	3		F
9	-	**Through A Big Country - Greatest Hits**	Big Country	Mercury	5		L
10	-	**A Pocketful Of Dreams**	Big Fun	Jive	2		FL

June 1990

This Mnth	Last Mnth	Title	Artist	Label	Wks in 10	US Pos	
1	-	**Vol II (A New Decade)**	Soul II Soul	10	7	21	
2	-	**Between The Lines**	Jason Donovan	PWL	7		
3	2	**...But Seriously**	Phil Collins	Virgin	42	1	2P
4	-	**The Essential Pavarotti**	Luciano Pavarotti	Decca	14		FP
5	-	**I'm Breathless**	Madonna	Sire	8	2	
6	-	**Natural History - The Very Best Of...**	Talk Talk	Parlophone	5		L
7	9	**Through A Big Country - Greatest Hits**	Big Country	Mercury	5		L
8	1	**Only Yesterday**	Carpenters	A&M	13		PL
9	-	**Summer Dreams**	Beach Boys	Capitol	10		L
10	-	**Greatest Hits**	Bangles	CBS	8	97	L

US 1990 APR-JUNE

April 1990

This Mnth	Last Mnth	Title	Artist	Label	Wks in 10	UK Pos	
1	8	**Nick Of Time**	Bonnie Raitt	Capitol	11	51	**F4P**
2	2	**Rhythm 1814**	Janet Jackson	A&M	35	4	**6P**
3	1	**Forever Your Girl**	Paula Abdul	Virgin	64	5	**F7P**
4	6	**Soul Provider**	Michael Bolton	Columbia	21	4	**F6P**
5	-	**I Do Not Want What I Haven't Got**	Sinead O'Connor	Ensign	16	1	**F2PL**
6	9	**Alannah Myles**	Alannah Myles	Atlantic	8	3	**FPL**
7	3	**...But Seriously**	Phil Collins	Atlantic	20	1	**4PL**
8	-	**Pump**	Aerosmith	Geffen	30	3	**5P**
9	-	**Please Hammer Don't Hurt 'Em**	MC Hammer	Capitol	52	8	**F10P**
10	4	**Cosmic Thing**	B-52's	Warner	22	8	**F2PL**

May 1990

This Mnth	Last Mnth	Title	Artist	Label	Wks in 10	UK Pos	
1	5	**I Do Not Want What I Haven't Got**	Sinead O'Connor	Ensign	16	1	**F2PL**
2	9	**Please Hammer Don't Hurt 'Em**	MC Hammer	Capitol	52	8	**F10P**
3	2	**Rhythm Nation 1814**	Janet Jackson	A&M	35	4	**6P**
4	4	**Soul Provider**	Michael Bolton	Columbia	21	4	**F6P**
5	-	**Brigade**	Heart	Capitol	11	3	**2PL**
6	1	**Nick Of Time**	Bonnie Raitt	Capitol	11	51	**F4P**
7	3	**Forever Your Girl**	Paula Abdul	Virgin	64	5	**F7P**
8	-	**Violator**	Depeche Mode	Sire	15	2	**F2P**
9	-	**Pretty Woman**	Soundtrack	EMI	17		**3P**
10	-	**Poison**	Bell Biv Devoe	MCA	27	35	**F2PL**

June 1990

This Mnth	Last Mnth	Title	Artist	Label	Wks in 10	UK Pos	
1	2	**Please Hammer Don't Hurt 'Em**	MC Hammer	Capitol	52	8	**F10P**
2	1	**I Do Not Want What I Haven't Got**	Sinead O'Connor	Ensign	16	1	**F2PL**
3	-	**Pretty Woman**	Soundtrack	EMI	17		**3P**
4	5	**Brigade**	Heart	Capitol	11	3	**2PL**
5	10	**Poison**	Bell Biv Devoe	MCA	27	35	**F2PL**
6	-	**I'm Breathless**	Madonna	Sire	11	2	**2P**
7	8	**Violator**	Depeche Mode	Sire	15	2	**F2P**
8	4	**Soul Provider**	Michael Bolton	Columbia	21	4	**F6P**
9	-	**Shut Up And Dance**	Paula Abdul	Virgin	4	40	**P**
10	-	**Step By Step**	New Kids On The Block	Columbia	12	1	**3PL**

• A record four female artists held the top four rungs on the US album chart: Bonnie Raitt, Sinead O'Connor, Paula Abdul and Janet Jackson. The first three were enjoying their debut hits. It was a similar situation on the singles chart where newcomers O'Connor, Jane Child and Lisa Stansfield took the Top 3 spots. O'Connor's album, **I Do Not Want What I Haven't Got**, which entered the UK chart at Number 1, had sold five million copies by the end of the quarter. O'Connor, the first Irish woman to reach Number 1 in the USA, simultaneously headed the single and LP chart on both sides of the Atlantic.

• There had been a 17-and-a-half year gap between Bonnie Raitt's US album chart debut and her first Number 1. In Britain, The Carpenters hit the top again after a gap of almost 15 years.

• Three quarters of a million fans watched an Earth Day concert in Central Park whose stars included Hall & Oates, Edie Brickell, The B-52's and Ben E. King

• The ever controversial rap act Public Enemy had their first transatlantic Top 10 entry with **Fear Of A Black Planet**; the album shipped over a million in its first week in the USA.

UK 1990 JULY-SEPT

• As Elvis Presley scored a record 94th chart album, Cliff Richard equaled Presley's record 55 Top 10 single hits and producers Stock Aitken & Waterman clocked up their 100th Top 75 single.

• An estimated one billion TV viewers saw The Wall show, organized by ex-Pink Floyd member Roger Walters. Appearing in front of 200,000 fans in Berlin were such acts as Bryan Adams, The Band, Cyndi Lauper, Joni Mitchell, Van Morrison, Sinead O'Connor and The Scorpions.

• Paul McCartney ended his 45-week, 102-show world tour in the USA, his last gig being in front of 53,000 fans at Chicago's Soldier Field. Other British acts on tour in the USA included Bad Company, ex-Iron Maiden vocalist Bruce Dickinson, Erasure, Billy Idol, The Moody Blues, Robert Plant and Soul II Soul.

• **Sleeping With The Past** gave Elton John his first Number 1 hit in his homeland for 16 years.

• Whitesnake, Aerosmith, Poison and Thunder appeared in the Monsters Of Rock festival at Castle Donington and Top 10 album acts The Inspiral Carpets and The Pixies were among the headliners at the Reading Festival. Britain's Wet Wet Wet, Lisa Stansfield and Yazz appeared alongside American acts Lenny Kravitz and Adeva at the Prince's Trust show at Wembley.

July 1990

This Mnth	Last Mnth	Title	Artist	Label	Wks in 10	US Pos	
1	4	**The Essential Pavarotti**	Luciano Pavarotti	Decca	14		**FP**
2	-	**Sleeping With The Past**	Elton John	Rocket	17	23	
3	9	**Summer Dreams**	Beach Boys	Capitol	10		**L**
4	-	**Hot Rocks 1964-1971**	Rolling Stones	London	7	4	
5	-	**Step By Step**	New Kids On The Block	CBS	12	1	
6	-	**Flesh And Blood**	Poison	Enigma	3	2	**FL**
7	10	**Greatest Hits**	Bangles	CBS	8	97	**L**
8	3	**...But Seriously**	Phil Collins	Virgin	42	1	**2P**
9	1	**Vol II (A New Decade)**	Soul II Soul	10	7	21	
10	5	**I'm Breathless**	Madonna	Sire	8	2	

August 1990

This Mnth	Last Mnth	Title	Artist	Label	Wks in 10	US Pos	
1	2	**Sleeping With The Past**	Elton John	Rocket	17	23	
2	1	**The Essential Pavarotti**	Luciano Pavarotti	Decca	14		**FP**
3	10	**I'm Breathless**	Madonna	Sire	8	2	
4	8	**...But Seriously**	Phil Collins	Virgin	42	1	**2P**
5	3	**Summer Dreams**	Beach Boys	Capitol	10		**L**
6	5	**Step By Step**	New Kids On The Block	CBS	12	1	
7	4	**Hot Rocks 1964-1971**	Rolling Stones	London	7	4	
8	-	**Blaze Of Glory/Young Guns II (Soundtrack)**	Jon Bon Jovi	Mercury	4	3	**FL**
9	-	**Bossanova**	Pixies	4AD	2	70	
10	-	**Lovegod**	Soup Dragons	Raw	2	88	**FL**

September 1990

This Mnth	Last Mnth	Title	Artist	Label	Wks in 10	US Pos	
1	-	**In Concert**	Luciano Pavarotti, Placido Domingo & Jose Carreras	Decca	22	43	**P**
2	1	**Sleeping With The Past**	Elton John	Rocket	17	23	
3	-	**Listen Without Prejudice Vol. 1**	George Michael	CBS	19	2	**PL**
4	-	**Soul Provider**	Michael Bolton	CBS	23	3	**FP**
5	-	**Graffiti Bridge**	Prince	Paisley Park	2	6	
6	-	**Look Sharp!**	Roxette	EMI	5	23	**F**
7	-	**Ooh La Vegas**	Deacon Blue	CBS	4		
8	8	**Blaze Of Glory/Young Guns II (Soundtrack)**	Jon Bon Jovi	Mercury	4	3	**FL**
9	-	**Boomania**	Betty Boo	Rhythm King	4		**FL**
10	6	**Step By Step**	New Kids On The Block	CBS	12	1	

US 1990

JULY-SEPT

July 1990

This Mnth	Last Mnth	Title	Artist	Label	Wks in 10	UK Pos	
1	1	**Please Hammer Don't Hurt 'Em**	MC Hammer	Capitol	52	8	**F10P**
2	9	**Step By Step**	New Kids On The Block	Columbia	12	1	**3PL**
3	5	**I'm Breathless**	Madonna	Sire	11	2	**2P**
4	10	**Wilson Phillips**	Wilson Phillips	SBK	52	7	**F5P**
5	1	**Pretty Woman**	Soundtrack	EMI	17		**3P**
6	4	**Poison**	Bell Biv Devoe	MCA	27	35	**F2PL**
7	2	**I Do Not Want What I Haven't Got**	Sinead O'Connor	Ensign	16	1	**F2PL**
8	-	**Violator**	Depeche Mode	Sire	15	2	**F2P**
9	-	**I'll Give All My Love To You**	Keith Sweat	Vintertainment	10	47	
10	-	**Johnny Gill**	Johnny Gill	Motown	4		**F2PL**

August 1990

This Mnth	Last Mnth	Title	Artist	Label	Wks in 10	UK Pos	
1	1	**Please Hammer Don't Hurt 'Em**	MC Hammer	Capitol	52	8	**F10P**
2	4	**Wilson Phillips**	Wilson Phillips	SBK	52	7	**F5P**
3	2	**Step By Step**	New Kids On The Block	Columbia	12	1	**3PL**
4	-	**Flesh And Blood**	Poison	Enigma	10	3	**3PL**
5	-	**Mariah Carey**	Mariah Carey	Columbia	49	6	**F8P**
6	3	**I'm Breathless**	Madonna	Sire	11	2	**2P**
7	9	**I'll Give All My Love To You**	Keith Sweat	Vintertainment	10	47	**F2P**
8	-	**Compositions**	Anita Baker	Elektra	9	7	
9	5	**Pretty Woman**	Soundtrack	EMI	17		**3P**
10	6	**Poison**	Bell Biv Devoe	MCA	27	35	**F2PL**

September 1990

This Mnth	Last Mnth	Title	Artist	Label	Wks in 10	UK Pos	
1	1	**Please Hammer Don't Hurt 'Em**	MC Hammer	Capitol	52	8	**F10P**
2	2	**Wilson Phillips**	Wilson Phillips	SBK	52	7	**F5P**
3	5	**Mariah Carey**	Mariah Carey	Columbia	49	6	**F8P**
4	-	**Blaze Of Glory/Young Guns II (Soundtrack)**	Jon Bon Jovi	Mercury	7	2	**F2PL**
5	4	**Flesh And Blood**	Poison	Enigma	10	3	**3PL**
6	10	**Poison**	Bell Biv Devoe	MCA	27	35	**F2PL**
7	8	**Compositions**	Anita Baker	Elektra	9	7	
8	-	**Graffiti Bridge**	Prince	Paisley Park	4	1	
9	7	**I'll Give All My Love To You**	Keith Sweat	Vintertainment	10	47	**F2P**
10	3	**Step By Step**	New Kids On The Block	Columbia	12	1	**3PL**

• New Kids On The Block, who went on to earn an unbelievable $115 million in 1990, had three of the Top 4 US music videos. They signed a $10 million sponsorship deal with McDonalds and joined the elite few who had grossed $1 million for one show. In July, Maurice Starr, the group's producer/manager, simultaneously had four of his discoveries in the singles Top 10; the others being Bell Biv Devoe, Johnny Gill and Bobby Brown.

• Noted guitarist Stevie Ray Vaughan was killed in a helicopter crash. Two other up-and-coming stars also died; rapper MC Trouble succumbed to fatal epileptic fit and Andrew Wood, leader of the critically acclaimed band Mother Love Bone, who evolved into Pearl Jam, reportedly overdosed on heroin.

• Controversial rap act 2 Live Crew's single 'Banned In The USA' amassed record (for the Atlantic label) advance orders of 500,000, and riots broke out during fellow rappers Public Enemy's performance in California.

UK 1990 OCT-DEC

• In December, for the first time, the UK Top 3 albums were double albums; **The Immaculate Collection** by Madonna, **The Very Best Of Elton John** and **Serious Hits...Live!** by Phil Collins.

• American headliners at Wembley included George Benson, Cher, Earth, Wind & Fire, Gloria Estefan and Janet Jackson. Among the other bill toppers were The Christians, INXS, The Pogues and The Sisters Of Mercy

• Two British acts which had been clocking up hits since the late Fifties were back in the album Top 10; Cliff Richard and The Shadows. Cliff clicked with **From A Distance...The Event** and his old backing group scored with **Reflection**.

• Seventies superstars Led Zeppelin, whose total album sales were said to be 39 million, returned to the Top 10 with **Remasters**, a 26 track set of their recordings digitally remastered by member Jimmy Page. In America, this UK group reached the Top 20 with a self-titled, 54 track $54 box set. Also climbing the US charts was a double album called **The Complete Recordings**, which contained all the recordings by blues legend Robert Johnson – whose work had influenced Led Zeppelin and many other early British blues-based bands. Although the tracks it contained were over fifty years old the album turned gold.

October 1990

This Mnth	Last Mnth	Title	Artist	Label	Wks in 10	US Pos	
1	1	**In Concert**	Luciano Pavarotti, Placido Domingo & Jose Carreras	Decca	22	43	P
2	3	**Listen Without Prejudice Vol. 1**	George Michael	CBS	19	2	L
3	-	**X**	INXS	Mercury	3	5	
4	4	**Soul Provider**	Michael Bolton	CBS	23	3	FP
5	-	**Rocking All Over The Years**	Status Quo	Vertigo	9		
6	-	**Some Friendly**	Charlatans	Situation Two	2	73	F
7	-	**Reflection**	Shadows	Polydor	5		L
8	-	**No Prayer For The Dying**	Iron Maiden	EMI	2	17	
9	-	**The Rhythm Of The Saints**	Paul Simon	Warner	10	4	L
10	2	**Sleeping With The Past**	Elton John	Rocket	17	23	

November 1990

This Mnth	Last Mnth	Title	Artist	Label	Wks in 10	US Pos	
1	9	**The Rhythm Of The Saints**	Paul Simon	Warner	10	4	L
2	-	**The Very Best Of Elton John**	Elton John	Rocket	20		2P
3	5	**Rocking All Over The Years**	Status Quo	Vertigo	9		
4	1	**In Concert**	Luciano Pavarotti, Placido Domingo & Jose Carreras	Decca	22	43	P
5	-	**Choke**	Beautiful South	Go! Discs	3		
6	-	**Serious Hits...Live!**	Phil Collins	Virgin	12	12	P
7	-	**Behaviour**	Pet Shop Boys	EMI	2	45	
8	-	**The Immaculate Collection**	Madonna	Sire	27	3	2P
9	-	**Cornerstones 1967-1970**	Jimi Hendrix	Polydor	2		
10	-	**Pills 'n' Thrills And Bellyaches**	Happy Mondays	Factory	1		FL

December 1990

This Mnth	Last Mnth	Title	Artist	Label	Wks in 10	US Pos	
1	8	**The Immaculate Collection**	Madonna	Sire	27	3	2P
2	2	**The Very Best Of Elton John**	Elton John	Rocket	20		2P
3	6	**Serious Hits...Live!**	Phil Collins	Virgin	12	12	P
4	4	**In Concert**	Luciano Pavarotti, Placido Domingo & Jose Carreras	Decca	22	43	P
5	-	**From A Distance...The Event**	Cliff Richard	EMI	8		
6	-	**The Singles Collection 1984-1990**	Jimmy Somerville	London	9		FL
7	-	**Soul Provider**	Michael Bolton	CBS	23	3	FP
8	3	**Rocking All Over The Years**	Status Quo	Vertigo	9		
9	-	**The Very Best Of The Bee Gees**	Bee Gees	Warner	4		L
10	1	**The Rhythm Of The Saints**	Paul Simon	Warner	10	4	L

US 1990 OCT-DEC

October 1990

This Mnth	Last Mnth	Title	Artist	Label	Wks in 10	UK Pos	
1	1	**Please Hammer Don't Hurt 'Em**	MC Hammer	Capitol	52	8	**F10P**
2	3	**Mariah Carey**	Mariah Carey	Columbia	49	6	**F8P**
3	-	**Listen Without Prejudice Vol. 1**	George Michael	Columbia	13	1	**2PL**
4	2	**Wilson Phillips**	Wilson Phillips	SBK	52	7	**F5P**
5	6	**Poison**	Bell Biv Devoe	MCA	27	35	**F2PL**
6	-	**The Razors Edge**	AC/DC	Atco	19	4	**3PL**
7	4	**Blaze Of Glory/Young Guns II (Soundtrack)**	Jon Bon Jovi	Mercury	7	2	**F2PL**
8	-	**X**	INXS	Atlantic	6	2	**PL**
9	-	**To The Extreme**	Vanilla Ice	SBK	26	9	**F7PL**
10	-	**Empire**	Queensryche	EMI	7	13	**F3P**

November 1990

This Mnth	Last Mnth	Title	Artist	Label	Wks in 10	UK Pos	
1	9	**To The Extreme**	Vanilla Ice	SBK	26	9	**F7PL**
2	1	**Please Hammer Don't Hurt 'Em**	MC Hammer	Capitol	52	8	**F10P**
3	2	**Mariah Carey**	Mariah Carey	Columbia	49	6	**F8P**
4	6	**The Razors Edge**	AC/DC	Atco	19	4	**3PL**
5	4	**Wilson Phillips**	Wilson Phillips	SBK	52	7	**F5P**
6	8	**X**	INXS	Atlantic	6	2	**PL**
7	-	**Rhythm Of The Saints**	Paul Simon	Warner	13	1	**PL**
8	3	**Listen Without Prejudice Vol. 1**	George Michael	Columbia	13	1	**2PL**
9	-	**Recycler**	ZZ Top	Warner	5	8	**P**
10	-	**Family Style**	Vaughan Brothers	Epic	4	63	**FPL**

December 1990

This Mnth	Last Mnth	Title	Artist	Label	Wks in 10	UK Pos	
1	1	**To The Extreme**	Vanilla Ice	SBK	26	9	**F7PL**
2	2	**Please Hammer Don't Hurt 'Em**	MC Hammer	Capitol	52	8	**F10P**
3	3	**Mariah Carey**	Mariah Carey	Columbia	49	6	**F8P**
4	-	**I'm Your Baby Tonight**	Whitney Houston	Arista	22	6	**3PL**
5	7	**Rhythm Of The Saints**	Paul Simon	Warner	13	1	**PL**
6	-	**The Immaculate Collection**	Madonna	Sire	13	1	**4P**
7	-	**Some People's Lives**	Bette Midler	Atlantic	18	5	**2PL**
8	5	**Wilson Phillips**	Wilson Phillips	SBK	52	7	**F5P**
9	4	**The Razors Edge**	AC/DC	Atco	19	4	**3PL**
10	9	**Recycler**	Zz Top	Warner	5	8	**P**

• Total shipments of record and tapes increased 14% to $7.5 billion. The sales of compact disks were up 33% as vinyl slipped 60%. It was also a year when Japan increased its share of the US record business. MCA was purchased by Matsushita and CBS was renamed Sony by their Japanese owners.

• The Righteous Brothers were back over a quarter of a century after they first charted. Their 1965 recording of 'Unchained Melody' was a transatlantic smash and the soundtrack from *Ghost*, on which it was the featured track, hit the US Top 10. Added to this, the veteran duo were also hitting with three albums of their own, on different labels.

• After 21 weeks at the summit, MC Hammer was dethroned by another rapper, Vanilla Ice, with his debut, **To The Extreme** – the first non-vinyl album to reach Number 1. Ice's album, which sold a staggering five million copies in 12 weeks, contained the first Number 1 rap single, 'Ice Ice Baby'.

UK 1991 JAN-MAR

• British groups making their first trip into the Top 10 included Carter – The Unstoppable Sex Machine with **30 Something**, dance music acts KLF with **The White Room** and 808 State with **Ex:El** plus the chart topping Jesus Jones with **Doubt** and The Farm with **Spartacus**.

• Madonna's **Immaculate Collection** topped the UK chart for two months with sales of over 2 million. It helped push her total worldwide album sales over 50 million.

• David Bowie was unimpressed by the Rock And Roll Hall Of Fame and asked for his name to be taken off a list of acts nominated for entry. Acts inducted this year included R&B performers The Impressions, Ike & Tina Turner, John Lee Hooker, Lavern Baker, Jimmy Reed, Wilson Pickett and Howlin' Wolf.

• Twenty nine years after she debuted on the US album chart and 28 years after her death in a plane crash, Patsy Cline had her first UK chart entry with **Sweet Dreams**. Belatedly she became one of Britain's biggest selling country acts. The top country artist in the UK was Irish singer Daniel O'Donnell, who at times had six albums in the country Top 10.

January 1991

This Mnth	Last Mnth	Title	Artist	Label	Wks in 10	US Pos	
1	1	**The Immaculate Collection**	Madonna	Sire	27	3	**2P**
2	2	**The Very Best Of Elton John**	Elton John	Rocket	20		**2P**
3	3	**Serious Hits...Live!**	Phil Collins	Virgin	12	12	**P**
4	-	**I'm Your Baby Tonight**	Whitney Houston	Arista	10	3	**L**
5	-	**MCMXC AD**	Enigma	Virgin International	7	6	**F**
6	-	**To The Extreme**	Vanilla Ice	SBK	4	1	**FL**
7	4	**In Concert**	Luciano Pavarotti, Placido Domingo & Jose Carreras	Decca	22	43	**P**
8	6	**The Singles Collection 1984-1990**	Jimmy Somerville	London	9		**FL**
9	7	**Soul Provider**	Michael Bolton	CBS	23	3	**FP**
10	-	**A Little Ain't Enough**	David Lee Roth	Warner	1	18	**FL**

February 1991

This Mnth	Last Mnth	Title	Artist	Label	Wks in 10	US Pos	
1	-	**Wicked Game**	Chris Isaak	Reprise	9		**FL**
2	1	**The Immaculate Collection**	Madonna	Sire	27	3	**2P**
3	2	**The Very Best Of Elton John**	Elton John	Rocket	20		**2P**
4	5	**MCMXC AD**	Enigma	Virgin International	7	6	**F**
5	-	**Innuendo**	Queen	Parlophone	4	30	
6	-	**Into The Light**	Gloria Estefan	Epic	6	5	
7	-	**All True Man**	Alexander O'Neal	Tabu	3	49	
8	-	**The Soul Cages**	Sting	A&M	2	2	
9	-	**Doubt**	Jesus Jones	Food	3	25	**F**
10	-	**Runaway Horses**	Belinda Carlisle	Virgin	6	37	

March 1991

This Mnth	Last Mnth	Title	Artist	Label	Wks in 10	US Pos	
1	-	**Auberge**	Chris Rea	East West	8	176	
2	-	**Spartacus**	Farm	Produce	3		**FL**
3	-	**The Complete Picture - Very Best Of**	Deborah Harry & Blondie	Chrysalis	7		**L**
4	-	**Circle Of One**	Oleta Adams	Fontana	3	20	**F**
5	-	**Listen Without Prejudice Vol. 1**	George Michael	Columbia	19	2	**L**
6	-	**Out Of Time**	R.E.M.	Warner	27	1	**FP**
7	2	**The Immaculate Collection**	Madonna	Sire	27	3	**2P**
7	3	**The Very Best Of Elton John**	Elton John	Rocket	20		**2P**
8	5	**Innuendo**	Queen	Parlophone	4	30	
10	1	**Wicked Game**	Chris Isaak	Reprise	9		**FL**

January 1991

This Mnth	Last Mnth	Title	Artist	Label	Wks in 10	UK Pos	
1	1	**To The Extreme**	Vanilla Ice	SBK	26	9	**F7PL**
2	2	**Please Hammer Don't Hurt 'Em**	MC Hammer	Capitol	52	8	**F10P**
3	6	**The Immaculate Collection**	Madonna	Sire	13	1	**4P**
4	3	**Mariah Carey**	Mariah Carey	Columbia	49	6	**F8P**
5	4	**I'm Your Baby Tonight**	Whitney Houston	Arista	22	6	**3PL**
6	-	**The Simpsons Sing The Blues**	Simpsons	Geffen	9	6	**FL**
7	7	**Some People's Lives**	Bette Midler	Atlantic	18	5	**2PL**
8	8	**Wilson Phillips**	Wilson Phillips	SBK	52	7	**F5P**
9	5	**Rhythm Of The Saints**	Paul Simon	Warner	13	1	**PL**
10	9	**The Razors Edge**	AC/DC	Atco	19	4	**3PL**

February 1990

This Mnth	Last Mnth	Title	Artist	Label	Wks in 10	UK Pos	
1	1	**To The Extreme**	Vanilla Ice	SBK	26	9	**F7PL**
2	4	**Mariah Carey**	Mariah Carey	Columbia	49	6	**F8P**
3	3	**The Immaculate Collection**	Madonna	Sire	13	1	**4P**
4	6	**The Simpsons Sing The Blues**	Simpsons	Geffen	9	6	**FL**
5	2	**Please Hammer Don't Hurt 'Em**	MC Hammer	Capitol	52	8	**F10P**
6	5	**I'm Your Baby Tonight**	Whitney Houston	Arista	22	6	**3PL**
7	8	**Wilson Phillips**	Wilson Phillips	SBK	52	7	**F5P**
8	10	**The Razors Edge**	AC/DC	Atco	19	4	**3PL**
9	7	**Some People's Lives**	Bette Midler	Atlantic	18	5	**2PL**
10	-	**The Soul Cages**	Sting	A&M	10	1	**P**

March 1991

This Mnth	Last Mnth	Title	Artist	Label	Wks in 10	UK Pos	
1	2	**Mariah Carey**	Mariah Carey	Columbia	49	6	**F8P**
2	10	**The Soul Cages**	Sting	A&M	10	1	**P**
3	1	**To The Extreme**	Vanilla Ice	SBK	26	9	**F7PL**
4	7	**Wilson Phillips**	Wilson Phillips	SBK	52	7	**F5P**
5	6	**I'm Your Baby Tonight**	Whitney Houston	Arista	22	6	**3PL**
6	-	**Into The Light**	Gloria Estefan	Epic	7	2	**2P**
7	5	**Please Hammer Don't Hurt 'Em**	MC Hammer	Capitol	52	8	**F10P**
8	-	**Gonna Make You Sweat**	C&C Music Factory	Columbia	29	8	**F5PL**
9	-	**Shake Your Money Maker**	Black Crowes	Enigma	17	36	**F4P**
10	9	**Some People's Lives**	Bette Midler	Atlantic	18	5	**2PL**

US 1991

JAN-MAR

• Female artists continued to ride high on both the singles and album chart. Over half of the Top 10 albums were sung by women and at times they held seven of the Top 10 rungs on the singles chart. Whitney Houston clocked up her ninth Number 1 single, equalling Madonna's record, newcomer Mariah Carey headed the album list and scored her third successive chart topping single, 'Someday'.

• New US rock bands Nelson, featuring the sons of top Fifties star Ricky Nelson, Queensryche and Damn Yankees scored their first US Top 20 entries with **After The Rain, Empire** and **Damn Yankees** respectively. R&B acts debuting on the Top 20 included Guy with **The Future**, Oletta Adams with **Circle Of One** and ex-New Edition member Ralph Tresvant with a self-titled set.

• No sooner had Janet Jackson signed a record breaking $50 million deal with Virgin, than her brother Michael smashed that record by re-signing to CBS/Sony in a deal reportedly worth between $500,000 and $1 billion!

UK 1991 APR-JUNE

April 1991

This Mnth	Last Mnth	Title	Artist	Label	Wks in 10	US Pos	
1	-	**Greatest Hits**	Eurythmics	RCA	21	72	**PL**
2	-	**Vagabond Heart**	Rod Stewart	Warner	8	10	
3	6	**Out Of Time**	R.E.M.	Warner	27	1	**FP**
4	-	**Joyride**	Roxette	EMI	10	12	
5	-	**Real Life**	Simple Minds	Virgin	5	74	
6	1	**Auberge**	Chris Rea	East West	8	176	
7	-	**Inspector Morse - Music From The TV Series**	Barrington Pheloung	Virgin	4		**FL**
8	3	**The Complete Picture - Very Best Of**	Deborah Harry & Blondie	Chrysalis	7		**L**
9	-	**God Fodder**	Ned's Atomic Dustbin	Furtive	1	91	**FL**
10	-	**The Simpsons Sing The Blues**	Simpsons	Geffen	7	3	**FL**

• The Eurythmics' **Greatest Hits** headed the UK charts for two months and sold over a million copies in Britain. Surprisingly, the record which also sold over a million in Europe, failed to reach the US Top 40.

• A record eight acts from continental Europe were in the UK singles chart. The latest European acts to crack the Top 20 album charts in Britain and the USA were Swedish duo Roxette and German-based dance outfit Enigma with **Joyride** and **MCMXC AD** respectively.

• Among the noteworthy new faces on the UK Top 10 were James with **Gold Mother**, Lenny Kravitz with **Mama Said**, and Kylie's sister Dannii Minogue with **Love And Kisses**. Also charting for the first time were singer/songwriter Beverley Craven and Electronic with self-titled albums.

• Steve Marriott, lead singer of Sixties hitmakers The Small Faces and the top Seventies act Humble Pie, died in a fire at his home.

May 1991

This Mnth	Last Mnth	Title	Artist	Label	Wks in 10	US Pos	
1	1	**Greatest Hits**	Eurythmics	RCA	21	72	**PL**
2	4	**Joyride**	Roxette	EMI	10	12	
3	-	**Time, Love & Tenderness**	Michael Bolton	Columbia	11	1	**P**
4	-	**Gold Mother**	James	Fontana	3		**F**
5	5	**Real Life**	Simple Minds	Virgin	5	74	
6	-	**Schubert Dip**	EMF	Parlophone	3	12	**FL**
7	3	**Out Of Time**	R.E.M.	Warner	27	1	**F**
8	-	**The White Room**	KLF	KLF Comms.	7	39	**FL**
9	-	**Best Of The Waterboys '81-'90**	Waterboys	Ensign	2		
10	-	**Sugar Tax**	OMD	Virgin	6		**FL**

June 1991

This Mnth	Last Mnth	Title	Artist	Label	Wks in 10	US Pos	
1	-	**Seal**	Seal	ZTT	19	24	**F**
2	1	**Greatest Hits**	Eurythmics	RCA	21	72	**PL**
3	7	**Out Of Time**	R.E.M.	Warner	27	1	**FP**
4	-	**Beverley Craven**	Beverley Craven	Columbia	14		**F**
5	-	**Fellow Hoodlums**	Deacon Blue	Columbia	8		
6	-	**Electronic**	Electronic	Factory	2	109	**FL**
7	3	**Time, Love & Tenderness**	Michael Bolton	Columbia	11	1	**P**
8	-	**Never Loved Elvis**	Wonder Stuff	Polydor	2		
9	-	**Love Hurts**	Cher	Geffen	13	48	
10	-	**Greatest Hits 1977-1990**	Stranglers	Epic	8		**L**

US 1991 APR-JUNE

April 1991

This Mnth	Last Mnth	Title	Artist	Label	Wks in 10	UK Pos	
1	1	**Mariah Carey**	Mariah Carey	Columbia	49	6	**F8P**
2	8	**Gonna Make You Sweat**	C&C Music Factory	Columbia	29	8	**F5PL**
3	4	**Wilson Phillips**	Wilson Phillips	SBK	52	7	**F5P**
4	9	**Shake Your Money Maker**	Black Crowes	Enigma	17	36	**F4P**
5	-	**Out Of Time**	R.E.M.	Warner	22	1	**4P**
6	-	**Heart Shaped World**	Chris Isaak	Reprise	7		**FPL**
7	2	**The Soul Cages**	Sting	A&M	10	1	**P**
8	5	**I'm Your Baby Tonight**	Whitney Houston	Arista	22	6	**3PL**
9	3	**To The Extreme**	Vanilla Ice	SBK	26	9	**F7PL**
10	-	**The Doors (Soundtrack)**	Doors	Elektra	3	43	**L**

May 1991

This Mnth	Last Mnth	Title	Artist	Label	Wks in 10	UK Pos	
1	1	**Mariah Carey**	Mariah Carey	Columbia	49	6	**F8P**
2	-	**Out Of Time**	R.E.M.	Warner	22	1	**4P**
3	2	**Gonna Make You Sweat**	C&C Music Factory	Columbia	29	8	**F5PL**
4	3	**Wilson Phillips**	Wilson Phillips	SBK	52	7	**F5P**
5	-	**New Jack City**	Soundtrack	Giant	9		**P**
6	4	**Shake Your Money Maker**	Black Crowes	Enigma	17	36	**F4P**
7	-	**MCMXC AD**	Enigma	Charisma	5	1	**F2P**
8	-	**Time, Love And Tenderness**	Michael Bolton	Columbia	38	2	**8P**
9	-	**No Fences**	Garth Brooks	Capitol	36		**F11P**
10	6	**Heart Shaped World**	Chris Isaak	Reprise	7		**FPL**

June 1991

This Mnth	Last Mnth	Title	Artist	Label	Wks in 10	UK Pos	
1	-	**Spellbound**	Paula Abdul	Captive/Virgin	16	4	**3PL**
2	2	**Out Of Time**	R.E.M.	Warner	22	1	**4P**
3	8	**Time, Love And Tenderness**	Michael Bolton	Columbia	38	2	**8P**
4	3	**Gonna Make You Sweat**	C&C Music Factory	Columbia	29	8	**F5PL**
5	1	**Mariah Carey**	Mariah Carey	Columbia	49	6	**F8P**
6	-	**Efil4zaggin**	N.W.A.	Profile	7	25	**FPL**
7	9	**No Fences**	Garth Brooks	Capitol	36		**F11P**
8	5	**New Jack City**	Soundtrack	Giant	9		**P**
9	-	**Coolin' At The Playground Ya' Know!**	Another Bad Creation	Motown	7		**FPL**
10	-	**Slave To The Grind**	Skid Row	Atlantic	6	5	**PL**

• At the end of May, *Billboard* introduced a new method of compiling their album charts, which better reflected actual sales. Instantly the positions of country and rap albums improved and the number of albums entering in high positions increased. As examples of the changes, Garth Brook's six-months-old **No Fences** leaped into the Top 10, N.W.A.'s controversial **Efil4zaggin** entered at Number 2 and Skid Row's **Slave To The Grind** bowed in at Number 1.

• The first of many **MTV Unplugged** albums to grace the US Top 20 was **Unplugged - The Official Bootleg** by Paul McCartney.

• Paula Abdul replaced her supposed one time baby sitter, Michael Bolton, on top of the UK chart. At the same time session singer Yvette Marine claimed she had sung lead on some of the tracks on Abdul's Number 1, **Spellbound**.

• American acts who headlined at Wembley included Gloria Estefan, MC Hammer, New Kids On The Block and Paul Simon. It was the final date of a 31-show, $9 million grossing European tour for New Kids On The Block.

• For the first time April's top four albums were all by new acts: Mariah Carey, C&C Music Factory, Wilson Phillips and The Black Crowes.

UK 1991

JULY-SEPT

• A variety of musical styles was heard at Number 1: opera singer Luciano Pavarotti scored his third chart topper in just over a year, heavy metal merchants Metallica repeated their US feat by entering at the top spot and the London cast album of **Joseph And The Amazing Technicolor Dreamcoat**, led by teen idol Jason Donovan, also reached the summit. Incidentally Donovan also joined The Stranglers, The Jam, Paul Young, T. Rex and The Specials, who all had **Greatest Hits** compilations in the Top 10.

• At the age of 74, blues man John Lee Hooker became the oldest ever resident of the Top 10 when the newly recorded **Mr. Lucky** gave him his biggest hit to date.

• Despite the fact that the soundtrack from **Robin Hood: Prince Of Thieves** was not a Number 1 hit on either side of the Atlantic, its most popular track '(Everything I Do) I Do It For You' by Bryan Adams was the world's top selling single in 1991. It sold over three million copies in America, and in Britain topped the chart for a record 16 weeks and became the first million seller since 1985. It also broke longevity records at the top of the charts in Holland and Norway.

July 1991

This Mnth	Last Mnth	Title	Artist	Label	Wks in 10	US Pos	
1	9	**Love Hurts**	Cher	Geffen	13	48	
2	3	**Out Of Time**	R.E.M.	Warner	27	1	FP
3	-	**Greatest Hits**	Jam	Polydor	4		L
4	1	**Seal**	Seal	ZTT	19	24	F
5	2	**Greatest Hits**	Eurythmics	RCA	21	72	PL
6	-	**Essential Pavarotti II**	Luciano Pavarotti	Decca	8		L
7	-	**Some People's Lives**	Bette Midler	Atlantic	3	6	F
8	-	**Into The Great White Open**	Tom Petty & The Heartbreakers	MCA	2	13	
9	10	**Greatest Hits 1977-1990**	Stranglers	Epic	8		L
10	4	**Beverley Craven**	Beverley Craven	Columbia	14		F

August 1991

This Mnth	Last Mnth	Title	Artist	Label	Wks in 10	US Pos	
1	6	**Essential Pavarotti II**	Luciano Pavarotti	Decca	8		L
2	1	**Love Hurts**	Cher	Geffen	13	48	
3	4	**Seal**	Seal	ZTT	19	24	F
4	-	**Sugar Tax**	OMD	Virgin	6		FL
5	-	**The Immaculate Collection**	Madonna	Sire	27	3	2P
6	10	**Beverley Craven**	Beverley Craven	Columbia	14		F
7	-	**Metallica**	Metallica	Vertigo	2	1	L
8	2	**Out Of Time**	R.E.M.	Warner	27	1	FP
9	-	**Move To This**	Cathy Dennis	Polydor	2	67	F
10	5	**Greatest Hits**	Eurythmics	RCA	21	72	PL

September 1991

This Mnth	Last Mnth	Title	Artist	Label	Wks in 10	US Pos	
1	-	**Joseph And The Amazing Technicolor Dreamcoat**	Jason Donovan/Cast	Really Useful	5		
2	-	**From Time To Time - The Singles Collection**	Paul Young	Columbia	15		L
3	8	**Out Of Time**	R.E.M.	Warner	27	1	F
4	-	**On Every Street**	Dire Straits	Vertigo	5	12	
5	2	**Love Hurts**	Cher	Geffen	13	48	
6	-	**C.M.B.**	Color Me Badd	Giant	5	3	FL
7	3	**Seal**	Seal	ZTT	19	24	F
8	-	**Mr. Lucky**	John Lee Hooker	Silvertone	2	101	FL
9	-	**Use Your Illusion II**	Guns N' Roses	Geffen	4	8	L
10	-	**Use Your Illusion I**	Guns N' Roses	Geffen	3	2	L

US 1991 JULY-SEPT

July 1991

This Mnth	Last Mnth	Title	Artist	Label	Wks in 10	UK Pos	
1	-	**For Unlawful Carnal Knowledge**	Van Halen	Warner	12	12	**3P**
2	10	**Slave To The Grind**	Skid Row	Atlantic	6	5	**PL**
3	1	**Spellbound**	Paula Abdul	Captive/Virgin	16	4	**3PL**
4	-	**Unforgettable**	Natalie Cole	Elektra	21	11	**5PL**
5	4	**Gonna Make You Sweat**	C&C Music Factory	Columbia	29	8	**F5PL**
6	2	**Out Of Time**	R.E.M.	Warner	22	1	**4P**
7	7	**No Fences**	Garth Brooks	Capitol	36		**F11P**
8	6	**Efil4zaggin**	N.W.A.	Profile	7	25	**FPL**
9	-	**Luck Of The Draw**	Bonnie Raitt	Capitol	17	38	**5P**
10	-	**Robin Hood: Prince Of Thieves**	Soundtrack	Morgan Creek	6		**P**

August 1991

This Mnth	Last Mnth	Title	Artist	Label	Wks in 10	UK Pos	
1	4	**Unforgettable**	Natalie Cole	Elektra	21	11	**5PL**
2	9	**Luck Of The Draw**	Bonnie Raitt	Capitol	17	38	**5P**
3	1	**For Unlawful Carnal Knowledge**	Van Halen	Warner	12	12	**3P**
4	5	**Gonna Make You Sweat**	C&C Music Factory	Columbia	29	8	**F5PL**
5	3	**Spellbound**	Paula Abdul	Captive/Virgin	16	4	**3PL**
6	-	**Cooleyhighharmony**	Boyz II Men	Motown	28	7	**F5P**
7	10	**Robin Hood: Prince Of Thieves**	Soundtrack	Morgan Creek	6		**P**
8	-	**C.M.B.**	Color Me Badd	Giant	12	3	**F3PL**
9	6	**Out Of Time**	R.E.M.	Warner	22	1	**4P**
10	-	**Time, Love And Tenderness**	Michael Bolton	Columbia	38	2	**8P**

September 1991

This Mnth	Last Mnth	Title	Artist	Label	Wks in 10	UK Pos	
1	-	**Metallica**	Metallica	Elektra	31	1	**7PL**
2	1	**Unforgettable**	Natalie Cole	Elektra	21	11	**5PL**
3	8	**C.M.B.**	Color Me Badd	Giant	12	3	**F3PL**
4	2	**Luck Of The Draw**	Bonnie Raitt	Capitol	17	38	**5P**
5	6	**Cooleyhighharmony**	Boyz II Men	Motown	28	7	**F5P**
6	3	**For Unlawful Carnal Knowledge**	Van Halen	Warner	12	12	**3P**
7	4	**Gonna Make You Sweat**	C&C Music Factory	Columbia	29	8	**F5PL**
8	10	**Time, Love And Tenderness**	Michael Bolton	Columbia	38	2	**8P**
9	-	**Ropin' The Wind**	Garth Brooks	Capitol	50	41	**10P**
10	-	**Roll The Bones**	Rush	Atlantic	2	10	

• Van Halen and Metallica were the latest acts to enter the US charts at Number 1 with **For Unlawful Carnal Knowledge** and **Metallica**.

• American groups in the news included Aerosmith, who signed a $40 million deal with Columbia, Motley Crue (above) who re-signed to Elektra for $35 million and R.E.M. who won a record six MTV awards.

• Hot new acts Boyz II Men, Color Me Badd and C&C Music Factory reached the Top 10 with **Cooleyhighharmony, C.M.B.** and **Gonna Make You Sweat** respectively. Close behind were fellow R&B stars Bell Biv Devoe with **WBBD – Boot City** and Luther Vandross with his eighth successive platinum album, **The Power Of Love**. Rap LPs in the Top 20 included: **Homebase** by DJ Jazzy Jeff & The Fresh Prince, **Derelicts Of Dialect** by 3rd Bass and the self titled debut by Naughty By Nature, whose single 'O.P.P.' went on to sell over two million copies.

UK 1991 OCT-DEC

• Simply Red's chart topping album **Stars** was the biggest seller of the early Nineties in Britain. It spent over 50 weeks in the Top 10 and sold three million copies in the UK alone. Although **Stars** failed to reach the American Top 40, it also sold over three million copies outside Britain.

• Primal Scream reached the Top 10 with **Screamadelica**. It was voted Album Of The Year by *NME* and the following September picked up the prestigious Mercury Music Prize.

• A guitar owned by Jimi Hendrix was sold to Motley Crue's drummer for $30,000 and Elvis Presley's first guitar fetched $180,000 at auction.

• Britain's top selling singles and albums act of the year were Queen, whose leader Freddie Mercury died in November. Their **Greatest Hits** album returned to the Top 10 and passed the three million sales mark while **Greatest Hits II** entered at Number 1. As the year ended, the group had five videos in the UK Top 30 and albums climbing the charts all around Europe.

• Irish singer/songwriter Enya became the first New Age act to top the charts. Her Number 1 album **Shepherd Moons** has been the most successful album of the genre with sales over seven million world-wide.

October 1991

This Mnth	Last Mnth	Title	Artist	Label	Wks in 10	US Pos	
1	-	**Waking Up The Neighbours**	Bryan Adams	A&M	6	6	
2	-	**Stars**	Simply Red	East West	51	76	**3PL**
3	-	**Simply The Best**	Tina Turner	Capitol	23	113	**P**
4	-	**Diamonds And Pearls**	Prince & The New Power Generation	Paisley Park	10	3	
5	2	**From Time To Time - The Singles Collection**	Paul Young	Columbia	15		**L**
6	4	**On Every Street**	Dire Straits	Vertigo	5	12	
7	9	**Use Your Illusion II**	Guns N' Roses	Geffen	4	8	**L**
8	-	**Chorus**	Erasure	Mute	3	29	**F**
10	-	**The Ultimate Collection**	Marc Bolan & T-Rex	Telstar	4		**L**

November 1991

This Mnth	Last Mnth	Title	Artist	Label	Wks in 10	US Pos	
1	2	**Stars**	Simply Red	East West	51	76	**3PL**
2	-	**Greatest Hits II**	Queen	Parlophone	18		**P**
3	3	**Simply The Best**	Tina Turner	Capitol	23	113	**P**
4	-	**Shepherd Moons**	Enya	WEA	7	17	**P**
5	5	**From Time To Time - The Singles Collection**	Paul Young	Columbia	15		**L**
6	-	**The Commitments (Soundtrack)**	Commitments	MCA	9	8	**FPL**
7	-	**We Can't Dance**	Genesis	Virgin	20	4	**P**
8	9	**Voices**	Kenny Thomas	Cooltempo	4		**F**
9	-	**Discography**	Pet Shop Boys	Parlophone	2	111	
10	8	**Chorus**	Erasure	Mute	3	29	

December 1991

This Mnth	Last Mnth	Title	Artist	Label	Wks in 10	US Pos	
1	2	**Greatest Hits II**	Queen	Parlophone	18		**P**
2	1	**Stars**	Simply Red	East West	51	76	**3PL**
3	-	**Dangerous**	Michael Jackson	Epic	24	1	**PL**
4	3	**Simply The Best**	Tina Turner	Capitol	23	113	**P**
5	-	**Performs Andrew Lloyd Webber**	Michael Crawford/RPO	Telstar	8	54	**FL**
6	-	**Time, Love & Tenderness**	Michael Bolton	Columbia	11	1	**P**
7	-	**Greatest Hits**	Queen	EMI	23	11	**3P**
8	7	**We Can't Dance**	Genesis	Virgin	20	4	**P**
9	-	**Achtung Baby**	U2	Island	5	1	**P**
10	-	**The Definitive Simon And Garfunkel**	Simon And Garfunkel	Columbia	3		**L**

US 1991 OCT-DEC

October 1991

This Mnth	Last Mnth	Title	Artist	Label	Wks in 10	UK Pos	
1	-	**Use Your Illusion II**	Guns N' Roses	Geffen	16	1	**5P**
2	9	**Ropin' The Wind**	Garth Brooks	Capitol	50	41	**10P**
3	-	**Use Your Illusion I**	Guns N' Roses	Geffen	9	2	**4P**
4	-	**Emotions**	Mariah Carey	Columbia	12	4	**4P**
5	1	**Metallica**	Metallica	Elektra	31	1	**7PL**
6	-	**Decade Of Decadence**	Motley Crue	Elektra	4	20	**P**
7	-	**Apocalypse 91...The Enemy Strikes Black**	Public Enemy	Def Jam	4	8	**8PL**
8	-	**Diamonds And Pearls**	Prince & The New Power Generation	Paisley Park	7	2	**2P**
9	2	**Unforgettable**	Natalie Cole	Elektra	21	11	**5PL**
10	-	**Waking Up The Neighbours**	Bryan Adams	A&M	4	1	**3P**

November 1991

This Mnth	Last Mnth	Title	Artist	Label	Wks in 10	UK Pos	
1	2	**Ropin' The Wind**	Garth Brooks	Capitol	50	41	**10P**
2	1	**Use Your Illusion II**	Guns N' Roses	Geffen	16	1	**5P**
3	5	**Metallica**	Metallica	Elektra	31	1	**7PL**
4	-	**Too Legit To Quit**	Hammer	Capitol	17	41	**3PL**
5	-	**Death Certificate**	Ice Cube	Priority	4		**FP**
6	8	**Diamonds And Pearls**	Prince & The New Power Generation	Paisley Park	7	2	**2P**
7	-	**Nevermind**	Nirvana	DGC	28	7	**F6P**
8	3	**Use Your Illusion I**	Guns N' Roses	Geffen	9	2	**4P**
9	6	**Decade Of Decadence**	Motley Crue	Elektra	4	20	**P**
10	4	**Emotions**	Mariah Carey	Columbia	12	4	**4P**

December 1991

This Mnth	Last Mnth	Title	Artist	Label	Wks in 10	UK Pos	
1	1	**Ropin' The Wind**	Garth Brooks	Capitol	50	41	**10P**
2	-	**Achtung Baby**	U2	Island	18	2	**5P**
3	4	**Too Legit To Quit**	Hammer	Capitol	17	41	**3PL**
4	-	**Dangerous**	Michael Jackson	Epic	18	1	**6PL**
5	-	**Time, Love And Tenderness**	Michael Bolton	Columbia	38	2	**8P**
6	7	**Nevermind**	Nirvana	DGC	28	7	**F6P**
7	2	**Use Your Illusion II**	Guns N' Roses	Geffen	16	1	**5P**
8	3	**Metallica**	Metallica	Elektra	31	1	**7PL**
9	-	**Unforgettable**	Natalie Cole	Elektra	21	11	**5PL**
10	-	**Cooleyhighharmony**	Boyz II Men	Motown	28	7	**F5P**

• The value of record and tape sales in the USA increased by 3.8% to $7.8 billion and 90 albums were certified platinum – the most since 1978. In Britain, for the first time compact disks outsold cassettes and 12" singles outsold 7".

• **Use Your Illusion I** and **II** by Guns N' Roses broke a record set by The Beatles when they entered the US chart in positions 1 and 2. They repeated this feat in the UK and Australia and came in at Numbers 2 and 3 in Japan. In total, the albums shipped a staggering 3.7 million in the USA.

• Garth Brooks' **Ropin' the Wind** shipped 2.6 million copies and was the first album certified quadruple platinum in its initial month on sale. It was also the first country album to enter the chart at Number 1. The album stayed there for 18 weeks and in total sold over ten million copies.

• **Two Rooms: The Songs Of Elton John & Bernie Taupin** became the first of several various artist tribute albums to crack the Top 20.

UK 1992 JAN-MAR

January 1992

This Mnth	Last Mnth	Title	Artist	Label	Wks in 10	US Pos	
1	2	**Stars**	Simply Red	East West	51	76	**3PL**
2	1	**Greatest Hits II**	Queen	Parlophone	18		**P**
3	4	**Simply The Best**	Tina Turner	Capitol	23	113	**P**
4	1	**Real Love**	Lisa Stansfield	Arista	19	43	
5	8	**We Can't Dance**	Genesis	Virgin	20	4	**P**
6	3	**Dangerous**	Michael Jackson	Epic	24	1	**PL**
7	7	**Greatest Hits**	Queen	EMI	23	11	**3P**
8	-	**Diamonds And Pearls**	Prince & The New Power Generation	Paisley Park	10	3	
9	9	**Achtung Baby**	U2	Island	5	1	**P**
10	6	**Time, Love & Tenderness**	Michael Bolton	Columbia	11	1	**P**

• Seal became the first act to win three BRIT awards in one year. Other winners included Beverley Craven (Best Newcomer) Simply Red and KLF (joint Best Group) and PM Dawn (Best International Newcomer). Freddie Mercury was given a posthumous award for his Outstanding Contribution to British Music.

• For a while, a record seventeen solo female singers were situated in the UK Top 75; among them was Diana Ross who clocked up a record-breaking 30th chart entry.

• **Dangerous** by Michael Jackson entered both charts at Number 1. It sold a record 200,000 in three days in the UK and shipped an unprecedented four million copies in both Europe and America. In its first four months it sold over 10 million copies globally – a better start than even **Thriller**. The first single taken from it, 'Black Or White', was the first US record to enter the British chart at Number 1 for 32 years.

February 1992

This Mnth	Last Mnth	Title	Artist	Label	Wks in 10	US Pos	
1	1	**Stars**	Simply Red	East West	51	76	**3PL**
2	5	**We Can't Dance**	Genesis	Virgin	20	4	**P**
3	-	**High On The Happy Side**	Wet Wet Wet	Precious	9		
4	4	**Real Love**	Lisa Stansfield	Arista	19	43	
5	-	**No Regrets - The Best Of ..1965-1976**	Scott Walker & The Walker Brothers	Fontana	3		**L**
6	2	**Greatest Hits II**	Queen	Parlophone	18		**P**
7	-	**Emotions**	Mariah Carey	Columbia	5	4	
8	-	**From The Heart - His Greatest Love Songs**	Elvis Presley	RCA	4		
9	3	**Simply The Best**	Tina Turner	Capitol	23	113	**P**
10	-	**Seven**	James	Fontana	3		

March 1992

This Mnth	Last Mnth	Title	Artist	Label	Wks in 10	US Pos	
1	-	**Divine Madness**	Madness	Virgin	12		**L**
2	1	**Stars**	Simply Red	East West	51	76	**3PL**
3	-	**Tears Roll Down (Greatest Hits 1982-1992)**	Tears For Fears	Fontana	8	53	
4	-	**Hormonally Yours**	Shakespears Sister	London	8	56	**L**
5	3	**High On The Happy Side**	Wet Wet Wet	Precious	9		
6	-	**After Hours**	Gary Moore	Virgin	2	145	
7	10	**Seven**	James	Fontana	3		
8	-	**Woodface**	Crowded House	Capitol	3	83	**F**
9	-	**Up**	Right Said Fred	Tug	12	46	**FL**
10	8	**From The Heart - His Greatest Love Songs**	Elvis Presley	RCA	4		

US 1992

JAN-MAR

January 1992

This Mnth	Last Mnth	Title	Artist	Label	Wks in 10	UK Pos	
1	1	**Ropin' The Wind**	Garth Brooks	Capitol	50	41	**10P**
2	4	**Dangerous**	Michael Jackson	Epic	18	1	**6PL**
3	3	**Too Legit To Quit**	Hammer	Capitol	17	41	**3PL**
4	6	**Nevermind**	Nirvana	DGC	28	7	**F6P**
5	2	**Achtung Baby**	U2	Island	18	2	**5P**
6	5	**Time, Love And Tenderness**	Michael Bolton	Columbia	38	2	**8P**
7	10	**Cooleyhighharmony**	Boyz II Men	Motown	28	7	**F5P**
8	8	**Metallica**	Metallica	Elektra	31	1	**7PL**
9	7	**Use Your Illusion II**	Guns N' Roses	Geffen	16	1	**5P**
10	-	**Emotions**	Mariah Carey	Columbia	12	4	**4P**

February 1992

This Mnth	Last Mnth	Title	Artist	Label	Wks in 10	UK Pos	
1	1	**Ropin' The Wind**	Garth Brooks	Capitol	50	41	**10P**
2	4	**Nevermind**	Nirvana	DGC	28	7	**F6P**
3	2	**Dangerous**	Michael Jackson	Epic	18	1	**6PL**
4	-	**No Fences**	Garth Brooks	Capitol	36	F	**11P**
5	3	**Too Legit To Quit**	Hammer	Capitol	17	41	**3PL**
6	7	**Cooleyhighharmony**	Boyz II Men	Motown	28	7	**F5P**
7	6	**Time, Love And Tenderness**	Michael Bolton	Columbia	38	2	**8P**
8	5	**Achtung Baby**	U2	Island	18	2	**5P**
9	-	**C.M.B.**	Color Me Badd	Giant	12	3	**F3PL**
10	8	**Metallica**	Metallica	Elektra	31	1	**7PL**

March 1992

This Mnth	Last Mnth	Title	Artist	Label	Wks in 10	UK Pos	
1	1	**Ropin' The Wind**	Garth Brooks	Capitol	50	41	**10P**
2	2	**Nevermind**	Nirvana	DGC	28	7	**F6P**
3	3	**Dangerous**	Michael Jackson	Epic	18	1	**6PL**
4	-	**Unforgettable**	Natalie Cole	Elektra	21	11	**5PL**
5	4	**No Fences**	Garth Brooks	Capitol	36		**F11P**
6	7	**Time, Love And Tenderness**	Michael Bolton	Columbia	38	2	**8P**
7	-	**Luck Of The Draw**	Bonnie Raitt	Capitol	17	38	**5P**
8	-	**Wayne's World**	Soundtrack	Reprise	9		**P**
9	6	**Cooleyhighharmony**	Boyz II Men	Motown	28	7	**F5P**
10	9	**C.M.B.**	Color Me Badd	Giant	12	3	**F3PL**

• Winners at the Grammy ceremonies included **Unforgettable** by Natalie Cole (Album of the Year), **Luck Of The Draw** by Bonnie Raitt (Best Rock Solo Performance), **For Unlawful Carnal Knowledge** by Van Halen (Best Rock Group Performance) and **Out Of Time** by R.E.M. (Best Alternative Music Album). Natalie Cole was the evening's big winner picking up seven awards.

• Capitol failed to push **Too Legit To Quit** by Hammer, previously MC Hammer, to the top, despite the amazing sales of its predecessor and the record breaking million dollar promotion campaign they put behind it. The label had better luck with Garth Brooks, whose first three albums were simultaneously situated in the Top 20 with two of them, at times, holding the first couple of rungs – a feat not previously equalled since the mid-Sixties when Herb Alpert was at his peak. Not surprisingly, Brooks, whose first TV special topped the ratings, held the first three rungs on the country chart.

• A recording engineer sued New Kids On The Block and accused them of singing only part of the vocals on their recordings. The case was settled out of court, but the bad press affected the group's sales as it had Paula Abdul's when she was similarly accused.

UK 1992 APR-JUNE

• Headliners at a tribute show to Queen's late leader Freddie Mercury included David Bowie, Def Leppard, Guns N' Roses, Elton John, Metallica, George Michael, Robert Plant and U2. The show, which raised a small fortune for AIDS awareness, was televised around the world. In America, Queen, who had not been in the Top 10 for 12 years, returned with **Classic Queen**. Simultaneously, their single 'Bohemian Rhapsody', which was featured on the chart topping soundtrack **Wayne's World**, returned to the US Top 10. Queen also had four albums on the American chart as well as the top selling video.

• Among the '**Greatest Hits**' albums charting were sets by Britain's Joe Cocker, Tom Jones, Madness, Queen, Squeeze and Tears For Fears. There were also hit collections from America's Four Seasons, Dr. Hook, Alexander O'Neal, Lionel Richie, Tina Turner and ZZ Top. The most surprising hit compilation was by Irish balladeer Josef Locke whose biggest sellers had been in the Forties.

• The Beatles classic **Sergeant Pepper** reached the UK Top 10 for the third time on its 25th anniversary.

• Annie Lennox, who had been voted Best Female Singer at the BRIT awards a record four times, entered first week at Number 1 with her solo debut, **Diva**.
It also returned to the top the following March.

April 1992

This Mnth	Last Mnth	Title	Artist	Label	Wks in 10	US Pos	
1	9	**Up**	Right Said Fred	Tug	12	46	**FL**
2	1	**Divine Madness**	Madness	Virgin	12		**L**
3	-	**Adrenalize**	Def Leppard	Bludgeon Riffola	4	1	
4	3	**Tears Roll Down (Greatest Hits 1982-1992)**	Tears For Fears	Fontana	8	53	
5	-	**Diva**	Annie Lennox	RCA	24	23	**FPL**
6	-	**Human Touch**	Bruce Springsteen	Columbia	3	2	
7	2	**Stars**	Simply Red	Eastwest	51	76	**3PL**
8	-	**Lucky Town**	Bruce Springsteen	Columbia	2	3	
9	-	**0898**	Beautiful South	Go! Discs	2		
10	-	**Volume III Just Right**	Soul II Soul	Virgin	3		

May 1992

This Mnth	Last Mnth	Title	Artist	Label	Wks in 10	US Pos	
1	7	**Stars**	Simply Red	East West	51	76	**3PL**
2	1	**Up**	Right Said Fred	Tug	12	46	**FL**
3	5	**Diva**	Annie Lennox	RCA	24	23	**FPL**
4	-	**Greatest Hits**	ZZ Top	Warner	5	9	
5	-	**1992 - The Love Album**	Carter - The Unstoppable Sex Machine	Chrysalis	2		
6	-	**Wish**	Cure	Fiction	2	2	**L**
7	-	**Fear Of The Dark**	Iron Maiden	EMI	2	12	
8	-	**Power Of Ten**	Chris De Burgh	A&M	2		
9	2	**Divine Madness**	Madness	Virgin	12		**L**
10	-	**Southern Harmony And Musical Companion**	Black Crowes	Def American	2	1	**F**

June 1992

This Mnth	Last Mnth	Title	Artist	Label	Wks in 10	US Pos	
1	-	**Back To Front**	Lionel Richie	Motown	24	1	**PL**
2	-	**Live At Wembley '86**	Queen	Parlophone	4	53	**L**
3	-	**Completely Hooked - The Best Of Dr. Hook**	Dr. Hook	Capitol	5		**L**
4	-	**This Thing Called Love - Greatest Hits**	Alexander O'Neal	Tabu	8		
5	1	**Stars**	Simply Red	Eastwest	51	76	**3PL**
6	-	**Change Everything**	Del Amitri	A&M	2	178	**L**
7	-	**Angel Dust**	Faith No More	Slash	2	10	**FL**
8	-	**The One**	Elton John	Rocket	5	8	
9	-	**Michael Ball**	Michael Ball	Polydor	3		**F**
10	2	**Up**	Right Said Fred	Tug	12	46	**FL**

US 1992 APR-JUNE

April 1992

This Mnth	Last Mnth	Title	Artist	Label	Wks in 10	UK Pos	
1	8	**Wayne's World**	Soundtrack	Reprise	9		**P**
2	1	**Ropin' The Wind**	Garth Brooks	Capitol	50	41	**10P**
3	2	**Nevermind**	Nirvana	DGC	28	7	**F6P**
4	-	**Adrenalize**	Def Leppard	Mercury	15	1	**3P**
5	-	**Human Touch**	Bruce Springsteen	Columbia	3	1	**P**
6	-	**As Ugly As They Want To Be**	Ugly Kid Joe	Star Dog	5	9	**FPL**
7	-	**Lucky Town**	Bruce Springsteen	Columbia	2	2	**PL**
8	5	**No Fences**	Garth Brooks	Capitol	36		**F11P**
9	-	**Wynonna**	Wynonna	Curb	5		**F4P**
10	-	**Metallica**	Metallica	Elektra	31	1	**7PL**

May 1992

This Mnth	Last Mnth	Title	Artist	Label	Wks in 10	UK Pos	
1	4	**Adrenalize**	Def Leppard	Mercury	15	1	**3P**
2	-	**Totally Krossed Out**	Kris Kross	Ruffhouse	25	31	**F4PL**
3	-	**Blood Sugar Sex Magik**	Red Hot Chili Peppers	Warner	19	25	**F3PL**
4	2	**Ropin' The Wind**	Garth Brooks	Capitol	50	41	**10P**
5	-	**Classic Queen**	Queen	Hollywood	7		**2PL**
6	-	**Wish**	Cure	Fiction	4	1	**FPL**
7	8	**No Fences**	Garth Brooks	Capitol	36		**F11P**
8	1	**Wayne's World**	Soundtrack	Reprise	9		**P**
9	3	**Nevermind**	Nirvana	DGC	28	7	**F6P**
10	-	**Southern Harmony And Musical Companion**	Black Crowes	Def American	7	2	**2PL**

June 1992

This Mnth	Last Mnth	Title	Artist	Label	Wks in 10	UK Pos	
1	-	**Some Gave All**	Billy Ray Cyrus	Mercury	43	9	**F8P**
2	2	**Totally Krossed Out**	Kris Kross	Ruffhouse	25	31	**F4PL**
3	3	**Blood Sugar Sex Magik**	Red Hot Chili Peppers	Warner	19	25	**F3PL**
4	10	**Southern Harmony And Musical Companion**	Black Crowes	Def American	7	2	**PL**
5	1	**Adrenalize**	Def Leppard	Mercury	15	1	**3P**
6	-	**Ten**	Pearl Jam	Epic Associated	35	18	**F8P**
7	-	**Shadows And Light**	Wilson Phillips	SBK	4	6	**PL**
8	4	**Ropin' The Wind**	Garth Brooks	Capitol	50	41	**10P**
9	-	**MTV Unplugged EP**	Mariah Carey	Columbia	12	3	**P**
10	-	**Revenge**	Kiss	Mercury	1	10	

• There was no shortage of rock groups on the Top 10. Def Leppard's **Adrenalize** entered at Number 1 and sold two million in its first week. Making their debut were British band The Cure, Seattle's latest hit makers Pearl Jam, Red Hot Chili Peppers, Slaughter and Ugly Kid Joe. There was also room for veteran bands Kiss, Queen and ZZ Top.

• On April 18, a record five albums entered the Top 10 in their first week; among them was the self-titled debut by the ex-Judds member Wynonna. **Wynonna** was also the first album by a female to enter the country chart at Number 1.

• Bruce Springsteen equaled Guns N' Roses recent feat when his albums **Human Touch** and **Lucky Town** entered the UK chart together in positions Number 1 and 2. In the USA, however, thanks to Def Leppard, they only managed to appear at Numbers 2 and 3.

UK 1992

JULY-SEPT

• Mike Oldfield's first hit **Tubular Bells** in 1973 spent 15 months on the chart before it hit Number 1. Nineteen years later the multi-instrumentalist's **Tubular Bells II** entered at the top spot.

• British stars Eric Clapton, Jeff Beck and Jimmy Page were inducted into the Rock And Roll Hall Of Fame alongside Americans Jimi Hendrix, Johnny Cash, The Isley Brothers and influential blues performers Bobby Bland and Elmore James.

• Elton John, Madonna and Morrissey all broke records set by The Beatles: Elton clocked up his 50th US Top 40 entry, the number of Madonna's UK Top 10 hits now surpassed the 'mop tops' and Morrissey sold out the L.A. Bowl in just 23 minutes.

• Several interesting artists made their UK Top 10 debuts including actor Jimmy Nail with **Growing Up In Public**, The Orb with **U.F. Orb**, Shamen with **Boss Drum**, Sonic Youth with **Dirty** and ex-Husker Du front-man Bob Mould's group Sugar with **Copper Blue**. Also debuting in the Top 10 were teen idols Take That with **Take That And Party**, heavy metal band Thunder with **Laughing On Judgement Day** and ex-Pink Floyd member Roger Waters with **Amused To Death**.

July 1992

This Mnth	Last Mnth	Title	Artist	Label	Wks in 10	US Pos	
1	1	**Back To Front**	Lionel Richie	Motown	24	19	**PL**
2	-	**The Greatest Hits 1966-1992**	Neil Diamond	Columbia	11	90	**L**
3	-	**The Legend - The Essential Collection**	Joe Cocker	Capitol	7		**F**
4	8	**The One**	Elton John	Rocket	5	8	
5	5	**Stars**	Simply Red	Eastwest	51	76	**3PL**
6	-	**MTV Unplugged EP**	Mariah Carey	Columbia	4	3	
7	-	**U.F.Orb**	Orb	Big Life	2		**F**
8	3	**Completely Hooked - The Best Of Dr. Hook**	Dr. Hook	Capitol	5		**L**
9	-	**Performs Andrew Lloyd Webber**	Michael Crawford/RPO	Telstar	8	54	**FL**
10	-	**A Life Of Surprises - The Best Of**	Prefab Sprout	Kitchenware	4		**L**

August 1992

This Mnth	Last Mnth	Title	Artist	Label	Wks in 10	US Pos	
1	2	**The Greatest Hits 1966-1992**	Neil Diamond	Columbia	11	90	**L**
2	5	**Stars**	Simply Red	East West	51	76	**3PL**
3	-	**Dangerous**	Michael Jackson	Epic	24	1	**PL**
4	-	**We Can't Dance**	Genesis	Virgin	20	4	**P**
5	1	**Back To Front**	Lionel Richie	Motown	24	19	**PL**
6	-	**Welcome To Wherever You Are**	INXS	Mercury	3	16	
7	-	**Growing Up In Public**	Jimmy Nail	East West	4		**F**
8	-	**Best...I**	Smiths	WEA	4	139	**L**
9	3	**The Legend - The Essential Collection**	Joe Cocker	Capitol	7		**F**
10	6	**MTV Unplugged EP**	Mariah Carey	Columbia	4	3	

September 1992

This Mnth	Last Mnth	Title	Artist	Label	Wks in 10	US Pos	
1	-	**Tubular Bells II**	Mike Oldfield	WEA	8		
2	-	**Kylie's Greatest Hits**	Kylie Minogue	PWL	4		
3	5	**Back To Front**	Lionel Richie	Motown	24	19	**L**
4	-	**Diva**	Annie Lennox	RCA	24	23	**FPL**
5	-	**The Best Of Belinda Vol. 1**	Belinda Carlisle	Virgin	8		
6	-	**Tourism**	Roxette	EMI	3	117	
7	8	**Best...I**	Smiths	WEA	4	139	**L**
8	-	**Unplugged**	Eric Clapton	Duck	11	1	
9	-	**Laughing On Judgement Day**	Thunder	EMI	1		**FL**
10	-	**III Sides To Every Story**	Extreme	A&M	2	10	**FL**

US 1992 JULY-SEPT

July 1992

This Mnth	Last Mnth	Title	Artist	Label	Wks in 10	UK Pos	
1	1	**Some Gave All**	Billy Ray Cyrus	Mercury	43	9	**F8P**
2	2	**Totally Krossed Out**	Kris Kross	Ruffhouse	25	31	**F4PL**
3	9	**MTV Unplugged EP**	Mariah Carey	Columbia	12	3	**P**
4	6	**Ten**	Pearl Jam	Epic Associated	35	18	**F8P**
5	3	**Blood Sugar Sex Magik**	Red Hot Chili Peppers	Warner	19	25	**F3PL**
6	8	**Ropin' The Wind**	Garth Brooks	Capitol	50	41	**10P**
7	-	**Boomerang**	Soundtrack	LaFace	12		**2P**
8	5	**Adrenalize**	Def Leppard	Mercury	15	1	**3P**
9	-	**No Fences**	Garth Brooks	Capitol	36	F	**11P**
10	7	**Shadows And Light**	Wilson Phillips	SBK	4	6	**PL**

August 1992

This Mnth	Last Mnth	Title	Artist	Label	Wks in 10	UK Pos	
1	1	**Some Gave All**	Billy Ray Cyrus	Mercury	43	9	**F8P**
2	2	**Totally Krossed Out**	Kris Kross	Ruffhouse	25	31	**F4PL**
3	4	**Ten**	Pearl Jam	Epic Associated	35	18	**F8P**
4	3	**MTV Unplugged EP**	Mariah Carey	Columbia	12	3	**P**
5	7	**Boomerang**	Soundtrack	LaFace	12		**2P**
6	-	**Countdown To Extinction**	Megadeth	Capitol	8	5	**F2P**
7	6	**Ropin' The Wind**	Garth Brooks	Capitol	50	41	**10P**
8	-	**Mo' Money**	Soundtrack	Perspective	3		**P**
9	-	**Shorty The Pimp**	Too Short	Jive	2		**F**
10	5	**Blood Sugar Sex Magik**	Red Hot Chili Peppers	Warner	19	25	**F3PL**

September 1992

This Mnth	Last Mnth	Title	Artist	Label	Wks in 10	UK Pos	
1	1	**Some Gave All**	Billy Ray Cyrus	Mercury	43	9	**F8P**
2	3	**Ten**	Pearl Jam	Epic Associated	35	18	**F8P**
3	-	**Unplugged**	Eric Clapton	Duck	38	2	**7P**
4	-	**Beyond The Season**	Garth Brooks	Capitol	11		**2P**
5	-	**Bobby**	Bobby Brown	MCA	5	11	**2PL**
6	2	**Totally Krossed Out**	Kris Kross	Ruffhouse	25	31	**F4PL**
7	5	**Boomerang**	Soundtrack	LaFace	12		**2P**
8	-	**Temple Of The Dog**	Temple Of The Dog	A&M	4		**FPL**
9	-	**What's The 411**	Mary J. Blige	Uptown	9		**F2P**
10	-	**Countdown To Extinction**	Megadeth	Capitol	8	5	**F2P**

• The first artist to enter the Top 5 with their debut album was Billy Ray Cyrus with **Some Gave All**. Other country albums in the Top 20 were **The Hard Way** by Clint Black, **I Still Believe In You** by Vince Gill and the most successful Christmas album in 20 years, **Beyond The Season** by Garth Brooks.

• Some of the acts involved in big money deals in 1992 were The Rolling Stones who signed to Virgin for $40 million, Barbra Streisand who re-signed with Columbia for $60 million and Madonna, whose contract guaranteed her at least $5 million per album. Prince was involved in a reported $100 million deal, and Elton John and U2 signed publishing contracts said to be worth $26 million and $15 million respectively.

• Among the various artist albums in the Top 20 were **MTV Party To Go Vol. 2** and the soundtracks from **Honeymoon In Vegas, Singles, Boomerang** and **Mo'Money**.

UK 1992 OCT-DEC

• More acts debuted on the UK singles chart in 1992 than in any previous year with records tending to enter higher and have shorter chart life spans. It was also reported that even though Britain only accounted for 8% of world sales, 25% of the records sold globally were by UK artists.

• The Number 1s for the last three months of 1992 were hit compilations: **Gold – Greatest Hits** by Abba, **Glittering Prize 81-92** by Simple Minds and **Cher's Greatest Hits: 1965-1992**.

• In Britain, both compact disk singles and albums were now outselling cassettes. Sales of records and tapes in the USA were up 15.2% to $9 billion.

• To celebrate their 30th anniversary all The Beatles albums were re-promoted in the USA and 11 of them re-entered the catalogue chart with **Sergeant Pepper** reaching Number 1.

• Bob Marley's 78-track boxed set **Songs Of Freedom** was reportedly the highest priced album yet to reach the UK Top 10.

• Dire Straits ended their worldwide two year megatour in Spain. They had played almost 300 concerts and were seen by over seven million people. U2 were the top live act in the USA in 1992, their 70 shows grossed over $60 million.

October 1992

This Mnth	*Last Mnth*	*Title*	*Artist*	*Label*	*Wks in 10*	*US Pos*	
1	-	**Gold - Greatest Hits**	Abba	Polydor	19	63	**PL**
2	-	**Automatic For The People**	R.E.M.	Warner	46	2	**P**
3	1	**Tubular Bells II**	Mike Oldfield	WEA	8		
4	-	**Timeless (The Classics)**	Michael Bolton	Columbia	13	1	
5	-	**Symbol**	Prince & The New Power Generation	Paisley Park	3	5	
6	-	**Glittering Prize 81/92**	Simple Minds	Virgin	13		**L**
7	-	**Erotica**	Madonna	Maverick	5	2	
8	5	**The Best Of Belinda Vol. 1**	Belinda Carlisle	Virgin	8		
9	3	**Back To Front**	Lionel Richie	Motown	24	19	**L**
10	-	**Us**	Peter Gabriel	Realworld	3	2	

November 1992

This Mnth	*Last Mnth*	*Title*	*Artist*	*Label*	*Wks in 10*	*US Pos*	
1	6	**Glittering Prize 81/92**	Simple Minds	Virgin	13		**L**
2	4	**Timeless (The Classics)**	Michael Bolton	Columbia	13	1	
3	1	**Gold - Greatest Hits**	Abba	Polydor	19	63	**PL**
4	-	**Cher's Greatest Hits: 1965-1992**	Cher	Geffen	11		**PL**
5	-	**Keep The Faith**	Bon Jovi	Jambco	6	5	
6	7	**Erotica**	Madonna	Maverick	5	2	
7	-	**Greatest Hits**	Gloria Estefan	Epic	11	15	
8	2	**Automatic For The People**	R.E.M.	Warner	46	2	**P**
9	-	**Pop! - The First 20 Hits**	Erasure	Mute	8		
10	-	**God's Great Banana Skin**	Chris Rea	East West	2		

December 1992

This Mnth	*Last Mnth*	*Title*	*Artist*	*Label*	*Wks in 10*	*US Pos*	
1	4	**Cher's Greatest Hits: 1965-1992**	Cher	Geffen	11		**PL**
2	9	**Pop! - The First 20 Hits**	Erasure	Mute	8		
3	-	**Live - The Way We Walk Vol. 1: The Shorts**	Genesis	Virgin	10	35	
4	7	**Greatest Hits**	Gloria Estefan	Epic	11	15	
5	2	**Timeless (The Classics)**	Michael Bolton	Columbia	13	1	
6	1	**Glittering Prize 81/92**	Simple Minds	Virgin	13		**L**
7	-	**The Freddie Mercury Album**	Freddie Mercury	Polydor	6		**L**
8	3	**Gold - Greatest Hits**	Abba	Polydor	19	63	**PL**
9	-	**Stars**	Simply Red	Eastwest	51	76	**3PL**
10	8	**Automatic For The People**	R.E.M.	Warner	46	2	**P**

US 1992 OCT-DEC

October 1992

This Mnth	Last Mnth	Title	Artist	Label	Wks in 10	UK Pos	
1	1	**Some Gave All**	Billy Ray Cyrus	Mercury	43	9	**F8P**
2	-	**The Chase**	Garth Brooks	Capitol	17		**5P**
3	3	**Unplugged**	Eric Clapton	Duck	38	2	**7P**
4	2	**Ten**	Pearl Jam	Epic Associated	35	18	**F8P**
5	-	**Automatic For The People**	R.E.M.	Warner	8	1	**3P**
6	4	**Beyond The Season**	Garth Brooks	Capitol	11		**2P**
7	-	**Us**	Peter Gabriel	Geffen	3	2	**PL**
8	-	**Timeless (The Classics)**	Michael Bolton	Columbia	20	3	**4P**
9	9	**What's The 411**	Mary J. Blige	Uptown	9		**F2P**
10	-	**Singles**	Soundtrack	Epic Soundtrax	3		**P**

November 1992

This Mnth	Last Mnth	Title	Artist	Label	Wks in 10	UK Pos	
1	2	**The Chase**	Garth Brooks	Capitol	17		**5P**
2	8	**Timeless (The Classics)**	Michael Bolton	Columbia	20	3	**4P**
3	3	**Unplugged**	Eric Clapton	Duck	38	2	**7P**
4	1	**Some Gave All**	Billy Ray Cyrus	Mercury	43	9	**F8P**
5	-	**Erotica**	Madonna	Maverick	4	2	**2P**
6	5	**Automatic For The People**	R.E.M.	Warner	8	1	**3P**
7	-	**Pure Country**	George Strait	MCA	6		**F3P**
8	-	**Love Deluxe**	Sade	Epic	7	10	**4P**
9	4	**Ten**	Pearl Jam	Epic Associated	35	18	**F8P**
10	-	**Keep The Faith**	Bon Jovi	Jambco	2	1	**2P**

December 1992

This Mnth	Last Mnth	Title	Artist	Label	Wks in 10	UK Pos	
1	-	**The Bodyguard**	Soundtrack	Arista	40		**13P**
2	2	**Timeless (The Classics)**	Michael Bolton	Columbia	20	3	**4P**
3	1	**The Chase**	Garth Brooks	Capitol	17		**5P**
4	3	**Unplugged**	Eric Clapton	Duck	38	2	**7P**
5	4	**Some Gave All**	Billy Ray Cyrus	Mercury	43	9	**F8P**
6	-	**Home For Christmas**	Amy Grant	A&M	5		**PL**
7	-	**The Predator**	Ice Cube	Priority	4	73	**P**
8	-	**A Very Special Christmas 2**	Various	A&M	4		**FPL**
9	-	**Breathless**	Kenny G	Arista	35	4	**7P**
10	-	**The Christmas Album**	Neil Diamond	MCA	2	50	**P**

• For the second year running Garth Brooks was America's top artist. **The Chase** was the first album certified quintuple platinum in its first month and it was one of four albums he had simultaneously in the Top 20.

• In November, 10 of the Top 25 albums were by country acts. Moreover, before 1992, there had never been as many as three country albums simultaneously in the Top 10; during that year it happened on over 20 occasions.

• As African-American acts held a record nine of the Top 10 placings on the singles chart, **The Predator** by Ice Cube became the first rap album to enter at Number 1. Ice Cube also made the headlines when seven people were injured during a shooting incident at one of his concerts. Several other rap acts also found themselves in the media's firing line after recording anti-police songs. The most notorious being 'Cop Killer', which came from Ice-T's rock rap group Body Count's self-titled debut album.

UK 1993

JAN-MAR

• Among the noteworthy British artists debuting in the Top 10 were: Dina Carroll with **So Close**, super-duo Coverdale/Page with **Coverdale/Page**, teen idols East 17 with **Walthamstow**, Little Angels with **Jam** and The Stereo MCs with **Connected**.

• The Rolling Stones leader Mick Jagger and ex-Beatle Paul McCartney each narrowly missed the Top 10 with their solo albums **Wandering Spirit** and **Off The Ground** respectively. Another relatively veteran British act, Duran Duran (above), also returned to the Top 20 with a self-titled album.

• Pink Floyd's **Dark Side Of The Moon** was reissued in a special compact disk box to commemorate its 20th anniversary, and a Buddy Holly compilation, **Words Of Love**, was released on the 34th anniversary of his death. Both albums made the Top 10.

• When Elton John's single 'The Last Song' reached the US Top 40, it meant that he had achieved at least one Top 40 entry for 24 consecutive years – breaking a record held by Elvis Presley.

January 1993

This Mnth	Last Mnth	Title	Artist	Label	Wks in 10	US Pos	
1	1	**Cher's Greatest Hits: 1965-1992**	Cher	Geffen	11		PL
2	-	**Take That And Party**	Take That	RCA	14		F
3	10	**Automatic For The People**	R.E.M.	Warner	46	2	P
4	2	**Pop! - The First 20 Hits**	Erasure	Mute	8		
5	4	**Greatest Hits**	Gloria Estefan	Epic	11	15	
6	-	**Boss Drum**	Shamen	One Little Indian	9		FL
7	-	**Live - The Way We Walk Vol. 2: The Longs**	Genesis	Virgin	3	20	
8	3	**Live - The Way We Walk Vol. 1: The Shorts**	Genesis	Virgin	10	35	
9	-	**Connected**	Stereo MCs	Gee Street	9	92	FL
10	-	**3 Years, 5 Months And 2 Days In The Life Of...**	Arrested Development	Cooltempo	10	3	FL

February 1993

This Mnth	Last Mnth	Title	Artist	Label	Wks in 10	US Pos	
1	3	**Automatic For The People**	R.E.M.	Warner	46	2	P
2	10	**3 Years, 5 Months And 2 Days In The Life Of...**	Arrested Development	Cooltempo	10	3	FL
3	-	**Pure Cult**	Cult	Beggars Banquet	3		L
4	-	**Funky Divas**	En Vogue	East West America	3	8	FL
5	-	**Words Of Love**	Buddy Holly & The Crickets	PolyGram TV	3		L
6	-	**So Close**	Dina Carroll	A&M	29		FPL
7	-	**Gorecki Symphony No. 3**	Dawn Upshaw/The London Sinfonietta c. David Zinman	Elektra Nonsuch	3		FL
8	-	**Walthamstow**	East 17	London	3		F
9	-	**Jam**	Little Angels	Polydor	1		FL
10	-	**Dusk**	The The	Epic	1	142	L

March 1993

This Mnth	Last Mnth	Title	Artist	Label	Wks in 10	US Pos	
1	-	**Unplugged**	Eric Clapton	Duck	11	1	
2	-	**Are You Gonna Go My Way**	Lenny Kravitz	Virgin	5	12	L
3	-	**Diva**	Annie Lennox	RCA	24	23	FPL
4	1	**Automatic For The People**	R.E.M.	Warner	46	2	P
5	-	**Ten Summoner's Tales**	Sting	A&M	15	2	
6	-	**Ingenue**	kd lang	Sire	4	18	FL
7	-	**Rod Stewart, Lead Vocalist**	Rod Stewart	Warner	2		
8	-	**Their Greatest Hits**	Hot Chocolate	EMI	3		L
9	-	**Dangerous**	Michael Jackson	Epic	24	1	PL
10	-	**Amazing Things**	Runrig	Chrysalis	1		L

US 1993 JAN-MAR

January 1993

This Mnth	Last Mnth	Title	Artist	Label	Wks in 10	UK Pos	
1	1	**The Bodyguard**	Soundtrack	Arista	40		13P
2	5	**Unplugged**	Eric Clapton	Duck	38	2	7P
3	4	**The Chase**	Garth Brooks	Capitol	17		5P
4	3	**Timeless (The Classics)**	Michael Bolton	Columbia	20	3	4P
5	10	**Breathless**	Kenny G	Arista	35	4	7P
6	6	**Some Gave All**	Billy Ray Cyrus	Mercury	43	9	F8P
7	-	**Ten**	Pearl Jam	Epic Associated	35	18	F8P
8	7	**Home For Christmas**	Amy Grant	A&M	5		PL
9	-	**If I Ever Fall In Love**	Shai	Gasoline Alley	6		F2PL
10	-	**It's Your Call**	Reba McEntire	MCA	4		F3P

February 1993

This Mnth	Last Mnth	Title	Artist	Label	Wks in 10	UK Pos	
1	1	**The Bodyguard**	Soundtrack	Arista	40		13P
2	5	**Breathless**	Kenny G	Arista	35	4	7P
3	-	**The Chronic**	Dr. Dre	Death Row	28		F3PL
4	2	**Unplugged**	Eric Clapton	Duck	38	2	7P
5	6	**Some Gave All**	Billy Ray Cyrus	Mercury	43	9	F8P
6	9	**If I Ever Fall In Love**	Shai	Gasoline Alley	6		F2PL
7	4	**Timeless (The Classics)**	Michael Bolton	Columbia	20	3	4P
8	-	**Aladdin**	Soundtrack	Walt Disney	6		3P
9	-	**Pocket Full Of Kryptonite**	Spin Doctors	Epic Associated	22	2	F4PL
10	7	**Ten**	Pearl Jam	Epic Associated	35	18	F8P

March 1993

This Mnth	Last Mnth	Title	Artist	Label	Wks in 10	UK Pos	
1	1	**The Bodyguard**	Soundtrack	Arista	40		13P
2	4	**Unplugged**	Eric Clapton	Duck	38	2	7P
3	2	**Breathless**	Kenny G	Arista	35	4	7P
4	3	**The Chronic**	Dr. Dre	Death Row	28	F	3PL
5	5	**Some Gave All**	Billy Ray Cyrus	Mercury	43	9	F8P
6	-	**19 Naughty III**	Naughty By Nature	Tommy Boy	4	40	FPL
7	9	**Pocket Full Of Kryptonite**	Spin Doctors	Epic Associated	22	2	F4PL
8	-	**Ten Summoner's Tales**	Sting	A&M	8	2	3P
9	-	**3 Years 5 Months & 2 Days In The Life Of...**	Arrested Development	Chrysalis	3		F3PL
10	-	**Live: Right Here, Right Now**	Van Halen	Warner	1		2PL

• The soundtrack album to Whitney Houston's film **The Bodyguard** sold a record breaking six million copies in just eight weeks. Her first single from the film, 'I Will Always Love You', topped the American chart for a record 14 weeks, selling three million copies in two months. In Britain, it became the biggest selling single ever by a female. It was one of three singles by Houston that, at times, were simultaneously situated in the US Top 15. On a personal note, Whitney, who was married to top star Bobby Brown, had her first baby, Bobbi Kristina.

• Eric Clapton won six trophies at the Grammy Awards including Album Of The Year for **Unplugged**, which then moved to the top after six months on the chart. Other major award winners included Arrested Development (Best New Artist), kd lang (Best Female Performance) and U2 (Best Group Rock Performance). Also walking away with trophies were such diverse acts as Chet Atkins, Tony Bennett, Boyz II Men, The Chieftains, Enya, Melissa Etheridge, Al Jarreau, Nine Inch Nails, Shabba Ranks, Jon Secada and Tom Waits. Little Richard received the Lifetime Achievement Award and Michael Jackson picked up the Grammy Legend Award.

UK 1993

APR-JUNE

• There were a lot of changes at the top of the UK chart with Depeche Mode, the critically acclaimed Suede, David Bowie, New Order, Cliff Richard, Dutch dance duo 2 Unlimited and Tina Turner all spending one week at the summit.

• R.E.M. were the hottest American group in the UK. Their album **Automatic For The People** returned to the top six months after originally entering in that position. In the prestigious *NME* Poll it was voted Album Of The Year and they were named Top Group. The latest US band to hit on both sides of the Atlantic were The Spin Doctors whose **Pocket Full Of Kryptonite** was a transatlantic Top 3 entry.

• Depeche Mode's transatlantic Number 1 album **Songs Of Faith And Devotion** was the first album from a British independent label to enter the US chart in the top spot. The group's tenth consecutive UK Top 10 album also entered the German, Italian and Swiss charts in pole position.

• Groups in the headlines included Iron Maiden, Deep Purple and U2. Lead vocalist Bruce Dickinson left Iron Maiden, Ian Gillan rejoined Deep Purple and U2 signed a six-album record deal reported to be worth $200 million.

April 1993

This Mnth	Last Mnth	Title	Artist	Label	Wks in 10	US Pos	
1	-	**Suede**	Suede	Nude	4		F
2	-	**Cover Shot**	David Essex	PolyGram TV	5		L
3	-	**Black Tie White Noise**	David Bowie	Arista	3	39	
4	-	**Songs Of Faith And Devotion**	Depeche Mode	Mute	2	1	L
5	4	**Automatic For The People**	R.E.M.	Warner	46	2	P
6	3	**Diva**	Annie Lennox	A&M	24	23	FPL
7	1	**Their Greatest Hits**	Hot Chocolate	EMI	3		L
8	1	**Unplugged**	Eric Clapton	Duck	11	1	
9	2	**Are You Gonna Go My Way**	Lenny Kravitz	Virgin	5	12	L
10	-	**Taxi**	Bryan Ferry	Virgin	1	79	L

May 1993

This Mnth	Last Mnth	Title	Artist	Label	Wks in 10	US Pos	
1	5	**Automatic For The People**	R.E.M.	Warner	46	2	P
2	-	**Ten Summoner's Tales**	Sting	A&M	15	2	
3	-	**Republic**	New Order	Centredate Co	3	11	
4	-	**The Album**	Cliff Richard	EMI	3		
5	-	**No Limits**	2 Unlimited	PWL Continental	7		F
6	-	**So Close**	Dina Carroll	A&M	29		FPL
7	-	**Duran Duran (The Wedding Album)**	Duran Duran	Parlophone	4	7	L
8	-	**Bang!**	World Party	Ensign	2	126	FL
9	-	**Get A Grip**	Aerosmith	Geffen	2	1	
10	-	**On The Night**	Dire Straits	Vertigo	2	116	L

June 1993

This Mnth	Last Mnth	Title	Artist	Label	Wks in 10	US Pos	
1	1	**Automatic For The People**	R.E.M.	Warner	46	2	P
2	5	**No Limits**	2 Unlimited	PWL Continental	7		F
3	-	**Janet**	Janet Jackson	Virgin	5	1	L
4	-	**Unplugged...And Seated**	Rod Stewart	Warner	13	2	L
5	-	**What's Love Got To Do With It (Soundtrack)**	Tina Turner	Parlophone	6	17	L
6	-	**Pocket Full Of Kryptonite**	Spin Doctors	Epic	17	3	F
7	-	**Kamakiriad**	Donald Fagen	Reprise	2	10	FL
8	-	**Emergency On Planet Earth**	Jamiroquai	Sony S2	10		F
9	-	**Too Long In Exile**	Van Morrison	Polydor	2	29	
10	-	**Dream Harder**	Waterboys	Geffen	2	171	L

US 1993 APR-JUNE

April 1993

This Mnth	Last Mnth	Title	Artist	Label	Wks in 10	UK Pos	
1	1	**The Bodyguard**	Soundtrack	Arista	40		13P
2	3	**Breathless**	Kenny G	Arista	35	4	7P
3	2	**Unplugged**	Eric Clapton	Duck	38	2	7P
4	7	**Pocket Full Of Kryptonite**	Spin Doctors	Epic Associated	22	2	F4PL
5	8	**Ten Summoner's Tales**	Sting	A&M	8	2	3P
6	-	**Songs Of Faith And Devotion**	Depeche Mode	Sire	4	1	PL
7	-	**12 Inches Of Snow**	Snow	Atco	8	41	FPL
8	4	**The Chronic**	Dr. Dre	Death Row	28	F	3PL
9	-	**Lose Control**	Silk	Keia	9		FPL
10	-	**Coverdale Page**	Coverdale/Page	Geffen	2	4	FL

May 1993

This Mnth	Last Mnth	Title	Artist	Label	Wks in 10	UK Pos	
1	1	**The Bodyguard**	Soundtrack	Arista	40		13P
2	2	**Breathless**	Kenny G	Arista	35	4	7P
3	-	**Get A Grip**	Aerosmith	Geffen	12	2	6P
4	4	**Pocket Full Of Kryptonite**	Spin Doctors	Epic Associated	22	2	F4PL
5	3	**Unplugged**	Eric Clapton	Duck	38	2	7P
6	8	**The Chronic**	Dr. Dre	Death Row	28		F3PL
7	7	**12 Inches Of Snow**	Snow	Atco Eastwest	8	41	FPL
8	-	**Porno For Pyros**	Porno For Pyros	Warner	1	13	FL
9	-	**It's About Time**	SWV	RCA	11	17	F2PL
10	9	**Lose Control**	Silk	Keia	9		FPL

June 1993

This Mnth	Last Mnth	Title	Artist	Label	Wks in 10	UK Pos	
1	-	**Janet**	Janet Jackson	Virgin	36	1	6PL
2	1	**The Bodyguard**	Soundtrack	Arista	40		13P
3	-	**Unplugged...And Seated**	Rod Stewart	Warner	12	2	2PL
4	2	**Breathless**	Kenny G	Arista	35	4	7P
5	6	**The Chronic**	Dr. Dre	Death Row	28		F3PL
6	3	**Get A Grip**	Aerosmith	Geffen	12	2	6P
7	4	**Pocket Full Of Kryptonite**	Spin Doctors	Epic Associated	22	2	F4PL
8	9	**It's About Time**	SWV	RCA	11	17	F2PL
9	-	**Core**	Stone Temple Pilots	Atlantic	17	27	F3P
10	-	**Tell Me Why**	Wynonna	Curb	2		PL

• White Canadian rapper Snow with **Information**, Run-D.M.C. with **Down With The King**, LL Cool J with **14 Shots To The Dome** and ex-N.W.A. member Dr. Dre with **The Chronic** were among the rap acts that reached the Top 10. Rappers who cracked the Top 20 included The Geto Boys with **Till Death Do Us Part**, Naughty By Nature with **19 Naughty III** and Body Count's leader Ice-T with **Home Invasion**.

• For 11 weeks Kenny G's album **Breathless** was in runner up position to his label-mate Whitney Houston's **The Bodyguard**. Amazingly the track 'Even If My Heart Would Break' by saxophonist G with vocalist Aaron Neville was included on both albums. For the record, **The Bodyguard** went on to sell 13 million copies in the USA alone and over 20 million globally.

• Country music continued to grow in popularity and at times 50 of the Top 200 albums were from that musical genre.

UK 1993 JULY-SEPT

• Ten years after reaching the UK and American Top 20 with **Labour Of Love**, UB40's **Promises And Lies** became their first transatlantic Top 10 entry. A single taken from it, 'Can't Help Falling In Love', gave the British reggae band their second transatlantic Number 1. Interestingly, the track, which had been rejected for inclusion in the film **Honeymoon In Vegas**, was now featured on the soundtrack of **Sliver**.

• Noteworthy Top 10 chart newcomers included Jamiroquai, The Manic Street Preachers and Bjork, with the chart topping **Emergency On Planet Earth**, **Gold Against The Soul** and **Debut** respectively.

• As **Zooropa**, which had advance orders of over 500,000, became the fifth album by U2 to enter at Number 1, Paul Weller clocked up the seventh No. 2 album of his career with **Wild Wood**.

• Duran Duran, whose new American tour was sponsored by Coca Cola, were given their star on the Hollywood Rock Walk Of Fame as were America's Steely Dan.

• The breakers chart, listing singles between positions 40-75, which was introduced at the beginning of the year to help increase sales, proved to be a complete failure, with only 3% of the records that made the chart going on into the Top 40.

July 1993

This Mnth	Last Mnth	Title	Artist	Label	Wks in 10	US Pos	
1	8	**Emergency On Planet Earth**	Jamiroquai	Sony S2	10		F
2	4	**Unplugged...And Seated**	Rod Stewart	Warner	13	2	L
3	6	**Pocket Full Of Kryptonite**	Spin Doctors	Epic	17	3	F
4	-	**Zooropa**	U2	Island	9	1	L
5	1	**Automatic For The People**	R.E.M.	Warner	46	2	P
6	-	**Promises And Lies**	UB40	DEP International	11	6	
7	-	**Always**	Michael Ball	Polydor	6		
8	-	**Ten Summoner's Tales**	Sting	A&M	15	2	
9	-	**Back To Broadway**	Barbra Streisand	Columbia	3	1	L
10	5	**What's Love Got To Do With It (Soundtrack)**	Tina Turner	Parlophone	6	17	L

August 1993

This Mnth	Last Mnth	Title	Artist	Label	Wks in 10	US Pos	
1	6	**Promises And Lies**	UB40	DEP International	11	6	
2	4	**Zooropa**	U2	Island	9	1	L
3	3	**Pocket Full Of Kryptonite**	Spin Doctors	Epic	17	3	F
4	5	**Automatic For The People**	R.E.M.	Warner	46	2	P
5	-	**River Of Dreams**	Billy Joel	Columbia	6	1	L
6	-	**Bigger Better, Faster, More!**	4 Non Blondes	Interscope	8		FL
7	7	**Always**	Michael Ball	Polydor	6		
8	1	**Emergency On Planet Earth**	Jamiroquai	Sony S2	10		F
9	-	**Keep The Faith**	Bon Jovi	Jambco	6	5	
10	-	**Take That And Party**	Take That	RCA	14		F

September 1993

This Mnth	Last Mnth	Title	Artist	Label	Wks in 10	US Pos	
1	1	**Promises And Lies**	UB40	DEP International	11	6	
2	-	**Music Box**	Mariah Carey	Columbia	38	1	PL
3	-	**Levellers**	Levellers	China	3		FL
4	-	**Bat Out Of Hell II: Back Into Hell**	Meat Loaf	Virgin	23	1	PL
5	3	**Pocket Full Of Kryptonite**	Spin Doctors	Epic	17	3	F
6	-	**Wild Wood**	Paul Weller	Go! Discs	3		L
7	5	**River Of Dreams**	Billy Joel	Columbia	6	1	L
8	-	**In Utero**	Nirvana	Geffen	3	1	
9	2	**Zooropa**	U2	Island	9	1	L
10	4	**Automatic For The People**	R.E.M.	Warner	46	2	P

US 1993 JULY-SEPT

July 1993

This Mnth	Last Mnth	Title	Artist	Label	Wks in 10	UK Pos	
1	1	**Janet**	Janet Jackson	Virgin	36	1	**6PL**
2	9	**Core**	Stone Temple Pilots	Atlantic	17	27	**F3P**
3	3	**Unplugged...And Seated**	Rod Stewart	Warner	12	2	**2PL**
4	-	**Back To Broadway**	Barbra Streisand	Columbia	5	4	**2P**
5	5	**The Chronic**	Dr. Dre	Death Row	28		**F3PL**
6	-	**It Won't Be The Last**	Billy Ray Cyrus	Mercury	5		**PL**
7	-	**Zooropa**	U2	Island	7	1	**2PL**
8	4	**Breathless**	Kenny G	Arista	35	4	**7P**
9	-	**Sleepless In Seattle**	Soundtrack	Epic	13		**3P**
10	-	**Last Action Hero**	Soundtrack	Columbia	4		**P**

August 1993

This Mnth	Last Mnth	Title	Artist	Label	Wks in 10	UK Pos	
1	-	**Black Sunday**	Cypress Hill	Ruffhouse	10	13	**FPL**
2	9	**Sleepless In Seattle**	Soundtrack	Epic	13		**3P**
3	7	**Zooropa**	U2	Island	7	1	**2PL**
4	1	**Janet**	Janet Jackson	Virgin	36	1	**6PL**
5	2	**Core**	Stone Temple Pilots	Atlantic	17	27	**F3P**
6	-	**Promises And Lies**	UB40	Virgin	6	1	**FPL**
7	4	**Back To Broadway**	Barbra Streisand	Columbia	5	4	**2P**
8	-	**The Bodyguard**	Soundtrack	Arista	40		**13P**
9	-	**River Of Dreams**	Billy Joel	Columbia	18	3	**4PL**
10	3	**Unplugged...And Seated**	Rod Stewart	Warner	12	2	**2PL**

September 1993

This Mnth	Last Mnth	Title	Artist	Label	Wks in 10	UK Pos	
1	9	**River Of Dreams**	Billy Joel	Columbia	18	3	**4PL**
2	2	**Sleepless In Seattle**	Soundtrack	Epic	13		**3P**
3	-	**Blind Melon**	Blind Melon	Capitol	11	53	**F2PL**
4	4	**Janet**	Janet Jackson	Virgin	36	1	**6PL**
5	-	**In Pieces**	Garth Brooks	Capitol	8	2	**5PL**
6	-	**Music Box**	Mariah Carey	Columbia	33	1	**8P**
7	1	**Black Sunday**	Cypress Hill	Ruffhouse	10	13	**FPL**
8	5	**Core**	Stone Temple Pilots	Atlantic	17	27	**F3P**
9	6	**Promises And Lies**	UB40	Virgin	6	1	**FPL**
10	8	**The Bodyguard**	Soundtrack	Arista	40		**13P**

• There was no shortage of new US rock bands in the Top 10. Stone Temple Pilots scored with **Core**, grunge rockers Smashing Pumpkins hit the heights with **Siamese Dream** as did Blind Melon with their eponymous album. Also selling remarkably well were **Bigger, Better, Faster, More!** by 4 Non Blondes and **Grave Dancers Union** from Minneapolis quartet Soul Asylum.

• A variety of acts entered the chart at Number 1: Janet Jackson with **Janet**, Barbra Streisand with **Back To Broadway**, U2 with **Zooropa**, rappers Cypress Hill with **Black Sunday**, Billy Joel (above) with **River Of Dreams** and Garth Brooks with **In Pieces**.

• Stars of a bygone era including Nat 'King' Cole, Jimmy Durante, Louis Armstrong and Gene Autry, found themselves at the top again thanks to their appearances on the soundtrack album **Sleepless In Seattle**. Other film soundtracks selling well were **Last Action Hero** and the Tina Turner bio-pic **What's Love Got To Do With It**.

UK 1993

OCT-DEC

• Comeback of the year was undoubtedly that of Meat Loaf. He rocketed to the top of the transatlantic charts with **Bat Out Of Hell II: Back Into Hell** – the fastest selling album worldwide since **Thriller.** It was the first American Number 1 album for the artist who had made his US chart debut over 22 years earlier. The initial single from the LP, 'I'd Do Anything For Love (But I Won't Do That)', also hit the top.

• Nirvana, arguably the most influential new rock group of the early Nineties, entered both the UK and US charts at Number 1 with **In Utero**.

• Take That entered in the top slot with **Everything Changes**, which amassed advance orders of almost 300,000. The top teen appeal act, who had recently completed a record breaking trio of hits that crashed straight in at Number 1, ended the year with three of the Top four videos.

• Both Elton John and Frank Sinatra released albums entitled **Duets**, both not surprisingly contained duets with other top acts. Sinatra took most of the honours, although worldwide his album sold only a quarter of the 20 million copies that his label prophesied.

October 1993

This Mnth	Last Mnth	Title	Artist	Label	Wks in 10	US Pos	
1	4	**Bat Out Of Hell II: Back Into Hell**	Meat Loaf	Virgin	23	1	**PL**
2	-	**Very**	Pet Shop Boys	Parlophone	3	20	
3	-	**Elegant Slumming**	M People	Deconstruction	17		**F**
4	-	**Everything Changes**	Take That	RCA	14		**PL**
5	-	**The Hits 2**	Prince	Paisley Park	5	54	
6	8	**In Utero**	Nirvana	Geffen	3	1	
7	-	**Vs.**	Pearl Jam	Epic	3	1	**F**
8	-	**The Beatles 1962-1966**	Beatles	Apple	16	3	
9	-	**Aces And Kings - The Best Of Go West**	Go West	Chrysalis	3		**L**
10	-	**Elements - The Best Of Mike Oldfield**	Mike Oldfield	Virgin	3		**L**

November 1993

This Mnth	Last Mnth	Title	Artist	Label	Wks in 10	US Pos	
1	1	**Bat Out Of Hell II: Back Into Hell**	Meat Loaf	Virgin	23	1	**PL**
2	-	**One Woman - The Ultimate Collection**	Diana Ross	EMI	18		**PL**
3	4	**Everything Changes**	Take That	RCA	14		**PL**
4	-	**Both Sides**	Phil Collins	Virgin	13	13	**L**
5	-	**So Far So Good**	Bryan Adams	A&M	13	6	**L**
6	-	**So Close**	Dina Carroll	A&M	29		**FPL**
7	-	**Experience The Divine - Greatest Hits**	Bette Midler	Atlantic	4	50	**L**
8	-	**The Red Shoes**	Kate Bush	EMI	2	28	**L**
9	-	**End Of Part One (Their Greatest Hits)**	Wet Wet Wet	Precious	22		**PL**
10	-	**Full Moon, Dirty Hearts**	INXS	Mercury	1	53	

December 1993

This Mnth	Last Mnth	Title	Artist	Label	Wks in 10	US Pos	
1	1	**Bat Out Of Hell II: Back Into Hell**	Meat Loaf	Virgin	23	1	**PL**
2	5	**So Far So Good**	Bryan Adams	A&M	13	6	**L**
3	4	**Both Sides**	Phil Collins	Virgin	13	13	**L**
4	2	**One Woman - The Ultimate Collection**	Diana Ross	EMI	18		**PL**
5	3	**Everything Changes**	Take That	RCA	14		**PL**
6	-	**Duets**	Elton John	Rocket	5	25	**L**
7	9	**End Of Part One (Their Greatest Hits)**	Wet Wet Wet	Precious	22		**PL**
8	-	**The Spaghetti Incident?**	Guns N' Roses	Geffen	2	4	**F**
9	-	**The One Thing**	Michael Bolton	Columbia	6	3	**L**
10	-	**So Close**	Dina Carroll	A&M	29		**FPL**

US 1993 OCT-DEC

October 1993

This Mnth	Last Mnth	Title	Artist	Label	Wks in 10	UK Pos	
1	5	**In Pieces**	Garth Brooks	Capitol	8	2	**5PL**
2	-	**Bat Out Of Hell II: Back Into Hell**	Meat Loaf	MCA	19	1	**F4PL**
3	6	**Music Box**	Mariah Carey	Columbia	33	1	**8P**
4	-	**In Utero**	Nirvana	DGC	6	1	**3P**
5	1	**River Of Dreams**	Billy Joel	Columbia	18	3	**4PL**
6	4	**Janet**	Janet Jackson	Virgin	36	1	**6PL**
7	3	**Blind Melon**	Blind Melon	Capitol	11	53	**F2PL**
8	-	**Greatest Hits Volume Two**	Reba McEntire	MCA	12		**3P**
9	-	**Easy Come, Easy Go**	George Strait	MCA	3		**2PL**
10	2	**Sleepless In Seattle**	Soundtrack	Epic	13		**3P**

November 1993

This Mnth	Last Mnth	Title	Artist	Label	Wks in 10	UK Pos	
1	-	**Vs.**	Pearl Jam	Epic	14	2	**5P**
2	2	**Bat Out Of Hell II: Back Into Hell**	Meat Loaf	MCA	19	1	**F4PL**
3	-	**Common Thread: The Songs Of The Eagles**	Various	Giant	11		**F3P**
4	3	**Music Box**	Mariah Carey	Columbia	33	1	**8P**
5	-	**Duets**	Frank Sinatra	Reprise	8	5	**2P**
6	5	**River Of Dreams**	Billy Joel	Columbia	18	3	**4PL**
7	6	**Janet**	Janet Jackson	Virgin	36	1	**6PL**
8	-	**It's On (Dr. Dre 187UM) Killa**	Eazy-E	Ruthless	3		**FPL**
9	-	**Counterparts**	Rush	Atlantic	1	14	**L**
10	-	**Get In Where Ya Fit In**	Too Short	Jive	2		**PL**

December 1993

This Mnth	Last Mnth	Title	Artist	Label	Wks in 10	UK Pos	
1	1	**Vs.**	Pearl Jam	Epic	14	2	**5P**
2	4	**Music Box**	Mariah Carey	Columbia	33	1	**8P**
3	-	**Doggystyle**	Snoop Doggy Dogg	Death Row	17	38	**F3PL**
4	2	**Bat Out Of Hell II: Back Into Hell**	Meat Loaf	MCA	19	1	**F4PL**
5	5	**Duets**	Frank Sinatra	Reprise	8	5	**2P**
6	-	**The One Thing**	Michael Bolton	Columbia	10	4	**3PL**
7	3	**Common Thread: The Songs Of The Eagles**	Various	Giant	11		**F3P**
8	-	**The Beavis & Butt-Head Experience**	Beavis & Butt-Head	Geffen	4		**FPL**
9	7	**Janet**	Janet Jackson	Virgin	36	1	**6PL**
10	-	**The Spaghetti Incident?**	Guns N' Roses	Geffen	2	2	**PL**

• The total sales of records and tapes in the USA passed the $10 billion mark for the first time, while in Britain sales increased by 13.5%. The arrival on the international scene of the MiniDisk and the Digital Compact Cassette made only a minor difference to sales.

• 1993, which had been another record year for rap, ended with the notorious Snoop Doggy Dogg becoming the first artist ever to enter the US chart in peak position with their debut album. He must surely have been the only person to head the chart whilst on a murder charge. However, he was not the only rapper to reach the Top 10, there was also Spice 1 with **187 He Wrote**, Eazy E with his short-form album **It's On Killa**, Too Short with **Get In Where Ya Fit In** and Ice Cube with **Lethal Injection**.

•Two of the most unusual Top 10 hits of the year were **Barney's Favorites Vol. 1** by TV's favourite dinosaur and **The Beavis & Butt-Head Experience** by MTV's favourite duo.

• Michael Jackson grossed a staggering $12 million from five shows in Mexico. However, the media were far more interested in a schoolboy scandal he was allegedly involved in.

UK 1994 JAN-MAR

• Among the winners at the BRIT awards were Sting (Male Solo), Dina Carroll (Female Solo), Stereo MCs (group) and Gabrielle (Newcomer). Awards for Best International artists went to Lenny Kravitz, Bjork and Crowded House.

• It was noticeable that many of Britain's top acts were no longer reaching the heights in the USA. In fact, 1994 proved to be the worst year for UK artists Stateside since the first British invasion thirty years earlier.

• Canadian rocker Bryan Adams' second British Number 1, **So Far So Good**, sold an estimated seven million copies around the globe in its first six weeks.

• The year's top selling act were the Swedish quartet Ace Of Base. Their debut album **Happy Nation** (titled **The Sign** in the US) was an international smash selling over 15 million copies. The album also spawned a string of huge global hit singles.

January 1994

This Mnth	Last Mnth	Title	Artist	Label	Wks in 10	US Pos	
1	10	**So Close**	Dina Carroll	A&M	29		FPL
2	2	**So Far So Good**	Bryan Adams	A&M	13	6	L
3	4	**One Woman - The Ultimate Collection**	Diana Ross	EMI	18		PL
4	5	**Everything Changes**	Take That	RCA	14		PL
5	-	**Elegant Slumming**	M People	Deconstruction	17		F
6	1	**Bat Out Of Hell II: Back Into Hell**	Meat Loaf	Virgin	23	1	PL
7	-	**Debut**	Bjork	One Little Indian	12	61	FL
8	3	**Both Sides**	Phil Collins	Virgin	13	13	L
9	-	**Tease Me**	Chaka Demus & Pliers	Mango	6		FL
10	-	**Music Box**	Mariah Carey	Columbia	38	1	PL

Feruary 1994

This Mnth	Last Mnth	Title	Artist	Label	Wks in 10	US Pos	
1	9	**Tease Me**	Chaka Demus & Pliers	Mango	6		FL
2	-	**Under The Pink**	Tori Amos	East West	4	12	FL
3	10	**Music Box**	Mariah Carey	Columbia	38	1	PL
4	-	**Cross Of Changes**	Enigma	Virgin	9	9	L
5	3	**One Woman - The Ultimate Collection**	Diana Ross	EMI	18		PL
6	-	**In Pieces**	Garth Brooks	Capitol	2	1	FL
7	7	**Debut**	Bjork	One Little Indian	12	61	FL
8	1	**So Close**	Dina Carroll	A&M	29		FPL
9	-	**D:ream On Vol 1**	D:ream	Magnet	5		FL
10	-	**Antenna**	ZZ Top	RCA	1	14	L

March 1994

This Mnth	Last Mnth	Title	Artist	Label	Wks in 10	US Pos	
1	3	**Music Box**	Mariah Carey	Columbia	38	1	L
2	4	**Cross Of Changes**	Enigma	Virgin International	9	9	L
3	-	**Elegant Slumming**	M People	Deconstruction	17		F
4	7	**Debut**	Bjork	One Little Indian	12	61	FL
5	-	**Everybody Else Is Doing It, So Why Can't We**	Cranberries	Island	16	18	F
6	-	**Ten Summoner's Tales**	Sting	A&M	15	2	
7	8	**So Close**	Dina Carroll	A&M	29		FPL
8	-	**Vauxhall And I**	Morrissey	Parlophone	2	18	L
9	-	**Brutal Youth**	Elvis Costello	Warner	1	34	L
10	-	**Happy Nation**	Ace Of Base	London	14	1	FL

US 1994 JAN-MAR

January 1994

This Mnth	Last Mnth	Title	Artist	Label	Wks in 10	UK Pos	
1	2	**Music Box**	Mariah Carey	Columbia	33	1	**8P**
2	1	**Vs.**	Pearl Jam	Epic	14	2	**5P**
3	3	**Doggystyle**	Snoop Doggy Dogg	Death Row	17	38	**F3PL**
4	6	**The One Thing**	Michael Bolton	Columbia	10	4	**3PL**
5	4	**Bat Out Of Hell II: Back Into Hell**	Meat Loaf	MCA	19	1	**F4PL**
6	9	**Janet**	Janet Jackson	Virgin	36	1	**6PL**
7	5	**Duets**	Frank Sinatra	Reprise	8	5	**2P**
8	-	**So Far So Good**	Bryan Adams	A&M	7	1	**3PL**
9	-	**Diary Of A Mad Band**	Jodeci	Uptown	6		**FPL**
10	7	**Common Thread: The Songs Of The Eagles**	Various	Giant	11		**F3P**

February 1994

This Mnth	Last Mnth	Title	Artist	Label	Wks in 10	UK Pos	
1	1	**Music Box**	Mariah Carey	Columbia	33	1	**8P**
2	3	**Doggystyle**	Snoop Doggy Dogg	Death Row	17	38	**F3PL**
3	-	**Kickin' It Up**	John Michael Montgomery	Atlantic	4		**F2PL**
4	-	**Jar Of Flies**	Alice In Chains	Columbia	3	4	**PL**
5	-	**Greatest Hits Volume Two**	Reba McEntire	MCA	12		**3P**
6	-	**Greatest Hits**	Tom Petty & The Heartbreakers	MCA	10	10	**3P**
7	9	**Diary Of A Mad Band**	Jodeci	Uptown	6		**FPL**
8	-	**Toni Braxton**	Toni Braxton	LaFace	11	15	**F5PL**
9	-	**Very Necessary**	Salt-N-Pepa	Next Plateau	8	36	**F3PL**
10	-	**12 Play**	R. Kelly	Jive	18	36	**F3PL**

March 1994

This Mnth	Last Mnth	Title	Artist	Label	Wks in 10	UK Pos	
1	10	**12 Play**	R. Kelly	Jive	18	36	**F3PL**
2	1	**Music Box**	Mariah Carey	Columbia	33	1	**8P**
3	8	**Toni Braxton**	Toni Braxton	Laface	11	15	**F5PL**
4	-	**The Sign**	Ace Of Base	Arista	31	1	**F7PL**
5	2	**Doggystyle**	Snoop Doggy Dogg	Death Row	17	38	**F3PL**
6	-	**The Colour Of My Love**	Celine Dion	550 Music	11	10	**F2PL**
7	-	**August & Everything After**	Counting Crows	Geffen	32	16	**F4PL**
8	9	**Very Necessary**	Salt-N-Pepa	Next Plateau	8	36	**F3PL**
9	-	**Superunknown**	Soundgarden	A&M	11	4	**F3PL**
10	-	**The Downward Spiral**	Nine Inch Nails	Nothing	1	9	**PL**

• The biggest selling new artist of the early Nineties, Mariah Carey, scored her first transatlantic Number 1, **Music Box**. The album sold over seven million in her homeland, in excess of one million in the UK and clocked up sales of almost 20 million worldwide. At times, Carey also had four singles simultaneously on the US singles chart.

• Whitney Houston swept the board at the Grammy and American Music Awards. Among her many trophies was one for Album Of The Year won by **The Bodyguard**. At the Grammy ceremony U2's Bono presented Frank Sinatra with a Lifetime Award.

• Noteworthy R&B acts who debuted on the Top 10 included vocal quartet Jodeci with **Diary Of A Mad Band**, song stylist Toni Braxton with her eponymous first album and the year's Number 1 R&B singer/songwriter/producer R. Kelly with **12 Play**.

• John Michael Montgomery became the latest country act to top the charts. His album **Kickin' It Up** contained the original version of the award winning song 'I Swear' – later a million selling single for R&B group All-4-One.

• Two more Seattle bands entered the charts first week in pole position: Alice In Chains with **Jar Of Flies** and Soundgarden with **Superunknown**.

UK 1994 APR-JUNE

• In 1994 several veteran acts hit the road again. One of the most successful was British group Pink Floyd whose tour broke box office records around the world. They grossed £55 million in Europe from 43 shows and in the USA their 57 dates took £70 million. The group, who had sold over 125 million albums in their 25-year career, simultaneously topped the UK and US pop charts with **The Division Bell**, which reached Number 1 in 15 countries, and held the top two places on the US Catalog chart with **Dark Side Of The Moon** and **The Wall**.

• The most unexpected international hit of the year was the transatlantic Top 10 entry **Chant** (titled **Canto Gregoriano** for UK consumption) by The Benedictine Monks Of Santo Domingo De Silos.

• Three noted British acts reached the US Top 20 for the first time; Morrissey with **Vauxhall & I**, Erasure with **I Say, I Say, I Say** and Seal with his second eponymous album.

• Two of the year's most acclaimed British albums charted. They were Blur's BRIT winning **Parklife** and the UK's most successful female quartet of all time, Eternal, with their hit packed album **Always & Forever**.

April 1994

This Mnth	Last Mnth	Title	Artist	Label	Wks in 10	US Pos	
1	-	**The Division Bell**	Pink Floyd	EMI	13	1	**L**
2	10	**Happy Nation**	Ace Of Base	London	14	1	**FL**
3	1	**Music Box**	Mariah Carey	Columbia	38	1	**PL**
4	-	**Our Town - Greatest Hits**	Deacon Blue	Columbia	14		**L**
5	-	**The Very Best Of**	Marvin Gaye	Motown	5		**L**
6	-	**Give Out But Don't Give Up**	Primal Scream	Creation	3		**L**
7	-	**Crash! Boom! Bang!**	Roxette	EMI	2		**L**
8	-	**Brother Sister**	Brand New Heavies	Acid Jazz	5	95	**FL**
9	-	**D:ream On Vol 1**	D:ream	Magnet	5		**FL**
10	3	**Elegant Slumming**	M People	Deconstruction	17		**F**

May 1994

This Mnth	Last Mnth	Title	Artist	Label	Wks in 10	US Pos	
1	4	**Our Town - Greatest Hits**	Deacon Blue	Columbia	14		**L**
2	1	**The Division Bell**	Pink Floyd	EMI	13	1	**L**
3	-	**Parklife**	Blur	Food	10		**L**
4	-	**Always & Forever**	Eternal	EMI	17	152	**FPL**
5	-	**God Shuffled His Feet**	Crash Test Dummies	RCA	6	9	**FL**
6	-	**Everybody Else Is Doing It, So Why Can't We**	Cranberries	Island	16	18	**F**
7	-	**Carnival Of Hits**	Judith Durham & The Seeekers	EMI	4		**L**
8	-	**Goin' Back - The Very Best Of**	Dusty Springfield	Phillips	3		**L**
9	-	**I Say I Say I Say**	Erasure	Mute	3	18	**L**
10	-	**Stacked Up**	Senser	Ultimate	1		**FL**

June 1994

This Mnth	Last Mnth	Title	Artist	Label	Wks in 10	US Pos	
1	6	**Everybody Else Is Doing It, So Why Can't We**	Cranberries	Island	16	18	**F**
2	1	**Our Town - Greatest Hits**	Deacon Blue	Columbia	14		**L**
3	-	**Seal**	Seal	ZTT	6	24	**L**
4	4	**Always & Forever**	Eternal	EMI	17	152	**FPL**
5	-	**Music Box**	Mariah Carey	Columbia	38	1	**PL**
6	2	**The Division Bell**	Pink Floyd	EMI	13	1	**L**
7	-	**Real Things**	2 Unlimited	PWL Continental	3		**L**
8	9	**I Say I Say I Say**	Erasure	Mute	3	18	**L**
9	-	**Pomme Fritz**	Orb	Inter-Modo	1		**L**
10	-	**The Last Temptation**	Alice Cooper	Epic	2	68	**L**

US 1994 APR-JUNE

April 1994

This Mnth	Last Mnth	Title	Artist	Label	Wks in 10	UK Pos	
1	4	**The Sign**	Ace Of Base	Arista	31	1	**F7PL**
2	-	**Above The Rim**	Soundtrack	Death Row	14		**2P**
3	-	**Longing In Their Hearts**	Bonnie Raitt	Capitol	7	26	**2PL**
4	7	**August & Everything After**	Counting Crows	Geffen	32	16	**F4PL**
5	1	**12 Play**	R. Kelly	Jive	18	36	**F3PL**
6	-	**The Division Bell**	Pink Floyd	Columbia	9	1	**2PL**
7	2	**Music Box**	Mariah Carey	Columbia	33	1	**8P**
8	-	**Not A Moment Too Soon**	Tim McGraw	Curb	17	F	**3PL**
9	-	**Far Beyond Driven**	Pantera	East West	2	3	**FL**
10	9	**Superunknown**	Soundgarden	A&M	11	4	**F3PL**

May 1994

This Mnth	Last Mnth	Title	Artist	Label	Wks in 10	UK Pos	
1	8	**Not A Moment Too Soon**	Tim McGraw	Curb	17		**F3PL**
2	6	**The Division Bell**	Pink Floyd	Columbia	9	1	**2PL**
3	1	**The Sign**	Ace Of Base	Arista	31	1	**F7PL**
4	-	**Chant**	Benedictine Monks Of Santo				
			Domingo De Silos	Angel	8	7	**F2PL**
5	-	**Read My Mind**	Reba McEntire	MCA	4		**2PL**
6	4	**August & Everything After**	Counting Crows	Geffen	32	16	**F4PL**
7	2	**Above The Rim**	Soundtrack	Death Row	14		**2P**
8	5	**12 Play**	R. Kelly	Jive	18	36	**F3PL**
9	3	**Longing In Their Hearts**	Bonnie Raitt	Capitol	7	26	**2PL**
10	-	**The Crow**	Soundtrack	Atlantic	7		**P**

June 1994

This Mnth	Last Mnth	Title	Artist	Label	Wks in 10	UK Pos	
1	3	**The Sign**	Ace Of Base	Arista	31	1	**F7PL**
2	10	**The Crow**	Soundtrack	Atlantic	7		**P**
3	1	**Not A Moment Too Soon**	Tim McGraw	Curb	17		**F3PL**
4	7	**Above The Rim**	Soundtrack	Death Row	14		**2P**
5	4	**Chant**	Benedictine Monks Of Santo				
			Domingo De Silos	Angel	8	7	**F2PL**
6	-	**Ill Communication**	Beastie Boys	Capitol	3	10	**PL**
7	6	**August & Everything After**	Counting Crows	Geffen	32	16	**F4PL**
8	-	**Purple**	Stone Temple Pilots	Atlantic	16	10	**3PL**
9	2	**The Division Bell**	Pink Floyd	Columbia	9	1	**2PL**
10	-	**Regulate... G Funk Era**	Warren G	Violator	13	25	**F2PL**

• Barbra Streisand's first tour for over 20 years smashed box-office records on both sides of the Atlantic. In America, she sold $30 million worth of tickets in a matter of hours and her seven shows at Madison Square Garden took a record $16.5 million. She also earned £5 million for four shows at Wembley Arena.

• Kurt Cobain and Henry Mancini died. Cobain was the controversial front man of the influential and innovative chart topping group Nirvana, and Mancini was an internationally renowned composer/conductor who in his long career had won 20 Grammy and four Oscar awards.

• Frank Sinatra's five shows at New York's Radio City Music Hall grossed $1.76 million. Elton John, Luciano Pavarotti, Sting, James Taylor and Tammy Wynette appeared at the fifth Rain Forest benefit concert at Carnegie Hall. Meanwhile in Russia, A-Ha, Patti LaBelle, Run-D.M.C. and Whitesnake performed at the White Nights International Cultural Festival.

UK 1994 JULY-SEPT

• Wet Wet Wet, whose **End Of Part One (Their Greatest Hits)** topped the chart, had the year's biggest single hit with a revival of The Troggs' song 'Love Is All Around'. It topped the chart for 15 weeks and sold over 1.8 million, putting it in the UK's all time Top 10 singles.

• Elton John and Billy Joel's joint tour sold $10 million worth of tickets in one day, and their five shows at the Giant Stadium grossed almost $15 million. As impressive was the $10 million that the Rolling Stones took for their four shows at the same venue. The re-formed British group Traffic's American tour with The Grateful Dead also broke several Stateside box office records.

• The Rolling Stones, whose **Voodoo Lounge** was their first UK Number 1 for 13 years, and Neil Young joined fellow veteran rocker Elton John at the top end of the transatlantic charts. However, they were relative newcomers compared to harmonica player Larry Adler whose **The Glory Of Gershwin** almost took the 80-year-old to the top of the UK chart.

• Greatest hits albums reaching the British Top 10 included those by UK artists Boomtown Rats, ELO, Wet Wet Wet and Whitesnake plus others by American acts The Eagles, Cyndi Lauper, Elvis Presley and Nina Simone.

July 1994

This Mnth	Last Mnth	Title	Artist	Label	Wks in 10	US Pos	
1	-	**Happy Nation**	Ace Of Base	London	14	1	FL
2	5	**Music Box**	Mariah Carey	Columbia	38	1	PL
3	-	**End Of Part One (Their Greatest Hits)**	Wet Wet Wet	Precious	22		PL
4	-	**Music For The Jilted Generation**	Prodigy	XL	11		FL
5	-	**Voodoo Lounge**	Rolling Stones	Virgin	5	2	L
6	-	**The Very Best Of The Electric Light Orchestra**	Electric Light Orchestra	Dino	5		L
7	1	**Everybody Else Is Doing It, So Why Can't We**	Cranberries	Island	16	18	F
8	-	**Greatest Hits**	Whitesnake	EMI	6		L
9	-	**Turn It Upside Down**	Spin Doctors	Epic	2	28	L
10	-	**The Very Best Of The Eagles**	Eagles	Elektra	5		L

August 1994

This Mnth	Last Mnth	Title	Artist	Label	Wks in 10	US Pos	
1	3	**End Of Part One (Their Greatest Hits)**	Wet Wet Wet	Precious	22		PL
2	-	**The Glory Of Gershwin**	Larry Adler/Various	Mercury	4		FL
3	4	**Music For The Jilted Generation**	Prodigy	XL	11		FL
4	5	**Voodoo Lounge**	Rolling Stones	Virgin	5	2	L
5	10	**The Very Best Of The Eagles**	Eagles	Elektra	5		L
6	2	**Music Box**	Mariah Carey	Columbia	38	1	PL
7	-	**Come**	Prince	Warner	2	15	L
8	-	**Sleeps With Angels**	Neil Young & Crazy Horse	Reprise	2	9	L
9	8	**Greatest Hits**	Whitesnake	EMI	6		L
10	-	**Always & Forever**	Eternal	EMI	17	152	FPL

September 1994

This Mnth	Last Mnth	Title	Artist	Label	Wks in 10	US Pos	
1	1	**End Of Part One (Their Greatest Hits)**	Wet Wet Wet	Precious	22		PL
2	-	**The 3 Tenors In Concert 1994**	Jose Carreras, Placido Domingo & Luciano Pavarotti with Mehta	Teldec	8	4	FL
3	-	**Definitely Maybe**	Oasis	Creation	7		FL
4	-	**Twelve Deadly Cyns...And Then Some**	Cyndi Lauper	Epic	11		L
5	-	**Crazy**	Julio Iglesias	Columbia	9	30	L
6	-	**Always & Forever**	Eternal	EMI	17	152	FPL
7	-	**The Essential Collection**	Elvis Presley	RCA	4		L
8	-	**From The Cradle**	Eric Clapton	Duck	4	1	L
9	-	**Brother Sister**	Brand New Heavies	Acid Jazz	5	95	FL
10	7	**Come**	Prince	Warner	2	15	L

US 1994 JULY-SEPT

July 1994

This Mnth	Last Mnth	Title	Artist	Label	Wks in 10	UK Pos	
1	8	**Purple**	Stone Temple Pilots	Atlantic	16	10	**3PL**
2	-	**The Lion King**	Soundtrack	Walt Disney	22		**7P**
3	1	**The Sign**	Ace Of Base	Arista	31	1	**F6PL**
4	10	**Regulate... G Funk Era**	Warren G	Violator	13	25	**F2PL**
5	3	**Not A Moment Too Soon**	Tim McGraw	Curb	17		**F4PL**
6	7	**August & Everything After**	Counting Crows	Geffen	32	16	**F4PL**
7	-	**Who I Am**	Alan Jackson	Arista	3		**F2PL**
8	-	**Voodoo Lounge**	Rolling Stones	Virgin	5	1	**PL**
9	-	**All-4-One**	All-4-One	Blitzz	7	25	**F2PL**
10	-	**When Love Finds You**	Vince Gill	MCA	3		**PL**

August 1994

This Mnth	Last Mnth	Title	Artist	Label	Wks in 10	UK Pos	
1	2	**The Lion King**	Soundtrack	Walt Disney	22		**7P**
2	-	**Forrest Gump**	Soundtrack	Epic Soundtrax	11		**3P**
3	3	**The Sign**	Ace Of Base	Arista	31	1	**F6PL**
4	1	**Purple**	Stone Temple Pilots	Atlantic	16	10	**3PL**
5	4	**Regulate... G Funk Era**	Warren G	Violator	13	25	**F2PL**
6	6	**August & Everything After**	Counting Crows	Geffen	32	16	**F4PL**
7	8	**Voodoo Lounge**	Rolling Stones	Virgin	5	1	**2PL**
8	-	**Superunknown**	Soundgarden	A&M	11	4	**F4PL**
9	-	**Candlebox**	Candlebox	Maverick	7		**F3PL**
10	-	**We Come Strapped**	MC Eiht Featuring CMW	Epic Street	1		**FL**

September 1994

This Mnth	Last Mnth	Title	Artist	Label	Wks in 10	UK Pos	
1	1	**The Lion King**	Soundtrack	Walt Disney	22		**7P**
2	2	**Forrest Gump**	Soundtrack	Epic Soundtrax	11		**3P**
3	4	**Purple**	Stone Temple Pilots	Atlantic	16	10	**3PL**
4	-	**Dookie**	Green Day	Reprise	16	35	**F6PL**
5	-	**II**	Boyz II Men	Motown	16	17	**7PL**
6	3	**The Sign**	Ace Of Base	Arista	31	1	**F8PL**
7	6	**August & Everything After**	Counting Crows	Geffen	32	16	**F5PL**
8	9	**Candlebox**	Candlebox	Maverick	7		**F3PL**
9	-	**The 3 Tenors In Concert 1994**	Jose Carreras, Placido Domingo & Luciano Pavarotti with Mehta	Atlantic	2	1	**F2PL**
10	5	**Regulate... G Funk Era**	Warren G	Violator	13	25	**F2PL**

• The top album act of the Seventies, Elton John, returned to the top spot with the soundtrack album of the Disney film **The Lion King**. It was Disney's biggest selling album of all time and their first Number 1 since **Mary Poppins** in 1965. Other soundtracks that reached the Top 20 were **Above The Rim**, **The Crow**, **Forrest Gump**, **Natural Born Killers** and **Reality Bites**.

• Woodstock's 25th anniversary was celebrated by several festivals being staged around the world. Woodstock '94, held in New York State, was arguably the best of them. Scores of rock greats from the last 30 years appeared. They ranged from past masters like The Allman Brothers, Bob Dylan and Crosby, Stills & Nash to recent hitmakers such as Cypress Hill, Green Day, Metallica (above) and Nine Inch Nails.

• Country newcomer Tim McGraw had a Number 1 with **Not A Moment Too Soon** and award winners Vince Gill and Alan Jackson also cracked the Top 10.

UK 1994 OCT-DEC

• Amazingly, Cliff Richard had albums on the first and last UK Top 10s in this book. Another long time favourite, Eric Clapton (above), who scored his first solo UK Number 1 with **From The Cradle**.

• For the first time BBC's Radio 1 had fewer listeners than commercial radio. MTV launched their VH-1 channel and digital radio was now available on cable.

• Sales of albums and singles in the UK were booming. The year's top single-artist albums were the million sellers **Cross Road – The Best Of Bon Jovi** and **Carry on Up The Charts – The Best Of The Beautiful South**. Compilation albums still accounted for a high percentage of total sales and the million selling **Now That's What I Call Music! 29** became the most successful album in the series.

• EMI underestimated the demand for **The Beatles At The BBC**, which was the group's first UK Number 1 for 17 years. In America, it came in at Number 3 – equaling their highest entry ever.

October 1994

This Mnth	Last Mnth	Title	Artist	Label	Wks in 10	US Pos	
1	-	**Monster**	R.E.M.	Warner	6	1	L
2	4	**Twelve Deadly Cyns...And Then Some**	Cyndi Lauper	Epic	11		L
3	-	**Songs**	Luther Vandross	Epic	4	5	L
4	2	**The 3 Tenors In Concert 1994**	Jose Carreras, Placido Domingo & Luciano Pavarotti with Mehta	Teldec	8	4	FL
5	-	**No Need To Argue**	Cranberries	Island	4	9	L
6	-	**Cross Road - The Best Of**	Bon Jovi	Vertigo	11	8	PL
7	-	**The Hit List**	Cliff Richard	EMI	8		L
8	8	**From The Cradle**	Eric Clapton	Duck	4	1	L
9	5	**Crazy**	Julio Iglesias	Columbia	9	30	L
10	-	**The Return Of The Space Cowboy**	Jamiroquai	Sony S2	2		L

November 1994

This Mnth	Last Mnth	Title	Artist	Label	Wks in 10	US Pos	
1	6	**Cross Road - The Best Of**	Bon Jovi	Vertigo	11	8	PL
2	-	**MTV Unplugged In New York**	Nirvana	Geffen	3	1	L
3	-	**Bedtime Stories**	Madonna	Maverick	3	3	L
4	-	**Greatest Hits**	INXS	Mercury	3	112	L
5	-	**Carry On Up The Charts - The Best Of**	Beautiful South	Go! Discs	7		PL
6	-	**Fields Of Gold - The Best Of**	Sting	A&M	7	7	L
7	-	**The Best Of Chris Rea**	Chris Rea	East West	3		L
8	-	**Labour Of Love - Volumes I & II**	UB40	DEP International	3		L
9	-	**Best Of Sade**	Sade	Epic	4	9	L
10	1	**Monster**	R.E.M.	Warner	6	1	L

December 1994

This Mnth	Last Mnth	Title	Artist	Label	Wks in 10	US Pos	
1	5	**Carry On Up The Charts - The Best Of**	Beautiful South	Go! Discs	7		PL
2	1	**Cross Road - The Best Of**	Bon Jovi	Vertigo	11	8	PL
3	-	**Live At The BBC**	Beatles	Apple	4	3	L
4	-	**Always & Forever**	Eternal	EMI	17	152	FPL
5	6	**Fields Of Gold - The Best Of**	Sting	A&M	7	7	L
6	-	**Crocodile Shoes**	Jimmy Nail	East West	3		L
7	-	**Steam**	East 17	London	6		L
8	-	**Bizarre Fruit**	M People	Deconstruction	6		L
9	-	**? (The Best Of)**	New Order	Centredate Co.	3		L
10	-	**The Hit List**	Cliff Richard	EMI	8		L

US 1994 OCT-DEC

October 1994

This Mnth	Last Mnth	Title	Artist	Label	Wks in 10	UK Pos	
1	5	II	Boyz II Men	Motown	16	17	7PL
2	-	From The Cradle	Eric Clapton	Duck	8	1	3PL
3	-	Rhythm Of Love	Anita Baker	Elektra	5	14	2PL
4	-	Monster	R.E.M.	Warner	6	1	3PL
5	1	The Lion King	Soundtrack	Walt Disney	22		7P
6	-	Smash	Offspring	Epitaph	17	38	F3PL
7	4	Dookie	Green Day	Reprise	16	35	F6PL
8	-	Songs	Luther Vandross	LV	3	1	PL
9	-	Tuesday Night Music Club	Sheryl Crow	A&M	4	22	F4PL
10	-	Pisces Iscariot	Smashing Pumpkins	Virgin	2		PL

November 1994

This Mnth	Last Mnth	Title	Artist	Label	Wks in 10	UK Pos	
1	-	Murder Was The Case	Soundtrack	Death Row	4		2P
2	1	II	Boyz II Men	Motown	16	17	7PL
3	6	Smash	Offspring	Epitaph	17	38	F3PL
4	-	MTV Unplugged In New York	Nirvana	DGC	7	1	3PL
5	-	The Diary	Scarface	Rap-A-Lot	2		PL
6	4	Monster	R.E.M.	Warner	6	1	3PL
7	-	Bedtime Stories	Madonna	Maverick	2	2	2PL
8	-	Hell Freezes Over	Eagles	Geffen	6	28	5PL
9	2	From The Cradle	Eric Clapton	Duck	8	1	3PL
10	-	Promised Land	Queensryche	EMI	1	13	PL

December 1994

This Mnth	Last Mnth	Title	Artist	Label	Wks in 10	UK Pos	
1	-	Miracles The Holiday Album	Kenny G	Arista	5		3PL
2	2	II	Boyz II Men	Motown	16	17	7PL
3	8	Hell Freezes Over	Eagles	Geffen	6	28	5PL
4	-	Merry Christmas	Mariah Carey	Columbia	5	32	3PL
5	4	MTV Unplugged In New York	Nirvana	DGC	7	1	3PL
6	-	Vitalogy	Pearl Jam	Epic	2	6	4PL
7	3	Smash	Offspring	Epitaph	17	38	F3PL
8	-	The Lion King	Soundtrack	Walt Disney	22		7P
9	-	Live At The BBC	Beatles	Capitol	2	1	4PL
10	-	Dookie	Green Day	Reprise	16	35	F6PL

• In 1994, rock, rap, country, R&B and pop albums regularly shared the Top 10 places. The value of American sales increased 20% to $12 billion and for the first time over one billion records were sold.

• The Eagles smashed box office records on their comeback tour, and their new album **Hell Freezes Over** entered in the top slot. Other Number 1 debut albums were **II** by Boyz II Men, **From The Cradle** by Eric Clapton, **Monster** by R.E.M., **MTV Unplugged In New York** from Nirvana and a 73-minute album of music inspired by the 18-minute film **Murder Was The Case**.

• At Pearl Jam's request **Vitalogy** was initially only available on vinyl. When the compact disk was released it leapt from No. 173 to Number 1.

• Sweden's Ace Of Base replaced Garth Brooks as the USA's top act of the year. However, Brooks quickly sold over four million copies of **The Garth Brooks Collection** which was available only through McDonalds and therefore ineligible for the chart.

• The early Nineties were very good for American acts worldwide. The future also looked bright with new bands like Green Day and Offspring looking set to join America's international hitmakers such as R.E.M., Mariah Carey, Madonna and Michael Bolton.

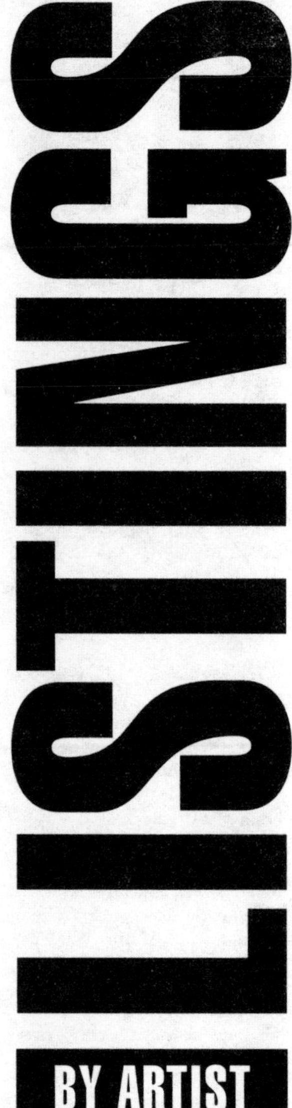

LISTING BY ARTIST

ABBA - Globally successful Swedish pop quartet. Anni-Frid Lyngstad, Benny Andersson, Bjorn Ulvaeus and Agnetha Faltskog. One of the world's biggest selling recording acts and top songwriting teams (Andersson and Ulvaeus) of the Seventies. They had eight successive Number 1 albums in Britain.

	US Top 10 Ent	UK Top 10 Ent
Greatest Hits		4/76
Arrival		12/76
The Album		2/78
Voulez-Vous		5/79
Greatest Hits Vol. 2		11/79
Super Trouper		11/80
The Visitors		12/81
The Singles -The First Ten Years		11/82
Gold - Greatest Hits		10/92

ABC - Fashion conscious pop/rock quintet from Yorkshire, England. Martin Fry, Mark White, Stephen Singleton, Mark Lickley, David Palmer.

	US Top 10 Ent	UK Top 10 Ent
The Lexicon Of Love		7/82

PAULA ABDUL - Noteworthy pop/dance vocalist and award winning choreographer, born 1962 in Los Angeles. Her debut album spent 68 consecutive weeks in the US Top 40 - a record for a female performer.

	US Top 10 Ent	UK Top 10 Ent
Forever Your Girl	3/89	5/89
Shut Up And Dance	6/90	
Spellbound	6/91	

AC/DC - Australian-based rock band. Angus Young, Malcolm Young, Bon Scott (died 1980), Mark Evans, Phillip Rudd. English vocalist Brian Johnson replaced Scott in 1980. They were one of the top selling LP acts of the Eighties.

	US Top 10 Ent	UK Top 10 Ent
Back In Black	11/80	8/80
Dirty Deeds Done Dirt Cheap	5/81	
For Those About To Rock We Salute You	12/81	12/81
Flick Of The Switch		9/83
Blow Up Your Video		2/88
The Razor's Edge	10/90	

ACE OF BASE - Swedish quartet who have become global pop stars. Siblings Jenny, Malin and Jonathan Bergren and Ulf Ekberg. Winners of the *Billboard* award for Best New Act of 1994, debut LP sold over 15 million copies worldwide.

	US Top 10 Ent	UK Top 10 Ent
The Sign (AKA Happy Nation)	3/94	3/94

BRYAN ADAMS - Internationally famous rock singer/songwriter born 1959 in Ontario, Canada. One of America's top LP acts in the Eighties, his 1991 single '(Everything I Do) I Do It For You' sold three million in the USA and topped the UK chart for a record 16 weeks.

	US Top 10 Ent	UK Top 10 Ent
Cuts Like A Knife	6/83	
Reckless	1/85	3/85
Into The Fire	5/87	
Waking Up The Neighbours	10/91	10/91
So Far So Good	1/94	11/93

OLETA ADAMS - Soulful singer/pianist/songwriter who was discovered by British duo Tears For Fears playing in a hotel bar in Kansas, USA.

	US Top 10 Ent	UK Top 10 Ent
Circle Of One		3/91

LARRY ADLER - Veteran American-born and British-based harmonica player who, together with an array of recent hit makers, made his chart debut when in his 80s.

	US Top 10 Ent	UK Top 10 Ent
The Glory Of Gershwin		8/94

AEROSMITH - Distinctive hard rock band from New Hampshire, USA, who have been regular US chart entrants since the early Seventies. Steven Tyler (born Steven Tallarico), Joe Perry, Brad Whitford, Tom Hamilton, Joey Kramer.

	US Top 10 Ent	UK Top 10 Ent
Rocks	6/76	
Pump	10/89	9/89
Get A Grip	5/93	5/93

A-HA - Pop trio who are Norway's most successful recording act. Morten Harket, Pal Waaktaar and Mags Furuholem. The group, whose videos have won several awards, were one of the top teen attractions in Britain in the Eighties.

	US Top 10 Ent	UK Top 10 Ent
Hunting High And Low		1/86
Scoundrel Days		10/86
Stay On These Roads		5/88

AIR SUPPLY - Australian-based AOR duo. Russell Hitchcock (born Melbourne, Australia) and Graham Russell (born Nottingham, England). Their first seven US singles all made the Top 5.

	US Top 10 Ent	UK Top 10 Ent
Greatest Hits	10/83	

ALICE IN CHAINS - International hard rock band. Jerry Cantrell, Sean Kinney, Layne Staley and Michael Starr. **Jar Of Flies** was the first EP to top the American LP chart.

	US Top 10 Ent	UK Top 10 Ent
Jar Of Flies	2/94	

ALL-4-ONE - Multi-racial R&B harmony vocal group from Los Angeles. Jamie Jones, Delious Kennedy, Tony Borowiak, Alfred Nevarez. Their 'I Swear' was the top single in the USA in 1994.

	US Top 10 Ent	UK Top 10 Ent
All-4-One	7/94	

ALLMAN BROTHERS BAND - Groundbreaking, influential southern rock band which included brothers Duane (died 1971) and Gregg Allman, Dickey Betts and Berry Oakley (died 1972). They were one of the top selling album acts in America in the early Seventies.

	US Top 10 Ent	UK Top 10 Ent
Eat A Peach	4/72	
Brothers And Sisters	9/73	
Win, Lose Or Draw	10/75	
Enlightened Rouges	4/79	

HERB ALPERT (& HIS TIJUANA BRASS) - Celebrated MOR/ R&B trumpet player/singer/band-leader/writer/producer/arranger and record and publishing company owner born 1935 in Los Angeles. America's most successful instrumental recording artist with eight successive Top 10 albums.

	US Top 10 Ent	UK Top 10 Ent
Going Places	11/65	2/66
Whipped Cream & Other Delights	7/65	
S.R.O.	12/66	3/67
South Of The Border	4/66	
What Now My Love	5/66	
Sounds Like	6/67	
Herb Alpert's Ninth	1/68	
The Beat Of The Brass	5/68	4/69
Rise	11/79	

AMERICA - American soft rock trio whose first taste of success came in the UK. Dan Peek, Gerry Beckley and Dewey Bunnell. They won the Grammy for Best New Artist in 1972.

	US Top 10 Ent	UK Top 10 Ent
America	3/72	
Homecoming	1/73	
Holiday	11/74	
Hearts	6/75	
History - America's Greatest Hits	12/75	

ED AMES - MOR vocalist. Real name Ed Urick, born 1927 in Massachusetts, USA. He was a member of the very successful Fifties vocal group, The Ames Brothers.

BIOGRAPHIES/ARTIST INDEX

Group members listed are those generally regarded as the original line-up unless otherwise stated.

	US Top 10 Ent	UK Top 10 Ent
My Cup Runneth Over	4/67	

TORI AMOS - Critically applauded singer/songwriter/pianist from North Carolina, USA, whose first success came in Britain.

	US Top 10 Ent	UK Top 10 Ent
Under The Pink		2/94

ANIMALS - Noted rock/R&B group from Newcastle, England. Eric Burdon, Alan Price, Bryan 'Chas' Chandler, Hilton Valentine and John Steel. The first UK group to top the US single charts after The Beatles.

	US Top 10 Ent	UK Top 10 Ent
The Animals	11/64	11/64
Animal Tracks		6/65
The Best Of The Animals	3/66	
Most Of The Animals		5/66
Animalisms		6/66

PAUL ANKA - Internationally famous pop vocalist born 1941 in Ottawa, Canada. He was the youngest transatlantic chart regular in the Fifties, and is one of the most successful singer/songwriters of the rock era.

	US Top 10 Ent	UK Top 10 Ent
Paul Anka Sings His Big 15	8/60	

ANOTHER BAD CREATION - Youthful R&B/rap group from Atlanta. Chris Sellers, Romell Chapman, Dave Shelton and brothers Demetrius and Marliss Pugh.

	US Top 10 Ent	UK Top 10 Ent
Coolin' At The Playground Ya' Know!	6/91	

ADAM ANT/ADAM & THE ANTS - Flamboyant pop/rock group led by Londoner Adam Ant (born Stuart Goddard), who composed the majority of the group's hits with member Marco Pirroni. Britain's top recording act of 1981.

	US Top 10 Ent	UK Top 10 Ent
Kings Of The Wild Frontier		11/80
Prince Charming		11/81

JOAN ARMATRADING - Distinctive folk-oriented vocalist/guitarist/pianist/composer born 1950 in St. Kitts, West Indies, and raised in Birmingham, England.

	US Top 10 Ent	UK Top 10 Ent
Me Myself I		6/80

LOUIS ARMSTRONG - Legendary jazz/MOR singer/trumpet player nicknamed 'Satchmo'. Born 1900 in New Orleans, USA. He has the longest singles chart span in both the US and Britain, and is also the oldest person to top the charts on both sides of the Atlantic.

	US Top 10 Ent	UK Top 10 Ent
Hello, Dolly!	5/64	

EDDY ARNOLD - Country singer born 1918 in Tennessee, USA, known as 'The Tennessee Ploughboy'. He is the top all time country artist with a tally of 136 country chart singles between 1945 and 1983.

	US Top 10 Ent	UK Top 10 Ent
My World	1/66	

ARRESTED DEVELOPMENT - Distinctive rap group from Georgia, USA, led by Speech (born Todd Thomas in Milwaukee) and including sixty-something-year-old Baba Oke. Won the Grammy For Best New Artist 1992.

	US Top 10 Ent	UK Top 10 Ent
3 Years 5 Months & 2 Days In The Life Of...	3/93	1/93

ASIA - Rock supergroup from the UK, who were more popular in America. Steve Howe (ex-Yes), Carl Palmer (ex-Emerson Lake & Palmer) Geoff Downes (ex-Yes, Buggles), John Wetton (ex-King Crimson, Uriah Heep, Roxy Music).

	US Top 10 Ent	UK Top 10 Ent
Asia	4/82	
Alpha	9/83	8/83

ASSOCIATION - Successful soft rock sextet from California. Terry Kirkman and Gary 'Jules' Alexander, Brian Cole (died 1972), Jim Yester, Ted Bluechel Jr. and Russ Giguere. They were American chart regulars in the late Sixties.

	US Top 10 Ent	UK Top 10 Ent
And Then...Along Comes The Association	10/66	
Greatest Hits Vol. 1	2/69	

RICK ASTLEY - Pop/R&B singer born 1966 in Warrington, England. He is the only act in the Eighties whose first two single releases topped the US chart.

	US Top 10 Ent	UK Top 10 Ent
Whenever You Need Somebody	3/88	11/87

ATLANTA RHYTHM SECTION - Noteworthy rock sextet from Georgia USA. J.R.Cobb, Dean Daughtry (both ex-Classics IV), Rodney Justo, Barry Bailey, Paul Goddard, Robert Nix.

	US Top 10 Ent	UK Top 10 Ent
Champagne Jam	5/78	

AVERAGE WHITE BAND - Acclaimed funk/rock vocal/instrumental sextet from Scotland. Alan Gorrie, Hamish Stuart, Onnie McIntyre, Malcolm Duncan, Roger Ball, Robbie McIntosh (died 1974).

	US Top 10 Ent	UK Top 10 Ent
AWB	2/75	
Cut The Cake	7/75	

BURT BACHARACH - World renowned composer/arranger/conductor born 1928 in Kansas City, USA. He is one of the most successful songwriters of the 20th century, with many Number 1 hits to his credit.

	US Top 10 Ent	UK Top 10 Ent
Hit Maker Burt Bacharach		6/65
Portrait In Music		4/71

BACHELORS - Top selling MOR/pop vocal trio from Dublin, Ireland. Brothers Declan and Con Cluskey and John Stokes. Arguably the most successful non-rock vocal group in Britain in the Sixties.

	US Top 10 Ent	UK Top 10 Ent
The Bachelors And 16 Great Songs		7/64
World Of The Bachelors		7/69

BACHMAN-TURNER OVERDRIVE - Well respected rock group from Vancouver, Canada. Brothers Randy (ex-Guess Who), Tim and Robbie Bachman and Fred Turner.

	US Top 10 Ent	UK Top 10 Ent
Bachman-Turner Overdrive II	8/74	
Not Fragile	10/74	
Four Wheel Drive	6/75	

BAD COMPANY - Rock supergroup from Britain. Paul Rodgers and Simon Kirke (both ex-Free), Mick Ralphs (ex-Mott The Hoople), and Boz Burrell (ex-King Crimson). In 1986 Brian Howe took over lead vocal chores.

	US Top 10 Ent	UK Top 10 Ent
Bad Company	8/74	6/74
Straight Shooter	5/75	4/75
Run With The Pack	3/76	2/76
Desolation Angels	4/79	

JOAN BAEZ - Legendary, pure-voiced folk singer born 1941 in New York City, USA. The Number 1 female folk music artist of the Sixties.

	US Top 10 Ent	UK Top 10 Ent
Joan Baez In Concert Part 2	1/64	8/65
Joan Baez No. 5		7/65
Farewell Angelina		12/65

ANITA BAKER - Grammy winning soul stylist born 1958 in Ohio, USA, who first recorded as lead vocalist of Chapter 8. Generally regarded as one of the best new female vocalist of the late Eighties.

	US Top 10 Ent	UK Top 10 Ent
Giving You The Best That I Got	11/88	
Compositions	8/90	
Rhythm Of Love	10/94	

KENNY BALL - Jazz trumpeter/vocalist born 1930 in Essex, England. He was a mainstay of the UK trad jazz music boom of the early Sixties.

	US Top 10 Ent	UK Top 10 Ent
Kenny Ball's Golden Hits		9/63
The Best Of Ball, Barber And Bilk		9/62

MICHAEL BALL - London-based actor/singer was one of the biggest stars in British musical theatre in the Nineties. He had his own TV series in 1994.

	US Top 10 Ent	UK Top 10 Ent
Michael Ball		6/92
Always		7/93

BANANARAMA - Female pop trio from London, England. Sarah Dallin, Siobhan Fahey and Keren Woodward. The most successful British girl group in both the UK and US.

	US Top 10 Ent	UK Top 10 Ent
Deep Sea Skiving		4/83
The Greatest Hits Collection		12/88

BAND - Critically acclaimed rock group formed at Woodstock, New York, USA. Robbie Robertson, Rick Danko, Richard Manuel (died 1986), Garth Hudson, Levon Helm (all Canadian except Helm who was from Arkansas, USA). The Band backed Bob Dylan in the mid-Seventies.

	US Top 10 Ent	UK Top 10 Ent
Stage Fright	9/70	
Rock Of Ages	11/72	

BANGLES - Famed female pop/rock quartet from Los Angles, USA. Susanna Hoffs, sisters Vicki and Debbi Peterson and Michael Steele. One of the biggest selling female groups of all time.

	US Top 10 Ent	UK Top 10 Ent
Different Light	1/87	1/87
Everything		5/89
Greatest Hits		6/90

CHRIS BARBER - Pioneer British trad jazz trombonist and band leader born 1930 in Welwyn Garden City, England. He had a million selling American hit with 'Petite Fleur' in 1959.

	US Top 10 Ent	UK Top 10 Ent
Best Of Barber And Bilk Vol. 1		6/61
The Best Of Ball, Barber And Bilk		9/62

COUNT BASIE - See FRANK SINATRA

SHIRLEY BASSEY - Celebrated song stylist and internationally renowned cabaret entertainer born 1937 in Cardiff, Wales. She has had more albums on the UK chart than any other British female artist.

	US Top 10 Ent	UK Top 10 Ent
Something		9/70
The Shirley Bassey Singles Album		3/75
25th Anniversary Album		11/78

BAY CITY ROLLERS - Teeny bop/pop group from Scotland. Les McKeown, brothers Alan and Derek Longmuir, Eric Faulkner and Stuart Wood. These tartan teen-idols were the UK's top selling singles act in the mid-Seventies.

	US Top 10 Ent	UK Top 10 Ent
Rollin'		10/74
Once Upon A Star		5/75
Wouldn't You Like It		12/75
Dedication		10/76

BEACH BOYS - Legendary rock/pop group from California, USA. Original line-up the Wilson Brothers Brian, Carl and Dennis (died 1983) plus cousin Mike Love and Al Jardine. Later members included Bruce Johnson, Glen Campbell and David Marks.This distinctive and innovative vocal harmony group were America's main rival to The Beatles in the mid-Sixties. They are one of the greats of the rock era.

	US Top 10 Ent	UK Top 10 Ent
Surfin' U.S.A.	6/63	
Surfer Girl	11/63	
Little Deuce Coupe	2/64	
All Summer Long	8/64	
Beach Boys Concert	11/64	
Beach Boys Party!	12/65	2/66
The Beach Boys Today!	5/65	5/66
Summer Days (And Summer Nights!!)	8/65	7/66

LISTING BY ARTIST

Album	US Top 10 Ent	UK Top 10 Ent
Pet Sounds		7/66
Best Of The Beach Boys	9/66	11/66
Best Of The Beach Boys Vol. 2		10/67
Wild Honey		4/68
20/20		4/69
Greatest Hits		10/70
Endless Summer	9/74	
20 Golden Greats		7/76
15 Big Ones	8/76	
The Very Best Of The Beach Boys		8/83
Summer Dreams		6/90

BEASTIE BOYS - Controversial white rap trio from New York, USA. King Ad-Rock (Adam Horovitz), MCA (Adam Yauch), Mike D (Diamond). They were the first rap act to top the US album chart.

Album	US Top 10 Ent	UK Top 10 Ent
Licensed To Ill	2/87	6/87
Ill Communication	6/94	

BEAT - Top notch ska/2-Tone group from Birmingham, England which included Dave Wakeling, Ranking Roger, Andy Cox and David Steele. Wakeling and Roger then formed General Public and Cox and Steele later formed Fine Young Cannibals.

Album	US Top 10 Ent	UK Top 10 Ent
Just Can't Stop It		5/80
Wha'ppen		5/81

BEATLES - World's all time top pop/rock group from Liverpool, England. John Lennon (died 1980), Paul McCartney, George Harrison and Ringo Starr. The results of their eight years recording together produced 15 US and 13 UK Number 1 albums and 21 US and 17 UK chart topping singles.

Album	US Top 10 Ent	UK Top 10 Ent
Please Please Me		4/63
With The Beatles		11/63
Meet The Beatles	2/64	
Introducing...The Beatles	2/64	
The Beatles' Second Album	5/64	
A Hard Day's Night	7/64	7/64
Something New	8/64	
The Beatles' Story	1/65	
Beatles For Sale		12/64
Beatles '65	1/65	
Rubber Soul	1/66	12/65
Beatles VI	7/65	
Help	9/65	8/65
'Yesterday'...And Today	7/66	
Revolver	9/66	8/66
Sergeant Pepper's Lonely Hearts Club Band	7/67	6/67
Magical Mystery Tour	1/68	
The Beatles (White Album)	12/68	12/68
Yellow Submarine	2/69	2/69
Abbey Road	10/69	10/69
Hey Jude	3/70	
Let It Be	6/70	5/70
The Beatles/1962-1966	5/73	5/73
The Beatles/1967-1970	5/73	5/73
Rock 'n' Roll Music	7/76	
The Beatles At The Hollywood Bowl	6/77	5/77
Love Songs		1/78
Live At The BBC	12/94	12/94

BEAUTIFUL SOUTH - Innovative pop group formed by ex-Housemartins Paul Heaton and Dave Hemmingway and featuring female vocalist Brianna Corragan.

Album	US Top 10 Ent	UK Top 10 Ent
Welcome To The Beautiful South		11/89
Choke		11/90
0898		4/92
Carry On Up The Charts - The Best Of		11/94

BEAVIS & BUTT-HEAD - Two rock loving cartoon chartacters who found international fame after being seen regularly on MTV.

Album	US Top 10 Ent	UK Top 10 Ent
The Beavis & Butt-Head Experience	12/93	

JEFF BECK - Critcically acclaimed rock guitarist born 1944 in Surrey, England, who had much success with The Yardbirds before forming his own group, which at times included Rod Stewart and Ron Wood.

Album	US Top 10 Ent	UK Top 10 Ent
Blow By Blow	5/75	

BEE GEES - Very successful trio from Manchester, England, who were raised in Australia. Brothers Barry and twins Maurice and Robin Gibb. They first hit in 1967 and were still charting in the mid-Nineties. They contributed the majority of the tracks on the **Saturday Night Fever** soundtrack which sold over 25 million worldwide. They are undoubtedly one of the top groups of all time.

Album	US Top 10 Ent	UK Top 10 Ent
Bee Gees First	11/67	
Idea		10/68
Best Of The Bee Gees		11/69
Children Of The World	11/76	
Saturday Night Fever (Soundtrack)	1/78	4/78
Spirits Having Flown	2/79	2/79
Bee Gees Greatest	12/79	1/80
Staying Alive (Soundtrack)	8/83	
The Very Best Of The Bee Gees		12/90

HARRY BELAFONTE - Internationally renowned singer/actor born 1927 in New York, USA, who led the calypso craze of the Fifties. His 1957 album **Calypso** spent seven months at Number 1 in the USA.

Album	US Top 10 Ent	UK Top 10 Ent
Belafonte At Carnegie Hall	3/60	
Belafonte Returns To Carnegie Hall	1/61	
Jump Up Calypso	10/61	
The Midnight Special	7/62	

BELL BIV DEVOE - Soulful vocal/songwriting trio from Boston, USA. Ricky Bell, Michael Bivens and Ronnie DeVoe (all ex-New Edition). Bivens also produced hits for Boyz II Men and Another Bad Creation.

Album	US Top 10 Ent	UK Top 10 Ent
Poison	5/90	

PAT BENATAR - Respected rock singer born Pat Andrzejewski in New York State, USA, in 1952. The ofttimes Grammy winner is one of the leading ladies of rock music.

Album	US Top 10 Ent	UK Top 10 Ent
Crimes Of Passion	10/80	
Precious Time	8/81	
Get Nervous	12/82	
Best Shots		11/87

BENEDICTINE MONKS OF SANTO DOMINGO DE SILOS (AKA MONKS CHORUS SILOS) - A Spanish monks chorus whose Gregorian chants made them reluctant international stars in 1994.

Album	US Top 10 Ent	UK Top 10 Ent
Chant (AKA Canto Gregoriano)	5/94	

TONY BENNETT - Aclaimed MOR/pop singer and entertainer, born Anthony Benedetto in New York, USA, in 1925. A top recording star of the early Fifties. He remained a leading cabaret performer and was re-discovered by the MTV generation in the Nineties.

Album	US Top 10 Ent	UK Top 10 Ent
I Left My Heart In San Francisco	10/62	
I Wanna Be Around	5/63	

GEORGE BENSON - Highly regarded R&B/jazz guitarist/vocalist born 1943 in Pittsburgh, USA, who is a very popular live act on both sides of the Atlantic.

Album	US Top 10 Ent	UK Top 10 Ent
Breezin'	6/76	
Weekend In L.A.	3/78	
Livin' Inside Your Love	4/79	
Give Me The Night	9/80	8/80
In Your Eyes		6/83
The Love Songs		10/85

SHELLEY BERMAN - Grammy winning, original comedian/actor born 1926 in Chicago, USA, who was very popular at the dawn of the Sixties.

Album	US Top 10 Ent	UK Top 10 Ent
Outside Shelley Berman	1/60	
Inside Shelley Berman	1/60	
The Edge Of Shelley Berman	8/60	

CHUCK BERRY - Generally accepted as the first rock'n'roll singer/songwriter/guitarist. Berry, from San Jose, California, USA, born in 1926, is rightfully regarded as one of the legends of rock music.

Album	US Top 10 Ent	UK Top 10 Ent
Chuck Berry On Stage		10/63
His Latest And Greatest		6/64
The London Chuck Berry Sessions	10/72	

B-52S - Quirky rock/new wave quintet from Georgia, USA. Kate Pierson, Fred Schneider, brother and sister Cindy and Ricky Wilson (died 1985), Keith Strickland.

Album	US Top 10 Ent	UK Top 10 Ent
Cosmic Thing	12/89	

BIG BROTHER AND THE HOLDING COMPANY - San Francisco-based rock group who gave the late Janis Joplin her first taste of success. Other members included Peter Albin, Sam Andrew, David Getz and James Gurley.

Album	US Top 10 Ent	UK Top 10 Ent
Cheap Thrills	9/68	

BIG COUNTRY - Distinctive folk-influenced rock quartet from Scotland. Stuart Adamson (ex-Skids), Bruce Watson, Mark Brzezicki, Tony Butler.

Album	US Top 10 Ent	UK Top 10 Ent
The Crossing		8/83
Steeltown		10/84
The Seer		7/86
Through A Big Country - Greatest Hits		5/90

BIG FUN - Pop trio from Scotland, who for a short while in 1989 were teen pin ups in Britain. Phil Cheswick, Jason John and Mark Gillespie.

Album	US Top 10 Ent	UK Top 10 Ent
A Pocketful Of Dreams		5/90

MR. ACKER BILK - Jazz clarinetist/vocalist/composer born 1929 in Somerset, England. A major star of the UK trad jazz scene of the early Sixties who was voted Top Instrumentalist in the USA in 1962.

Album	US Top 10 Ent	UK Top 10 Ent
Seven Ages Of Acker		3/60
Best Of Barber And Bilk Vol. 1		6/61
Stranger On The Shore	6/62	7/62
The Best Of Ball, Barber And Bilk		9/62
Sheer Magic		6/77

BJORK - Unmistakable BRIT award winning singer/songwriter born 1966 in Iceland, who first came to fame as lead singer of The Sugarcubes.

Album	US Top 10 Ent	UK Top 10 Ent
Debut		1/94

BLACK CROWES - Hard rock group from Atlanta, USA. Brothers Chris and Rich Robinson, Jeff Cease, Steve Gorman and Johnny Colt. They are regarded as one of rock music's brightest prospects for the Nineties.

Album	US Top 10 Ent	UK Top 10 Ent
Shake Your Money Maker	3/91	
Southern Harmony And		

	US Top 10 Ent	UK Top 10 Ent
Musical Companion	5/92	5/92

BLACK - Pop/rock singer/songwriter from Liverpool, England, born Colin Vearncombe in 1962.

	US Top 10 Ent	UK Top 10 Ent
Wonderful Life		10/87

CILLA BLACK - Pop vocalist born Priscilla White in Liverpool, England, in 1943. The only female singer managed by Brian Epstein. She is now one of Britain's leading TV personalities.

	US Top 10 Ent	UK Top 10 Ent
Cilla		2/65
Cilla Sings A Rainbow		5/66

BLACK LACE - British pop duo who had a big following with pre-teens. Alan Barton and Colin Routh.

	US Top 10 Ent	UK Top 10 Ent
Party Party - 16 Great Party Icebreakers		12/84

BLACK SABBATH - Outstanding heavy metal group from Birmingham, England. Ozzy Osbourne, Tony Iommi, William Ward and Terry 'Geezer' Butler. Later members included Ronnie James Dio, Ian Gillan and Cozy Powell.

	US Top 10 Ent	UK Top 10 Ent
Paranoid		10/70
Master Of Reality		8/71
Black Sabbath Vol. 4		10/72
Sabbath Bloody Sabbath		12/73
Black Sabbath Live At Last		7/80

MARY J. BLIGE - Trend setting hip hop R&B vocalist born 1971 in Atlanta, Georgia, USA. She was the most successful new female R&B artist of 1992 in America.

	US Top 10 Ent	UK Top 10 Ent
What's The 411	9/92	

BLIND FAITH - Short lived British rock/blues supergroup. Eric Clapton (ex-Yardbirds, Cream), Steve Winwood (ex-Spencer Davis, Traffic), Ginger Baker (ex-Cream), Rick Grech (ex-Family, Traffic - died 1990). The group's only album topped the chart on both sides of the Atlantic.

	US Top 10 Ent	UK Top 10 Ent
Blind Faith	8/69	9/69

BLIND MELON - Self contained rock band fronted by Shannon Hoon from Indiana, USA. Other members; Brad Smith, Roger Stevens, Christopher Thorn and Glen Graham.

	US Top 10 Ent	UK Top 10 Ent
Blind Melon	9/93	

BLONDIE - Noted new wave pop group from New York, USA, led by vocalist Debbie Harry. Chris Stein, Frank Infante, Jimmy Destri, Gary Valentine, Clem Burke. They were one of the top selling acts of 1979-1981. See also Debbie Harry.

	US Top 10 Ent	UK Top 10 Ent
Parallel Lines	4/79	1/79
Eat To The Beat		10/79
Autoamerican	1/81	12/80
Best Of Blondie		11/81

BLOOD, SWEAT & TEARS - Groundbreaking jazz-rock band based in New York, USA. Included Al Kooper (replaced by David Clayton-Thomas in 1969), Steve Katz, Bobby Colomby and Jim Fielder. They were one of the top US LP sellers in the early Seventies.

	US Top 10 Ent	UK Top 10 Ent
Blood Sweat & Tears	2/69	
Blood, Sweat & Tears 3	7/70	

BLUES BROTHERS - Joliet 'Jake' (John Belushi - died 1982) from Illinois, USA, and Elwood Blues (Dan Aykroyd) from Ottawa, Canada. Duo formed for TV's *Saturday Night Live* and became successful in their own right.

	US Top 10 Ent	UK Top 10 Ent
Briefcase Full Of Blues	1/79	

BLUR - Well regarded British rock band. Damon Albarn, Graham Coxon, Alex James and Dave Rowntree. They were one of the most successful UK acts of the mid-Nineties.

	US Top 10 Ent	UK Top 10 Ent
Parklife		5/94

MARC BOLAN - See T. REX

MICHAEL BOLTON - Soulful rock singer born Michael Bolotin in New Haven, Connecticut, USA, in 1954. He was one of the top selling male artists of the late Eighties and early Nineties.

	US Top 10 Ent	UK Top 10 Ent
Soul Provider	3/90	9/90
Time, Love And Tenderness	5/91	5/91
Timeless (The Classics)	10/92	10/92
The One Thing	12/93	12/93

BON JOVI - Leading heavy rock band from New Jersey, USA. Jon Bon Jovi, Richie Sambora, Dave Bryan, Alec John Such, Tico Torres. They were one of the world's most successful rock bands in the late Eighties-early Nineties.

	US Top 10 Ent	UK Top 10 Ent
Slippery When Wet	10/86	11/86
New Jersey	10/88	10/88
Keep The Faith	11/92	11/92
Cross Road - The Best Of		10/94

JON BON JOVI - Hard rock singer (real name Bongiovi) born 1962 in New Jersey, USA. Leader of the very successful band Bon Jovi.

	US Top 10 Ent	UK Top 10 Ent
Blaze Of Glory/Young Guns II	9/90	8/90

GARY (U.S.) BONDS - Distinctive rock/R&B singer born Gary Anderson in Jacksonville, Florida, USA, in 1939. Early Sixties star who had a new lease of chart life in the Eighties when produced by fan Bruce Springsteen.

	US Top 10 Ent	UK Top 10 Ent
Dance 'Til Quarter To Three	9/61	

BONEY M - West Indian pop quartet assembled in Germany by producer Frank Farian. Marcia Barrett, Maizie Williams, Liz Mitchell, Bobby Farrell. Their single 'Rivers Of Babylon/Brown Girl In The Ring' sold over two million in the UK, where they were one of the top selling acts in the late Seventies.

	US Top 10 Ent	UK Top 10 Ent
Night Flight To Venus		8/78
Oceans Of Fantasy		10/79
The Magic Of Boney M		5/80

BETTY BOO - Pop/dance singer born Alison Clarkson in London, England, in 1970. She first found fame as a featured vocalist with the Beatmasters and was voted Best New Artist of 1990 at the BRIT awards.

	US Top 10 Ent	UK Top 10 Ent
Boomania		9/90

DEBBY BOONE - Pop-turned-contemporary-gospel singer. Daughter of Pat Boone, born 1956 in Hackensack, New Jersey. Her single 'You Light Up My Life' topped the US chart for ten weeks.

	US Top 10 Ent	UK Top 10 Ent
You Light Up My Life	12/77	

BOSTON - Critcially aclaimed session rock group masterminded by Boston born Tom Scholz and also featuring Brad Delph. Their albums come infrequently but are always successful .

	US Top 10 Ent	UK Top 10 Ent
Boston	11/76	
Don't Look Back	9/78	
Third Stage	10/86	

DAVID BOWIE - Trend setting and unique pop/rock singer/actor born David Jones in London, England, in 1947. He was one of the most successful, important and influential recording artists of the rock era.

	US Top 10 Ent	UK Top 10 Ent
The Rise And Fall Of Ziggy Stardust And The Spiders From Mars		8/72
Aladdin Sane		5/73
Hunky Dory		8/73
Pin Ups		11/73
Diamond Dogs	7/74	6/74
David Live		11/74
Young Americans		4/75
Station To Station	2/76	2/76
Changesonebowie		6/76
Low		2/77
Heroes		11/77
Stage		10/78
Lodger		6/79
Scary Monsters And Super Creeps		9/80
Very Best Of David Bowie		1/81
Let's Dance	5/83	4/83
Tonight		10/84
Changesbowie		3/90
Black Tie White Noise		4/93

MAX BOYCE - Humorous Welsh entertainer who specialized in material about rugby football.

	US Top 10 Ent	UK Top 10 Ent
We All Had Doctors' Papers		11/75
I Know Cos I Was There		6/78

BOYZ II MEN - Soulful R&B quartet from Philadelphia, USA. Michael McCary, Nathan Morris, Wayne Morris and Shawn Stockman. Both their singles 'End Of The Road' and 'I'll Make Love To You' topped the US chart for three months. Their two hit LPs are the biggest selling R&B albums of all time.

	US Top 10 Ent	UK Top 10 Ent
Cooleyhighharmony	8/91	
II	9/94	

WILFRID BRAMBELL & HARRY H. CORBETT - British character actors Brambell (1912-1985) and Corbett (1925-1982) who charted with soundtrack albums from their very successful British comedy TV show, *Steptoe & Son.*

	US Top 10 Ent	UK Top 10 Ent
Steptoe And Son		9/63

BRAND NEW HEAVIES - Innovative dance/R&B act based in London, England which includes N'Dea Davenport, Simon Bartholomew, Andrew Levy, Jan Kincaid.

	US Top 10 Ent	UK Top 10 Ent
Brother Sister		4/94

TONI BRAXTON - Highly acclaimed soulful female vocalist born 1968 in Maryland, USA. She won two Grammy Awards in 1993. She is regarded as one of the brightest new R&B acts of the Nineties.

	US Top 10 Ent	UK Top 10 Ent
Toni Braxton	2/94	

BREAD - World renowned AOR quartet from Los Angeles, USA. Members included David Gates, James Griffin, Robb Royer, Jim Gordon. The latter two being replaced early on by Larry Knechtel and Mike Botts repectively. They were one of the Seventies top selling acts, who made a very successful comeback in 1994.

	US Top 10 Ent	UK Top 10 Ent
Baby I'm-A Want You	3/72	
The Best Of Bread	4/73	11/72
The Sound Of Bread		11/77

EDIE BRICKELL & THE NEW BOHEMIANS - Texas rock band. Edie Brickell, John Bush, Brad Houser, Kenny Withrow. Vocalist Brickell was married to Paul Simon in 1992. He co-produced her first solo album in 1994.

	US Top 10 Ent	UK Top 10 Ent
Shooting Rubberbands At The Stars	2/89	

BRONSKI BEAT - British techno-pop trio. Jimmy Somerville, Steve Bronski, Larry Steinbachek. Somerville went on to form The Communards and then to a solo career.

	US Top 10 Ent	UK Top 10 Ent
The Age Of Consent		10/84

ELKIE BROOKS - Pop/MOR singer born Elaine Bookbinder in 1945 in Manchester, England. Despite her many years at the top in Britain she is, as yet, without a hit Stateside.

	US Top 10 Ent	UK Top 10 Ent
Pearls		12/81

	US Top 10 Ent	UK Top 10 Ent
Pearls II		12/82
No More The Fool		2/87

GARTH BROOKS - The biggest selling country singer of all-time was born Oklahoma, USA, in 1962. He was the top selling artist (in any musical field) in America in 1992 and 1993 and has sold over 50 million albums during his short career.

	US Top 10 Ent	UK Top 10 Ent
No Fences	5/91	
Ropin' The Wind	9/91	
Beyond The Season	9/92	
The Chase	10/92	
In Pieces	9/93	2/94

NIGEL BROOKS SINGERS - Noted British session group who were often seen and heard on UK television in the Seventies.

	US Top 10 Ent	UK Top 10 Ent
Songs Of Joy		12/75

BROS - London-based pop trio were the UK's top teen idols in the late Eighties. Twin brothers Matt and Luke Goss with Craig Logan.

	US Top 10 Ent	UK Top 10 Ent
Push		4/88
The Time		10/89

BROTHERHOOD OF MAN - British pop group who originally included Tony Burrows (ex-Edison Lighthouse, White Plains, Pipkins, First Class), John Goddison and Sunny. The mid-Seventies line-up included Martin Lee and Lee Sheriden.

	US Top 10 Ent	UK Top 10 Ent
Brotherhood Of Man		11/78

BROTHERS FOUR - Folk/pop quartet of fraternity brothers from University of Washington. Bob Flick, Dick Foley, Mike Kirkland and John Paine.

	US Top 10 Ent	UK Top 10 Ent
B.M.O.C. (Best Music On/Off Campus)	3/61	

BROTHERS JOHNSON - Well regarded R&B/funk duo from Los Angles, USA. Comprised George and Louis Johnson.

	US Top 10 Ent	UK Top 10 Ent
Blam!	9/78	
Light Up The Night	4/80	

CRAZY WORLD OF ARTHUR BROWN - Rock band fronted by outrageously outfitted Brown. Real name Arthur Wilton, born 1944 in Yorkshire, England.

	US Top 10 Ent	UK Top 10 Ent
The Crazy World Of Arthur Brown	11/68	7/68

BOBBY BROWN - Leading R&B/dance music singer from Boston, born 1969. The ex-New Edition member was one of the late Eighties top selling acts. He married Whitney Houston in 1992.

	US Top 10 Ent	UK Top 10 Ent
Don't Be Cruel	10/88	3/89
Dance!...Ya Know It	2/90	
Bobby	9/92	

JAMES BROWN - The most successful soul/ R&B singer of all time was born Macon, Georgia, USA in 1928. Rightfully known as 'Soul Brother Number 1' and 'Godfather of Soul'. He has had over 100 singles on the R&B chart and only Elvis Presley has had more pop chart entries.

	US Top 10 Ent	UK Top 10 Ent
Live At The Apollo	7/63	

JOE BROWN - 'Cockney' pop singer/guitarist from London born 1941. He was one of the most original British rock acts in the pre-Beatles years.

	US Top 10 Ent	UK Top 10 Ent
A Picture Of You		9/62

SAM BROWN - Pop singer/songwriter born 1964 in London, England, the daughter of Joe Brown (above). Her single 'Stop' sold two million globally.

	US Top 10 Ent	UK Top 10 Ent
Stop		3/89

JACKSON BROWNE - Critically lauded, L.A.-based vocalist/musician/composer/producer was born in Germany in 1948.

	US Top 10 Ent	UK Top 10 Ent
The Pretender	12/76	
Running On Empty	2/78	
Hold Out	8/80	
Lawyers In Love	9/83	

DAVE BRUBECK QUARTET - Jazz quartet led by pianist Brubeck (real name David Warren) from California, USA. Quartet included Paul Desmond, Joe Morello and Eugene Wright. Most commercially successful modern jazz act of their time.

	US Top 10 Ent	UK Top 10 Ent
Time Out Featuring 'Take Five'	11/61	

B.T. EXPRESS - Eight-strong funk/R&B group from Brooklyn, New York, whose members included the later hit producer/composer Kashif. They were one of the first, and most respected disco acts of the Seventies.

	US Top 10 Ent	UK Top 10 Ent
Do It ('Til You're Satisfied)	2/75	

KATE BUSH - Distinctive singer/songwriter from Bexley, Kent, England, born 1958. Despite her enormous popularity in the UK, her records have never sold in vast quantities in the USA.

	US Top 10 Ent	UK Top 10 Ent
The Kick Inside		3/78
Lionheart		12/78
Never For Ever		9/80
Hounds Of Love		9/85
The Whole Story		11/86
The Sensual World		10/89
The Red Shoes		11/93

MAX BYGRAVES - Veteran London-based MOR singer/entertainer/comedian. He has been one of Britain's most popular stage performers since the early Fifties.

	US Top 10 Ent	UK Top 10 Ent
Sing Along With Max		11/72
Singalongamax Vol. 3		5/73
100 Golden Greats		11/76

CHARLIE BYRD See STAN GETZ

BYRDS - Legendary Los Angeles-based folk/country/rock quintet whose members have included Roger McGuinn, David Crosby, Mike Clarke, Gene Clark (died 1991), Chris Hillman, Gram Parsons (died 1973) and Clarence White. They are one of the most innovative and imitated acts of the rock era.

	US Top 10 Ent	UK Top 10 Ent
Mr. Tambourine Man	8/65	9/65
The Byrds' Greatest Hits	10/67	

C&C MUSIC FACTORY - R&B/dance act assembed by producer/songwriter/musicians Robet Clivilles and David Cole (died 1995). Their featured vocalists include Freedom Williams, Zelma Davis and Martha Wash (ex-Weather Girls).

	US Top 10 Ent	UK Top 10 Ent
Gonna Make You Sweat	3/91	

JOHN CAFFERTY & THE BEAVER BROWN BAND - Rock sextet from Rhode Island, USA. John Cafferty, Michael Antunes, Bob Cotoia, Gary Gramolini, Pat Lupo, Kenny Jo Silva.

	US Top 10 Ent	UK Top 10 Ent
Eddie And The Cruisers	10/84	

CAMEO - Unmistakable 13-piece funk band from New York, USA, who were led by innovative singer/songwriter Larry Blackmon. Act have since slimmed down to a trio.

	US Top 10 Ent	UK Top 10 Ent
Word Up!	12/86	10/86

GLEN CAMPBELL - Pop/country singer and one-time noted session guitarist born Arkansas, USA, in 1936. The one-time singer with the Beach Boys was also one of America's top selling artists in the late Sixties.

	US Top 10 Ent	UK Top 10 Ent
Gentle On My Mind	10/68	
Wichita Lineman	12/68	
Galveston	4/69	
20 Golden Greats		11/76

CANDLEBOX - Noteworthy new Seattle hard rock quartet. Kevin Martin, Scott Mercado, Peter Kleit and Bardi Martin. Signed to Madonna's Maverick label.

	US Top 10 Ent	UK Top 10 Ent
Candlebox	8/94	

CANNED HEAT - Seminal blues/rock group from Los Angeles, USA. Bob Hite (died 1981), Al Wilson (died 1970), Henry Vestine, Larry Taylor, Frank Cook.

	US Top 10 Ent	UK Top 10 Ent
Boogie With Canned Heat		9/68

FREDDY CANNON - Pop/rock singer born Frederick Picariello in 1939 in Massachusetts, USA. Freddy 'Boom Boom' Cannon is regarded by many as the last of the Fifties styled rock'n'roll singers.

	US Top 10 Ent	UK Top 10 Ent
The Explosive Freddy Cannon		3/60

CAPTAIN & TENNILLE - Successful pop/MOR duo. Daryl 'Captain' Dragon (ex-Beach Boys keyboard player) from Los Angeles, USA, and wife, Toni Tennille, from Montgomery, Alabama, USA.

	US Top 10 Ent	UK Top 10 Ent
Love Will Keep Us Together	7/75	

MARIAH CAREY - Outstanding soulful pop vocalist born New York, USA, in 1970. The Grammy winning artist was one of the Nineties top acts worldwide with LP sales of over 40 million. She was the first artist to put their first five singles at the top of the US chart.

	US Top 10 Ent	UK Top 10 Ent
Mariah Carey	8/90	
Emotions	10/91	2/92
MTV Unplugged EP	6/92	7/92
Music Box	9/93	9/93
Merry Christmas	12/94	

BELINDA CARLISLE - Rock singer from Hollywood, USA, born in 1958. The ex-Go-Go's vocalist had an even more successful career as a solo artist in the UK.

	US Top 10 Ent	UK Top 10 Ent
Heaven On Earth		6/88
Runaway Horses		11/89
The Best Of Belinda Vol. 1		9/92

KIM CARNES - Distinctive singer/songwriter and pianist was born Los Angeles, USA, in 1945. She also had hits duetting with fellow ex-New Christy Minstrels singer Kenny Rogers. Her single, 'Bette Davis Eyes', topped the US singles chart for nine weeks.

	US Top 10 Ent	UK Top 10 Ent
Mistaken Identity	5/81	

CARPENTERS - World famous pop/MOR act were the most successful family duo of all time. Richard Carpenter and sister Karen from New Haven, Connecticut, USA. They were one of the biggest selling LP acts of the early Seventies. Karen died from anorexia nervosa in 1983.

	US Top 10 Ent	UK Top 10 Ent
Close To You	11/70	
Carpenters	6/71	
A Song For You	8/72	
The Singles 1969-1973	12/73	2/74
Now & Then	7/73	7/73
Horizon		6/75
A Kind Of Hush		7/76
The Singles 1974-78		12/78
Voice Of The Heart		10/83
Only Yesterday		4/90

JOSE CARRERAS - See LUCIANO PAVAROTTI, PLACIDO DOMINGO & JOSE CARRERAS

DINA CARROLL - Britain's most succesful black female singer of the Nineties was born in Suffolk, England. The BRIT award winning vocalist's debut LP sold over a million copies in the UK.

	US Top 10 Ent	UK Top 10 Ent
So Close		2/93

CARS - Successful rock band from Boston, USA. Ric Ocasek, Ben Orr, Elliot Easton, Greg Hawkes, David Robinson. Lead singer Ocasek was also group's main songwriter.

	US Top 10 Ent	UK Top 10 Ent
Candy-O	7/79	
Panorama	9/80	
Heartbeat City	4/84	

CARTER - THE UNSTOPPABLE SEX MACHINE - London based rock act were the British music media's darlings of the early Nineties. James Morrison (Jimbob) and Leslie Carter (Fruitbat).

	US Top 10 Ent	UK Top 10 Ent
1992 - The Love Album		5/92

JOHNNY CASH - Legendary country singer/songwriter born 1932 in Arkansas, USA. The 'Man In Black' who, like Elvis, started with Sun Records, is arguably the best known country performer in the world.

	US Top 10 Ent	UK Top 10 Ent
Johnny Cash At San Quentin	8/69	9/69
Hello I'm Johnny Cash	3/70	3/70

DAVID CASSIDY - Pop singer/actor born New York, USA, in 1950. The star of top Seventies TV show *The Partridge Family* was, for a time, a Number 1 teen idol on both sides of the Atlantic.

	US Top 10 Ent	UK Top 10 Ent
Cherish		5/72
Rock Me Baby		2/73
Dreams Are Nothin' More Than Wishes		12/73

SHAUN CASSIDY - Pop singer/TV actor born 1959 in Los Angeles, USA . The half-brother of David Cassidy (above) was also a top selling teen star in the USA.

	US Top 10 Ent	UK Top 10 Ent
Shaun Cassidy	9/77	
Born Late	1/78	

RICHARD CHAMBERLAIN - Pop/MOR singer/actor born 1935 in Los Angeles, USA. His recording success came via his role as Dr. Kildare in the top-rated Sixties TV series.

	US Top 10 Ent	UK Top 10 Ent
Richard Chamberlain Sings	3/63	

CHAMBERS BROTHERS - Gospel-based rock band comprised four Mississipi-born brothers George, Joe, Lester and Willie Chambers and English drummer Brian Keenan.

	US Top 10 Ent	UK Top 10 Ent
The Time Has Come	10/68	

HARRY CHAPIN - Well respected folk/rock singer/songwriter born 1942 in New York, USA. Chapin, who helped raise much money for international famine relief, died in a car crash in 1981.

	US Top 10 Ent	UK Top 10 Ent
Verities & Balderdash	12/74	

TRACY CHAPMAN - Distinctive black folk singer/songwriter born 1964 in Cleveland, USA. Her appearance at Nelson Mandela's 70th Birthday Tribute in 1988 helped rocket her to international fame.

	US Top 10 Ent	UK Top 10 Ent
Tracy Chapman	7/88	6/88
Crossroads	11/89	10/89

CHARLATANS - Cheshire, England-based retro-oriented rock band. Tim Burgess, Jon Baker, Martin Blunt, Rob Collins, Jon Brookes.

	US Top 10 Ent	UK Top 10 Ent
Some Friendly		10/90

RAY CHARLES - Foremost soul/jazz/R&B singer/songwriter and musician was born Ray Charles Robinson in Albany, Georgia, in 1930. With chart records spanning six decades, he is undoubtedly one of the legends of the rock music era.

	US Top 10 Ent	UK Top 10 Ent
Genius Plus Soul Equals Jazz	6/61	
Modern Sounds In Country And Western Music	5/62	
Ray Charles' Greatest Hits	9/62	
Modern Sounds In Country And Western Music (Vol. 2)	11/62	
Ingredients In A Recipe For Soul	9/63	

CHAS & DAVE - Music hall styled pub-rock duo from London, England. Chas Hodges and Dave Peacock.

	US Top 10 Ent	UK Top 10 Ent
Chas & Dave's Knees Up Jamboree Bag No 2		12/83

CHEAP TRICK - Top selling rock band from Rockford, Illinois, USA. Rick Nielsen, Tom Petersson, Bun E. Carlos, Robin Zander. Act were successful in Japan before breaking in their homeland.

	US Top 10 Ent	UK Top 10 Ent
Cheap Trick At Budokan	6/79	
Dream Police	10/79	

CHUBBY CHECKER - The 'King of the Twist' was born Ernest Evans in Philadelphia in 1941. At times he had four albums simultaneously in the US Top 10.

	US Top 10 Ent	UK Top 10 Ent
Your Twist Party	1/62	
Twist With Chubby Checker	1/62	
Chubby Checker/Bobby Rydell (with Bobby Rydell)	1/62	
For Twisters Only	2/62	

CHEECH & CHONG - Drug culture rock comedians Richard 'Cheech' Marin from California, USA and Thomas Chong from Alberta, Canada.

	US Top 10 Ent	UK Top 10 Ent
Big Bambu	8/72	
Los Cochinos	9/73	
Cheech & Chong's Wedding Album	11/74	

CHER - Singer/actress born Cherilyn LaPierre in California, USA, in 1946. She has been a frequent visitor to the chart, both on her own and initially with former husband Sonny Bono, since the mid-Sixties. She was one of the all time top female artists.

	US Top 10 Ent	UK Top 10 Ent
Love Hurts		6/91
Cher's Greatest Hits: 1965-1992		11/92

NENEH CHERRY - Rock/R&B vocalist born Stockholm, Sweden in 1964 and raised in New York. She was a double winner at the 1990 BRIT awards.

	US Top 10 Ent	UK Top 10 Ent
Raw Like Sushi		6/89

CHIC - Disco/R&B group from New York formed by (later) top producers/songwriters Nile Rodgers and Bernard Edwards. Also included Norma Jean Wright, Luci Martin, Tony Thompson.

	US Top 10 Ent	UK Top 10 Ent
C'est Chic	12/78	3/79
Risque	9/79	

CHICAGO - Foremost AOR rock/jazz group from Chicago. Peter Cetera, Terry Kath (died 1978), Robert Lamm, Lee Loughnane, James Pankow, Danny Seraphine, Walt Parazaider. They are one of the most successful album acts of all time.

	US Top 10 Ent	UK Top 10 Ent
Chicago II	3/70	4/70
Chicago III	2/71	
At Carnegie Hall	12/71	
Chicago V	8/72	
Chicago VI	7/73	
Chicago VII	4/74	
Chicago VIII	4/75	
Chicago IX - Chicago's Greatest Hits	12/75	
Chicago X	7/76	
Chicago XI	11/77	
Chicago 17	1/85	

CHI-LITES - Chicago R&B/soul quartet. Marshall Thompson, Eugene Record, Robert Lester and Creadel Jones were one of the top soul acts of the Seventies on both sides of the Atlantic.

	US Top 10 Ent	UK Top 10 Ent
A Lonely Man	6/72	

CHIPMUNKS - Prime time TV cartoon characters created by David Seville (Ross Bagdasarian, died 1972). Alvin, Simon and Theodore. Seville's son, Ross Jr., took over the trio after his father's death.

	US Top 10 Ent	UK Top 10 Ent
Let's All Sing With The Chipmunks	1/60	

CHRISTIANS - Pop group from Liverpool, England. Gary, Russell and Roger Christian plus singer/composer/multi-instrumentalist Henry Priestman.

	US Top 10 Ent	UK Top 10 Ent
The Christians		1/88
Colour		1/90

SIR WINSTON CHURCHILL - Britain's best known politician of the 20th century.

	US Top 10 Ent	UK Top 10 Ent
The Voice Of Churchill		3/65

CINDERELLA - Heavy metal group from Pennsylvania, USA. Tom Keifer, Eric Brittingham, Fred Coury, Jeff LaBar.

	US Top 10 Ent	UK Top 10 Ent
Night Songs	1/87	

CLANNAD - Folk-oriented family quintet from Ireland. Maire Brennan and her brothers Pol and Ciaran, and twin uncles Noel and Padraig Duggan. Singer, Enya (Brennan's sister) was a member 1980-82.

	US Top 10 Ent	UK Top 10 Ent
Pastpresent		5/89

ERIC CLAPTON - Legendary rock guitarist born 1945 in Surrey, England. Ex-Yardbirds, John Mayall's Bluesbreakers, Cream, Blind Faith, Derek & The Dominos. Arguably the most famous guitarist of the rock era. See also John Mayall.

	US Top 10 Ent	UK Top 10 Ent
History Of Eric Clapton	6/72	
461 Ocean Boulevard	8/74	8/74
Slowhand	3/78	
Backless	1/79	
Just One Night	5/80	5/80
Another Ticket	4/81	
August		2/87
The Cream Of Eric Clapton		10/87
Journeyman		11/89
Unplugged	9/92	9/92
From The Cradle	10/94	9/94

DAVE CLARK FIVE - Very successful pop/rock group from London, England. Dave Clark, Lenny Davidson, Rick Huxley, Mike Smith, Dennis Payton. They were one of the most popular UK acts in America during the Sixties.

	US Top 10 Ent	UK Top 10 Ent
Glad All Over	5/64	
A Session With The Dave Clark Five		5/64
The Dave Clark Five Return!	7/64	
Coast To Coast	2/65	
Catch Us If You Can		8/65

LOUIS CLARK & THE ROYAL PHILHARMONIC ORCHESTRA - Well known British classical orchestra, who had a major medley hit under the baton of Birmingham, England born conductor Louis Clark.

	US Top 10 Ent	UK Top 10 Ent
Hooked On Classics	1/82	10/81

CLASH - Controversial punk/new wave band from London, England. Joe Strummer, Mick Jones, Topper Headon, Paul Simonon. Leading lights of the British punk music scene.

	US Top 10 Ent	UK Top 10 Ent
Give 'Em Enough Rope		11/78
Combat Rock	1/83	5/82

RICHARD CLAYDERMAN - Popular MOR/light classical pianist from France, born Phillipe Pages in 1954 and has sold millions of albums around the globe.

	US Top 10 Ent	UK Top 10 Ent
Richard Clayderman		1/83

CLUB NOUVEAU - Dance/disco group from Sacramento, USA. Jay King (producer, ex-Timex Social Club), Denzil Foster, Thomas McAlroy, Valerie Watson, Samuelle Prater.

	US Top 10 Ent	UK Top 10 Ent
Life, Love And Pain	3/87	

JOE COCKER - Distinctive gravel-voiced rock singer from Sheffield, England, born 1944. He was one of the stars of Woodstock whose success has spanned four decades.

	US Top 10 Ent	UK Top 10 Ent
Mad Dogs & Englishmen	9/70	
The Legend - The Essential Collection		7/92

COCKNEY REBEL - See STEVE HARLEY

LEONARD COHEN - Downbeat singer/songwriter and poet born 1934 in Montreal, Canada, whose unique style has earned him a big cult following.

	US Top 10 Ent	UK Top 10 Ent
Songs From A Room		5/69
Songs Of Love And Hate		5/71

NAT 'KING' COLE - Very successful, velvet-voiced, MOR/jazz singer/pianist from Montgomery, Alabama, USA, born in 1917, died 1965. Regarded as one of the finest song stylists of the 20th century.

	US Top 10 Ent	UK Top 10 Ent
Wild Is Love	11/60	
Ramblin' Rose	10/62	
L-O-V-E	3/65	
20 Golden Greats		4/78
Greatest Love Songs		12/82

NATALIE COLE - Soulful MOR vocalist born 1950 in Los Angeles, California. The daughter of Nat 'King' Cole (above) has earned her own place in music's Who's Who.

	US Top 10 Ent	UK Top 10 Ent
Unpredictable	4/77	
Unforgettable	7/91	

JUDY COLLINS - Distinctive folk singer/songwriter born 1939 in Seattle, USA. She was one of the Sixties leading folk music performers.

	US Top 10 Ent	UK Top 10 Ent
Wild Flowers	12/68	

PHIL COLLINS - Singer/songwriter/producer/drummer and actor from London, England, born 1951. This multi-talented solo performer and member of Genesis is one of the top selling artists of the last 15 years.

	US Top 10 Ent	UK Top 10 Ent
Face Value	6/81	2/81
Hello, I Must Be Going!	2/83	11/82
No Jacket Required	3/85	3/85
...But Seriously	12/89	12/89
Serious Hits...Live!		11/90
Both Sides		11/93

COLOR ME BADD - Retro R&B/dance quartet from Oklahoma City, USA who re-located to New York. Bryan Abrams, Mark Calderon, Kevin Thornton and Sam Watters.

	US Top 10 Ent	UK Top 10 Ent
C.M.B.	8/91	9/91

COMMITMENTS - Blue-eyed Irish soul band put together for the successful film of the same name. Robert Arkins, Angeline Ball, Maria Doyle, Bronagh Gallagher, Andrew Strong.

	US Top 10 Ent	UK Top 10 Ent
The Commitments (Soundtrack)		11/91

COMMODORES - Successful R&B band from Alabama, USA. Lionel Richie, William King, Ronald LaPread, Thomas McClary, Walter Orange and Milan Williams. Thanks to singer/songwriter Richie's input they were one of the top selling groups late-Seventies and early-Eighties.

	US Top 10 Ent	UK Top 10 Ent
Commodores	5/77	
Commodores Live!	11/77	
Natural High	7/78	
Midnight Magic	9/79	
Heroes	7/80	
Love Songs		8/82

COMMUNARDS - British synth pop duo conisting of distinctive ex-Bronski Beat vocalist Jimmy Somerville and multi-instrumentalist Richard Coles. Sarah Jane Morris was the co-lead vocalist on their UK Number 1 single 'Don't Leave Me This Way'.

	US Top 10 Ent	UK Top 10 Ent
Communards		10/86

PERRY COMO - Highly successful MOR singer/entertainer born Canonsburg, Pennsylvania, USA, in 1912. This relaxed performer, who first charted in 1940, topped the British LP chart in 1975, aged 63. He is a legend of American popular music.

	US Top 10 Ent	UK Top 10 Ent
And I Love You So		7/73
40 Greatest Hits		11/75

RAY CONNIFF - Unmistakable arranger/conductor/trombonist from Massachusetts, USA, born 1916. Coniff's distinctive multi-tracked vocal sound helped make him one of the top selling album acts in the early days of stereo recordings.

	US Top 10 Ent	UK Top 10 Ent
Say It With Music (A Touch Of Latin)	12/60	
Hi-Fi Companion Album		12/60
Memories Are Made Of This	3/61	
Somewhere My Love	8/66	
His Orchestra, His Chorus, His Singers, His Sound		6/69

BILLY CONNOLLY - Scottish born comedian/TV entertainer and one time folk singer.

	US Top 10 Ent	UK Top 10 Ent
Get Right Intae Him		12/75

RUSS CONWAY - Pop/honky tonk pianist/songwriter born Trevor Stanford in 1927 in Bristol, England. He was the top selling singles artist in the UK in 1959.

	US Top 10 Ent	UK Top 10 Ent
My Concerto For You		4/60
Party Time		12/60

RITA COOLIDGE - Rock singer born Nashville, USA, in 1944. Worked with Delaney & Bonnie, Joe Cocker and Eric Clapton, and was married to Kris Kristofferson.

	US Top 10 Ent	UK Top 10 Ent
Anytime...Anywhere	10/77	6/78
Very Best Of Rita Coolidge		3/81

ALICE COOPER - Ghoulish horror-rock performer from Detroit, USA, was born Vincent Furnier in 1948, and is one of rock music's best recognized characters.

	US Top 10 Ent	UK Top 10 Ent
School's Out	8/72	8/72
Billion Dollar Babies	4/73	3/73
Welcome To My Nightmare	5/75	
Trash		8/89
The Last Temptation		6/94

BILL COSBY - Top US comedian/TV actor for over 25 years, born 1938 in Philadelphia. He has amassed a collection of Grammys, Emmys and million sellers.

	US Top 10 Ent	UK Top 10 Ent
Wonderfulness	7/66	
Revenge	5/67	
To Russell, My Brother, Whom I Slept With	5/68	

ELVIS COSTELLO - Highly regarded rock/new wave singer/songwriter, born Declan McManus in Liverpool, England, in 1954.

	US Top 10 Ent	UK Top 10 Ent
This Year's Model		4/78
Armed Forces		1/79
Get Happy		2/80
Punch The Clock		8/83
Brutal Youth		3/94

COUNTING CROWS - San Francsico rock band were one of 1994's most successful new acts in the USA. Matt Malley, Dave Bryson, Dan Vickrey, Charlie Gillingham, Adam Duritz, Steve Bowman.

	US Top 10 Ent	UK Top 10 Ent
August & Everything After	3/94	

COVERDALE/PAGE - Major heavy metal masters, David Coverdale (ex-Whitesnake) and Jimmy Page (ex-Led Zeppelin) proved a successful, but short-lived team.

	US Top 10 Ent	UK Top 10 Ent
Coverdale Page	4/93	

CRANBERRIES - Ireland's most successful new group of the mid-Nineties. Dolores O'Riordan, Noel Hogan Mike Hogan, Feargal Lawler.

	US Top 10 Ent	UK Top 10 Ent
Everybody Else Is Doing It, So Why Can't We		3/94
No Need To Argue		10/94

CRASH TEST DUMMIES - Distinctive rock group from Manitoba, Canada, were globally successful in 1994. Brad Roberts, Ellen Reid, Benjamin Darvill, Dan Roberts and Mitch Dorge.

	US Top 10 Ent	UK Top 10 Ent
God Shuffled His Feet		5/94

BEVERLEY CRAVEN - British-based, Sri Lanka born singer/songwriter/pianist who was voted Top British Newcomer of 1991 at the BRIT awards.

	US Top 10 Ent	UK Top 10 Ent
Beverley Craven		6/91

MICHAEL CRAWFORD - Popular stage/TV actor/singer, born 1942 in Salisbury, England, who has been very successful in both TV sitcoms and stage musicals.

	US Top 10 Ent	UK Top 10 Ent
Performs Andrew Lloyd Webber		12/91

RANDY CRAWFORD - Soul/jazz singer born 1952 in Macon, Georgia, USA. Found fame as a featured vocalist with The Crusaders.

	US Top 10 Ent	UK Top 10 Ent
Secret Combination		7/81

CRAZY HORSE - See NEIL YOUNG

CREAM - Influential and innovative British rock/blues trio, often considered to be the first supergroup. Eric Clapton, Jack Bruce and Ginger Baker. They were one of the most important acts of the rock era.

	US Top 10 Ent	UK Top 10 Ent
Fresh Cream		2/67
Disraeli Gears	1/68	11/67
Wheels Of Fire	7/68	9/68
Goodbye	3/69	3/69
Best Of Cream	8/69	11/69
Live Cream		7/70
The Cream Of Eric Clapton		9/87

CREEDENCE CLEARWATER REVIVAL - Retro rock'n'roll group from California, USA. Brothers John and Tom Fogerty (died 1990), Doug Clifford and Stu Cook. They were one of the top selling artists in America at the end of the Sixties.

	US Top 10 Ent	UK Top 10 Ent
Bayou Country	5/69	
Green River	9/69	
Willy And The Poor Boys	12/69	
Cosmo's Factory	8/70	9/70
Pendulum	1/71	

KID CREOLE AND THE COCONUTS - New York based Latin-oriented pop/dance band, formed by August 'Kid Creole' Darnell and Andy 'Coati Mundi' Hernandez. This unique act were far more successful in the UK than in North America.

	US Top 10 Ent	UK Top 10 Ent
Tropical Gangsters		6/82

CRICKETS - See BUDDY HOLLY and BOBBY VEE.

JIM CROCE - Noted singer/songwriter/guitarist born 1943 in Philadelphia, USA. His American recording future looked very bright before he was killed in a plane crash in 1973. Shortly after his death he held the top two places on the US LP chart.

	US Top 10 Ent	UK Top 10 Ent
Life And Times	12/73	
You Don't Mess Around With Jim	11/73	
I Got A Name	1/74	
Photographs & Memories - His Greatest Hits	11/74	

CROSBY, STILLS & NASH (& YOUNG) - Soft rock

supergroup which consisted of David Crosby (ex-Byrds), Stephen Stills (ex-Buffalo Springfield), British musician Graham Nash (ex-Hollies) and sometimes Neil Young (ex-Buffalo Springfield).

	US Top 10 Ent	UK Top 10 Ent
Crosby, Stills & Nash	7/69	
Deja Vu	4/70	6/70
4 Way Street	5/71	5/71
So Far	10/74	
CSN	7/77	
Daylight Again	8/82	

DAVID CROSBY/GRAHAM NASH - Crosby, Stills & Nash members David Crosby (born Los Angeles, USA) and Graham Nash (born Blackpool, England) also recorded successfully as a duo.

	US Top 10 Ent	UK Top 10 Ent
Graham Nash/David Crosby	5/72	
Wind On The Water	11/75	

CHRISTOPHER CROSS - Grammy winning pop/rock singer/songwriter from San Antonio, Texas, USA, who was born Christopher Geppert in 1951.

	US Top 10 Ent	UK Top 10 Ent
Christopher Cross	5/80	
Another Page		2/83

SHERYL CROW - St. Louis, Missouri,USA, born rock singer/songwriter who previously sang background vocals for such greats as Michael Jackson, Rod Stewart and Stevie Wonder.

	US Top 10 Ent	UK Top 10 Ent
Tuesday Night Music Club	10/94	

CROWDED HOUSE - Internationally popular Antipodean rock band whose members have included brothers Neil and Tim Finn (both ex-Split Enz), Paul Hester, Nick Seymour.

	US Top 10 Ent	UK Top 10 Ent
Woodface		3/92

CULT - Celebrated guitar-driven rock group. Ian Astbury, Billy Duffy, Jamie Stewart and Matt Sorum (who joined Guns N' Roses). First known as The Southern Death Cult.

	US Top 10 Ent	UK Top 10 Ent
Electric		4/87
Sonic Temple	6/89	
Pure Cult		2/93

CULTURE CLUB - Image-conscious pop/rock band from London, England, led by gender-bender Boy George (born George O'Dowd in 1961). Other members were Michael Craig, Roy Hay, Jon Moss. George is one of the best known characters of early Eighties music.

	US Top 10 Ent	UK Top 10 Ent
Colour By Numbers	12/83	10/83
Waking Up With The House On Fire		11/84

CURE - BRIT winning group from Sussex, England fronted by the charismatic Robert Smith. Other early members included producer Michael Dempsey and Lol Tolhurst. After a slow start The Cure became as popular in the USA as they were in their homeland.

	US Top 10 Ent	UK Top 10 Ent
The Head On The Door		9/85
Standing On A Beach - The Singles		6/86
Wish	5/92	5/92

CURIOSITY KILLED THE CAT - Teen appeal pop/rock group from London, England. Ben Volpeliere-Pierrot, Julian Brookhouse, Nick Thorp, Miguel Drummond. The most publicized new pop act in Britain in 1987.

	US Top 10 Ent	UK Top 10 Ent
Keep Your Distance		5/87

CURVED AIR - British progressive rock band who were fronted by Sonja Kristina. Group's ever changing personnel has included Darryl Way, Eddie Jobson (later Roxy Music, Jethro Tull) and American Stewart Copeland (later Police). Group claim to have released the first LP picture disc.

	US Top 10 Ent	UK Top 10 Ent
Air Conditioning		2/71

CYPRESS HILL - Hard-hitting, drug-promoting rap trio based in Los Angeles, USA. Sen Dog (Sen Reyes), B-Real (Louis Freeze), DJ Muggs (Lawrence Muggerud).

	US Top 10 Ent	UK Top 10 Ent
Black Sunday	8/93	

BILLY RAY CYRUS - Country singer born 1961 in Kentucky, USA. He became the first artist to top the pop album chart in just two weeks with his debut release and spent a record (for a first hit) 17 weeks at the top.

	US Top 10 Ent	UK Top 10 Ent
Some Gave All	6/92	
It Won't Be The Last	7/93	

D:REAM - British dance music duo formed by Peter Cunnah and Al McKenzie. The latter returned to DJ work just prior to D:Ream's commercial breakthrough.

	US Top 10 Ent	UK Top 10 Ent
D:ream On Vol. 1		2/94

BILL DANA (JOSE JIMENEZ) - Funny man Bill Dana, born William Szarthmary, 1924, in Quincy, Massachusetts, USA, had American record success as the Latin American comic character he invented, Jose Jimenez.

	US Top 10 Ent	UK Top 10 Ent
Jose Jiminez At The Hungry I	10/61	

CHARLIE DANIELS BAND - Country fiddle player/guitarist and Nashville session musician was born 1936 in North Carolina, USA. Among his band members were Tom Crain, Joe DiGregorio, Charles Hayward, James Marshall.

	US Top 10 Ent	UK Top 10 Ent
Million Mile Reflections	8/79	

TERENCE TRENT D'ARBY - British-based soul/pop singer/songwriter born 1962 in New York, USA. This outstanding live performer was the first American artist to enter the UK chart at Number 1 with their debut album.

	US Top 10 Ent	UK Top 10 Ent
Introducing The Hardline According To...	4/88	7/87

BOBBY DARIN - Multi-faceted singer/songwriter/actor, who was born Walden Robert Cassotto, in the Bronx, New York, USA, in 1936, died from heart failure in 1973. He was one of the biggest talents to come from the early rock'n'roll years.

	US Top 10 Ent	UK Top 10 Ent
That's All	3/60	
This Is Darin	4/60	3/60

SPENCER DAVIS GROUP - Respected R&B influenced rock group from Birmingham, England. Spencer Davis led the band which included brothers, Steve and Muff Winwood, and Pete York. Steve Winwood went on to write his own chapter in rock history.

	US Top 10 Ent	UK Top 10 Ent
Their 1st LP		2/66
The 2nd LP		2/66
Autumn '66		10/66

DEACON BLUE - Top selling pop/rock group from Glasgow, whose British success never spread to the USA. They were fronted by singer/songwriter Ricky Ross (born 1957) and included the future Mrs. Ross, Lorraine McIntosh.

	US Top 10 Ent	UK Top 10 Ent
When The World Knows Your Name		4/89
Ooh La Vegas		9/90
Fellow Hoodlums		6/91
Our Town - Greatest Hits		4/94

CHRIS DE BURGH - British-based pop/MOR singer/songwriter born 1948 in Argentina. Real name Chris Davidson. He has been a regular entrant to the UK album chart since the early Eighties.

	US Top 10 Ent	UK Top 10 Ent
The Very Best Of Chris De Burgh		2/85
Into The Light		8/86
Flying Colours		10/88
From A Spark To A Flame - The Very Best Of Chris De Burgh		11/89
Power Of Ten		5/92

JOEY DEE & THE STARLITERS - This energetic New York rock band helped make the twist a worldwide dance craze in 1962. Dee was born Joseph DiNicola in New Jersey in 1940. At times, band included Jimi Hendrix and three of the (Young) Rascals.

	US Top 10 Ent	UK Top 10 Ent
Doin' The Twist At The Peppermint Lounge	1/62	

DEEP PURPLE - Trail-blazing English heavy metal band, who were a hugely successful live act in the Seventies. Members have included Ritchie Blackmore, Rod Evans, Jon Lord, Ian Gillan, Roger Glover, David Coverdale, Glenn Hughes, Tommy Bolin (died 1976) and Joe Lynn Turner.

	US Top 10 Ent	UK Top 10 Ent
Deep Purple In Rock		6/70
Fireball		9/71
Machine Head	8/73	4/72
Made In Japan	7/73	
Burn		3/74
Deepest Purple		7/80
Perfect Strangers		11/84

DEF LEPPARD - Very successful heavy metal band from Sheffield, England. Joe Elliott, Rick Allen, Steve Clark (died 1991), Rick Savage, Pete Willis. Hysteria is the biggest selling LP ever by a UK group in America. It was the first metal LP to sell a million CDs.

	US Top 10 Ent	UK Top 10 Ent
Pyromania	3/83	
Hysteria	9/87	8/87
Adrenalize	4/92	4/92

DEL AMTRI - Acoustic/electric rock group from Glasgow, Scotland. Justin Currie, Iain Harvie, David Cummings, Brian McDermott.

	US Top 10 Ent	UK Top 10 Ent
Change Everything		6/92

CHAKA DEMUS & PLIERS - Jamaican reggae duo consisted of DJ Chaka Demus and singer Pliers. The first reggae act to have three consecutive Top 5 hit singles in the UK.

	US Top 10 Ent	UK Top 10 Ent
Tease Me		1/94

CATHY DENNIS - Dance/pop vocalist from Norwich, England, born in 1970. In 1991, she was *Billboard*'s Top New Female Artist in the USA, as well as Britain's most successful singles artist in America.

	US Top 10 Ent	UK Top 10 Ent
Move To This		8/91

JOHN DENVER - Pop/folk singer/songwriter, born John Deutschendorf in Roswell, New Mexico, in 1943. He was one of the biggest selling album acts in America in the mid-Seventies.

	US Top 10 Ent	UK Top 10 Ent
Rocky Mountain High	3/73	
John Denver's Greatest Hits	1/74	
Back Home Again	7/74	9/74
An Evening With John Denver	4/75	
Windsong	10/75	
Live In London		5/76
Spirit	9/76	
John Denver's Greatest Hits Vol. 2	3/77	

KARL DENVER - Distinctive folk/country/pop singer/yodeller from Glasgow, Scotland, born in 1934. He was one of the most unique UK artists in the pre-Beatles era.

	US Top 10 Ent	UK Top 10 Ent
Wimoweh		1/62

DEODATA - Musician/composer/producer/arranger born Eumir Deodata in Rio De Janeiro, Brazil, in 1942. Later produced a string of hits for Kool & The Gang.

	US Top 10 Ent	UK Top 10 Ent
Prelude	3/73	

DEPECHE MODE - Synthesizer-rock quartet from Essex, England,whose members have included David Gahan, Martin Gore, Andy Fletcher and Vince Clarke (replaced by Alan Wilder). They were one of Britain's most successful bands of the Eighties and became the first UK indie act to top the US chart.

	US Top 10 Ent	UK Top 10 Ent
Construction Time Again		9/83
Black Celebration		3/86
Violator	5/90	
Songs Of Faith And Devotion	4/93	4/93

DEXY'S MIDNIGHT RUNNERS - Multi-faceted band fronted by singer/songwriter Kevin Rowland, born 1953 in Wolverhampton, England. Their transatlantic Number 1, 'Come On Eileen', sold over a million copies in Britain.

	US Top 10 Ent	UK Top 10 Ent
Searching For The Young Soul Rebels		8/80
Too-Rye-Ay		8/82

NEIL DIAMOND - Enormously successful singer/songwriter born Noah Kaminsky in New York, USA, in 1941. Only Elvis Presley has amassed more American gold albums.

	US Top 10 Ent	UK Top 10 Ent
Moods	8/72	9/72
Hot August Night	2/73	
Jonathan Livingston Seagull (Soundtrack)	12/73	
Serenade	12/74	
Beautiful Noise	7/76	
Love At The Greek	4/77	7/77
I'm Glad You're Here With Me Tonight	1/78	
20 Golden Greats		12/78
You Don't Bring Me Flowers	1/79	
The Jazz Singer (Soundtrack)	1/81	3/81
The Greatest Hits 1966-1992		7/92
The Christmas Album	12/92	

BARBARA DICKSON - Scottish born pop/MOR singer started on the folk circuit. Although unknown in the USA she had been a regular visitor to the British album chart.

	US Top 10 Ent	UK Top 10 Ent
All For A Song		3/82
The Barbara Dickson Songbook		2/85

DIO - Heavy metal act fronted by Ronnie James Dio (ex-Black Sabbath and Rainbow), born Ronald Padavona in 1949 in New Hampshire, USA. Other members: Vivian Campbell, Claude Schnell, Jimmy Bain, Vinny Appice.

	US Top 10 Ent	UK Top 10 Ent
The Last In Line		7/84

CELINE DION - French Canadian pop singer born 1968 in Quebec, Canada. She won the Eurovison Song Contest for Switzerland in 1988 and in 1993 received a record seven JUNO (Canadian Grammy) nominations.

	US Top 10 Ent	UK Top 10 Ent
The Colour Of My Love	3/94	

DIRE STRAITS - One of the biggest selling British rock bands hail from London, England. Formed by brothers Mark and David Knopfler, John Illsley and Pick Withers. **Brothers In Arms** is Britain's second best-selling album of all time.

	US Top 10 Ent	UK Top 10 Ent
Dire Straits	2/79	4/79
Communique		6/79
Makin' Movies		2/81
Love Over Gold		10/82
Alchemy - Dire Straits Live		3/84
Brothers In Arms	8/85	5/85
Money For Nothing		11/88
On Every Street		9/91
On The Night	5/93	

DJ JAZZY JEFF & THE FRESH PRINCE - Popular rap act from Philadelphia, USA. DJ Jeff Townes and rapper Will Smith, the star of the very successfull international TV sitcom *The Fresh Prince Of Bel Air.*

	US Top 10 Ent	UK Top 10 Ent
He's The DJ I'm The Rapper	8/88	

DR. DRE - Seminal west coast gangsta rapper born Andre Young, Los Angeles, USA. Founder member of multi-platinum rap act, N.W.A., who remained a top album seller when he went solo. He was *Billboard's*Top New Pop Act in 1993.

	US Top 10 Ent	UK Top 10 Ent
The Chronic	2/93	

DR. FEELGOOD - Pub rock band, named after earlier US R&B act, were fronted by Wilko Johnson from Essex, England. Other members included Lee Brilleaux, The Figure (born John Martin) and John B. Sparks.

	US Top 10 Ent	UK Top 10 Ent
Stupidity		10/76

DR. HOOK - Good time pop/country/rock band from New Jersey, USA, formed by Ray Sawyer, Dennis Locorriere and Bil Francis.

	US Top 10 Ent	UK Top 10 Ent
A Little Bit More		8/76
Dr. Hook's Greatest Hits		12/80
Completely Hooked - The Best Of Dr. Hook		6/92

KEN DODD - Veteran comedian/MOR singer from Liverpool, England, born in 1927. His single 'Tears' sold over a million in the UK alone.

	US Top 10 Ent	UK Top 10 Ent
Tears Of Happiness		1/66

PLACIDO DOMINGO - See LUCIANO PAVAROTTI, PLACIDO DOMINGO & JOSE CARRERAS

LONNIE DONEGAN - The 'King of Skiffle', was born Anthony Donegan in Glasgow, Scotland, in 1931. Britain's most successful singles act 1956-1960, also the first UK artist in the rock age to reach the US Top 10 with two separate singles.

	US Top 10 Ent	UK Top 10 Ent
The Golden Age Of Donegan		9/62

DONOVAN - Britain's premiere pop/folk artist in the Sixties, was born Donovan Leitch in Glasgow, Scotland, in 1946. This 'flower child' proved to be far more talented than his early tag, 'The British Dylan', suggested.

	US Top 10 Ent	UK Top 10 Ent
What's Bin Did And What's Bin Hid		6/65
Universal Soldier		11/67
Donovan's Greatest Hits	4/69	

JASON DONOVAN - Teen idol singer/actor born 1968 in Melbourne, Australia. The Photogenic soap-opera star became one of the biggest selling artists in Britain. **Ten Good Reasons** sold one million cassettes in the UK.

	US Top 10 Ent	UK Top 10 Ent
Ten Good Reasons		5/89
Between The Lines		6/90
Joseph And The Amazing Technicolor Dreamcoat (Original Cast)		9/91

DOOBIE BROTHERS - Highly regarded rock/R&B-oriented band from San Jose, California, USA, were among America's top LP acts in the mid-Seventies. Members included Tom Johnston, Jeff 'Skunk' Baxter (ex-Steely Dan), Michael McDonald and Pat Simmons.

	US Top 10 Ent	UK Top 10 Ent
The Captain And Me	7/73	
What Were Once Vices Are Now Habits	4/74	
Stampede	6/75	
The Best Of The Doobies	1/77	
Minute By Minute	3/79	
One Step Closer	10/80	

DOOLEYS - Clean-cut British family pop group who appealed mainly to a young audience. Included siblings Jim, John, Frank, Kathy, Anne and Helen Dooley.

	US Top 10 Ent	UK Top 10 Ent
The Best Of The Dooleys		8/79

VAL DOONICAN - MOR/country singer born 1928 in Ireland. Relaxed vocalist whose own TV show was very popular in the UK in the late Sixties.

	US Top 10 Ent	UK Top 10 Ent
Lucky 13 Shades Of Val Doonican		1/65
Gentle Shades Of Val Doonican		12/66
Val Doonican Rocks But Gently		12/67
Val		12/68
World Of Val Doonican		6/69

DOORS - Vastly influential rock group from Los Angeles, USA, was led by the colourful and controversial singer/songwriter Jim Morrison (born 1943, Florida, USA; died 1971, Paris, France). Other members were John Densmore, Robby Kreiger, Ray Manzarek.

	US Top 10 Ent	UK Top 10 Ent
The Doors	7/67	
Strange Days	11/67	
Waiting For The Sun	8/68	
The Soft Parade	8/69	
Morrison Hotel/Hard Rock Cafe	3/70	
The Doors (Soundtrack)	4/91	

DRIFTERS - Very successful R&B/pop group originally formed in 1953 by Clyde McPhatter (ex-Dominoes). Group, who were still performing in the mid-Nineties, have had many personnel changes. Noted members include Ben E. King, Johnny Moore, Bill Pinkney and Rudy Lewis (died 1963).

	US Top 10 Ent	UK Top 10 Ent
24 Original Hits		12/75

DUBLINERS - Long running traditional Irish folk band led by Ronnie Drew. Their good time pub music has kept them in demand.

	US Top 10 Ent	UK Top 10 Ent
A Drop Of The Hard Stuff		6/67

DURAN DURAN - Leading New Romantic synth-pop group from Birmingham, England. Simon Le Bon, Nick Rhodes, Andy Taylor, John Taylor, Roger Taylor (none related). They were one of Britain's most successful Eighties groups.

	US Top 10 Ent	UK Top 10 Ent
Duran Duran		7/81
Rio	3/83	5/82
Seven And The Ragged Tiger	2/84	12/83
Arena	12/84	12/84
Duran Duran (The Wedding Album)		5/93

JUDITH DURHAM - See THE SEEKERS

IAN DURY & THE BLOCKHEADS - Pub rock/punk outfit fronted by singer/composer Ian Dury (born 1942, Essex, England). A very popular live act in the UK in the late Seventies.

	US Top 10 Ent	UK Top 10 Ent
New Boots And Panties!!		2/79
Do It Yourself		6/79

BOB DYLAN - Legendary folk/rock pioneer, born Robert Zimmerman in Duluth, Minnesota in 1941. Innovative and amazingly influential singer/songwriter/guitarist/harmonica player, who led the Sixties folk-protest movement. Deservedly won Grammy Lifetime Achievement Award in 1991.

	US Top 10 Ent	UK Top 10 Ent
The Freewheelin' Bob Dylan		4/65
The Times They Are A-Changin'		4/65
Bringing It All Back Home	6/65	5/65
Highway 61 Revisited	10/65	10/65
Blonde On Blonde		8/66
Greatest Hits		2/67
John Wesley Harding	2/68	3/68
Nashville Skyline	5/69	5/69
Self Portrait	7/70	7/70
New Morning		11/70

	US Top 10 Ent	UK Top 10 Ent
Planet Waves	2/74	3/74
Before The Flood	7/74	
Blood On The Tracks	2/75	2/75
The Basement Tapes	9/75	
Desire	2/76	2/76
Street Legal		7/78
Bob Dylan At Budokan		6/79
Slow Train Coming	9/79	9/79
Saved		6/80

EAGLES - Foremost country rock band from Los Angeles, USA, whose members have included Glenn Frey, Don Henley, Bernie Leadon, Randy Meisner, Don Felder, Joe Walsh and Timothy B. Schmit. They were one of the most respected and imitated acts of the rock era. The first group to have two LPs sell over 10 million copies in the USA.

	US Top 10 Ent	UK Top 10 Ent
One Of These Nights	7/75	7/75
Eagles - Their Greatest Hits 1971-1975	3/76	3/76
Hotel California	12/76	12/76
The Long Run	10/79	10/79
Eagles Live	12/80	
The Very Best Of The Eagles		7/94
Hell Freezes Over	11/94	

EARTH, WIND & FIRE - Best selling, L.A.-based R&B/funk band formed by producer/multi-instrumentalist/songwriter Maurice White (born 1941, Memphis Tennessee,USA). Philip Bailey is this large group's best known vocalist.

	US Top 10 Ent	UK Top 10 Ent
That's The Way Of The World (Soundtrack)	4/75	
Gratitude	12/75	
Spirit	10/76	
All 'n All	12/77	
The Best Of Earth, Wind & Fire Vol. 1	1/79	2/79
I Am	6/79	7/79
Raise!	11/81	
The Collection		5/86

EAST 17 - East 17 is the London postcode for Walthamstow, the home town of Tony Mortimer, Brian Harvey, Terry Coldwell and John Hendy.

	US Top 10 Ent	UK Top 10 Ent
Walthamstow		2/93
Steam		12/94

EAZY-E - Rapper/producer born 1973 in Compton, California, died in 1985 of AIDS-related illness. Real name Eric Wright. A member of gangsta-rap outfit N.W.A before achieving a string of platinum solo albums.

	US Top 10 Ent	UK Top 10 Ent
It's On (Dr. Dre 187um) Killa	11/93	

ECHO & THE BUNNYMEN - Respected rock group from Liverpool led by Ian McCulloch. Other members; Will Sergeant, Les Pattinson, Pete De Freitas.

	US Top 10 Ent	UK Top 10 Ent
Porcupine		2/83
Ocean Rain		5/84
Echo & The Bunnymen		7/87

DUANE EDDY - The King of the 'Twangy' guitar was born 1938 in New York, USA. He was the most successful solo instrumentalist of the early rock era.

	US Top 10 Ent	UK Top 10 Ent
The Twang's The Thang		3/60
A Million Dollars' Worth Of Twang		5/61
Twistin' & Twangin'		9/62

VINCENT EDWARDS - Actor/singer, real name Vincent Eduardo Zoine, born 1928 in New York, USA. He played the title role in the popular US TV series *Ben Casey.*

	US Top 10 Ent	UK Top 10 Ent
Vincent Edwards Sings	8/62	

ELECTRIC LIGHT ORCHESTRA - Original rock band from Birmingham, England, which featured an orchestral string section. Founder members included Roy Wood, Bev Bevan and Jeff Lynne (all ex-Move).

	US Top 10 Ent	UK Top 10 Ent
A New World Record	12/76	6/77
Out Of The Blue	12/77	11/77
Discovery	7/79	6/79
ELO's Greatest Hits		12/79
Xanadu (Soundtrack)	9/80	7/80
Time		8/81
Secret Messages		7/83
The Very Best Of The Electric Light Orchestra		7/94

ELECTRONIC - Temporary super-group featuring Bernard Sumner (New Order), Johnny Marr (The Smiths) plus Neil Tennant (Pet Shop Boys) and Anne Dudley (Art Of Noise).

	US Top 10 Ent	UK Top 10 Ent
Electronic		6/91

EMERSON, LAKE & PALMER - Progressive rock super-trio with classical overtones. Keith Emerson (ex-Nice), Greg Lake (ex-King Crimson) and Carl Palmer (ex-Crazy World of Arthur Brown). They were one of the world's top selling album artists in the Seventies.

	US Top 10 Ent	UK Top 10 Ent
Emerson, Lake And Palmer		12/70
Tarkus		6/71
Pictures At An Exhibition		12/71
Trilogy	9/72	7/72
Brain Salad Surgery		1/74
Welcome Back, My Friends, To The Show That Never Ends - Ladies & Gentlemen: Emerson Lake & Palmer	10/74	8/74

EMF - Transatlantically successful pop band from the Forest of Dean, England. James Atkin, Derry Brownson, Mark Decloedt, Ian Dench, Zac Foley.

	US Top 10 Ent	UK Top 10 Ent
Schubert Dip		5/91

EMOTIONS - Noteworthy soulful trio from Chicago, USA, which comprised sisters Wanda, Sheila and Jeanette Hutchinson.

	US Top 10 Ent	UK Top 10 Ent
Rejoice	8/77	

EN VOGUE - Female R&B/dance vocal quartet from San Francisco, USA. Terry Ellis, Cindy Herron, Maxine Jones, Dawn Robinson. They were one of the most successful female groups of the early Nineties.

	US Top 10 Ent	UK Top 10 Ent
Funky Divas		2/93

ENGLAND FOOTBALL WORLD CUP SQUAD - The 1970 English soccer team had more success with their album than they had in that year's World Cup.

	US Top 10 Ent	UK Top 10 Ent
The World Beaters Sing The World Beaters		5/70

ENIGMA - Unique world music/dance act featuring producer Michael Cretu (born 1957 in Bucharest, Romania) and his wife Sandra. **MCMXC AD** sold over 12 million copies worldwide.

	US Top 10 Ent	UK Top 10 Ent
MCMXC A.D.	5/91	1/91
Cross Of Changes		2/94

ENYA - Grammy winning new age/folk performer from Donegal, Ireland, who was born Eithne Ni Bhraonain. The internationally successful ex-Clannad vocalist was America's Top New Age Artist of 1993.

	US Top 10 Ent	UK Top 10 Ent
Watermark		11/88
Shepherd Moons		11/91

ERASURE - Self-contained London-based synth-pop duo, formed by ex-Depeche Mode member Vince Clark and vocalist Andy Bell. Act have had more British Top 10 singles than any other recording duo.

	US Top 10 Ent	UK Top 10 Ent
The Innocents		4/88
Wild!		10/89
Chorus		10/91
Pop! - The First 20 Hits		11/92
I Say I Say I Say		5/94

DAVID ESSEX - Pop singer/actor/composer from London, born David Cook in 1947. He was one of the top selling acts in Britain in the mid Seventies.

	US Top 10 Ent	UK Top 10 Ent
David Essex		11/74
All The Fun Of The Fair		10/75
Cover Shot		4/93

GLORIA ESTEFAN (& THE MIAMI SOUND MACHINE) - Latin American pop/dance group fronted by vocalist/songwriter Estefan (born Gloria Fajardo, 1957 in Cuba). The most successful Latin-American act around the globe in recent years.

	US Top 10 Ent	UK Top 10 Ent
Let It Loose	5/88	1/89
Cuts Both Ways	9/89	8/89
Into The Light	3/91	2/91
Greatest Hits		11/92

ETERNAL - Britain's most successful female foursome in the USA. The London, England, R&B act consists of Louise Nurding, Kelle Bryan, and sisters Vernie and Easther Bennett.

	US Top 10 Ent	UK Top 10 Ent
Always & Forever		5/94

EUROPE - Rock band from Sweden led by singer/writer Joey Tempest. Ian Haughland, John Leven, Kee Marcello, Mic Michaeli.

	US Top 10 Ent	UK Top 10 Ent
The Final Countdown	3/87	

EURYTHMICS - Distinctive, innovative and internationally successful synth/pop duo. Annie Lennox and Dave Stewart (both ex-Tourists). Most charted British male/female duo of all time.

	US Top 10 Ent	UK Top 10 Ent
Sweet Dreams (Are Made Of This)	3/83	
Touch	3/84	1/84
Be Yourself Tonight		5/85
Revenge		7/86
We Two Are One		9/89
Greatest Hits		4/91

EVERLY BROTHERS - The early rock era's biggest selling duo are singer/songwriters and guitarists Don and Phil Everly born 1937 and 1939 respectively. They were the first non-solo act in the Rock'n'Roll Hall of Fame.

	US Top 10 Ent	UK Top 10 Ent
It's Everly Time		7/60
Fabulous Style Of The Everly Brothers		10/60
A Date With The Everly Brothers		3/61
Original Greatest Hits		11/70

EXTREME - Boston-based rock band. Gary Cherone, Nuno Bettencourt, Pat Badger and Paul Geary. Metal band whose biggest hit single was the acoustic 'More Than Words'.

	US Top 10 Ent	UK Top 10 Ent
III Sides To Every Story		9/92

FABIAN - Top teen idol of the late Fifties was born Fabiano Forte in 1943 in Philadelphia, USA.

	US Top 10 Ent	UK Top 10 Ent
Fabulous Fabian	1/60	

FACES - Noted rock band from London, England, which evolved from mod/R&B group, The Small Faces. Rod Stewart, Ron Wood (both ex-Jeff Beck band), Kenny Jones, Ronnie Lane, Ian McLagen.

	US Top 10 Ent	UK Top 10 Ent
A Nod Is As Good As A Wink... To A Blind Horse	2/72	1/72

	US Top 10 Ent	UK Top 10 Ent
Ooh-La-La		4/73
Overture And Beginners		2/74

DONALD FAGEN - Best known for his work with Steely Dan this soft rock singer/songwriter was born 1948 in Passaic, New Jersey, USA.

	US Top 10 Ent	UK Top 10 Ent
Kamakiriad		6/93

FAIRGROUND ATTRACTION - English/Scottish folk-flavoured rock group comprised vocalist Eddi (Sadenia) Reader and composer Mark Nevin plus members Roy Dodds and Simon Edwards. BRIT winners in 1988 for Best Single and Album.

	US Top 10 Ent	UK Top 10 Ent
The First Of A Million Kisses		8/88

FAITH NO MORE - Credible Nineties rock band from San Francisco, USA, who have a large international cult following. Vlad Dracula aka Michael Patton (who replaced Chuck Mosley in 1988), Mike Bordin, Roddy Bottum, Billy Gould, Jim Martin.

	US Top 10 Ent	UK Top 10 Ent
Angel Dust		6/92

ADAM FAITH - Top British teen idol in the early Sixties was born Terry Nelhams in 1940 in London, England. Later turned to acting, production and management.

	US Top 10 Ent	UK Top 10 Ent
Adam		1/61

PERCY FAITH - Orchestra leader from Toronto, Canada born 1908, died 1976. Conductor/arranger in the Fifties for Columbia Records' stars like Tony Bennett, Rosemary Clooney, Doris Day and Johnny Mathis. His was one of the biggest selling orchestras of the Fifties.

	US Top 10 Ent	UK Top 10 Ent
Camelot	2/61	

FALCO - Austria's most successful recent recording artist. Real name Johann Holzel, born 1957 in Vienna, Austria.

	US Top 10 Ent	UK Top 10 Ent
Falco 3	4/86	

GEORGIE FAME - Pop/R&B/jazz singer/pianist who was born Clive Powell, in 1943 in Lancashire, England. He was one of the major figures in the early Sixties British R&B boom.

	US Top 10 Ent	UK Top 10 Ent
Sweet Things		6/66

FAMILY - Well respected progressive rock group from Leicester, England, fronted by Roger Chapman. Members have included noteworthies John Wetton (King Crimson, Uriah Heep, Asia), Tony Ashton and Rick Grech (Blind Faith).

	US Top 10 Ent	UK Top 10 Ent
A Song For Me		2/70

FARM - Alternative indie band from Liverpool, England who were highly touted by the British music media. Peter Hooten, Steve Grimes, Roy Boulter, Carl Hunter, Ben Leach and Keith Mullen.

	US Top 10 Ent	UK Top 10 Ent
Spartacus		3/91

FAT BOYS - One of the first successful rap trios hailed from the Bronx, New York, USA. The Human Beat Box (Darren Robinson), Prince Markie Dee (Mark Morales) and Kool Rockski (Damon Wimbley).

	US Top 10 Ent	UK Top 10 Ent
Crushin'	9/87	

JOSE FELICIANO - Latin-American/pop singer and guitarist, born blind in Puerto Rico in 1945. He won the Grammy for Best New Artist in 1968.

	US Top 10 Ent	UK Top 10 Ent
Feliciano!	9/68	2/69

BRYAN FERRY - Stylish pop/rock singer born 1945 in Durham, England. Also fronted Roxy Music, he occupied a pivitol role in the Seventies British music scene.

	US Top 10 Ent	UK Top 10 Ent
These Foolish Things		11/73
Another Time, Another Place		7/74
In Your Mind		3/77
Boys And Girls		6/85
Street Life - 20 Great Hits (with Roxy Music)		4/86
The Ultimate Collection (with Roxy Music)		12/88
Taxi		4/93

5TH DIMENSION - Smooth pop/R&B vocal group based in Los Angeles, USA. Billy Davis Jr. and Marilyn McCoo (husband and wife), Florence LaRue, Lamont McLemore and Ron Townson. A leading recording act of the late Sixties in the USA.

	US Top 10 Ent	UK Top 10 Ent
Up, Up And Away	8/67	
The Age Of Aquarius	6/69	
The 5th Dimension - Greatest Hits	6/70	

FINE YOUNG CANNIBALS - Pop/rock group from Birmingham, England. David Steele, Andy Cox (both ex-Beat) and singer/actor Roland Gift.

	US Top 10 Ent	UK Top 10 Ent
The Raw & The Cooked	4/89	2/89

FIVE STAR - Top British brother/sister R&B/pop act. Deniece, Delroy, Doris, Lorraine and Stedman Pearson. Winners of Top British Group at the 1986 BRIT awards.

	US Top 10 Ent	UK Top 10 Ent
Silk And Steel		9/86

FIXX - London-based synth-rock quintet led by Cy Curnin, which included Dan Brown, Rupert Greenall, Jamie West-Oram, Adam Woods.

	US Top 10 Ent	UK Top 10 Ent
Reach The Beach	9/83	

ROBERTA FLACK - Grammy winning, classy and distinctive jazz/R&B vocalist/pianist born 1939 in North Carolina, USA.

	US Top 10 Ent	UK Top 10 Ent
First Take	4/72	
Roberta Flack & Donny Hathaway	6/72	
Killing Me Softly	9/73	

FLEETWOOD MAC - Top Anglo-American AOR group, who started as a British blues band, were formed by Peter Green (ex-John Mayall's Bluesbreakers), Mick Fleetwood and John McVie. Members have included Christine McVie, Stevie Nicks and Lindsey Buckingham.

	US Top 10 Ent	UK Top 10 Ent
Fleetwood Mac	2/76	4/68
Then Play On		10/69
Rumours	3/77	8/77
Tusk	11/79	11/79
Mirage	7/82	7/82
Tango In The Night	5/87	5/87
Greatest Hits		12/88
Behind The Mask		4/90

FOCUS - Internationally successful progressive rock group from Holland led by highly regarded guitarist Jan Akkerman and organist/flautist Thijs van Leer.

	US Top 10 Ent	UK Top 10 Ent
Moving Waves		2/73

DAN FOGELBERG - Folk/country/rock singer/songwriter from Peoria, Illinois, USA, born 1951. He was a regular visitor to the US charts in the early Eighties.

	US Top 10 Ent	UK Top 10 Ent
Phoenix	2/80	
The Innocent Age	10/81	
Twin Sons Of Different Mothers (with Tim Weisberg)	10/78	

JOHN FOGERTY - Multi-instrumentalist/composer born 1945 in Berkeley, California, USA. Lead vocalist of Creedence Clearwater Revival, who went solo in 1972.

	US Top 10 Ent	UK Top 10 Ent
Centerfield	2/85	

FRANK FONTAINE - Comedian/singer/actor born 1920 in Cambridge, Massachusetts, USA, whose regular appearences on Jackie Gleason's TV show brought him short-lived record fame.

	US Top 10 Ent	UK Top 10 Ent
Songs I Sing On The Jackie Gleason Show	3/63	

FOREIGNER - Top-line Anglo-American heavy rock band formed in New York, USA. Mick Jones (ex-Spooky Tooth), Lou Gramm, Dennis Elliott, Ed Gagliardi, Al Greenwood, Ian McDonald (ex-King Crimson).

	US Top 10 Ent	UK Top 10 Ent
Foreigner	7/77	
Double Vision	8/78	
Head Games	10/79	
4	8/81	2/82
Agent Provocateur	2/85	1/85

4 NON BLONDES - Internationally successful female fronted rock band from San Francisco, USA. Linda Perry, Roger Rocha, Christa Hillhouse and Dawn Richardson.

	US Top 10 Ent	UK Top 10 Ent
Bigger Better, Faster, More!		8/93

FOUR SEASONS - Pop/doo-wop vocal group from New Jersey, USA. 1961 line-up was falsetto-voiced Frankie Valli (Francis Castelluccio), Bob Gaudio, Nick Massi and Tommy DeVito. Arguably, the biggest selling American vocal group in the early Sixties. They have a record US singles hit span of over 38 years.

	US Top 10 Ent	UK Top 10 Ent
Sherry & 11 Others	11/62	
Big Girls Don't Cry & 12 Others	4/63	
Dawn (Go Away) And 11 Other Great Songs	4/64	
Rag Doll	9/64	
Greatest Hits		12/76

FOUR TOPS - Veteran R&B vocal group from Detroit, USA. Levi Stubbs, Renaldo Benson, Lawrence Payton amd Abdul Fakir. Quartet has remained unchanged since their formation in 1954.

	US Top 10 Ent	UK Top 10 Ent
The Four Tops' Greatest Hits	11/67	2/68
The Four Tops Live!		3/67
Reach Out		1/68
Magnificent Seven (with The Supremes)		7/71

PETER FRAMPTON - Noted rock singer/guitarist and composer from Kent, England, born in 1950. Youthful member of The Herd, left to form Humble Pie, then Frampton's Camel, and went solo in 1974. **Frampton Comes Alive** was the biggest selling live album of all time.

	US Top 10 Ent	UK Top 10 Ent
Frampton Comes Alive!	2/76	6/76
I'm In You	6/77	

CONNIE FRANCIS - Born Concetta Franconero in New Jersey, USA, in 1938. She was the top US female vocalist in the late-Fifties/early-Sixties, and was the first female to top the UK LP charts in 1977.

	US Top 10 Ent	UK Top 10 Ent
Italian Favorites	3/60	
20 All Time Greats		8/77

FRANKIE GOES TO HOLLYWOOD - Pop/dance group from Liverpool, England. Holly Johnson, Paul Rutherford, Peter Gill, Brian Nash, Marc O'Toole. The first act to sell a million with their first two singles in the UK. They were the top act of 1984, selling over four million singles.

	US Top 10 Ent	UK Top 10 Ent
Welcome To The Pleasuredome		11/84

ARETHA FRANKLIN - Gospel-based R&B singer known as the 'Queen of Soul', born 1942 in Memphis. One of the most successful female artists of the rock era. In 1987, Franklin was the first woman inducted into Rock and Roll Hall Of Fame. She also won the prestigious Grammy Legends Award in 1990.

	US Top 10 Ent	UK Top 10 Ent
I Never Loved A Man The Way I Love You	5/67	
Aretha Arrives	9/67	
Aretha: Lady Soul	3/68	
Aretha Now	8/68	10/68
Aretha Live At Fillmore West	6/71	

FREDDIE AND THE DREAMERS - Fun pop group from Manchester, England, led by Freddie Garrity. The Dreamers were Peter Birrell, Roy Crewsdon, Bernie Dwyer and Derek Quinn.

	US Top 10 Ent	UK Top 10 Ent
Freddie And The Dreamers		11/63

FREE - Acclaimed London-based rock/blues outfit. Paul Rodgers, Paul Kossoff (died 1976), Simon Kirke, Andy Fraser. Their 'All Right Now' is regarded as one of the classic rock records. Rodgers and Kirke later formed Bad Company.

	US Top 10 Ent	UK Top 10 Ent
Fire And Water		7/70
Free Live!		6/71
The Free Story		3/74

FUN BOY THREE - Pop/2-Tone trio of Lynval Golding, Terry Hall and Neville Staples (all ex-Specials). Short-lived act had a handful of UK hit singles and helped launch the career of Bananarama.

	US Top 10 Ent	UK Top 10 Ent
Fun Boy Three		3/82

BILLY FURY - Premiere British rock'n'roll singer/song-writer and teen idol from Liverpool, England. Born Ron Wycherley in 1941 and died 1983. The first successful UK rocker to pen his own hits.

	US Top 10 Ent	UK Top 10 Ent
Halfway To Paradise		10/61
Billy		6/63

FUZZBOX - Enjoyably amateurish female rock band from Birmingham, England. Victoria Perks, sisters Jo and Maggie Dunne and Tina O'Neill. Moniker shortened from We've Got A Fuzzbox And We're Gonna Use It.

	US Top 10 Ent	UK Top 10 Ent
Big Bang		8/89

KENNY G - Top selling R&B/pop saxophonist. Real name Kenny Gorelick, born 1956 in Seattle, USA. His album **Breathless** is the biggest selling instrumental LP of all time.

	US Top 10 Ent	UK Top 10 Ent
Duotones	7/87	
Silhouette	11/88	
Breathless	12/92	
Miracles: The Holiday Album	12/94	

WARREN G - Rapper born Warren Griffin III in California, USA, in 1971. A half-brother of Dr. Dre, and a founder member of Dre's Dogg Pound collective.

	US Top 10 Ent	UK Top 10 Ent
Regulate...G Funk Era	6/94	

PETER GABRIEL - Celebrated rock singer, known for his award winning videos. Born 1950 in London, England. He was lead singer of Genesis from 1966-75 before embarking on his solo career.

	US Top 10 Ent	UK Top 10 Ent
Peter Gabriel		6/80
So	7/86	5/86
Us	10/92	10/92

JAMES GALWAY - Internationally renowned classical flautist, born 1939 in Belfast, Ireland. He has worked with many of the top British orchestras.

	US Top 10 Ent	UK Top 10 Ent
James Galway Plays Songs For Annie		9/78

DAVE GARDNER - Late American comedian, better known as 'Brother Dave' Gardner, was born 1926 in Jackson, Tennessee.

	US Top 10 Ent	UK Top 10 Ent
Kick Thy Own Self	10/60	
Rejoice, Dear Hearts!	10/60	

ART GARFUNKEL - Folk/pop singer-turned-actor from New York, USA, born in 1942. Half of the record-breaking duo Simon & Garfunkel. He had two Number 1 solo singles in Britain: 'I Only Have Eyes For You' and 'Bright Eyes'.

	US Top 10 Ent	UK Top 10 Ent
Angel Clare	10/73	
Fate For Breakfast	5/79	

JUDY GARLAND - Legendary vocalist/entertainer and actress, who was born Francis Gumm in 1922 in Minnesota. She appeared in many MGM movies including the classic *The Wizard Of Oz* (1939).

	US Top 10 Ent	UK Top 10 Ent
Judy At Carnegie Hall	9/61	

MARVIN GAYE - Internationally celebrated soul singer/songwriter born 1939 in Washington DC, USA. Among his many hits was the transatlantic chart topper 'I Heard It Through The Grapevine' (1968) and 'Sexual Healing' which spent a record 10 weeks on top of the R&B chart. He was shot and killed by his father in 1984.

	US Top 10 Ent	UK Top 10 Ent
What's Going On	7/71	
Let's Get It On	10/73	
Diana & Marvin (with Diana Ross)		4/74
I Want You	5/76	
Marvin Gaye Live At The London Palladium	5/77	
Midnight Love	12/82	
The Very Best Of Marvin Gaye		4/94

GLORIA GAYNOR - Disco diva born 1949 in New Jersey, USA. Best known for her transatlantic Number 1 hit 'I Will Survive' in 1979.

	US Top 10 Ent	UK Top 10 Ent
Love Tracks	3/79	

J. GEILS BAND - Rock band from Boston, USA. Jerome Geils, Stephen Bladd, Seth Justman, Danny Klein, Dick Salwitz and lead vocalist Peter Wolf (Blankfield).

	US Top 10 Ent	UK Top 10 Ent
Freeze Frame	1/82	

GENESIS - Successful British rock group originally led by Peter Gabriel. Tony Banks, Anthony Phillips, Mike Rutherford, Chris Stewart. Drummer Phil Collins joined in 1970 and took over vocals when Gabriel left in 1975. One of the most successful bands of the Eighties.

	US Top 10 Ent	UK Top 10 Ent
Selling England By The Pound		10/73
A Trick Of The Trail		3/76
Seconds Out		11/77
And Then There Were Three		4/78
Duke		4/80
Abacab	11/81	9/81
3 Sides Live		6/82
Genesis		10/83
Invisible Touch	7/86	6/86
We Can't Dance		11/91
Live - The Way We Walk Vol. 1: The Shorts		12/92
Live - The Way We Walk Vol. 2: The Longs		1/93

BOBBIE GENTRY - Pop/country singer/songwriter and multi-instrumentalist born Roberta Streeter (1944) in Mississippi, USA. Grammy winning performer married singer Jim Stafford in 1978.

	US Top 10 Ent	UK Top 10 Ent
Ode To Billie Joe	9/67	

GEORGIA SATELLITES - Atlanta based rock band led by Dan Baird and Rick Richards with Mauro Magellan and Rich Price.

	US Top 10 Ent	UK Top 10 Ent
Georgia Satellites	2/87	

GERRY AND THE PACEMAKERS - Liverpudlian pop group led by Gerry Marsden with brother Freddie, Les Chadwick and Leslie Maguire. The Brian Epstein managed band were the first act to see their initial three singles reach Number 1 in the UK.

	US Top 10 Ent	UK Top 10 Ent
How Do You Like It?		11/63

STAN GETZ - Jazz saxophonist from Philadelphia, USA, was born Stan Gayetsky in 1927. This leading exponent of bossa nova music died in 1991.

	US Top 10 Ent	UK Top 10 Ent
Jazz Samba (with Charlie Byrd)	10/62	
Getz/Gilberto (with Joao Gilberto)	7/64	

ANDY GIBB - Pop singer born 1958 in Manchester, England, raised in Australia. The youngest brother of the Bee Gees topped the American chart with his first three single releases. He died from drug-related heart problems in 1988.

	US Top 10 Ent	UK Top 10 Ent
Shadow Dancing	7/78	

DEBBIE GIBSON - Hugely successful teenage pop singer/songwriter/pianist and producer from Long Island, USA (born 1970). First female teenager to top the US album and single charts simultaneously.

	US Top 10 Ent	UK Top 10 Ent
Out Of The Blue	2/88	
Electric Youth	2/89	

JOAO GILBERTO - See STAN GETZ

JOHNNY GILL - R&B styled singer born 1965 in Washington, DC, USA. Replaced Bobby Brown in the successful Boston group New Edition in 1988.

	US Top 10 Ent	UK Top 10 Ent
Johnny Gill	7/90	

VINCE GILL - Hugely popular country singer/guitarist, born 1957 in Oklahoma, USA. This ex-member of the Pure Prairie League has collected five platinum albums and has won scores of country awards in the Nineties, including the much coveted CMA Entertainer of the Year.

	US Top 10 Ent	UK Top 10 Ent
When Love Finds You	7/94	

GILLAN - Heavy rock band fronted by renowned vocalist Ian Gillan (born 1945 in London, England) who has also been a member of Deep Purple and Black Sabbath.

	US Top 10 Ent	UK Top 10 Ent
Glory Road		8/80
Future Shock		5/81

GARY GLITTER - The 'King of Glitter Rock' was born Paul Gadd in 1944 in Banbury, England. This singer/songwriter, who first recorded, aged 15, as Paul Raven, was one of Britain's top selling artists in the Seventies. His first nine hit singles all reached the Top 5.

	US Top 10 Ent	UK Top 10 Ent
Touch Me		6/73
Remember Me This Way		7/74

GODLEY & CREME - See 10CC

GO WEST - British pop duo consisting of Peter Cox and Richard Drummie. They won the BRIT award for Best Newcomers in 1986.

	US Top 10 Ent	UK Top 10 Ent
Go West/Bangs And Crashes		4/85
Aces And Kings - The Best Of Go West		10/93

GO-GO'S - First successful all-girl rock group were formed in Los Angeles, USA. Belinda Carlisle, Jane Wiedlin, Charlotte Caffey, Gina Schock, Kathy Valentine. Disbanded in 1984 but re-united for tours in 1990 and 1994. Wiedlin and Carlisle both persued solo careers.

	US Top 10 Ent	UK Top 10 Ent
Beauty And The Beat	2/82	
Vacation	8/82	

BOBBY GOLDSBORO - Pop singer/songwriter and guitarist born 1941 in Florida, USA. Member of Roy Orbison's backing group in the Sixties which led him to solo success and own TV show in the Seventies.

	US Top 10 Ent	UK Top 10 Ent
Honey	6/68	

ROBERT GOULET - Stage/film/TV actor and MOR singer born 1933 in Lawrence, Massachusetts, USA. Won a Grammy for Best New Artist of 1962.

	US Top 10 Ent	UK Top 10 Ent
My Love Forgive Me	2/65	

GRAND FUNK RAILROAD/GRAND FUNK - Critcally ignored though ultra-successful heavy rock group from Flint, Michigan, USA. Don Brewer, Mark Farner, Mel Schacher. Stadium filling act were one of America's top selling acts of the early Seventies.

	US Top 10 Ent	UK Top 10 Ent
Closer To Home	9/70	
Live Album	12/70	
Survival	5/71	
E Pluribus Funk	12/71	
We're An American Band	9/73	
Shinin' On	5/74	

AMY GRANT - Commercially successful contemporary Christian singer was born 1960 in Augusta, Georgia, USA. America's top inspirational recording artist of the Eighties.

	US Top 10 Ent	UK Top 10 Ent
Home For Christmas	12/92	

GRATEFUL DEAD - Premier psychedelic rock group from San Francisco, USA, led by Jerry Garcia and Bob Weir. Other original members were Bill Kreutzmann, Phil Lesh, Ron McKernan (died 1973). They are one of the most successful live acts of the rock era.

	US Top 10 Ent	UK Top 10 Ent
In The Dark	8/87	

AL GREEN - Distinctive soul/gospel singer/songwriter born 1946 in Arkansas, USA. He was one of the top selling recording artists of the early Seventies and now pastor of a church in Memphis.

	US Top 10 Ent	UK Top 10 Ent
Let's Stay Together	4/72	
I'm Still In Love With You	12/72	

GREEN DAY - Grammy winning, punk-influenced rock trio from San Francisco, USA. Billie Joe, Mike Dirnt and Tre Cool. After two critically acclaimed albums on the indie label Lookout, they joined Reprise and instantly jumped from cult heroes to commercial superstars.

	US Top 10 Ent	UK Top 10 Ent
Dookie	9/94	

GROUNDHOGS - Archetypal British heavy rock band whose success never spread to the USA. Tony McPhee, Pete Cruickshank and drummer Ken Pustelnik (later replaced by Clive Brooks).

	US Top 10 Ent	UK Top 10 Ent
Split		5/71

GUESS WHO - One of Canada's most successful rock groups. Randy Bachman, Burton Cummings, Jim Kale, Garry Peterson. Bachman went on to form the Bachman-Turner Overdrive.

	US Top 10 Ent	UK Top 10 Ent
American Woman	5/70	

GUNS N' ROSES - Enormously successful and influential heavy rock group from Los Angeles, USA, led by W. Axl Rose (real name Bill Bailey). Steven Adler, Michael 'Duff' McKagan, Slash (real name Saul Hudson), Izzy Stradlin (real name Jeffrey Isbell). They were one of the top selling acts of the Nineties.

	US Top 10 Ent	UK Top 10 Ent
Appetite For Destruction	5/88	4/89
G N' R Lies	1/89	
Use Your Illusion I	10/91	9/91
Use Your Illusion II	10/91	9/91
The Spaghetti Incident?	12/93	12/93

HAIRCUT 100 - Teen appeal pop group from Kent, England, fronted by Nick Heyward. Other members - Graham Jones, Les Nemes, Phil Smith, Mark Fox and Blair Cunningham.

	US Top 10 Ent	UK Top 10 Ent
Pelican West		3/82

DARYL HALL & JOHN OATES - Soulful rock duo from Philadelphia. USA. Daryl Hohl (born 1948) and John Oates (born 1949) joined forces in 1972. The most successful singles duo in the rock era in the USA.

	US Top 10 Ent	UK Top 10 Ent
Private Eyes	11/81	
H2O	12/82	
Rock 'n Soul, Part 1	1/84	
Big Bam Boom	11/84	

MARVIN HAMLISCH - Grammy-winning composer/arranger/conductor and pianist, born 1944 in New York, USA. He penned the Academy Award winning 'The Way We Were' and many film soundtracks.

	US Top 10 Ent	UK Top 10 Ent
The Sting (Soundtrack)	4/74	4/74

HAMMER - The biggest selling rap artist of the early Nineties was born Stanley Burrell, California, USA in 1962. In the pre-gangsta rap days his award winning **Please Hammer Don't Hurt 'Em** topped the US chart for 21 weeks and sold 10 million in the USA and over four million overseas.

	US Top 10 Ent	UK Top 10 Ent
Please Hammer Don't Hurt 'Em	4/90	
Too Legit To Quit	11/91	

TONY HANCOCK - Highly regarded British radio and TV comedian born 1924. Had much record success with recordings of his top rated shows. He committed suicide in 1968.

	US Top 10 Ent	UK Top 10 Ent
This Is Hancock		4/60

HAPPY MONDAYS - Indie dance group from Manchester, England, fronted by Shaun Ryder. Other members - Mark 'Cow' Day, Paul Davis, Paul Ryder, Gary 'Gaz' Whelan and Mark 'Bez' Berry. At one time they had six singles in the UK Indie Top 30.

	US Top 10 Ent	UK Top 10 Ent
Pills 'n' Thrills And Bellyaches		11/90

STEVE HARLEY/COCKNEY REBEL - London-based pop rock band fronted by distinctive singer/songwriter Steve Harley (born Steven Nice in 1951). For a period in mid-Seventies this act had a big UK following.

	US Top 10 Ent	UK Top 10 Ent
The Psychomodo		9/74
The Best Years Of Our Lives		3/75

EDDIE HARRIS - Jazz saxophonist born 1936 in Chicago, USA, who successfully experimented with electronic reed instruments. He also had Top 40 albums with keyboard player Les McCann.

	US Top 10 Ent	UK Top 10 Ent
Exodus To Jazz	8/61	

EMMYLOU HARRIS - Foremost contemporary country vocalist born Alabama, USA, in 1947. After working in the country/rock field, she notched up more than 50 country chart singles. On **Trio** she teamed with rock star Linda Ronstadt and country superstar Dolly Parton.

	US Top 10 Ent	UK Top 10 Ent
Trio (with Dolly Parton & Linda Ronstadt)	5/87	

RICHARD HARRIS - Stage and film actor born 1930 in Limerick, Ireland, whose recording of 'MacArthur Park' and its parent album briefly took him into the pop spotlight.

	US Top 10 Ent	UK Top 10 Ent
A Tramp Shining	7/68	

GEORGE HARRISON - Guitar playing, singer/songwriting, ex-Beatle was born 1943 in Liverpool, England. First Beatle to have a solo Number 1 single in America. He was the first person to receive *Billboard*'s 'Century Award'.

	US Top 10 Ent	UK Top 10 Ent
All Things Must Pass	12/70	1/71
The Concert For Bangla Desh	1/72	1/72
Living In The Material World	6/73	7/73
Dark Horse	1/75	
Extra Texture (Read All About It)	11/75	

DEBORAH HARRY - New wave/pop singer born 1945 in New York, USA, who fronted the very successful group Blondie until she went solo in the mid-Eighties.

	US Top 10 Ent	UK Top 10 Ent
The Complete Picture - The Very Best Of (with Blondie)		3/91

DONNY HATHAWAY - See ROBERTA FLACK

ISAAC HAYES - Soul singer-rapper/songwriter/producer/pianist and actor was born 1942 in Covington, Tennessee, USA. Stax Records' best known songwriter in the Sixties who became their biggest selling solo act in the Seventies.

	US Top 10 Ent	UK Top 10 Ent
The Isaac Hayes Movement	6/70	
Shaft (Soundtrack)	9/71	

JUSTIN HAYWARD - Lead singer of The Moody Blues, born 1946 in Swindon, England. Also had record success with fellow group member John Lodge.

	US Top 10 Ent	UK Top 10 Ent
Bluejays		4/75

HEART - Top selling AOR rock group from Seattle, USA, fronted by sisters Ann and Nancy Wilson. Also included Michael DeRosier, Roger Fisher, Steve Fossen, Howard Leese. Arguably the biggest selling female-fronted band of the rock era.

	US Top 10 Ent	UK Top 10 Ent
Bebe Le Strange	3/80	
Heart	9/85	
Bad Animals	7/87	8/87
Brigade	5/90	4/90

HEAVEN 17 - Electro-pop trio from Sheffield, England, formed by ex-Human league members Ian Craig Marsh and Martin Ware with vocalist Glenn Gregory, .

	US Top 10 Ent	UK Top 10 Ent
The Luxury Gap	5/83	

JIMI HENDRIX - Innovative and influential psychedelic rock guitarist/singer/composer born 1942 in Seattle, USA, died 1970 in London, England, of a drug overdose. He was one of the true greats of rock who helped shape the future of the music.

	US Top 10 Ent	UK Top 10 Ent
Axis: Bold As Love	2/68	12/67
Are You Experienced?	12/67	6/67
Electric Ladyland	11/68	12/68
Smash Hits	9/69	5/68
Band Of Gypsys	5/70	7/70
The Cry Of Love	3/71	3/71
Hendrix In The West		2/72
Crash Landing	5/75	
Cornerstones 1967-1970		11/90

DON HENLEY - Country/rock singer/composer and drummer born 1947 in Texas, USA. A co-founder of The Eagles who successfully went solo in 1982.

	US Top 10 Ent	UK Top 10 Ent
The End Of The Innocence	9/89	

HERMAN'S HERMITS - Hugely successful pop group from Manchester, England, fronted by Peter 'Herman' Noone, born 1947. Karl Green, Keith Hopwood, Derek Leckenby (died 1974), Barry Whitwam. They were one of the biggest selling British acts in the USA in the Swinging Sixties.

	US Top 10 Ent	UK Top 10 Ent
Introducing Herman's Hermits	4/65	
Herman's Hermits On Tour	7/65	
The Best Of Herman's Hermits	12/65	

AL HIRT - Dixieland jazz trumpeter born 1922 in New Orleans, USA. The ex-member of the Dorsey Brothers Band was one of the major instrumental artists of the early Sixties.

	US Top 10 Ent	UK Top 10 Ent
Honey In The Horn	2/64	
Cotton Candy	6/64	
Sugar Lips	11/64	

GERARD HOFFNUNG - Comedian, cartoonist and multi-instrumentalist born 1925. The performer, who was very popular with the British college crowd, died of a heart attack in 1959.

	US Top 10 Ent	UK Top 10 Ent
At The Oxford Union		9/60

HOLLIES - Highly respected pop/rock group from Manchester, England, noted for their unmistakable harmonies. Allan Clarke, Graham Nash (later of Crosby, Stills & Nash), Eric Haydock, Tony Hicks and Bobby Elliott. They were one of the Sixties most distinctive and successful groups.

	US Top 10 Ent	UK Top 10 Ent
Stay With The Hollies		3/64
Hollies		10/65
Greatest Hits		8/68
Hollies Sing Dylan		5/69
Hollies Live Hits		4/77
20 Golden Greats		7/78

BUDDY HOLLY (& THE CRICKETS) - Texas-born (1936) Charles Holley was one of the foremost singer/songwriters of the rock era. Even though he died in a plane crash in 1959, his influence has been felt on pop music ever since.

	US Top 10 Ent	UK Top 10 Ent
Buddy Holly Story Vol. 2		11/60
Buddy Holly Story		2/61
That'll Be The Day		11/61
Reminiscing		4/63
Buddy Holly Showcase		6/64
20 Golden Greats		3/78
Words Of Love		2/93

HONEYDRIPPERS - Short-lived Anglo-American super-group comprised Robert Plant (Led Zeppelin), Jeff Beck (The Yardbirds), Nile Rodgers (Chic) and Jimmy Page (The Yardbirds, Led Zeppelin).

	US Top 10 Ent	UK Top 10 Ent
Volume One	11/84	

JOHN LEE HOOKER - Perennially successful and influential blues singer and guitarist born 1917 in Mississippi, USA. He first charted in 1949 and was still hitting in the Nineties when he was in his 70s.

	US Top 10 Ent	UK Top 10 Ent
Mr. Lucky		9/91

MARY HOPKIN - Folky-pop singer born 1950 in Pontardawe, Wales. Spotted by model, Twiggy, and with a little help from Paul McCartney, had three years of record success.

	US Top 10 Ent	UK Top 10 Ent
Postcard		3/69

BRUCE HORNSBY & THE RANGE - Grammy winning rock/pop act led by singer/songwriter and pianist Bruce Hornsby, born 1954 in Virginia, USA. The Range: David Mansfield. George Marinelli, John Molo, Joe Puerta.

	US Top 10 Ent	UK Top 10 Ent
The Way It Is	12/86	
Scenes From The Southside	6/88	

HOT CHOCOLATE - Soul/pop group from London, England, led by Jamaican-born (1948) Errol Brown. Multi-racial members consisted of Tony Connor, Larry Ferguson, Harvey Hinsley, Patrick Olive, Tony Wilson. Act were seldom off the UK singles chart in the Seventies and early-Eighties.

	US Top 10 Ent	UK Top 10 Ent
20 Hottest Hits		12/79
The Very Best Of Hot Chocolate		2/87
Their Greatest Hits		3/93

HOUSEMARTINS - Innovative pop group from Hull, England. Paul Heaton, Norman Cook, Dave Hemmingway with Stan Cullimore. They were regular UK hitmakers in the late Eighties. Heaton later formed Beautiful South; Cook, Beats International.

	US Top 10 Ent	UK Top 10 Ent
London 0 Hull 4		7/86

WHITNEY HOUSTON - Record breaking soul singer born 1963 in Newark, New Jersey, USA. She has had a record seven successive US Number1 singles and is the only woman to enter US LP chart at Number 1 (**Whitney**). She is also the only US female to sell a million of her first two albums in the UK and her recording of 'I Will Always Love You' (from **The Bodyguard** soundtrack) is one of the world's biggest selling singles of all time.

	US Top 10 Ent	UK Top 10 Ent
Whitney Houston	9/85	2/86
Whitney	6/87	6/87
I'm Your Baby Tonight	12/90	1/91

HUMAN LEAGUE - Pioneer synth rock group from Sheffield, England. Martin Ware, Ian Marsh, Adrian Wright & Philip Oakey. Ian Burden, Joanne Catherall and Suzanne Sulley replaced Ware and Marsh, who went on to form Heaven 17.

	US Top 10 Ent	UK Top 10 Ent
Dare	6/82	10/81
Love And Dancing (as League Unlimited Orchestra)		7/82
Hysteria		5/84
Greatest Hits		11/88

HUMBLE PIE - Heavy rock group formed by leaders of two top British bands of the Sixties - Peter Frampton (ex-Herd) and Steve Marriott (ex-Small Faces). Other members were Jerry Shirley and Greg Ridley (ex-Spooky Tooth).

	US Top 10 Ent	UK Top 10 Ent
Smokin'	5/72	

ENGELBERT HUMPERDINCK - Celebrated British MOR singer and cabaret entertainer, real name Gerry Dorsey, born 1936 in Madras, India. He was one of the top earning acts of the late Sixties, who was still a headliner three decades later.

	US Top 10 Ent	UK Top 10 Ent
Release Me	8/67	6/67
The Last Waltz		12/67
A Man Without Love		8/68
Engelbert Humperdinck	1/70	12/69
Engelbert		3/69
Engelbert Humperdinck - His Greatest Hits		12/74

JANIS IAN - Acclaimed singer/songwriter and musician born 1951 in New York, USA. Real name Janis Fink, who first charted as a 16-year-old.

	US Top 10 Ent	UK Top 10 Ent
Between The Lines	8/75	

ICE CUBE - Controversial hardcore rapper who was born O'Shea Jackson, Los Angeles, USA, in 1969. The ex-N.W.A. mainstay was the first rap artist to enter the US LP chart at Number 1 (**The Predator**).

	US Top 10 Ent	UK Top 10 Ent
Death Certificate	11/91	
The Predator	12/92	

BILLY IDOL - Punk rocker, real name William Broad, born 1955, Middlesex, England. He was lead singer of successful British band Generation X before finding international success as a solo artist in 1982.

	US Top 10 Ent	UK Top 10 Ent
Rebel Yell	7/84	
Whiplash Smile	12/86	
Idol Songs: 11 Of The Best		7/88

FRANK IFIELD - Yodelling MOR/country/pop vocalist born 1936, Coventry, England, and raised in Australia. He managed a trio of successive UK chart topping singles with revivals of American oldies in the early Sixties.

	US Top 10 Ent	UK Top 10 Ent
I'll Remember You		2/63
Born Free		10/63

JULIO IGLESIAS - Spain's biggest selling pop artist was born 1943 in Madrid, Spain. Multi-lingual MOR vocalist has reportedly sold over 165 million records around the globe.

	US Top 10 Ent	UK Top 10 Ent
Begin The Beguine		12/81
Julio		7/83
1100 Bel Air Place	9/84	
Crazy		9/94

IMAGINATION - London-based soul/dance trio. Leee John, Ashley Ingram and Errol Kennedy. They were one of the most popular black British acts in the Eighties.

	US Top 10 Ent	UK Top 10 Ent
In The Heat Of The Night		9/82
Imagination		9/89

IMPRESSIONS - Legendary soul group from Chicago whose original line-up was Jerry Butler, Curtis Mayfield, Sam Gooden and brothers Arthur and Richard Brooks. Pioneer soul group were US chart regulars in the Sixties. Afte leaving, both Butler and Mayfield had successful solo careers.

	US Top 10 Ent	UK Top 10 Ent
The Impressions Keep On Pushing	10/64	

INCREDIBLE STRING BAND - Scottish folk group who combined original and traditional material. Mike Heron and Robin Williamson were the nucleus of the group.

	US Top 10 Ent	UK Top 10 Ent
Hangman's Beautiful Daughter		4/68

INNER CITY - Detroit-based funk/dance act masterminded by producer/mixer/songwriter and keyboard player Kevin Saunderson with vocalist Paris Grey.

	US Top 10 Ent	UK Top 10 Ent
Paradise		5/89

INSPIRAL CARPETS - Self-contained Manchester indie band who were one of the most successful acts in Britain during the early Nineties. Tom Hingley, Clint Boon, Graham Lambert, Martyn Walsh and Craig Gill.

	US Top 10 Ent	UK Top 10 Ent
Life		5/90

INXS - Internationally acclaimed AOR rock band from Sydney, Australia, fronted by Michael Hutchence. Other members are Garry Beers, brothers Andy, Jon and Tim Farris, and Kirk Pengilly.

	US Top 10 Ent	UK Top 10 Ent
Kick	1/88	
X	10/90	10/90
Welcome To Wherever You Are		8/92
Full Moon, Dirty Hearts		11/93
The Greatest Hits		11/94

IRON BUTTERFLY - American heavy metal pioneers from San Diego, USA. Members have included Doug Ingle, Eric Braunn, Ron Bushy, Lee Dorman and Mike Pinera (ex-Blues Image). Their **In-A-Gadda-Da-Vida** is regarded as one of the classic rock albums of its time.

	US Top 10 Ent	UK Top 10 Ent
In-A-Gadda-Da-Vida	10/68	
Ball	3/69	

IRON MAIDEN - Leading lights of the early-Eighties New Wave of British Heavy Metal. The London-based act has had numerous personnel changes; members have included vocalists Paul Di'Anno and Bruce Dickinson, Steve Harris and Clive Burr. In 1990, they had an amazing ten records on the UK LP chart in just two months.

	US Top 10 Ent	UK Top 10 Ent
Iron Maiden		4/80
The Number Of The Beast		4/82
Piece Of Mind		5/83
Powerslave		9/84
Live After Death		10/85
Somewhere In Time		10/86
Seventh Son Of A Seventh Son		4/88
No Prayer For The Dying		10/90
Fear Of The Dark		5/92

CHRIS ISAAK - Distinctive rockabilly-based brooding pop singer/songwriter born California, USA, in 1956. Photogenic performer who brought a breath of Fifties air to the Nineties charts.

	US Top 10 Ent	UK Top 10 Ent
Wicked Game		1/91
Heart Shaped World	4/91	2/91

ISLEY BROTHERS - World-famous R&B/soul group from Cincinnati, USA, consisted of brothers Rudolph, Ronald and O'Kelly (died 1986) Isley. Brothers Ernie and Marvin Isley and brother-in-law Chris Jasper were members from 1969-84.

	US Top 10 Ent	UK Top 10 Ent
The Heat Is On	8/75	
Go For Your Guns	5/77	
Showdown	6/78	
Go All The Way	5/80	

ALAN JACKSON - Major new country singer/songwriter born 1958 in Georgia, USA. One of the most successful artists in the country field, who had 10 Number 1 country singles, four platinum albums and can boast a shelf-full of awards.

	US Top 10 Ent	UK Top 10 Ent
Who Am I	7/94	

JANET JACKSON - Award-winning and record breaking pop/dance singer/songwriter, born 1966 in Gary, Indiana, USA. The youngest of the Jackson family that included the Jackson 5 and Michael Jackson.

	US Top 10 Ent	UK Top 10 Ent
Control	5/86	
Rhythm Nation 1814	10/89	
Janet	6/93	6/93

JERMAINE JACKSON - Pop/dance vocalist/guitarist born 1954 in Gary, Indiana, USA. He was a member of the ultra-successful Jackson 5 and also had several successful solo recordings.

	US Top 10 Ent	UK Top 10 Ent
Let's Get Serious	7/80	

JOE JACKSON - Multi-faceted singer/songwriter and pianist born 1955 in Burton-on-Trent, England. He built up a large transatlantic cult following.

	US Top 10 Ent	UK Top 10 Ent
Night And Day	11/82	2/83

MICHAEL JACKSON - Arguably the world's most successful male solo artist of all time, whose every move makes international headlines. This innovative pop/dance singer/songwriter was born 1958 in Gary, Indiana, USA. He was the first entertainer to earn $100 million in one year and his **Thriller** has sold more copies than any other record. Debuted aged 5 with The Jackson 5.

	US Top 10 Ent	UK Top 10 Ent
Ben	11/72	
Off The Wall	9/79	10/79
18 Greatest Hits (with The Jackson 5)		8/83
Thriller	1/83	2/83
Bad	9/87	9/87
Dangerous	12/91	12/91

JACKSONS/JACKSON 5 - World's most successful family recording act are brothers Jackie, Tito, Jermaine, Marlon and Michael Jackson, from Gary, Indiana, USA. They were one of the most popular live acts of the rock era whose first four singles topped the US chart.

	US Top 10 Ent	UK Top 10 Ent
Diana Ross Presents The Jackson 5	2/70	
ABC	7/70	
Third Album	10/70	
Lookin' Through The Windows	8/72	
Victory (as The Jacksons)	8/84	7/84
18 Greatest Hits (with The Jackson 5)		8/83

JAM - British mod-inspired new wave-punk trio consisted of Paul Weller, Bruce Foxton, Rick Buckler. Although unsuccessful Stateside, they were one of Britain's top acts of the Eighties. They quit at their peak in 1982 and soon after 15 re-issued singles simultaneously reached the UK Top 100. Weller went on to form The Style Council.

	US Top 10 Ent	UK Top 10 Ent
Sound Affects		12/80
The Gift		3/82
Dig The New Breed		12/82
Snap		10/83
Greatest Hits		7/91

JAMES - Well regarded Manchester rock band. Tim Booth, Jim Glennie, Larry Gott, Mark Hunter, Saul Davies and David Power. Formed in the early Eighties, they finally captured the UK public's imagination in the early Nineties.

	US Top 10 Ent	UK Top 10 Ent
Gold Mother		5/91
Seven		2/92

RICK JAMES - Singer/songwriter/guitarist and successful producer, who pioneered the punk funk sound. From Buffalo, USA, was born James Johnson in 1952. The oft-sampled singer was sentenced to four years imprisonment in 1992 for assault.

	US Top 10 Ent	UK Top 10 Ent
Street Songs	7/81	

TOMMY JAMES & THE SHONDELLS - Successful pop group fronted by James (born Tommy Jackson in 1947 in Ohio, USA) and including Eddie Gray, Pete Lucia, Ronnie Rosman, Mike Vale. They were one of America's most popular singles acts in the Sixties.

	US Top 10 Ent	UK Top 10 Ent
Crimson & Clover	3/69	

JAMIROQUAI - Initially highly touted London-based R&B styled group fronted by fur-hatted Jason Kay. Other members: Stuart Zender, Toby Smith and Nick van Gelder.

	US Top 10 Ent	UK Top 10 Ent
Emergency On Planet Earth		6/93
The Return Of The Space Cowboy		10/94

JAPAN - Prominent New Romantic pop group from London who were David Sylvian, Steve Jansen (actually brothers David and Steve Batt), Mick Karn, Rob Dean and Richard Barbieri.

	US Top 10 Ent	UK Top 10 Ent
Oil On Canvas		6/83

JEAN-MICHEL JARRE - World renowned synthesizer player who was born 1948 in Lyon, France. He is famed for his spectacular outdoor concerts.

	US Top 10 Ent	UK Top 10 Ent
Oxygene		9/77
Magnetic Fields		6/81
Revolutions		10/88

AL JARREAU - Grammy-winning soul/jazz singer born 1940 in Milwaukee, USA. He is one of the top selling jazz oriented acts in recent years.

	US Top 10 Ent	UK Top 10 Ent
Breakin' Away	10/81	

JEFFERSON AIRPLANE/STARSHIP - San Francisco rock band whose success spanned three decades, albeit with several personnel changes. Group members have included Grace Slick, Mickey Thomas, Marty Balin, Paul Kantner and Papa John Creach (died 1994).

	US Top 10 Ent	UK Top 10 Ent
Surrealistic Pillow	6/67	
Crown Of Creation	10/68	
Red Octopus (as Jefferson Starship)	8/75	
Spitfire (as Jefferson Starship)	7/76	
Earth (as Jefferson Starship)	4/78	
Knee Deep In The Hoopla (as Starship)	1/86	

JESUS JONES - Pop/rock group from London, England, led by singer/songwriter Mike Edwards and including Barry D (Iain Baker), Jerry De Borg, Gen (Simon Matthews) and Al Jaworski. They were one of the few new UK acts to have American success in the early Nineties.

	US Top 10 Ent	UK Top 10 Ent
Doubt		2/91

JETHRO TULL - Conceptual heavy rock-to-folk group from Blackpool, England, led by eccentric singer/flautist Ian Anderson. Other members Mick Abrahams, Clive Bunker, Glenn Cornick. They were one of the top selling UK album acts of the early Seventies.

	US Top 10 Ent	UK Top 10 Ent
Stand Up		8/69
Benefit		5/70
Aqualung	6/71	4/71
Thick As A Brick	5/72	3/72
Living In The Past	12/72	
A Passion Play	8/73	
War Child	12/74	
Minstrel In The Gallery	10/75	
Songs From The Wood	5/77	

JOAN JETT & THE BLACKHEARTS - Rock group fronted by photogenic singer/guitarist Jett, born Joan Larkin, 1960 in Philadelphia, USA. While still at school, she was a member of the noted L.A. group, The Runaways.

	US Top 10 Ent	UK Top 10 Ent
I Love Rock-N-Roll	3/82	

JOSE JIMENEZ - See BILL DANA

JIVE BUNNY - Club DJs Les Hemstock, John and Andy Pickles and Ian Morgan from Yorkshire, England, who sampled their way to success in the late Eighties. Their first three singles all headed the UK chart.

	US Top 10 Ent	UK Top 10 Ent
Jive Bunny - The Album		12/89

JODECI - Soulful vocal group consisting of two pairs of brothers from North Carolina, USA. Joel and Gedric Hailey (known as Jo-Jo and K-Ci) with Dalvin and Donald DeGrate Jr (known as Mr. Dalvin and DeVante Swing).

	US Top 10 Ent	UK Top 10 Ent
Diary Of A Mad Band	1/94	

BILLY JOEL - Foremost rock/pop singer/songwriter and pianist born 1949 in Hicksville, Long Island, USA. This performer, who married model Christie Brinkley in 1985, is one of the all time top album sellers with four of his LPs passing the five million sales mark.

	US Top 10 Ent	UK Top 10 Ent
The Stranger	2/78	
52nd Street	11/78	
Glass Houses	4/80	
Songs In The Attic	10/81	
The Nylon Curtain	11/82	
An Innocent Man	9/83	11/83
Greatest Hits Vol. 1 & Vol. 2	9/85	7/85
The Bridge	9/86	
Storm Front	11/89	
River Of Dreams	8/93	8/93

ELTON JOHN - Piano-playing pop/rock singer/songwriting superstar was born Reg Dwight in 1947 in Pinner, Middlesex, England. He is Britain's biggest selling solo artist and was the first act to enter the US LP chart at Number 1 (which he has done twice). He is also the only recording artist to crack the US Top 40 singles for 26 successive years (1970-1995).

	US Top 10 Ent	UK Top 10 Ent
Tumbleweed Connection	2/71	2/71
Elton John	2/71	
Madman Across The Water	2/72	
Honky Chateau	7/72	6/72
Don't Shoot Me I'm Only The Piano Player	2/73	2/73
Goodbye Yellow Brick Road	10/73	11/73
Caribou	7/74	7/74
Elton John - Greatest Hits	11/74	11/74
Captain Fantastic And The Brown Dirt Cowboy	6/75	6/75
Rock Of The Westies	11/75	11/75
Here And There	5/76	
Blue Moves	11/76	11/76
Greatest Hits Vol. 2		1/78
Breaking Hearts		7/84
Ice On Fire		11/85
Sleeping With The Past		7/90
The Very Best Of Elton John		11/90
The One		6/92
Duets		12/93

JOHNNY HATES JAZZ - London-based pop/rock act who were short-lived teen idols in the late Eighties. Britishers Clark Datchler, Calvin Hayes (Mickie Most's son) with American Mike Nocito.

	US Top 10 Ent	UK Top 10 Ent
Turn Back The Clock		1/88

HOLLY JOHNSON - Pop/rock/dance singer born 1960 Kartoum, Sudan, and raised in Liverpool, England. He was lead singer of the record-breaking Frankie Goes To Hollywood before turning solo in 1989.

	US Top 10 Ent	UK Top 10 Ent
Blast		5/89

JON & VANGELIS - Lancashire born vocalist Jon Anderson (of Yes fame) and Greek keyboardist Evangelos Papathanassiou (who was in Aphrodite's Child with Demis Roussos).

	US Top 10 Ent	UK Top 10 Ent
Short Stories		2/80
The Friends Of Mr. Cairo		2/82

ALED JONES - Choirboy from Wales who found fame in Britain thanks to a TV talent show. He retired from show business aged 16 to concentrate on school work.

	US Top 10 Ent	UK Top 10 Ent
All Through The Night		7/85

GRACE JONES - Model/film actress and dance music singer born 1952 in Spanishtown, Jamaica. Built up a cult following on both sides of the Atlantic.

	US Top 10 Ent	UK Top 10 Ent
Island Life		1/86

HOWARD JONES - Pop singer/songwriter and synth virtuoso born 1955 in Southampton, England. He was one of the most popular singles acts in Britain during the mid-Eighties.

	US Top 10 Ent	UK Top 10 Ent
Human's Lib		3/84
Dream Into Action		3/85

JACK JONES - MOR singer born 1938 in Los Angeles, USA, the son of noted vocalist Allan Jones. He was one of the last of the 'old school' of balladeers to crack the pop charts.

	US Top 10 Ent	UK Top 10 Ent
Bread Winners		6/72

QUINCY JONES - Composer/producer and record label MD (Mercury and own label Qwest), born 1933 in Chicago, USA. Produced and arranged many successful records, most notably Michael Jackson's **Thriller**. He holds the record for Grammy nominations and has won 25 including the prestigious Legends Award in 1990.

	US Top 10 Ent	UK Top 10 Ent
Back On The Block	2/90	

RICKIE LEE JONES - Jazz influenced pop singer/songwriter born 1954 in Chicago, USA. She won the Grammy Award for Best New Artist of 1979 thanks in part to her hit single 'Chuck E.'s In Love'.

	US Top 10 Ent	UK Top 10 Ent
Rickie Lee Jones	6/79	
Pirates	9/81	

TOM JONES - Pop/MOR superstar was born Tom Woodward, South Wales, in 1940. In the Sixties, this ever popular performer went from local club singer to Las Vegas star. He has remained a top headliner for four decades.

	US Top 10 Ent	UK Top 10 Ent
Green Green Grass Of Home		4/67
Live At The Talk Of The Town		9/67
13 Smash Hits		1/68
Delilah		8/68
Help Yourself	4/69	1/69
This Is Tom Jones	7/69	6/69
Tom Jones Live In Las Vegas	12/69	11/69
Tom		5/70
20 Greatest Hits		3/75

JANIS JOPLIN - Rock'n'blues singer born 1943 in Texas, USA, who started as vocalist with Big Brother And The Holding Company before going solo in 1968. This much revered performer died in 1970 after a drug overdose.

	US Top 10 Ent	UK Top 10 Ent
I Got Dem Ol' Kozmic Blues Again Mama	11/69	
Pearl	2/71	
Joplin In Concert	6/72	

JOURNEY - AOR group from San Francisco, USA. Members have included Gregg Rolie, Neal Schon (both ex-Santana), George Tickner, Ross Valory, Aynsley Dunbar (ex-John Mayall, Mothers of Invention), Steve Perry and Jonathan Cain. They were one of the biggest selling LP acts of the Eighties.

	US Top 10 Ent	UK Top 10 Ent
Departure	4/80	
Captured	3/81	
Escape	8/81	
Frontiers	2/83	
Raised On Radio	5/86	

JUDAS PRIEST - Noteworthy heavy metal band from Birmingham, England. Rob Halford, K.K. Downing, Ian Hill, Dave Holland, Glenn Tipton,

	US Top 10 Ent	UK Top 10 Ent
British Steel		4/80

BERT KAEMPFERT - Bandleader/musician born 1923 in Hamburg, Germany. He composed 'Strangers In The Night' (Frank Sinatra) and 'Wooden Heart' (Elvis Presley) and was first producer of The Beatles. He died in 1980.

	US Top 10 Ent	UK Top 10 Ent
Wonderland By Night	1/61	
Blue Midnight	4/65	
Bye Bye Blues		3/66

KANSAS - Successful AOR rock group from Topeka, Kansas, USA, led by Steve Walsh. Phil Ehart, Dave Hope, Kerry Livgren, Robby Steinhart and Rich Williams completed the group.

	US Top 10 Ent	UK Top 10 Ent
Leftoverture	4/77	
Point Of Know Return	12/77	

KC & THE SUNSHINE BAND - Multi-racial disco group from Florida, USA, formed by singer/writer/producers Harry Casey (KC) and Richard Finch. One of the top selling singles acts of the disco era.

	US Top 10 Ent	UK Top 10 Ent
KC & The Sunshine Band	12/75	

HOWARD KEEL - Noted MOR singer/actor and stage star. He appeared in many top Fifties musicals and starred in the top soap opera *Dallas.*

	US Top 10 Ent	UK Top 10 Ent
And I Love You So		5/84

R. KELLY - Chicago based R&B singer/composer and producer, born Robert Kelly. He was the most successful R&B artist/producer in 1994. His single 'Bump N' Grind' topped the R&B chart for a record 12 weeks.

	US Top 10 Ent	UK Top 10 Ent
12 Play	2/94	

NIGEL KENNEDY - British virtuoso violinist born 1956, brought classical violin music to a youthful audience.

	US Top 10 Ent	UK Top 10 Ent
Vivaldi Four Seasons		3/90

NIK KERSHAW - Pop singer/songwriter born 1958 in Bristol, England. In the mid-Eighties had a big teen following in the UK. In the Nineties, he had chart success as a writer for acts such as Chesney Hawkes and Let Loose.

	US Top 10 Ent	UK Top 10 Ent
Human Racing		7/84

KIDS FROM FAME - Members from the cast of US TV series *Fame*, plus studio musicians. They were one of 1982's top selling acts in the UK but found little fame in their homeland.

	US Top 10 Ent	UK Top 10 Ent
Kids From Fame		7/82
Kids From Fame Again		10/82

KING - Fashion conscious pop group led by Paul King from Coventry, England. Other members were Tony Wall, Jim Jackall and Mick Roberts. King is now a VJ on MTV Europe.

	US Top 10 Ent	UK Top 10 Ent
Steps In Time		2/85

CAROLE KING - Grammy winning songwriter and pop singer/pianist born 1942 in Brooklyn, USA (real name Carol Klein). She is one of the most successful female songwriters of all time, penning many of her numerous hits with ex-husband Gerry Goffin.

	US Top 10 Ent	UK Top 10 Ent
Tapestry	5/71	9/71
Music	12/71	
Rhymes & Reasons	11/72	
Fantasy	7/73	
Wrap Around Joy	10/74	
Thoroughbred	3/76	

KING CRIMSON - Well respected, all-star British progressive rock group. Members have included Robert Fripp, Greg Lake (later ELP), Ian McDonald (later Foreigner), Bill Bruford (later Yes), Boz Burrell (later Bad Company), John Wetton (later Asia), Adrian Belew and Pete Sinfield (later a top pop composer).

	US Top 10 Ent	UK Top 10 Ent
In The Court Of The Crimson King		11/69
In The Wake Of Poseidon		6/70

KINGSTON TRIO - Influential San Francisco-based folk/pop trio, were America's top selling album group in the early Sixties. Dave Guard (died 1991), Bob Shane, Nick Reynolds. John Stewart replaced Guard in 1961.

	US Top 10 Ent	UK Top 10 Ent
Here We Go Again!	1/60	
The Kingston Trio At Large	1/60	
Sold Out	5/60	
String Along	9/60	
Make Way!	3/61	
Goin' Places	8/61	
Close-Up	11/61	
College Concert	3/62	
The Kingston Trio No. 16	4/63	
Sunny Side!	9/63	

KINKS - Distinctive pop/rock group from London, England, which featured singer/songwriter Ray Davies with brother, Dave, Mike Avory and Peter Quaife. The long running group were inducted into the Rock And Roll Hall Of Fame in 1990.

	US Top 10 Ent	UK Top 10 Ent
Kinks		10/64
Kinda Kinks		3/65
Well Respected Kinks		10/66

KISS - Heavily made up glam rock band were one of America's top selling LP acts of the late-Seventies. Gene Summers, Paul Stanley, Ace Frehley and Peter Criss. Major British sales came after they removed their make up in the early-Eighties.

	US Top 10 Ent	UK Top 10 Ent
Love Gun	7/77	
Alive II	1/78	
Crazy Nights		11/87
Revenge	6/92	

KLF - Eccentric British act whose mainstays were Scottish-born Bill Drummond and Bill Cauty. In 1991, they won the BRIT award for Top Group and outsold all other UK bands worldwide that year. They stopped recording while at their peak.

	US Top 10 Ent	UK Top 10 Ent
The White Room		5/91

KNACK - Rock group from Los Angeles, USA, who had a brief fling with fame in 1979. Doug Fieger, Berton Averre, Bruce Gary, Prescott Niles.

	US Top 10 Ent	UK Top 10 Ent
Get The Knack	8/79	

GLADYS KNIGHT & THE PIPS - World famous R&B group fronted by Knight, born 1944 in Georgia, USA. For most of their career, The Pips were Gladys' brother 'Bubba' plus her cousins William Guest and Edward Patten. Gladys, who was a winner on Ted Mack's *Amateur Hour* in 1951 (aged 6), was still a top line act in the mid Nineties.

	US Top 10 Ent	UK Top 10 Ent
Neither One Of Us	5/73	
The Best Of Gladys Knight And The Pips		6/76
30 Greatest		12/77

KOOL & THE GANG - Jazz based R&B group from New Jersey, USA, led by Robert 'Kool' Bell (born 1950). They were R&B chart regulars for ten years before being international pop stars in 1983. Most noteworthy member was vocalist James 'J.T.' Taylor, who joined in 1979.

	US Top 10 Ent	UK Top 10 Ent
Twice As Kool		5/83

KRAFTWERK - Innovative German electronic group formed by Ralf Hutter and Florian Schneider. Their music has greatly influenced both the rock and dance music fields.

	US Top 10 Ent	UK Top 10 Ent
Autobahn	4/75	6/75

LENNY KRAVITZ - Critically lauded, dreadlock-wearing, multi-faceted American rock/R&B singer/songwriter and musician was born in 1964. He was voted Top International Male Singer in the 1993 BRIT awards.

	US Top 10 Ent	UK Top 10 Ent
Are You Gonna Go My Way		3/93

KRIS KROSS - Back-to-front clothes-wearing teen rap duo from Georgia, USA. Chris 'Mack Daddy' Kelly and Chris 'Daddy Mack' Smith.

	US Top 10 Ent	UK Top 10 Ent
Totally Krossed Out	5/92	

LABELLE - Female R&B vocal group which evolved from Patti LaBelle & The Blue Belles. Patti LaBelle, Sarah Dash and Nona Hendryx. LaBelle (see below) is generally regarded as one of the all time great female R&B vocalists.

	US Top 10 Ent	UK Top 10 Ent
Nightbirds	3/75	

PATTI LABELLE - Pop/R&B singer born Patricia Holt in 1944 in Philadelphia, USA. Had hits with her groups, The Blue Belles and LaBelle, before successfully going solo in the late Seventies.

	US Top 10 Ent	UK Top 10 Ent
Winner In You	6/86	

KD LANG - Grammy winning, multi-faceted vocalist born Kathryn Dawn Lang 1961 in Canada. After initial success in country music, Lang moved successfully into the mainstream.

	US Top 10 Ent	UK Top 10 Ent
Ingenue		3/93

MARIO LANZA - Revered operatic tenor born Alfredo Cocozza in 1921 in Philadelphia, USA, died in 1959. He was one of the most popular operatic performers of the century with many pop hits to his credit.

	US Top 10 Ent	UK Top 10 Ent
Mario Lanza Sings Caruso Favorites	6/60	8/60

JAMES LAST - Orchestra leader/producer/arranger born 1929 in Bremen, Germany. One of Europe's top selling album acts of all time. Only Elvis Presley has amassed more British LP chart entries.

	US Top 10 Ent	UK Top 10 Ent
This Is James Last		5/67
Ten Years Non-Stop Jubilee		8/75
Make The Party Last		12/75
Last The Whole Night Long		5/79

CYNDI LAUPER - Striking singer/songwriter born 1953 in New York, USA. Winner of the Best New Artist Grammy in 1984, who for a while gave Madonna a run for her money.

	US Top 10 Ent	UK Top 10 Ent
She's So Unusual	5/84	
True Colors	11/86	
Twelve Deadly Cyns... And Then Some		9/94

LEAGUE UNLIMITED ORCHESTRA - See HUMAN LEAGUE

LED ZEPPELIN - Record shattering British heavy metal/rock group. Robert Plant, Jimmy Page (ex-Yardbirds), John Bonham (died 1980) and John Paul Jones. One of the top drawing acts of all time, whose tally of ten multi-platinum albums is only bettered by The Beatles.

	US Top 10 Ent	UK Top 10 Ent
Led Zeppelin		5/69
Led Zeppelin II	11/69	11/69
Led Zeppelin III	10/70	11/70
Led Zeppelin IV (Four Symbols)	12/71	12/71
Houses Of The Holy	5/73	4/73
Physical Graffiti	3/75	3/75
Presence	4/76	4/76
The Soundtrack From The Film 'The Song Remains The Same'	11/76	11/76
In Through The Out Door	9/79	9/79
Coda	12/82	12/82

BRENDA LEE - The most successful female teenager in the rock era was born Brenda Tarpley in 1944 in Georgia, USA. With a long string on pop hits behind her 'Little Miss Dynamite' returned to country music in the Seventies.

	US Top 10 Ent	UK Top 10 Ent
Brenda Lee	9/60	
This Is...Brenda	12/60	
All Alone Am I		5/63

JOHN LENNON - The singer/songwriter and ex-Beatle, who wrote his own chapter in the history of rock, was born 1940 in Liverpool, England, and was killed 1980 in New York. In the two months following his murder, he had three UK Number 1 singles. One of the greatest musical talents of the century.

	US Top 10 Ent	UK Top 10 Ent
John Lennon/Plastic Ono Band	1/71	
Imagine	10/71	11/71
Mind Games	12/73	
Walls And Bridges	11/74	10/74
Rock 'n' Roll	4/75	
Double Fantasy	12/80	12/80
The John Lennon Collection		12/82
Milk And Honey		2/84

ANNIE LENNOX - Pop/rock vocalist born 1954 in Aberdeen, Scotland. The oft-times BRIT award winner, was the lead singer of The Tourists and Eurythmics prior to embarking on a solo career.

	US Top 10 Ent	UK Top 10 Ent
Diva		4/92

LETTERMEN - Smooth MOR/pop vocal trio from Los Angeles. Tony Butala, Bob Engemann, Jim Pike. The act, who amassed 32 American chart albums, surprisingly never dented the UK chart.

	US Top 10 Ent	UK Top 10 Ent
A Song For Young Love	4/62	

LEVEL 42 - Noted funk/pop group from Manchester, England, led by Mark King. Other members included Brothers Phil and Boon Gould and Mike Lindup.

	US Top 10 Ent	UK Top 10 Ent
World Machine		1/86
Running In The Family		3/87
Staring At The Sun		10/88

LEVELLERS - Alternative rock band formed in Brighton, England, were one of the UK's most popular acts in the Nineties. Mark Chadwick, Jeremy Cunningham, Simon Friend, Charlie Heather, Jon Sevink.

	US Top 10 Ent	UK Top 10 Ent
Levellers		9/93

HUEY LEWIS & THE NEWS - Top selling pop/rock group from San Francisco, USA, led by Huey Lewis (real name Hugh Cregg III) born 1950 in New York, USA. Mario Cipollina, Johnny Colla, Bill Gibson, Chris Hayes, Sean Hopper. One of America's most successful acts in the Eighties.

	US Top 10 Ent	UK Top 10 Ent
Sports	3/84	
Fore!	9/86	

RAMSEY LEWIS - Jazz pianist born 1935 in Chicago, USA. His band at times included Maurice White (Earth, Wind & Fire) and Eldee Young and Isaac Holt (Young-Holt Unlimited). A regular US album chart entrant for twenty years.

	US Top 10 Ent	UK Top 10 Ent
The In Crowd	9/65	

GORDON LIGHTFOOT - Folk/country/pop singer/songwriter and guitarist born 1938 in Ontario, Canada. His songs 'For Loving Me' and 'Early Morning Rain' have become folk and country standards.

	US Top 10 Ent	UK Top 10 Ent
Sundown	6/74	

LIMELITERS - Folk vocal group formed in Hollywood, USA. Lou Gottlieb, Alex Hassilev and Glen Yarbrough (who later had solo successes).

	US Top 10 Ent	UK Top 10 Ent
Tonight: In Person	3/61	

LINDISFARNE - Folk/rock group from Tyne And Wear, England, who were popular in the UK in the early Seventies. Members included Rod Clements, Simon Cowe, Alan Hull, Ray Laidlaw and Ray Jackson.

	US Top 10 Ent	UK Top 10 Ent
Fog On The Tyne		3/72
Dingly Dell		10/72

LIPPS INC. - Disco act from Minneapolis masterminded by producer/composer and musician Steven Greenberg with vocals by Cynthia Johnson. Their single 'Funkytown' was a US Number 1.

	US Top 10 Ent	UK Top 10 Ent
Mouth To Mouth	6/80	

LISA LISA & CULT JAM - R&B/dance act from Harlem, New York, USA, who were produced by Full Force. Lisa Velez, Mike Hughes, Alex 'Spanador' Moseley. They had two US Number 1 singles in 1987, 'Head To Toe' and 'Lost In Emotion'.

	US Top 10 Ent	UK Top 10 Ent
Spanish Fly	6/87	

LITTLE ANGELS - Youthful British heavy rock band from Scarborough, England. Toby Jepson, Mark Plunkett, Jim and Bruce Dickinson (no relation to the former Iron Maiden frontman) and Mark Richardson.

	US Top 10 Ent	UK Top 10 Ent
Jam		2/93

LIVING COLOUR - The most successful black rock group from New York, USA. Vernon Reid (born in London, England), Corey Glover, Muzz Skillings and William Calhoun. They won a batch of video awards in 1989.

	US Top 10 Ent	UK Top 10 Ent
Vivid	5/89	

LL COOL J - Groundbreaking rapper, born James Todd Smith 1969 in New York, USA, whose stage name stands for 'Ladies Love Cool James'. One of rap's most successful soloists with five platinum albums.

	US Top 10 Ent	UK Top 10 Ent
Bigger And Deffer	7/87	
Walking With A Panther	7/89	

ANDREW LLOYD WEBBER - Britain's foremost composer of stage musicals was born London, England, in 1948. He has penned such hits as Jesus Christ Superstar, Evita, Cats and Phantom Of The Opera.

	US Top 10 Ent	UK Top 10 Ent
Variations		2/78
Requiem		4/85

LOGGINS & MESSINA - West Coast rock duo, which consisted of Kenny Loggins (see below) and Jim Messina (ex-Buffalo Springfield and Poco). Notched up six US Top 40 albums.

	US Top 10 Ent	UK Top 10 Ent
On Stage	8/74	
Mother Lode	12/74	

KENNY LOGGINS - Talented Califonia-based rock singer/songwriter and guitarist born 1947 in Washington, USA. He had a string of hits with Jim Messina before starting a similarly impressive run of solo successes.

	US Top 10 Ent	UK Top 10 Ent
Nightwatch	10/78	

LONDON BOYS - Hi-NRG duo Dennis George and Edem Phillips from London, England, who found short-lived British fame after relocating to Germany.

	US Top 10 Ent	UK Top 10 Ent
The Twelve Commandments Of Dance	7/89	

LONDON SYMPHONY ORCHESTRA - World renowned British orchestra who have on occasions found themselves on the pop charts.

	US Top 10 Ent	UK Top 10 Ent
The Strauss Family		1/73
Classic Rock		9/78

TRINI LOPEZ - Latin-American pop singer/guitarist and actor born 1937 in Dallas, Texas, USA. After several small selling singles Lopez had a run of international hits in the mid-Sixties.

	US Top 10 Ent	UK Top 10 Ent
Trini Lopez At PJ's	8/63	12/63
Trini Lopez In London		4/67

SOPHIA LOREN - See PETER SELLERS

LOS INDIOS TABAJARAS - Instrumental duo, which comprised Brazilian Indian brothers, Antenor and Natalicio Lima, had a brief flirtation with international fame thanks to the old Tommy Dorsey hit 'Maria Elena'.

	US Top 10 Ent	UK Top 10 Ent
Maria Elena	1/64	

LOVE UNLIMITED - Female soul vocal trio from California, USA, were protegees of Barry White, who managed and produced them. Sisters Glodean (married to White) and Linda James and Diane Taylor.

	US Top 10 Ent	UK Top 10 Ent
Under The Influence Of...	2/74	

LOVERBOY - Canadian rock group who had several US hits in the Eighties. Mike Reno, Paul Dean, Doug Johnson, Scott Smith and Matt Frenette.

	US Top 10 Ent	UK Top 10 Ent
Get Lucky	4/82	
Keep It Up	7/83	

LOVIN' SPOONFUL - Influential good time rock group from New York, USA, led by John Sebastian. Steve Boone, Joe Butler and Zal Yanovsky completed the quartet, who helped put US groups back on the musical map after the British Invasion.

	US Top 10 Ent	UK Top 10 Ent
The Best Of The Lovin' Spoonful	4/67	

LYNYRD SKYNYRD - Celebrated southern-rock group from Florida, USA, who lost several members, including lead singer Ronnie Van Zant, in a plane crash in 1977. Other members included Gary Rossington and Allen Collins (died 1990). Van Zant's brother Johnny re-formed the group in 1987.

	US Top 10 Ent	UK Top 10 Ent
One More From The Road	11/76	
Street Survivors	11/77	

MC EIHT FEATURING CMW - Hard hitting rapper (whose name stands for 'experienced in hardcore thumpin') first hit the headlines as leader of the fierce West Coast outfit Compton's Most Wanted.

	US Top 10 Ent	UK Top 10 Ent
We Come Strapped	8/94	

MC HAMMER - See HAMMER

M PEOPLE - Award winning, self-contained soulful dance act from Manchester, England. Masterminded by Mike Pickering with Paul Heard and vocals from Heather Small.

	US Top 10 Ent	UK Top 10 Ent
Elegant Slumming		10/93
Bizarre Fruit		12/94

MADNESS - Foremost 2 Tone/pop band from North London, England, led by Graham 'Suggs' McPherson. Also included Mike Barson, Chris Foreman, Mark Bedford, Lee Thompson, Dan Woodgate and Carl Smythe. No group spent longer on the UK singles chart in the Eighties.

	US Top 10 Ent	UK Top 10 Ent
One Step Beyond		1/80
Absolutely		10/80
Madness 7		10/81
Complete Madness		5/82
Divine Madness		3/92

MADONNA - Record breaking pop/rock/dance singer/songwriter and actress born Madonna Ciccone in 1958 in Michigan, USA. The most successful female singer of all time whose amazing transatlantic chart record is only bettered by Elvis and The Beatles.

	US Top 10 Ent	UK Top 10 Ent
Like A Virgin	12/84	8/85
Madonna (AKA The First Album)	10/84	8/85
True Blue	8/86	7/86
Who's That Girl (Soundtrack)	9/87	8/87
Like A Prayer	4/89	4/89
I'm Breathless	6/90	6/90
The Immaculate Collection	12/90	11/90
Erotica	11/92	10/92
Bedtime Stories	11/94	11/94

MAMAS & THE PAPAS - Very successful flower power/pop foursome from New York, USA. John Phillips and Michelle Phillips (ex husband and wife), Dennis Doherty, and 'Mama Cass' Elliot (died 1974). John Phillips, the group's main songwriter, also penned the hippie anthem 'San Francisco (Be Sure To Wear Some Flowers In Your Hair)'.

	US Top 10 Ent	UK Top 10 Ent
If You Can Believe Your Eyes And Ears	5/66	
The Mamas And The Papas	10/66	7/66
The Mamas & The Papas Deliver	4/67	8/67
Farewell To The First Golden Era	12/67	

HENRY MANCINI - World renowned composer/conductor/arranger born 1924 in Cleveland, USA, and died 1994. He has won more Oscars and Grammy Awards than any other artist.

	US Top 10 Ent	UK Top 10 Ent
Music From Mr. Lucky	5/60	
Breakfast At Tiffany's (Soundtrack)	12/61	
Hatari!	10/62	
Charade	3/64	
A Warm Shade Of Ivory	7/69	

MANFRED MANN - London-based R&B/pop group, led by South African Michael 'Manfred Mann' Lubowitz. Others members included vocalist Paul Jones (replaced by Mike D'Abo), Mike Hugg, Tom McGuinness and Michael Vickers. One of the most enduring groups of the Sixties.

	US Top 10 Ent	UK Top 10 Ent
Five Faces Of Manfred Mann		9/64
Mann Made		11/65

CHUCK MANGIONE - Grammy winning jazz/pop flugelhorn player and composer born 1940 in New York, USA.

	US Top 10 Ent	UK Top 10 Ent
Feels So Good	5/78	

BARRY MANILOW - MOR/pop singer/songwriter and entertainer from Brooklyn, USA, born Barry Pincus in 1946. Internationally successful recording artist, who has been one of the world's most successful live attractions since the mid-Seventies.

	US Top 10 Ent	UK Top 10 Ent
Tryin' To Get The Feeling	1/76	
This One's For You	4/77	
Barry Manilow Live	6/77	
Even Now	3/78	
Greatest Hits	2/79	
Manilow Magic		3/79
Barry		1/81
If I Should Love Again		10/81
Barry Live In Britain		5/82

MANTOVANI - World famous British-based orchestra leader, who was born Annunzio Mantovani in Venice, Italy in 1905 and died in 1980. His lush string sound was hugely successful in the USA throughout the Fifties and Sixties.

	US Top 10 Ent	UK Top 10 Ent
Mantovani Plays Music From Exodus And Other Great Themes	1/61	
Mantovani Magic		5/66
World Of Mantovani		6/69
World Of Mantovani Vol. 2		10/69

MANUEL & HIS MUSIC OF THE MOUNTAINS - British session orchestra led by the noted EMI Records A&R man Geoff Love, who was born 1917 in Yorkshire, England and died in 1991.

	US Top 10 Ent	UK Top 10 Ent
Carnival		3/76

MARILLION - Respected rock group from Aylesbury, England, originally led by Fish (real name Derek Dick). Steve Rothery, Mark Kelly, Peter Trewavas and Andy Ward. Fish went solo in 1988 and was replaced by Steve Hogarth.

	US Top 10 Ent	UK Top 10 Ent
Misplaced Childhood		7/85
Clutching At Straws		7/87

BOB MARLEY & THE WAILERS - The West Indies' best known performer was born 1945 in Jamaica, and died in 1981. Marley's influence was inestimable and more than anyone else he put reggae on the world's musical map. The Wailers included Bunny Wailer (born Neville O'Riley) and Peter Tosh (born Winston McIntosh - died 1987).

	US Top 10 Ent	UK Top 10 Ent
Rastaman Vibration	7/76	
Kaya		4/78
Uprising		7/80
Confrontation		6/83
Legend		5/84

LENA MARTELL - Glasgow, Scotland, born country-influenced MOR singer, who had been recording for 18 years before she debuted on the singles chart with the UK Number 1, 'One Day At A Time'.

	US Top 10 Ent	UK Top 10 Ent
Lena's Music Album		11/79

DEAN MARTIN - Acclaimed MOR singer/actor was born Dino Crocetti in 1917 in Ohio, USA. After ending his successful partnership with comedian Jerry Lewis in 1956, this member of Frank Sinatra's renowned Rat Pack remained at the top of his profession for many years.

	US Top 10 Ent	UK Top 10 Ent
Everybody Loves Somebody	9/64	
Gentle On My Mind		4/69
20 Original Dean Martin Hits		11/76

STEVE MARTIN - Internationally famous film and TV comedian/actor and comedy writer, born 1945 in Waco, Texas, USA. He won the Grammy for Best Comedy Performance in 1977 and 1978.

	US Top 10 Ent	UK Top 10 Ent
A Wild And Crazy Guy	11/78	

AL MARTINO - MOR singer and actor from Philadelphia, USA, born Alfred Cini in 1927. Martino's 'Here In My Heart' was Number 1 on the first UK chart in 1952. He was one of the few pre-rock acts to continue scoring big hits into the Sixties.

	US Top 10 Ent	UK Top 10 Ent
I Love You Because	7/63	

RICHARD MARX - Talented rock/pop singer/songwriter born 1963 in Chicago, USA. He had 12 consecutive US Top 20 singles, the first six of which reached the Top 3.

	US Top 10 Ent	UK Top 10 Ent
Richard Marx	9/88	
Repeat Offender	8/89	

MASSED WELSH CHOIRS - A collection of the best known male voice choirs from the valleys of Wales.

	US Top 10 Ent	UK Top 10 Ent
Cymansa Gann		8/69

JOHNNY MATHIS - Jazz influenced MOR/pop singer born 1935 in San Francisco, USA. Distinctive and perennially successful vocalist whose **Greatest Hits** was on the charts for almost 10 years - a record for a solo act.

	US Top 10 Ent	UK Top 10 Ent
Heavenly	1/60	
Faithfully	2/60	
Johnny's Moods	9/60	
Rhythms And Ballads Of Broadway		12/60
Portrait Of Johnny	9/61	
The Johnny Mathis Collection		6/77
You Light Up My Life		5/78
Tears And Laughter		3/80

PAUL MAURIAT - French orchestra leader and composer born 1925. He penned the chart topping single 'I Will Follow Him' and had his own Number 1 with 'Love Is Blue', a cover of an unsuccessful Eurovision entry.

	US Top 10 Ent	UK Top 10 Ent
Blooming Hits	2/68	

JOHN MAYALL - Well respected pioneer British R&B/blues performer was born 1943 in Macclesfield, England. His band members read like a British blues who's who including Eric Clapton, Jack Bruce, Mick Fleetwood, John McVie, MickTaylor and Peter Green.

	US Top 10 Ent	UK Top 10 Ent
Bare Wires		7/68
Blues Breakers (with Eric Clapton)		9/66

CURTIS MAYFIELD - Critcally acclaimed soul singer/songwriter/producer and record label owner born 1942 in Chicago, USA. He fronted hit-making trio The Impressions during the Sixties, before starting an equally successful solo career. Despite being paralyzed in a bad stage accident in 1990, he is still making music.

	US Top 10 Ent	UK Top 10 Ent
Superfly (Soundtrack)	10/72	

PAUL McCARTNEY/WINGS - Ex-Beatle and world's most successful songwriter in the rock era was born 1942 in Liverpool, England. One of the few undisputed greats of pop and rock music who has packed stadiums around the world for thirty years. He won the Grammy for Lifetime Achievement in 1990, and is the only owner of a Rhodium Record (presented by Guinness for his outstanding sales achievements).

	US Top 10 Ent	UK Top 10 Ent
McCartney	5/70	5/70
Ram (with Linda McCartney)	6/71	6/71
Red Rose Speedway (as Paul McCartney & Wings)	6/73	5/73
Band On The Run (as Paul McCartney & Wings)	1/74	1/74
Venus And Mars (as Wings)	6/75	6/75
Wings At The Speed Of Sound (as Wings)	4/76	4/76
Wings Over America (as Wings)	1/77	
London Town (as Wings)	4/78	4/78
Wings Greatest Hits (as Wings)		2/79
Back To The Egg (as Wings)	7/79	
McCartney II	6/80	5/80
Tug Of War	5/82	5/82
Pipes Of Peace		1/84
Give My Regards To Broad Street		11/84
All The Best!		11/87
Flowers In The Dirt		6/89

MICHAEL McDONALD - Noted singer/songwriter born 1952 in St. Louis, USA, had been a member of Steely Dan and the Doobie Brothers before going solo. Among his hit singles were duets with James Ingram and Patti LaBelle.

	US Top 10 Ent	UK Top 10 Ent
If That's What It Takes	10/82	

REBA McENTIRE - Country music's first lady was born 1954 in Oklahoma, USA. She was the first female country performer to amass five multi-platinum albums, and among female vocalists, only Barbara Streisand and Linda Ronstadt have earned more gold LPs.

	US Top 10 Ent	UK Top 10 Ent
It's Your Call	1/93	
Greatest Hits Volume Two	10/93	
Read My Mind	5/94	

BOBBY McFERRIN - Jazz based singer born 1950 in New York, USA. Although little known to the public before his chart topping 'Don't Worry Be Happy' in 1988, he had already collected a shelf-full of Grammy awards.

	US Top 10 Ent	UK Top 10 Ent
Simple Pleasures	10/88	

TIM McGRAW - Arguably the brightest new country act of 1994 was born 1967 in Louisiana, USA. The controversy stirred up by the single 'Indian Outlaw' (which allegedly promoted bigotry) helped take his album to the Number 1 slot.

	US Top 10 Ent	UK Top 10 Ent
Not A Moment Too Soon	4/94	

DON McLEAN - Acclaimed singer/songwriter born 1945 in New York, USA. His chart topping debut recording, 'American Pie', is regarded as a classic of the rock era.

	US Top 10 Ent	UK Top 10 Ent
American Pie	1/71	6/72
The Very Best Of Don Mclean		10/80

VAUGHN MEADER - President John F. Kennedy impersonator born 1936 in Boston, USA. **The First Family** hit the top in just two weeks and was the fastest selling album of its time. Not unexpectedly, sales of his LPs slumped dramatically after the President's assassination.

	US Top 10 Ent	UK Top 10 Ent
The First Family	12/62	
The First Family Vol. 2	6/63	

MEAT LOAF - Unmistakable rock singer and actor born Marvin Lee Aday 1947 in Dallas, Texas, USA. **Bat Out Of Hell**, the result of his partnership with producer/writer Jim Steinman, spent over 400 weeks on the UK chart (yet only one week in the Top 10) and sold over 25 million around the globe.

	US Top 10 Ent	UK Top 10 Ent
Dead Ringer		9/81
Hits Out Of Hell		2/85
Bat Out Of Hell II : Back Into Hell	10/93	9/93

MEGADETH - Top selling thrash metal outfit from California, USA, fronted by singer/songwriter/guitarist Dave Mustaine (ex-Metallica). Other members of the band, that went from cult status to stardom, include Dave Ellefson and recent recruits Marty Friedman and Nick Menzer.

	US Top 10 Ent	UK Top 10 Ent
Countdown To Extinction	8/92	

MEL & KIM - Pop/dance duo of sisters Kim (born 1961) and Mel Appleby (born 1966) were one of the top transatlantic dance acts of the late Eighties. Mel died from cancer in 1990. Kim had some solo success later.

	US Top 10 Ent	UK Top 10 Ent
F.L.M.		4/87

MELANIE - Folk singer/songwriter born Melanie Safka in 1947 in New York, USA. One of the stars of Woodstock, she was the last of the original hippie hitmakers.

	US Top 10 Ent	UK Top 10 Ent
Candles In The Rain		11/70

JOHN COUGAR MELLENCAMP - Acclaimed rock singer/songwriter was born 1951 in Indiana, USA, started his recording career as Johnny Cougar. He has been a regular American chart visitor since 1979.

	US Top 10 Ent	UK Top 10 Ent
American Fool (as John Cougar)	7/92	
Scarecrow	10/85	
The Lonesome Jubilee	10/87	
Big Daddy	6/89	

MEN AT WORK - Rock group from Melbourne, Australia, led by Scotsman Colin Hay. Other members - Greg Ham, John Rees, Jerry Speiser, Ron Strykert. Their debut LP topped the US chart for 15 weeks - then a record for a rookie act.

	US Top 10 Ent	UK Top 10 Ent
Business As Usual	10/82	1/83
Cargo	5/83	

SERGIO MENDES & BRASIL '66 - Latin-American group led by pianist Sergio Mendes, born 1941 in Brazil, who were US chart regulars in the Sixties.

	US Top 10 Ent	UK Top 10 Ent
Look Around	6/68	
Fool On The Hill	1/69	

FREDDIE MERCURY - Celebrated lead singer of the premier rock band Queen, born Frederick Bulsara in 1946 in Zanzibar, Tanzania. The highly acclaimed singer/songwriter died of an AIDS-related illness in 1991.

	US Top 10 Ent	UK Top 10 Ent
Mr Bad Guy		5/85
The Freddie Mercury Album		12/92

METALLICA - Top selling speed metal band from Los Angeles, USA. Original line-up James Hetfield, Lars Ulrich, Cliff Burton (died 1986) and Dave Mustaine (who was replaced by Kirk Hammett when he left to form Megadeth in 1982).

	US Top 10 Ent	UK Top 10 Ent
...And Justice For All	10/88	9/88
Metallica	9/91	8/91

MFSB - Mothers Fathers Sisters Brothers is a large multi-racial studio band from Philadelphia, USA, masterminded by producers Kenny Gamble and Leon Huff with arranger Thom Bell.

	US Top 10 Ent	UK Top 10 Ent
Love Is The Message	4/74	

MIAMI SOUND MACHINE - See GLORIA ESTEFAN

GEORGE MICHAEL - Highly acclaimed pop/rock singer/songwriter and ex-front man of Wham!, was born George Panayiotou in 1963 in Bushey, England. **Faith**, which he produced, arranged, composed, sung and played on, was the first LP by a solo male to sell a million CDs. It was also the first album by a UK male to top the US chart for 11 weeks, and the first by a white act to top the US R&B chart.

	US Top 10 Ent	UK Top 10 Ent
Faith	12/87	11/87
Listen Without Prejudice Vol. 1	10/90	9/90

BETTE MIDLER - Top notch singer/entertainer and film/stage actress was born 1945 in New Jersey, USA. She is one of America's best known celebrities of the last 20 years.

	US Top 10 Ent	UK Top 10 Ent
Bette Midler	1/74	
Beaches (Soundtrack)	5/89	
Some People's Lives	12/90	7/91
Experience The Divine - Greatest Hits		11/93

MIKE & THE MECHANICS - British rock band led by Mike Rutherford (of Genesis) with singer Paul Carrack (ex-Ace and Squeeze). Other Mechanics - Adrian Lee, Peter Van Hooke (ex-Van Morrison) and Paul Young (ex-Sad Cafe).

	US Top 10 Ent	UK Top 10 Ent
The Living Years		2/89

BUDDY MILES - See CARLOS SANTANA

GLENN MILLER ORCHESTRA - The world's most popular big band were led by trombone-playing, band leader/arranger Miller, who was born 1904 in Iowa, USA, and died in 1944. The 'Glenn Miller Sound' became famous around the world in the late Thirties and has remained popular ever since.

Album	US Top 10 Ent	UK Top 10 Ent
The Best Of Glenn Miller		7/69
The Unforgettable Glenn Miller		4/77

MITCH MILLER - Multi-talented band leader/producer/arranger and A&R man who was born 1911 in New York, USA. He was the most successful record producer of the Fifties, and had a string of top selling 'Sing Along' albums.

Album	US Top 10 Ent	UK Top 10 Ent
Sentimental Sing Along With Mitch	7/60	
TV Sing Along With Mitch	7/61	
Holiday Sing Along With Mitch	1/62	

ROGER MILLER - Distinctive country singer/songwriter born 1936 in Fort Worth, Texas, USA, died 1992. He was a regular transatlantic hit maker in the mid-Sixties and won six Grammy Awards in 1965.

Album	US Top 10 Ent	UK Top 10 Ent
The Return Of Roger Miller	4/65	
Golden Hits	2/66	

STEVE MILLER BAND - Consistently successful rock band fronted by singer/songwriter Miller, born 1943 in Milwaukee, USA. One of America's top selling album acts in the Seventies.

Album	US Top 10 Ent	UK Top 10 Ent
The Joker	12/73	
Fly Like An Eagle	10/76	
Book Of Dreams	6/77	
Abracadabra	8/82	

MILLI VANILLI - Pop/dance act masterminded by producer Frank Farian (of Boney M fame). John Davis, Brad Howe and Charles Shaw recorded the vocals, which Rob Pilatus and Fabrice Morvan mimed. When Rob and Fab admitted to this situation, they had to return their Grammy for Best New Act of 1990.

Album	US Top 10 Ent	UK Top 10 Ent
Girl You Know It's True	7/89	
All Or Nothing/2 X 2		11/89

MILLICAN & NESBIT - Singing coalminers from the North of England, whose five minutes of fame came courtesy of TV's *Opportunity Knocks* show.

Album	US Top 10 Ent	UK Top 10 Ent
Millican And Nesbit		4/74

KYLIE MINOGUE - Star of Australian TV soap opera, *Neighbours*, who turned successful singer, was born 1968 in Melbourne, Australia. She broke the existing British record when her first seven singles all made the Top 4. She was the youngest female to top the British album chart, and had the biggest selling debut album by a female artist in the UK.

Album	US Top 10 Ent	UK Top 10 Ent
Kylie		7/88
Enjoy Yourself		10/89
Kylie's Greatest Hits		9/92

MIRACLES - See SMOKEY ROBINSON & THE MIRACLES

MIRAGE - Dance act put together by very successful UK producer Nigel Wright, which featured vocalist Kiki Billy from Liverpool, England.

Album	US Top 10 Ent	UK Top 10 Ent
The Best Of Mirage - Jack Mix '88		2/88

MR. MISTER - AOR group formed in Los Angeles, USA. Richard Page, Steve Farris, Steve George and Pat Mastelotto.

Album	US Top 10 Ent	UK Top 10 Ent
Welcome To The Real World	2/86	4/86

GEORGE MITCHELL MINSTRELS - Britain's most successful album act in the pre-Beatles years were a 'blacked-up' minstel chorus formed by noted Scottish arranger George Mitchell (born 1917). The best known soloists were Dai Francis, Tony Mercer and John Boulter. The act is now deemed to be racially offensive.

Album	US Top 10 Ent	UK Top 10 Ent
The Black And White Minstrel Show		12/60
Another Black And White Minstrel Show		10/61
On Stage With The George Mitchell Minstrels		11/62
On Tour With The George Mitchell Minstrels		1/64

JONI MITCHELL - Unmistakable folk singer/songwriter and musician, born Roberta Joan Anderson in 1943 in Alberta, Canada. One of the best known female folk artists in the rock era.

Album	US Top 10 Ent	UK Top 10 Ent
Blue		7/71
Court And Spark	3/74	
Miles Of Aisles	1/75	
The Hissing Of Summer Lawns	12/75	

MONKEES - Pop quartet, formed in Los Angeles for a TV series, achieved instant worldwide fame. Britisher Davy Jones and Americans Peter Tork, Micky Dolenz and Michael Nesmith. They had a record four Number 1 LPs in the USA in 1967 - the year in which they replaced The Beatles as the world's most successful act.

Album	US Top 10 Ent	UK Top 10 Ent
The Monkees	11/66	1/67
Pisces, Aquarius, Capricorn & Jones Ltd	12/67	2/68
More Of The Monkees	2/67	4/67
Headquarters	6/67	7/67
The Birds, The Bees & The Monkees	5/68	

MATT MONRO - Sinatra-styled MOR singer born Terry Parsons in 1932 in London, England, died 1985. Voted Most Promising Artist in America by *Billboard* in 1961.

Album	US Top 10 Ent	UK Top 10 Ent
Heartbreakers		3/80

LOU MONTE - Italian-American singer/guitarist, born 1917 in New Jersey, USA, popular in the USA in the early rock years.

Album	US Top 10 Ent	UK Top 10 Ent
Pepino The Italian Mouse & Other Italian Fun Songs	1/63	

JOHN MICHAEL MONTGOMERY - Kentucky, USA, born country singer who was one of of America's top selling new artists in 1994. His original version of 'I Swear' (a worldwide pop hit for All-4-One) earned him a gold disc.

Album	US Top 10 Ent	UK Top 10 Ent
Kickin' It Up	2/94	

MOODY BLUES - Highly regarded rock quintet from Birmingham, England. Mike Pinder, Ray Thomas, Graeme Edge, Justin Hayward and John Lodge (the latter two replacing Denny Laine and Clint Warwick in 1966). Innovative band who have sold over 50 million albums worldwide.

Album	US Top 10 Ent	UK Top 10 Ent
In Search Of The Lost Chord		9/68
On The Threshold Of A Dream		5/69
To Our Children's Children's Children		12/69
A Question Of Balance	10/70	8/70
Every Good Boy Deserves Favour	9/71	8/71
Days Of Future Passed	10/72	
Seventh Sojourn	12/72	12/72
Octave		7/78
Long Distance Voyager	7/81	
The Other Side Of Life	7/86	

GARY MOORE - Respected blues guitarist born 1954 in Belfast, Ireland. He was a mainstay of Skid Row, Colosseum and Thin Lizzy before starting a successful solo career.

Album	US Top 10 Ent	UK Top 10 Ent
After Hours		3/92

MORMON TABERNACLE CHOIR - Church choir with 375 members, conducted by Richard Condie. They were the largest act to hit the charts.

Album	US Top 10 Ent	UK Top 10 Ent
The Lord's Prayer	1/60	

VAN MORRISON - World renowned performer, who started as lead singer of R&B/rock band Them, was born George Ivan in 1945 in Belfast, Ireland. He is one of the most respected singer/songwriters of the rock era.

Album	US Top 10 Ent	UK Top 10 Ent
The Best Of Van Morrison		4/90
Too Long In Exile		6/93

MORRISSEY - Unmistakable indie rock singer/songwriter from Manchester, England, born Stephen Morrissey in 1959. A unique act of the rock era and originally the leader of ground-breaking group The Smiths.

Album	US Top 10 Ent	UK Top 10 Ent
Vauxhall And I		3/94

MOTLEY CRUE - Platinum plated heavy rock group from Los Angeles, USA. Vince Neil (Vince Wharton), Nikki Sixx (Frank Ferranno), Tommy Lee (Thomas Bass) and Mick Mars (Bob Deal). Few acts have sold more albums since 1985.

Album	US Top 10 Ent	UK Top 10 Ent
Girls Girls Girls	6/87	
Dr. Feelgood	10/89	
Decade Of Decadence	10/91	

MOTORHEAD - Famed British heavy metal act featuring Lemmy Kilminster (ex-Hawkwind), 'Fast Eddie' Clarke and Phil 'Philthy Animal' Taylor.

Album	US Top 10 Ent	UK Top 10 Ent
Ace Of Spades		11/80
No Sleep Til Hammersmith		6/81

NANA MOUSKOURI - Internationally celebrated MOR singer and entertainer, born 1936 in Athens, Greece.

Album	US Top 10 Ent	UK Top 10 Ent
Passport		8/76

ALISON MOYET - Acclaimed pop/rock vocalist born 1961 in Essex, England, also known as 'Alf'. Creative partnership with Vince Clarke in the hitmaking duo Yazoo (Yaz in USA) led to solo success - she won the BRIT award for Top UK Female Artist of 1984 and 1987.

Album	US Top 10 Ent	UK Top 10 Ent
Alf		11/84
Raindancing		4/87

MUD - Rock'n'roll-styled pop quartet led by Les Gray. Other founder members; Rob Davis, Dave Mount and Ray Stiles. They were one of the most successful singles acts in Britain during the Seventies.

Album	US Top 10 Ent	UK Top 10 Ent
Mud Rock Vol. 2		8/75

MARIA MULDAUR - Folk/pop performer born Maria Grazia Rosa Domenica D'Amato in 1943 in New York, USA. The ex-member of Jim Kweskin's Jug Band is best known for her 1974 hit single 'Midnight At The Oasis'.

Album	US Top 10 Ent	UK Top 10 Ent
Maria Muldaur	5/74	

MUPPETS - Well-loved puppets, whose TV series has delighted two generations of children around the world. They were masterminded by Mississippi-born Jim Henson (1936-1990).

Album	US Top 10 Ent	UK Top 10 Ent
The Muppet Show		6/77

ALANNAH MYLES - Award winning rock singer, born in Toronto, Canada, whose debut album reportedly sold a staggering million copies in her homeland.

Album	US Top 10 Ent	UK Top 10 Ent
Alannah Myles	3/90	4/90

N.W.A. - Notorious and often controversial rap group, whose name stands for Niggers With Attitude. Dr. Dre (Andre Young), DJ Yella (Antoine Carraby), MC Ren (Lorenzo Patterson), Eazy-E (Eric Wright) and Ice Cube

(Oshea Jackson). This groundbreaking group, and its spin-offs, provided the template for rap in the Nineties.

	US Top 10 Ent	UK Top 10 Ent
Efil4zaggin	6/91	

JIMMY NAIL - British TV actor (star of *Auf Wiederseh'n Pet, Spender* and *Crocodile Shoes*) born 1955 in Newcastle, England.

	US Top 10 Ent	UK Top 10 Ent
Growing Up In Public		8/92
Crocodile Shoes		12/94

NAUGHTY BY NATURE - Rap trio from New Jersey, USA. Treach (Anthony Criss), Vinnie (Vincent Brown), DJ Kay Gee (Keir Gist). Their singles 'O.P.P.' and 'Hip Hop Hooray' both sold over a million in the USA.

	US Top 10 Ent	UK Top 10 Ent
19 Naughty III	3/93	

NED'S ATOMIC DUSTBIN - Critically praised British rock band led by Jonathan Penney. Matthew Cheslin, Alexander Griffin, Garath Pring, Daniel Worton.

	US Top 10 Ent	UK Top 10 Ent
God Fodder		4/91

RICK(Y) NELSON - Top Fifties pop idol/vocalist/actor from New Jersey, USA, who was virtually raised on TV in his parents' show, *The Adventures Of Ozzie & Harriet.* The sales of his singles, EPs and albums in the early rock years were second only to Elvis. He died in a plane crash in 1985.

	US Top 10 Ent	UK Top 10 Ent
Rick Is 21	8/61	

SANDY NELSON - Acclaimed rock drummer born 1938 in Santa Monica, California, USA, who played on numerous chart records by other people and has had a handful of his own hits.

	US Top 10 Ent	UK Top 10 Ent
Let There Be Drums	3/62	

WILLIE NELSON - Famed country singer/songwriter and founder 'Outlaw' born 1933 in Fort Worth, Texas, USA. The Legendary performer, who has been a country hit-maker for four decades, was elected into the Country Music Hall Of Fame in 1993.

	US Top 10 Ent	UK Top 10 Ent
Always On My Mind	6/82	

NEW EDITION - Five teenage R&B vocalists from Boston, USA, brought together and produced by Maurice Starr. Act included Bobby Brown (who went solo in 1986 and married Whitney Houston in 1992), Ralph Tresvant, Ricky Bell, Michael Bivins and Ronald DeVoe (latter three formed Bell Biv DeVoe in 1990).

	US Top 10 Ent	UK Top 10 Ent
New Edition	2/85	

NEW KIDS ON THE BLOCK - Record breaking teen pop idols from Boston, USA, formed by producer Maurice Starr as a white version of New Edition. Brothers Jon and Jordan Knight, Joe McIntyre, Donny Wahlberg, Danny Wood. The first US group to get six US Top 10 entries in one year (1989), and the first group to score eight UK Top 10s in a year (1990). Their earnings in 1990-91 were over $100 million.

	US Top 10 Ent	UK Top 10 Ent
Hangin' Tough	4/89	1/90
Merry Merry Christmas	12/89	
Step By Step	6/90	7/90

NEW ORDER - Multi-faceted, dance-oriented rock act from Manchester, England (evolved from Joy Division). Bernard Sumner. Gillian Gilbert, Peter Hook and Stephen Morris.

	US Top 10 Ent	UK Top 10 Ent
Power, Corruption And Lies		5/83
Substance		8/87
Technique		2/89
Republic		5/93
? (The Best Of)		12/94

NEW SEEKERS - Successful pop group formed by ex-Seeker Keith Potger. Eve Graham, Lyn Paul, Peter Doyle, Paul Layton and Marty Kristian.

	US Top 10 Ent	UK Top 10 Ent
We'd Like To Teach The World To Sing		4/72

NEW VAUDEVILLE BAND - Twenties-styled session band put together by producer/composer/vocalist Geoff Stevens. However, singer Allen Klein fronted the live act.

	US Top 10 Ent	UK Top 10 Ent
Winchester Cathedral	1/67	

BOB NEWHART - Unique American comedian born 1929 in Illinois, USA. He was one of the top album-selling acts in the early Sixties, and later had several long-running US TV series.

	US Top 10 Ent	UK Top 10 Ent
The Button Down Mind Of Bob Newhart	5/60	11/60
The Button Down Mind Strikes Back!	11/60	

ANTHONY NEWLEY - Acclaimed singer/actor/composer born 1951 in London, England, was once married to actress Joan Collins. He was among the top singles acts in Britain in the early rock years and successfully moved into stage musicals, movies and cabaret.

	US Top 10 Ent	UK Top 10 Ent
Tony		7/61

OLIVIA NEWTON-JOHN - Successful singer/actress born 1948 in Cambridge, England, raised in Australia. She became one of the top female vocalists on both sides of the Atlantic in the Seventies, and starred in the box office smash *Grease.* Her single 'Physical' topped the US chart for 10 weeks.

	US Top 10 Ent	UK Top 10 Ent
If You Love Me, Let Me Know	9/74	
Have You Never Been Mellow	3/75	
Grease (Soundtrack)	7/78	7/78
Totally Hot	3/79	
Xanadu (Soundtrack)	9/80	7/80
Physical	12/81	

NICE - Visually exciting British classical-rock act led by Keith Emerson prior to Emerson, Lake & Palmer's success. Other members: Brian Davison, Lee Jackson and David O'List.

	US Top 10 Ent	UK Top 10 Ent
Five Bridges		7/70
Elegy		4/71

STEVIE NICKS - Top AOR singer born 1948 in Phoenix, USA. Apart from her solo successes she was also a featured member of hitmaking act Fleetwood Mac between 1975 and 1993.

	US Top 10 Ent	UK Top 10 Ent
Bella Donna	8/81	
The Wild Heart	7/83	
The Other Side Of The Mirror		6/89

NILSSON - Singer/songwriter from Brooklyn, New York, USA, born Harry Nelson III in 1941 and died 1994. He is best remembered for his transatlantic Number 1 'Without You' in 1972.

	US Top 10 Ent	UK Top 10 Ent
Nilsson Schmilsson	3/72	3/72

NINE INCH NAILS - Barrier-breaking industrial rock act which is basically a one-man band fronted by singer/songwriter/synth player Trent Reznor from Pennysylvania, USA.

	US Top 10 Ent	UK Top 10 Ent
The Downward Spiral	3/94	

NIRVANA - Hugely popular Seattle-based alternative rock band fronted by acclaimed singer/songwriter Kurt Cobain (died 1994) and including Chris Novoselic, Jason Everman and Chad Channing. One of the most important and imitated groups of the Nineties.

	US Top 10 Ent	UK Top 10 Ent
Nevermind	11/91	
In Utero	10/93	9/93
MTV Unplugged In New York	11/94	11/94

NOLANS - Pop/MOR singing sisters from Ireland. The popular cabaret act were the Nolan Sisters - Ann, Bernice, Colleen, Denise, Linda and Maureen.

	US Top 10 Ent	UK Top 10 Ent
20 Giant Hits		8/78

NOT THE NINE O'CLOCK NEWS CAST - Humorous British TV series which starrred Rowan Atkinson, Griff Rhys Jones, Mel Smith and Pamela Stephenson.

	US Top 10 Ent	UK Top 10 Ent
Not The 9 O'Clock News		11/80

NOTTING HILLBILLIES - Team of guitarists having some rock'n'roll fun. Mark Knopfler, Guy Fletcher (both Dire Straits) with Brendan Croker and Steve Phillips. Named after Notting Hill, an area of London where they recorded.

	US Top 10 Ent	UK Top 10 Ent
Missing...Presumed Having A Good Time		3/90

ALDO NOVA - Noted Candian AOR/pomp metal singer/songwriter and multi-instrumentalist who was born Aldo Scarporuscio in Montreal.

	US Top 10 Ent	UK Top 10 Ent
Aldo Nova	5/82	

GARY NUMAN/TUBEWAY ARMY - Electro/synth new wave rocker from London, England, born Gary Webb in 1958. Dropped band name after first hit. He had a remarkable 23 solo singles in the UK chart in the Eighties.

	US Top 10 Ent	UK Top 10 Ent
Replicas (as Tubeway Army)		7/79
The Pleasure Principal		9/79
Telekon		9/80
Living Ornaments 1979-1980		5/81
Dance		9/81

OASIS - Manchester-based alternative rock band. Liam and Noel Gallagher, Paul Arthurs, Paul McGuigan and Tony McCarroll. Darlings of the UK music media in 1994.

	US Top 10 Ent	UK Top 10 Ent
Definitely Maybe		9/94

BILLY OCEAN - R&B/pop singer/songwriter born Leslie Charles in Trindiad in 1950. He was the most successful British-based R&B artist in the Eighties and America's most successful male R&B vocalist in 1986.

	US Top 10 Ent	UK Top 10 Ent
Love Zone	6/86	5/86
Tear Down These Walls		3/88
Greatest Hits		11/89

SINEAD O'CONNOR - Distinctive and often controversial singer/songwriter born 1967 in Dublin. She was the first Irish-born female singer to top the transatlantic album charts.

	US Top 10 Ent	UK Top 10 Ent
I Do Not Want What I Haven't Got	4/90	3/90

ESTHER & ABI OFARIM - Israeli husband and wife team of Esther Zaled (born 1943) and Abi Reichstadt (born 1939). Best known for the UK chart topping single 'Cinderella Rockafella' in 1968.

	US Top 10 Ent	UK Top 10 Ent
2 In 3		4/68

OFFSPRING - Top-selling West Coast band who helped turn punk rock to platinum in the mid-1990s. Bryan Holland, Kevin Wasserman, Ron Welty and Greg Kriesel. After five years of recording and playing in relative obscurity, the California quartet became one of the hottest acts in the business in 1994.

	US Top 10 Ent	UK Top 10 Ent
Smash	10/94	

OHIO PLAYERS - Respected R&B/funk group, who became one of the top soul acts of the Seventies. Billy Beck, Leroy Bonner, Marshall Jones, Ralph Middlebrook, Marvin Pierce, Clarence Satchell, Jimmy Williams.

	US Top 10 Ent	UK Top 10 Ent
Fire	12/74	
Honey	9/75	

O'JAYS - Perennially successful R&B vocal group from Ohio, USA. Eddie Levert, Bill Isles, Bobby Massey, William Powell (died 1977), Walter Williams. One of the acts that put the Philly Sound on the musical map in the Seventies.

	US Top 10 Ent	UK Top 10 Ent
Family Reunion	1/76	
So Full Of Love	6/78	

MIKE OLDFIELD - Critically acclaimed classical rock multi-instumentalist and composer from Reading, England, born 1953. His **Tubular Bells** sold over 1.8 million in the UK and 16 million worldwide.

	US Top 10 Ent	UK Top 10 Ent
Tubular Bells	3/74	9/73
Hergest Ridge		9/74
Ommadawn		11/75
Crisis		7/83
Tubular Bells II		9/92
Elements - The Best Of Mike Oldfield		10/93

OMD - See ORCHESTRAL MANOEUVRES IN THE DARK

ONE HUNDRED & ONE STRINGS - Session orchestra (often recorded in Europe) masterminded by US record company boss Dave Miller, who earlier had helped such artists as Bill Haley and Al Martino on their way to fame.

	US Top 10 Ent	UK Top 10 Ent
Down Drury Lane To Memory Lane		9/60

ALEXANDER O'NEAL - Soulful R&B/dance singer born 1953 in Mississippi, USA, who previously sang in Flyte Time with his later producers/composers, Jimmy Jam and Terry Lewis. Hearsay sold over 500,000 in Briitain and contained five UK Top 30 singles.

	US Top 10 Ent	UK Top 10 Ent
Hearsay/All Mixed Up		3/88
All True Man		2/91
This Thing Called Love - Greatest Hits		6/92

ORB - Unique British Alternative dance act formed by ex A&R man and Club DJ Alex Paterson and Jimmy Cauty (who left in 1989 to concentrate on KLF). They were the first act to ask for their name to be removed from the BRIT award nominations.

	US Top 10 Ent	UK Top 10 Ent
U.F.Orb		7/92
Pomme Fritz		6/94

ROY ORBISON - Legendary singer/songwriter born 1936 in Vernon, Texas, USA, died of a heart attack in 1988. He had an enviable string of transatlantic hit singles that covered five decades. The most successful US act in Britain in the early Beatles era.

	US Top 10 Ent	UK Top 10 Ent
In Dreams		12/63
Oh Pretty Woman		1/65
The Best Of Roy Orbison		1/76
The Legendary Roy Orbison		1/89
Mystery Girl	3/89	2/89

ORCHESTRAL MANOEUVRES IN THE DARK - Synth-led rock band from Liverpool, England, formed by Andy McCluskey and Paul Humphreys. One of Britain's most consistently successful acts of the Eighties, returned to the charts in the Nineties, minus Humphreys and long time members Martin Cooper and Martin Holmes.

	US Top 10 Ent	UK Top 10 Ent
Organisation		11/80
Architecture And Morality		11/81
Dazzle Ships		3/83
The Best Of OMD		3/88
Sugar Tax		5/91

ORIGINAL CAST

	US Top 10 Ent	UK Top 10 Ent
My Fair Lady		3/60
Flower Drum Song		4/60
The Sound Of Music	1/60	7/61
Camelot	1/61	
Wildcat	3/61	
Carnival	7/61	
West Side Story	5/62	3/62
No Strings	6/62	
Stop The World-I Want To Get Off	1/63	
Hello, Dolly!	3/64	
Fiddler On The Roof	2/65	
Hair	4/69	
Aspects Of Love		9/89

ORIGINAL LONDON CAST

	US Top 10 Ent	UK Top 10 Ent
Follow That Girl		5/60
Oliver		9/60
Music Man		6/61
Sound Of Music		8/61
Blitz		7/62
Fiddler On The Roof		5/67
Hair		2/69
Phantom Of The Opera		2/87

CYRIL ORNADEL - See LONDON SYMPHONY ORCHESTRA

OZZY OSBOURNE - Grammy-winning heavy metal hero (ex-Black Sabbath vocalist) born 1948 in Birmingham, England. Platinum-plated performer is one of the legends of the genre.

	US Top 10 Ent	UK Top 10 Ent
The Ultimate Sin	3/86	
Tribute	6/87	

DONNY OSMOND - Top transatlantic teen idol in the Seventies, born 1957 in Utah, USA. He was was lead singer of family act The Osmonds and also had hits duetting with sister Marie.

	US Top 10 Ent	UK Top 10 Ent
Portrait Of Donny	7/72	12/72
Too Young		12/72
Alone Together		6/73
A Time For Us		12/73

OSMONDS - One of the most successful and best supported groups of the Seventies were The Osmond Brothers, Donny, Alan, Wayne, Merrill and Jay from Utah, USA. The family had an enviable collection of hit singles and albums.

	US Top 10 Ent	UK Top 10 Ent
The Plan		9/73
Our Best To You		9/74

GILBERT O'SULLIVAN - Piano-playing singer/songwriter from Waterford, Ireland, born Raymond O'Sullivan in 1946. Managed by Gordon Mills (Tom Jones, Engelbert Humperdinck), whom he later sued for £2 ($3.5) million.

	US Top 10 Ent	UK Top 10 Ent
Himself		4/72
Back To Front		11/72
I'm A Writer Not A Fighter		10/73

OUTFIELD - British AOR trio who were far more successful in the USA. Alan Jackman, Tony Lewis, John Spinks.

	US Top 10 Ent	UK Top 10 Ent
Play Deep	6/86	

PABLO CRUISE - Smooth rock group from San Francisco, USA. Dave Jenkins, Cory Lerios and Stephen Price (all ex-Stoneground), Bud Cockrell (ex-It's A Beautiful Day).

	US Top 10 Ent	UK Top 10 Ent
Worlds Away	8/78	

ELAINE PAIGE - British MOR singer and actress born 1948. First found fame playing the lead in the musical *Evita.* She was a regular chart visitor in the Eighties.

	US Top 10 Ent	UK Top 10 Ent
Stages		12/83

ROBERT PALMER - Grammy-winning rock vocalist born 1949 in Yorkshire, England. The internationally known artist was also lead singer of the one-album super-group, Power Station.

	US Top 10 Ent	UK Top 10 Ent
Riptide	5/86	8/86

PANTERA - Rough-edged thrash metal outfit from Texas, USA, who have built up a large and loyal US following. Philip Anselmo, Dimebag Darrell, brothers Rex and Vinnie Paul.

	US Top 10 Ent	UK Top 10 Ent
Far Beyond Driven	4/94	

MICA PARIS - Soulful singer born Michelle Wallen in 1969 in London, England. One of the most outstanding British-born black vocalists.

	US Top 10 Ent	UK Top 10 Ent
So Good		9/88

ALAN PARSONS PROJECT - London-based producer/musician/engineer Alan Parsons and his songwriter/musician manager Eric Woolfson led this successful team of session musicians and vocalists.

	US Top 10 Ent	UK Top 10 Ent
Eye In The Sky	10/82	

DOLLY PARTON - See EMMYLOU HARRIS

PARTRIDGE FAMILY - Transatlantically successful TV family, who on record featured Mrs Partridge (Shirley Jones) and eldest son Keith Partridge (her real life stepson David Cassidy). Cassidy, one of the top teen idols of the Seventies, also had a successful solo career.

	US Top 10 Ent	UK Top 10 Ent
The Partridge Family Album	1/71	
Up To Date	4/71	

PASADENAS - Well choreographed British R&B vocal group are 'Rockin' Jeff Brown, John Andrew Banfield, brothers David and Michael Milliner and Hammish Seelochan.

	US Top 10 Ent	UK Top 10 Ent
To Whom It May Concern		10/88

LUCIANO PAVAROTTI - Internationally successful operatic tenor born 1935 in Modena, Italy. He is arguably the best known classical performer in the world today.

	US Top 10 Ent	UK Top 10 Ent
The Essential Pavarotti		6/90
Essential Pavarotti II		7/91

LUCIANO PAVAROTTI, PLACIDO DOMINGO & JOSE CARRERAS - Three of the world's best-known opera singers. Their first album is the top selling classical album of all time and proved that operatic music could be a commercial proposition in the Nineties

	US Top 10 Ent	UK Top 10 Ent
In Concert		9/90
The 3 Tenors In Concert 1994	9/94	9/94

PEACHES & HERB - Soul/dance duo from Washington, D.C., USA, were originally Herb Fame and Francine Barker. Latter-day Peaches were Marlene Mack (1968-69) and Linda Green (1977 on).

	US Top 10 Ent	UK Top 10 Ent
2 Hot!	3/79	

PEARL JAM - Highly rated modern rock group from Seattle, USA, who evolved from Mother Love Bone. Eddie Vedder, Jeff Ament, Stone Gossard, Dave Krusen, Mike McCready. America's top selling album group in 1993 and 1994.

	US Top 10 Ent	UK Top 10 Ent
Ten	6/92	
Vs.	11/93	10/93
Vitalogy	12/94	

TEDDY PENDERGRASS - Smooth R&B/soul singer was born 1950 in Philadelphia, USA, who became one of the best known soul sex symbols. He fronted Harold Melvin's Blue Notes before going solo in 1976. He was paralyzed after a car crash in 1982.

	US Top 10 Ent	UK Top 10 Ent
Teddy	8/79	

PENTANGLE - Acclaimed British acoustic folk act whose members included vocalist Jacqui McShee and noted musicians Bert Jansch and John Renbourn.

	US Top 10 Ent	UK Top 10 Ent
Basket Of Light		2/70

PET SHOP BOYS - One of Britain's most successful pop duos of all time are vocalist Neil Tennant and keyboard wizard Chris Lowe. The BRIT winning act had 16 consecutive UK Top 20 singles.

	US Top 10 Ent	UK Top 10 Ent
Please	6/86	4/86
Pet Shop Boys, Actually		9/87
Introspective		10/88
Behaviour		11/90
Discography		11/91
Very		10/93

PETER, PAUL & MARY - Foremost sixties folk trio were based in New York, USA. Peter Yarrow, Paul Stookey and Mary Travers. They gave Bob Dylan his first hit as a writer and were one of the biggest selling album acts of the Sixties, who at times held the top two chart rungs simultaneously.

	US Top 10 Ent	UK Top 10 Ent
Peter, Paul & Mary	7/62	
(Moving)	2/63	
In The Wind	11/63	
Peter, Paul And Mary In Concert	9/64	
A Song Will Rise	5/65	

PETERS & LEE - MOR duo of Lennie Peters and Di Lee hit the big-time after winning *Opportunity Knocks* - a British TV talent contest. Veteran performer Peters, uncle of Rolling Stone Charlie Watts, had been blind from the age of 16.

	US Top 10 Ent	UK Top 10 Ent
We Can Make It		7/73
Rainbow		10/74
Favourites		10/75

TOM PETTY & THE HEARTBREAKERS - Famed rock band formed in Los Angeles, USA, by Tom Petty (born 1953 in Florida, USA). Other members: Ron Blair, Mike Campbell, Stan Lynch, Benmont Tench. The group have been regular chart entrants since the late Seventies.

	US Top 10 Ent	UK Top 10 Ent
Damn The Torpedoes	12/79	
Hard Promises	6/81	
Southern Accents	5/85	
Full Moon Fever	6/89	
Into The Great White Open		7/91
Greatest Hits	2/94	

BARRINGTON PHELOUNG - Conductor/composer born 1955 in Sydney, Australia, who relocated to the UK in 1977. He wrote music for several British TV shows including *Beyond The Pale, Lovebirds* and *Inspector Morse.*

	US Top 10 Ent	UK Top 10 Ent
Inspector Morse - Music From The TV Series		4/91

PHOTOS - Blondie-influenced British group fronted by Wendy Wu. Other members: Steve Eagles, Olly Harrison and Dave Sparrow.

	US Top 10 Ent	UK Top 10 Ent
The Photos		6/80

PINK FLOYD - British progressive rock band who specialize in extravagant live shows. Syd Barrett (replaced by Dave Gilmour in 1968), Nick Mason, Roger Waters (left in 1986), Rick Wright. **Dark Side Of The Moon**, which has sold 25 million world-wide, spent a record 14 years on the US Top 200. In all, the act have sold over 125 million records and have played to countless millions of fans around the world.

	US Top 10 Ent	UK Top 10 Ent
Piper At The Gates Of Dawn		9/67
Ummagumma		11/69
Atom Heart Mother		10/70
Meddle		11/71
Dark Side Of The Moon	4/73	3/73
Wish You Were Here	10/75	9/75
Animals	3/77	2/77
The Wall	1/80	12/79
The Final Cut	4/83	4/83
A Momentary Lapse Of Reason	10/87	9/87
The Division Bell	4/94	4/94

GENE PITNEY - Enduring and distinctive pop singer/songwriter born 1941 in Connecticut, USA. One of the most successful American male singers of the Sixties, who also penned hits for other artists including 'Hello Mary Lou', 'He's A Rebel' and 'Rubber Ball'.

	US Top 10 Ent	UK Top 10 Ent
Blue Gene		5/64

PIXIES - Critically acclaimed Boston-based alternative rock band fronted by Black Francis (born Charles Kitridge Thompson IV). Other members: Kim Deal, David Lovering, Joey Santiago. They were voted Best New American Band by *Rolling Stone* in 1989.

	US Top 10 Ent	UK Top 10 Ent
Bossanova		8/90

ROBERT PLANT - World renowned rock singer born 1948 in West Bromwich, England. Lead vocalist of the record-shattering Led Zeppelin (1968-80) and The Honeydrippers (1984).

	US Top 10 Ent	UK Top 10 Ent
Pictures At Eleven	8/82	7/82
The Principle Of Moments	10/83	
Now And Zen	4/88	

PLATTERS - The most successful vocal group of the early rock years were based in Los Angeles, USA, and fronted by Tony Williams (died 1992). The group's best known line-up also included David Lynch (died 1981), Herb Reed, Paul Robi (died 1989), and Zola Taylor.

	US Top 10 Ent	UK Top 10 Ent
Encore Of Golden Hits	5/60	
20 Classic Hits		5/78

POGUES - Eight-member Celtic punk band led by the outrageous Shane MacGowan. Other members have included Cait O'Riordan, Jem Finer, Spider Stacy and Joe Strummer (ex-Clash).

	US Top 10 Ent	UK Top 10 Ent
If I Should Fall From Grace With God		2/88

POINTER SISTERS - Multi-faceted trio of singing sisters from Oakland, California, USA. Anita, Bonnie and Ruth. Youngest sister, June, joined in early Seventies while Bonnie quit for a solo career in 1978. They are one of only a few acts to have had hits in the pop, R&B, MOR and country music fields.

	US Top 10 Ent	UK Top 10 Ent
Break Out		8/84

POISON - Successful heavy rock band from Pennsylvania, USA. Bret Michaels, Bobby Dall, CC DeVille and Rikki Rockett. They were one of the late Eighties top selling rock bands.

	US Top 10 Ent	UK Top 10 Ent
Look What The Cat Dragged In	4/87	
Open Up And Say Ahh	6/88	
Flesh And Blood	8/90	7/90

POLICE - World famous British-based rock trio consisted of English born Sting (Gordon Sumner) and Andy Summers plus Egyptian-born American, Stewart Copeland (ex-Curved Air). Five of their albums entered the UK chart in peak position and they had Number 1 singles on both sides of the Atlantic. The award winning group disbanded in the mid-Eighties, while still at the top. Sting has since pursued a solo career.

	US Top 10 Ent	UK Top 10 Ent
Outlandos D'amour		8/79
Reggatta De Blanc		10/79
Zenyatta Mondatta	12/80	10/80
Ghost In The Machine	11/81	10/81
Synchronicity	7/83	6/83
Every Breath You Take - The Singles	12/86	11/86

PORNO FOR PYROS - Rock band formed by Perry Farrell (ex-Jane's Addiction), who instigated the successful Lollapalooza tours. Other members were Peter DiStefano, Martyn Le Noble and Stephen Perkins.

	US Top 10 Ent	UK Top 10 Ent
Porno For Pyros	5/93	

POWER STATION - Short-lived rock supergroup led by Robert Palmer with Andy Taylor and John Taylor (both Duran Duran) and Tony Thompson (Chic).

	US Top 10 Ent	UK Top 10 Ent
The Power Station	6/85	

PREFAB SPROUT - Noteworthy pop/rock act from Newcastle, England, featuring singer/songwriter Paddy McAloon with brother Martin, Neil Conti and Wendy Smith.

	US Top 10 Ent	UK Top 10 Ent
A Life Of Surprises - The Best Of ..		7/92

ELVIS PRESLEY - World's most famous rock singer and most successful solo recording artist of all time (sales reported to be over one billion) was born 1935 in Tupelo, Mississippi, USA, and died 1977. He broke and set countless records, won hundreds of awards, endlessly collected gold and platinum records and influenced thousands of performers. Among his many feats was having 10 tracks simultaneously in the US Top 100 singles, and 27 albums simultaneously in the UK Top 100.

	US Top 10 Ent	UK Top 10 Ent
Elvis Is Back!	5/60	7/60
Elvis' Golden Records Vol. 2		7/60
G.I. Blues (Soundtrack)	11/60	12/60
His Hand In Mine		5/61
Something For Everybody	8/61	11/61
Blue Hawaii (Soundtrack)	11/61	12/61
Girls! Girls! Girls! (Soundtrack)	12/62	2/63
Pot Luck	8/62	7/62
Rock 'n' Roll No. 2		12/62
Elvis' Golden Records, Vol. 3	10/63	4/64
It Happened At The World's Fair (Soundtrack)	5/63	5/63
Fun In Acapulco (Soundtrack)	1/64	2/64
Kissin' Cousins (Soundtrack)	5/64	7/64
Roustabout (Soundtrack)	12/64	
Girl Happy (Soundtrack)	6/65	5/65
Elvis For Everybody		12/65
Paradise Hawaiian Style (Soundtrack)		8/66
Elvis	2/69	5/69
Flaming Star		7/69
From Elvis In Memphis		8/69
From Memphis To Vegas - From Vegas To Memphis		3/70
On Stage		8/70
Elvis Country		4/71
C'mon Everybody		8/71
Elvis At Madison Square Garden		7/72
Aloha From Hawaii Via Satellite	4/73	
Moody Blue	9/77	9/77
40 Greatest Hits		9/77
Elvis In Concert	11/77	
Love Songs		12/79
Inspiration		12/80
Presley - The All Time Greatest Hits		9/87
From The Heart - His Greatest Love Songs		2/92
The Essential Collection		9/94

PRETENDERS - Popular Anglo-American rock band led by Ohio-born singer/songwriter and guitarist Chrissie Hynde, who married Jim Kerr of Simple Minds in 1984. Other members included Martin Chambers, Pete Farndon (died 1983) and James Honeyman-Scott (died 1982).

	US Top 10 Ent	UK Top 10 Ent
Pretenders		1/80

	US Top 10 Ent	UK Top 10 Ent
Pretenders II	9/81	8/81
Learning To Crawl	2/84	
The Singles		11/87

PRETTY THINGS - Revered Sixties British rock band, whose hair made The Rolling Stones seem clean-cut, and whose rock opera, *S.F. Sorrow*, pre-dated The Who's *Tommy*. Members included Phil May, Dick Taylor and Viv Prince.

	US Top 10 Ent	UK Top 10 Ent
Pretty Things		4/65

CHARLEY PRIDE - By far the most successful black country singer of all time was born 1938 in Mississippi, USA. His 29 Number 1 country hit singles spanned 1969-1983.

	US Top 10 Ent	UK Top 10 Ent
Golden Collection		2/80

PRIMAL SCREAM - Critically praised British rock/dance group whose **Screamadelica** was voted Top Album of 1992 by NME and won the Mercury Music Prize. Bobby Gillespie, Denise Johnson, Robert Young, Andrew Innes and Martin Duffy.

	US Top 10 Ent	UK Top 10 Ent
Give Out, But Don't Give Up		4/94

PRINCE - World renowned rock/funk performer from Minneapolis, USA, born Prince Rogers Nelson in 1958. This singer/songwriter/multi-instrumentalist/ producer and label-owner is one of the most prolific and successful recording artists in the world. His soundtrack album **Purple Rain** topped the US charts for 24 weeks. One of the true greats of the rock era.

	US Top 10 Ent	UK Top 10 Ent
1999	6/83	
Purple Rain (Soundtrack)	7/84	
Around The World In A Day	5/85	5/85
Parade - Music From 'Under The Cherry Moon'	5/86	4/86
Sign 'O' The Times	5/87	4/87
Lovesexy		5/88
Batman (Soundtrack)	7/89	7/89
Graffiti Bridge	9/90	9/90
Diamonds & Pearls	10/91	10/91
Symbol		10/92
The Hits 2		10/93
Come		8/94

PROCUL HARUM - Classical rock band from Southend, England. Members included Gary Booker, Matthew Fisher, Bobby Harrison, Dave Knights, Keith Reid, Ray Royer and Robin Trower. Best known for their multi-million selling single 'Whiter Shade Of Pale'.

	US Top 10 Ent	UK Top 10 Ent
Procol Harum Live In Concert With The Edmonton Symphony Orchestra	7/72	

PRODIGY - Very successful self-contained rave music act masterminded by keyboard player Liam Howlett (born 1972). Britain's top-selling hardcore dance act.

	US Top 10 Ent	UK Top 10 Ent
Music For The Jilted Generation		7/94

DOROTHY PROVINE - Actress/singer born 1937 in Deadwood, South Dakota, USA. Her starring role in US TV series *The Roaring Twenties* led to a couple of hit records.

	US Top 10 Ent	UK Top 10 Ent
The Roaring Twenties - Songs From The TV Series		12/61

PUBLIC ENEMY - Controversial and ground breaking rap group who greatly influenced the direction of the genre in the Nineties. Chuck D. (Carlton Ridenhauer) plus DJ Terminator X (Norman Rogers), MC Flavor-Flave (William Drayton) and Professor Griff (Richard Griffin).

	US Top 10 Ent	UK Top 10 Ent
Apocalypse 91... The Enemy Strikes Black	10/91	

QUARTERFLASH - Rock group from Portland, Oregon, USA, who had a brief fling with fame. Marv and Lindy Ross (husband and wife), Jack Charles, Rick DiGiallonardo, Brian David Willis and Rick Gooch.

	US Top 10 Ent	UK Top 10 Ent
Quarterflash	3/82	

SUZI QUATRO - Trend-setting female rock singer/guitarist born Suzi Quatrocchio in 1950 in Detroit, USA. She became one of the top singles acts in Britain during the Seventies - thanks in part to the songs and productions of Nicky Chinn and Mike Chapman.

	US Top 10 Ent	UK Top 10 Ent
Suzi Quatro's Greatest Hits		5/80

QUEEN - Legendary rock group, whose transatlantic hits covered three decades, were fronted by supreme showman Freddie Mercury (died 1991). Brian May, John Deacon and Roger Taylor completed the award winning quartet. Their single 'Bohemian Rhapsody' earned them a US gold record on two occasions, and is the only record to top the UK charts twice. Their **Greatest Hits** was the first album certified 11 times platinum in the UK (3.3 million sales).

	US Top 10 Ent	UK Top 10 Ent
Queen 2		4/74
Sheer Heart Attack		11/74
A Night At The Opera	3/76	12/75
A Day At The Races	2/77	1/77
News Of The World	1/78	11/77
Jazz	12/78	12/78
Live Killers		7/79
The Game	8/80	7/80
Greatest Hits		11/81
Hot Space		5/82
The Works		3/84
A Kind Of Magic		6/86
Live Magic		12/86
The Miracle		6/89
Innuendo		2/91
Greatest Hits II		11/91
Classic Queen	5/92	
Live At Wembley '86		6/92

QUEENSRYCHE - Top selling heavy metal band from Washington, USA. Geoff Tate, Chris DeGarmo, Eddie Jackson, Scott Rockenfield, Michael Wilton.

	US Top 10 Ent	UK Top 10 Ent
Empire	10/90	
Promised Land	11/94	

QUIET RIOT - Heavy metal group from Los Angeles, USA, who owed something to British group Slade. Kevin DuBrown, Frankie Banali, Carlos Cavazo and Rudy Sarzo. An earlier line-up included noted guitarist Randy Rhoads (died 1982), who was later in Ozzy Osbourne's band.

	US Top 10 Ent	UK Top 10 Ent
Metal Health	10/83	

QUIREBOYS - Seventies-influenced hard rock band, origianally called themselves The Queerboys, who built up a solid UK following. Spike, Nigel Mogg, Guy Bailey, Guy Griffin, Chris Johnstone and Ian Wallace.

	US Top 10 Ent	UK Top 10 Ent
A Bit Of What You Fancy		2/90

R.E.M.

	US Top 10 Ent	UK Top 10 Ent
Out Of Time	4/90	3/91
Automatic For The People	10/92	10/92
Monster	10/94	10/94

GERRY RAFFERTY - Folk/pop singer/songwriter and guitarist born 1947 in Paisley, Scotland. After leaving folk duet The Humblebums (with comedian Billy Connolly), he fronted the hit pop group Stealers Wheel and in 1978 had transatlantic solo succcess.

	US Top 10 Ent	UK Top 10 Ent
City To City	6/78	4/78

RAINBOW - Well respected hard rock group formed by Ritchie Blackmore (ex-Deep Purple). Members have included Roger Glover (ex-Deep Purple) Ronnie James Dio, Graham Bonnet (ex-Marbles), Joe Lynn Turner and noted drummer Cozy Powell.

	US Top 10 Ent	UK Top 10 Ent
On Stage		8/77
Long Live Rock 'n' Roll		5/78
Difficult To Cure		2/81

BONNIE RAITT - Veteran blues-rock vocalist and guitarist born 1949 in Burbank, California, USA, whose career really took off after 17 years when **Nick Of Time** was voted Best Album of 1989 at the Grammy awards.

	US Top 10 Ent	UK Top 10 Ent
Nick Of Time	• 3/90	
Luck Of The Draw	7/91	
Longing In Their Hearts	4/94	

RASCALS - Top selling pop/blue-eyed soul group from New York first recorded as The Young Rascals. Felix Cavaliere, Eddie Brigati, Gene Cornish (all ex-Joey Dee's Starliters) and Dino Danelli. One of the most popular American groups of the late Sixties.

	US Top 10 Ent	UK Top 10 Ent
Groovin'	9/67	
Time Peace/The Rascals' Greatest Hits	8/68	

RATT - Successful mid-Eighties heavy rock band from Los Angeles, USA. Stephen Pearcy. Bobby Blotzer, Robin Crosby, Juan Croucier, Warren DeMartini.

	US Top 10 Ent	UK Top 10 Ent
Out Of The Cellar	8/84	
Invasion Of Your Privacy	7/85	

LOU RAWLS - Grammy winning jazz-based soul vocalist was born 1935 in Chicago, USA. After many years in the business, this one-time professional gospel singer, found pop fame when he joined Philly International Records.

	US Top 10 Ent	UK Top 10 Ent
Lou Rawls Live!	7/66	
Lou Rawls Soulin'	11/66	
All Things In Time	9/76	

CHRIS REA - Acclaimed pop/rock performer born 1951 in Middlesborough, England, who was a huge European star before eventually cracking the British Top 10. One of the UK's top selling singer/songwriters since the late Eighties.

	US Top 10 Ent	UK Top 10 Ent
Dancing With Strangers		10/87
New Light Through Old Windows		11/88
The Road To Hell		11/89
Auberge		3/91
God's Great Banana Skin		11/92
The Best Of Chris Rea		11/94

OTIS REDDING - Unique soul vocalist/songwriter born 1941 in Georgia, USA, died 1967 in an airplane crash. One of the first, and arguably the most important and influential, soul singers in the Sixties. Voted World's Top Male Singer in Britain in 1967.

	US Top 10 Ent	UK Top 10 Ent
Otis Blue		3/66
History Of Otis Redding		3/68
The Dock Of The Bay	4/68	6/68

HELEN REDDY - Top Australian singer born 1941 in Melbourne, relocated to USA in 1966, where she had a string of hit singles and albums in the Seventies.

	US Top 10 Ent	UK Top 10 Ent
Helen Reddy's Greatest Hits	1/76	2/76

RED HOT CHILI PEPPERS - Rock funk act from Los Angeles, USA. Michael 'Flea' Balzary, Jack Irons, Anthony Kiedis, Hillel Slovak (died 1988). They moved from cult heroes to chart regulars in the Nineties when they earned both Grammy and MTV awards.

	US Top 10 Ent	UK Top 10 Ent
Blood Sugar Sex Magik	5/92	

JIM REEVES - Internationally famous country/MOR singer who was born 1924 in Texas, USA, and died in an airplane crash in 1964. He is one of the biggest selling country artists of all time. Reeves had a record eight albums simultaneously in the UK Top 20 in 1964, and even manged to chart in Britain 30 years after his death.

Album	US Top 10 Ent	UK Top 10 Ent
Gentleman Jim		8/64
Moonlight And Roses		9/64
Twelve Songs Of Christmas		12/64
Best Of Jim Reeves		2/65
Distant Drums		11/66
According To My Heart		7/69
40 Golden Greats		10/75

NEIL REID - When this British singer was 11 years old he became the youngest person to top the UK LP chart. His short-lived success was due to his regular wins on the TV talent show *Opportunity Knocks.*

Album	US Top 10 Ent	UK Top 10 Ent
Neil Reid		2/72

REO SPEEDWAGON - Very popular AOR power rock band from Illinois, USA. Kevin Cronin, Neal Doughty, Alan Gratzer, Bruce Hall, Gary Richrath. They have earned eight platinum albums in their homeland, including **Hi-Infidelity**, which was a Number 1 for 15 weeks selling over seven million copies.

Album	US Top 10 Ent	UK Top 10 Ent
Hi Infidelity	2/81	8/81
Good Trouble	8/82	
Wheels Are Turnin'	3/85	

PAUL REVERE & THE RAIDERS - 'Revolutionary'-styled teen pop/rock group from Portland, Oregon, USA. Fronted by keyboardist Paul Revere (born 1942 in Boise, Idaho, USA) and lead vocalist Mark Lindsay. They were among America's top teen idols of the Sixties when they were seldom off the American charts.

Album	US Top 10 Ent	UK Top 10 Ent
Just Like Us!	4/66	
The Spirit Of '67	2/67	

CHARLIE RICH - Versatile singer/songwriter and pianist born 1932 in Arkansas, USA, also known as 'The Silver Fox'. The jazz/blues/rockabilly/MOR performer first recorded for Sun Records.

Album	US Top 10 Ent	UK Top 10 Ent
Behind Closed Doors	2/74	5/74

CLIFF RICHARD - Britain's most successful solo artist of all time was born Harry Webb in 1940 in Lucknow, India. This award winning pop/rock singer has been at the top of his profession for five decades and despite relatively little US success has sold over 80 million records. He has had 33 Top 10 albums in the UK and no artist (Elvis included) has beaten his 64 Top 10 singles.

Album	US Top 10 Ent	UK Top 10 Ent
Cliff Sings		3/60
Me And My Shadows		10/60
Listen To Cliff		4/61
21 Today		11/61
The Young Ones (Soundtrack)		1/62
32 Minutes And 17 Seconds		10/62
Summer Holiday (Soundtrack)		1/63
Cliff's Hit Album		7/63
When In Spain		10/63
Wonderful Life (Soundtrack)		7/64
Finders Keepers (Soundtrack)		1/67
Best Of Cliff		7/69
I'm Nearly Famous		6/76
Every Face Tells A Story		4/77
40 Golden Greats		10/77
Thank You Very Much - Reunion Concert At The London Palladium		3/79
Rock 'n' Roll Juvenile		9/79
I'm No Hero		9/80
Love Songs		7/81
Wired For Sound		10/81
Now You See Me, Now You Don't		9/82
Private Collection		11/88
From A Distance...The Event		12/90
The Album		5/93
The Hit List		10/94

LIONEL RICHIE - R&B/pop singer/songwriter born 1949 in Alabama, USA. Lead singer of The Commodores from 1970-82. He was arguably the most successful songwriter of the Eighties with 13 successive US Top 10 singles. He wrote a US chart topper every year for a record eight years in a row.

Album	US Top 10 Ent	UK Top 10 Ent
Lionel Richie	11/82	
Can't Slow Down	11/83	11/83
Dancing On The Ceiling	9/86	8/86
Back To Front		6/92

RIGHT SAID FRED - Zany pop/rock trio from London, England. Brothers Fred and Richard Fairbrass with Rob Manzoli. Their debut single 'I'm Too Sexy' sold over a million in the USA.

Album	US Top 10 Ent	UK Top 10 Ent
Up		3/92

RIGHTEOUS BROTHERS - Celebrated blue-eyed soul duo of Bill Medley (from California) and Bobby Hatfield (from Wisconsin). One of the Sixties most popular acts whose Phil Spector-produced recordings, including 'You've Lost That Lovin' Feelin" and the two-time transatlantic hit 'Unchained Melody', are regarded as rock classics.

Album	US Top 10 Ent	UK Top 10 Ent
You've Lost That Lovin' Feelin'	2/65	
Just Once In My Life...	8/65	
Soul & Inspiration	5/66	

WALDO DE LOS RIOS - Conductor/composer/arranger born 1934 in Buenos Aires, Argentina and died 1977. Noted film score composer who relocated to Spain in 1982 after working in the USA since 1958.

Album	US Top 10 Ent	UK Top 10 Ent
Symphonies For The Seventies		5/71

MINNIE RIPERTON - R&B/pop song stylist born 1947 in Chicago, USA, died 1979. Before successfuly going solo in 1974, she had recorded in The Gems, Rotary Connection and in Stevie Wonder's backing group, Wonderlove.

Album	US Top 10 Ent	UK Top 10 Ent
Perfect Angel	3/75	

JOHNNY RIVERS - Top Sixties rock singer/songwriter born Johnny Ramistella in 1942 in New York, USA. After a successful recording career he later owned the hit label, Soul City, which scored with acts like Fifth Dimension.

Album	US Top 10 Ent	UK Top 10 Ent
Realization	8/68	

MARTY ROBBINS - DistinctiveTex-Mex country singer/songwriter and guitarist from Arizona, USA, born Martin Robinson in 1925, died 1982. He was one of the first country artists to regularly reach the US Top 20 pop singles charts, and one of the first to find international success.

Album	US Top 10 Ent	UK Top 10 Ent
Gunfighter Ballads And Trail Songs	2/60	
Marty Robbins Collection		2/79

SMOKEY ROBINSON & THE MIRACLES - Outstanding R&B group from Detroit, USA, led by distinctive singer/songwriter William 'Smokey' Robinson. Other members of the very sucessful group included Warren 'Pete' Moore, Bobby Rogers, Ronnie White and Smokey's wife Claudette. Robinson started a successful solo career in 1972.

Album	US Top 10 Ent	UK Top 10 Ent
Greatest Hits Vol. 2	3/68	

TOM ROBINSON BAND - Critically applauded rock band fronted by Tom Robinson, born 1950 in Cambridge, England. Robinson is also famous for being a gay rights spokesperson.

Album	US Top 10 Ent	UK Top 10 Ent
Power In The Darkness		6/78

KENNY ROGERS - Internationally famous pop/country singer/actor born 1938 in Houston, Texas, USA. After leaving the New Christy Minstrels, he formed the hitmaking First Edition and went solo in 1976. Rogers, who has earned more American Music Awards than any other act, joined RCA in 1983 for the then record advance of $20 million.

Album	US Top 10 Ent	UK Top 10 Ent
Kenny	1/80	
Kenny Rogers' Greatest Hits	11/80	
Share Your Love	8/81	
Eyes That See In The Dark	11/83	
The Kenny Rogers Story		8/85

ROLLING STONES - 'The World's greatest rock band' were formed in 1962 in London, England. Mick Jagger, Brian Jones (died 1969), Keith Richards, Charlie Watts, Bill Wyman. No other group has had more British or American album hits, and thirty years after their formation their live shows were still breaking box office records around the world.

Album	US Top 10 Ent	UK Top 10 Ent
Rolling Stones		5/64
12 X 5	12/64	
Rolling Stones No.2		1/65
The Rolling Stones, Now!	4/65	
Out Of Our Heads	8/65	10/65
December's Children (And Everbody's)	1/66	
Aftermath	8/66	4/66
Big Hits (High Tide And Green Grass)	5/66	11/66
Got Live If You Want It!	1/67	
Between The Buttons	3/67	2/67
Flowers	8/67	
Their Satanic Majesties Request	1/69	1/68
Beggars Banquet	1/69	1/69
Through The Past Darkly (Big Hits Vol. 2)	10/69	10/69
Let It Bleed	12/69	12/69
Get Yer Ya-Ya's Out!	10/70	9/70
Stone Age		4/71
Sticky Fingers	5/71	5/71
Hot Rocks 1964-1971	2/72	7/90
Exile On Main Street	6/72	6/72
Goat's Head Soup	10/73	9/73
It's Only Rock 'n' Roll	11/74	11/74
Metamorphosis	7/75	
Made In The Shade	7/75	
Black And Blue	5/76	5/76
Love You Live	10/77	10/77
Some Girls	7/78	7/78
Emotional Rescue	7/80	7/80
Tattoo You	9/81	9/81
Still Life (American Concert 1981)	7/82	6/82
Undercover	12/83	11/83
Dirty Work	5/86	4/86
Steel Wheels	10/89	9/89
Voodoo Lounge	7/94	7/94

LINDA RONSTADT - Consistently successful multi-faceted singer who was born 1946 in Tucson, Arizona, USA. The oft-times Grammy winner has amassed 17 gold albums in the USA and has been a chart regular for four decades. See also Emmylou Harris.

	US Top 10 Ent	UK Top 10 Ent
Heart Like A Wheel	1/75	
Prisoner In Disguise	10/75	
Hasten Down The Wind	9/76	
Greatest Hits	1/77	
Simple Dreams	10/77	
Living In The USA	10/78	
Mad Love	3/80	
What's New	11/83	
Cry Like A Rainstorm, Howl Like The Wind	1/90	

ROSE ROYCE - Successful soul/dance octet from Los Angeles, USA. Group started as a backing band for acts like Edwin Starr and The Temptations before adding lead vocalist Gwen Dickey in 1976.

	US Top 10 Ent	UK Top 10 Ent
Strikes Again		10/78
Greatest Hits		3/80

DAVID ROSE - US-based orchestral conductor born 1910 in London, England, died 1990. This noted composer/arranger also had film and TV score success (including *Little House On The Prairie, High Chaparral* and *Bonanza*). The Grammy winning performer was once married to Judy Garland (1941-43).

	US Top 10 Ent	UK Top 10 Ent
The Stripper And Other Fun Songs For The Family	8/62	

DIANA ROSS - The most consistently successful female singer of the rock era was born Diane Earle in 1944 in Detroit, USA. The R&B/pop vocalist fronted the Sixties most successful female group, The Supremes, before going solo in 1970. No other American female singer has put so many albums into the UK chart and few artists can claim such a large and loyal worldwide following. See also The Supremes.

	US Top 10 Ent	UK Top 10 Ent
Lady Sings The Blues	2/73	
Touch Me In The Morning	8/73	
Diana & Marvin (with Marvin Gaye)		4/74
Diana Ross	6/76	4/76
Greatest Hits 2		8/76
20 Golden Greats		11/79
Diana	8/80	
Love Songs		12/82
Portrait		1/84
One Woman - The Ultimate Collection		11/93

DAVID LEE ROTH - Extrovert heavy metal vocalist born 1955 in Bloomington, Indiana, USA. He was the lead singer of the top selling group Van Halen before going solo in 1985.

	US Top 10 Ent	UK Top 10 Ent
Eat 'Em And Smile	8/86	
Skyscraper	2/88	
A Little Ain't Enough		1/91

DEMIS ROUSSOS - Very popular Greek MOR singer/musician born 1947 in Alexandria, Egypt. A member of Aphrodite's Child (with Vangelis) before finding European success as a solo performer.

	US Top 10 Ent	UK Top 10 Ent
Forever And Ever		7/76
Happy To Be		7/76

ROXETTE - Top selling rock/pop duo from Sweden. Marie Fredriksson and Per Gessle. They had four Number 1 singles in America between 1989 and 1991 - making them the most successful Scandinavian act to date in the USA.

	US Top 10 Ent	UK Top 10 Ent
Look Sharp!		9/90
Joyride		4/91
Tourism		9/92
Crash! Boom! Bang!		4/94

ROXY MUSIC - Influential avant garde art/rock band from Durham, England, led by stylish vocalist/keyboardist Bryan Ferry. Other members included Andy Mackay, Brian Eno and Phil Manzanera. A major act in Britain throughout the Seventies and early-Eighties, who never broke through Stateside. See also Bryan Ferry.

	US Top 10 Ent	UK Top 10 Ent
For Your Pleasure		4/73
Stranded		12/73
Country Life		12/74
Siren		11/75
Viva Roxy Music		8/76
Manifesto		6/79
Flesh And Blood		6/80
Avalon		6/82
Street Life - 20 Great Hits (with Bryan Ferry)		4/86
The Ultimate Collection (with Bryan Ferry)		12/88

ROYAL PHILHARMONIC ORCHESTRA - See LOUIS CLARK.

RUFUS FEATURING CHAKA KHAN - Soul group from Chicago formed by Al Ciner, Charles Colbert and Lee Graziano (all ex-American Breed). Success came thanks mainly to later members Chaka Khan and Andre Fisher. Act had a string of successful records and Khan went on to worldwide solo fame.

	US Top 10 Ent	UK Top 10 Ent
Rags To Rufus	9/74	
Rufus Featuring Chaka Khan	3/76	

RUN-D.M.C. - Groundbreaking rap act from Queens, New York, USA. Joseph Simmons (Run), Darryl McDaniels (DMC) and DJ Jason Mizell (Jam Master Jay). These very influential rap pioneers were the first act in the genre to earn both gold and platinum albums.

	US Top 10 Ent	UK Top 10 Ent
Raising Hell	8/86	

RUNRIG - Scottish folk/rock band who are among the top selling acts in their homeland. Donnie Munro, Rory MacDonald, Malcolm Jones, Calum MacDonald, Peter Wishart and Iain Bayne.

	US Top 10 Ent	UK Top 10 Ent
Amazing Things		3/93

RUSH - Internationally acclaimed rock band from Toronto, Canada, fronted by Geddy Lee with Alex Lifeson and John Rutsey (replaced by Neil Peart after their first album in 1974). The consistently succcessful trio have earned a dozen platinum albums in the USA.

	US Top 10 Ent	UK Top 10 Ent
Permanent Waves	3/80	2/80
Moving Pictures	3/81	2/81
Exit Stage Left		11/81
Signals		9/82
Grace Under Pressure		4/84
Roll The Bones	9/91	
Counterparts	11/93	

LEON RUSSELL - Well respected rock singer/songwriter and multi-instrumentalist born 1941 in Oklahoma, USA. Not only has he had several hits of his own, but he has also (as a session musician) played on countless other top sellers.

	US Top 10 Ent	UK Top 10 Ent
Carney	9/72	

S'EXPRESS - Dance/disco act masterminded by keyboard-playing club DJ Mark Moore, born 1965 in London, England. Their debut single 'Theme From S Express' was a groundbreaking UK Number 1.

	US Top 10 Ent	UK Top 10 Ent
Original Soundtrack		4/89

SADE - Acclaimed British-based jazz-styled R&B/pop band named after their singer/songwriter (born Helen Folasade Adu in Ibadan, Nigeria in 1958). Other group members: Stewart Matthewman, Paul Denman, Andrew Hale and Paul Cook. The group, who have sold close to 30 million albums, won the Grammy for Best New Artist in 1985.

	US Top 10 Ent	UK Top 10 Ent
Diamond Life	4/85	7/84
Promise	1/86	11/85
Stronger Than Pride	7/88	5/88
Love Deluxe	11/92	
Best Of Sade		11/94

SSGT. BARRY SADLER - Singer/songwriting veteran of the Green Berets in Vietnam. Born 1940 in New Mexico, USA, and died 1989. The Staff Sergeant topped the album and single chart with his patriotic songs.

	US Top 10 Ent	UK Top 10 Ent
Ballads Of The Green Berets	3/66	

SALT'N'PEPA - Foremost female rap crew from Queens, New York, USA. Cheryl 'Salt' James (from Jamaica) and Sandy 'Pepa' Denton, and 'DJ Spinderella' LaToya Roper. The most consistently successful female rap act on both sides of the Atlantic.

	US Top 10 Ent	UK Top 10 Ent
Very Necessary	2/94	

SANTANA - Influential and innovative jazz-fusion/Latin-rock band formed in San Francisco, USA, by Carlos Santana (see below). Other members included David Brown, Gregg Rolie, Michael Shrieve and Neil Schon. They were regular Top 40 entrants in the Seventies, and their first 11 LPs all turned gold.

	US Top 10 Ent	UK Top 10 Ent
Santana	11/69	
Abraxas	10/70	12/70
Santana III	10/71	11/71
Caravanserai	12/72	
Zebop!	6/81	

CARLOS SANTANA - Jazz-fusion and Latin-rock guitarist born 1947 in Mexico. He has also had several successful recording projects outside of his group, Santana.

	US Top 10 Ent	UK Top 10 Ent
Carlos Santana & Buddy Miles! Live!	9/72	

SAXON - English heavy metal band led by Yorkshireman Biff Byford. Other members included Steve Dawson, Pete Gill (replaced by Nigel Glocker in 1981), Graham Oliver and Paul Quinn.

	US Top 10 Ent	UK Top 10 Ent
Wheels Of Steel		4/80

LEO SAYER - Distinctive pop singer/songwriter from Shoreham, England, born Gerard Sayer in 1948. Sayer, who was managed by ex-British pop idol Adam Faith, was a transatlantic chart regular in the Seventies.

	US Top 10 Ent	UK Top 10 Ent
Silver Bird		2/74
Just A Boy		11/74
Another Year		10/75
Endless Flight		2/77
The Very Best Of Leo Sayer		4/79

BOZ SCAGGS - Critically lauded soulful rock singer/songwriter born 1944 in Ohio, USA. He worked with the Steve Miller Band intermittently from late Fifties until 1969 whilst also pursuing solo career. His 'Lowdown' won the Grammy for Best R&B Song at the 1977 Grammy awards.

	US Top 10 Ent	UK Top 10 Ent
Silk Degrees	9/76	
Middle Man	6/80	

SCARFACE - Hardcore rapper from Houston, Texas, USA, born Brad Jordan. A member of the notorious Geto Boys before successfully going solo in 1991.

	US Top 10 Ent	UK Top 10 Ent
The Diary	11/94	

MICHAEL SCHENKER GROUP - Hard rock group led by West German-born Michael Schenker (ex-Scorpions and UFO). Members have included Gary Barden, Cozy

Powell (ex-Rainbow, etc.) and Graham Bonnet.

	US Top 10 Ent	UK Top 10 Ent
One Night At Budokan		3/82

SCORPIONS - Top selling heavy metal band from Germany fronted by Klaus Meine with Rudolf Schenker. Among their members were Rudolf's brother Michael Schenker (see above), Ulrich Roth, Francis Buchholz, Matthias Jabs and Herman Rarebell. The veteran band are arguably the most successful rock group from continental Europe.

	US Top 10 Ent	UK Top 10 Ent
Love At First Sting	4/84	
Savage Amusement	6/88	

SCOTLAND FOOTBALL WORLD CUP SQUAD 1974 - Like their 'old enemies', the English World Cup Squad, Scotland's top soccer players also had top selling records.

	US Top 10 Ent	UK Top 10 Ent
Easy Easy		6/74

JACK SCOTT - Successful rockabilly singer/songwriter who was born Jack Scafone Jr. in 1935 in Ontario, Canada. He was a regular singles chart entrant in the late Fifties and is still active on the club circuit.

	US Top 10 Ent	UK Top 10 Ent
I Remember Hank Williams		6/60

SCRITTI POLITTI - Quality pop act masterminded by Welsh singer/songwriter Green Strohmeyer-Gartside. Other members: David Gamson, Fred Maher. Gartside songs have been recorded by Al Jarreau, Chaka Khan and Madness and the act has recorded with such notables as Shabba Ranks and Roger Troutman.

	US Top 10 Ent	UK Top 10 Ent
Cupid And Psyche '85		6/85

SEAL - Multi-award-winning singer/songwriter from London, England, born Seal Henry Samuel in 1963. He first came to prominence as vocalist with Adamski and is now one of the most successful new UK acts on the American chart.

	US Top 10 Ent	UK Top 10 Ent
Seal		6/91
Seal		6/94

SEALS & CROFTS - Top selling pop partnership of singing-songwriting multi-instrumentalists Dan Seals and Dash Crofts, both from Texas, USA. They tasted success as members of The Champs (after the chart topping 'Tequila' in 1958) and as a duo were US chart regulars in the early Seventies.

	US Top 10 Ent	UK Top 10 Ent
Summer Breeze	12/72	
Diamond Girl	6/73	

SEARCHERS - Famed harmony pop/rock group from Liverpool, England. John McNally, Mike Pender, Chris Curtis and Tony Jackson (replaced in 1964 by Frank Allen).

	US Top 10 Ent	UK Top 10 Ent
Meet The Searchers		8/63
Sugar And Spice		11/63
It's The Searchers		6/64

HARRY SECOMBE - Veteran singer, entertainer and comedian born 1921 in Swansea, Wales. He has been one of Brtiain's best known radio and TV personalities since the early-Fifties, and was a member of the revered comedy act, The Goons (with Peter Sellers).

	US Top 10 Ent	UK Top 10 Ent
Secombe's Personal Choice		5/67

NEIL SEDAKA - Very successful pop singer/songwriter and pianist born 1939 in New York, USA. Apart from having a string of hit singles in the late-Fifties and again in the early-Seventies, he has also penned major hits for such acts as Connie Francis, Captain and Tennille and Andy Williams.

	US Top 10 Ent	UK Top 10 Ent
Laughter And Tears - The Best Of Neil Sedaka		7/76

SEEKERS - Distinctive folk-pop quartet were the first Australian act to top either the UK singles or album charts. Judith Durham, Athol Guy, Keith Potger, Bruce Woodley. They were one of the top selling mixed groups of the Sixties.

	US Top 10 Ent	UK Top 10 Ent
A World Of Our Own		7/65
Come The Day		12/66
Live At The Talk Of The Town		10/68
The Best Of The Seekers		11/68
Carnival Of Hits (as Judith Durham & The Seekers)		5/94

BOB SEGER & THE SILVER BULLET BAND - Veteran rock band vocalist Seger, born 1945 in Michigan, USA, formed The Silver Bullet Band in 1976. Original band line-up: Drew Abbott, Chris Campbell, Charlie Martin, Alto Reed, Robyn Robbins. Only bassist Campbell's membership has endured.

	US Top 10 Ent	UK Top 10 Ent
Night Moves	3/77	
Stranger In Town	7/78	
Against The Wind	3/80	
Nine Tonight	10/81	
The Distance	2/83	
Like A Rock	5/86	

PETER SELLERS - World famous British comedian/actor born 1925 and died 1980. He was a member of the renowned radio comedy team The Goons, and had several chart records before finding international fame in the *Pink Panther* movies.

	US Top 10 Ent	UK Top 10 Ent
Songs For Swinging Sellers		5/60
The Best Of Sellers		9/60
Peter & Sophia (with Sophia Loren)		1/61

SENSER - British rock band formed by Nick Michaelson and James Barrett. Other members: Heitham Al-Sayed, Kerstin Haigh, John Morgan and Andy Clinton.

	US Top 10 Ent	UK Top 10 Ent
Stacked Up		5/94

SEX PISTOLS - Ever controversial, ground-breaking London-based band were the foremost British punk act. Their best known line-up was Johnny Rotten (John Lydon), Paul Cook, Steve Jones and Sid Vicious (died 1979). Malcolm McLaren put together the group that shook up the British recording industry in the late-Seventies. They are arguably one of the most important and influential acts of the rock era.

	US Top 10 Ent	UK Top 10 Ent
Never Mind The Bollocks Here's The Sex Pistols		11/77
The Great Rock 'n' Roll Swindle		3/79
Some Product - Carri On Sex Pistols		8/79

SHADOWS - The most successful British instrumental act of all time started as Cliff Richard's backing band. On their first hit single the line-up was Hank Marvin, Bruce Welch, Jet Harris and Tony Meehan. Although yet to debut on the US charts, they have scored British hits for five decades.

	US Top 10 Ent	UK Top 10 Ent
The Shadows		9/61
Out Of The Shadows		10/62
Greatest Hits		6/63
Dance With The Shadows		5/64
Sound Of The Shadows		8/65
Shadow Music		6/66
Jigsaw		8/67
20 Golden Greats		2/77
String Of Hits		10/79
Reflection		10/90

SHAI - Smooth soulful vocal group formed at Howard University, Washington D.C., USA. Carl 'Groove' Martin, Garfield Bright, Marc Gay and Darnell Van Rensalier. Martin penned and produced their million selling single 'If I Ever Fall In Love'.

	US Top 10 Ent	UK Top 10 Ent
If I Ever Fall In Love	1/93	

SHAKATAK - British jazz funk group masterminded by keyboardists Bill Sharpe and Nigel Wright often featuring vocalist Jill Saward. Act had much success in Japan as well as in Britain. Sharpe has also worked as a duo with Gary Numan and Wright became a top UK producer.

	US Top 10 Ent	UK Top 10 Ent
Night Birds		5/82

SHAKESPEARS SISTER - Anglo-American pop/rock duo of Siobhan Fahey (ex-Bananarama) from London and ex-session singer/composer Marcella Detroit (real name Marcy Levy) from Detroit. Fahey is married to Eurythmics' Dave Stewart.

	US Top 10 Ent	UK Top 10 Ent
Hormonally Yours		3/92

SHALAMAR - Trend-setting trio, masterminded by Don Cornelius of US TV's *Soul Train*. Best known line-up was Jody Watley, Jeffrey Daniels and Howard Hewett. They all left to start solo careers in the mid-Eighties.

	US Top 10 Ent	UK Top 10 Ent
The Greatest Hits		5/86

SHAMEN - Psychedelic/rave/dance act formed in Aberdeen, Scotland, in 1985 by Colin Angus and Will Sinnot. Critically acclaimed act only found real commercial success after the death (at a video shoot) of Sinnot in 1990, at which point rapper Mr. 'C' was introduced.

	US Top 10 Ent	UK Top 10 Ent
Boss Drum		1/93

DEL SHANNON - Pop/rock singer/songwriter from Michigan, USA, born Charles Westover in 1934. His debut record 'Runaway' was a transatlantic Number 1, and he was one of the most consistent hitmakers of the early-Sixties. He committed suicide in 1990.

	US Top 10 Ent	UK Top 10 Ent
Hats Off To Del Shannon		6/63

HELEN SHAPIRO - Celebrated pop singer/actress born 1946 in London. She had two UK Number 1s while still at school and was the first British female recording star of the Sixties. For three years she was one of the UK's top selling acts, and was once supported on tour by The Beatles.

	US Top 10 Ent	UK Top 10 Ent
Tops With Me		3/62

SANDIE SHAW - Sixties role-model/vogueish pop singer from Essex, England, born Sandra Goodrich in 1947. Discovered by Adam Faith, she was the first British act to win the Eurovision Song Contest (in 1967 with 'Puppet On A String'). She made an Eighties comeback in the company of The Smiths.

	US Top 10 Ent	UK Top 10 Ent
Sandie		3/65

ALLAN SHERMAN - Top American comedian/comic script writer from Chicago, born Allan Copelon in 1924, died 1973. The man, who created and produced the US TV show *I've Got A Secret*, was one of the biggest selling LP acts of the early Sixties thanks to his My Son.. series.

	US Top 10 Ent	UK Top 10 Ent
My Son, The Folk Singer	11/62	
My Son, The Celebrity	2/63	
My Son, The Nut	8/63	

SHOWADDYWADDY - Good time rock'n'roll revival band from Leicester, England. Members included Dave Bartram, Buddy Gask, Malcolm Allured, Romeo Challenger, Russ Fields, Al James, Trevor Oakes and Rod Teas. They had seven successive UK Top 10 hits in the mid-Seventies.

	US Top 10 Ent	UK Top 10 Ent
Step Two		7/75
Greatest Hits		1/77
Greatest Hits		12/78

SILK - Polished R&B vocal group produced by hitmaker Keith Sweat. Timothy Cameron, Jimmy Gates Jr., Gary Glenn, Gary Jenkins and Jonathan Rasboro. Their Sweat composed 'Freak Me' topped the US chart and sold over a million.

	US Top 10 Ent	UK Top 10 Ent
Lose Control	4/93	

SIMON & GARFUNKEL - The biggest selling album duo of all time are the folk/rock partnership of Paul Simon and Art Garfunkel from New York, USA. Only The Beatles have spent more weeks on the UK album chart than the duo, who at times had three LPs in the US Top 5.

	US Top 10 Ent	UK Top 10 Ent
Parsley Sage Rosemary And Thyme	12/66	
The Graduate (Soundtrack)	3/68	11/68
Bookends	5/68	8/68
Bridge Over Troubled Water	2/70	2/70
Simon & Garfunkel's Greatest Hits	8/72	7/72
The Simon And Garfunkel Collection		12/81
The Concert In Central Park	4/82	
The Definitive Simon And Garfunkel		12/91

CARLY SIMON - Celebrated pop singer/songwriter born 1945 in New York, USA. She won the Grammy for Best New Artist in 1971, married James Taylor in 1972 and is a member of the Songwriters Hall of Fame.

	US Top 10 Ent	UK Top 10 Ent
No Secrets	1/73	1/73
Hotcakes	3/74	

PAUL SIMON - World renowned singer/songwriter and guitarist born 1941 in New Jersey, USA. He had a very successful solo career after working with Art Garfunkel (see above) for many years. The Grammy winner has been a chart artist for five decades.

	US Top 10 Ent	UK Top 10 Ent
Paul Simon	3/72	2/72
There Goes Rhymin' Simon	6/73	6/73
Still Crazy After All These Years	11/75	1/76
Greatest Hits, Etc.		12/77
Graceland	11/86	9/86
Rhythm Of The Saints	11/90	10/90

SIMPLE MINDS - Top British rock group from Scotland, fronted by Jim Kerr. Other members: Charles Burchill, Mel Gaynor, John Giblin, Michael MacNeil. Five of the act's albums entered the UK chart at Number 1.

	US Top 10 Ent	UK Top 10 Ent
New Gold Dream (81,82,83,84)		10/82
Sparkle In The Rain		2/84
Once Upon A Time	3/86	11/85
Live In The City Of Light		6/87
Street Fighting Years		5/89
Real Life		4/91
Glittering Prize 81/92		10/92

SIMPLY RED - Distinctive and innovative pop/R&B group from Manchester, England, fronted by the flame-haired Mick Hucknall. Other members: Tony Bowers, Chris Joyce, Tim Kellett, Fritz McIntyre, Sylvan Richardson. Both **A New Flame** and **Stars** (the biggest selling album in the UK in the Nineties) sold over five million copies worldwide.

	US Top 10 Ent	UK Top 10 Ent
Picture Book		6/86
Men And Women		3/87
A New Flame		2/89
Stars		10/91

SIMPSONS - Oddball American cartoon family; Homer Simpson (voice of Dan Castellaneta), Marge (Julie Kavner), Bart (Nancy Cartwright), Lisa (Yeardley Smith) and Maggie (Matt Groening, the Simpsons' creator). R&B performer Bryan Loren produced, sang backing vocals on and composed much of their hit album.

	US Top 10 Ent	UK Top 10 Ent
The Simpsons Sing The Blues	1/91	4/91

JOYCE SIMS - Noted dance music singer/songwriter/pianist and producer from New York, USA, who found more chart success in Britain than her homeland.

	US Top 10 Ent	UK Top 10 Ent
Come Into My Life		2/88

FRANK SINATRA - One of the century's best known singer/entertainers who was born 1915 in New Jersey, USA. He was the vocalist on the first ever US Number 1 single (1940) and has seldom been off the charts since. 'Ol' Blue Eyes' was the first singer to attract screaming fans and is regarded by many as the greatest song stylist of all time.

	US Top 10 Ent	UK Top 10 Ent
Nice 'n' Easy	9/60	1/61
Come Back To Sorrento		8/60
Swing Easy		11/60
Sinatra's Swingin' Session!!!	2/61	
Ring-A-Ding Ding!	5/61	1/62
All The Way	5/61	
Sinatra Swings	9/61	11/61
When Your Lover Has Gone		9/61
I Remember Tommy...	11/61	
Sinatra And Strings		6/62
Sinatra - Basie (with Count Basie)		3/63
Concert Sinatra		8/63
September Of My Years	1/66	
A Man And His Music	2/66	3/66
Strangers In The Night	7/66	7/66
That's Life	2/67	
My Way		6/69
Greatest Hits Vol. 2		1/71
Portrait Of Sinatra		3/77
20 Golden Greats		5/78
Duets	11/93	

NANCY SINATRA - Pop singing daughter of Frank Sinatra (see above), born 1940 in New Jersey, USA. She first recorded for her father's Reprise label in 1961 and had a run of transatlantic hits in the latter half of that decade including 'Somethin' Stupid', a duet with Frank.

	US Top 10 Ent	UK Top 10 Ent
Boots	4/66	

SINGING NUN - Belgian nun Soeur Sourire (Sister Smile) who was also known as Sister Luc-Gabrielle, was born Jeanine Deckers in 1933. She was the first female and the first white act to simultaneously top the US single and album charts. In 1985 she committed suicide.

	US Top 10 Ent	UK Top 10 Ent
The Singing Nun	11/63	

SIOUXSIE & THE BANSHEES - Consistently successful London-based punk band led by Susan 'Siouxsie Sioux' Dallion (born 1957). Among The Banshees have been Steve Severin, Robert Smith (also of The Cure) and Budgie (whom she married).

	US Top 10 Ent	UK Top 10 Ent
Kaleidoscope		8/80

SISTER SLEDGE - Successful R&B/dance act consisted of sisters Debra, Joan, Kim and Kathy Sledge from Philadelphia, USA. They started out as backing singers for Gamble & Huff, before composer/producers Nile Rodgers and Bernard Edwards helped them to stardom.

	US Top 10 Ent	UK Top 10 Ent
We Are Family	5/79	

SKID ROW - Chart-topping heavy metal band from New York, USA, fronted by Canadian Sebastian 'Bach' Bierk. Other members: Rob Affuso, Rachel Bolan, Scott Hill, Dave Sabo.

	US Top 10 Ent	UK Top 10 Ent
Skid Row	8/89	
Slave To The Grind	6/91	

SKY - Popular classically-oriented soft rock instrumental group who had a string of top selling LPs in the UK during the early-Eighties. John Williams, Herbie Flowers, Francis Monkman, Tristan Fry and Kevin Peek.

	US Top 10 Ent	UK Top 10 Ent
Sky 2		5/80
Sky 3		4/81
Sky 4 - Forthcoming		4/82

SLADE - Highly successful stompin' rock/pop group from Wolverhampton, England, led by Noddy Holder with Dave Hill, Jim Lea and Don Powell. Holder and Lea penned most of the act's British hit singles including their six Number 1s in the Seventies.

	US Top 10 Ent	UK Top 10 Ent
Slade Alive		4/72
Slayed		12/72
Sladest		10/73
Old New Borrowed And Blue		2/74
Slade In Flame		12/74

SLY & THE FAMILY STONE - Groundbreaking multi-racial funk rock band from San Francisco, USA, formed by vocalist/keyboardist and former A&R man Sylvester 'Sly' Stewart. Freddie Stone and Rosie Stone (Sly's brother and sister), Larry Graham (cousin) plus Gregg Errico, Jerry Martini and Cynthia Robinson. One of the most influential acts of the Seventies.

	US Top 10 Ent	UK Top 10 Ent
Greatest Hits	11/70	
There's A Riot Goin' On	11/71	
Fresh	8/73	

SMALL FACES - Revered mod rock/R&B band from London, England. Steve Marriott, and Ronnie Lane (the act's co-writers), Ian McLagen, Kenny Jones (later of The Who). Marriott, who left in 1969 to form Humble Pie, died in 1991. The group evolved into The Faces when joined by vocalist Rod Stewart.

	US Top 10 Ent	UK Top 10 Ent
Small Faces		5/66
Ogden's Nut Gone Flake		6/68

SMASHING PUMPKINS - Critically acclaimed grunge rock band formed in Chicago, USA, in 1987. Billy Corgan, James Iha, D'Arcy and Jimmy Chamberlain. **Pisces Iscariot**, an album of 'rarities' was not released in Britain.

	US Top 10 Ent	UK Top 10 Ent
Pisces Iscariot	10/94	

SMITHS - Innnovative and original indie group from Manchester, England, led by distinctive singer/songwriter Morrissey and co-writer and guitarist Johnny Marr. Other members: Mike Joyce and Andy Rourke. The group is regarded by many as one of the most important acts of the Eighties.

	US Top 10 Ent	UK Top 10 Ent
The Smiths		3/84
Meat Is Murder		2/85
The Queen Is Dead		6/86
The World Won't Listen		3/87
Strangeways Here We Come		10/87
Rank		9/88
Best...1		8/92

SMOKIE - Recognizable English pop/rock quartet who had a string of UK hit singles in the late Seventies. Chris Norman. Alan Silson, Pete Spencer, Terry Utley. Distinctive vocalist Norman was a star in his own right in Germany in the Eighties.

	US Top 10 Ent	UK Top 10 Ent
Greatest Hits		5/77

SNOOP DOGGY DOGG - Controversial rapper born Calvin Broadus in 1971 in California, USA. The publicity from a shooting murder case he was involved in helped. amass advance orders of 1.5 million for **Doggystyle**, the first debut album in history to enter the US chart at Number 1.

	US Top 10 Ent	UK Top 10 Ent
Doggystyle	12/93	

SNOW - White Canadian reggae-styled rapper born

Damen O'Brien in Toronto. His single 'Informer' became one of the biggest international hits of 1993.

	US Top 10 Ent	UK Top 10 Ent
12 Inches Of Snow	4/93	

PHOEBE SNOW - Versatile jazz/folk pop singer/songwriter and guitarist from New York, USA. Born Phoebe Laub in 1952, she is held in high esteem by many of her peers.

	US Top 10 Ent	UK Top 10 Ent
Phoebe Snow	3/75	

SOFT CELL - Top selling synth-pop duo of Marc Almond and David Ball from Leeds, England. The visually distinctive duo were one of the most consistent singles sellers in the UK in the early-Eighties. Their 'Tainted Love' was on the US Top 100 chart for a (then) record 43 weeks. After splitting in 1984, Almond continued with a solo career while Ball formed dance outfit The Grid.

	US Top 10 Ent	UK Top 10 Ent
Non-Stop Erotic Cabaret		2/82

JIMMY SOMERVILLE - Falsetto-voiced pop/dance vocalist born 1961 in Glasgow, Scotland, who previously had hits as front man of Bronski Beat and The Communards.

	US Top 10 Ent	UK Top 10 Ent
The Singles Collection 1984/1990		12/90

SONNY & CHER - The world's most successful musical husband and wife team are Salvatore 'Sonny' Bono and Cherilyn 'Cher' LaPier. The duo, who were married from 1963-74, were one of the best known recording acts of the mid-Sixties on both sides of the Atlantic.

	US Top 10 Ent	UK Top 10 Ent
Look At Us	9/65	10/65

SOUL II SOUL - London-based soul/dance collective masterminded by Jazzie B (Beresford Romeo) and Nellee Hooper, whose best known lead vocalist was Caron Wheeler. They were the first black act to top the UK single and album charts simultaneously, and were arguably the most successful British act ever on the US R&B scene.

	US Top 10 Ent	UK Top 10 Ent
Club Classics Vol. One		4/89
Vol II (1990 A New Decade)		6/90
Volume III Just Right		4/92

DAVID SOUL - Transatlantically famous TV actor/pop singer from Chicago, USA, born David Solberg in 1943. He is best known for his role as Ken Hutchinson in the TV cop series *Starsky and Hutch.*

	US Top 10 Ent	UK Top 10 Ent
David Soul		1/77

SOUNDGARDEN - Successful alternative rock band from Seattle, USA. Chris Cornell, Matt Cameron (both ex-Temple Of The Dog), Kim Thayil and Hiro Yamamoto. Their fourth A&M album **Superunknown** entered at Number 1 in the USA, Canada and New Zealand.

	US Top 10 Ent	UK Top 10 Ent
Superunknown	3/94	

SOUNDTRACK

	US Top 10 Ent	UK Top 10 Ent
South Pacific		3/60
The Five Pennies		3/60
The King And I		3/60
Gigi		3/60
Oklahoma		6/60
Can-Can	6/60	5/60
Exodus	1/61	
The Alamo	1/61	
Song Without End		3/61
Never On Sunday	6/61	
Seven Brides For Seven Brothers		5/61
West Side Story	3/62	3/62
It's Trad Dad		5/62
Rome Adventure	7/62	
The Music Man	9/62	
Lawrence Of Arabia	5/63	
Bye Bye Birdie	8/63	
Mary Poppins	12/64	4/65
My Fair Lady	12/64	
Goldfinger	2/65	
The Sound Of Music	5/65	5/65
Doctor Zhivago	6/66	8/67
The Good, The Bad And The Ugly	4/68	11/68
The Jungle Book		6/68
Oliver		3/69
Romeo & Juliet	5/69	
2001 - A Space Odyssey		8/69
Easy Rider		1/70
Paint Your Wagon		3/70
Love Story	2/71	
Clockwork Orange		3/73
Tommy	5/75	
Rocky	5/77	
Star Wars	8/77	
Saturday Night Fever	1/78	4/78
The Stud		5/78
FM	6/78	
Grease	7/78	8/78
Sergeant Pepper's Lonely Hearts Club Band	8/78	
American Gigolo	4/80	
Empire Strikes Back	6/80	
Xanadu	9/80	7/80
Fame	8/80	7/82
Urban Cowboy	7/80	
Dance Craze		2/81
Flashdance	5/83	
Staying Alive	8/83	
Footloose	3/84	5/84
Breakin'	7/84	
Ghostbusters	8/84	
Beverly Hills Cop	3/85	
Rocky IV		2/86
Pretty In Pink	4/86	
Top Gun	7/86	11/86
Dirty Dancing	10/87	4/88
Beverly Hills Cop II	8/87	
La Bamba	8/87	
Cocktail	9/88	
Pretty Woman	5/90	
New Jack City	5/91	
Robin Hood: Prince Of Thieves	7/91	
Wayne's World	3/92	
Boomerang	7/92	
Mo' Money	8/92	
Singles	10/92	
The Bodyguard	12/92	
Aladdin	2/93	
Sleepless In Seattle	7/93	
Last Action Hero	7/93	
Above The Rim	4/94	
The Crow	5/94	
The Lion King	7/94	
Forrest Gump	8/94	
Murder Was The Case	11/94	

SOUNDTRACK (COMPILATION)

	US Top 10 Ent	UK Top 10 Ent
Great Motion Picture Themes	2/61	

SOUNDTRACK (TV)

	US Top 10 Ent	UK Top 10 Ent
All In The Family	1/72	
Rock Follies		4/76
Miami Vice	10/85	
Jonathan King's Entertainment USA		3/86
Moonlighting		10/88

SOUP DRAGONS - Indie rock group from Glasgow, Scotland. Sean Dickinson with Sushil Dade, Jim McCulloch and Ross Sinclair. They were voted Best New Foreign Band by *Rolling Stone* readers.

	US Top 10 Ent	UK Top 10 Ent
Lovegod		8/90

SPANDAU BALLET - Foremost new romantic band. Tony Hadley, John Keeble, brothers Gary and Martin Kemp and Steve Norman. Trend-setting act were regular UK chart entrants in the early Eighties. The Kemp brothers have since turned to acting, portraying the notorious Kray twins on film.

	US Top 10 Ent	UK Top 10 Ent
Journey To Glory		3/81
True		4/83
Parade		7/84
The Singles Collection		12/85

SPARKS - Popular rock/dance band fronted by the visually memorable brothers Ron and Russell Mael from California, USA. Act, whose main success came in Britain during the mid-Seventies, still have a loyal following in the mid-Nineties.

	US Top 10 Ent	UK Top 10 Ent
Kimono My House		6/74

SPECIALS - Leading 2-Tone band from Coventry, England (aka The Special AKA). Members included Jerry Dammers (real name Gerald Dankin), Lynval Golding, Terry Hall and Neville Staples, the latter three went on to become Fun Boy Three in 1981. The group scored seven UK Top 10 singles between 1979-1981.

	US Top 10 Ent	UK Top 10 Ent
Specials		11/79
More Specials		10/80

SPIN DOCTORS - Internationally known New York-based boogie rock foursome. Christopher Barron, Aaron Comess, Eric Schenkman, Mark White.

	US Top 10 Ent	UK Top 10 Ent
Pocket Full Of Kryptonite	2/93	6/93
Turn It Upside Down		7/94

SPINNERS - Veteran R&B group from Detroit, USA, known as the Detroit Spinners in Britain. Members have included Billy Henderson, Henry Fambrough, Pervis Jackson, Bobbie Smith, G. C. Cameron, Phillipe Wynne (died in 1984) and John Edwards.

	US Top 10 Ent	UK Top 10 Ent
Pick Of The Litter	10/75	

DUSTY SPRINGFIELD - Multi-faceted vocalist from London, England, born Mary O'Brien in 1939. She fronted the award winning folk/pop trio The Springfields before going solo with success in 1963. One of the best known female singers of the swinging sixties.

	US Top 10 Ent	UK Top 10 Ent
A Girl Called Dusty		5/64
Everything Comes Up Dusty		11/65
Golden Hits		11/66
Goin' Back - The Very Best Of		5/94

RICK SPRINGFIELD - Noted pop/rock singer/songwriter and actor born 1949 in Sydney, Australia. This regular early Eighties American hitmaker also starred in the US TV series' *The Young & The Restless* and *General Hospital.*

	US Top 10 Ent	UK Top 10 Ent
Working Class Dog	9/81	
Success Hasn't Spoiled Me Yet	4/82	

BRUCE SPRINGSTEEN - Hugely popular rock singer/songwriter and guitarist known as 'The Boss', was born 1949 in New Jersey, USA. This outstanding live performer broke numerous records when a five-album box set of his live recordings entered the US chart at Number 1. He is undoubedly one of the legendary figures of the rock era.

Album	US Top 10 Ent	UK Top 10 Ent
Born To Run	9/75	
Darkness On The Edge Of Town	7/78	
The River	11/80	10/80
Nebraska	10/82	10/82
Born In The U.S.A.	6/84	6/84
Bruce Springsteen & The E Street Band Live/1975-1985	11/86	
Tunnel Of Love	10/87	10/87
Human Touch	4/92	4/92
Lucky Town	4/92	4/92

SQUEEZE - Well regarded new wave pop/rock group from London, England. Members included singer/songwriters Chris Difford and Glenn Tilbrook, keyboardist 'Jools' Holland and Paul Carrack (ex-Ace and later Mike & The Mechanics).

Album	US Top 10 Ent	UK Top 10 Ent
Singles - 45's And Under		11/82

BILLY SQUIER - Noted hard-rocking singer/songwriter and guitarist born 1950 in Massachusetts, USA. After more than ten years performing, Squier had a string of US chart records in the early-Eighties.

Album	US Top 10 Ent	UK Top 10 Ent
Don't Say No	9/81	
Emotions In Motion	9/82	

LISA STANSFIELD - Soulful white vocalist born 1966 in Rochdale, England. The BRIT-winning Best Newcomer of 1989 was the only white British female to top the American R&B chart - a feat she has accomplished on three occassions.

Album	US Top 10 Ent	UK Top 10 Ent
Affection		12/89
Real Love		1/92

STARSHIP - See JEFFERSON STARSHIP

RINGO STARR - Beatles drummer from Liverpool, England, born Richard Starkey in 1940. As well as solo album projects (he first recorded solo in 1970 before group split), he has carved out a film and TV career. He is also the only Beatle to have two consecutive US Number 1 singles.

Album	US Top 10 Ent	UK Top 10 Ent
Sentimental Journey		4/70
Ringo	11/73	12/73

STARS ON - Dutch session group, masterminded by producer Jaap Eggermont (ex-Golden Earring), who started a worldwide craze for segued medley hits. Group was known as Starsound in the UK.

Album	US Top 10 Ent	UK Top 10 Ent
Stars On Long Play	7/81	5/81

STARSOUND - See STARS ON

STATUS QUO - Headbanging hard rock/boogie band from London, who are Britain's best kept secret from US record buyers. Francis Rossi, Rick Parfitt, John Coghlan and Alan Lancaster. The veteran band, who have had more hit singles in the UK than any other group, have yet to make a lasting mark on the US scene.

Album	US Top 10 Ent	UK Top 10 Ent
Hello		10/73
Quo		5/74
On The Level		3/75
Blue For You		3/76
Live		3/77
Rockin' All Over The World		12/77
Can't Stand The Heat		11/78
Whatever You Want		10/79
12 Gold Bars		4/80
Just Supposin'		10/80
Never Too Late		3/81
1982		4/82
From The Makers Of...		11/82
In The Army Now		9/86
Rocking All Over The Years		10/90

STEELY DAN - Critically acclaimed jazzy pop studio band from Los Angeles, USA. Formed by Walter Becker and Donald Fagen (both ex-Jay & The Americans). Other one-time members have included Michael McDonald and Jeff Baxter (who both joined the Doobie Brothers). Act has amassed seven platinum albums in the US.

Album	US Top 10 Ent	UK Top 10 Ent
Aja	10/77	10/77
Gaucho	1/81	

STEPPENWOLF - Top selling heavy metal band from Los Angeles, USA. John Kay (real name Joachim Krauldat), Goldy McJohn, Michael Monarch, Nick St. Nicholas and brothers Mars Bonfire (Dennis Edmonton) and Jerry Edmonton. The band are best known internationally for their recording of Bonfire's classic composition 'Born To Be Wild'.

Album	US Top 10 Ent	UK Top 10 Ent
Steppenwolf	9/68	
The Second	11/68	
Steppenwolf 'Live'	5/70	

STEREO MCs - Award-winning self-contained dance/rap/rock act from Nottingham, England. Rob Birch, Nick Hallam and Owen Rossiter. One of the few new British acts to chart Stateside in the Nineties.

Album	US Top 10 Ent	UK Top 10 Ent
Connected		1/93

CAT STEVENS - Internationally renowned singer/songwriter from London, England, born Steven Georgiou in 1947, now known as Yusef Islam since his conversion to the Islamic faith. Stevens was a regular Top 10 entrant on both sides of the Atlantic between 1971-75.

Album	US Top 10 Ent	UK Top 10 Ent
Matthew And Son		5/67
Tea For The Tillerman	4/71	
Teaser And The Firecat	10/71	10/71
Catch Bull At Four	11/72	10/72
Foreigner	8/73	7/73
Buddah And The Chocolate Box	5/74	4/74
Greatest Hits	8/75	9/75
The Very Best Of Cat Stevens		2/90

SHAKIN' STEVENS - Retro rock'n'roll singer born Michael Barratt in 1948 in Wales. He was one of Britain's most regular UK singles chart visitors in the Eighties, clocking up 14 Top 10 singles.

Album	US Top 10 Ent	UK Top 10 Ent
This Ole House		4/81
Shaky		10/81
Give Me Your Heart Tonight		10/82
Greatest Hits		12/84

AL STEWART - Respected folk/rock singer/songwriter and guitarist born 1945 in Glasgow, Scotland, who was more successful in the USA than his homeland.

Album	US Top 10 Ent	UK Top 10 Ent
Year Of The Cat	2/77	

ROD STEWART - World famous rock vocalist was born 1945 in London, England. Apart from countless solo successes, he has had hits as singer with The Jeff Beck Group and The Faces. The award-winning performer has 17 US gold LPs and seven British Number 1 albums to his credit. He is one of the legends of rock and was arguably the most successful British act in the USA during the early Nineties.

Album	US Top 10 Ent	UK Top 10 Ent
Every Picture Tells A Story	8/71	7/71
Never A Dull Moment	9/72	8/72
Sing It Again Rod		8/73
Smiler		10/74
Atlantic Crossing		8/75
A Night On The Town	11/76	7/76
Foot Loose & Fancy Free	12/77	11/77
Blondes Have More Fun	2/79	12/78
Greatest Hits		11/79
Tonight I'm Yours		11/81
Body Wishes		7/83
Every Beat Of My Heart		7/86
The Best Of Rod Stewart		12/89
Vagabond Heart		4/91
Rod Stewart, Lead Vocalist		3/93
Unplugged...And Seated	6/93	6/93

STEPHEN STILLS - Renowned singer/songwriter/musician was born 1945 in Dallas, Texas, USA. Also scored as a member of Buffalo Springfield and Crosby, Stills & Nash. See also Crosby, Stills & Nash.

Album	US Top 10 Ent	UK Top 10 Ent
Stephen Stills	12/70	
Stephen Stills 2	8/71	
Manassas	5/72	

STING - Globally famous rock singer/songwriter from Newcastle, England, born Gordon Sumner in 1951. Lead vocalist and bass guitarist of The Police throughout their career. This philanthropic performer has had considerable solo success since leaving and has earned both BRIT and Grammy awards.

Album	US Top 10 Ent	UK Top 10 Ent
The Dream Of The Blue Turtles	8/85	7/85
Nothing Like The Sun	11/87	10/87
The Soul Cages	2/91	2/91
Ten Summoner's Tales	3/93	3/93
Fields Of Gold - The Best Of		11/94

STONE TEMPLE PILOTS - San Diego, California-based hard rock group fronted by a vocalist simply known as Weiland. The DeLeo brothers, Dean & Robert and Eric Kretz complete the quartet.

Album	US Top 10 Ent	UK Top 10 Ent
Core	6/93	
Purple	6/94	

GEORGE STRAIT - One of the biggest selling country acts of all time was born 1952 in Texas, USA. Since first charting in the early Eighties, Strait has had more than two dozen Number 1 country singles and collected 17 gold albums (10 of which turned platinum).

Album	US Top 10 Ent	UK Top 10 Ent
Pure Country	11/92	
Easy Come, Easy Go	10/93	

STRANGLERS - Revered new wave/punk rock group from Surrey, England, led by Hugh Cornwall with Jet Black, Jean Jacques Burnel and Dave Greenfield.

Album	US Top 10 Ent	UK Top 10 Ent
Stranglers IV (Rattus Norvegicus)		5/77
No More Heroes		10/77
Black And White		6/78
Feline		1/83
Greatest Hits 1977-1990		6/91

STRAWBS - Leicester-based progressive folk/rock band fronted by David Cousins. Other members have included Richard Hudson, John Ford (who went on to become Hudson-Ford), Rick Wakeman (later with Yes) and Blue Weaver.

Album	US Top 10 Ent	UK Top 10 Ent
Bursting At The Seams		3/73

STRAY CATS - Top selling rockabilly revival act from Long Island, New York, USA, recorded and launched in the UK. Slim Jim Phantom (real name Jim McDonell), Lee Rocker (real name Leon Drucher) and Brian Setzer. Without doubt one of the better retro rock acts, they were produced by Dave Edmunds.

Album	US Top 10 Ent	UK Top 10 Ent
Stray Cats		3/81
Built For Speed	11/82	

BARBRA STREISAND - The world's most successful female MOR singer/actress was born 1942 in Brooklyn, New York, USA. Since first hitting in 1963, she has been a regular chart entrant on both sides of the Atlantic. The multi-award winning performer has a record 36 US gold albums (21 going platinum), making her the biggest selling female album act of all time.

	US Top 10 Ent	UK Top 10 Ent
The Barbra Streisand Album	7/63	
The Second Barbra Streisand Album	10/63	
The Third Album	3/64	
Funny Girl	5/64	
People	10/64	
My Name Is Barbra	6/65	
My Name Is Barbra, Two...	11/65	2/66
Color Me Barbra	4/66	
Je M'appelle Barbra	12/66	
The Way We Were	3/74	
Funny Lady (Soundtrack)	5/75	
A Star Is Born (Soundtrack)	1/77	5/77
Streisand Superman	7/77	
Barbra Streisand's Greatest Hits Vol 2	12/78	3/79
Wet	11/79	
Guilty	10/80	10/80
Love Songs		1/82
Yentl	1/84	
The Broadway Album	12/85	1/86
Back To Broadway	7/93	7/93

STUDIO CAST

	US Top 10 Ent	UK Top 10 Ent
Evita		2/77
South Pacific		10/86

STYLE COUNCIL - One of the most consistently successful British groups of the Eighties was formed by Paul Weller (after he left regular chart toppers Jam) and Mick Talbot (ex-Merton Parkas).

	US Top 10 Ent	UK Top 10 Ent
Cafe Bleu		3/84
Our Favourite Shop		6/85
Singular Adventures Of The Style Council		3/89

STYLISTICS - Distinctive soft soul vocal group from Philadelphia, USA, led by falsetto-voiced Russell Thompkins Jr. with James Dunn, Airron Love, Herbie Murrell and James Smith. The stylish act were more successful with their albums in the UK than in America.

	US Top 10 Ent	UK Top 10 Ent
The Best Of The Stylistics		4/75
Thank You Baby		8/75
Best Of The Stylistics Vol 2		9/76

STYX - Top selling pomp rock band based in Chicago, USA, led by Dennis DeYoung and Tommy Shaw, the act's main songwriters. Other members were twin brothers Chuck and John Panozzo and James Young. One of America's most consistent album acts between 1977 and 1983.

	US Top 10 Ent	UK Top 10 Ent
The Grand Illusion	2/78	
Pieces Of Eight	11/78	
Cornerstone	10/79	
Paradise Theater	2/81	
Kilroy Was Here	4/83	

SUEDE - Much hyped British alternative rock band. Brett Anderson, Bernard Butler, Matt Osman and Simon Gilbert. The group were voted Best New Band of 1992 by NME, and **Suede** won the prestigious Mercury Music Prize for Best LP of 1993. Co-songwriter, Butler, left in 1994 to be replaced by Richard Oakes.

	US Top 10 Ent	UK Top 10 Ent
Suede		4/93

DONNA SUMMER - The 'Queen of Disco' was born Adrian Donna Gaines in Boston, USA, in 1948. Her first recording successes came in Germany where she was produced by Giorgio Moroder. She has an enviable string of transatlantic hits and was the first female singer to achieve three consecutive US Number 1 albums.

	US Top 10 Ent	UK Top 10 Ent
I Remember Yesterday		7/77
Greatest Hits		1/78
Live And More	10/78	
Bad Girls	5/79	
On The Radio - Greatest Hits - Vols 1 & 2	11/79	

SUNDAYS - British indie/pop group. Harriet Wheeler, Paul Brindley, Dave Gavurin and Pat Hannan who had a brief flirtation with fame on both sides of the Atlantic.

	US Top 10 Ent	UK Top 10 Ent
Reading Writing & Arithmetic		1/90

SUPERTRAMP - Famed progressive rock group from London, England. Richard Davies, Roger Hodgson, John Helliwell, Bob Siebenberg and Dougie Thompson. One of the top selling British groups in the early Eighties.

	US Top 10 Ent	UK Top 10 Ent
Breakfast In America	5/79	4/79
Paris	11/80	
...Famous Last Words...	12/82	11/82

SUPREMES - The biggest selling girl group of all time consisted of Diana Ross, Mary Wilson and Florence Ballard (died 1976). The R&B/pop trio clocked up 12 American Number 1 singles in the Sixties before Diana Ross went solo. (Act billed as Diana Ross and the Supremes from mid-1967)

	US Top 10 Ent	UK Top 10 Ent
Where Did Our Love Go	12/64	
More Hits By The Supremes	10/65	
I Hear A Symphony	5/66	
The Supremes A Go-Go	10/66	
The Supremes Sing Holland-Dozier-Holland	3/67	
Diana Ross & The Supremes' Greatest Hits	10/67	2/68
Live At The Talk Of The Town		4/68
Diana Ross & The Supremes Join The Temptations (with The Temptations)	1/69	2/69
TCB (with The Temptations)	1/69	
Magnificent Seven (with The Four Tops, but no Ross credit)		7/71
20 Golden Greats		9/77

SURVIVOR - Noted rock group from the American Midwest, led by singer/songwriter Dave Bickler and keyboardist/composer Jim Peterik (ex-Ides Of March). Other original members: Dennis Johnson, Gary Smith, Frank Sullivan.

	US Top 10 Ent	UK Top 10 Ent
Eye Of The Tiger	7/82	

KEITH SWEAT - Acclaimed R&B singer/songwriter and producer from Harlem, New York, USA, who had one of the Nineties biggest selling singles with 'I'll Give All My Love To You'. He also wrote and produced hits for Entouch, Silk and Kut Klose.

	US Top 10 Ent	UK Top 10 Ent
I'll Give All My Love To You	7/90	

SWING OUT SISTER - Jazzy pop trio formed by Andy Cornell and Martin Jackson and fronted by the stylish Corrine Drewery. For a while they were the 'flavour of the month' and their debut LP entered at Number 1 in the UK and earned them an American gold disc.

	US Top 10 Ent	UK Top 10 Ent
It's Better To Travel		5/87

SWV - Top selling new jill swing trio from New York, USA, whose name stands for Sisters With Voices. Cheryl 'Coko' Gamble, Leanne 'LeeLee' Lyons and Tamara 'Taj' Johnson. They were the most successful new singles group in America in 1993, and at times had two records simultaneously in the Top 10.

	US Top 10 Ent	UK Top 10 Ent
It's About Time	5/93	

T. REX - Groundbreaking glam rock act formed and fronted by singer/songwriter Marc Bolan (born Marc Feld in 1948 in London, England). Original partner Steve Peregrine was replaced by Mickey Finn in 1969. Bolan, whose image and music influenced many later acts, died in a car crash in 1977.

	US Top 10 Ent	UK Top 10 Ent
Electric Warrior		10/71
Prophets, Seers And Sages The Angels Of The Ages/My People Were Fair And Had Sky In Their Hair But Now They're Content To Wear Stars On Their Brows		4/72
Bolan Boogie		5/72
The Slider		8/72
Tanx		4/73
Best Of The 20th Century Boy		6/85
The Ultimate Collection		10/91

TAKE THAT - The most successful British group of the early Nineties consisted of Gary Barlow, Jason Orange, Robbie Williams, Mark Owen and Howard Donald. They were the first act since The Beatles to have four consecutive UK Number 1 singles, and the first ever to have three in a row enter at Number 1. They have so far sold over four million singles in the UK without causing even a ripple in the US.

	US Top 10 Ent	UK Top 10 Ent
Take That And Party		1/93
Everything Changes		10/93

TALK TALK - London-based synth rock band consisted of singer/keyboard player Mark Hollis (brother of producer Ed Hollis), Paul Webb and Lee Harris.

	US Top 10 Ent	UK Top 10 Ent
Natural History - The Very Best Of..		6/90

TASTE OF HONEY - R&B/dance act from Los Angeles, USA, fronted by Janice Marie Johnson and Hazel Payne with Donald Johnson and Perry Kimble. They won a Grammy for Best New Artist in 1978.

	US Top 10 Ent	UK Top 10 Ent
A Taste Of Honey	9/78	

JAMES TAYLOR - World famous folk/pop singer/songwriter and guitarist born 1948 in Boston, USA, who was once married to singer Carly Simon. He was one of the top selling album artists of the Seventies, and is regarded as one of the leading artists in his genre.

	US Top 10 Ent	UK Top 10 Ent
Sweet Baby James	10/70	2/71
Mud Slide Slim And The Blue Horizon	5/71	6/71
One Man Dog	1/73	
Gorilla	8/75	
JT	8/77	

JOHNNIE TAYLOR - Top soul/blues singer, born 1938 in Arkansas, USA. This one-time gospel performer recorded for Sam Cooke's Sar label before starting a string of R&B hits on Stax. His 'Disco Lady' was the first single certified platinum (two million seller).

	US Top 10 Ent	UK Top 10 Ent
Eargasm	4/76	

TEARS FOR FEARS - Innovative pop/rock duo from Bath, England. Curt Smith and Roland Orzabal previously recorded as Graduate. One of the leading acts of the mid-Eighties British Invasion of the US charts.

	US Top 10 Ent	UK Top 10 Ent
The Hurting		3/83
Songs From The Big Chair	6/85	3/85
The Seeds Of Love	11/89	10/89
Tears Roll Down (Greatest Hits 1981-1992)		3/92

TECHNOTRONIC - Belgian dance music project produced by Thomas De Quincy (real name Jo Bogaert).

Act's first hit, 'Pump Up The Jam', was composed and performed by Ya Kid K (Zaire-born real name Manuella Kamosi Maoso Djogi), although credited to Felly, a model who fronted the group for videos.

	US Top 10 Ent	UK Top 10 Ent
Pump Up The Jam		2/90

TEMPERANCE SEVEN - Tongue-in-cheek, nine-man novelty band who played late-Twenties jazz-influenced pop. They were guided by Captain Cephas Howard and featured the (megaphoned) vocals of Paul MacDowell. Act were producer George Martin's last major success before The Beatles.

	US Top 10 Ent	UK Top 10 Ent
Temperance Seven 1961		2/62

TEMPLE OF THE DOG - Tribute band to Andrew Wood, the late lead singer of Mother Love Bone (died of drug overdose 1990). Comprised six Seattle musicians: Jeff Ament and Stone Gossard (both Mother Love Bone/Pearl Jam), Matt Cameron and Chris Cornell (both Soundgarden), Mike McCready and Eddie Vedder (both Pearl Jam).

	US Top 10 Ent	UK Top 10 Ent
Temple Of The Dog	9/92	

TEMPTATIONS - World's most successful male soul vocal group from Detroit, USA. Members have included Eddie Kendricks (died 1992), Paul Williams (died 1973) Melvin Franklin, Otis Williams, David Ruffin (died 1991), Dennis Edwards and Damon Harris. The group were seldom out of the US charts between 1964-1986. See also The Supremes.

	US Top 10 Ent	UK Top 10 Ent
The Temptations' Greatest Hits	2/67	
With A Lot O' Soul	9/67	
Cloud Nine	4/69	
Puzzle People	11/69	
All Directions	10/72	
Masterpiece	4/73	

10 C.C. - Commercially successful British art rock/pop group. Lol Creme, Kevin Godley, Graham Gouldman (hit songwriter for The Yardbirds, Herman's Hermits, The Hollies etc.), Eric Stewart (ex-Mindbenders). Godley and Creme later continued as a duo and video producers.

	US Top 10 Ent	UK Top 10 Ent
The Original Soundtrack		4/75
How Dare You?		2/76
Deceptive Bends		5/77
Bloody Tourists		10/78
Greatest Hits 1972-1978		11/79
Changing Faces - The Very Best Of 10 CC (with Godley & Creme)		9/87

TEN YEARS AFTER - Acclaimed blues/rock band from Nottingham, England, fronted by guitar wizard Alvin Lee. Other members: Chick Churchill, Ric Lee and Leo Lyons.

	US Top 10 Ent	UK Top 10 Ent
Stonedhenge		2/69
Ssssh		10/69
Cricklewood Green		5/70

TEXAS - Noteworthy country/blues/rock group from Glasgow, Scotland. Sharleen Spiteri, Ally McErlaine, John McElhone (ex-Altered Images) and Stuart Kerr.

	US Top 10 Ent	UK Top 10 Ent
Southside		3/89

THE THE - Adventurous indie rock act, the brainchild of songwriter/producer Matt Johnson. Members have included Johnny Marr (ex-Smiths), David Palmer and James Eller.

	US Top 10 Ent	UK Top 10 Ent
Dusk		2/93

THEN JERICO - British rock band led by Mark Shaw, who were on the verge of major success in the late Eighties. Other members: Scott Taylor, Rob Downes, Jasper Stanthorpe, Keith Airey and Steve Wren.

	US Top 10 Ent	UK Top 10 Ent
The Big Area		3/89

THIN LIZZY - Acclaimed heavy rock group from Dublin, Ireland, built around distinctive singer/guitarist Phil Lynott (died 1986). Other members have included Brian Downey, Gary Moore, Brian Robertson, Scott Gorham, Snowy White and Midge Ure.

	US Top 10 Ent	UK Top 10 Ent
Live And Dangerous		6/78
Black Rose (A Rock Legend)		5/79
Thunder And Lightning		3/83

KENNY THOMAS - Blue-eyed soul singer born 1968 in London, England. He had a handful of UK hits (mostly cover versions) in the early-Nineties. His debut LP sold over half a million copies in Britain.

	US Top 10 Ent	UK Top 10 Ent
Voices		10/91

THOMPSON TWINS - Successful British-based synth-led pop/dance trio consisted of Tom Bailey (from Yorkshire, England) with Alannah Currie (from New Zealand) and Londoner Joe Leeway. They were one of the acts involved in the second major British Invasion of the US charts.

	US Top 10 Ent	UK Top 10 Ent
Quick Step And Side Kick		3/83
Into The Gap	5/84	2/84

THREE DEGREES - Leading pop/soul vocal trio from Philadelphia, USA, whose best known line-up was Fayette Pinkney, Sheila Ferguson and Valerie Holiday. Act were especially popular in the UK, where it was claimed that they were Prince Charles' favourite group.

	US Top 10 Ent	UK Top 10 Ent
Take Good Care Of Yourself		6/75
A Collection Of Their 20 Greatest Hits		4/79

THREE DOG NIGHT - Top selling pop/rock group from Los Angeles, USA. Danny Hutton, Chuck Negron and Cory Wells. Although they were almost unknown in the UK, the group were one of America's most consistent hit-makers in the early Seventies.

	US Top 10 Ent	UK Top 10 Ent
Was Captured Live At The Forum	1/70	
Golden Bisquits	4/71	
Harmony	11/71	
Seven Separate Fools	9/72	

THUNDER - Raw British blues-based rock group who evolved from Terraplane. Danny Bowes, Luke Morley, Ben Matthews, Mark Luckhurst and Garry James.

	US Top 10 Ent	UK Top 10 Ent
Laughing On Judgement Day		9/92

TIFFANY - Teenage pop singer born 1971 in Oklahoma (real name Tiffany Darwisch), who kick-started her career with a shopping-mall tour. For a short while, she was the hottest female act on the US singles scene.

	US Top 10 Ent	UK Top 10 Ent
Tiffany	12/87	

TANITA TIKARAM - Distinctive British-based singer/songwriter born 1969 in West Germany, of Malaysian/Fijian parents, who has not, as yet, reached the heights many critics prophesied.

	US Top 10 Ent	UK Top 10 Ent
Ancient Heart		2/89
The Sweetkeeper		2/90

JOHNNY TILLOTSON - Hit making pop/country singer/songwriter born 1939 in Jacksonville, Florida, USA. He was a regular visitor to the US singles chart in the early Sixties.

	US Top 10 Ent	UK Top 10 Ent
It Keeps Right On A-Hurtin'	9/62	

TIN MACHINE - Relatively short-lived rock group formed by David Bowie. Other members were Reeves Gabrels and brothers Hunt and Tony Sales (both ex-Utopia and sons of noted funny man Soupy Sales).

	US Top 10 Ent	UK Top 10 Ent
Tin Machine		6/89

TINY TIM - Novelty singer and ukulele player from New York, USA, born Herbert Khaury in 1930. He was one of the most unique acts of the rock era and for a brief time was an international celebrity.

	US Top 10 Ent	UK Top 10 Ent
God Bless Tiny Tim	7/68	

TONE LOC - Hoarse-voiced Los Angeles-based rapper (nickname Antonio Loco, real name Anthony Smith). He was the first black rap artist to have a US Number 1 LP, and his humour-laced 'Wild Thing' and 'Funky Cold Medina' are among the biggest selling rap singles ever.

	US Top 10 Ent	UK Top 10 Ent
Loc-Ed After Dark	3/89	

TOO SHORT - Diminutive rapper from Los Angeles, USA, born Todd Shaw in 1966, whose main lyrical topic is his sexual prowess.

	US Top 10 Ent	UK Top 10 Ent
Shorty The Pimp	8/92	
Get In Where Ya Fit In	11/93	

TOTO - Critically acclaimed rock act from Los Angeles, USA, formed by top session musicians. Members have included David Hungate, Bobby Kimball (real name Robert Toteaux), Steve Lukather, David Paich, brothers Steve, Jeff (died 1992) and, later, Mike Porcaro. They won a record five Grammy Awards in 1983.

	US Top 10 Ent	UK Top 10 Ent
Toto IV	6/82	3/83

PETE TOWNSEND - Legendary rock guitarist/songwriter born 1945 in London, England. He was The Who's main composer and, along with the other group members, started an additional solo career in 1972.

	US Top 10 Ent	UK Top 10 Ent
Empty Glass	7/80	

TOYAH - Punk-styled singer/actress, born 1958 in Birmingham, England. One of the few females to find UK success in the punk/new wave era. Toyah, whose films include *Jubilee* and *Quadrophenia*, married Robert Fripp (King Crimson) in 1986.

	US Top 10 Ent	UK Top 10 Ent
Anthem		6/81
The Changeling		6/82

T'PAU - Late-Eighties hitmaking pop/rock sextet from Shrewsbury, England, fronted by Carol Decker. Other members: Ronnie Rogers, Dean Howard, Michael Chetwood, Paul Jackson and Tim Burgess.

	US Top 10 Ent	UK Top 10 Ent
Bridge Of Spies		11/87
Rage		11/88

TRAFFIC - Revered British progressive rock group formed by Steve Winwood (ex-Spencer Davis Group) with Jim Capaldi, Dave Mason and Chris Wood (died 1983). Top selling act from the early Seventies made a moderately successful comeback in 1994.

	US Top 10 Ent	UK Top 10 Ent
John Barleycorn Must Die	8/70	
The Low Spark Of High Heeled Boys	2/72	
Shoot Out At The Fantasy Factory	3/73	

TRANSVISION VAMP - London-based pop/rock group fronted by the controversial glam-pop princess Wendy James. Other members: Ted Axile, Pol Burton, Dave Parsons and Nick Sayer.

	US Top 10 Ent	UK Top 10 Ent
Velveteen		7/89

TRAVELING WILBURYS - Rock supergroup consisted of 'Wilbury brothers' Lucky/Boo (Bob Dylan), Nelson/Spike (George Harrison), Otis/Clayton (Jeff Lynne), Charlie T. Junior/Muddy (Tom Petty) and Lefty (Roy Orbison). The latter member died as the first of their two albums hit the Top 10.

	US Top 10 Ent	UK Top 10 Ent
Traveling Wilburys	12/88	

JOHN TRAVOLTA - Internationally famous actor/singer/dancer born 1954 in New Jersey, USA. He was arguably the best known personality in the disco era. His film successes include *Saturday Night Fever*, *Urban Cowboy* and *Grease* and several of his singles have passed the million sales mark.

Title	US Top 10 Ent	UK Top 10 Ent
Grease (Soundtrack)	7/78	7/78

TROGGS - Distinctive British rock band from Hampshire, England, fronted by Reg Presley (real name Reg Ball). Other members: Chris Britton, Ronnie 'Bond' Bullis (died 1992) and Pete Staples. Best known for their chart topping single 'Wild Thing', they also first recorded and wrote 1994's biggest hit song, 'Love Is All Around'.

Title	US Top 10 Ent	UK Top 10 Ent
From Nowhere...The Troggs		8/66

ROBIN TROWER - Highly rated rock guitarist born 1945 in London, England, who was a member of Procol Harum before successfully going solo. He worked with vocalist James Dewar on his own albums.

Title	US Top 10 Ent	UK Top 10 Ent
Bridge Of Sighs	8/74	
For Earth Below	4/75	

TUBEWAY ARMY - See GARY NUMAN

TINA TURNER - World renowned R&B/rock singer born Anna Mae Bullock in 1938 in Tennessee, USA. She had a successful musical partnership with husband Ike, 1960-1976. In the Eighties Tina went to much greater heights as a solo performer; she sold countless millions of albums and packed stadiums worldwide.

Title	US Top 10 Ent	UK Top 10 Ent
Private Dancer	8/84	8/84
Break Every Rule	11/86	9/86
Foreign Affair		9/89
Simply The Best		10/91
What's Love Got To Do With It (Soundtrack)		6/93

TURTLES - Noted pop/rock/folk act from Los Angeles, USA, whose nucleus was Mark Volman and Howard Kaylan (real name Kaplan). The act, who had many personnel changes, were one of America's biggest selling groups in the late-Sixties.

Title	US Top 10 Ent	UK Top 10 Ent
The Turtles! Golden Hits	2/68	

2 UNLIMITED - Top selling Dutch techno/Euro pop act are Ray Slijngaard and Anita Dels. The duo were the brainchild of producer/songwriters Jean-Paul De Coster and Phil Wilde and sold millons of singles in Europe during the early-Nineties.

Title	US Top 10 Ent	UK Top 10 Ent
No Limits		5/93
Real Things		6/94

BONNIE TYLER - Gruff-voiced rock singer from Swansea, Wales, born Gaynor Hopkins in 1953. Tyler, who suprisingly had a US country Top 10 hit ('It's A Heartache'), was the first Welsh act to top the US pop chart ('Total Eclipse Of The Heart').

Title	US Top 10 Ent	UK Top 10 Ent
Faster Than The Speed Of Night	10/83	4/83

UB40 - Consistently successful multi-racial reggae group from Birmingham, England. Brothers Ali and Robin Campbell, Astro, James Brown, Earl Falconer, Norman Hassan, Brian Travers and Michael Virtue. The only reggae act to have two US Number 1 singles, 'Red Red Wine' and 'Can't Help Falling In Love'.

Title	US Top 10 Ent	UK Top 10 Ent
Signing Off		9/80
Present Arms		6/81
UB44		10/82
Labour Of Love		9/83
Geffrey Morgan		10/84
The Best Of UB40 Vol. I		11/87
Labour Of Love II		4/90
Promises And Lies	8/93	7/93
Labour Of Love - Volumes I & II		11/94

UFO - Well-rated hard rock group from Britain whose first success came in Germany. Best known line-up was Phil Mogg, Michael Schenker (ex-Scorpions), Pete Way and Andy Parker.

Title	US Top 10 Ent	UK Top 10 Ent
Strangers In The Night		2/79

UGLY KID JOE - Hard rock band from California, USA, fronted by Whitfield Crane with Cordell Crockett, Mark Davis, Klaus Eichstadt, Roger Lahr (replaced by Dave Fortman).

Title	US Top 10 Ent	UK Top 10 Ent
As Ugly As They Want To Be	4/92	

ULTRAVOX - Acclaimed electro-rock band led by Midge Ure (ex-Slik and Visage, who replaced John Foxx) with Canadian Warren Cann, Chris Cross and Billy Currie. A groundbreaking early-Eighties act.

Title	US Top 10 Ent	UK Top 10 Ent
Vienna		2/81
Rage In Eden		9/81
The Collection		11/84

MIDGE URE - Respected rock singer/songwriter born 1953 in Glasgow, Scotland. The one-time member of hit acts Slik, Visage and Ultravox (see above), who co-wrote and produced Band Aid's 'Do They Know It's Christmas' and helped organize Live Aid and the Nelson Mandela 70th Birthday Tribute show.

Title	US Top 10 Ent	UK Top 10 Ent
The Gift		10/85

URIAH HEEP - Successful British heavy-rock group whose members have included David Byron, Mick Box, Ken Henlsey, Pete Goalby, Gary Thain and noted session man Nigel Olsson. They were, arguably, more successful in the USA and Germany than in their homeland.

Title	US Top 10 Ent	UK Top 10 Ent
Return To Fantasy		7/75

USA FOR AFRICA - All-star American ensemble who combined their talents solely to raise money for famine relief. Their four million selling 'We AreThe World' was the biggest selling single of the Eighties in America. In total, an estimated $50 million was raised by the project.

Title	US Top 10 Ent	UK Top 10 Ent
We Are The World	4/85	

U2 - One of the most popular rock acts of all time. Paul 'Bono' Hewson, Dave 'The Edge' Evans, Adam Clayton and Larry Mullen Jr. From Dublin, Ireland, the quartet have been breaking sales and box office records around the world since the late-Eighties. Four of their albums have topped the US chart and four have entered at Number 1 in the UK.

Title	US Top 10 Ent	UK Top 10 Ent
War		3/83
U2 Live: Under A Blood Red Sky		12/83
The Unforgettable Fire		10/84
The Joshua Tree	4/87	3/87
Rattle And Hum	11/88	10/88
Achtung Baby	12/91	12/91
Zooropa	7/93	7/93

FRANKIE VALLI - See FOUR SEASONS

VAN HALEN - Hugely popular hard rock band from Pasadena, California, USA. David Lee Roth (replaced as lead singer in 1985 by Sammy Hagar), Dutch-born brothers Eddie and Alex Van Halen and Michael Anthony. One of the biggest selling LP acts of the Eighties, who are still adding to their total of 10 US platinum albums.

Title	US Top 10 Ent	UK Top 10 Ent
Van Halen II	5/79	
Women And Children First	5/80	
Fair Warning	6/81	
Diver Down	5/82	
1984 (MCMLXXXIV)	2/84	
5150	4/86	
OU812	6/88	
For Unlawful Carnal Knowledge	7/91	
Live: Right Here, Right Now	3/93	

LUTHER VANDROSS - Superior soul singer/songwriter and producer born 1951 in New York, USA. The internationally renowned ex-session singer has had his last 10 albums all pass the platinum sales mark in the USA.

Title	US Top 10 Ent	UK Top 10 Ent
Give Me The Reason		3/88
Songs	10/94	10/94

VANGELIS - Well known keyboard player/composer born Evangelos Papathanassiou in 1943 in Greece. Apart from his solo successes, he has had chart success with Demis Roussos in Aphrodite's Child and with Jon Anderson (ex-Yes).

Title	US Top 10 Ent	UK Top 10 Ent
Chariots Of Fire (Soundtrack)	3/82	6/81

VANILLA FUDGE - Trail-blazing psychedelic rock group from New York, USA. Mark Stein, Vinnie Martell, Carmine Appice and Tim Bogert. One of the more inventive US groups of the late-Sixties, whose members Appice and Bogert later worked with Rod Stewart and Jeff Beck.

Title	US Top 10 Ent	UK Top 10 Ent
Vanilla Fudge	10/67	

VANILLA ICE - White rapper, born Robert Van Winkle in 1968 in Florida, USA. His debut LP headed the US charts for four months and sold a record five million copies in only 12 weeks. He received a lot of flak from the media and other rap acts and soon lost his place at the forefront of the genre.

Title	US Top 10 Ent	UK Top 10 Ent
To The Extreme	10/90	1/91

VARIOUS

Title	US Top 10 Ent	UK Top 10 Ent
60 Years Of Music America Loves Best	1/60	
60 Years Of Music America Loves Best Vol. II	11/60	
Stars For A Summer Night	7/61	
Sixty Years Of Music America Loves Best Vol. 3 (Red Seal)	10/61	
Sixty Years Of Music America Loves Best Vol. 3 (Black Seal)	10/61	
All Star Festival		3/63
Shut Down	8/63	
Welcome To The LBJ Ranch!	12/65	
Stars Charity Fantasia Save The Children		10/66
British Motown Chartbusters		11/67
Breakthrough		10/67
British Motown Chartbusters Vol. 3		10/69
Woodstock	6/70	
Motown Chartbusters Vol. 4		10/70
Jesus Christ Superstar	12/70	
Motown Chartbusters Vol. 5		4/71
Hot Hits 6		8/71
Top Of The Pops Vol. 18		8/71
Motown Chartbusters Vol. 6		10/71
Hot Hits 7		10/71
Top Of The Pops Vol. 19		10/71
Top Of The Pops Vol. 20		11/71
Hot Hits 8		12/71
20 Dynamic Hits		6/72
20 Fantastic Hits		8/72
20 All Time Hits Of The Fifties		10/72
20 Star Tracks		10/72
20 Fantastic Hits Vol. 2		11/72
25 Dynamic Hits Vol. 2		11/72
25 Rockin' & Rollin' Greats		12/72
Tommy	1/73	
20 Flashback Greats Of The Sixties		3/73

	US Top 10 Ent	UK Top 10 Ent
40 Fantastic Hits From The 50s And 60s		4/73
Believe In Music		4/73
20 Fantastic Hits Vol. 3		5/73
Pure Gold		6/73
That'll Be The Day		6/73
Disco Hits '75		12/75
Music Express		2/76
Juke Box Jive		4/76
Hit Machine		5/76
Instrumental Gold		5/76
Soul Motion		10/76
Disco Rocket	12/76	
Dance To The Music		3/77
Heartbreakers		2/77
Feelings		12/77
Disco Fever		12/77
Disco Stars		3/78
Boogie Nights		3/78
Star Party		8/78
Big Wheels Of Motown		10/78
Emotions		11/78
Midnight Hustle		12/78
Don't Walk Boogie		1/79
Action Replay		2/79
Country Life		4/79
This Is It		6/79
The Best Disco Album In The World		7/79
Rock 'n' Roller Disco		11/79
Peace In The Valley		12/79
Video Stars		1/80
The Last Dance		2/80
Star Tracks		4/80
Hot Wax		6/80
Mounting Excitement		10/80
Chartbusters 81		5/81
Roll On		5/81
Disco Daze And Disco Nites		6/81
Themes		6/81
The Official BBC Album Of The Royal Wedding		8/81
Super Hits 1 & 2		10/81
Chart Hits 81		11/81
Hits Hits Hits		1/82
Modern Dance		1/82
Dreaming		2/82
Action Trax		3/82
James Bond's Greatest Hits		4/82
Chartbusters		5/82
Breakout		9/82
Chartbeat/Chartheat		9/82
Reflections		10/82
Raiders Of The Pop Charts		1/83
Visions		2/83
Chart Runners		4/83
Hotline		3/83
Chart Encounters Of The Hit Kind		6/83
The Hit Squad - Chart Tracking		10/83
The Two Of Us		11/83
Formula 30		12/83
Now That's What I Call Music		12/83
Now That's What I Call Music 2		4/84
American Heartbeat		6/84
Hungry For Hits		6/84
Then Came Rock 'n' Roll		6/84
Now That's What I Call Music 3		8/84
Hits Hits Hits - 18 Smash Originals		10/84
The Hits Album		12/84
Now That's What I Call Music 4		12/84
Hits 2		4/85
Out Now!		5/85
Now Dance		6/85
Now That's What I Call Music 5		8/85
Out Now! 2		11/85
The Greatest Hits Of 1985		11/85
Now - The Christmas Album		12/85
Now That's What I Call Music 6		12/85
Hits 3		12/85
The Love Album		12/85
Hits For Lovers		3/86
Hits 4		3/86
Now - The Summer Album		7/86
Now That's What I Call Music 7		8/86
Hits 5		11/86
Now Dance '86		11/86
Now That's What I Call Music 8		12/86
Move Closer		3/87
Now That's What I Call Music 9		4/87
Hits 6		7/87
Sixties Mix		8/87
Hits 7		12/87
Now That's What I Call Music 10		12/87
Unforgettable		3/88
Hip Hop And Rapping In The House		4/88
Now That's What I Call Music 11		4/88
More Dirty Dancing	4/88	5/88
Nite Flite		6/88
Motown Dance Party		6/88
Hits 8		8/88
Now That's What I Call Music 12		7/88
The Greatest Ever Rock 'n' Roll Mix		8/88
Rap Trax		9/88
Hot City Nights		9/88
Smash Hits Party '88		11/88
The Premiere Collection		12/88
The Hits Album		12/88
Now That's What I Call Music 13		12/88
A Very Special Christmas 2	12/92	
Common Thread: The Songs Of The Eagles	11/93	

VAUGHAN BROTHERS - Celebrated blues/rock guitarist Stevie Ray Vaughan born 1954 in Dallas, Texas, USA. He had his biggest hit album when he teamed with brother Jimmie (ex-Fabulous Thunderbirds). It was Stevie's first album released after his death in a helicopter crash.

	US Top 10 Ent	UK Top 10 Ent
Family Style	11/90	

BILLY VAUGHN - Top selling orchestra leader/arranger/producer born 1919 in Kentucky, USA (died 1991). He produced a string of hits in the Fifties for acts like Pat Boone, The Fontane Sisters and Gale Storm. His orchestra had one of the most distinctive sounds of their era.

	US Top 10 Ent	UK Top 10 Ent
Theme From A Summer Place	4/60	

BOBBY VEE - Top teen idol of the early-Sixties was born Robert Velline in 1943 in North Dakota. The Buddy Holly influenced act had numerous hit singles on both sides of the Atlantic. On his biggest album he was backed by Holly's backing band, The Crickets.

	US Top 10 Ent	UK Top 10 Ent
Bobby Vee Meets The Crickets		11/62

SUZANNE VEGA - Notable folk singer/songwriter and guitarist who was born 1959 in New York, USA. The award-winning transatlantic star has been heard on record with such varied acts as The Smithereens, Luciano Pavarotti and DNA.

	US Top 10 Ent	UK Top 10 Ent
Solitude Standing		5/87

VILLAGE PEOPLE - Visually unmistakable 'camp' disco act formed by producer Jacques Morali (died 1991). Lead vocalist Victor Willis with Alexander Briley, Randy Jones, David Hodo, Glenn Hughes, Felipe Rose. Ray Simpson replaced Willis at the end of 1979.

	US Top 10 Ent	UK Top 10 Ent
Cruisin'	2/79	
Go West	5/79	

VILLAGE STOMPERS - One-hit wonder trad-jazz-styled instrumental octet, based in Greenwich Village, New York, USA. Members included Frank Hubbell and Joe Muranyi.

	US Top 10 Ent	UK Top 10 Ent
Washington Square	12/63	

BOBBY VINTON - Very successful pop/MOR singer born 1935 in Pennsylvania, USA. Arguably America's top selling male solo artist in the early-Sixties, whose 30 single hits that decade included four Number1s.

	US Top 10 Ent	UK Top 10 Ent
Roses Are Red	9/62	
There! I've Said It Again	3/64	

VISAGE - New romantic dance act fronted by cult figure Steve Strange (real name Steve Harrington). Other members included Midge Ure, Billy Currie (both Ultravox) and Rusty Egan (ex Rich Kids).

	US Top 10 Ent	UK Top 10 Ent
The Anvil		4/82

RICK WAKEMAN - Celebrated rock keyboardist born 1949 in London, England. Worked with The Strawbs and Yes before going solo and finding success on both sides of the Atlantic.

	US Top 10 Ent	UK Top 10 Ent
Journey To The Centre Of The Earth	7/74	5/74
The Myths And Legends Of King Arthur And The Knights Of The Round Table		4/75

WALKER BROTHERS - Top teen appeal act consisted of Scott Engel, Gary Leeds and John Maus. Success came to the image-conscious American trio after they relocated to Britain. They were one of the most popular groups in the UK during the late-Sixties.

	US Top 10 Ent	UK Top 10 Ent
Take It Easy		1/66
Portrait		9/66
Images		4/67
No Regrets - The Best Of ... 1965-1976 (with Scott Walker)		2/92

SCOTT WALKER - Distinctive pop balladeer from Ohio, USA, born Noel Scott Engel in 1944. He found stardom as front man of the Walker Brothers, had several hits as a soloist and still has a large cult following.

	US Top 10 Ent	UK Top 10 Ent
Scott		9/67
Scott 2		5/68
Scott 3		4/69
No Regrets - The Best Of ...1965-1976 (with Walker Brothers)		2/92

JOE WALSH - Well known rock singer/songwriter and guitarist born 1947 in Wichita, Kansas, USA. The ex-member of The James Gang and The Eagles formed his own band in 1972.

The Smoker You Drink,

	US Top 10 Ent	UK Top 10 Ent
The Player You Get	11/73	

WAR - Innovative R&B/funk band from Long Beach, California, USA. Members included Lonnie Jordan, Morris 'B.B.' Dickerson, Charles Miller (died 1980), Lee Oskar and Howard Scott. The group first charted as Eric Burdon's backing band.

	US Top 10 Ent	UK Top 10 Ent
The World Is A Ghetto	1/73	
Deliver The Word	10/73	
Greatest Hits	9/76	

ANITA WARD - Chart topping disco/R&B singer born 1957 in Memphis, Tennessee, USA. The ex-school teacher and session singer had a transatlantic Number 1 with her only hit single, 'Ring My Bell'.

	US Top 10 Ent	UK Top 10 Ent
Songs Of Love	7/79	

RUSTY WARREN - Slightly risque comedienne from New York, USA, born Ilene Goldman in 1931. The only female humorist to crack the US Top 10.

	US Top 10 Ent	UK Top 10 Ent
Knockers Up!	8/61	

DIONNE WARWICK - Internationally renowned soul/MOR singer born 1940 in New Jersey, USA. The one time session singer was discovered by Burt Bacharach, who penned many of her hits. She is one of the most respected and consistently successful female singers of the rock era.

	US Top 10 Ent	UK Top 10 Ent
Valley Of The Dolls	4/68	
Heartbreaker		11/82

GENO WASHINGTON - Indiana, USA born soul singer who settled in the UK. He was a very popular live act in Britain, who sold more albums than singles. A tribute record, 'Geno' by Dexy's Midnight Runners, topped the UK chart in 1980.

	US Top 10 Ent	UK Top 10 Ent
Hand Clappin' - Foot Stompin' - Funky Butt - Live!		1/67

GROVER WASHINGTON JR. - Stylish and successful jazz/R&B tenor sax player born 1943 in Buffalo, USA. He was the top selling jazz instrumentalist in the early-Eighties.

	US Top 10 Ent	UK Top 10 Ent
Winelight	4/81	

WATERBOYS - Noteworthy celtic-folk-rock band formed by Scottish-born singer/songwriter Mike Scott. Other members have included Anthony Thistlethwaite (English), Trevor Hutchinson (Irish) and Karl Wallinger (Welsh). The latter left in 1985 to form the equally well-regarded World Party.

	US Top 10 Ent	UK Top 10 Ent
Best Of The Waterboys '81-'90		5/91
Dream Harder		6/93

JEFF WAYNE - Multi-talented American born producer/musician/composer who found success when he relocated to the UK, producing a string of hit singles for David Essex. The all-star **War Of The Worlds** album was on the UK charts for over 200 weeks.

	US Top 10 Ent	UK Top 10 Ent
War Of The Worlds		7/78

MARTI WEBB - Popular British MOR/pop singer/actress whose main claim to fame was her starring role in Andrew Lloyd Webber's staged-for-TV musical *Tell Me On A Sunday.*

	US Top 10 Ent	UK Top 10 Ent
Tell Me On A Sunday		3/80

BERT WEEDON - Britain's best known guitarist in the Fifties was born 1921 in London. An *NME* poll winner in 1954, he played on dozens of early UK rock hits, and had his own biggest chart record 20 years later.

	US Top 10 Ent	UK Top 10 Ent
22 Golden Guitar Greats		11/76

ERIC WEISSBERG - Respected New York-based multi-instrumentalist, who was a top session musician in the Sixties and Seventies (playing for Bob Dylan, Jim Croce and Billy Joel). He worked with Steve Mandell and Marshall Brickman on his hit album.

	US Top 10 Ent	UK Top 10 Ent
Dueling Banjos/Deliverance (Soundtrack)	3/73	

TIM WEISBERG - See DAN FOGELBERG

LAWRENCE WELK - Very successful accordionist/band-leader, whose sweet polka-based sound was tagged 'Champagne Music'. He was born 1903 in North Dakota, USA, and died 1992. Welk's 50-year recording career produced many top sellers. He also hosted a long running TV show and headed a music publishing company.

	US Top 10 Ent	UK Top 10 Ent
Last Date	1/61	
Calcutta!	2/61	
Yellow Bird	9/61	

PAUL WELLER - Highly regarded singer/songwriter born 1958 in Surrey, England. One of the most regular UK chart artists since the late-Seventies, fronting top selling acts The Jam and The Style Council before going solo in 1992.

	US Top 10 Ent	UK Top 10 Ent
Wild Wood		9/93

WET WET WET - One-time UK teen idols who have maintained their popularity. The pop/soul group from Glasgow, Scotland, are fronted by Marti Pellow (real name Mark McLoughlin). Other members: Graeme Clark, Tom Cunningham and Neil Mitchell. Their cover of the Troggs' 'Love Is All Around' topped the UK singles chart for 15 weeks in 1994.

	US Top 10 Ent	UK Top 10 Ent
Popped In Souled Out		10/87
The Memphis Sessions		11/88
Holding Back The River		11/89
High On The Happy Side		2/92
End Of Part One (Their Greatest Hits)		11/93

WHAM! - World renowned pop duo of George Michael (real name Georgios Panayiotou) and Andrew Ridgeley, sold 40 million records in their short career. No duo has scored more UK Number 1 singles than Wham! George Michael stayed at the top after act disbanded. See also George Michael.

	US Top 10 Ent	UK Top 10 Ent
Fantastic		7/83
Make It Big	2/85	11/84
The Final		7/86

WHISPERS - Top soul vocal group from Los Angeles, USA. Nicolas Caldwell, Gordy Harmon (replaced by Leaveil Degree), Marcus Hutson and twins Walter and Wallace Scott. Act had recorded for 16 years before their first major pop success came in 1980.

	US Top 10 Ent	UK Top 10 Ent
The Whispers	3/80	

BARRY WHITE - Distinctive deep-voiced Los Angeles-based soul singer/songwriter/producer and pianist born 1944 in Texas, USA. This one time A&R man, who formed Love Unlimited and fronted the Love Unlimited Orchestra, had an enviable string of top selling transatlantic singles and albums in the Seventies and was still going strong in the Nineties.

	US Top 10 Ent	UK Top 10 Ent
Can't Get Enough	10/74	11/74
The Collection		7/88

WHITESNAKE - Famed heavy metal band formed by lead singer David Coverdale (ex-Deep Purple). Members have included Jon Lord, Ian Paice (both ex Deep Purple), Aynsley Dunbar (ex-Jefferson Starship) and noted musicians Cozy Powell and Steve Vai.

	US Top 10 Ent	UK Top 10 Ent
Ready And Willing		6/80
Come And Get It		4/81
Whitesnake	5/87	
Greatest Hits		7/94

SLIM WHITMAN - Yodelling country singer born 1924 in Tampa, Florida, USA. Despite only moderate US success, he became a top UK act in the Fifties, and had a string of big selling albums there twenty years later.

	US Top 10 Ent	UK Top 10 Ent
The Very Best Of Slim Whitman		2/76
Red River Valley		1/77
Home On The Range		10/77

ROGER WHITTAKER - Unique singer/guitarist/whistler born 1936 in Nairobi, Kenya. He made a name for himself on both sides of the Atlantic before settling in Germany, where he is still a massive album seller.

	US Top 10 Ent	UK Top 10 Ent
The Very Best Of Roger Whittaker		9/75

WHO - Legendary rock band from London, England. Roger Daltrey, songwriter/guitarist Peter Townshend, John Entwistle and Keith Moon (died 1978). Moon replaced by Kenny Jones (ex-Small Faces). One of the most innovative and important acts of the rock era.

	US Top 10 Ent	UK Top 10 Ent
My Generation		1/66
A Quick One		1/67
Tommy	7/69	6/69
Live At Leeds	6/70	6/70
Who's Next	9/71	9/71
Quadrophenia	11/73	11/73
The Story Of The Who		10/76
Who Are You	9/78	9/78
The Kids Are Alright	8/79	
Face Dances	4/81	4/81
It's Hard	11/82	

WILD CHERRY - White funk band from Ohio, USA, who had five minutes of fame in 1976 thanks to their single 'Play That Funky Music'. Bob Parissi with Mark Avsec, Bryan Bassett, Ron Beitle and Allen Wentz.

	US Top 10 Ent	UK Top 10 Ent
Wild Cherry	9/76	

KIM WILDE - Pop singer from London, England, born Kim Smith in 1960. Daughter of British Fifties/Sixties star Marty Wilde, she is the only UK female vocalist to top the chart in America without repeating the feat in Britain.

	US Top 10 Ent	UK Top 10 Ent
Kim Wilde		7/81

ANDY WILLIAMS - Internationally famous MOR/pop singer/entertainer born 1928 in Iowa, USA. A late-Fifties chart regular, whose own TV show in the Sixties helped make him one of that decade's top selling album artists. He is still one of America's top cabaret performers.

	US Top 10 Ent	UK Top 10 Ent
Moon River & Other Great Movie Themes	7/62	
Days Of Wine And Roses	5/63	
'Call Me Irresponsible' And Other Hit Songs	6/64	
The Great Songs From 'My Fair Lady' And Other Broadway Hits	11/64	
Dear Heart	5/65	
Almost There		8/65
The Shadow Of Your Smile	6/66	
Born Free	6/67	
Love Andy		6/68
Happy Heart	6/69	
Greatest Hits		4/70
Can't Help Falling In Love		1/71
Love Story	3/71	
Home Loving Man		3/71
Solitaire		2/74
Reflections		2/78

DON WILLIAMS - Country singer/songwriter and guitarist born 1939 in Texas, USA. Scored 17 country Number 1s in the Sixties and Seventies and also found pop success on the other side of the Atlantic.

Album	US Top 10 Ent	UK Top 10 Ent
Images		9/78

JOHN WILLIAMS - British-based acoustic guitarist, born 1941 in Melbourne, Australia. As the solo LP **Bridges** climbed the UK chart, he was scoring the first of several hits as part of the classic-based soft rock band Sky.

Album	US Top 10 Ent	UK Top 10 Ent
Bridges		7/79

ROGER WILLIAMS - Top selling MOR pianist born Louis Weertz in 1925 in Nebraska, USA. A TV talent show win gained him a recording contract which led to a series of US chart albums spanning three decades.

Album	US Top 10 Ent	UK Top 10 Ent
Temptation	1/61	
Born Free	1/67	

BRUCE WILLIS - Famous film star/singer born 1955 in New Jersey, USA. The role of David Addison in the transatlantically successful TV series *Moonlighting* led to chart success for would-be soul singer Willis.

Album	US Top 10 Ent	UK Top 10 Ent
The Return Of Bruno		7/87

WILSON PHILLIPS - Commercially successful singing/songwriting trio. Chynna Phillips (daughter of John & Michelle Phillips of The Mamas & The Papas) and sisters Carnie and Wendy Wilson (daughters of Brian Wilson of the Beach Boys). Their eponymous LP was one of the top selling debut albums in the Nineties

Album	US Top 10 Ent	UK Top 10 Ent
Wilson Phillips	7/90	
Shadows And Light	6/92	

NANCY WILSON - Stylish jazz/R&B/MOR singer/entertainer born 1937 in Ohio, USA. Consistently popular performer who was seldom away from the US album chart in the Sixties.

Album	US Top 10 Ent	UK Top 10 Ent
Yesterday's Love Songs/Today's Blues	3/64	
How Glad I Am	10/64	

EDGAR WINTER GROUP - Well regarded rock/blues singer/musician born 1946 in Texas, USA (Johnny Winter is his older brother). Among his group members have been such notables as Rick Derringer (ex- McCoys), Dan Hartman (later a top disco composer) and Ronnie Montrose (later Montrose).

Album	US Top 10 Ent	UK Top 10 Ent
They Only Come Out At Night	5/73	

STEVE WINWOOD - Respected rock singer/songwriter and keyboard player born 1948 in Birmingham, England. Before finding solo success, Winwood fronted hit acts The Spencer Davis Group, Blind Faith and Traffic.

Album	US Top 10 Ent	UK Top 10 Ent
Arc Of A Diver	4/81	
Talking Back To The Night		8/82
Back In The High Life	8/86	
Roll With It	7/88	7/88

WISHBONE ASH - Noteworthy British progressive rock band. Members have included brothers Martin & Ted Turner, Laurie Wisefield, Andy Powell, Steve Upton, Trevor Bolder, John Wetton (Asia, Roxy Music, Uriah Heep), Claire Hamill.

Album	US Top 10 Ent	UK Top 10 Ent
Argus		5/72

BILL WITHERS - Unique folk-styled soul singer/songwriter and guitarist born 1938 in West Virginia, USA. Fame came late in life for the talented performer who penned such classics as 'Ain't No Sunshine', 'Lean On Me' and 'Lovely Day'.

Album	US Top 10 Ent	UK Top 10 Ent
Still Bill	7/72	

WOMACK AND WOMACK - Soulful American husband and wife duo. Cecil Womack (brother of Bobby Womack) and wife Linda (Sam Cooke's daughter). Act were more popular in the UK than their homeland.

Album	US Top 10 Ent	UK Top 10 Ent
Conscience		10/88

WONDER STUFF - Well-rated British rock quartet from Birmingham fronted by Miles Hunt. Other members: Malcolm Treece, Rob Jones (died 1993) and Martin Gilks. They had a UK Number 1 single in 1991 when teamed with comedian Vic Reeves ('Dizzy').

Album	US Top 10 Ent	UK Top 10 Ent
Never Loved Elvis		6/91

STEVIE WONDER - Legendary soul singer/songwriter/keyboard player born Steveland Judkins in 1950 in Michigan, USA. Multi-talented performer, who has been a regular transatlantic chart entrant since the late-Sixties, was the first act to simultaneously top the US single and album chart, which he did aged just 13.

Album	US Top 10 Ent	UK Top 10 Ent
Little Stevie Wonder/ The 12 Year Old Genius	8/63	
Talking Book	2/73	
Innervisions	9/73	
Fulfillingness' First Finale	8/74	8/74
Songs In The Key Of Life	10/76	10/76
Journey Through The Secret Life Of Plants	11/79	
Hotter Than July	11/80	11/80
Stevie Wonder's Original Musiquarium I	6/82	
The Woman In Red (Soundtrack)	10/84	9/84
In Square Circle	11/85	10/85

WORLD PARTY - Ecologically-slanted rock act masterminded by Welsh singer/songwriter and multi-instrumentalist Karl Wallinger (ex-Waterboys). Act has a cult following on both sides of the Atlantic.

Album	US Top 10 Ent	UK Top 10 Ent
Bang!		5/93

GARY WRIGHT - Hit rock singer/songwriter and keyboardist, born 1943 in New Jersey, USA. He co-fronted British rock band Spooky Tooth before going solo in 1974.

Album	US Top 10 Ent	UK Top 10 Ent
The Dream Weaver	4/76	

TAMMY WYNETTE - Country singer from Mississippi, USA, born Virginia Wynette Pugh in 1942, known as the 'First Lady Of Country Music'. Apart from dozens of solo country chart entries, she also had many hit duets with fellow country superstar George Jones, to whom she was once married.

Album	US Top 10 Ent	UK Top 10 Ent
The Best Of Tammy Wynette		6/75
20 Country Classics		1/78

WYNONNA - Foremost female country singer born Christina Cimenella in 1964 in Kentucky, USA. Until her mother Naomi's enforced retirement in 1991, they recorded together as The Judds and were the most successful female country duo of all time. However, it was Wynonna's solo recordings that introduced her to the US Top 40 pop album chart.

Album	US Top 10 Ent	UK Top 10 Ent
Wynonna	4/92	
Tell Me Why	6/93	

XTC - Noted left-field new wave British rock act which featured singer/songwriter Andy Partridge (born Malta in 1953). Other members: Dave Gregory, Terry Chambers and Colin Moulding.

Album	US Top 10 Ent	UK Top 10 Ent
English Settlement		2/82

YAZOO - Top selling, London-based synth-pop duo of Vince Clarke (ex-Depeche Mode) and Alison 'Alf' Moyet. Moyet went on to solo fame and Clarke formed another hitmaking duo, Erasure. Act known as Yaz in the USA.

Album	US Top 10 Ent	UK Top 10 Ent
Upstairs At Eric's		9/82
You And Me Both		7/83

YAZZ - Ex-model Yasmin Evans was born in London, England, in 1963. She first found fame as a featured singer with Coldcut followed by a run of solo hit singles.

Album	US Top 10 Ent	UK Top 10 Ent
Wanted		12/88

YES - Top progressive rock band from London, England. Jon Anderson, Peter Banks, Bill Bruford, Tony Kaye, Chris Squire. Other noted Yes-men have included Steve Howe, Rick Wakeman (ex-Strawbs), Trevor Horn and Geoff Downes (both ex-Buggles).

Album	US Top 10 Ent	UK Top 10 Ent
The Yes Album		3/71
Fragile	2/72	
Close To The Edge	11/72	10/72
Tales From Topographic Oceans	3/74	1/74
Relayer	1/75	12/74
Going For The One		7/77
Drama		9/80
90125	12/83	

NEIL YOUNG - Revered rock singer/songwriter and guitarist born 1945 in Toronto, Canada. Formed Buffalo Springfield with Steve Stills (1966) and in 1969 joined forces with Crosby, Stills & Nash, whilst also pursuing a solo career. He is one of the most consistently successful artists of the last four decades.

Album	US Top 10 Ent	UK Top 10 Ent
After The Gold Rush	11/70	
Harvest	3/72	3/72
Comes A Time	12/78	
Sleeps With Angels		8/94

PAUL YOUNG - Best selling soulful rock singer/songwriter born 1956 in Luton, England. Lead singer of band The Q-Tips before turning solo. The oft-times BRIT winner sold a million copies of **No Parlez** in the UK alone.

Album	US Top 10 Ent	UK Top 10 Ent
No Parlez		8/83
The Secret Of Association		4/85
From Time To Time - The Singles Collection		9/91

YOUNG RASCALS - See THE RASCALS

WARREN ZEVON - Critically acclaimed rock singer/songwriter and pianist born 1947 in Chicago, USA, of Russian parentage. Jackson Browne produced **Excitable Boy** which gave the cult artist his only commercial success. Early in the Nineties, Zevon was featured in the R.E.M. offshoot, The Hindu Love Gods.

Album	US Top 10 Ent	UK Top 10 Ent
Excitable Boy	5/78	

DAVID ZINMAN - Respected classical conductor born 1936 in New York, USA. The one-time musical director of The Netherlands Chamber Orchestra and The Rotterdam Philharmonic Orchestra had a UK hit with his interpretation of a Gorecki symphony which featured soprano Dawn Upshaw and the London Sinfonietta.

Album	US Top 10 Ent	UK Top 10 Ent
Gorecki Symphony No. 3		2/93

ZZ TOP - Unmistakable long-bearded boogie rock band from Houston Texas, USA. Billy Gibbons, Dusty Hill and Frank Beard. One of the Eighties top selling album acts, they signed a multi-million dollar deal with RCA in 1994.

Album	US Top 10 Ent	UK Top 10 Ent
Eliminator		9/84
Afterburner	11/85	11/85
Recycler	11/90	
Greatest Hits		5/92
Antenna		2/94

LISTINGS

BY TITLE

ALBUM TOP 10 TITLE INDEX

Alphabetical listing of every album that reached the monthly Top 10s. If an album had a slightly different title in the US and UK, the American title is listed. If the titles are very different, both are listed.

LISTINGS BY TITLE

Title	Artist
Abacab	Genesis
Abbey Road	Beatles
ABC	Jackson 5
Above The Rim	Soundtrack
Abracadabra	Steve Miller Band
Abraxas	Santana
Absolutely	Madness
According To My Heart	Jim Reeves
Ace Of Spades	Motorhead
Aces And Kings - The Best Of Go West	Go West
Achtung Baby	U2
Action Replay	Various
Action Trax	Various
Adam	Adam Faith
Adrenalize	Def Leppard
Affection	Lisa Stansfield
After Hours	Gary Moore
After The Gold Rush	Neil Young
Afterburner	ZZ Top
Aftermath	Rolling Stones
Against The Wind	Bob Seger & The Silver Bullet Band
The Age Of Aquarius	5th Dimension
The Age Of Consent	Bronski Beat
Agent Provocateur	Foreigner
Air Conditioning	Curved Air
Aja	Steely Dan
Aladdin	Soundtrack
Aladdin Sane	David Bowie
The Alamo	Soundtrack
Alannah Myles	Alannah Myles
The Album	Abba
The Album	Cliff Richard
Alchemy - Dire Straits Live	Dire Straits
Aldo Nova	Aldo Nova
Alf	Alison Moyet
Alive II	Kiss
All 'n All	Earth, Wind & Fire
All Alone Am I	Brenda Lee
All Directions	Temptations
All For A Song	Barbara Dickson
All In The Family	TV Soundtrack
All Or Nothing/2 X 2	Milli Vanilli
All Star Festival	Various
All Summer Long	Beach Boys
All The Best!	Paul McCartney
All The Fun Of The Fair	David Essex
All The Way	Frank Sinatra
All Things In Time	Lou Rawls
All Things Must Pass	George Harrison
All Through The Night	Aled Jones
All True Man	Alexander O'Neal
All-4-One	All-4-One
Almost There	Andy Williams
Aloha From Hawaii Via Satellite	Elvis Presley
Alone Together	Donny Osmond
Alpha	Asia
Always	Michael Ball
Always & Forever	Eternal
Always On My Mind	Willie Nelson
Amazing Things	Runrig
America	America
American Fool	John Cougar Mellencamp
American Gigolo	Soundtrack
American Heartbeat	Various
American Pie	Don McLean
American Woman	Guess Who
Ancient Heart	Tanita Tikaram
And I Love You So	Perry Como
And I Love You So	Howard Keel
...And Justice For All	Metallica
And Then There Were Three	Genesis
And Then...Along Comes The Association	Association
Angel Clare	Art Garfunkel
Angel Dust	Faith No More
Animal Tracks	Animals
Animalisms	Animals
Animals	Pink Floyd
The Animals	Animals
Another Black and White Minstrel Show	George Mitchell Minstrels
Another Page	Christopher Cross
Another Ticket	Eric Clapton
Another Time, Another Place	Bryan Ferry
Another Year	Leo Sayer
Antenna	ZZ Top
Anthem	Toyah
The Anvil	Visage
Anything For You	Gloria Estefan & The Miami Sound Machine
Anytime...Anywhere	Rita Coolidge
Apocalypse 91...The Enemy Strikes Black	Public Enemy
Appetite For Destruction	Guns N' Roses
Aqualung	Jethro Tull
Arc Of A Diver	Steve Winwood
Architecture And Morality	Orchestral Manoeuvres In The Dark
Are You Experienced?	Jimi Hendrix Experience
Are You Gonna Go My Way	Lenny Kravitz
Arena	Duran Duran
Aretha Arrives	Aretha Franklin
Aretha Live At Fillmore West	Aretha Franklin
Aretha Now	Aretha Franklin
Aretha: Lady Soul	Aretha Franklin
Argus	Wishbone Ash
Armed Forces	Elvis Costello
Around The World In A Day	Prince & The Revolution
Arrival	Abba
As Ugly As They Want To Be	Ugly Kid Joe
Asia	Asia
Aspects Of Love	Original Cast
At Carnegie Hall	Chicago
At The Oxford Union	Gerard Hoffnung
Atlantic Crossing	Rod Stewart
Atom Heart Mother	Pink Floyd
Auberge	Chris Rea
August	Eric Clapton
August & Everything After	Counting Crows
Autoamerican	Blondie
Autobahn	Kraftwerk
Automatic For The People	R.E.M.
Autumn '66	Spencer Davis Group
Avalon	Roxy Music
AWB	Average White Band
Axis: Bold As Love	Jimi Hendrix Experience
B.M.O.C. (Best Music On/Off Campus)	Brothers Four
Baby I'm-A Want You	Bread
The Bachelors And 16 Great Songs	Bachelors
Bachman-Turner Overdrive II	Bachman-Turner Overdrive
Back Home Again	John Denver
Back In Black	AC/DC
Back In The High Life	Steve Winwood
Back On The Block	Quincy Jones
Back To Broadway	Barbra Streisand
Back To Front	Gilbert O'Sullivan
Back To Front	Lionel Richie
Back To The Egg	Wings
Backless	Eric Clapton
Bad	Michael Jackson
Bad Animals	Heart
Bad Company	Bad Company
Bad Girls	Donna Summer
Ball	Iron Butterfly
Ballads Of The Green Berets	Ssgt Barry Sadler
Band Of Gypsys	Jimi Hendrix
Band On The Run	Paul McCartney & Wings
Bang!	World Party
The Barbara Dickson Songbook	Barbara Dickson

Barbra Streisand's Greatest Hits Vol. 2 — Barbra Streisand
The Barbra Streisand Album — Barbra Streisand
Bare Wires — John Mayall
Barry — Barry Manilow
Barry Live In Britain — Barry Manilow
Barry Manilow Live — Barry Manilow
The Basement Tapes — Bob Dylan
Basket Of Light — Pentangle
Bat Out Of Hell II: Back Into Hell — Meat Loaf
Batman (Soundtrack) — Prince
Bayou Country — Creedence Clearwater Revival
Be Yourself Tonight — Eurythmics
Beach Boys Concert — Beach Boys
Beach Boys Party! — Beach Boys
The Beach Boys Today! — Beach Boys
Beaches (Soundtrack) — Bette Midler
The Beat Of The Brass — Herb Alpert & The Tijuana Brass
Beatles '65 — Beatles
The Beatles (White Album) — Beatles
The Beatles At The Hollywood Bowl — Beatles
Beatles For Sale — Beatles
Beatles VI — Beatles
The Beatles' Second Album — Beatles
The Beatles — Beatles
The Beatles/1962-1966 — Beatles
The Beatles/1967-1970 — Beatles
Beautiful Noise — Neil Diamond
Beauty And The Beat — Go-Go's
The Beavis & Butt-Head Experience — Beavis & Butt-Head
Bebe Le Strange — Heart
Bedtime Stories — Madonna
Bee Gees First — Bee Gees
Bee Gees Greatest — Bee Gees
Before The Flood — Bob Dylan
Beggars Banquet — Rolling Stones
Begin The Beguine — Julio Iglesias
Behaviour — Pet Shop Boys
Behind Closed Doors — Charlie Rich
Behind The Mask — Fleetwood Mac
Belafonte At Carnegie Hall — Harry Belafonte
Belafonte Returns To Carnegie Hall — Harry Belafonte
Believe In Music — Various
Bella Donna — Stevie Nicks
Ben — Michael Jackson
Benefit — Jethro Tull
The Best Disco Album In The World — Various
The Best Of Ball, Barber And Bilk — Kenny Ball, Chris Barber & Acker Bilk
Best Of Barber And Bilk Vol. 1 — Chris Barber And Acker Bilk
The Best Of Belinda Vol. 1 — Belinda Carlisle
Best Of Blondie — Blondie
The Best Of Bread — Bread
The Best Of Chris Rea — Chris Rea
Best Of Cliff — Cliff Richard
Best Of Cream — Cream
Best Of John Denver Vol. 2 — John Denver
The Best Of Earth, Wind & Fire Vol. 1 — Earth, Wind & Fire
The Best Of Gladys Knight And The Pips — Gladys Knight & The Pips
The Best Of Glenn Miller — Glenn Miller
The Best Of Herman's Hermits — Herman's Hermits
The Best Of Helen Reddy — Helen Reddy
Best Of Jim Reeves — Jim Reeves
The Best Of Mirage-Jack Mix '88 — Mirage
? (The Best Of) — New Order
The Best Of OMD — Orchestral Manoeuvres In The Dark
The Best Of Rod Stewart — Rod Stewart
The Best Of Roy Orbison — Roy Orbison
Best Of Sade — Sade
The Best Of Sellers — Peter Sellers
The Best Of Tammy Wynette — Tammy Wynette
Best Of The 20th Century Boy — T. Rex
Best Of The Beach Boys — Beach Boys
Best Of The Beach Boys Vol. 2 — Beach Boys
Best Of The Bee Gees — Bee Gees
Best Of The Stylistics Vol. 2 — Stylistics
Best Of The Waterboys '81-'90 — Waterboys
The Best Of The Animals — Animals
The Best Of The Doobies — Doobie Brothers
The Best Of The Dooleys — Dooleys
The Best Of The Lovin' Spoonful — Lovin' Spoonful
The Best Of The Seekers — Seekers
The Best Of The Stylistics — Stylistics
The Best Of UB40 Vol. I — UB40
The Best Of Van Morrison — Van Morrison
Best Shots — Pat Benatar
The Best Years Of Our lives — Steve Harley & Cockney Rebel
Best..1 — Smiths
Bette Midler — Bette Midler
Between The Buttons — Rolling Stones
Between The Lines — Jason Donovan
Between The Lines — Janis Ian
Beverley Craven — Beverley Craven
Beverly Hills Cop — Soundtrack
Beverly Hills Cop II — Soundtrack
Beyond The Season — Garth Brooks
The Big Area — Then Jerico
Big Bam Boom — Daryl Hall & John Oates
Big Bambu — Cheech & Chong
Big Bang — Fuzzbox
Big Daddy — John Cougar Mellencamp
Big Girls Don't Cry & 12 Others — Four Seasons
Big Hits (High Tide And Green Grass) — Rolling Stones
Big Wheels Of Motown — Various
Bigger And Deffer — LL Cool J
Bigger Better, Faster, More! — 4 Non Blondes
Billion Dollar Babies — Alice Cooper
Billy — Billy Fury
The Birds, The Bees & The Monkees — Monkees
A Bit Of What You Fancy — Quireboys
Bizarre Fruit — M People
Black And Blue — Rolling Stones
Black And White — Stranglers
The Black And White Minstrel Show — George Mitchell Minstrels
Black Celebration — Depeche Mode
Black Rose (A Rock Legend) — Thin Lizzy
Black Sabbath Live At Last — Black Sabbath
Black Sabbath Vol. 4 — Black Sabbath
Black Sunday — Cypress Hill
Black Tie White Noise — David Bowie
Blam! — Brothers Johnson
Blast — Holly Johnson
Blaze Of Glory/Young Guns II — Jon Bon Jovi
Blind Faith — Blind Faith
Blind Melon — Blind Melon
Blitz — Original London Cast
Blonde On Blonde — Bob Dylan
Blondes Have More Fun — Rod Stewart
Blood On The Tracks — Bob Dylan
Blood Sugar Sex Magik — Red Hot Chili Peppers
Blood Sweat & Tears — Blood, Sweat & Tears
Blood Sweat & Tears 3 — Blood, Sweat & Tears
Bloody Tourists — 10 C.C.
Blooming Hits — Paul Mauriat
Blow By Blow — Jeff Beck
Blow Up Your Video — AC/DC
Blue — Joni Mitchell
Blue For You — Status Quo
Blue Gene — Gene Pitney
Blue Hawaii (Soundtrack) — Elvis Presley
Blue Midnight — Bert Kaempfert
Blue Moves — Elton John
Bluejays — Justin Hayward & John Lodge
Blues Breakers — John Mayall & Eric Clapton
Bob Dylan At Budokan — Bob Dylan
Bobby — Bobby Brown
Bobby Vee Meets The Crickets — Bobby Vee & The Crickets
Body Wishes — Rod Stewart
The Bodyguard — Soundtrack
Bolan Boogie — T. Rex
Boogie Nights — Various
Boogie With Canned Heat — Canned Heat
Book Of Dreams — Steve Miller Band
Bookends — Simon & Garfunkel
Boomania — Betty Boo
Boomerang — Soundtrack
Boots — Nancy Sinatra
Born Free — Frank Ifield
Born Free — Andy Williams
Born Free — Roger Williams
Born In The U.S.A. — Bruce Springsteen
Born Late — Shaun Cassidy
Born To Run — Bruce Springsteen
Boss Drum — Shamen
Bossanova — Pixies
Boston — Boston
Both Sides — Phil Collins
Boys And Girls — Bryan Ferry
Brain Salad Surgery — Emerson, Lake & Palmer
Bread Winners — Jack Jones
Break Every Rule — Tina Turner
Break Out — Pointer Sisters
Breakfast At Tiffany's (Soundtrack) — Henry Mancini
Breakfast In America — Supertramp
Breakin' — Soundtrack
Breakin' Away — Al Jarreau
Breaking Hearts — Elton John
Breakout — Various
Breakthrough — Various
Breathless — Kenny G
Breezin' — George Benson
Brenda Lee — Brenda Lee
Bridge Of Sighs — Robin Trower
Bridge Of Spies — T'Pau
Bridge Over Troubled Water — Simon & Garfunkel
The Bridge — Billy Joel
Bridges — John Williams
Briefcase Full Of Blues — Blues Brothers
Brigade — Heart
Bringing It All Back Home — Bob Dylan
British Motown Chartbusters — Various
British Motown Chartbusters Vol. 3 — Various
British Steel — Judas Priest
The Broadway Album — Barbra Streisand
Brother Sister — Brand New Heavies
Brotherhood Of Man — Brotherhood Of Man
Brothers And Sisters — Allman Brothers Band
Brothers In Arms — Dire Straits
Bruce Springsteen & The E Street Band Live/1975-1985 — Bruce Springsteen
Brutal Youth — Elvis Costello
Buddah And The Chocolate Box — Cat Stevens
Buddy Holly Showcase — Buddy Holly
Buddy Holly Story — Buddy Holly
Buddy Holly Story Vol. 2 — Buddy Holly
Built For Speed — Stray Cats
Burn — Deep Purple
Bursting At The Seams — Strawbs
Business As Usual — Men At Work
...But Seriously — Phil Collins
The Button Down Mind Of Bob Newhart — Bob Newhart
The Button Down Mind Strikes Back! — Bob Newhart
Bye Bye Birdie — Soundtrack
Bye Bye Blues — Bert Kaempfert
The Byrds' Greatest Hits — Byrds
C'est Chic — Chic

C'mon Everybody — Elvis Presley
C.M.B. — Color Me Badd
Cafe Bleu — Style Council
Calcutta! — Lawrence Welk
'Call Me Irresponsible' And Other Hit Songs — Andy Williams
Camelot — Original Cast
Camelot — Percy Faith
Can't Get Enough — Barry White
Can't Help Falling In Love — Andy Williams
Can't Slow Down — Lionel Richie
Can't Stand The Heat — Status Quo
Can-Can — Soundtrack
Candlebox — Candlebox
Candles In The Rain — Melanie
Candy-O — Cars
The Captain And Me — Doobie Brothers
Captain Fantastic And The Brown Dirt Cowboy — Elton John
Captured — Journey
Caravanserai — Santana
Cargo — Men At Work
Caribou — Elton John
Carlos Santana & Buddy Miles! Live! — Carlos Santana
Carney — Leon Russell
Carnival — Manuel & His Music Of The Mountains
Carnival — Original Cast
Carnival Of Hits — Judith Durham/The Seeekers
Carpenters — Carpenters
Carry On Up The Charts - The Best Of — Beautiful South
Catch Bull At Four — Cat Stevens
Catch Us If You Can — Dave Clark Five
Centerfield — John Fogerty
Champagne Jam — Atlanta Rhythm Section
Change Everything — Del Amitri
The Changeling — Toyah
Changesbowie — David Bowie
Changesonebowie — David Bowie
Changing Faces - The Very Best Of 10 CC & Godley & Creme — 10 C.C. & Godley & Creme
Chant — Benedictine Monks Of Santo Domingo De Silos
Charade — Henry Mancini
Chariots Of Fire (Soundtrack) — Vangelis
Chart Encounters Of The Hit Kind — Various
Chart Hits 81 — Various
Chart Runners — Various
Chartbeat/Chartheat — Various
Chartbusters — Various
Chartbusters 81 — Various
Chas & Dave's Knees Up-Jamboree Bag No 2 — Chas & Dave
The Chase — Garth Brooks
Cheap Thrills — Big Brother & The Holding Company
Cheap Trick At Budokan — Cheap Trick
Cheech & Chong's Wedding Album — Cheech & Chong
Cher's Greatest Hits: 1965-1992 — Cher
Cherish — David Cassidy
Chicago — Chicago
Chicago II — Chicago
Chicago III — Chicago
Chicago V — Chicago
Chicago VI — Chicago
Chicago VII — Chicago
Chicago VIII — Chicago
Chicago IX - Chicago's Greatest Hits — Chicago
Chicago X — Chicago
Chicago XI — Chicago
Chicago 17 — Chicago
Children Of The World — Bee Gees
Choke — Beautiful South
Chorus — Erasure
The Christians — Christians
The Christmas Album — Neil Diamond
Christopher Cross — Christopher Cross
The Chronic — Dr. Dre
Bobby Rydell/Chubby Checker — Chubby Checker/Bobby Rydell
Chuck Berry On Stage — Chuck Berry
Cilla — Cilla Black
Cilla Sings A Rainbow — Cilla Black
Circle Of One — Oleta Adams
City To City — Gerry Rafferty
Classic Queen — Queen
Classic Rock — London Symphony Orchestra
Cliff Sings — Cliff Richard
Cliff's Hit Album — Cliff Richard
Clockwork Orange — Soundtrack
Close To The Edge — Yes
Close To You — Carpenters
Close-Up — Kingston Trio
Closer To Home — Grand Funk Railroad
Cloud Nine — Temptations
Club Classics Vol. 1 — Soul II Soul
Clutching At Straws — Marillion
Coast To Coast — Dave Clark Five
Cocktail — Soundtrack
Coda — Led Zeppelin
A Collection Of Their 20 Greatest Hits — Three Degrees
The Collection — Earth, Wind & Fire
The Collection — Ultravox
The Collection — Barry White
College Concert — Kingston Trio
Color Me Barbra — Barbra Streisand
Colour — Christians
Colour By Numbers — Culture Club
The Colour Of My Love — Celine Dion
Combat Rock — Clash
Come — Prince
Come And Get It — Whitesnake
Come Back To Sorrento — Frank Sinatra
Come Into My Life — Joyce Sims
Come The Day — Seekers
Comes A Time — Neil Young
The Commitments (Soundtrack) — Commitments
Commodores — Commodores
Commodores Live! — Commodores
Common Thread: The Songs Of The Eagles — Various
Communards — Communards
Communique — Dire Straits
Complete Madness — Madness
The Complete Picture - Very Best Of — Deborah Harry & Blondie
Completely Hooked - The Best Of Dr. Hook — Dr. Hook
Compositions — Anita Baker
The Concert For Bangla Desh — George Harrison & Friends
The Concert In Central Park — Simon & Garfunkel
Concert Sinatra — Frank Sinatra
Confrontation — Bob Marley & The Wailers
Connected — Stereo MCs
Conscience — Womack And Womack
Construction Time Again — Depeche Mode
Control — Janet Jackson
Cooleyhighharmony — Boyz II Men
Coolin' At The Playground Ya' Know! — Another Bad Creation
Core — Stone Temple Pilots
Cornerstone — Styx
Cornerstones 1967-1970 — Jimi Hendrix
Cosmic Thing — B-52's
Cosmo's Factory — Creedence Clearwater Revival
Cotton Candy — Al Hirt
Countdown To Extinction — Megadeth
Counterparts — Rush
Country Life — Roxy Music
Country Life — Various
Court And Spark — Joni Mitchell
Cover Shot — David Essex
Coverdale Page — Coverdale/Page
Crash! Boom! Bang! — Roxette
Crash Landing — Jimi Hendrix
Crazy — Julio Iglesias
Crazy Nights — Kiss
The Crazy World Of Arthur Brown — Crazy World Of Arthur Brown
The Cream Of Eric Clapton — Eric Clapton & Cream
Cricklewood Green — Ten Years After
Crimes Of Passion — Pat Benatar
Crimson & Clover — Tommy James & The Shondells
Crisis — Mike Oldfield
Crocodile Shoes — Jimmy Nail
Crosby, Stills & Nash — Crosby, Stills & Nash
Cross Of Changes — Enigma
The Crossing — Big Country
Crossroad - The Best Of — Bon Jovi
Crossroads — Tracy Chapman
The Crow — Soundtrack
Crown Of Creation — Jefferson Airplane
Cruisin' — Village People
Crushin' — Fat Boys
Cry Like A Rainstorm, Howl Like The Wind — Linda Ronstadt
The Cry Of Love — Jimi Hendrix
CSN — Crosby, Stills & Nash
Cupid And Psyche '85 — Scritti Politti
Cut The Cake — Average White Band
Cuts Both Ways — Gloria Estefan
Cuts Like A Knife — Bryan Adams
Cymansa Gann — Massed Welsh Choirs

D:ream On Vol. 1 — D:ream
Damn The Torpedoes — Tom Petty & The Heartbreakers
Dance — Gary Numan
Dance 'til Quarter To Three — Gary (U.S.) Bonds
Dance Craze — Soundtrack
Dance To The Music — Various
Dance With The Shadows — Shadows
Dance!...Ya Know It — Bobby Brown
Dancing On The Ceiling — Lionel Richie
Dancing With Strangers — Chris Rea
Dangerous — Michael Jackson
Dare — Human League
Dark Horse — George Harrison
Dark Side Of The Moon — Pink Floyd
Darkness On The Edge Of Town — Bruce Springsteen
A Date With The Everly Brothers — Everly Brothers
The Dave Clark Five Return! — Dave Clark Five
David Essex — David Essex
David Live — David Bowie
David Soul — David Soul
Dawn (Go Away) And 11 Other Great Songs — Four Seasons
A Day At The Races — Queen
Daylight Again — Crosby, Stills & Nash
Days Of Future Passed — Moody Blues
Days Of Wine And Roses — Andy Williams
Dazzle Ships — Orchestral Manoeuvres In The Dark
Dead Ringer — Meat Loaf
Dear Heart — Andy Williams
Death Certificate — Ice Cube
Debut — Bjork
Decade Of Decadence — Motley Crue
December's Children (And Everbody's) — Rolling Stones
Deceptive Bends — 10 C.C.
Dedication — Bay City Rollers
Deep Purple In Rock — Deep Purple
Deep Sea Skiving — Bananarama
Deepest Purple — Deep Purple
Definitely Maybe — Oasis
The Definitive Simon And Garfunkel — Simon And Garfunkel
Deja Vu — Crosby, Stills, Nash & Young
Delilah — Tom Jones
Deliver The Word — War
Departure — Journey

Title	Artist
Desire	Bob Dylan
Desolation Angels	Bad Company
Diamond Dogs	David Bowie
Diamond Girl	Seals & Crofts
Diamond Life	Sade
Diamonds & Pearls	Prince & The New Power Generation
Diana	Diana Ross
Diana & Marvin	Diana Ross & Marvin Gaye
Diana Ross	Diana Ross
Diana Ross & The Supremes Greatest Hits	Diana Ross & The Supremes
Diana Ross & The Supremes Join The Temptations	Diana Ross & The Supremes With The Temptations
Diana Ross Presents The Jackson 5	Jackson 5
Diary Of A Mad Band	Jodeci
The Diary	Scarface
Different Light	Bangles
Difficult To Cure	Rainbow
Dig The New Breed	Jam
Dingly Dell	Lindisfarne
Dire Straits	Dire Straits
Dirty Dancing	Soundtrack
Dirty Deeds Done Dirt Cheap	AC/DC
Dirty Work	Rolling Stones
Disco Daze And Disco Nites	Various
Disco Fever	Various
Disco Hits '75	Various
Disco Rocket	Various
Disco Stars	Various
Discography	Pet Shop Boys
Discovery	Electric Light Orchestra
Disraeli Gears	Cream
The Distance	Bob Seger & The Silver Bullet Band
Distant Drums	Jim Reeves
Diva	Annie Lennox
Diver Down	Van Halen
Divine Madness	Madness
The Division Bell	Pink Floyd
Do It ('til You're Satisfied)	B.T. Express
Do It Yourself	Ian Dury & The Blockheads
The Dock Of The Bay	Otis Redding
Doctor Zhivago	Soundtrack
Doggystyle	Snoop Doggy Dogg
Doin' The Twist At The Peppermint Lounge	Joey Dee & The Starliters
Don't Be Cruel	Bobby Brown
Don't Look Back	Boston
Don't Say No	Billy Squier
Don't Shoot Me I'm Only The Piano Player	Elton John
Don't Walk Boogie	Various
Donovan's Greatest Hits	Donovan
Dookie	Green Day
The Doors	Doors
The Doors (Soundtrack)	Doors
Double Fantasy	John Lennon
Double Vision	Foreigner
Doubt	Jesus Jones
Down Drury Lane To Memory Lane	One Hundred & One Strings
The Downward Spiral	Nine Inch Nails
Dr. Feelgood	Motley Crue
Dr. Hook's Greatest Hits	Dr. Hook
Drama	Yes
Dream Harder	Waterboys
Dream Into Action	Howard Jones
The Dream Of The Blue Turtles	Sting
Dream Police	Cheap Trick
The Dream Weaver	Gary Wright
Dreaming	Various
Dreams Are Nothin' More Than Wishes	David Cassidy
A Drop Of The Hard Stuff	Dubliners
Dueling Banjos/Deliverance (Soundtrack)	Eric Weissberg
Duets	Elton John
Duets	Frank Sinatra
Duke	Genesis
Duotones	Kenny G
Duran Duran	Duran Duran
Duran Duran (The Wedding Album)	Duran Duran
Dusk	The The
E Pluribus Funk	Grand Funk Railroad
Eagles Live	Eagles
Eagles/Their Greatest Hits 1971-1975	Eagles
Eargasm	Johnnie Taylor
Earth	Jefferson Starship
Easy Come, Easy Go	George Strait
Easy Easy	Scotland Football World Cup Squad
Easy Rider	Soundtrack
Eat 'em And Smile	David Lee Roth
Eat A Peach	Allman Brothers Band
Eat To The Beat	Blondie
Echo & The Bunnymen	Echo & The Bunnymen
Eddie And The Cruisers	John Cafferty & The Beaver Brown Band
The Edge Of Shelley Berman	Shelley Berman
Efil4zaggin	N.W.A.
18 Greatest Hits	Michael Jackson & Jackson Five
Electric	Cult
Electric Ladyland	Jimi Hendrix Experience
Electric Warrior	T. Rex
Electric Youth	Debbie Gibson
Electronic	Electronic
Elegant Slumming	M People
Elegy	Nice
Elements - The Best Of Mike Oldfield	Mike Oldfield
1100 Bel Air Place	Julio Iglesias
Eliminator	ZZ Top
ELO's Greatest Hits	Electric Light Orchestra
Elton John	Elton John
Elton John - Greatest Hits	Elton John
Elvis	Elvis Presley
Elvis At Madison Square Garden	Elvis Presley
Elvis Country	Elvis Presley
Elvis For Everybody	Elvis Presley
Elvis In Concert	Elvis Presley
Elvis Is Back!	Elvis Presley
Elvis - NBC TV Special	Elvis Presley
Elvis' Golden Records Vol. 2	Elvis Presley
Elvis' Golden Records Vol. 3	Elvis Presley
Emergency On Planet Earth	Jamiroquai
Emerson, Lake And Palmer	Emerson, Lake & Palmer
Emotional Rescue	Rolling Stones
Emotions	Mariah Carey
Emotions	Various
Emotions In Motion	Billy Squier
Empire	Queensryche
Empire Strikes Back	Soundtrack
Empty Glass	Pete Townsend
Encore Of Golden Hits	Platters
End Of Part One (Their Greatest Hits)	Wet Wet Wet
The End Of The Innocence	Don Henley
Endless Flight	Leo Sayer
Endless Summer	Beach Boys
Engelbert	Engelbert Humperdinck
Engelbert Humperdinck	Engelbert Humperdinck
Engelbert Humperdinck - His Greatest Hits	Engelbert Humperdinck
English Settlement	XTC
Enjoy Yourself	Kylie Minogue
Enlightened Rouges	Allman Brothers Band
Erotica	Madonna
Escape	Journey
The Essential Collection	Elvis Presley
The Essential Pavarotti	Luciano Pavarotti
The Essential Pavarotti II	Luciano Pavarotti
Even Now	Barry Manilow
An Evening With John Denver	John Denver
Every Beat Of My Heart	Rod Stewart
Every Breath You Take - The Singles	Police
Every Face Tells A Story	Cliff Richard
Every Good Boy Deserves Favour	Moody Blues
Every Picture Tells A Story	Rod Stewart
Everybody Else Is Doing It So Why Can't We	Cranberries
Everybody Loves Somebody	Dean Martin
Everything	Bangles
Everything Changes	Take That
Everything Comes Up Dusty	Dusty Springfield
Evita	Studio Cast
Excitable Boy	Warren Zevon
Exile On Main Street	Rolling Stones
Exit Stage Left	Rush
Exodus	Soundtrack
Exodus To Jazz	Eddie Harris
Experience The Divine - Greatest Hits	Bette Midler
The Explosive Freddy Cannon	Freddy Cannon
Extra Texture (Read All About It)	George Harrison
Eye In The Sky	Alan Parsons Project
Eye Of The Tiger	Survivor
Eyes That See In The Dark	Kenny Rogers
F.L.M.	Mel & Kim
Fabulous Fabian	Fabian
Fabulous Style Of The Everly Brothers	Everly Brothers
Face Dances	Who
Face Value	Phil Collins
Fair Warning	Van Halen
Faith	George Michael
Faithfully	Johnny Mathis
Falco 3	Falco
Fame	Soundtrack
Family Reunion	O'Jays
Family Style	Vaughan Brothers
...Famous Last Words...	Supertramp
Fantastic	Wham!
Fantasy	Carole King
Far Beyond Driven	Pantera
Farewell Angelina	Joan Baez
Farewell To The First Golden Era	Mamas & The Papas
Faster Than The Speed Of Night	Bonnie Tyler
Fate For Breakfast	Art Garfunkel
Favourites	Peters & Lee
Fear Of The Dark	Iron Maiden
Feelings	Various
Feels So Good	Chuck Mangione
Feliciano!	Jose Feliciano
Feline	Stranglers
Fellow Hoodlums	Deacon Blue
Fiddler On The Roof	Original Cast
Fiddler On The Roof	Original London Cast
Fields Of Gold - The Best Of	Sting
15 Big Ones	Beach Boys
The 5th Dimension/Greatest Hits	5th Dimension
52nd Street	Billy Joel
The Final	Wham!
The Final Countdown	Europe
The Final Cut	Pink Floyd
Finders Keepers (Soundtrack)	Cliff Richard
Fire	Ohio Players
Fire And Water	Free
Fireball	Deep Purple
The First Family	Vaughn Meader
The First Family Vol. 2	Vaughn Meader
The First Of A Million Kisses	Fairground Attraction
First Take	Roberta Flack
Five Bridges	Nice
Five Faces Of Manfred Mann	Manfred Mann
5150	Van Halen
The Five Pennies	Soundtrack
Flaming Star	Elvis Presley
Flashdance	Soundtrack
Fleetwood Mac	Fleetwood Mac
Flesh And Blood	Poison

Title	Artist
Flesh And Blood	Roxy Music
Flick Of The Switch	AC/DC
Flower Drum Song	Original Broadway Cast
Flowers	Rolling Stones
Flowers In The Dirt	Paul McCartney
Fly Like An Eagle	Steve Miller Band
Flying Colours	Chris De Burgh
FM	Soundtrack
Fog On The Tyne	Lindisfarne
Follow That Girl	Original London Cast
Fool On The Hill	Sergio Mendes & Brasil '66
Foot Loose & Fancy Free	Rod Stewart
Footloose	Soundtrack
For Earth Below	Robin Trower
For Those About To Rock We Salute You	AC/DC
For Twisters Only	Chubby Checker
For Unlawful Carnal Knowledge	Van Halen
For Your Pleasure	Roxy Music
Fore!	Huey Lewis & The News
Foreign Affair	Tina Turner
Foreigner	Foreigner
Foreigner	Cat Stevens
Forever And Ever	Demis Roussos
Forever Your Girl	Paula Abdul
Formula 30	Various
Forrest Gump	Soundtrack
40 Fantastic Hits From The 50s And 60s	Various
40 Golden Greats	Jim Reeves
40 Golden Greats	Cliff Richard
40 Greatest Hits	Perry Como
40 Greatest Hits	Elvis Presley
4	Foreigner
461 Ocean Boulevard	Eric Clapton
Four Symbols (Led Zeppelin IV)	Led Zeppelin
The Four Tops Greatest Hits	Four Tops
Four Tops Live!	Four Tops
4 Way Street	Crosby, Stills, Nash & Young
Four Wheel Drive	Bachman-Turner Overdrive
Fragile	Yes
Frampton Comes Alive!	Peter Frampton
Freddie And The Dreamers	Freddie And The Dreamers
The Freddie Mercury Album	Freddie Mercury
Free Live!	Free
The Free Story	Free
The Freewheelin' Bob Dylan	Bob Dylan
Freeze Frame	J. Geils Band
Fresh	Sly & The Family Stone
Fresh Cream	Cream
The Friends Of Mr. Cairo	Jon & Vangelis
From A Distance...The Event	Cliff Richard
From A Spark To A Flame - The Very Best Of Chris De Burgh	Chris De Burgh
From Elvis In Memphis	Elvis Presley
From Memphis To Vegas - From Vegas To Memphis	Elvis Presley
From Nowhere...The Troggs	Troggs
From The Cradle	Eric Clapton
From The Heart - His Greatest Love Songs	Elvis Presley
From The Makers Of...	Status Quo
From Time To Time - The Singles Collection	Paul Young
Frontiers	Journey
Fulfillingness' First Finale	Stevie Wonder
Full Moon Fever	Tom Petty
Full Moon, Dirty Hearts	INXS
Fun In Acapulco (Soundtrack)	Elvis Presley
Fun Boy Three	Fun Boy Three
Funky Divas	En Vogue
Funny Girl	Barbra Streisand
Funny Lady (Soundtrack)	Barbra Streisand
Future Shock	Gillan
G N' R Lies	Guns N' Roses
G.I. Blues (Soundtrack)	Elvis Presley
Galveston	Glen Campbell
The Game	Queen
Gaucho	Steely Dan
Geffrey Morgan	UB40
Genesis	Genesis
Genius Plus Soul Equals Jazz	Ray Charles
Gentle On My Mind	Glen Campbell
Gentle On My Mind	Dean Martin
Gentle Shades Of Val Doonican	Val Doonican
Gentleman Jim	Jim Reeves
Georgia Satellites	Georgia Satellites
Get A Grip	Aerosmith
Get Happy	Elvis Costello
Get In Where Ya Fit In	Too Short
Get Lucky	Loverboy
Get Nervous	Pat Benatar
Get Right Intae Him	Billy Connolly
Get The Knack	Knack
Get Yer Ya-Ya's Out!	Rolling Stones
Getz/Gilberto	Stan Getz/Joao Gilberto
Ghost In The Machine	Police
Ghostbusters	Soundtrack
The Gift	Jam
The Gift	Midge Ure
Gigi	Soundtrack
A Girl Called Dusty	Dusty Springfield
Girl Happy (Soundtrack)	Elvis Presley
Girl You Know It's True	Milli Vanilli
Girls Girls Girls	Motley Crue
Girls! Girls! Girls! (Soundtrack)	Elvis Presley
Give 'em Enough Rope	Clash
Give Me The Night	George Benson
Give Me The Reason	Luther Vandross
Give Me Your Heart Tonight	Shakin' Stevens
Give My Regards To Broad Street	Paul McCartney
Give Out, But Don't Give Up	Primal Scream
Giving You The Best That I Got	Anita Baker
Glad All Over	Dave Clark Five
Glass Houses	Billy Joel
Glittering Prize 81/92	Simple Minds
The Glory Of Gershwin	Larry Adler
Glory Road	Gillan
Go All The Way	Isley Brothers
Go For Your Guns	Isley Brothers
Go West	Village People
Go West/Bangs And Crashes	Go West
Goat's Head Soup	Rolling Stones
God Bless Tiny Tim	Tiny Tim
God Fodder	Ned's Atomic Dustbin
God Shuffled His Feet	Crash Test Dummies
God's Great Banana Skin	Chris Rea
Goin' Back - The Very Best Of	Dusty Springfield
Goin' Places	Kingston Trio
Going For The One	Yes
Going Places	Herb Alpert & The Tijuana Brass
Gold - Greatest Hits	Abba
Gold Mother	James
The Golden Age Of Donegan	Lonnie Donegan
Golden Bisquits	Three Dog Night
Golden Collection	Charley Pride
Golden Hits	Roger Miller
Golden Hits	Dusty Springfield
Goldfinger	Soundtrack
Gonna Make You Sweat	C&C Music Factory
Good Trouble	REO Speedwagon
The Good, The Bad And The Ugly	Soundtrack
Goodbye	Cream
Goodbye Yellow Brick Road	Elton John
Gorecki Symphony No. 3	David Zinman
Gorilla	James Taylor
Got Live If You Want It!	Rolling Stones
Grace Under Pressure	Rush
Graceland	Paul Simon
The Graduate (Soundtrack)	Simon & Garfunkel
Graffiti Bridge	Prince
Graham Nash/David Crosby	David Crosby/Graham Nash
The Grand Illusion	Styx
Gratitude	Earth, Wind & Fire
Grease	Soundtrack
The Great Caruso	Mario Lanza
Great Motion Picture Themes	Soundtrack (Compilation)
The Great Rock 'n' Roll Swindle	Sex Pistols
The Great Songs From 'My Fair Lady' And Other Broadway Hits	Andy Williams
The Greatest Ever Rock 'n' Roll Mix	Various
Greatest Hits	Abba
Greatest Hits	Air Supply
Greatest Hits	Bangles
Greatest Hits	Beach Boys
Greatest Hits	Bob Dylan
Greatest Hits	Gloria Estefan
Greatest Hits	Eurythmics
Greatest Hits	Fleetwood Mac
Greatest Hits	Four Seasons
Greatest Hits	Four Tops
Greatest Hits	Hollies
Greatest Hits	Human League
Greatest Hits	Jam
Greatest Hits	Barry Manilow
Greatest Hits	Billy Ocean
Greatest Hits	Tom Petty & The Heartbreakers
Greatest Hits	Queen
Greatest Hits	Linda Ronstadt
Greatest Hits	Rose Royce
Greatest Hits	Diana Ross & The Supremes
Greatest Hits	Shadows
Greatest Hits	Showaddywaddy
Greatest Hits	Simon & Garfunkel
Greatest Hits	Sly & The Family Stone
Greatest Hits	Smokie
Greatest Hits	Cat Stevens
Greatest Hits	Shakin' Stevens
Greatest Hits	Rod Stewart
Greatest Hits	Donna Summer
Greatest Hits	War
Greatest Hits	Whitesnake
Greatest Hits	Andy Williams
Greatest Hits	ZZ Top
Greatest Hits 1972-1978	10 C.C.
Greatest Hits (1976-1978)	Showaddywaddy
Greatest Hits 1977-1990	Stranglers
Greatest Hits II	Queen
Greatest Hits 2	Diana Ross
Greatest Hits Vol. 1	Association
Greatest Hits Vol. 1 & Vol. 2	Billy Joel
Greatest Hits Vol. 2	Abba
Greatest Hits Vol. 2	Elton John
Greatest Hits Vol. 2	Reba McEntire
Greatest Hits Vol. 2	Smokey Robinson & The Miracles
Greatest Hits Vol. 2	Frank Sinatra
Greatest Hits Vol. 2	Barbra Streisand
Greatest Hits, Etc.	Paul Simon
The Greatest Hits	INXS
The Greatest Hits	Shalamar
The Greatest Hits 1966-1992	Neil Diamond
The Greatest Hits Collection	Bananarama
The Greatest Hits Of 1985	Various
Greatest Love Songs	Nat 'King' Cole
Green Green Grass Of Home	Tom Jones
Green River	Creedence Clearwater Revival
Groovin'	Young Rascals
Growing Up In Public	Jimmy Nail
Guilty	Barbra Streisand
Gunfighter Ballads And Trail Songs	Marty Robbins
H2O	Daryl Hall & John Oates
Hair	Original Cast
Hair	Original London Cast
Halfway To Paradise	Billy Fury

Hand Clappin' - Foot Stompin' - Funky Butt - Live! Geno Washington
Hangin' Tough New Kids On The Block
Hangman's Beautiful Daughter Incredible String Band
Happy Heart Andy Williams
Happy Nation Ace Of Base
Happy To Be Demis Roussos
A Hard Day's Night Beatles
Hard Promises Tom Petty & The Heartbreakers
Harmony Three Dog Night
Harvest Neil Young
Hasten Down The Wind Linda Ronstadt
Hatari! Henry Mancini
Hats Off To Del Shannon Del Shannon
Have You Never Been Mellow Olivia Newton-John
He's The DJ I'm The Rapper DJ Jazzy Jeff & The Fresh Prince
Head Games Foreigner
The Head On The Door Cure
Headquarters Monkees
Hearsay/All Mixed Up Alexander O'Neal
Heart Heart
Heart Like A Wheel Linda Ronstadt
Heart Shaped World Chris Isaak
Heartbeat City Cars
Heartbreaker Dionne Warwick
Heartbreakers Matt Monro
Heartbreakers Various
Hearts America
The Heat Is On Isley Brothers
Heaven On Earth Belinda Carlisle
Heavenly Johnny Mathis
Helen Reddy's Greatest Hits Helen Reddy
Hell Freezes Over Eagles
Hello Status Quo
Hello I'm Johnny Cash Johnny Cash
Hello, Dolly! Louis Armstrong
Hello, Dolly! Original Cast
Hello, I Must Be Going! Phil Collins
Help Beatles
Help Yourself Tom Jones
Hendrix In The West Jimi Hendrix
Herb Alpert's Ninth Herb Alpert & The Tijuana Brass
Here And There Elton John
Here We Go Again! Kingston Trio
Hergest Ridge Mike Oldfield
Herman's Hermits On Tour Herman's Hermits
Heroes David Bowie
Heroes Commodores
Hey Jude Beatles
Hi Infidelity REO Speedwagon
Hi-Fi Companion Album Ray Conniff
High On The Happy Side Wet Wet Wet
Highway 61 Revisited Bob Dylan
Himself Gilbert O'Sullivan
Hip Hop And Rapping In The House Various
His Hand In Mine Elvis Presley
His Latest And Greatest Chuck Berry
His Orchestra, His Chorus, His Singers, His Sound Ray Conniff
The Hissing Of Summer Lawns Joni Mitchell
History Of Eric Clapton Eric Clapton
History Of Otis Redding Otis Redding
History/America's Greatest Hits America
The Hit List Cliff Richard
Hit Machine Various
Hit Maker - Burt Bacharach Burt Bacharach
The Hit Squad - Chart Tracking Various
Hits 2 Various
The Hits 2 Prince
Hits 3 Various
Hits 4 Various
Hits 5 Various
Hits 6 Various
Hits 7 Various
Hits 8 Various
The Hits Album Various
The Hits Album Various
Hits For Lovers Various
Hits Hits Hits Various
Hits Hits Hits - 18 Smash Originals Various
Hits Out Of Hell Meat Loaf
Hold Out Jackson Browne
Holding Back The River Wet Wet Wet
Holiday America
Holiday Sing Along With Mitch Mitch Miller
Hollies Hollies
Hollies Live Hits Hollies
Hollies Sing Dylan Hollies
Home For Christmas Amy Grant
Home Loving Man Andy Williams
Home On The Range Slim Whitman
Homecoming America
Honey Bobby Goldsboro
Honey Ohio Players
Honey In The Horn Al Hirt
Honky Chateau Elton John
Hooked On Classics Royal Philharmonic Orchestra cond. by Louis Clark
Horizon Carpenters
Hormonally Yours Shakespears Sister
Hot August Night Neil Diamond
Hot City Nights Various
Hot Hits 6 Various
Hot Hits 7 Various
Hot Hits 8 Various
Hot Rocks 1964-1971 Rolling Stones
Hot Space Queen
Hot Wax Various
Hotcakes Carly Simon
Hotel California Eagles
Hotline Various
Hotter Than July Stevie Wonder
Hounds Of Love Kate Bush
Houses Of The Holy Led Zeppelin
How Dare You? 10 C.C.
How Do You Like It? Gerry And The Pacemakers
How Glad I Am Nancy Wilson
Human Racing Nik Kershaw
Human Touch Bruce Springsteen
Human's Lib Howard Jones
Hungry For Hits Various
Hunky Dory David Bowie
Hunting High And Low A-Ha
The Hurting Tears For Fears
Hysteria Def Leppard
Hysteria Human League

I Am Earth, Wind & Fire
I Do Not Want What I Haven't Got Sinead O'Connor
I Got A Name Jim Croce
I Got Dem Ol' Kozmic Blues Again Mama Janis Joplin
I Hear A Symphony Supremes
I Know Cos I Was There Max Boyce
I Left My Heart In San Francisco Tony Bennett
I Love Rock-N-Roll Joan Jett & The Blackhearts
I Love You Because Al Martino
I Never Loved A Man The Way I Love You Aretha Franklin
I Remember Hank Williams Jack Scott
I Remember Tommy... Frank Sinatra
I Remember Yesterday Donna Summer
I Say I Say I Say Erasure
I Wanna Be Around Tony Bennett
I Want You Marvin Gaye
I'll Give All My Love To You Keith Sweat
I'll Remember You Frank Ifield
I'm A Writer Not A Fighter Gilbert O'Sullivan
I'm Breathless Madonna
I'm Glad You're Here With Me Tonight Neil Diamond
I'm In You Peter Frampton
I'm Nearly Famous Cliff Richard
I'm No Hero Cliff Richard
I'm Still In Love With You Al Green
I'm Your Baby Tonight Whitney Houston
Ice On Fire Elton John
Idea Bee Gees
Idol Songs: 11 Of The Best Billy Idol
If I Ever Fall In Love Shai
If I Should Fall From Grace With God Pogues
If I Should Love Again Barry Manilow
If That's What It Takes Michael McDonald
If You Can Believe Your Eyes And Ears Mamas & The Papas
If You Love Me, Let Me Know Olivia Newton-John
Ill Communication Beastie Boys
Images Walker Brothers
Images Don Williams
Imagination Imagination
Imagine John Lennon
The Immaculate Collection Madonna
The Impressions Keep On Pushing Impressions
In Concert Luciano Pavarotti, Placido Domingo & Jose Carreras
The In Crowd Ramsey Lewis
In Dreams Roy Orbison
In Pieces Garth Brooks
In Search Of The Lost Chord Moody Blues
In Square Circle Stevie Wonder
In The Army Now Status Quo
In The Court Of The Crimson King King Crimson
In The Dark Grateful Dead
In The Heat Of The Night Imagination
In The Wake Of Poseidon King Crimson
In The Wind Peter, Paul & Mary
In Through The Out Door Led Zeppelin
In Utero Nirvana
In Your Eyes George Benson
In Your Mind Bryan Ferry
In-A-Gadda-Da-Vida Iron Butterfly
Ingenue kd lang
Ingredients In A Recipe For Soul Ray Charles
Innervisions Stevie Wonder
The Innocent Age Dan Fogelberg
An Innocent Man Billy Joel
The Innocents Erasure
Innuendo Queen
Inside Shelley Berman Shelley Berman
Inspector Morse - Music From The TV Series Barrington Pheloung
Inspiration Elvis Presley
Instrumental Gold Various
Into The Fire Bryan Adams
Into The Gap Thompson Twins
Into The Great White Open Tom Petty & The Heartbreakers
Into The Light Chris De Burgh
Into The Light Gloria Estefan
Introducing Herman's Hermits Herman's Hermits
Introducing The Hardline According To... Terence Trent D'arby
Introducing...The Beatles Beatles
Introspective Pet Shop Boys
Invasion Of Your Privacy Ratt
Invisible Touch Genesis
Iron Maiden Iron Maiden
The Isaac Hayes Movement Isaac Hayes
Island Life Grace Jones
It Happened At The World's Fair (Soundtrack) Elvis Presley
It Keeps Right On A-Hurtin' Johnny Tillotson
It Won't Be The Last Billy Ray Cyrus
It's About Time SWV
It's Better To Travel Swing Out Sister
It's Everly Time Everly Brothers

Title	Artist
It's Hard	Who
It's On (Dr. Dre 187um) Killa	Eazy-E
It's Only Rock 'n' Roll	Rolling Stones
It's The Searchers	Searchers
It's Trad Dad	Soundtrack
It's Your Call	Reba McEntire
Italian Favorites	Connie Francis
Jam	Little Angels
James Bond's Greatest Hits	Various
James Galway Plays Songs For Annie	James Galway
Janet	Janet Jackson
Jar Of Flies	Alice In Chains
Jazz	Queen
Jazz Samba	Stan Getz/Charlie Byrd
The Jazz Singer	Neil Diamond
Je M'appelle Barbra	Barbra Streisand
Jesus Christ Superstar	Various
Jigsaw	Shadows
Jive Bunny - The Album	Jive Bunny & The Mastermixers
Joan Baez In Concert Part 2	Joan Baez
Joan Baez No. 5	Joan Baez
John Barleycorn Must Die	Traffic
John Denver's Greatest Hits	John Denver
John Denver's Greatest Hits Vol. 2	John Denver
The John Lennon Collection	John Lennon
John Lennon/Plastic Ono Band	John Lennon
John Wesley Harding	Bob Dylan
Johnny Cash At San Quentin	Johnny Cash
Johnny Gill	Johnny Gill
The Johnny Mathis Collection	Johnny Mathis
Johnny's Moods	Johnny Mathis
The Joker	Steve Miller Band
Jonathan King's Entertainment USA	Various
Jonathan Livingston Seagull (Soundtrack)	Neil Diamond
Joplin In Concert	Janis Joplin
Jose Jiminez At The Hungry I	Bill Dana
Joseph And The Amazing Technicolor Dream Coat	Jason Donovan/Cast
The Joshua Tree	U2
Journey Through The Secret Life Of Plants	Stevie Wonder
Journey To Glory	Spandau Ballet
Journey To The Centre Of The Earth	Rick Wakeman
Journeyman	Eric Clapton
Joyride	Roxette
JT	James Taylor
Judy At Carnegie Hall	Judy Garland
Juke Box Jive	Various
Julio	Julio Iglesias
Jump Up Calypso	Harry Belafonte
The Jungle Book	Soundtrack
Just A Boy	Leo Sayer
Just Can't Stop It	Beat
Just Like Us!	Paul Revere & The Raiders
Just Once In My Life...	Righteous Brothers
Just One Night	Eric Clapton
Just Supposin'	Status Quo
Kaleidoscope	Siouxsie & The Banshees
Kamakiriad	Donald Fagen
Kaya	Bob Marley & The Wailers
KC & The Sunshine Band	KC & The Sunshine Band
Keep It Up	Loverboy
Keep The Faith	Bon Jovi
Keep Your Distance	Curiosity Killed The Cat
Kenny	Kenny Rogers
Kenny Ball's Golden Hits	Kenny Ball
Kenny Rogers' Greatest Hits	Kenny Rogers
The Kenny Rogers Story	Kenny Rogers
Kick	INXS
The Kick Inside	Kate Bush
Kick Thy Own Self	Dave Gardner
Kickin' It Up	John Michael Montgomery
The Kids Are Alright	Who
Kids From Fame	Kids From Fame
Kids From Fame Again	Kids From Fame
Killing Me Softly	Roberta Flack
Kilroy Was Here	Styx
Kim Wilde	Kim Wilde
Kimono My House	Sparks
A Kind Of Hush	Carpenters
A Kind Of Magic	Queen
Kinda Kinks	Kinks
The King And I	Soundtrack
Kings Of The Wild Frontier	Adam & The Ants
The Kingston Trio 16	Kingston Trio
The Kingston Trio At Large	Kingston Trio
Kinks	Kinks
Kissin' Cousins (Soundtrack)	Elvis Presley
Knee Deep In The Hoopla	Starship
Knockers Up!	Rusty Warren
Kylie	Kylie Minogue
Kylie's Greatest Hits	Kylie Minogue
L-O-V-E	Nat 'King' Cole
La Bamba	Soundtrack
Labour Of Love	UB40
Labour Of Love II	UB40
Labour Of Love - Volumes I & II	UB40
Lady Sings The Blues (Soundtrack)	Diana Ross
Last Action Hero	Soundtrack
The Last Dance	Various
Last Date	Lawrence Welk
The Last In Line	Dio
The Last Temptation	Alice Cooper
Last The Whole Night Long	James Last
The Last Waltz	Engelbert Humperdinck
Laughing On Judgement Day	Thunder
Laughter And Tears - The Best Of Neil Sedaka	Neil Sedaka
Lawrence Of Arabia	Soundtrack
Lawyers In Love	Jackson Browne
Learning To Crawl	Pretenders
Led Zeppelin	Led Zeppelin
Led Zeppelin II	Led Zeppelin
Led Zeppelin III	Led Zeppelin
Led Zeppelin IV (Four Symbols)	Led Zeppelin
Leftoverture	Kansas
Legend	Bob Marley & The Wailers
The Legend - The Essential Collection	Joe Cocker
The Legendary Roy Orbison	Roy Orbison
Lena's Music Album	Lena Martell
Let It Be	Beatles
Let It Bleed	Rolling Stones
Let It Loose	Gloria Estefan & The Miami Sound Machine
Let There Be Drums	Sandy Nelson
Let's All Sing With The Chipmunks	Chipmunks
Let's Dance	David Bowie
Let's Get It On	Marvin Gaye
Let's Get Serious	Jermaine Jackson
Let's Stay Together	Al Green
Levellers	Levellers
The Lexicon Of Love	ABC
Licensed To Ill	Beastie Boys
Life	Inspiral Carpets
Life And Times	Jim Croce
A Life Of Surprises - The Best Of Prefab Sprout	Prefab Sprout
Life, Love And Pain	Club Nouveau
Light Up The Night	Brothers Johnson
Like A Prayer	Madonna
Like A Rock	Bob Seger & The Silver Bullet Band
Like A Virgin	Madonna
The Lion King	Soundtrack
Lionel Richie	Lionel Richie
Lionheart	Kate Bush
Listen To Cliff	Cliff Richard
Listen Without Prejudice Vol. 1	George Michael
A Little Ain't Enough	David Lee Roth
A Little Bit More	Dr. Hook
Little Deuce Coupe	Beach Boys
Little Stevie Wonder/The 12 Year Old Genius	Stevie Wonder
Live	Status Quo
Live After Death	Iron Maiden
Live Album	Grand Funk Railroad
Live And Dangerous	Thin Lizzy
Live And More	Donna Summer
Live At Leeds	Who
Live At The Apollo	James Brown
Live At The BBC	Beatles
Live At The Talk Of The Town	Tom Jones
Live At The Talk Of The Town	Seekers
Live At The Talk Of The Town	Supremes
Live At Wembley '86	Queen
Live Cream	Cream
Live In London	John Denver
Live In The City Of Light	Simple Minds
Live Killers	Queen
Live Magic	Queen
Live: Right Here, Right Now	Van Halen
Live - The Way We Walk Vol. 1: The Shorts	Genesis
Live - The Way We Walk Vol. 2: The Longs	Genesis
Livin' Inside Your Love	George Benson
Living In The Material World	George Harrison
Living In The Past	Jethro Tull
Living In The USA	Linda Ronstadt
Living Ornaments 1979-1980	Gary Numan
The Living Years	Mike & The Mechanics
Loc-Ed After Dark	Tone Loc
Lodger	David Bowie
London 0 Hull 4	Housemartins
The London Chuck Berry Sessions	Chuck Berry
London Town	Wings
A Lonely Man	Chi-Lites
The Lonesome Jubilee	John Cougar Mellencamp
Long Distance Voyager	Moody Blues
Long Live Rock 'n' Roll	Rainbow
The Long Run	Eagles
Longing In Their Hearts	Bonnie Raitt
Look Around	Sergio Mendes & Brasil '66
Look At Us	Sonny & Cher
Look Sharp!	Roxette
Look What The Cat Dragged In	Poison
Lookin' Through The Windows	Jackson 5
The Lord's Prayer	Mormon Tabernacle Choir
Los Cochinos	Cheech & Chong
Lose Control	Silk
Lou Rawls Live!	Lou Rawls
Lou Rawls Soulin'	Lou Rawls
The Love Album	Various
Love And Dancing	League Unlimited Orchestra
Love Andy	Andy Williams
Love At First Sting	Scorpions
Love At The Greek	Neil Diamond
Love Deluxe	Sade
Love Gun	Kiss
Love Hurts	Cher
Love Is The Message	MFSB
Love Over Gold	Dire Straits
Love Songs	Beatles
Love Songs	Commodores
Love Songs	Elvis Presley
Love Songs	Cliff Richard
Love Songs	Diana Ross
Love Songs	Barbra Streisand
The Love Songs	George Benson
Love Story	Soundtrack
Love Story	Andy Williams
Love Tracks	Gloria Gaynor
Love Will Keep Us Together	Captain & Tennille
Love You Live	Rolling Stones
Love Zone	Billy Ocean

Title	Artist
Lovegod	Soup Dragons
Lovesexy	Prince
Low	David Bowie
The Low Spark Of High Heeled Boys	Traffic
Luck Of The Draw	Bonnie Raitt
Lucky 13 Shades Of Val Doonican	Val Doonican
Lucky Town	Bruce Springsteen
The Luxury Gap	Heaven 17
Machine Head	Deep Purple
Mad Dogs & Englishmen	Joe Cocker
Mad Love	Linda Ronstadt
Made In Japan	Deep Purple
Made In The Shade	Rolling Stones
Madman Across The Water	Elton John
Madness 7	Madness
Madonna	Madonna
Madonna/The First Album	Madonna
The Magic Of Boney M	Boney M
Magical Mystery Tour	Beatles
Magnetic Fields	Jean-Michel Jarre
Magnificent Seven	Supremes & Four Tops
Make It Big	Wham!
Make The Party Last	James Last
Make Way!	Kingston Trio
Makin' Movies	Dire Straits
The Mamas & The Papas Deliver	Mamas & The Papas
The Mamas And The Papas	Mamas & The Papas
A Man And His Music	Frank Sinatra
A Man Without Love	Engelbert Humperdinck
Manassas	Stephen Stills
Manifesto	Roxy Music
Manilow Magic	Barry Manilow
Mann Made	Manfred Mann
Mantovani Magic	Mantovani
Mantovani Plays Music From Exodus And Other Great Themes	Mantovani
Maria Elena	Los Indios Tabajaras
Maria Muldaur	Maria Muldaur
Mariah Carey	Mariah Carey
Mario Lanza Sings Caruso Favorites	Mario Lanza
Marty Robbins Collection	Marty Robbins
Marvin Gaye Live At The London Palladium	Marvin Gaye
Mary Poppins	Soundtrack
Master Of Reality	Black Sabbath
Masterpiece	Temptations
Matthew And Son	Cat Stevens
McCartney	Paul McCartney
McCartney II	Paul McCartney
MCMXC AD	Enigma
Me And My Shadows	Cliff Richard
Me Myself I	Joan Armatrading
Meat Is Murder	Smiths
Meddle	Pink Floyd
Meet The Beatles	Beatles
Meet The Searchers	Searchers
Memories Are Made Of This	Ray Conniff
The Memphis Sessions	Wet Wet Wet
Men And Women	Simply Red
Merry Christmas	Mariah Carey
Merry Merry Christmas	New Kids On The Block
Metal Health	Quiet Riot
Metallica	Metallica
Metamorphosis	Rolling Stones
Miami Vice	TV Soundtrack
Michael Ball	Michael Ball
Middle Man	Boz Scaggs
Midnight Hustle	Various
Midnight Love	Marvin Gaye
Midnight Magic	Commodores
The Midnight Special	Harry Belafonte
Miles Of Aisles	Joni Mitchell
Milk And Honey	John Lennon
Millican And Nesbit	Millican And Nesbit
A Million Dollars' Worth Of Twang	Duane Eddy
Million Mile Reflections	Charlie Daniels Band
Mind Games	John Lennon
Minstrel In The Gallery	Jethro Tull
Minute By Minute	Doobie Brothers
The Miracle	Queen
Miracles The Holiday Album	Kenny G
Mirage	Fleetwood Mac
Misplaced Childhood	Marillion
Missing...Presumed Having A Good Time	Notting Hillbillies
Mistaken Identity	Kim Carnes
Mo' Money	Soundtrack
Modern Dance	Various
Modern Sounds In Country And Western Music	Ray Charles
Modern Sounds In Country And Western Music (Vol. 2)	Ray Charles
A Momentary Lapse Of Reason	Pink Floyd
Money For Nothing	Dire Straits
The Monkees	Monkees
Monster	REM
Moods	Neil Diamond
Moody Blue	Elvis Presley
Moon River & Other Great Movie Themes	Andy Williams
Moonlight And Roses	Jim Reeves
Moonlighting	TV Soundtrack
More Dirty Dancing	Various
More Hits By The Supremes	Supremes
More Of The Monkees	Monkees
More Specials	Specials
Morrison Hotel/Hard Rock Cafe	Doors
Most Of The Animals	Animals
Mother Lode	Loggins & Messina
Motown Chartbusters Vol. 4	Various
Motown Chartbusters Vol. 5	Various
Motown Chartbusters Vol. 6	Various
Motown Dance Party	Various
Mounting Excitement	Various
Mouth To Mouth	Lipps Inc.
Move Closer	Various
Move To This	Cathy Dennis
Moving Pictures	Rush
Moving Waves	Focus
(Moving)	Peter, Paul & Mary
Mr. Bad Guy	Freddie Mercury
Mr. Lucky	John Lee Hooker
Mr. Tambourine Man	Byrds
MTV Unplugged EP	Mariah Carey
MTV Unplugged In New York	Nirvana
Mud Rock Vol. 2	Mud
Mud Slide Slim And The Blue Horizon	James Taylor
The Muppet Show	Muppets
Murder Was The Case	Soundtrack
Music	Carole King
Music Box	Mariah Carey
Music Express	Various
Music For The Jilted Generation	Prodigy
Music From Mr. Lucky	Henry Mancini
Music Man	Original London Cast
The Music Man	Soundtrack
My Concerto For You	Russ Conway
My Cup Runneth Over	Ed Ames
My Fair Lady	Original Broadway Cast
My Fair Lady	Soundtrack
My Generation	Who
My Love Forgive Me	Robert Goulet
My Name Is Barbra	Barbra Streisand
My Name Is Barbra, Two...	Barbra Streisand
My Son, The Celebrity	Allan Sherman
My Son, The Folk Singer	Allan Sherman
My Son, The Nut	Allan Sherman
My Way	Frank Sinatra
My World	Eddy Arnold
Mystery Girl	Roy Orbison
The Myths And Legends Of King Arthur And The Knights Of The Round Table	Rick Wakeman
Nashville Skyline	Bob Dylan
Natural High	Commodores
Natural History - The Very Best Of..	Talk Talk
Nebraska	Bruce Springsteen
Neil Reid	Neil Reid
Neither One Of Us	Gladys Knight & The Pips
Never A Dull Moment	Rod Stewart
Never For Ever	Kate Bush
Never Loved Elvis	Wonder Stuff
Never Mind The Bollocks Here's The Sex Pistols	Sex Pistols
Never On Sunday	Soundtrack
Never Too Late	Status Quo
Nevermind	Nirvana
New Boots And Panties!!	Ian Dury & The Blockheads
New Edition	New Edition
A New Flame	Simply Red
New Gold Dream (81,82,83,84)	Simple Minds
New Jack City	Soundtrack
New Jersey	Bon Jovi
New Light Through Old Windows	Chris Rea
New Morning	Bob Dylan
A New World Record	Electric Light Orchestra
News Of The World	Queen
Nice 'n' Easy	Frank Sinatra
Nick Of Time	Bonnie Raitt
Night And Day	Joe Jackson
A Night At The Opera	Queen
Night Birds	Shakatak
Night Flight To Venus	Boney M
Night Moves	Bob Seger & The Silver Bullet Band
A Night On The Town	Rod Stewart
Night Songs	Cinderella
Nightbirds	LaBelle
Nightwatch	Kenny Loggins
Nilsson Schmilsson	Nilsson
90125	Yes
Nine Tonight	Bob Seger & The Silver Bullet Band
1982	Status Quo
1984 (MCMLXXXIV)	Van Halen
19 Naughty III	Naughty By Nature
1992 - The Love Album	Carter - The Unstoppable Sex Machine
Nite Flite	Various
No Fences	Garth Brooks
No Jacket Required	Phil Collins
No Limits	2 Unlimited
No More Heroes	Stranglers
No More The Fool	Elkie Brooks
No Need To Argue	Cranberries
No Parlez	Paul Young
No Prayer For The Dying	Iron Maiden
No Regrets - The Best Of ...1965-1976	Scott Walker & The Walker Brothers
No Secrets	Carly Simon
No Sleep Til Hammersmith	Motorhead
No Strings	Original Cast
A Nod Is As Good As A Wink...To A Blind Horse	Faces
Non-Stop Erotic Cabaret	Soft Cell
Not A Moment Too Soon	Tim McGraw
Not Fragile	Bachman-Turner Overdrive
Not The 9 O'Clock News	Not The 9 O'Clock News Cast
Nothing Like The Sun	Sting
Now & Then	Carpenters
Now And Zen	Robert Plant
Now Dance	Various
Now Dance '86	Various
Now That's What I Call Music	Various
Now That's What I Call Music 2	Various
Now That's What I Call Music 3	Various
Now That's What I Call Music 4	Various
Now That's What I Call Music 5	Various

Title	Artist
Now That's What I Call Music 6	Various
Now That's What I Call Music 7	Various
Now That's What I Call Music 8	Various
Now That's What I Call Music 9	Various
Now That's What I Call Music 10	Various
Now That's What I Call Music 11	Various
Now That's What I Call Music 12	Various
Now That's What I Call Music 13	Various
Now - The Christmas Album	Various
Now - The Summer Album	Various
Now You See Me, Now You Don't	Cliff Richard
The Number Of The Beast	Iron Maiden
The Nylon Curtain	Billy Joel
0898	Beautiful South
Ocean Rain	Echo & The Bunnymen
Oceans Of Fantasy	Boney M
Octave	Moody Blues
Ode To Billie Joe	Bobbie Gentry
Off The Wall	Michael Jackson
The Official BBC Album Of The Royal Wedding	Various
Ogden's Nut Gone Flake	Small Faces
Oh Pretty Woman	Roy Orbison
Oil On Canvas	Japan
Oklahoma	Soundtrack
Old New Borrowed And Blue	Slade
Oliver	Original London Cast
Oliver	Soundtrack
Ommadawn	Mike Oldfield
On Every Street	Dire Straits
On Stage	Loggins & Messina
On Stage	Elvis Presley
On Stage	Rainbow
On Stage With The George Mitchell Minstrels	George Mitchell Minstrels
On The Level	Status Quo
On The Night	Dire Straits
On The Radio - Greatest Hits Volumes I & 2	Donna Summer
On The Threshold Of A Dream	Moody Blues
On Tour With The George Mitchell Minstrels	George Mitchell Minstrels
Once Upon A Star	Bay City Rollers
Once Upon A Time	Simple Minds
100 Golden Greats	Max Bygraves
One Man Dog	James Taylor
One More From The Road	Lynyrd Skynyrd
One Night At Budokan	Michael Schenker Group
One Of These Nights	Eagles
One Step Beyond	Madness
One Step Closer	Doobie Brothers
The One	Elton John
The One Thing	Michael Bolton
One Woman - The Ultimate Collection	Diana Ross
Only Yesterday	Carpenters
Ooh Las Vegas	Deacon Blue
Ooh-La-La	Faces
Open Up And Say Ahh	Poison
Organisation	Orchestral Manoeuvres In The Dark
Original Greatest Hits	Everly Brothers
Original Soundtrack	S'Express
The Original Soundtrack	10 C.C.
The Other Side Of Life	Moody Blues
The Other Side Of The Mirror	Stevie Nicks
Otis Blue	Otis Redding
OU812	Van Halen
Our Best To You	Osmonds
Our Favourite Shop	Style Council
Our Town - Greatest Hits	Deacon Blue
Out Now!	Various
Out Now! 2	Various
Out Of Our Heads	Rolling Stones
Out Of The Blue	Electric Light Orchestra
Out Of The Blue	Debbie Gibson
Out Of The Cellar	Ratt
Out Of The Shadows	Shadows
Out Of Time	R.E.M.
Outlandos D'amour	Police
Outside Shelley Berman	Shelley Berman
Overture And Beginners	Faces
Oxygene	Jean-Michel Jarre
Paint Your Wagon	Soundtrack
Panorama	Cars
Parade	Spandau Ballet
Parade - Music From 'Under The Cherry Moon' (Soundtrack)	Prince & The Revolution
Paradise	Inner City
Paradise Hawaiian Style (Soundtrack)	Elvis Presley
Paradise Theater	Styx
Parallel Lines	Blondie
Paranoid	Black Sabbath
Paris	Supertramp
Parklife	Blur
Parsley Sage Rosemary And Thyme	Simon & Garfunkel
The Partridge Family Album	Partridge Family
Party Party - 16 Great Party Icebreakers	Black Lace
Party Time	Russ Conway
A Passion Play	Jethro Tull
Passport	Nana Mouskouri
Pastpresent	Clannad
Paul Anka Sings His Big 15	Paul Anka
Paul Simon	Paul Simon
Peace In The Valley	Various
Pearl	Janis Joplin
Pearls	Elkie Brooks
Pearls II	Elkie Brooks
Pelican West	Haircut 100
Pendulum	Creedence Clearwater Revival
People	Barbra Streisand
Pepino The Italian Mouse & Other Italian Fun Songs	Lou Monte
Perfect Angel	Minnie Riperton
Perfect Strangers	Deep Purple
Performs Andrew Lloyd Webber	Michael Crawford/RPO
Permanent Waves	Rush
Pet Shop Boys, Actually	Pet Shop Boys
Pet Sounds	Beach Boys
Peter & Sophia	Peter Sellers & Sophia Loren
Peter Gabriel	Peter Gabriel
Peter, Paul & Mary	Peter, Paul & Mary
Peter, Paul & Mary In Concert	Peter, Paul & Mary
Phantom Of The Opera	Original London Cast
Phoebe Snow	Phoebe Snow
Phoenix	Dan Fogelberg
Photographs & Memories/His Greatest Hits	Jim Croce
The Photos	Photos
Physical	Olivia Newton-John
Physical Graffiti	Led Zeppelin
Pick Of The Litter	Spinners
Picture Book	Simply Red
A Picture Of You	Joe Brown
Pictures At An Exhibition	Emerson, Lake & Palmer
Pictures At Eleven	Robert Plant
Piece Of Mind	Iron Maiden
Pieces Of Eight	Styx
Pills 'n' Thrills And Bellyaches	Happy Mondays
Pin Ups	David Bowie
Piper At The Gates Of Dawn	Pink Floyd
Pipes Of Peace	Paul McCartney
Pirates	Rickie Lee Jones
Pisces Iscariot	Smashing Pumpkins
Pisces, Aquarius, Capricorn & Jones Ltd	Monkees
The Plan	Osmonds
Planet Waves	Bob Dylan
Play Deep	Outfield
Please	Pet Shop Boys
Please Hammer Don't Hurt 'em	MC Hammer
Please Please Me	Beatles
The Pleasure Principal	Gary Numan
Pocket Full Of Kryptonite	Spin Doctors
A Pocketful Of Dreams	Big Fun
Point Of Know Return	Kansas
Poison	Bell Biv Devoe
Pomme Fritz	Orb
Pop! - The First 20 Hits	Erasure
Popped In Souled Out	Wet Wet Wet
Porcupine	Echo & The Bunnymen
Porno For Pyros	Porno For Pyros
Portrait	Diana Ross
Portrait	Walker Brothers
Portrait In Music	Burt Bacharach
Portrait Of Donny	Donny Osmond
Portrait Of Johnny	Johnny Mathis
Portrait Of Sinatra	Frank Sinatra
Postcard	Mary Hopkin
Pot Luck	Elvis Presley
Power, Corruption And Lies	New Order
Power In The Darkness	Tom Robinson Band
Power Of Ten	Chris De Burgh
The Power Station	Power Station
Powerslave	Iron Maiden
Precious Time	Pat Benatar
The Predator	Ice Cube
Prelude	Deodato
The Premiere Collection	Various
Presence	Led Zeppelin
Present Arms	UB40
Presley - The All Time Greatest Hits	Elvis Presley
The Pretender	Jackson Browne
Pretenders	Pretenders
Pretenders II	Pretenders
Pretty In Pink	Soundtrack
Pretty Things	Pretty Things
Pretty Woman	Soundtrack
Prince Charming	Adam Ant
Prince **1999**	Prince
The Principle Of Moments	Robert Plant
Prisoner In Disguise	Linda Ronstadt
Private Collection	Cliff Richard
Private Dancer	Tina Turner
Private Eyes	Daryl Hall & John Oates
Procol Harum Live In Concert With The Edmonton Symphony Orchestra	Procol Harum
Promise	Sade
Promised Land	Queensryche
Promises And Lies	UB40
Prophets, Seers And Sages The Angels Of The Ages/My People Were Fair And Had Sky In Their Hair But Now They're Content To Wear Stars On Their Brows	T. Rex
The Psychomodo	Cockney Rebel
Pump	Aerosmith
Pump Up The Jam	Technotronic
Punch The Clock	Elvis Costello
Pure Country	George Strait
Pure Cult	Cult
Pure Gold	Various
Purple	Stone Temple Pilots
Purple Rain (Soundtrack)	Prince & The Revolution
Push	Bros
Puzzle People	Temptations
Pyromania	Def Leppard
Quadrophenia	Who
Quarterflash	Quarterflash
Queen 2	Queen
The Queen Is Dead	Smiths
A Question Of Balance	Moody Blues
A Quick One	Who
Quick Step And Side Kick	Thompson Twins
Quo	Status Quo
Rag Doll	Four Seasons

Title	Artist
Rage	T'Pau
Rage In Eden	Ultravox
Rags To Rufus	Rufus Featuring Chaka Khan
Raiders Of The Pop Charts	Various
Rainbow	Peters & Lee
Raindancing	Alison Moyet
Raise!	Earth, Wind & Fire
Raised On Radio	Journey
Raising Hell	Run-D.M.C.
Ram	Paul & Linda McCartney
Ramblin' Rose	Nat 'King' Cole
Rank	Smiths
Rap Trax	Various
Rastaman Vibration	Bob Marley & The Wailers
Rattle And Hum	U2
The Raw & The Cooked	Fine Young Cannibals
Raw Like Sushi	Neneh Cherry
Ray Charles' Greatest Hits	Ray Charles
The Razors Edge	AC/DC
Reach Out	Four Tops
Reach The Beach	Fixx
Read My Mind	Reba McEntire
Reading Writing & Arithmetic	Sundays
Ready And Willing	Whitesnake
Real Life	Simple Minds
Real Love	Lisa Stansfield
Real Things	2 Unlimited
Realization	Johnny Rivers
Rebel Yell	Billy Idol
Reckless	Bryan Adams
Recycler	ZZ Top
Red Octopus	Jefferson Starship
Red River Valley	Slim Whitman
Red Rose Speedway	Paul McCartney & Wings
The Red Shoes	Kate Bush
Reflection	Shadows
Reflections	Various
Reflections	Andy Williams
Reggatta De Blanc	Police
Regulate...G Funk Era	Warren G
Rejoice	Emotions
Rejoice, Dear Hearts!	Dave Gardner
Relayer	Yes
Release Me	Engelbert Humperdinck
Remember Me This Way	Gary Glitter
Reminiscing	Buddy Holly
Repeat Offender	Richard Marx
Replicas	Tubeway Army
Republic	New Order
Requiem	Andrew Lloyd Webber
The Return Of Bruno	Bruce Willis
The Return Of Roger Miller	Roger Miller
The Return Of The Space Cowboy	Jamiroquai
Return To Fantasy	Uriah Heep
Revenge	Bill Cosby
Revenge	Eurythmics
Revenge	Kiss
Revolutions	Jean-Michel Jarre
Revolver	Beatles
Rhymes & Reasons	Carole King
Rhythm Nation 1814	Janet Jackson
Rhythm Of Love	Anita Baker
Rhythm Of The Saints	Paul Simon
Rhythms And Ballads Of Broadway	Johnny Mathis
Richard Chamberlain Sings	Richard Chamberlain
Richard Clayderman	Richard Clayderman
Richard Marx	Richard Marx
Rick Is 21	Rick Nelson
Rickie Lee Jones	Rickie Lee Jones
Ring-A-Ding Ding!	Frank Sinatra
Ringo	Ringo Starr
Rio	Duran Duran
Riptide	Robert Palmer
Rise	Herb Alpert
The Rise And Fall Of Ziggy Stardust And The Spiders From Mars	David Bowie
Risque	Chic
River Of Dreams	Billy Joel
The River	Bruce Springsteen
The Road To Hell	Chris Rea
The Roaring Twenties - Songs From The TV Series	Dorothy Provine
Roberta Flack & Donny Hathaway	Roberta Flack
Robin Hood: Prince Of Thieves	Soundtrack
Rock Follies	TV Soundtrack
Rock Me Baby	David Cassidy
Rock 'n' Roll	John Lennon
Rock 'n' Roll Juvenile	Cliff Richard
Rock 'n' Roll Music	Beatles
Rock 'n' Roll No. 2	Elvis Presley
Rock 'n' Roller Disco	Various
Rock 'n Soul Part 1	Daryl Hall & John Oates
Rock Of Ages	Band
Rock Of The Westies	Elton John
Rockin' All Over The World	Status Quo
Rocking All Over The Years	Status Quo
Rocks	Aerosmith
Rocky	Soundtrack
Rocky IV	Soundtrack
Rocky Mountain High	John Denver
Rod Stewart, Lead Vocalist	Rod Stewart
Roll On	Various
Roll The Bones	Rush
Roll With It	Steve Winwood
Rollin'	Bay City Rollers
Rolling Stones	Rolling Stones
Rolling Stones No. 2	Rolling Stones
The Rolling Stones, Now!	Rolling Stones
Rome Adventure	Soundtrack
Romeo & Juliet	Soundtrack
Ropin' The Wind	Garth Brooks
Roses Are Red	Bobby Vinton
Roustabout (Soundtrack)	Elvis Presley
Rubber Soul	Beatles
Rufus Featuring Chaka Khan	Rufus Featuring Chaka Khan
Rumours	Fleetwood Mac
Run With The Pack	Bad Company
Runaway Horses	Belinda Carlisle
Running In The Family	Level 42
Running On Empty	Jackson Browne
S.R.O.	Herb Alpert & The Tijuana Brass
Sabbath Bloody Sabbath	Black Sabbath
Sandie	Sandie Shaw
Santana	Santana
Santana III	Santana
Saturday Night Fever	Soundtrack
Savage Amusement	Scorpions
Saved	Bob Dylan
Say It With Music (A Touch Of Latin)	Ray Conniff
Scarecrow	John Cougar Mellencamp
Scary Monsters And Super Creeps	David Bowie
Scenes From The Southside	Bruce Hornsby & The Range
School's Out	Alice Cooper
Schubert Dip	EMF
Scott	Scott Walker
Scott 2	Scott Walker
Scott 3	Scott Walker
Scoundrel Days	A-Ha
Seal	Seal
Seal	Seal
Searching For The Young Soul Rebels	Dexy's Midnight Runners
Secombe's Personal Choice	Harry Secombe
The Second Barbra Streisand Album	Barbra Streisand
The 2nd LP	Spencer Davis Group
The Second	Steppenwolf
Seconds Out	Genesis
Secret Combination	Randy Crawford
Secret Messages	Electric Light Orchestra
The Secret Of Association	Paul Young
The Seeds Of Love	Tears For Fears
The Seer	Big Country
Self Portrait	Bob Dylan
Selling England By The Pound	Genesis
The Sensual World	Kate Bush
Sentimental Journey	Ringo Starr
Sentimental Sing Along With Mitch	Mitch Miller
September Of My Years	Frank Sinatra
Serenade	Neil Diamond
Sergeant Pepper's Lonely Hearts Club Band	Beatles
Sergeant Pepper's Lonely Hearts Club Band	Soundtrack
Serious Hits...Live!	Phil Collins
A Session With The Dave Clark Five	Dave Clark Five
Seven	James
Seven Ages Of Acker	Mr. Acker Bilk
Seven And The Ragged Tiger	Duran Duran
Seven Brides For Seven Brothers	Soundtrack
Seven Separate Fools	Three Dog Night
Seventh Sojourn	Moody Blues
Seventh Son Of A Seventh Son	Iron Maiden
Shadow Dancing	Andy Gibb
Shadow Music	Shadows
The Shadow Of Your Smile	Andy Williams
Shadows And Light	Wilson Phillips
The Shadows	Shadows
Shaft (Soundtrack)	Isaac Hayes
Shake Your Money Maker	Black Crowes
Shaky	Shakin' Stevens
Share Your Love	Kenny Rogers
Shaun Cassidy	Shaun Cassidy
She's So Unusual	Cyndi Lauper
Sheer Heart Attack	Queen
Sheer Magic	Mr. Acker Bilk
Shepherd Moons	Enya
Sherry & 11 Others	Four Seasons
Shinin' On	Grand Funk
The Shirley Bassey Singles Album	Shirley Bassey
Shoot Out At The Fantasy Factory	Traffic
Shooting Rubberbands At The Stars	Edie Brickell & The New Bohemians
Short Stories	Jon & Vangelis
Shorty The Pimp	Too Short
Showdown	Isley Brothers
Shut Down	Various
Shut Up And Dance	Paula Abdul
Sign 'O' The Times	Prince
The Sign	Ace Of Base
Signals	Rush
Signing Off	UB40
Silhouette	Kenny G
Silk And Steel	Five Star
Silk Degrees	Boz Scaggs
Silver Bird	Leo Sayer
Simon & Garfunkel's Greatest Hits	Simon & Garfunkel
The Simon And Garfunkel Collection	Simon & Garfunkel
Simple Dreams	Linda Ronstadt
Simple Pleasures	Bobby McFerrin
Simply The Best	Tina Turner
The Simpsons Sing The Blues	Simpsons
Sinatra - Basie	Frank Sinatra & Count Basie
Sinatra And Strings	Frank Sinatra
Sinatra Swings	Frank Sinatra
Sinatra's Swingin' Session!!!	Frank Sinatra
Sing Along With Max	Max Bygraves
Sing It Again Rod	Rod Stewart
Singalongamax Vol. 3	Max Bygraves
The Singing Nun	Singing Nun
Singles	Soundtrack
The Singles - The First Ten Years	Abba
The Singles 1969-1973	Carpenters

Title	Artist
The Singles 1974-78	Carpenters
The Singles Collection	Spandau Ballet
The Singles Collection 1984/1990	Jimmy Somerville
The Singles	Pretenders
Singles-45's And Under	Squeeze
Singular Adventures Of The Style Council	Style Council
Siren	Roxy Music
Sixties Mix	Various
60 Years Of Music America Loves Best	Various
60 Years Of Music America Loves Best Vol.II	Various
Sixty Years Of Music America Loves Best Vol. 3 (Black Seal)	Various
Sixty Years Of Music America Loves Best Vol. 3 (Red Seal)	Various
Skid Row	Skid Row
Sky 2	Sky
Sky 3	Sky
Sky 4 - Forthcoming	Sky
Skyscraper	David Lee Roth
Slade Alive	Slade
Slade In Flame	Slade
Sladest	Slade
Slave To The Grind	Skid Row
Slayed	Slade
Sleeping With The Past	Elton John
Sleepless In Seattle	Soundtrack
Sleeps With Angels	Neil Young & Crazy Horse
The Slider	T. Rex
Slippery When Wet	Bon Jovi
Slow Train Coming	Bob Dylan
Slowhand	Eric Clapton
Small Faces	Small Faces
Smash	Offspring
Smash Hits	Jimi Hendrix
Smash Hits Party '88	Various
Smiler	Rod Stewart
The Smiths	Smiths
The Smoker You Drink, The Player You Get	Joe Walsh
Smokin'	Humble Pie
Snap	Jam
So	Peter Gabriel
So Close	Dina Carroll
So Far	Crosby, Stills, Nash & Young
So Far So Good	Bryan Adams
So Full Of Love	O'Jays
So Good	Mica Paris
The Soft Parade	Doors
Sold Out	Kingston Trio
Solitaire	Andy Williams
Solitude Standing	Suzanne Vega
Some Friendly	Charlatans
Some Gave All	Billy Ray Cyrus
Some Girls	Rolling Stones
Some People's Lives	Bette Midler
Some Product - Carri On Sex Pistols	Sex Pistols
Something	Shirley Bassey
Something For Everybody	Elvis Presley
Something New	Beatles
Somewhere In Time	Iron Maiden
Somewhere My Love	Ray Conniff
A Song For Me	Family
A Song For You	Carpenters
A Song For Young Love	Lettermen
The Song Remains The Same	Led Zeppelin
A Song Will Rise	Peter, Paul & Mary
Song Without End	Soundtrack
Songs	Luther Vandross
Songs For Swinging Sellers	Peter Sellers
Songs From A Room	Leonard Cohen
Songs From The Big Chair	Tears For Fears
Songs From The Wood	Jethro Tull
Songs I Sing On The Jackie Gleason Show	Frank Fontaine
Songs In The Attic	Billy Joel
Songs In The Key Of Life	Stevie Wonder
Songs Of Faith And Devotion	Depeche Mode
Songs Of Joy	Nigel Brooks Singers
Songs Of Love	Anita Ward
Songs Of Love And Hate	Leonard Cohen
Sonic Temple	Cult
Soul & Inspiration	Righteous Brothers
The Soul Cages	Sting
Soul Motion	Various
Soul Provider	Michael Bolton
Sound Affects	Jam
The Sound Of Bread	Bread
Sound Of Music	Original London Cast
The Sound Of Music	Original Cast
The Sound Of Music	Soundtrack
Sound Of The Shadows	Shadows
Sounds Like	Herb Alpert & The Tijuana Brass
The Soundtrack From The Film 'The Song Remains The Same'	Led Zeppelin
South Of The Border	Herb Alpert & The Tijuana Brass
South Pacific	Soundtrack
South Pacific	Studio Cast
Southern Accents	Tom Petty & The Heartbreakers
Southern Harmony And Musical Companion	Black Crowes
Southside	Texas
The Spaghetti Incident?	Guns N' Roses
Spanish Fly	Lisa Lisa & Cult Jam
Sparkle In The Rain	Simple Minds
Spartacus	Farm
Specials	Specials
Spellbound	Paula Abdul
Spirit	John Denver
Spirit	Earth, Wind & Fire
The Spirit Of '67	Paul Revere & The Raiders
Spirits Having Flown	Bee Gees
Spitfire	Jefferson Starship
Split	Groundhogs
Sports	Huey Lewis & The News
Ssssh	Ten Years After
Stacked Up	Senser
Stage	David Bowie
Stage Fright	Band
Stages	Elaine Paige
Stampede	Doobie Brothers
Stand Up	Jethro Tull
Standing On A Beach - The Singles	Cure
A Star Is Born (Soundtrack)	Barbra Streisand
Star Party	Various
Star Tracks	Various
Star Wars	Soundtrack
Staring At The Sun	Level 42
Stars	Simply Red
Stars Charity Fantasia Save The Children	Various
Stars For A Summer Night	Various
Stars on 45	Starsound (AKA Stars On)
Stars On Long Play	Stars On (AKA Starsound)
Station To Station	David Bowie
Stay On These Roads	A-Ha
Stay With The Hollies	Hollies
Staying Alive	Soundtrack
Steam	East 17
Steel Wheels	Rolling Stones
Steeltown	Big Country
Step By Step	New Kids On The Block
Step Two	Showaddywaddy
Stephen Stills	Stephen Stills
Stephen Stills 2	Stephen Stills
Steppenwolf	Steppenwolf
Steppenwolf 'Live'	Steppenwolf
Steps In Time	King
Steptoe And Son	Wilfrid Brambell & Harry H. Corbett
Stevie Wonder's Original Musiquarium I	Stevie Wonder
Sticky Fingers	Rolling Stones
Still Bill	Bill Withers
Still Crazy After All These Years	Paul Simon
Still Life (American Concert 1981)	Rolling Stones
The Sting (Soundtrack)	Marvin Hamlisch
Stone Age	Rolling Stones
Stonedhenge	Ten Years After
Stop	Sam Brown
Stop The World - I Want To Get Off	Original Cast
Storm Front	Billy Joel
The Story Of The Who	Who
Straight Shooter	Bad Company
Stranded	Roxy Music
Strange Days	Doors
Stranger In Town	Bob Seger & The Silver Bullet Band
Stranger On The Shore	Mr. Acker Bilk
The Stranger	Billy Joel
Strangers In The Night	Frank Sinatra
Strangers In The Night	UFO
Strangeways Here We Come	Smiths
Stranglers IV (Rattus Norvegicus)	Stranglers
The Strauss Family	London Symphony Orchestra
Stray Cats	Stray Cats
Street Fighting Years	Simple Minds
Street Legal	Bob Dylan
Street Life - 20 Great Hits	Bryan Ferry/Roxy Music
Street Songs	Rick James
Street Survivors	Lynyrd Skynyrd
Streisand Superman	Barbra Streisand
Strikes Again	Rose Royce
String Along	Kingston Trio
String Of Hits	Shadows
The Stripper And Other Fun Songs For The Family	David Rose
Stronger Than Pride	Sade
The Stud	Soundtrack
Stupidity	Dr. Feelgood
Substance	New Order
Success Hasn't Spoiled Me Yet	Rick Springfield
Suede	Suede
Sugar And Spice	Searchers
Sugar Lips	Al Hirt
Sugar Tax	Orchestral Manoeuvres In The Dark
Summer Breeze	Seals & Crofts
Summer Days (And Summer Nights!!)	Beach Boys
Summer Dreams	Beach Boys
Summer Holiday (Soundtrack)	Cliff Richard
Sundown	Gordon Lightfoot
Sunny Side!	Kingston Trio
Super Hits 1 & 2	Various
Super Trouper	Abba
Superfly (Soundtrack)	Curtis Mayfield
Superunknown	Soundgarden
The Supremes A Go-Go	Supremes
The Supremes Sing Holland-Dozier-Holland	Supremes
Surfer Girl	Beach Boys
Surfin' U.S.A.	Beach Boys
Surrealistic Pillow	Jefferson Airplane
Survival	Grand Funk Railroad
Suzi Quatro's Greatest Hits	Suzi Quatro
Sweet Baby James	James Taylor
Sweet Dreams (Are Made Of This)	Eurythmics
Sweet Things	Georgie Fame
The Sweetkeeper	Tanita Tikaram
Swing Easy	Frank Sinatra
Symbol	Prince & The New Power Generation
Symphonies For The Seventies	Waldo De Los Rios
Synchronicity	Police
Take Good Care Of Yourself	Three Degrees
Take It Easy	Walker Brothers
Take That And Party	Take That
Tales From Topographic Oceans	Yes
Talking Back To The Night	Steve Winwood
Talking Book	Stevie Wonder
Tango In The Night	Fleetwood Mac
Tanx	T. Rex
Tapestry	Carole King

Tarkus Emerson, Lake & Palmer
A Taste Of Honey Taste Of Honey
Tattoo You Rolling Stones
Taxi Bryan Ferry
TCB Diana Ross & The Supremes With The Temptations
Tea For The Tillerman Cat Stevens
Tear Down These Walls Billy Ocean
Tears And Laughter Johnny Mathis
Tears Of Happiness Ken Dodd
Tears Roll Down (Greatest Hits 1981-1992) Tears For Fears
Tease Me Chaka Demus & Pliers
Teaser And The Firecat Cat Stevens
Technique New Order
Teddy Teddy Pendergrass
Telekon Gary Numan
Tell Me On A Sunday Marti Webb
Tell Me Why Wynonna
Temperance Seven 1961 Temperance Seven
Temple Of The Dog Temple Of The Dog
Temptation Roger Williams
The Temptations Greatest Hits Temptations
Ten Pearl Jam
Ten Good Reasons Jason Donovan
Ten Summoner's Tales Sting
Ten Years Non-Stop Jubilee James Last
Thank You Baby Stylistics
Thank You Very Much - Reunion Concert At The London Palladium Cliff Richard
That'll Be The Day Buddy Holly
That'll Be The Day Various
That's All Bobby Darin
That's Life Frank Sinatra
That's The Way Of The World (Soundtrack) Earth, Wind & Fire
Theatre Of Pain Motley Crue
Their 1st LP Spencer Davis Group
Their Greatest Hits Hot Chocolate
Their Satanic Majesties Request Rolling Stones
Theme From A Summer Place Billy Vaughn
Themes Various
Then Came Rock 'n' Roll Various
Then Play On Fleetwood Mac
There Goes Rhymin' Simon Paul Simon
There! I've Said It Again Bobby Vinton
There's A Riot Goin' On Sly & The Family Stone
These Foolish Things Bryan Ferry
They Only Come Out At Night Edgar Winter Group
Thick As A Brick Jethro Tull
Third Album Jackson 5
The Third Album Barbra Streisand
Third Stage Boston
13 Smash Hits Tom Jones
30 Greatest Gladys Knight & The Pips
32 Minutes And 17 Seconds Cliff Richard
This Is...Brenda Brenda Lee
This Is Darin Bobby Darin
This Is Hancock Tony Hancock
This Is It Various
This Is James Last James Last
This Is Tom Jones Tom Jones
This Ole House Shakin' Stevens
This One's For You Barry Manilow
This Thing Called Love - Greatest Hits Alexander O'Neal
This Year's Model Elvis Costello
Thoroughbred Carole King
3 Sides Live Genesis
III Sides To Every Story Extreme
The 3 Tenors In Concert 1994 Jose Carreras, Placido Domingo & Luciano Pavarotti with Mehta
3 Years 5 Months & 2 Days In The Life Of... Arrested Development
Thriller Michael Jackson
Through A Big Country - Greatest Hits Big Country
Through The Past Darkly (Big Hits Vol. 2) Rolling Stones
Thunder And Lightning Thin Lizzy
Tiffany Tiffany
Time Electric Light Orchestra
A Time For Us Donny Osmond
The Time Has Come Chambers Brothers
Time Out Featuring 'Take Five' Dave Brubeck Quartet
Time Peace/The Rascals' Greatest Hits Rascals
The Time Bros
Time, Love And Tenderness Michael Bolton
Timeless (The Classics) Michael Bolton
The Times They Are A-Changin' Bob Dylan
Tin Machine Tin Machine
To Our Children's Children's Children Moody Blues
To Russell, My Brother, Whom I Slept With Bill Cosby
To The Extreme Vanilla Ice
To Whom It May Concern Pasadenas
Tom Tom Jones
Tom Jones Live In Las Vegas Tom Jones
Tommy Soundtrack
Tommy Various
Tommy Who
Toni Braxton Toni Braxton
Tonight David Bowie
Tonight I'm Yours Rod Stewart
Tonight: In Person Limeliters
Tony Anthony Newley
2 Hot! Peaches & Herb
Too Legit To Quit Hammer
Too Long In Exile Van Morrison
Too Young Donny Osmond
Too-Rye-Ay Dexy's Midnight Runners
Top Gun Soundtrack
Top Of The Pops Vol. 18 Various
Top Of The Pops Vol. 19 Various
Top Of The Pops Vol. 20 Various
Tops With Me Helen Shapiro
Totally Hot Olivia Newton-John
Totally Krossed Out Kris Kross
Toto IV Toto
Touch Eurythmics
Touch Me Gary Glitter
Touch Me In The Morning Diana Ross
Tourism Roxette
Tracy Chapman Tracy Chapman
A Tramp Shining Richard Harris
Trash Alice Cooper
Traveling Wilburys Traveling Wilburys
Tribute Ozzy Osbourne
A Trick Of The Trail Genesis
Trilogy Emerson, Lake & Palmer
Trini Lopez At PJ's Trini Lopez
Trini Lopez In London Trini Lopez
Trio Dolly Parton, Emmylou Harris & Linda Ronstadt
Tropical Gangsters Kid Creole & The Coconuts
True Spandau Ballet
True Blue Madonna
True Colors Cyndi Lauper
Tryin' To Get The Feeling Barry Manilow
Tubular Bells Mike Oldfield
Tubular Bells II Mike Oldfield
Tuesday Night Music Club Sheryl Crow
Tug Of War Paul McCartney
Tumbleweed Connection Elton John
Tunnel Of Love Bruce Springsteen
Turn Back The Clock Johnny Hates Jazz
Turn It Upside Down Spin Doctors
The Turtles! Golden Hits Turtles
Tusk Fleetwood Mac
TV Sing Along With Mitch Mitch Miller
The Twang's The Thang Duane Eddy
12 X 5 Rolling Stones
The Twelve Commandments Of Dance London Boys
Twelve Deadly Cyns...And Then Some Cyndi Lauper
12 Gold Bars Status Quo
12 Inches Of Snow Snow
12 Play R. Kelly
Twelve Songs Of Christmas Jim Reeves
20 All Time Greats Connie Francis
20 All Time Hits Of The Fifties Various
20 Classic Hits Platters
20 Country Classics Tammy Wynette
20 Dynamic Hits Various
20 Fantastic Hits Various
20 Fantastic Hits Vol. 2 Various
20 Fantastic Hits Vol. 3 Various
20 Flashback Greats Of The Sixties Various
20 Giant Hits Nolans
20 Golden Greats Beach Boys
20 Golden Greats Glen Campbell
20 Golden Greats Nat 'King' Cole
20 Golden Greats Neil Diamond
20 Golden Greats Hollies
20 Golden Greats Buddy Holly & The Crickets
20 Golden Greats Diana Ross & The Supremes
20 Golden Greats Diana Ross
20 Golden Greats Shadows
20 Golden Greats Frank Sinatra
20 Greatest Hits Tom Jones
20 Hottest Hits Hot Chocolate
20 Original Dean Martin Hits Dean Martin
20 Star Tracks Various
20/20 Beach Boys
21 Today Cliff Richard
22 Golden Guitar Greats Bert Weedon
24 Original Hits Drifters
25 Dynamic Hits Vol. 2 Various
25 Rockin' & Rollin' Greats Various
25th Anniversary Album Shirley Bassey
Twice As Kool Kool & The Gang
Twin Sons Of Different Mothers Dan Fogelberg & Tim Weisberg
Twist With Chubby Checker Chubby Checker
Twistin' & Twangin' Duane Eddy
II Boyz II Men
2 In 3 Esther & Abi Ofarim
The Two Of Us Various
2001 - A Space Odyssey Soundtrack

U.F.Orb Orb
U2 Live: Under A Blood Red Sky U2
UB44 UB40
The Ultimate Collection Bryan Ferry/Roxy Music
The Ultimate Collection Marc Bolan & T. Rex
The Ultimate Sin Ozzy Osbourne
Ummagumma Pink Floyd
Under The Influence Of ... Love Unlimited
Under The Pink Tori Amos
Undercover Rolling Stones
The Unforgettable Fire U2
The Unforgettable Glenn Miller Glenn Miller
Unforgettable Natalie Cole
Unforgettable Various
Universal Soldier Donovan
Unplugged Eric Clapton
Unplugged...And Seated Rod Stewart
Unpredictable Natalie Cole
Up Right Said Fred
Up To Date Partridge Family
Up, Up And Away 5th Dimension
Uprising Bob Marley & The Wailers
Upstairs At Eric's Yazoo
Urban Cowboy Soundtrack
Us Peter Gabriel
Use Your Illusion I Guns N' Roses
Use Your Illusion II Guns N' Roses

Vacation Go-Go's
Vagabond Heart Rod Stewart

Title	Artist
Val	Val Doonican
Val Doonican Rocks But Gently	Val Doonican
Valley Of The Dolls	Dionne Warwick
Van Halen II	Van Halen
Vanilla Fudge	Vanilla Fudge
Variations	Andrew Lloyd Webber
Vauxhall And I	Morrissey
Velveteen	Transvision Vamp
Venus And Mars	Wings
Verities & Balderdash	Harry Chapin
Very	Pet Shop Boys
The Very Best Of Cat Stevens	Cat Stevens
The Very Best Of Chris De Burgh	Chris De Burgh
Very Best Of David Bowie	David Bowie
The Very Best Of Don McLean	Don McLean
The Very Best Of Eagles	Eagles
The Very Best Of Elton John	Elton John
The Very Best Of Hot Chocolate	Hot Chocolate
The Very Best Of Leo Sayer	Leo Sayer
The Very Best Of Marvin Gaye	Marvin Gaye
Very Best Of Rita Coolidge	Rita Coolidge
The Very Best Of Roger Whittaker	Roger Whittaker
The Very Best Of Slim Whitman	Slim Whitman
The Very Best Of The Beach Boys	Beach Boys
The Very Best Of The Bee Gees	Bee Gees
The Very Best Of The Electric Light Orchestra	Electric Light Orchestra
Very Necessary	Salt-N-Pepa
A Very Special Christmas 2	Various
Victory	Jacksons
Video Stars	Various
Vienna	Ultravox
Vincent Edwards Sings	Vincent Edwards
Violator	Depeche Mode
Visions	Various
The Visitors	Abba
Vitalogy	Pearl Jam
Viva Roxy Music	Roxy Music
Vivaldi Four Seasons	Nigel Kennedy With The English Chamber Orchestra
Vivid	Living Colour
The Voice Of Churchill	Sir Winston Churchill
Voice Of The Heart	Carpenters
Voices	Kenny Thomas
Vol II (1990 A New Decade)	Soul II Soul
Volume III Just Right	Soul II Soul
Volume One	Honeydrippers
Voodoo Lounge	Rolling Stones
Voulez-Vous	Abba
Vs.	Pearl Jam
Waiting For The Sun	Doors
Waking Up The Neighbours	Bryan Adams
Waking Up With The House On Fire	Culture Club
Walking With A Panther	L.L. Cool J
The Wall	Pink Floyd
Walls And Bridges	John Lennon
Walthamstow	East 17
Wanted	Yazz
War	U2
War Child	Jethro Tull
War Of The Worlds	Jeff Wayne
A Warm Shade Of Ivory	Henry Mancini
Was Captured Live At The Forum	Three Dog Night
Washington Square	Village Stompers
Watermark	Enya
The Way It Is	Bruce Hornsby & The Range
The Way We Were	Barbra Streisand
Wayne's World	Soundtrack
We All Had Doctors' Papers	Max Boyce
We Are Family	Sister Sledge
We Are The World	USA For Africa
We Can Make It	Peters & Lee
We Can't Dance	Genesis
We Come Strapped	MC Eiht Featuring CMW
We Two Are One	Eurythmics
We'd Like To Teach The World To Sing	New Seekers
We're An American Band	Grand Funk
Weekend In L.A.	George Benson
Welcome Back, My Friends, To The Show That Never Ends - Ladies And Gentlemen: Emerson, Lake And Plamer	Emerson, Lake & Palmer
Welcome To My Nightmare	Alice Cooper
Welcome To The Beautiful South	Beautiful South
Welcome To The LBJ Ranch!	Various - Comedy
Welcome To The Pleasure Dome	Frankie Goes To Hollywood
Welcome To The Real World	Mr. Mister
Welcome To Wherever You Are	INXS
Well Respected Kinks	Kinks
West Side Story	Original Cast
West Side Story	Soundtrack
Wet	Barbra Streisand
Wha'ppen	Beat
What Now My Love	Herb Alpert & The Tijuana Brass
What Were Once Vices Are Now Habits	Doobie Brothers
What's Bin Did And What's Bin Hid	Donovan
What's Going On	Marvin Gaye
What's Love Got To Do With It (Soundtrack)	Tina Turner
What's New	Linda Ronstadt
What's The 411	Mary J. Blige
Whatever You Want	Status Quo
Wheels Are Turnin'	REO Speedwagon
Wheels Of Fire	Cream
Wheels Of Steel	Saxon
When In Spain	Cliff Richard
When Love Finds You	Vince Gill
When The World Knows Your Name	Deacon Blue
When Your Lover Has Gone	Frank Sinatra
Whenever You Need Somebody	Rick Astley
Where Did Our Love Go	Supremes
Whiplash Smile	Billy Idol
Whipped Cream & Other Delights	Herb Alpert & The Tijuana Brass
The Whispers	Whispers
The White Room	KLF
Whitesnake	Whitesnake
Whitney	Whitney Houston
Whitney Houston	Whitney Houston
Who Are You	Who
Who I Am	Alan Jackson
Who's Next	Who
Who's That Girl (Soundtrack)	Madonna
The Whole Story	Kate Bush
Wichita Lineman	Glen Campbell
Wicked Game	Chris Isaak
A Wild And Crazy Guy	Steve Martin
Wild Cherry	Wild Cherry
Wild Flowers	Judy Collins
The Wild Heart	Stevie Nicks
Wild Honey	Beach Boys
Wild Is Love	Nat 'King' Cole
Wild Wood	Paul Weller
Wild!	Erasure
Wildcat	Original Cast
Willy And The Poor Boys	Creedence Clearwater Revival
Wilson Phillips	Wilson Phillips
Wimoweh	Karl Denver
Win, Lose Or Draw	Allman Brothers Band
Winchester Cathedral	New Vaudeville Band
Wind On The Water	David Crosby/Graham Nash
Windsong	John Denver
Winelight	Grover Washington Jr.
Wings At The Speed Of Sound	Wings
Wings Greatest Hits	Wings
Wings Over America	Wings
Winner In You	Patti LaBelle
Wired For Sound	Cliff Richard
Wish	Cure
Wish You Were Here	Pink Floyd
With A Lot O' Soul	Temptations
With The Beatles	Beatles
The Woman In Red (Soundtrack)	Stevie Wonder
Women And Children First	Van Halen
Wonderful Life	Black
Wonderful Life (Soundtrack)	Cliff Richard
Wonderfulness	Bill Cosby
Wonderland By Night	Bert Kaempfert
Woodface	Crowded House
Woodstock	Various
Word Up!	Cameo
Words Of Love	Buddy Holly & The Crickets
Working Class Dog	Rick Springfield
The Works	Queen
The World Beaters Sing The World Beaters	England Football World Cup Squad
The World Is A Ghetto	War
World Machine	Level 42
The World Of Mantovani	Mantovani
The World Of Mantovani Vol. 2	Mantovani
A World Of Our Own	Seekers
World Of The Bachelors	Bachelors
World Of Val Doonican	Val Doonican
The World Won't Listen	Smiths
Worlds Away	Pablo Cruise
Wouldn't You Like It	Bay City Rollers
Wrap Around Joy	Carole King
Wynonna	Wynonna
X	INXS
Xanadu (Soundtrack)	Olivia Newton-John
Year Of The Cat	Al Stewart
Yellow Bird	Lawrence Welk
Yellow Submarine	Beatles
Yentl (Soundtrack)	Barbra Streisand
The Yes Album	Yes
Yesterday's Love Songs - Today's Blues	Nancy Wilson
'Yesterday'...And Today	Beatles
You And Me Both	Yazoo
You Don't Bring Me Flowers	Neil Diamond
You Don't Mess Around With Jim	Jim Croce
You Light Up My Life	Debby Boone
You Light Up My Life	Johnny Mathis
You've Lost That Lovin' Feelin'	Righteous Brothers
Young Americans	David Bowie
The Young Ones (Soundtrack)	Cliff Richard
Your Twist Party	Chubby Checker
Zebop!	Santana
Zenyatta Mondatta	Police
Zooropa	U2